BURIED VALUES:

THE ROOKIES

JOSHUA ADAM WEISELBERG

To Timothy,
Happy Father's Day!
Joshua Adam Weiselberg
June 19, 2020

BURIED VALUES: The Rookies

ISBN 978-0-9913732-6-0

Published by Buried Values Media Group
Cover painting by Monte Moore, Maverick Arts, www.mavarts.com
Editing by Adrienne Moch, Adrienne@AdrienneMoch.com
Interior formatting by Yvonne Betancourt, www.ebook-format.com
Exterior design by Linda Boulanger, http://telltalebookcovers.weebly.com/
Legal representation by Steins & Associates, http://steins-patents.com/

with special thanks to:

The Gambling Cowboy Chophouse and Saloon: operated by the Ehmcke Family and Staff, Old Town, Temecula, CA - for reservations call: (951) 699-2895

Richard Beck & Chris Greer of The Hotel Temecula, an 1891 Old West experience - for hotel reservation and western show information, call: (951) 972-8500
The Old Town Temecula Gunfighters
Marty "Doc Holliday" Kimble
The 69th Pennsylvania Infantry (re-enactors)
The San Diego Civil War Roundtable
Long Beach Shoreline Village Marina boutique shops, w/western Raindance store, Long Beach, CA
Jed Hoyer, Executive VP and General Manager, Chicago Cubs, a MLB organization

www.baseball-almanac.com to which a percentage of the proceeds of this novel will be donated! — an invaluable baseball resource for all fans of Major League Baseball

This book contains multiple references which are graphically violent, misogynistic, racist, anti-Semitic, and suggestive of the illegal manipulation of Major League Baseball. While these incidents do not necessarily reflect the views or preferences of the author, *they are meant to be highly offensive or distasteful to the reader*. It is the author's hope that each individual reader will recognize buried values within themselves and develop a better manner in which to view the world and conduct themselves towards others they will encounter in it, than do the characters within the following pages. This is a tale of reprehensible people and *their* true buried values.

www.BuriedValues.com

Also enjoy these other provocative titles by Joshua Adam Weiselberg:

BURIED VALUES: The Outlaws – *In the middle of the horror that's Bleeding Kansas, witness the start of Daniel Winthrop's criminal career. In 1857, the North begins to arm the South in a stolen weapons trafficking scandal that really happened with a conspiracy that reached all the way up to the Buchanan White House. Whether it grew from personal convictions or desperation for cash, the direct consequences were felt in the shape of the Civil War! Constance May betrays the young Winthrop's love and even her own father, the General, on behalf of the Abolitionist cause. And Sgt. Robert Masterson finds himself front and center with all the hell that's being raised as he winds up incriminated with Jack Talbot and his dirty crew. While somebody's getting paid, at least somebody else is really going to receive payback! As all attempt to escape their fate, take a guns-blazing ride on the trail to high treason 'western-style' with John Brown, William Quantrill, and Robert E. Lee, along with many more who sought to forever change the course of American history.*

BURIED VALUES: The Treasure – *In the maelstrom of the Civil War that now rages across the bloody landscapes of 19th Century America, the Buried Values legacy truly begins with treasonous acts of larceny and murder, and Robert Masterson and his future beloved are forever ensnared by events that will affect their families for generations. A robbery and key assassinations are plotted by dirty Daniel Winthrop, and President Abraham Lincoln's star witnesses to John Buchanan Floyd's arms trafficking conspiracy are targeted for termination without remorse. Abigail Hutchinson saves patriot Christopher Pratt's very existence, but the cost of his life might have been too high of price to pay! Now all her family members' lives are on the line when she and Winthrop get into bed together over dubious hopes for an escape – with a profit. But Pratt's betrayal demands he seek revenge! Now the originally contemptible Abigail's priorities change as the feisty Southern Belle realizes she'll have to rise up to be the better human being or no one will survive. Will the gold, the silver, at the very least some increment of justice – let alone the truth – ever be recovered?*

BURIED VALUES: The Fall – *The Rookies make the plays in a lot of extra innings that the Cubs were surely never planning on. Now in the middle of their killer 1918 season, Taddeo Villetti is murder on the mound serving up his special kind of cutters and Arlene Masterson will be the mother of all vengeance on the streets. The fire for women's rights has turned into a one-woman vicious crossburn that can run from the cornfields of the Midwest to the corrupt Congress in the capitol. And the Villetti Family with its part in gambling, drug dealing, and Big Jim Colosimo's bordellos is right in its path of devastation. And there's no going back to how things used to be, especially with Arnold Rothstein's agents on hand to practice their particular brand of playing hardball. Dark money is lining all the wrong people's pockets. Now Taddeo is a man who's losing control and can only hope he has enough balls to be that one pitcher who can finish the game. He struggles to form an alliance with Johnny Torrio's enforcer, the young Al Capone, while his last true love is torn between strengthening her ties to the infamous suffragette Katherine McCormick or The Windy City's favorite Madam, Victoria Moresco, ally of the fledgling Outfit. Blood's being let into the Chicago River from Little Italy to Rogers Park and in its backwards flow, it is painting everyone's true buried values in red. And now it is the new players' turn to witness some strikes up close. But all it will take is one now-veteran man to be called off the bench, for he to become the real game-changer.*

BURIED VALUES: The Library – *In 2016, several young women's futures will hang on the choices these rivals make in a deadly hunt for Civil War treasure so valuable, that as evidence, it's powerful enough to end a government insider conspiracy to take over control of Homeland Security – or see to it that the plot succeeds! Entering the adventure, are over a half-dozen men with special skills ranging from officers of the law, politicians, gangsters, the daring archaeologist Dr. Darren Hughes, and LSU freshman, Tony Porter, who's just smitten with the ladies. At stake is the highly profitable fast and furious flow of guns going south and drugs flowing north, and one woman's mission to foil the restructuring of a new Villetti crime family that's forming some very dangerous alliances south of the U.S. border. Going down amidst all the sex trafficking, prohibited weapons exchanges, illegal immigration, and the ever-present corruption in the failed war with the Mexican drug cartels – and with the shootings of police officers, clashes between the races,* *and the U.S. Presidential Election all in the mix – is a nail-biting mystery who the triumphant femme fatale really is, and how Naomi or Davina will react when in the aftermath of the Gulf's catastrophic flooding, the survivor's tempted with an unexpected and irresistible opportunity to take full control over everything! Now the past continues to haunt not just the true heirs of the bounty – but instead, its influence runs full circle back into the swirling winds of just one more very real hurricane that's bearing down, in tandem with one political maelstrom that no one foresaw – to join forces so as to blow the entire cover off of our whole country's true buried values – in our present.*

BURIED VALUES: The Recovery – *In the shocking sequel to Buried Values: The Library, will it be Naomi or Davina who has survived to now have to attempt to run the new Louisiana Mafia? The young woman will form the uncomfortable but necessary alliances that might barely keep her afloat in what's left of a sinking criminal empire, trying to rebuild in hurricane devastated flood lands. There's no electricity, no chance to call for any help, not even many roads still above water, and there will be no rescue coming for quite a long time. It is only the worst of the prison gangs – who escaped drowning behind bars – who now rise to surface and seek to satiate their all-consuming thirst for revenge – who can still hold even the slightest grip on any tangible real power. A shaky alliance with the street boss Demetrius Lamont appears to be the only way to push on and complete one thoroughly-soul-consuming quest for a fortune in lost treasure, now the sole currency of any real authority. But who will turn on whom first? One young woman, now ultimately corrupted, will relentlessly compete to capture unimaginable reserves of the real kind of tender she'll need to secure her status as power shifts drastically in America, following the wake of the controversial 2016 Presidential Election. What are the real values which lie beneath the surface, waiting for her to find? And could they save a lot more people from dying? The legacy of Buried Values continues – but only for the last carriers of enough personal fortitude to still remain breathing, when everything else purportedly held dear, seems destined to drown!*

Find Buried Values online at **www.BuriedValues.com**
for exclusive story excerpts, book tour news,
and the Buried Values store.
T-shirts, hats, and posters are now available!

Like Buried Values on Facebook:
www.Facebook.com/BuriedValues
for exclusive videos, contests, and up-to-the-minute news about live battle reenactment shows!

Follow Buried Values on www.Twitter.com/BuriedValues

It's hoped that aspiring storytellers might find useful writing tips and stimulating debates online at all the official Buried Values social media sources.

for Barry W. Benecke II
and my
Grandfather – that's you Poppa,
the greatest Cubs fans that I know!

Congratulations to the 2016 Chicago Cubs!!

with thanks to David Eckstein and Ashley Eckstein,
the world's greatest inspirational baseball family,
and to Trevor Hoffman – because every fan has his hero in this game!

May The Force be with you

Chapter 1

The intersection of West Addison and North Clark streets,
Chicago, Illinois, May 21, 1918:
4:02 pm CST

Ray Schmandt took a lunging swing at Vaughn the very first chance he got! The air swooshed with the all the power he could muster with his bat — and Schmandt connected against leathery skin with a vengeance, splitting stiches. The impact on the bat vibrated up his arms.

Screaming so all could hear him, The Reverend cried foul.

Killefer retrieved the ball from the dirt and tossed it back to the mound, and Hippo Vaughn stared down Brooklyn's 2nd baseman before he stepped back up the soft incline to find his footing on the rubber. He got started ahead of Schmandt and the count was "oh-and-one."

Now an audible number of fans of the visiting team roared, the New Yorkers cheering on Brooklyn, hoping they could bust open a game where thus far, both teams had been tied at zero for five frustrating innings. On the 3rd base line, Taddeo watched with urgent anticipation from the Cubs' bench. Alongside him, were George "The Hoff" Hoffman and Michael "Trip" Everston, both more than eager to contribute to Chicago's victory ever since they'd been called up to play with the pros. Now Vaughn's catcher signaled for Hippo's number four pitch. It was time to see if Schmandt could be fooled by Chicago's ace hurler's slider. A lefty against a right-handed batter, The Hippo had to be careful how he handled the first plate appearance of this early middle inning at Weeghman Park. The Robins' tough approach at the dish was tiring him earlier than usual. But having reached the higher end of what was still around the average age for players these days, he'd become one of the game's most talented pitchers on any active roster. And he had a winning record to prove it. So Hippo was rarely intimidated. And he was never going to be scared by some rookie kid the Robins sent out to face him.

He wound up and launched his slider that broke toward the inside. Too far inside. Or Schmandt made a great show of jumping back from the plate. But Hank O'Day called out, "Ball one!" and the count was even. Vaughn thought he'd get that one in the zone, or he'd have jammed up the less-experienced Schmandt trying to swing at any pitch that was close, but Killefer's plan didn't work.

Schmandt batted seventh in Brooklyn's order, though he'd proven as capable of hitting for multiple bases in the minors as the rest of his pro teammates hoped he'd do now. The Robins had a shaky start but their record could always evolve into something a little more respectable in the second month of the 1918 season. Considering Brooklyn's lineup and their close matchup to Chicago with their own prior year's *losing* statistics, the smart strategy to deal with the visiting club's offensive potential lay in pitching to them very carefully. The Cubs, way more successful than Brooklyn thus far, still eyed them as dangerously competitive rivals. Nobody wanted to rank dead last, after all. *Twelve more outs to go — if the guys can provide me with some offense*, Hippo thought. With a lot of the men off doing what the papers described as their patriotic duty to fight the German Kaiser, this was a year of opportunity for many new young players. But Hippo didn't know if that just meant he'd have to fight all of Brooklyn's lineup by himself for far too many innings this season, since Chicago's own rookies might not be able to handle the pressure. So he set in to focus hard on getting out the first three batters in the top of the sixth.

Now his last pitch had brushed the Robins' 2nd baseman back off the dish. While the batter's reach with his stick was limited, the veteran southpaw Vaughn struck. The Hippo set and released a circle-change that went low and outside, but Schmandt swung out ahead of it, missed, and The Reverend called "Steee-rike Two!"

Vaughn breathed in the smell of the grass, the dust from the gravel and the scent of cigar smoke from the stands that wafted over the field under the bright sunlight. He thought he could smell alcohol too, and the idea occurred to him that he might just want a drink right about then. But his work wasn't done yet and his senses were just as experienced in sniffing out another win for himself, and Chicago. The triumph would be his.

Killefer signaled for the one-and-two pitch to come in tight and inside again, since the batter had resumed closing his distance to the plate after losing range on that last outside toss. Keeping both hands on his bat, Schmandt raised it above his head and flattened his profile as Vaughn sped an 86-mph four-seam fastball inside on the batter. "Ball two!" O'Day officiated.

Now Vaughn knew that ever since 1st bagman Fred Merkle's base-running "boner" incident in a prior season, the Cubs' old manager-turned-umpire would show his former team no favoritism. This *Reverend* liked to demonstrate he was above that, and Hippo would have to work hard to get the calls he wanted out of each and every pitch. Taddeo bit his lower lip, watching from his seat among the Cubs' reserves.

The count was two-and-two now, but Brooklyn had no runners on and Vaughn still had room to fool around with Schmandt. Behind the plate, Killefer had reasoned their opponent would now move in and crowd the dish again, expecting The Hippo to attack the outside side of the zone once more. They had a chance to surprise the batter when Schmandt came back in on the plate, just to confuse him. So Killefer ordered another one up and inside. Jamming up, with an exasperated look on his face, the Robins' 2nd baseman still managed to tip this one backwards and into the stands. Killefer spun around, tossing off his mask, hustling after it, his effort great but nevertheless futile, while the fans dove for the foul ball hoping to get a souvenir. A gruff member of security in a dark suit located it immediately and took it away from a teary-eyed, small blonde-haired boy who'd been watching the game with his father, and only seconds ago had been excited to snag a foul. But the stadium's employee tossed the ball back to Killefer, who showed it to the umpire, and O'Day let him air-mail it back to Vaughn.

Dead-ball rules. The pitcher felt relieved, as he didn't want a new sphere. This one was scuffed up enough that the shreds in the leather would help him further slow his curveball and drop it down something good — and Hippo was not the least bit surprised when Killefer signaled for that pitch next.

But Schmandt anticipated the delivery and was prepared to swing where he just knew Vaughn would throw it. Nevertheless, his timing was off and another one was fouled along the home team's line as Brooklyn's batter was still slightly too far out ahead of this pitch. Out of play it ricocheted off the left field bricks then rolled all the way toward the demolition site of the old Lutheran seminary just beyond the outfield wall. The Reverend signaled for it to be retrieved to be put back into play and the ball was immediately sent back to the pitcher.

The count was still two-and-two, but Hippo Vaughn was through messing around with this batter. He'd thrown the rookie six offers already. Behind the plate, Killefer knew his shooter well, and because of that, the Cubs' catcher had already known what his battery-mate wanted to strike with next. Vaughn wound up and made it almost look like he shot put his fastball. But his arm didn't come down far enough before the release and the ball hurtled to the plate just above the letters and Schmandt was behind it — but not altogether *too* late. The bat did connect, and coming down on top of the pitch like it did, Brooklyn's hitter drove a chopper hard into the grass in front of the mound that bounced high into the air upon impact and looked like it would jump out toward right field, high over and in between the gap separating Kilduff, Chicago's 2nd baseman, and Merkle at 1st. But The Hippo made a jungle leap high in the air and swatted the ball down with his glove — straight into his bare left hand. Off balance and stumbling as he came down hard on his right foot first, he still managed to fire off the ball to Merkle, just ahead of the streaking Schmandt. The Hippo got another one! A triumphant Vaughn smiled as he made it all happen only to grimace a second later as he felt his ankle bend funny as he fell into the grass in front of the pitcher's mound.

A ballplayer can learn to hate it when he is in pain and the audience cheers. There's an infinite number of possibilities in the sport for why an audience erupts like this, and from the field, one couldn't be sure if it was mostly because Brooklyn's fans were hoping the play would remove an ace like Vaughn from continuing to be any threat to their winning the game. Making an effort to quell a persecution complex, Vaughn tried to convince himself the Cubs' fans cheered because of his great defense, getting Schmandt out; also since he didn't have the luxury of worrying about anything more than that. Right then the only thing Hippo became very sure about was his injury. His manager, Mr. Mitchell came running out of Chicago's dugout as Killefer, 3rd baseman Charlie Deal, and shortstop Charlie Hollocher all ran up to be at his side. The pain was almost too difficult to bear and his teammates were trying to help Hippo stand. "Great play!" they all pronounced, patting him on his white-but-soiled uniform's back as each arrived to the mound.

"It's no good. I mean my ankle. I need a minute to walk on this." Vaughn shook his head and looked around at his teammates, and could not control his eyes from pleading with his manager. "I just need a minute or two, Coach… Please."

But Mitchell had assessed the situation already and made up his mind. "I'm sorry. The Robins trail us by only six and a half games. I gotta keep us ahead. We're halfway through this series and behind. It's not fair to everyone else. We lost to these guys yesterday and I can't jerk around with your bench-mates' record only so you can record a shutout. You're plenty capable and will have many other opportunities this season. I'm sure of that. I'm going to bring out Taddeo."

"That rookie? *Again?* You got to be kidding me! C'mon Coach," the young twenty-two-year-old Hollocher exclaimed. "This is not a game."

"Oh really?" Mitchell's mouth moved and he covered his involuntary smile with his hand, but as he turned his face, he must have seen the fifty-nine-year-old Hank O'Day making his way out to the mound to see if the Cubs were changing pitchers. Mitchell's smile disappeared. It was decision time. "I'll go talk to the kid." But Hollocher grimaced and glanced at Deal for some support. Vaughn was going to start to protest again as well, but decided to bite his tongue. The manager had made up his mind and took the baseball.

O'Day approached. "Are you going to make a substitution? I need to know if you're warming someone up." The Reverend nodded toward Vaughn. "If so, you need to get this one off the field. We're burning daylight. I needed your new lineup. Yesterday."

Mitchell nodded, respectful of his immediate predecessor who had actually controlled the Cubs' bench only two years ago. He passed the game ball to Killefer who'd ran up to the mound to join them. "Hold on to this while I'll get a move on then. And I'll let you know in just a minute — if I'm sending in Carter — or Villetti."

And now, BURIED VALUES
is proud to bring you, in a first appearance up at the plate:

THE ROOKIES

"When you're forced to slide home, don't *ever* count on being safe."
—Taddeo Villetti, RHP, Chicago Cubs MLB Organization, from the South Side, May 21, 1918

Chapter 2

Tuesday, May 21, 1918
4:11 pm CST
Weeghman Park, Chicago, Illinois

6th Inning
Brooklyn – 0, Cubs – 0

0 Outs, 0 On

AB: The Brooklyn Robins (10 W – 16 L):
Ray Schmandt (2B, Bats: right, Throws: right) AVG .000, OBP .000
Age: 22, Games: < 20, Status: sophomoric rookie,
1st full season in The Show

On the mound:
Chicago Cubs (17 W – 10 L)
(Fighting to not be in last place in the National League)
P: James Leslie "Hippo" Vaughn (SP)
(Bats: Switch, Throws: Left) 6 W – 2 L, PCT: .617, ERA: 2.01, SO: 1,114,
HB: 59 x (in 6 years)
Age: 30, Games: 187, Status: 6-year veteran

AND THEN:

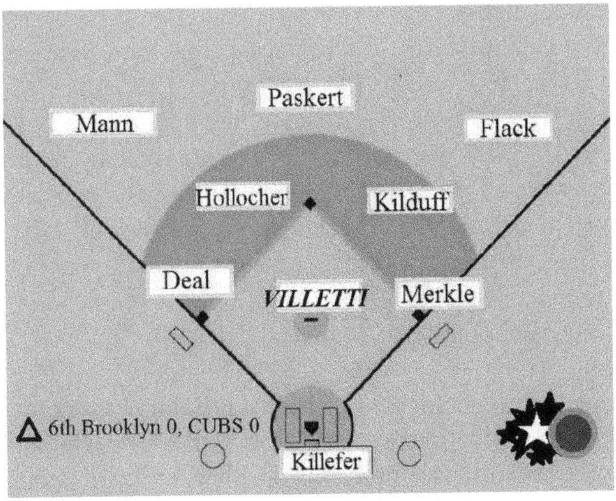

"Well, alright. I've been so seriously ready to win this thing!" Taddeo, already standing — and painfully, obviously, *hoping* — announced to his coach who'd just run up, entering Chicago's dugout. The Cubs' boss paused to scrutinize the dark-haired nineteen-year-old. Mitchell held his chin between his thumb and index finger while he had only seconds to think. He moved his hands to lift his ball cap and scratch his graying hair while his eyes darted over to right-handed reliever Paul Carter. Going with the more experienced pitcher would be the smarter move to make. Taddeo knew that as well. "Please Coach. I haven't pitched in six days," he pleaded.

"When you gave up three runs, sacrificed all Hippo's work, and buried Claude in a hole our bats couldn't ever dig him out of. Thank you very much."

"I've been throwing with Hoffman — even more since Boston. Sometimes three workout sessions a day. I'd never have been brought up from the minors if you'd not backed the request for me, personally. You believed in me, Sir. Now please let me on the field!"

"You're right about that. I *do* know what you can do, Villetti," Coach Mitchell said. He closed his eyes and exhaled audibly. "And there is that the Robins have never seen you." Brooklyn had already been using rookie batters like Schmandt to attempt to trip up Chicago.

"Then me and Hoff?" Taddeo glanced back to his teammate and best friend whose own eyes lit up glowing from where he sat on the bench. They were a match for the young pitcher's.

"No. You'll throw to Killefer." Taddeo looked down at his cleats as the Cubs' manager continued. "I'm not intentionally supplying Robinson and Charlie Ebbets with anything *more* to gloat over. How I'd love to wipe the sneers off their faces. Now mind your lessons I've been trying to teach you. *Obey* Billy when he signals you out there. It's quickly come to my attention that your teammates are still doubting you, Villetti. But alright. *I'm* going to rest my faith with you, Tad. So you go on and bring them home a win, and restore their confidence and at the same time you prove them wrong — you prove *me* right. I'm here to coach the Cubs to one hell of a winning season. So don't let me down, Villetti."

"I won't Coach. I promise you. And thanks!"

Bursting out of the dugout to barely a lukewarm welcome from Chicago's fans, Taddeo Villetti ran faster than all the wind in Chi-Town to take that hill. It appeared like he was trying to beat the tag.

Of course in his mind, Tad imagined he was climbing the mound to thunderous applause, trumpets playing, angels singing — and also that he'd better hurry and get there before Coach came to his senses and called him out of there, sending in Carter to take his place instead. The rookie breathed a deep sigh of relief when his first foot hit the rubber and Reverend O'Day nodded, acknowledging the umpire had seen him relieve Vaughn. He could distinctly single out the voices of Hoff and Trip encouraging him from the home team's bench. Of course that wasn't too hard. The stadium wasn't even close to filling to capacity these days, with a huge swath of his generation and the one immediately preceding it, off and overseas in France, still fighting the Germans. But Taddeo's war was at home, versus the Robins. And he was in the middle of it right now.

Killefer looked as impatient and unyielding as any Hun soldier Taddeo could've possibly envisioned, but the veteran catcher got settled behind the plate, first tossing Chicago's relief pitcher the game sphere. Good. It was the same one the teams had already been using into the 6th. Dead-ball rules were always a pleasure to count on. Taddeo pretended to drop Killefer's pitch as a fake late reaction, but he'd been rubbing down his hair under his cap and gathering up some styling grease on his throwing fingers. He let the ball drop so he could rub a greased sphere in the dust, and Taddeo did likewise with his left hand which he picked the ball up with, then brought that to his right as he also let his glove fall out of its position, clutched between his left elbow and the pitcher's side, faking more clumsiness. Tad kicked his mitt with his shoe while he stooped down and picked up a little extra dirt. The Robins fans called out a Bronx cheer while Chicago's loyalists immediately yelled back at them to shut the hell up already. A tide of brown, black, and white fedoras were in motion under the fog of cigar smoke. O'Day ignored all the goings-on and allowed for this show to get chalked up to the nervousness of a rookie. So with a smirk on his face, Taddeo fired his first warm-up pitch so hard into Killefer's waiting mitt that it produced a resounding slap. He'd thrown that ball like he'd show everyone in the stadium exactly who could play up to this level. But the seasoned catcher knew Taddeo had let the hecklers get to him already — and he hadn't even thrown his first pitch for the record. Killefer shook his head, got up from his crouch behind home plate, then jogged out to the mound, holding up his hand and raising his mask with the other to offer the sternest look that froze Taddeo. His backstop's gesture made it clear he didn't want the young arm to talk.

"Okay, Villetti. Don't you ever throw *me* sand. And don't you say anything. Just be quiet and listen. Here's how the rest of the inning's going to play. You're coming in facing off with Ernie Krueger. I guess it's baptism by fire for you today, Kid. But first base is open, so don't feel any pressure to sit this guy down. I'd walk him. Coombs is next in the order. Easy out if you don't do anything stupid. Their pitcher's not going to hit. Just throw him light cheese and sit *him* down. Then you'll have the second out — or maybe we can turn two. We both watch Krueger when he gets to First. Trust Merkle to be there as you may have to check the runner. The smart money is on Coombs trying to lay down the bunt. I've been watching Robinson signal from Brooklyn's bench. Charlie will move in shallow because Krueger's not even thinking about going all the way to Third. But I need you to bring the heat. If he doesn't think Coombs can put the wood on it, their Coach *Robber* is definitely sending Krueger to get him into scoring position. Even with one out. But I *know* I can pick him if you can get it to me in time. So now you just do your part by playing it *exactly* how I tell you, Rookie. And everything goes down exactly as I have planned."

O'Day had started marching out to break up their conference on the mound as Killefer continued to aggravate Taddeo by never showing any trust in him, and as Hollocher called out from shortstop, "Alright. Let's go Rookie."

That got under Taddeo's skin too, since almost immediately the visiting team's fans turned into hecklers all parroting him, *Taddeo's own teammate*, also calling Taddeo out as a rookie. And it was so hypocritical that it first came out of Hollocher's big mouth. *It's his first season, too, dammit.* Then that one guy Taddeo could hear all the way from left field got particularly annoying when he also capitalized on it. And this guy, a regular, who claimed to be a Cubs fan, was really loud. A Villetti would show them all who owned Chicago.

So after a few more warm-up tosses, Ernie Krueger stepped into the batter's box, boasting a .287 average and a .319 OBP. He wasn't a threat for the long ball with no home runs — so far — but the Robin had been known to stretch the ropes hitting into the gaps for doubles and even a few three-baggers. But that wasn't going to happen on Villetti's watch. Taddeo knew he could get this guy. Of course, Killefer was signaling for him to throw the safe junk, high and outside, coinciding with the catcher's plan for the rookie to pitch around Krueger and put him on 1st, so Villetti could get to Coombs. But Villetti shook off his catcher.

Killefer rocked on his ankles in his squat and hit his mitt into the ground twice while Krueger took some slow-motion practice swings, lining his bat up to connect. The Cubs' catcher continued to call for a ball high and outside. Angered by the continuing lack of confidence in him offered by just about everyone else, Taddeo wound up and brought the heat, sending Krueger *and the Cubs' defense* a message with his brushback. Taddeo could feel Killefer staring daggers at him from under his mask after Krueger dodged the pitch. He slammed the ball back to the mound and grabbed some dirt behind the dish, spit, and threw the dust down. The audience booed. A glance back at the dugout on the 3rd base line and Mitchell had sat down, combed his hair back under his cap, and began spreading his fingers out over his knees, shaking his head from side to side in disapproval. But Hoff and Trip had leapt to their feet and were clapping and gesturing until their coach shot them a look that was all it took to set their asses back on the bench. But his friends had inspired Taddeo who couldn't stop himself from grinning from ear to ear. He was going to be the rookie who takes down Ernie Kruger, Taddeo decided.

At one-and-oh, Chicago's young reliever really did want to see if he could cheat the Robbin out of his first chance at making a connection. Ignoring Killefer again, Taddeo threw a slurve, low and toward the outside, but with a good effort made to slide in the bottom of the box. The Reverend called it a ball. *God I hate that guy*, Taddeo thought. Two-and-nothing. The audience continued jeering him and demonstrating their frustration with the entire game thus far.

Krueger swung his bat, positioning it to connect with his sweet spot, as if the Robin imagined sending a roper into the gap and making the rookie Villetti look like he only had as much experience as he actually did. The fan in the left field box would just not shut up. Other members of the crowd began verbally assaulting him. Then Killefer signaled for a high slider way outside again to continue deceiving Brooklyn about the actual speed Villetti could strike with. His own plans not working, Taddeo decided to trust his team's veteran catcher, who looked like he was miserable behind the plate with Villetti on the mound, and the rookie moved his thumb and middle fingers' grip on the ball around the laces to position his hand to deliver that slider, which he'd been continually practicing his delivery on with Hoffman. Suddenly, Charlie Hollocher bolted from shortstop and ran onto the grass to approach the mound. "Hey! Don't you blow this, Rookie. We all can see what's going on here. Throw exactly what Billy calls for. I'm backing up Pete, so if you just put Krueger on, we'll get you your damned out. Trust your teammates, New Fish. Now just get us through the sixth, and maybe Coach will have the sense to put Carter out on the mound to go the final distance with these guys." He turned to run back to his position.

Incensed, Villetti could actually feel his anger burning through his shoulders and his arms. A fire was building in his neck and its angry flames climbed up his spine and got into his head. He imagined getting away with firing one — just one — right into *Hollocher's back.* Instead, Taddeo spit in the shortstop's direction while the middle infielder ran, the mound still behind him for a second. Hollocher wouldn't see that anyway, and Taddeo did need all his fielders backing him up as it were. Then a glance back toward the bench, but further beyond Mitchell's scowl he'd adopted to aim at the reliever, where Taddeo saw Hoff, Trip, and now even Trevor Bass clenching and unclenching their fists, all smiles directed toward him, while they tried to clandestinely nod their heads and pump their arms so Coach couldn't see them rooting on Taddeo. Between their enthusiasm and Taddeo's anger with the fans, his veteran teammates, and even Coach Mitchell, not to forget Hank O'Day's officiating, Taddeo drew upon all the emotional energy he was feeling. He went into his windup now, readjusting his fingers, and with absolutely zero intention of throwing that outside slider Killefer had called for. But the pitch came out of his hand with too much push from his shoulder and that cannonball that the shooter fired did break outside, anyway. And it traveled too low — once more. A professional, Krueger knew better than to swing at a two-and-oh delivery, and of course The Reverend called it a ball. The impatience of the spectators permeated the atmosphere.

It would be an easy matter to award Krueger a free base now and then face Coombs as the Cubs' catcher had planned. But at three-and-oh, Brooklyn's infielder was never going to swing. Taddeo knew he could blow a fastball by him, right down the center of the zone, and work the count back toward a position where at least the batter and Chicago's pitcher had more equal standing. Killefer was signaling again for high-and-outside. Audibly, Taddeo groaned — not that anyone could hear him against the noise of even less-than-half-full stands — booing him. *Maybe the United States* is *at war — and there are rumors of an influenza epidemic — but my hometown team has earned a lot more support than this city has decided to show us*, Taddeo thought. *The seats should be full. We're 17 and 10.* So he would attract his club some more attention. He'd be the new rookie sensation everyone was talking about. In his only other game appearance, he'd already become the media's darling for style and attitude, in his mind anyway, and the young pitcher remembered his father's personal operandi for achieving the higher status he so desired. Again, Taddeo ignored Killefer and didn't even bother shaking off his signs. And again, trumpets played, angels sang, and the Roman gods stopped everything else going on in the universe in order to watch Taddeo Villetti pitch a baseball. He wound up to throw his fastball. But he also had decided right then and there, that the catcher's strategy was sound — and the Cubs needed another win. So he'd play for his team record and put Krueger on after all. But he would do it on *his* terms. The rookie pitcher aimed the hardest thrown fastball that he had released yet, and threw it directly at Krueger's head!

When the ball's impact smashed right through the Robins' 2nd baseman's blue-billed soft cap, everyone in attendance at the stadium gasped as Brooklyn's Krueger was dropped like a sack of krout cabbage. The impact of baseball colliding with bone making a resounding crack. Villetti sneered as he watched the batter crumple, not paying any attention to his peripheral vision as he should have been when Ivy Olson, Brooklyn's shortstop and teammate of Krueger since they'd both played for Cleveland, broke from the 1st base sideline and careened into the Chicago reliever knocking him to the ground. He'd already been at the steps mentally preparing to bat after Coombs left the on-deck circle. And although Olson was first to strike back, defending his friend, and beginning to score hits on Villetti, within seconds, all the angry Robins took to flight from their dugout to dive onto every Cubbie they could catch as Chicago's players cleared their own bench racing to defend their teammate.

"Oh shit!" George Hoffman watched as Brooklyn's shortstop tackled Taddeo and then another one of the Robins' fielders pounced on him and pummeled his fist into the side of the Cubs' pitcher's head. "Tad's in trouble!" With all the velocity he could manage he took two steps at a time to launch himself out of the 3rd base dugout, and with Michael Everston right beside him, maneuvered at top speed to his best friend Villetti's defense. More of the Robbins' players hurled themselves across the diamond — and straight at them. White and blue streaks crossed green and tan ground, eager to paint it red. The audience roared with cries of exhilaration as the fight began.

"God dammit!" Mr. Mitchell expelled his exact feeling about the situation and threw his hat down as Trevor Bass, Turner Barber, Bob O'Farrell, and Rollie Zeider bounded after their youthful teammates mouthing every known expletive. Bill McCabe, Phil Douglas, Claude Hendrix and more of the Cubs pursued them. A reluctant Grover Alexander moved onto the field behind them. All the Cubs already on the field vaulted themselves towards the infield grass and ran right into the Robins as the brawl erupted.

Hoffman reached Tad first, grabbed the Robins' Olson by the back of his shoulders and threw him off the Cubs' pitcher. Running right behind him, Everston connected a haymaker with Brooklyn's shortstop's face as he was flung past him and the dark-haired youth Trevor Bass was one red-pinstripe streak on a graying uniform's blur just beyond him, as he sped into Jim Hickman and fell on top of him driving the twenty-six-year-old Robin left-fielder into the ground.

Taddeo got up off the dirt and spun around to find Olson for himself. It was payback time, but Brooklyn's 280-pound pitcher Dan Griner broke through the lines formed by his teammates for the Robins' pitcher's own protection and caught Villetti by his uniform collar and turned him straight into his right cross — knocking down Taddeo hard to land on his tailbone stunned, as the large Robin bore down on him. Other Brooklyners encircled their clash as the Cubs did the same, while many of the other position players tried to shield their pitchers. Now Mann, Paskert, and Flack had made it in from the Cubs' outfield, and looked to help Chicago's veteran infielders who already found themselves engaged. But the extra-large Griner could never be kept out of this fray if he didn't want to be and he even threw Ray Schmandt from his own team out of his path so he could personally continue exacting his punishment on Chicago's rookie reliever. Swearing, the injured Vaughn even attempted to limp past Mitchell trying to stop him, as Hippo was nearly the only Cub large enough to take on Griner.

The crowd roared in excitement as one Brooklyn fan shouted one insult at another Chicago Cubs fan, then one more after another came back, with the result being that those insults began getting traded for blows and the once-steady surface of brown, white, and black hats rocked like colliding waves as members of the audience blew into their own conflagration in the stands. The motions of their violent movement created such a rush of wind that even the ever-present cloud of cigar smoke cleared to reveal a new layer of carnage. Men struggled to defend themselves from the forthcoming onslaught of attacks ignited by other men at the same time as they also tried to stomp out the burning embers that fell onto any sections of dry wooden infrastructure that stood integrated with the steel as parts to the newly expanding sections of the stadium. Every man experienced a brief moment of fear that Weeghman Park itself would ignite. The beer that spilled everywhere actually did serve as an unintended preventative measure. Then the hint of metallic smell of fresh-drawn blood added to the pulsating air of tobacco, alcohol, and sweat.

In the middle of the melee, four seemingly brave Chicago peace enforcers raced down from the stadium's inside field-level's landing deck to descend upon the chaos in the seats. They too were punched and kicked before spectators-turned-participants of the battle could even take notice of *who* they were hitting. Rookie want-to-be detective-in-training Will Sweeney went down, struck by a two-fisted spin-thrusted into his gut and someone else's wallop to the side of the young man's head, his hat falling off under half-a-dozen stomping feet. He wasn't in an official uniform and it would have been reasonable for one of the combative fans to mistake the plainclothes junior for another spectator. Two had already been thrown completely off the terrace level, falling all the way onto the brawling crowd that clashed on beneath them. There was no escaping it. In fact Sweeney wasn't even sure what the hell the police were supposed to be accomplishing there. And how or why it got started. *Can't the medics sort this all out later?* Even small boys watching the game with their fathers were given no quarter. Not that Sweeney's particular group of lawmen worried about it. They had a different agenda altogether. But it was now a free-for-all and Cubs fans struck at Robins fans as well as the reverse with little care who they fought as long as they could fight alongside their favored ball team, feeling elated that they now got to participate in the contest as well. This ally of law-enforcement "Chicago-style" could only raise his arms in an attempt to protect his head as the rest of his body suffered a pummeling.

Then Sweeney's mentor "Chi-Town's Finest" junior Detective Michael Conway threw Brooklyn and Chicago partisans to either side of him as he forced an advance to his would-be protégé. Yanking him back on his feet and to momentary safety, he commanded, "Get to a telephone and call the Clark station. Then get word to the house by Monroe. We need backup! And after you make contact, you know who else to call. Move, Kid." Patrolmen trainees Charles Walsh and Harold Olsen tried to separate the combative fans so Sweeney had a clear path out of the seats.

Conway turned around and advanced down the steps toward the field, hoping he had a solid reason for stopping combat. "This had better be worth the money they said they'd pay me — or else they won't ever see me get involved in any more shit like this," he said under his breath. He reached the brick wall outside the 3rd baseline, untangling from the struggling throngs and threw one leg up over the short separator to make his quick descent onto the playing grass. But copying the plainclothes man's lead, both Chicago's and Brooklyn's frenzied spectators followed suit. The colors that clashed looked as if the riot would immediately spread out onto the green where the professional teams were still locked in their own violent competition. The blue-uniformed Olsen and Walsh turned around and set a fast course to defend their boss.

Hank O'Day saw the crazed mob and motioned for field umpire Lord Byron to take the nearest two available Weeghman Park security team members and rush across the grass to corral the frenzied fans back toward their seats. These riled-up one-time spectators fell on the guards and tumbled over them, pushing them into the dirt in a tangle of legs and arms, flailing as they rushed at agitated fans now coming across the field from the 1st base side.

Out on the main concourse, Sweeney forced his way in-between all the fans who'd torn out of the snack vending lines so they could also rush up the steps and out of the tunnels to join in the ruckus taking place outdoors. A glance in the other direction, outside and through the gates, away from Weeghman Park toward North Clark Street, the protégé-investigator observed about a dozen more boys and men wearing anything from suits and ties to just coveralls breaking apart wooden A-frames that had been positioned for traffic control. They saw their opportunity — probably in response to someone Sweeney heard shouting only to their own street crew: "Heads up. There's a riot I tell yous! Riot in the ballpark! Now's our chance, Boys. C'mon and get some!" But just about everyone and their makeshift striking weapons, accompanied by only everybody else, were now bearing down on the main entrance gate, clearly looking to enjoy creating the most violent type of mischief. Immediately, once aware of this, all the more sensible pedestrians started to scatter, running away down Addison toward Sheffield or straight back into the ballpark, adding their numbers to really overwhelm the sparse crowd control. Some sought safety, others sought different opportunities. The security and the police present, turned to the defense of where the most money was at: inside the stadium, with the wealthiest spectators who financed the team. The streets were abandoned to now succumb to anarchy.

As fast as he could, Sweeney reached a phone inside the front security office he was granted entry to with his provisional badge and then placed his first emergency call. Suddenly the glass window he looked out onto the street from was shattered by some kind of hurled debris or another. That caused him to jump and almost drop the microphone stand. But the telephone switchboard operator got through to the closest substation. The youngest member of Chicago's law enforcement's ad-hoc intel team could now only plea for assistance as he witnessed a throng of rough-looking characters swarm the neighboring ticket office and break open the entry to steal the cash box and raid the ticket rolls, hoping to illicitly acquire their admittance to the remaining games of this Chicago home-stand. Of course the looters then instantly took to fighting among themselves, fans competing with opportunistic thugs who hoped to resell their score.

Right about this time on the field, Taddeo was smashed back down under Dan Griner's impacting force, with all the large Robin's significant weight behind him. The Cubs' pitcher opened his mouth to cry out only to scoop up a newly created stew of soil and bloodied grass that his teeth clasped onto as his jaw clenched in pain as he rolled on the field while his ribs got pummeled on both sides. Suddenly, the blows stopped as Tad looked above him to see his friend Trip flying overhead. He had pushed off with his feet into a diving tackle of Griner, but then Mikey's own teammates Les Mann and Max Flack grabbed him and yanked him backward so Killefer caught him only to get in Everston's face as Fred Merkle covered the backup infielder's six by punching down Robin center-fielder Hy Myers before he could move in on Trip or Killefer himself. They were sure yelling at each other about something but Taddeo couldn't hear anything over his ears ringing from what the opposing pitcher had thrown him. The Hoff was suddenly there checking on Tad and exchanging thumbs up, then spinning about to go rescue Trip from their own teammates. Trevor Bass swept in, also backing up his friends and pulling Tad off the ground. Turner Barber had just rushed Griner along with Dode Paskert to help hold the largest Robin back. Having just got back to a secure standing thanks to his outfielder's assist, the current Cubs' pitcher's now-clearing vision let him see Robin 1st bagman "Gentleman Jake" Daubert sprinting in to finally settle things with Chicago. This would be some serious trouble. The rest of the Cubs players were distracted.

"Oh no you don't Everston! You haven't earned any right to touch Griner, New Boy!" Killefer's voice finally became audible, scolding Trip who grew red in the face as he got dressed-down before everyone on the field that day. "Rookies do not punch veterans — even the other team's. Not ever. Now back the hell off and Deal and I will have to handle this mess that your idiot pal Villetti's made." Max Flack finally spotted the opposing baseman and turned to face Daubert.

Just then, and down the street from Weeghman's main gate, the sound of their roaring engines attracting his attention, Sweeney saw two of the black Nash-LaFayette Motors cars speeding toward the massive stadium melee. Each prototype vehicle could carry four more officers and then some on their running boards who belonged to Chi-Town's Finest, adding more than a dozen other policemen to reinforce the authority's manpower on the scene. As if that alone would do any good, considering the size of the crowd that had gotten into it. But Chicago's Volunteer Fire Engine Company followed, some water tanks being maneuvered in on wagons drawn by visibly frightened horses, their blinders slipping in the mad rush as their masters' hastened towards what they hoped would become a flood of compensation. They labored fast, too eager to get their steamers ahead of the city's mainline personnel who were coming in on larger motor-driven trucks that were slowed by the melees in the streets. That figured. The city could be sued for running over pedestrians with their heavy American LaFrance engines — but wild horses could not. Women were not even safe from those rushing in under the impression they were there to save them. Because some first-responders would use the opportunity to assault *the ladies* as their first response *to them.* But when the regular line firefighters could actually reach the fray, some of these new combatants would assert control over the volunteers for certain. There was money in it. So to his relief, Sweeney would expect them all to turn their water hoses on the violators of the peace at any moment. But he smiled to himself as he imagined that very soon his own comrades would brandish their night sticks and also get *their chance* to beat this anarchy into submission — and make their own little profit while they were at it.

A very worried-looking small and older man who Sweeney never regarded as being up to the task of keeping the stadium's security, struggled with his arms outstretched to the fullest extension as he tried to dig his feet into the cement flooring and hold the door to the security office shut to protect the acting-peacekeeper as he'd made his urgent phone calls. This guy's boss, also in the little room, was busy holding a reddening handkerchief over his eye that had been cut by the flying glass. Sweeney estimated he had but only seconds. The frenzied mob on the other side was doing its best to force its way in as its members had with the ticket office. Switching his widened eyes from the door back through the broken window, he had to use all his strength to push a rioter from trying to climb through the jagged opening. Ignored had to be every bloody scrape and even deeper cut, which couldn't be allowed to interfere with even higher additional profits. That's when Sweeney saw that even Acting Police Chief John Alcock had arrived on the scene to rush out of one of the new cars. It would seem that *all hands* were needed as the unmistakably dark skin of the well-known Officer Grace Wilson moved into motion directly behind him trying to defend *her* commander, and the infamous Alice Clements burst from another car, also immediately following after them. The last would spell more trouble for Conway as that one had a reputation for not tolerating her fellow officers earning anything on the side from Chicago's *leading families* that always sought to order the police into what they determined as their proper place in The Windy City's hierarchy. It was all right. The majority of the profit would always make it to the very top and those who were there would threaten any integrity beneath them to keep secret, those values buried *that way*. The low ranks could keep any tickets they could confiscate from the looters they busted, and the fire department's men would get theirs, too. But Sweeney's unit had to earn a larger paycheck. He turned away from the amazing view of all that action and grabbed the older security man's shoulders to pull him from the exit where the acting-peacekeeper would then fight his way back up the tunnels to reach his mentor on the playing field. He had to tip off Conway that the supervisors from the department were here or there was going to be even more trouble than there was already, if he could imagine that. But he and his boss wouldn't jeopardize their opportunity to bring themselves even more green. So once the door fell open, he threw the old man to the mob using him in a sacrifice play so Sweeney could escape past them. Weeghman's security man's screams chased after him.

"I don't give a shit. You'll have him back out there to see him *at the very least* finish this inning. That's what's been paid for." Det. Conway was ordering the Cubs' Fred Mitchell and the game's governing official Hank O'Day just as soon as Sweeney was able to come within earshot of his very loud and vocal boss. "And *I'll* see to it that you won't be mistakenly picked up with any of the others who are going to finish this game — in jail."

"Christ," Mitchell exclaimed while O'Day gritted his teeth and shook his head at the ranking detective — still quite some years younger than he was — while Sweeney finally made his way through the brawling fans security that the lake city's other police were trying to grab and force to hold their hands behind their backs while they corralled them off the field. Walsh and Olsen circled Conway while he held his impromptu conference with the Cubs game officials. Sweeney also passed many a player from Chicago's bench who were likewise being held back by others amongst their own team members to keep the hot-heads out of any more trouble as additional cops entered onto the grass.

Damn!

Chief Alcock's puffed-up blue-coated chest decorated with ribbons and medals bore down on them with Clements and Wilson hustling in tow and his big mouth announcing to his men, the acting-commander proclaiming from still several dozen feet away, "That's right gentlemen — and ladies — once we take control of the field, the rest of them in the stands should all settle down, losing their inspiration *or influence* to fight this fight *inside* of Weeghman, and then with the help of the fire department we'll eventually be able to retake control of the streets."

The immediate plan seemed like it just might possibly work and Sweeney's mentor Conway didn't need the very green and wishful-detective's help noting his superior had arrived. The slightly older copper involuntarily gulped, and then nodded and with his jaw tight, his eyes intense, he stiffly shook hands with the still much older Mitchell and O'Day right before Alcock reached them and gained any knowledge about their conversation on the infield grass. "Everything seems under control now here, Boss-*men*. So then I must insist, let us finish the game."

"Indeed. And so we shall."

Trevor Bass was the only one of Tad's teammates available to offer him a hand getting up, while Hoffman glared after Dan Griner, making sure the tough guy allowed stadium security, accompanied by several more of his own teammates, to guide him back and away from the Cubs' relief pitcher. Chicago's larger outfielders also stood guard and made sure that's what happened. The fight was nearly over but Taddeo enjoyed seeing Mickey Doolin and Jake Daubert gang up on Charlie Hollocher and punch his own team's shortstop in the gut so hard, Holly dropped to his knees as the wind was knocked out of him — and Tad could only hope — maybe some of his attitude. The Robins were laughing. The rookie should not have engaged Brooklyn's veterans. Deal and Paskert came upon the Cubs' other rookies and passed them quickly to now go and help Hollocher. Then Trip drew Tad's attention as he shook himself free of Leslie Mann and Max Flack while simultaneously Hoff spun away from Merkle's control and took custody of Michael Everston so that together they advanced to group up with the closest of their friends. "Somebody-he-knew" was usually needed to settle Trip down. In that second was when another glance back revealed Brooklyn's still-brawling fielders finally discovering all the Cubs had reverted their attention toward those guys specifically, so Daubert and Doolin got the heck off of Hollocher, and summarily retreated toward their dugout by 1st, backing up so as to maintain their defense between their teammates and Chicago's. Deal helped the team's other Charlie. Concurrent with this, Brooklyn's manager Robinson was scolding his boys all the way along their return to their dugout. Trip had only just reached out smiling as he placed a reassuring hand on Tad's shoulder when their own manager started screaming at them from behind. Turner Barber got behind Taddeo and gently but firmly turned him to face his coach and make sure Tad listened to the instructions given him.

"You three, rookies! Get the hell off this field, right now! — or so help me." Coach jabbed his pointing finger at Bass-Man, Trip, and Hoff. "And Villetti — ." The lanky outfielder made sure Tad could not look away from their manager. "You stay right where you are. You. Yeah, you smart guy. You fucking stay! Can you finish this inning?"

Taddeo's eyes found Fred Mitchell through his still slightly blurred vision. Dan Griner had done a good job on him but he was still so excited he got to play. "Sure Coach, I — ."

"Then do it. I didn't ask you to say more than one word back to me. All I wanted was a 'yes' or a 'no.' I've heard enough about too many other peoples' assessment of your pitching. Miraculously it's been agreed upon to not toss you out of this game, or out of this stadium and into a jail cell where I think you belong. So now you'll just get me two more outs and then sit your butt back down on the bench while Carter finishes the game and then I *will* spend a lot more time paying attention to *you* Villetti. And that won't be a good thing. Of that you can be really sure you little shit. Now move!"

A little while still had to pass and all the cops finally exited the playing area before the Cubs and the Robins would retake their former positions on the field to finish out the top of this sixth inning. There was obviously enough money in play to ensure that this contest would go on. Few if any arrests were made in the stands and the audience was never evacuated, unless acute medical attention required it. Krueger also decided he could still play and took his position as the runner at 1st base, his teammates giving him high-fives or patting him on his shoulder or his butt. With even all the old hands experiencing fresh new pains, the next three and a half innings were to then play out like one really long game everyone longed to retire from.

Chapter 3

"Okay. Let's go! You, *you*, and you. C'mon." George Hoffman pointed while directing his voice toward some of the youngest men changing their clothes in the Cubs' locker room.

"Yeah? *Where* are we going again, Boss?" Trip asked, tossing him a smile.

The Hoff returned it back to him. "Just *out*. We need to blow off some of that post-game steam." He buttoned his shirt and gathered his gray sportscoat, fedora, and tie off the bench.

Michael "Trip" Everston laughed. "Yeah, that's one way to describe it. So, have you got somewhere *else* in mind, yet?"

"Nope. We're going to Villetti's."

Trip sighed. "Shit. You *still* want to talk to Pitch *right now*? Don't ya?" the backup 3rd baseman asked him, scratching his blonde hair, nodding his head, and then rolling his eyes.

"Well, that's not *all* there is to do around south of the Levee District," his friend grinned. "There's blowing off steam. But, yeah. We're his teammates, Mike. We're going to talk to him. And somebody's got to," George said.

Killefer overheard them and snorted. "Yeah rookies. You go on and do that. And I hope you enjoy your trip to the wrong side of town. Don't say I didn't warn you, either."

George turned to regard him as Michael spun around and closed in on the veteran leader of the team asking him, "What? You mean *you're not coming*?" feigning curiosity, very poorly, and pretty much only for appearances' sake. At least Trip could say he tried to *seem* respectful of Chicago's real "number one" behind the plate. *A professional* is *owed that*, George supposed. Killefer was the league's No. 1 rated defensive catcher. *Even if he is a jerk.*

"I've got my Maggie and a family in Pennsylvania that I hope to go home to, New Boy. You just got here from Marshalltown — and about almost yesterday. My guess is your eyes are so full of Big League dreams, you don't even have another job yet. Your backup game plan. Yeah. Anything else to do before they call you up to go fight in the war? Any *other* responsibility to take care of? Nu-huh?

Thought so. Well, you thought the Robins were something today? Then good luck with the Germans." He winked. "They're even tougher competition.

"But you make sure you go on and talk to the new pitch, first. You *really* should do that. Cause that's *you* being responsible," Killefer delivered an intentionally fake smile he sent over Trip and on to his backup-for-his-backup catcher. "Isn't that right, *Coach*? Huh. Well I really have a young wife, a true young love to feed there. And in order to do that, I've got to increase my value in The Show. That is a lot easier to do if I play for a winning team. And a team that's got some *skill* and some men — yeah *men* — who can stand tall and handle the top tier pressure, and not make me look like *I'm the one* calling for that amateur crap I witnessed from behind the plate today."

"Really? Well we all *do* have second jobs here, Golden Glove," Mike retorted, continuing to stalk right into the senior player's face, but one of the younger-though-veteran outfielders Leslie Mann quickly moved to intercept him. Still, from past the regular player's shoulder, Trip continued his declarations, "*And* we *all* want to make baseball our full-time career." He laughed, "We all want to be just like *you*, Killefer. But we all are going about it like we're *on* a *team* and not just in this for ourselves." Everston's intense blue eyes sought out Vaughn who'd just limped in to gather his personal things on the other side of the narrow locker room. "And just because you're mad at Villetti, you don't need to take it out on the rest of us. We all fought hard to get here."

"Alright, quit it. That's enough," Hoff told Everston walking up to place a calming hand on his shoulder. But Trip rather aggressively shook himself free of his friend's hold. Adopting a softer tone, George said, "Hey. We're still the new guys, Mikey, remember?"

"Well, you new guys should know this: we *all have* fought hard. In our many and some quite personal ways," the *real veteran* Grover Cleveland "Pete" Alexander said, backing up his own catcher. "And maybe in different arenas than some of you others. But this is a new season, and we have to come together and start all over again. And yes, adjust to playing with each other as a team. Now consider what being a good *teammate* actually means." There was a moment of silence paid to respect *him*. Of course there would be.

Then Les Mann, easily hearing every one of them as he was much too close to this, having already stepped in to end this argument, spoke over Trip's shoulder to address The Hoff, "Now *we're* going to handle this from here, *Captain*," he said. He referred the rookie to all the veteran ballplayers who'd assembled around the new guys, but he also specifically directed his voice over his own shoulder toward Killefer, while the large defender put his hand on the young new infielder's shoulder, hoping his intervention would help settle Everston down, as well as the rest of the excited emotions flying around the locker room that afternoon. The Cubs had already been through one big brawl with the Robins. There was no need to start another amongst themselves in their own clubhouse. But many other players *had* started gathering around, tempted to see or even participate in yet another fight. Their loss that day having further energized their anger that now motivated them.

All the while George had seen Mann start to look uncomfortable as soon as this group had begun to collect around Killefer's locker. But Mann wound up being the one large enough — and brave enough — to step in between Trip and the starting catcher. *Or was he just stupid enough?*

"We're just going to talk to the new kid. That's it. I'll go along. See what's going on in his mind." This time Mann overtly steered his voice back toward Killefer, while involuntarily trying to see over his own shoulder, hoping he'd catch some glimpse of approval. Mann had obviously decided that adding his voice to back Hoff's plan would lessen the perception of the rookies all being isolated, and all too-easy targets to be picked on to vent the senior players' frustration. Or for the rookies directing their impatience and alienation they were experiencing since being brought up to the Big Leagues back upon the veterans, who were supposed to be mentoring them in the first place. And George knew Mann was young enough to probably remember his just-being-brought-up like it was yesterday. The outfielder could empathize with the rookies. And this season especially, there were more new additions to the roster than was customary. On almost every team. The War's effect on life at home. It certainly made its impact in the Cubs' clubhouse that afternoon.

"We're happy to have you come along, Les," George told him.

"Then *you* set him straight," Paul Carter the relief pitcher spoke to Les Mann from a safer position, halfway across the narrow locker room. His choice of words were picked deliberately such that they'd help, but also so they would not give away any perception that he'd take his lead from anyone but a fellow veteran like Killefer. All the other players had stopped what they were doing and were now watching. He lit up a cigarette and took a puff. "I always like coming in with a lead — never taking the mound to come on and clean up some rookie's mess," he explained for everyone to hear. "And so does Hendrix — especially since he's 'sposed to be a starter. But boy is he *not* happy today. But when has he ever been happy about Villetti? Now as to the both of *you*?" Carter looked from Everston to Killefer. He shrugged his shoulders and turned the palms of his hands outward. He knew everyone was paying him their full attention. The reliever's performance would now bring some relief to the tension. "Well, maybe you're both right," he said, "but only partly. That's the dilemma. See, I *do* play for the team, and *we*, I mean those of us in this clubhouse right now, *are* all the real team. But I also have to stand behind a *personal* record to help me achieve some success in this profession. I have to make a living. And I don't need that screwed with. Ever."

"Well, every game, we all want to go out and play our best," George replied to him.

Fred Merkle's and Charlie Deal's slight nods signaled their reserved approval. Max Flack rolled his eyes and looked up at the ceiling.

"Speaking for *all* of us vets, I wouldn't expect any less," Les Mann tossed a smile around the horn. "But I can see that we all still have plenty to teach you youngsters."

"But hey. Would everyone please stop for a minute? Isn't this dangerous? I mean this plan to travel to the South Side. You said it's not so smart — us all crossing the river to go talk to Villetti." Trevor Bass, still in only the shower towel he'd wrapped around his waist since rookies had to let veterans use the facilities first, interrupted, only to bring up another angle to the subject. He stood looking for Killefer's guidance to still be extended to any of the other rookies who would listen to him. "I mean I want us to play well, but I also want us to play smart."

Silence ensued again as his teammates paused to regard this youngster on the roster, each full of their own thoughts, but all absent of any expression.

"Well, I don't see a better choice. I gotta do this," George said, interrupting the quiet.

"Yeah. Uh. Well then, I guess you can count me in too," The Bass-Man echoed the leader he was still most used to following. "I'll back you up like I've always."

Looking at his teammates, Trip nodded to indicate he was participating. "Yeah. Of course. Me as well."

Then Killefer shook his blonde head and looking down at his feet said, "Yup. It figures. And all of you had to know that this is exactly what would happen, now that they've let the Italians into the game."

Chapter 4

"Really. Well, we're not going to *kill* him. He's gonna live — to pay."

"C'mon Greg. Don't let that bonehead waylay this fella right in front of all my friends. Let me keep what little respect I have with my team."

"Relax there, Tad." The middle brother in a gentleman's hat, suit, and tie offered his similarly dressed but much younger sibling a reassuring pat on the shoulder, while his voice conveyed his usual condescending tone. "The lesson we're going to teach the butcher is *all about* respect. Then all those micks Papa lets you throw away your time with, are only going to respect you more. Urso's *Family*. Now, you respect your eldest brother's play."

"Uh-huh. And yah believe that they even respect *you*?" Taddeo never even waited one beat to retort. He addressed a thinner, shorter, slightly older version of himself. "They're afraid of our family. That's fear, Greg. Not respect. What you're doing is intimidating. There's a difference."

"We call it earning. And the people here respect us, even thank us, for easy lending, and thereby helping create businesses, income, jobs, classing it up around here. Providing some actual entertainment a man can appreciate. Trying to make something more out on the South Side. That's more than what I can say for what the shamrocks have built then left to rot up north of here. Now that Merlo has conned that green prude O'Banion into standing still. Stagnating and getting old while he arranges flowers, Hymie and Bugs lose patience with him, and the Genna Brothers eye the Irish real estate from the Near West Side. It's only a matter of time before this whole town explodes. And now the little leprechauns have gotten all jealous of the party we've been throwing south 'da Levees District. So our family is staying sharp. We could find ourselves targeted as well. Instead of playing defense, we need to play offense. So you better watch your back when you're uptown. But what do *you* do about it, Sport?" Greggorio laughed. "You play the same child's game without a care in the world like you always have — all your short little naïve-from-being-sheltered life. I suppose you think throwing it away in a stadium instead of on the street is going to make you famous? Isn't that right, *Tadpole*? Build yourself a legacy? *Papa* is going to be famous, have a legacy. One day, he's going to be the mayor of all Chicago. You might have one good season, Pitch. But you're a joke. Don't believe me? Come with me. Right now. *Papa* wants to explain it to you. Very clearly."

Greggorio shoved Taddeo in the direction of a window booth that looked out onto Taylor Street, near the entrance to the modest-sized green, red, and dark cherry-wood lounge. The young pitcher got in a quick glance behind him over at the smoky bar where his friends had just started to gather. Changed into their street clothes, they'd already begun ordering their drinks. He really didn't want them here, but nevertheless, Taddeo felt flattered and proud that his teammates — even a few of the starters — had all rallied to come support him after the argument with Mr. Mitchell that had resulted in his tantrum and storming out of the Cubs' locker room that afternoon. But because he believed in his dream — to one day become the leader of this squad — Taddeo felt all too embarrassed by the way his family was now treating him right in front of his teammates, and even some of their gawking fans who were gathering around, trying to approach a few of the players, hoping for an autograph. Weren't all the regulars *here* White Sox partisans? It was rare for folks to see so many of Chicago's National League team on the South Side, but Taddeo was relieved to also see that no one was actually watching *him*. In this moment anyway. A lot more eyes were concentrated on the scantily clad cocktail waitresses his father had dressed in salacious approximations of that late-breaking flapper fashion that had started to make its appearance among the youth. As long as their costumes showed a lot of cleavage and leg. So who could blame the men? He had to admit he too found the liberated appearance of the women enticing and he should have guessed his teammates would've been all too preoccupied with the girls and their revealing quite a lot of pink flesh for *some skin show*. But Taddeo was already used to seeing the almost bare-naked ladies, as he lived among them and returned to be around them nearly every waking hour he wasn't on a baseball diamond. So he did not plan to pay them much mind in this particular moment, not with another confrontation with his father only seconds away. But then a stunning red-haired girl caught Taddeo's eye and held it frozen, at least for a second, until his brother gave him a forceful shove along — Greggorio also having noticed his youngest sibling's fascination with someone who appeared to be a new philly in the family stable. His brother stole a second glance at *her*. And he smiled.

Brought up to the booth where Sigñor Villetti was sitting with three other businessmen, more specifically other Family members, intently staring out the window onto Taylor Street, his father instantly turned around at their approach and offered up a warm grin, delighted over discovering the presence his two younger sons. His color seemed a little pale while he straightened his charcoal suitcoat and tie, and as Greggorio removed a cigar and a tool from his pocket, cut his smoke and lit it. Taddeo's brother seemed to be gloating about something.

"There he is! There's my boy." Beaming with renewed energy, the athlete's progenitor reached out to squeeze Taddeo's arm. "Fine work you did out there today, Shooter. Fine work."

"But we lost," Taddeo voiced a different assessment to his Mustache Pete style-sporting, salt-and-pepper haired father, with matching chin-whiskers that'd so far survived in his own game so as to see the end of his fifties. His wrinkled face testified to it all taking its toll on him far too early. But his papa looked as if he would also turn green in that moment and grabbed for an empty wine glass, the only convenient receptacle immediately on hand in case he was going to vomit. He coughed instead. Maybe he wasn't expecting his youngest son's battered appearance after the fight.

"That's alright. You're new to playing at this level. But that arm of yours is like a gun! And I can see you've finally been taking to my lessons I've been trying to teach you all these years — about how I'm wielding *my* guns — making my own way out here in Chicago — and now you're applying what you learned from me, into one hell of a performance at *your* game; you make a father proud." His old man took a deep puff off his cigar and broadly smiled with sincere satisfaction while he studied his boy, swollen lip, puffy cheek, and two black eyes; a true brawler at last.

Taddeo looked at his father incredulously while he could almost feel Greggorio frowning behind him, obviously disappointed that the Villetti patriarch might hold no plans whatsoever to give his youngest son a good dressing down, and surely jealous of his sibling receiving so much of his father's affection. Greggorio and Urso had always been treated only as well as underlings in The Family organization.

"You know, I have the little nigger Lamont report in every now and then so I can check on how you are doing," Rinaldo Villetti explained. "The child loves it when I don't make him work and instead, I treat him to passage all the way across the town so he can take in your ball games. As any eight-year-old should. I can be quite generous that way. And now, for today at least, you have really earned my approval. My favor. But, oh," Villetti suddenly seemed to remember something and pointed toward nothing out in the dirty air he blew in front of him. "Remind me to pay a personal visit to that all-too-opinionated sportscaster they have chippering away over there at Weeghman. It came to my attention that some things were said about our family — and your fortitude on the mound — that I did not approve of. And I will correct that. Plus we will make sure The Family has final approval on what they print in tomorrow's *Examiner, The Herald, The Times*, and *The Tribune*. But oh-no. Actually, I'm too busy to go across the river. You'll see to that, Greggorio."

The middle son shifted, digging his shoes into the green carpeting, having to make an effort to contain his irritation over his new orders. "Yes, Papa," he reflexively mumbled with no enthusiasm.

"Now what I heard that I liked, is that when things got tough, you took your competition *out*, Taddeo. You ignored all the ignorant hecklers and everyone else who doubted you, and you threw at that Robin's crown, sending a message to all the New Yorkers, and proving to an audience that without question, you *are* your father's son." He took another puff from his cigar again, as the other gentlemen sitting with him did with theirs. A dark cloud of smoke hung above Taddeo's patriarch's table, as everyone evaluated the young athlete. "You really did make me proud today, Boy. Really proud."

Greggorio's scowl grew even deeper and his eyes narrowed. Taddeo blinked and his mouth dropped open. The smallest motion now hurt his bruised face.

"But right now I want you to feel proud about your family. Please. Watch *me* throw a pitch," Villetti said. He puffed on his cigar once more then nodded to outside the window, where a group of men in suits and fedoras led by Taddeo's oldest brother were moving at the quickstep, storming down upon a merchant dressed in bloody meat carver's coveralls and a crumpled chef's hat and walking exactly the opposite way — meaning directly toward them. The gap between the men rapidly closed as they came upon each other. They threw their cigarettes down on the ground. "I've been staging my own rookie tryouts," the senior Villetti laughed. "Ya see, Colosimo has bestowed his compliments on the way our family's been handling our streets that he made *us* in charge of taking up the collections from. D'Andrea approves. And even while he's been in prison in Atlanta, New York's Sigñor Peter Morello has stayed significant, powerful — and rather impressed as he follows the news regarding Colosimo's entertainment enterprises coming out of Chicago. And so it would seem that *we* have been entertaining the Don while he serves what he says will be only a temporary sentence. He's getting out and he agreed to help Big Jim defend us against The Black Hand — an unfortunate business consideration we all must be wary of in these times — and who knows? Maybe even a racket his lieutenant Masseria is running himself, passing orders to Cardinella. But from this late-breaking progress, your new Godfather in Chicago is generously allowing me to expand The Family's operations outward, just through the South Side — and just another few blocks for right now. Managing it for Colosimo so he looks good, above-board. And though it's one step at a time, your papa will be made a capo eventually. Maybe soon. But everything about the rates we actually charge for our protection business has to be kept quiet right now, while on the side, and thanks to your uncle here," Rinaldo Villetti nodded at the middle-aged man he sat with, "we'll continue to collect even more than anyone realizes — *quietly*. No big demonstrations of bluster. No. Not in the least. Not at all. Because what I'm really collecting — along with a promotion — is power — more power for *our* immediate family. Today I subtly took back complete control over Taylor Street. And shored up *our* levees where the Irish tide had been slowly eroding Colosimo's holding back of that green mold that drifts across the river. But as you can see, some people still need to drink in that idea." Tad's father motioned outside the window.

Taddeo saw the gentlemen conversing, their hats moving in turn when each would speak, and some of his oldest brother's muscle move around and behind Mr. Kean O'Rourke. The butcher looked furious and had obviously dropped everything at his work to storm down Taylor and confront Taddeo's father. He would never get that far. All the while the men had started arguing, pointing their fingers, his patriarch continued briefing his youngest son. "Meanwhile, as our earnings will once more grow, so too must the payroll. Fortunately, my other secret enterprise affords me the ability to hire more men, and not let that increasingly higher tribute our house must pay forward to eventually the Don, interfere with my maintaining my capable and ever-ready personnel here. Urso's going to test out this new goombah Dulio and see if he's got the balls to take on our old friend the butcher. Show *him* how *we* tenderize our meat."

Taddeo sighed. Well aware of how embarrassed he was to have all his new friends watching firsthand the way his family made their living. He spoke weakly, motivated to try and change his father's mind about continuing this course of action, well aware it was far beyond too late to stop the shakedown from happening. Taddeo wished he knew even less about his papa's operations. But wishing for something *from this family* never made it a reality in Taddeo's experience. Still, and unfortunately, he was compelled to say something. He couldn't figure if his father was being cruel — or senile. However, Taddeo knew that if it were both, things could get even worse. He chose his words carefully. "Papa, remember you squeezed the butcher *last* week? This is really none of my business, but *he* is not going to pay again. After Urso saw him, I don't know if Mister O'Rourke's even got anything left in his till."

Villetti snorted. "We only squeezed him a little bit. He qualified for our insurance at the new *re-introductory rate special*. That's exactly why I know he *can* pay more, but that's also the reason why I know he'll resist paying more. Kean's a proud, stubborn fool. His is one of the last Irish-owned businesses to remain in my territory. And I've had previous dealings with him. If I allow him to grow even an inkling of confidence that he can stand up to me *now*, he could lead the rest of the shopkeepers in a revolt. I need to slam O'Rourke down hard, immediately, publicly, and dispel any notion of his that he'll win any fight for independence on my newly reclaimed turf. Maintain our house's control permanently this time."

"Yeah, real quiet-like."

His papa ignored the comment. "And now one of my other new rookies can get a little on-the-job-training in the process." But Taddeo wasn't sure if his father had really been thinking about his new man, Dulio, or perhaps Taddeo himself with that comment. His old man went on. "You just watch. The butcher is about to fight back. He still carries them brass knuckles under his cap. Some while back, your brother found out the hard way 'bout that."

Taddeo saw Greggorio smile to himself and he recollected the men dragging a bloodied and unconscious Urso back to the family home two years ago. His father had come to tend to his injured son immediately. He displayed his concern by throwing a bucket of cold water onto Urso where he'd laid sprawled out, bleeding on the floor, and asked him where it hurt. When Urso came to his senses and pointed at his jaw, his father summarily kicked him there, hard, and in triplicate, then lifted him up and threw him out their back door. He instructed his oldest son not to return until he had collected what was owed by the butcher. It had taken days before Taddeo saw his brother again while Urso recovered, and then, somehow, finally became successful with that assignment. After his brother's eventual return with some real money, his father had then personally gone to pay the butcher a visit himself, and following their meeting, that particular butcher shop had been shuttered for over a month. Taddeo remembered having to ride his bicycle quite a few extra blocks when he helped his mother by going to fetch her fresh cuts when she was still well enough to help prepare the family's supper. His trip back into nostalgia ended abruptly when his eyes refocused outside the window, and locked onto the back of Urso. All the men were less than a bit of a distance away now. They'd stepped off the sidewalk and into the middle of the street. Cars had to either stop or maneuver around the men, honking their horns. His oldest brother pushed another young man in a suit and a fedora forward, and made impatient gestures between the recent recruit and the butcher. "You're going sit and watch while you let your new guy go and get his jaw broke? That's big of you." Taddeo couldn't help but risk the comment escaping him and irritating his father.

"Well, if it comes to that, then he deserves it. I need men who can take care of themselves. *This* isn't a game." Villetti, un-angered at all, responded with soft spoken words to his youngest son. Then he coughed, involuntarily.

Taddeo let out a grunt. "So where'd you find the new guy?"

"I hired him to fix the plumbing," his father now laughed. "The man complained he wasn't earning enough. I know making it these days is tough. So by my generous compassion I'm already so famous for, I offered him a better job. So we'll all see if he can find a more creative use for his two-and-a-half-foot basin wrench." Villetti nodded out the window toward the man who wore a long coat in spite of it being one of the warmer spring evenings in what passed for "downtown" South Chicago. But the times were growing colder with each passing hour. "He's a horrible plumber anyway," Sigñor Villetti commented. "Now when the butcher goes to make as if to scratch his head, he'll reach under his hat. Watch for Dulio to see if he suspects what's coming and then reach under his own coat. I don't want O'Rourke to think he can disrespect our family if I put someone new on the Taylor Street insurance payments just because I need your brother to move over into other, newer territories to continue on with some of the more lucrative kind of newer-yet-still-older collections that will really impress the Don when he gets free to go back to New York. Plus we need a cover story for our house's own more-profitable side-businesses, which I don't need none of them knowing anything about anyway. For one thing, it allows me to hire more men. But it was the praises Morello lavished on the Chicago operation that were what convinced Colosimo to consider promoting *me* in the first place. As far as Big Jim is concerned, I earned them to *his* benefit. And D'Andrea listens to him whenever they're drinking together. Which is often. So I can't waste a better-timed, more interesting opportunity to serve my own benefit — our house's benefit — now that *I've* finally got one."

But Taddeo wasn't feeling interested. What he felt was disgust — and hatred for Morello — this Peter the Clutch character he'd heard mentioned more than a few times before — and whomever else he didn't even know of that originated out of the powerful and elite of New York's underworld, and commanded so much clout that they could manipulate his father's life — and thereby Taddeo's entire family's life, even in Chicago — all the way from an Atlanta prison cell. Not to forget how angry he was with his *dear old Paps* — and even more so — for being involved in this in the first place. Just by even being in business in The Windy City, his father had to ally himself with Colosimo whose well-known easy-going appeasing nature might bring about the selling out of all of their lots to the Easterners, especially this extremely ambitious Masseria, while Taddeo knew his father had deliberately relocated their family to Chicago in order to escape all of that in the first place. Even Taddeo knew that the members of the older generation who still did things the way his papa counted on them being done, like Mr. Morello, could be on their way out. The talk was there because after all, The Clutch had been in prison for a while. And the status quo had angered those who would step in to take his place. They were rumored to have a different sort of way they wanted to do things. And now Rinaldo Villetti's son was angry, at least enough to embarrass his father in front of his uncle, his father's uncle, and a teenage cousin around Tad's own age, who sat with his family's patriarch, all dressed to appear like they were legitimate businessmen. Taddeo didn't really know them, and even though he'd get curious about who comprised the rest of his family, he'd more often prefer not to know them. His mother had warned him about that. "Screw this, Papa. You're the one who needs to wake up to a new idea. Colosimo's platitudes come with you getting to pay Morello's bill. Anyone can see that they're given away for free as long as the money keeps coming out of here. It's not making *our family* any richer. And I don't have to stand at your side and watch this shit. I have my own career to worry about. And Greg, just back the fuck off! Now everyone, get the hell out of my way!" Taddeo shoved aside the middle brother and started to storm off. However, his curiosity had already gotten the better of him and he had barely taken three steps away from his family's table, when he heard their laughter. That agitated Taddeo to become just curious enough to turn around and see what all the noise had been about.

It turned out the laughter had nothing to do with him.

O'Rourke had indeed gone for his set of brass knuckles underneath the butcher's hat and swung them in a roundhouse aimed at Dulio's skull. The plumber caught his arm at his opponent's fulcrum point and wrapped his elbow up so fast that the new worker's wrench glanced off the Irishman's wrist bone before his eyes could register the tool-turned-weapon had even appeared. His body bent down reflexively as the butcher winced in pain, losing his weapon and grabbing his superficial wound while Dulio dropped his wrench to grab O'Rourke by both shoulders and push the meat-man's wide face down into the plumber's rising knee and throw him backward. The pair of goombahs behind him were in the process of catching the ricochet of Villetti's plumber, but O'Rourke used them to bounce off of in the reverse direction from Gervasio and Vitale, grabbing up and swinging the goombah's own wrench into Dulio's skull and then kicking him, bending his leg down awkward from the knee as the plumber connected with the street. O'Rourke took another shot at him before Gino picked up the Irishman's brass knuckles and caught their former owner with a right cross to the meat chopper's jaw. Between that strike from the his left and Urso's punch he laid into on the right side of his back, O'Rourke started spinning right into the path of oncoming traffic. A driver blared his car horn and tried to swerve and at the same time cut his speed. But the butcher careened into the common Model-T and as his teeth connected, three were extracted on its raised headlight mounting as he fell down with his chest barely brushing the car's front engine grill. The vehicle raised on aftermarket replacement wheels traveled almost safely right over him, only the low hanging differential smacking him in between his legs as he screamed. But Kean O'Rourke survived and the scattered Villetti enforcers who dodged the car regrouped to gang up on the man who was down for the count clutching his balls and erupting blood from his mouth where the automobile had very visibly wounded him. Urso led Vitale, Gervasio, and Gino in kicking him until the Irishman lay motionless. Tad could see his brother then yelling at the injured Dulio, who managed with some considerable trouble to pick himself off of the street and at Urso's vigorous beckoning, helped Vitale scrape O'Rourke off the road and begin to move him around some now more cautious traffic and back toward the Villetti's establishment. Drops of blood glistened even from a distance as they leaked out of the most active participants of this fight onto the street.

Even more disgusted and sorry he'd now have a hard time forgetting what he'd seen, Taddeo made his way back toward the bar where his friends from his ball club sat. The entire team wasn't there but those who had come had very nearly taken up every seat around the bar. Many of the scantily wardrobed flapper girls pawed at them, adding their soft kisses to some of the roughed-up baseball players' new wounds, waitressing being only their *second* skilled occupation.

But as Taddeo feared, most of the guys had been watching the latest fight. "Holy shit! Did you see that? The meat packer just got turned into ground beef!" Charlie Hollocher said, moving his head for a better view outside the window and around a particularly youthful looking blonde wearing pink, the material almost so thin, that everything about her could be seen right through it.

"Guess the ways of the world had to be explained to him *Chicago-style*. Ain't that right, Pitch?" Tad's friend Trip smirked, then took a drag off his cigarette.

"Huh." Taddeo growled as he ranged back to the barstool the rookies saved him and joined the other members of his team he was the closest with. Meanwhile, he kept his eyes busy looking around everywhere else except outside the front windows, trying to locate the saucy redhead he'd noticed earlier. He'd love something *that interesting* to distract him right about now. However, he could not find her again among all the other working girls in his father's establishment that evening. Instead, he was immediately poured a glass of wine by the dark-haired lady bartender who smiled at him.

"So is *that* what you were trying to emulate when you threw to Brooklyn what you offered from the mound today?" Charlie Deal asked, taking a drag from his cigarette, his face squished into a critical expression reflecting displeasure and glancing around for any backup that could be awarded by some of the other veterans from the team who had joined them for libations. "I know Killefer didn't call for that headhunter you fired into Krueger."

"No. *He* wouldn't. At least he wouldn't call it from me." He could feel Hollocher watching for his reaction. The shortstop holding his position like his stock was so valuable as to earn him a seat with the veterans. Tad coughed a little from the smoke and tried not to inhale.

"That is for sure. He only wants conformity out of you right now. And so?" the starting 3rd baseman pressed him. Behind him, smoking, Les Mann looked on.

"So? So I threw what I had to throw him. There was one out but first base was open and with the Robins' pitcher coming to the plate next. Killefer wanted me to put Krueger on anyway. *I was trying to* save *the game*. But no one thought I was ready to face another Major Leaguer, especially our catcher, or *you* Hollocher." Taddeo squinted his eyes at the young shortstop. "*I remember*. That, and Killefer thinking Krueger would hit off me. As you made it clear that you thought that, too. Plus The Reverend wasn't going to give me any fair calls. Nope. Not a rookie. And on top of that, do you think *Krueger* actually cares if it's in the strike zone? I'm familiar with his reputation. He wanted to jump out on top of a new fish. So Killefer was right. First base *was* open. But the last thing I wanted to do was look like I was pussying-out — confirming what just about everyone in the stadium already thought of me being the new guy, unable to handle any pressure in only my second appearance with the Pros. So I had to put that Brooklyn bastard on no matter what, and I counted on you guys to back me up and not let him or anyone else get any farther. So I hit him."

"Yeah. That worked real well," Hollocher spoke up. He'd been letting his actual veteran teammate take the lead in Taddeo's debriefing since he knew the rookie pitcher didn't care much for him. He'd been right since Taddeo had decided to start off by verbally attacking the Cubs' shortstop the first chance he got, anyway, carrying over their non-overt dispute from on the field that afternoon. Now he'd fight to defend his position.

"Well Tad, you gotta admit things didn't go as *you* planned them. Instead, Robinson advanced Krueger and shook you up good while you were busy getting Coombs out, and after you threw that headhunter and caused a bench-clearing brawl that spreads from the field to the seats to the streets. And *that* shook us all up. Literally — man, you just gotta love that part," Trip announced. "And so the Cubs have our very own rebel son."

"No Everston. *I* did not love that part. Instead of encouraging him, try seeing that stunt Villetti pulled today as almost getting *me* put on the disabled list in the first month of my first professional season!" Hollocher let his anger burst. "Justify that," he said to Mike. Then he turned toward the rookie pitcher. "You're a real wise guy, Taddeo. You know that? You obviously *do* take after your family in the end, don't you? A *true* Villetti. The vets do wanna win — and they've already established themselves. Meanwhile, I'm sure you've had it in your head to prove you can just instantly play up to their level since all the way back to your last season in the mud fields," Hollocher continued. "Throwing like you did out there today? But you haven't earned that right. This isn't Iowa, goddammit! And it's definitely *not* all about you, Taddeo. What about me? This is my rookie season, too. I don't have a golden arm like you do, Villetti. I only get so many at-bats and so many fielding opportunities to prove *myself* to Coach or I'm not going to get to stay on the team. I need to find my way to some kind of record-setting season, not Cook County Hospital."

"Will you take it easy, Hollocher?" Trip tried to calm Chicago's agitated shortstop. "I'm sure you'll make a record debut. We're going to go all the way this season, right guys?"

"Yeah Team! Go Cubs Go!" Turner Barber and Leslie Mann rallied in unison, clanking their hi-ball glasses. They'd been rather quiet thus far, the more senior players observing the rookies working their issues out. They came along to guide their thinking, but only when necessary. Their other teammates and Villettis' patrons alike applauded and whistled, lending their support to the cheer.

"That's the spirit," said a new voice. George Hoffman, the Chicago Cubs' new backup-for-the-backup catcher had only just re-appeared. Tad smiled upon seeing his best friend.

"So where were you?" Mann asked him. "I thought it was your idea for us all to go out drinking tonight, *as a team*, together, after the game? And at Villetti's, especially."

"I was here," The Hoff smirked and stole Turner Barber's shot of whiskey the bartender had just poured before the outfielder could snatch it. He raised the small glass up in a salute aimed toward one of the blonde girls who had joined her lady friends smoking by the back wall. She smiled with her eyes to kindly acknowledge his gesture. "I was practicing my game — *with Chastity upstairs*. But when you all had *just* left, Coach wanted *me* to hold up."

"You sure that's who held you up?" Turner Barber asked, shrugging off Hoff's act of entitlement toward his drink with a good-natured smile and signaling the bartender that he needed a new beverage. Hoffman offered him a light for his cigarette in order to show him the deserved respect.

"Yeah. *He* wanted to talk to *me*." Hoff knew what Barber was alluding to. "And he was asking about *you*." Hoffman nodded toward Taddeo. His face reflected a more serious change of demeanor. "And Bill Killefer was also there, waiting to ambush me." Hoff paused and glanced out the window, nodding in that general direction and raising a finger to point. His mouth hung open for a second then puckered to let a single whistle escape it. But then his hazel eyes changed their focus and the large blonde man spoke directly to the Cub's youngest pitcher. "He really doesn't like you, Tad."

"This season's already just full of surprises, George. You can see that *I'm* truly shocked."

"Sure you are. But what won't your new good buddy go through for all of you guys? — though we'll get to that. So," he said, "I actually did still arrive here before the rest of you screwed up the nerve to cross the river, and that's how I also came up with the time to find some fine recreation and relaxation, upstairs." He smiled. "Stress relief. Great place your Papa has here, Tad. Yet before we're done speaking about ambushes, I gotta ask just what the hell just happened out on the street?" Hoff still tried to see out the window and nodded in that direction again.

"That's just another part of the entertainment the South Side provides," Trip said.

"Well, I went outside and down the back stairs before I re-entered the building through the front foyer. At least I was being discreet — just like Mister Mitchell coached us to be. That's one lesson I'll leave this season with. But someone left some blood smear from Taylor to the door, and then tracked it all the way around and back into the alley."

The other fellows' shoulders shook as they exchanged glances and snickered. But Taddeo didn't join them. Displaying the exact opposite reaction of his teammates, the pitcher explained, "Just never mind that. So now the rest of you all have seen? This is exactly why I wanted to drink at *any other joint* instead of here! I really need to get out of this place. But now I'll let that be your choice." He looked around at all his assembled teammates who were there. "If you actually want me to listen to you while you run any more of this unnecessary post-game analysis by me, then we can be honest with each other *there*, instead of even have to think that you owe my family anything for your recreation." Taddeo now also nodded in the direction out the window to the bloodied street. "I couldn't have that on my conscience."

"But this *is* your papa's place? And would you look at the women!" Trip replied, almost all the other members of their team nodding in agreement.

Hoff smiled broadly. "Oh I have been doing more than looking!"

While the others laughed, Taddeo allowed himself to sneak a smile that he hid by glancing around for a second, secretly agreeing with his friends while shaking his head. "Yeah. It is definitely my papa's place, but you of all people should know, when you have to slide home, you should *never* count on being safe." He was about to continue the conversation, his words aimed directly toward The Hoff, hoping his best friend would relent and help him out *here*, when Tad finally spotted that fascinating little redhead again. Distracting him once more, she looked amazingly tantalizing. And she gave Taddeo an idea. With his thought to make some good use of *her*, Taddeo could also win his struggle to gain control over *all* his immediate priorities and that brought him back to his conversation with his teammates. He had a just come up with a new plan, only now their outfielder was speaking to him. Taddeo made a little more effort and found himself able to impatiently listen to what Turner Barber had to say, faking his respect for the veteran, while in actuality, he impatiently waited to throw this next pitch in his own signature style.

"Well, it's not just *my* post-game analysis," Barber said to Taddeo, "What is known for a fact is, there are a lot of guys that just do not like you, Villetti."

"So I've heard. But how many times do I have to apologize to everyone, Turner?" he angrily asked the outfielder. "And for what? Being Italian?"

"No. For being a rookie. But I think you're learning a lesson, New Boy. Then you can affect some changes. Make an adjustment. Play for your teammates' priorities. Understand they're different from what's expected to be *the team's* priorities. That's the owner's priorities, not the players.' But what you also really need to learn is that behind your back, a lot of members of our club are always talking pretty bad about your entire family. And it's not the Italian thing. It's that some are saying it was only because of your father, and who *he* is, that you even got called up in the first place."

Taddeo had previously overheard mumblings in the locker room to the effect of "how they now they have to let the dagos play." But that also, he got his spot on the roster since he was "one special wop," and it was an offensive reputation that he preferred to do without.

Yet Hoff was quick to contribute to his friend's defensive record. "I caught for Taddeo in the Minors. He — all of us — are a little nervous when we're just called up and new to playing here. So were you vets at one time. But while on the Ansons, it's what we all worked so hard for, and I saw — and Coach saw, what Taddeo did out on there on all those mud fields. He was an ace."

So Barber continued, "Hey. *I* know you earned it, Tad. You've been developing your skills. Some of us just want to see you — and you too, Hoffman — develop some better judgment. This isn't Marshalltown. Some things are going to have to change. We're going to play on a lot of diamonds — and most of them not in your family's neighborhood," the outfielder explained. "So Coach is going to be most comfortable giving the relief duties to Carter. He also doesn't want to hold Alexander back from his wartime duty and then have him over here just to further damage his psyche and expend his arm too early in the schedule — especially if we get our bats going and rank this year so as to contend for the postseason. The papers are even predicting this season as *ours*."

"Chicago's papers," Charlie Deal got away with saying, unacknowledged.

"But Killefer hating your guts, Villetti? That's one fact that's never going to change. Still, that you've got talent is undeniable, by that Minor League record anyway. And they all must admit that their first thought had been that they'll need you in the pen. Hope that remains the truth for you. So make it happen and just do what we're all counting on you to do out there."

"Well, you can count on this as being undeniable, too. The feelings between me and Killefer are mutual, Pal. And every pitcher can only throw his best with his preferred partner in a battery. I graduated the farm system with *you*, Boss," Tad nodded toward The Hoff. "And you're the one I gotta play with 'cause when a crusher like Olson comes up to the dish and we have a situation like this afternoon, you already know what *I* want to throw."

"Yeah, throw us all into some deep need for medical attention."

Hollocher scowled, adding in his dry commentary before the catcher responded.

"Hey. Take it easy already. We'll beat those Robins down." And Trip added, "They haven't got anything on *us*. Look at their record so far. *We're* definitely not in the sewer. I've really got a good feeling about this year, too. Us Cubbies are still five and a half games ahead of them. We've got the right young energy and if we only get our veterans to accept us," he shot a glance toward Leslie Mann, "they already play professional — and with all that combined, all of us *will* get the job done and keep raising our value in the standings. At least it's not us that's in last place."

"Be mindful of who you're calling *us* Cubbies. So far, you've gotten to hang around here only a few weeks. Just keep hoping that Mitchell and Weeghman let you stay. And don't go telling *us* how we should *get it*," Pete Kilduff, the proven star 2nd baseman spoke up, rebuking him. He took a drag off his cigarette. "Rookies don't own that privilege. And we all have to be doing it *right* this season. No question about *any* call." He flicked a bright red ember off the tip that bounced on the bar top. "When we win, we have to win a fair ballgame. Not with more of this shit like what we played out there today," the infielder finished. "Maybe we even deserved to lose this one? And it's exactly all this kind of bull that's making my insides ache." He started back on his cigarette again when his speech ended. The lady bartender slid an ashtray over to him along with a cold stare.

"Well, what do Merkle and Paskert think?" Mike asked the veterans.

But Charlie Hollocher answered Trip. "Huh. They're both vets now. And Merkle made history with *his* rookie error with New York the other year. That means he did learn something and both he and Paskert are also smart enough now to *think* whatever Coach thinks," Charlie reasoned. "So is Flacky."

"So they pretend to be," Les Mann educated him.

"And are *you* not learning anything, Holly?" Barber asked him. He glanced at Deal.

"Well maybe they deliberately try and just seem like they're agreeing with Mitchell," Hollocher equivocated. "And so does *this* rookie." Turning on his barstool, he hopped off his seat to position himself right in Taddeo's face to save his own and jab his finger in the young pitcher's chest. "As for you — ." Then suddenly his eyes darted back and forth nervously and his lip trembled as he caught sidelong glimpses over at the front booth that were just long enough to observe Villetti's next older brother, Greggorio, in motion, turning in his chair he'd brought over to his father's table, and glaring in Hollocher's direction. The shortstop swallowed, remembering where he was, and stepped back toward his barstool. "Uh. Yeah. Well I forgot what else I was going to say." The very young-looking blonde that Charlie had been consorting with also looked toward the front booth and receiving an almost imperceptible nod from the Villetti brother, then walked around the bar to return to occupying herself with once more affectionately pawing at the Cubs' shortstop. Their almost-married shortstop.

Also having noticed — and expected — Greggorio's ever-so-subtle interference in what was to be his teammates' private affair, an irritated Taddeo interjected. "Well, *I* am sure Merkle and Paskert *are* thinking about their families. *That's hard to avoid.*" The pitcher cleared his throat as he too looked in the direction of his papa's table. "And no one can afford to be benched or worse yet, fired by the team. So what I've learned is I'll just have to watch myself and put you all, my teammates, as individuals, and my real friends, my real family, even ahead of our collective record. I 'spose I shouldn't even ruin any more of our wunderkind Killefer's great stats, as I know some of you guys *do* have kids to feed. That's why some of our other boys aren't here right now and already working their second jobs. I know that and I know I don't want them also working at hating me. So I hope this is settled and I agree to play in the best interests of both all our personal records, and subsequently the team's record, all at the same time, as much as both are possible. But from now on, I *will* play for *you*, my teammates, before I play for our owner or any of our fans."

"Yeah? Then this *is settled* as far as I'm concerned. I mean I guess — with you thinking like that. All *is* settled then, right? And that's all *they* wanted to hear. Right?" Trip made a sweeping gesture with his arm to indicate the other players, hoping his declaration was good enough for the veterans. Hoff looked on with interest to observe the others' reactions as well. So did Trevor Bass. "As for me? I was lucky my boss at the mill let me have this evening off to hang out with all of you. He's a fan and I'd asked if I could make the phone call as soon as I'd learned we had post-game plans," Mikey said. "He's encouraging me to bond with my new team. And so I'm also fortunate enough to also be able to bond with another beer. Maybe find a woman — a real *South Side girl*." He grinned.

"I've heard about *them*. But you're one real lucky man, Tad. Your Pa owns a place like this. You can *settle* for the truly good life. And you don't even have to work. Not many of us could live off just what Weeghman pays this team."

"Me neither," Taddeo shot back. He'd been wanting the others to know this about himself. "So let me tell you all something. I am *not* just hanging around waiting to collect my father's handouts. Soon as something works out, I've also been looking to hire on for a second job myself. Make it on my own like everybody else in our lineup does. I'm not going to be any different from the rest of you. You're my *true* family now," he repeated. Trevor Bass nodded at him in a warmly offered approval. But Taddeo's eyes kept straying to the pretty redhead. She, along with some of the other ladies, were leaning against the food service counter where the black cooks placed the rather simple dishes on Villettis' menu when they were ready to be delivered to their waiting customers. But the establishment had already seen its busiest hour for the evening following the game, while the players had still been at Weeghman being yelled at by Mr. Mitchell. The girls appeared to now have some time on their hands.

Hoff grabbed him around the shoulders and raised his hands to grab Tad's hat and mess up his hair. "Aww. Ain't that swell, Tad? But I've had my eye on the ball and noticed that it now looks clear to me like you've already got *your eye* on where you'd like to start *another* family," his friend quipped. He'd obviously noticed Taddeo struggling to stay focused on the conversation while his attention kept drifting back to the pretty redhead.

"Yeah. You caught me." Taddeo now rolled his eyes. "Listen fellas, I just *gotta* go and meet her. I wouldn't mean for it to go that far, in the family sense George, but that girl is like — whoa!"

While his teammates chuckled, some raising their glasses in toasts to his success, Taddeo strode forward toward the unavoidable object of his attention, even surprised with himself that he was *this* confident, in front of his teammates, and especially his brother, and even his father. But in spite of his teammates' intervention meeting, Taddeo was still feeling pretty good about *all* his decision-making skills since well before this evening got started. He *did* have self-confidence and trust in his own judgment. And that new plan to get the guys far away from his father's bar. Meeting with this girl was part of it. Over his shoulder he tossed a last word to his friends, "You know, I'll go invite her for a night out on the town with *all of us*.

Finish your drinks and pay what you owe, then we'll *all* get far away from here. And," he added conspiratorially, "I'll be asking if she'll bring along the majority of her girlfriends with her." That earned him a roar of approval from the bench.

Chapter 5

As he crossed the room, Taddeo felt relieved his cross-examinations were over and he was all the more eager to forget about this day and greet such an amazing and exotic Celtic fairy like the red-haired girl now before him. He still felt plenty restless and anxious to persuade his teammates to leave his demonic father's drinking hole. However, he was also very unprepared for how forward this mythical Irish enchantress — or spellcaster — would be upon his now hastened approach. The girl, barely covered by a tiny red body-glove of a sequin romper with a black form-fitting top with tassels, sensed his proximity before he arrived, reached in her oversized blood-red, sparkly purse for what she required to light up a new cigarette, and took a puff. And when Tad could finally pull his now-blackening, puffy eyes up from their travels over her long, trim pink legs, the two of them made direct eye contact. And neither one of them could look away.

The girl's lady friends dispersed as if on cue, leaving the two alone. Taddeo swallowed, then closed within comfortable speaking distance. The girl was so seductively dressed, as if she was apparently prepared just for him, and exhaled a ring of smoke. She started with the greetings first. "I can do something for you Mister Villetti?" she said, though it didn't sound like she phrased her words like they were a question. Her sentence was spoken quickly and her speech was feminine but sharp, delivered with a signature Irish accent.

"You know my name?"

"Did you think I was just going to wait around here, feigning ignorance to *pretend* that I'd actually enjoy *your* making a proper introduction? I know who you are, Mister Villetti."

Taddeo's wished-for-dream of gaining fame as the new hometown hero on the mound came to sudden focus as he imagined this girl was impressed with his work out of the Cubs' pen that afternoon. "You've seen me pitch?" He ignored the pain as his eyes widened with excitement.

But the lenses that would magnify his yearning for glory were quickly shattered when the girl with the hair of fire snapped back most directly, "No. But I heard you're a loser." Then she exhaled. "Although I could care less about the sports page. I'm not here for *my* entertainment, Mister Villetti. Ha," she laughed without smiling. "That's for sure." She looked at her almost bare feet while she paused. "I work for your father's paper." She raised her green eyes to pierce her protective cloud of smoke and meet with Taddeo's confusion.

Wait. Taddeo's father didn't own a newspaper. The Family's business associates were always running around at night, still trying to control them, and *who* published *what*, and who was able to sell it. Taddeo's father just ran a bar and restaurant the local "businessmen" would sometimes use as a gathering place. Then Taddeo realized the girl meant she worked for his father's money when she referred to his paper. "Oh. You mean you're a waitress. I get it."

"I'm a hostess," she corrected him. "And no. Clearly you don't *get it*."

"Ah-hah," he paused. "That's very progressive of you." She was gorgeous, in fact exotically intoxicating to Taddeo, and confusing, but sardonic and pointedly disrespectful even if she could deny it and explain it was just her poor choice of words that made her also so instantly irritating. All at once Taddeo felt fascinated by her and at the same time was feeling all the confidence he wanted to display in front of his brother, his father, and especially his friends, rapidly dissipating. And he knew he looked like a mess after that intimate introduction to the Robins. So now, whatever would come from his meeting with this girl — no, in fact something more closely resembling his *confrontation* with this young woman, he'd rather the rest of it not be going down under *their* watchful eyes. But he didn't have that choice.

What Taddeo really desired was to escape away from all of them right now, even if he had to back off, not getting the gal, and instead getting himself intimidated by only one little red-headed hostess. In his papa's own place. Truly embarrassing. *I could tell them she is married. But my family would know the truth and none of the guys on the team would buy that, what with the way she is dressed and where she is working.* And Taddeo didn't even know the young lady's name yet. On the other hand, he hadn't formally introduced himself either. *But what good is being a known name around here if I can't make the most of it?* So when he offered his invitation to her, this *hostess* reminded him of that fact. And even when the hapless Taddeo had so carefully phrased his dialogue: "Say, it's kind of emptying out around here, and I'm sort of friendly with the owner. So, if I could get you the rest of the evening off, would you and your lady friends want to go out with me and my teammates over there?" Taddeo gestured back toward the bar. All the ballplayers *were* definitely watching the rookie, and all of them now smiled, saluted with their drinks, or started winking and waving, black eyes and swollen, bloodied knuckles. *At me or the ladies?* Taddeo resisted a quick impulse to seek the comfort of his teammates' support by meekly waving back. Which was good, for he noted that Hoffman especially, was indeed waving *at the women*, his eyes now on a brunette who'd joined a lot of the gals on the other side of the bar where they had resettled themselves to mix drinks and gossip, after having departed to let Taddeo and the new hostess converse alone.

"You don't waste any time with your predictable delivery. I'll give you that. Only got *one pitch* in your arsenal, Ball Jockey? You still haven't even asked *my* name," she said.

"Oh. Right you are," Taddeo blushed. "I'm — ."

"Mister Villetti. I said I knew that. Remember?" she interrupted him. While she smoked her cigarette, her eyes glanced over toward Taddeo's father's table. Her jade irises in motion, the young man didn't need a look to confirm that when her pupils paused and expanded as they focused, they likely had connected with someone still seated over in that devil's den by the window. His papa or his brother? Taddeo sighed. He didn't even care to know. But what he did want, was to have some fun after one really long afternoon at the ballpark. So far, only the Robins' fans had surely done that. It had supposed to have been Tad's glorious second chance to pitch. But his day just wouldn't go as he had planned. The rest of Taddeo's family wouldn't bother him over what he did now — and with whom, to them, was probably — and only — just another saloon girl that he did it with. But this young woman was his best immediate option, her friends a distraction for his teammates to get them to leave, plus she *was* extremely enticing to the young player, and had been since he'd first spotted her. Taddeo sensed that somehow she was special. He needed to win this duel and get at least her smallest interest in him on the record. It was a place to begin.

"Call me Tad," he said, shrugging his shoulders. "That's what my friends call me."

"Well, *Tad*, don't you usually know *your friends'* names?" she quipped back.

"Uh. Yeah. So are you going to tell me your name or will I have to guess? You should know I'm a relentless pitcher." Through his fat lip, he smiled weakly.

"I'm called Arlene, *Tad*." She introduced herself with a very much intended tone of insolence. He cautiously took her hand in his.

"Well, uh, that's great. Do you also have a proper last name, Arlene?"

"If I did, you don't need to know it. Besides, there's nothing proper about me and my lady friends going out for a night on the town with you and these other ball jockey friends of yours you have over there." The woman withdrew from their brief contact.

"Okay. So you're *not* going to accept my invitation?"

"I didn't say that," Arlene responded. She blew her smoke in Tad's face and he blinked.

"But you're worried about what my father might say?" He coughed, choking on her smoke.

"No. I'm not at all worried about what your father will say, *Tad*. I'll collect my coat and my friends now. So let's go."

Quickly, a full-toothed smile of relief broadened into an open-mouthed one of anticipating excitement that Tad hurled across the bar to his ever-ready catcher, along with beaming wide eyes and two thumbs up. With a new spring in his gait, he crossed the saloon heading back toward his elders' table.

"Papa. I'm going out with the guys. Some of the ladies will be going with us. Okay?" He announced to Rinaldo Villetti, though his short speech ended with a question. He felt the eyes of his relatives he really didn't know, scrutinizing him.

"I don't mind," his father said. The patriarch reached for a pocket inside his coat and brought out a money clip. Peeling some paper bills from it, he started to pass the money to his youngest son. Then he snatched it away as Taddeo reached for it. "What I do mind is your insolence. I do not have to tolerate that, even from my own son, and no doubt because you think you're just so special. There will be a penance to pay. But for now — here." He then placed the cash in his son's hands. "This will entertain the boys. As they entertained more than just Chicago this afternoon. By that, I meant I was thinking about New York. Hah. You all showed them. And so I'll demonstrate my appreciation, to you and your teammates now that all our family has gotten a good look at them. And you'll tell them I'd enjoy seeing them back across the river again. They are always welcome at Villetti's."

"So I can drive them in the car?"

"Uh. No. I don't think so," his father answered.

Suspicious, Taddeo asked, "Yeah? And this money? Is this a loan or a gift?"

"It's cab fare. That's one thing it is."

Taddeo caught his brother using his cuff to wipe his mouth, most likely only dirtied by his expression he'd been hiding. "Just remember where that money comes from. That way you'll remember to also entertain your family some more by doing a little *actual work* for them now and then," Greggorio stated, as he inhaled from his own cigar and then dropped that hand. His other rose again as he pointed with his finger. "Not only your friends' amusement, but their very safety tonight, is bought and paid for by your brothers' sweat and blood, literally, to say nothing of our papa's." He nodded toward their father.

Yeah, well I gave up sweat — and blood — today too, Taddeo thought. He then realized that by favoring a window seat, Rinaldo Villetti must have enjoyed taunting the Irish, in the event Hymie Weiss, Bugs Moran, or one of O'Banion's other goons dared to come across the bridge and drive past The Family's establishment. He admitted to himself that his security, the very roof over his head, the food on his table, and even his personal protection as a player called up by a team from Chicago's North Side that required his safe passage across the river nearly every day — depended all upon the fortitude of his papa. Competition for territory was deadly. And Taddeo worried a little about the strength of the latest fragile truce and even for the senior Villetti's health — and his current safety — if his papa was nearly half as important as he liked to imagine he was. Moran probably wouldn't even bother with the old man, as Villetti was small time in the much larger Chicago Italian organization. Plus Hymie Weiss supposedly held a strong leash on him. But Tad still worried about his father, his only parent he had left. Until his papa spoke, once more annoying him.

"But your brother's right of course," Villetti pronounced. "Very soon I want you to start going out with your *other* teammates, your *real* siblings, and learn to be a part of what this family is all about." His father spread out his hands to indicate The Family members seated with him. "Your being *my* offspring has provided me much amusement over the years, but now that you've become an adult, you must be reminded that as talented a ballplayer as you may be, your family has provided you with all you've ever had, and all you ever will receive. To my credit, I am seeing to it that will be more than you will ever want for."

Taddeo wasn't sure what his papa meant by that, but that ever-expanding smirk on Greg's face only added to the pitcher's irritation that he wasn't running this home game.

"Well you should go on and have some fun with your little friends," Villetti said. "I'll worry about business for now — and how I'm going to exploit the opportunities and weaknesses given up by our dear Colosimo. You had an instinct for this, Taddeo. You see that Big Jim knows not what he did — getting in bed with New York. Your brother here has been working on setting up a meeting between your papa and the Unione Siciliana's favorite talking heads of Chicago. I'm making sure Mister Merlo and Mister D'Andrea see *my name* rising on *their* roster. So I'll let you know how and when you can play ball for your papa." Rinaldo Villetti smoked from his cigar while his eyes continued to assess his youngest son, as did his great-uncle's, his Uncle Delasandro's, and his cousin's.

This all now sounding more alarming than reassuring, Taddeo excused himself from standing before his father's court. He thought even handling another interaction with Arlene would be far simpler than managing even the smallest detail in The Windy City's complicated politics.

"See what I just did?" Rinaldo asked of his other son once Taddeo had passed beyond earshot. Greg nodded and Villetti continued. "He accepted my money as a gift, and now he will owe us. He will owe me."

"We all already owe you, Papa. We always will."

"Yes, but I've come to realize that your little brother's perception between fantasy and reality has never matured as fast as his suggested golden pitching arm. Yet all his skills need to be honed."

"I think the first would be most useful to cultivate," Greg said dryly.

"There's time. So we will see," said his father.

"Yes. We *will* see." Greg smoked his cigar.

Chapter 6

Now how are we going to play this, Villetti?" Hoff asked the reliever, who let out his breath he didn't know he'd been holding once he and eight of his teammates plus the eleven lady members from Villetti's more-than-full-service staff came out to join him while their afternoon ended on the plank-boards that formed the temporary sidewalk outside his father's saloon. There were some reparations that still needed to be made.

Taddeo found he could recall his ability to smile. "Now we get ourselves to the next party! And so there's what, twenty of us? We'll need to signal for at least four taxis."

"Oh my. This is so-oh outrageous," said one of the youngest and most-beautiful dark-haired girls with some kind of silver head chain. Trevor Bass squeezed her matching bracelet-adorned arm and when she looked up at him, his bright smile reflected similar sparkles. With the enthusiasm of someone a little toward the youngest end of the spectrum of ages for all these fairly youthful girls, she exclaimed in a Brooklyn accent, "I can't wait! I feel like I get to be in a parade."

"Yes. I'll bet it's your first time in a car that doesn't stay parked," Arlene retorted. "But trust me, Darling, this will be more comparable to a funeral procession," the redhead mumbled as she joined the rookie pitcher by his side. "Just give it a few more minutes."

"What?" Taddeo thought he misheard her.

"Never mind."

"Good. Now let's have some fun!"

"Is the circus in town?" Trip asked.

"Yeah. And you're starring in it, Junior," Pete Kilduff told him.

"You two stop," Mann interjected. "This is a team bonding night."

A brown-haired girl wearing a feathered hat, gray tied-coat and who-knew-what-if-anything underneath, folded her arm under his. "Great. I'm on your team now, Handsome."

"Well, the circus acts are lit up at night. They go on for much later than our games. Past dark. There's fire dancing and Joe Skelton's clown-family act. And Peter Taylor then bravely steps into cages with real lions and tigers."

Nineteen heads turned to stare at Mike. "Do you have a second job as their announcer or something that we didn't know about?"

"What? I'm a big patron of the arts."

"Yeah. You've established bench-warming at Weeghman as an art," Hollocher teased him. The girls giggled and Trip turned red.

Then he slid over and stole his prize from the inattentive shortstop who was preoccupied with taunting his own teammate and seeing if everyone else was paying him their attention, rather than on Michael, who had just appropriated his date. Trip hooked his arm under hers saying, "If I'm allowed to play, I can definitely get on."

"What? The disabled list?" The shortstop turned it around, reacting late to the play which Mike just executed. His face reddened as the others tried their best to keep their laughter to themselves over Everston stealing on him.

"I said stop it," Mann told the rookie. "*You're* very lucky you *did* make it onto the field as a starter Charlie — and that you aren't the one just called upon to be a pinch-hitter yourself. Don't embarrass your teammate."

"Yeah. Why don't *you* get on base more often instead?"

The veteran scowled in disapproval at the rookie who overestimated his place.

"Well, at least Charlie and Trip are both now turning a bright enough shade of scarlet that maybe a passing driver will see one of them," Hoff interjected. "*All* my teammates still need a ride. So do we just stand here taking shots at each other or did anyone call for cab service?"

"Do they have a dispatch for that?" Trevor asked.

"This is Chicago. We're in the big city. Horses and buggies now have a number at the switchboard. I'm sure that someone who can afford a car has a phone extension."

"I have a phone extension," another considerably young and medium brown-haired girl in a rich white coat and matching hat piped up.

"Everyone in Chi-Town knows that, Honey," Arlene quipped. But the girl took the ribbing with a sense of humor and giggled.

Then the brunette took Turner Barber's hand in hers and smiled at him. "You can reach me at Villetti's," she told him.

"We are still *at* Villetti's right now," he responded as if announcing the box score from out of left field. The sun had sunk fairly low between the buildings of southern Chicago's skyline.

"Yeah. Um, oops. So I'll just go back in for a minute and make the call," Taddeo offered.

Then five black cars appeared down Taylor Street. Tad wasn't sure if they'd been there or not as he only noticed them when their headlights attracted his attention. Had they been there already, their lights *off*, engines *on*, waiting? It felt suspicious. But the vehicles approached the walk outside his father's nightclub and slowed down, the driver of the lead car waving, his sign he was an incoming friendly — with a dark gloved hand. This made the reliever uneasy all over again, but a gentleman who appeared to be approaching middle-age offered a kind of forced smile as he became visible through the window when an impressive Studebaker touring car stopped in front of their group. He raised his voice so he could be heard above its growling engine and asked, "You boys must be the baseball team I got a call about. And these ladies must be your friends?" as if this new fella already didn't know the answer.

"You got a call? About *us*?" Taddeo asked him.

"That's great," the always too good-natured Hoffman offered from their group. Tad wished his friend hadn't spoken up so soon, so he could figure out who these newcomers were and what might be happening.

"I heard it from my little brother. So I thought I'd help him out a little. I'm Salvatore Genna. But you can just call me Sam." Tad gulped upon hearing the family name. "Some of my family's about to relocate here and I suppose we are going to be neighbors now. My brothers and I," he nodded over his shoulder while using their Americanized names, "especially James back there, have been interested in a piece of real estate down street from you, over toward Halstead." Genna smiled more genuinely. "We were in your part of town to look our new investment over. Is one of you Villetti?"

Tad had to respond since all his friends' eyes went to him. He felt the tension of the older players — who would know enough to become tense — increase its presence. "I am," he announced himself.

"Your brother is a friend and thought you might have more fun if you didn't burn up all your recently acquired fortune with cab fares. We happen to be headed your direction. And my siblings Michele and Angelo are about your age." He nodded back behind his car. "We're all big fans of Chicago baseball, especially the youngsters, and I'm sure they'd like to meet you. Why don't you go say hello to them? They're in the last car. Meanwhile, all of you kids can come along. We can take you out for a good time on the town. Want to head into The Loop? You'll be safe traveling with us." He studied

Taddeo's bruised face, evaluating him and his friends, all quite obviously wounded from the fight with the Robins. "It looks like you could use the protection."

"That'd be great!" Hoffman exclaimed. "Show us the way and we'll show you a party."

Taddeo groaned. Deal and Kilduff turned to the reliever for him to stop his buddy the rookie backstop from calling their game, but it was already too late. The Hoff caught one of the Villetti hostesses on each arm, and made to enter the first car. "Thanks Mister Genna. I'm George Hoffman and this is Jasmine and Delilah. We're the life in this party." Behind him he yelled back, "C'mon Kilduff. Grab a gal and show us all you still know how to have a good game." Tad knew better than to underestimate his best friend. And still this was happening.

Arlene stayed by his side and took his hand, to Taddeo's surprise and pleasure, while they watched the rest of Tad's teammates and their girl co-hostesses each board another of the Gennas' vehicles. He caught an exasperated look from Turner Barber, who abandoned his formerly reluctant look and then returned nods with Les Mann. At that point the outfielder and his lady friend for the night hung back, almost as if Mann had determined Barber would enforce some adult supervision over the relief pitcher and *his* new lady-friend; as they walked down the line of vehicles to board that final car, this black Oldsmobile 1910 Limited, which was the only one to generously offer a ride with *two* Genna brothers. Tad saw Mann following his buddy Trip and his new date. Then the athlete paused as he overlooked the youngest of the newcomers.

"Well get in," said a man barely older than Taddeo with a sharp chiseled-flat face, sitting behind the wheel. His skin was shaved smooth and his forehead stuck out further than his small chin while the muscles in his cheeks were taut and seemed to be held in place with as much pressure as his near perfectly ridged shirt and suit coat collars. His hair was oiled without a flaw into place. He had the appearance of someone intent on doing a job, not going out to have a good time like his oldest brother had suggested. Taddeo didn't feel right about he and Arlene sitting up front with him and moved ahead of Barber and his girl to take the back seat. Now one position to the vehicle's rear was already occupied. The youngest man they'd seen — one just about Tad's same age — sat in the back wearing a dark flat cap. He had large intense eyes, set close together, and his eyebrows nearly met above an angular nose. His beard growth was maybe several days old, unshaven after his sideburns ended at the bottom of his earlobes. He was not dressed in finer clothing like his brother and his posture and the most minute movements of his chest and arms conveyed an angry impatience. Then the Genna Brother who'd first greeted them from the Oldsmobile stopped his glaring at the newcomers long enough to blink as he nodded toward the back, but otherwise didn't emote. "This is my youngest brother Angelo, and I'm Michele but you call me Mike," said their driver.

"I'm Turner and this is Rose."

"Taddeo. I'm with Arlene." Tad wished he was in the same car with at least one of his closest friends. But Turner was an established veteran. He'd be just as good of backup for the pitcher. Wouldn't he?

So with its new passengers now seated, their car pulled out and followed the Gennas' older brothers. "So what do our new pals want to do tonight?" Mike asked them.

"We were just talking about the circus," Rose said. "Hagenbeck and Wallace," she added as if there was a better one.

"They don't come back to Chicago until September. They're touring the East this month, in Massachusetts about now, and Detroit's probably the closest they'll get to our town this summer, but not until June," Angelo spoke for the first time.

Even his brother looked over his shoulder from the driver's seat to stare at him.

"What?" Ang asked. "I like going to the show because I fancy spending a long time observing those exotic predators."

That figures, Tad thought. The younger Genna Brothers were starting to get a reputation in Chicago, and it wasn't a good one.

"But if you want to observe some wild animals right now, we should all go to White City. We're near enough to Woodlawn. They have electricity to keep the party wild well into the night. If we get hungry we can eat at the College Inn — they're always open late, as we uh, often work late." Angelo laughed to himself at that one. "They have a coaster doing the figure-eight and a roller rink, plus we like to shoot the chutes. We *really* like that. My brothers and I don't mind getting a little wet." Tad noticed Angelo couldn't help himself from grinning. He'd deliberately made sure that he sat in the center of the back seat, and squeezed in next to Genna, so that Arlene could not. "Would you girls like to get a little wet on a hot summer night?" Angelo asked her, leaning over Taddeo to also make sure she noticed him smile.

Arlene might have growled, but had otherwise continued to not speak one word. Taddeo rolled his eyes, but Rose said, "Oh, that sounds so exciting!"

"Here's to a little excitement then," Mike said and pushed down the gas pedal while he changed into the oncoming traffic lane and shot their vehicle ahead, passing most of the procession until he paced side-by-side with his eldest brother Sam's car. "They want to go to White City," he shouted over the roaring engine and the honking horn of another vehicle that was forced to pull over to the curb.

"Yeah, alright," his brother said. "Now drive on the right side of the road. We don't want anyone to get killed accidentally tonight."

From the front seat, Turner looked over his shoulder at Tad, and his eyes conveyed his worry. Taddeo tightened his jaw. *Accidentally*, but what about *intentionally*? Michele Genna's car fell back in line behind the sights of all their friends' automobiles. "Hey, you people who like to be scared by those big predatory animals? Huh. Want to make an unscheduled stop somewheres else that's kind of scary?" Mike Genna asked them.

"What do you mean?" Turner inquired, again looking back at Tad who could do nothing but shrug.

"Well, you wanted to visit the circus before, right? Showmen's Rest is close by Woodlawn. We'll go walking amongst the graves of the circus' best. You can imagine what it would be like to cavort with the most talented — among the dead," Angelo finished his brother's thought. "I've found the idea fascinating."

I'm sure you have, Tad thought.

"That's it — ," Turner started.

Arlene cut him off. "That is so funny. I've also always had something like this in mind."

Tad suddenly looked from Angelo to her with his eyes moving but his mouth frozen open, tasting smoke and gasoline particles that drifted in under the canopy of their cramped vehicle as if this Oldsmobile were a speeding coffin with an engine.

"I don't get out much," Arlene explained, with less than a second's offering of an obviously faked smile.

She had yet to really let their new companions hear her speak. They recognized the accent immediately. Their reaction was curious. Michele Genna turned uncomfortably in his seat at the wheel to look all the way over his left shoulder — at his brother — who responded to Arlene first. "You're a North-sider. An Irish lass, aren't ya? Huh. Well ain't that real interesting. Well you know, that graveyard was begun by Buffalo Bill Cody only a few months back," Angelo informed them. "And the dead the gunman will leave there is rumored to include some of the wildest animals whose spirits along with Cody's may still haunt the place. But you can stay close to me, Arlene. You may feel the need to." He smiled.

"But I feel the need to always know what I'm doing — and that includes having the right allies with the correct information," she said. "Now Buffalo Bill Cody wasn't any great gunman, he was a veteran who after the war could only make a living shooting a bunch of dumb animals only to then become a rodeo cowboy who died only the other year, peacefully in bed — and in Colorado. It's a little ways further from here," she said adding what Tad now knew to be customary sarcasm to her speech, "*and the timings not at all convenient for me*. But it was with the kindest of spirits that he donated for an expansion of the cemetery you're heading toward, in order to honor other performers going about their traveling show craft. Then again his passing and the others' passing wasn't of the kind of death some people might be familiar with."

Most of the company Tad kept paused to consider her words, and then awkwardly re-start their chatting as their car left the other Gennas' progression toward White City after they navigated around the Old Post Office to continue *west* on 22nd Street, *alone*. But neither he nor Turner seemed to have any thoughts they wanted to say out loud. At their speed, which only the Gennas and Rose demonstrated they found exhilarating, they were soon to arrive at the newly dedicated celebrity graveyard. The young people continued talking as Mike parked the car and they got out on foot to walk about and enter the cemetery as the sun began to disappear in a nearly dark red, western sky.

"How do you know so much about this place, and *on the South Side*, Arlene?" Taddeo asked, trying to keep the girl interested in conversing with him instead of Angelo. *Am I actually feeling jealous of some scrappy, low-life Genna now? I just met Arlene and I've been trying to tell myself that she's so irritating that it's intolerable. And once I found* that *out, I was just using her to help me get my teammates out of my father's hellhole. When did I actually let myself start caring about her?* He cautioned himself, *And definitely do not start to compete with a member of the* Genna Family *over some girl you just met, Tad. Besides, it's going to be plenty of fun watching Angelo try and figure out how to handle* her.

"I don't know about this place so much as I know about William

Cody, Taddeo," she replied, intriguing him.

"What, you saw one of his shows before? Became a fan?"

"Actually, he was a friend of a friend of my family's. My real family's."

Tad paused to wonder about this next bit of new information. Arlene was full of surprises. She really did fascinate him. But she didn't divulge anything more. And she had already walked on ahead of them and among the graves with Angelo Genna. *Perfect.* Tad jogged to catch up with them, his feet slipping a little on the moist grass. Up on the cemetery lawn ahead of them was Turner Barber and Rose, with Michele or "Mike" Genna, as he told them to address him by. "Hey, wait for me."

"Death does not wait," Arlene quipped. They walked around reading the often quirky performers' stage names engraved on the tombstones now. "Death arrives when it arrives. Sometimes even later than those who are suffering would actually prefer. The challenge is to do everything you set out to do before it gets you," she said.

"Yeah. Exactly," Angelo agreed. "You understand."

"Well, we're all in the right place to see that very clearly, aren't we now?" the lady asked.

That was creepy, Tad thought.

"Then I must inquire. Would you like to dance with me?" Angelo asked her.

Wait a minute. She's my *girl.*

"Do the Dance of the Dead, like the Mexicans do? And in a graveyard?" Arlene asked with a muted laugh. "That sounds appealing. But if you don't know how to do that one particularly well, I could teach it to you." She was reaching in her purse as though she were searching for something.

This time maybe Genna was finally and really puzzled by her. Or frightened? "No. Uh, I uh — well, maybe we should catch up with the others at White City? They have a regular Scottish band playing in just this incredible dance hall. It's kind of interesting music. Would you fancy seeing it?"

"I'm not Scottish. I'm *Irish.* I told you that already. And I thought you'd fancy paying closer attention to me."

This time Tad laughed as he observed even Angelo Genna react, indicating the woman had *him* miffed. You couldn't ever say the right thing for *her*. But mutual understandings between Italians and the Irish were hard to come by in Chicago, let alone those between men and women.

At least Angelo couldn't find any easier way to deal with the situation the Irish woman's presence had elicited. "Yeah, I uh definitely didn't forget that. But yes. As we're all supposed to be Americans now, I just originally had thought we'd all like to get to know one another a little closer by, you know, gathering around the headstones and telling a few ghost stories."

"I too had similar thoughts as you. How amazing, Angelo. But I've only just started rehearsing mine. When I'm ready to lay down my tale, it's going to be incredibly real. Perhaps unforgettable."

"Oh? Well, then perhaps we'll come back here — another time — when we're all settled in for the trip?"

"You know, I could see us ending up here again," she said.

"Uh, I think we should go on and catch up with my brothers now. The sun's down and they're all probably parked at White City quite a'ways east of us now, and have gone in ahead wondering where the hell we are. I've been curious to see the Midget City show anyway."

"After wanting to imagine the touch of death, I wouldn't suspect it would be nearly as difficult for you to imagine yourself feeling so small," Arlene responded to Angelo. "But I'd like to see that, too."

Tad covered his laugh over all her words spoken, surely with double-meanings, by faking that a new round of coughing started ailing him. "Yeah. Um, I'm starting to feel it getting colder by the minute out here."

After arriving at Chicago's most popular amusement park, this unlikely and unique company of professional girls, Mafia-styled gang enforcers, and Major League Baseball players rejoined their larger group of more of the same and now the twenty-six of them had to take turns so each of them had a chance to ride the six-car Ferris wheel while the others ate carnival snack foods and enjoyed a much-needed laugh as they watched the comical act of the Garden Follies Dancers. Then they all had a great-humored time catching the spray from racing in the water chutes ride and making at least an attempt to roller skate and falling all over one another.

Finally, this specific crowd exited the park to go to eat a proper meal at The College Inn, before Antonio Genna, who had only enjoyed the company of one of the Villetti girls with restraint offered, "Now I think we can go enjoy a last dance back at *another club* that should still be open — at least to us. Let me cover that bill."

"No. No. No," Tad protested. "I've got this. You were kind

enough to offer us all rides and I think…"

Hoff cut him off, with a new pair of ladies snuggled up in his big arms, "… that my teammates and I had a wonderful time. Thanks!"

Tad shot his friend a warning with his glance.

But Antonio spoke. "Good. Enough of this nonsense about the bill. Your father offered you this great night on the town to no doubt buy your family influence with our friendly and winning team on the North Side." He nodded toward several players on the Cubs' roster. But his brother Angelo was still allowing himself sidelong glances at Arlene. "That is fine. I pride myself on being a gentleman so I will not claim to have any better intentions, but you may keep his money and enjoy the next night out it may provide you all. Courtesy of your neighbors." He smiled around the extra-long tables the group had made by adjoining several together. "On *this night*, you can show your appreciation for your new friends on the Near West Side by letting us host your further great change of fortune. That would namely be meeting *us*. But please, we should leave now, as my dear Gladys awaits me at home. And I don't want to be too late." Several of Antonio's brothers rolled their eyes and groaned but he continued. "I do need to get back to her. I'm so sorry already that there just wasn't time for her to prepare and come along and join us as well." Looking directly at Taddeo he then said, "You must always be considerate of the feelings of your woman-friend. Am I right my young man?" His eyes flickered to Arlene, as now did both Angelo's and Michele's.

What is going on? Taddeo wondered. *And why did Greg — it has to be Greg since I only have two brothers – call these guys down on him?*

"Well, this all sounds like another great idea to me," Hoff said. It was Tad's turn to groan.

Tad had plenty of more opportunities to grind his teeth soon. Turner Barber didn't like their cemetery play and got Charlie Deal and Peter Kilduff to gang up on Taddeo and return to the subject matter of baseball, as a piano player and another performer quick with his violin, struck up the music in an unusually bright-lit small dive. Meanwhile, Angelo had gotten Arlene to take up his offer to dance with him once they were back to the Genna House's little operation. *Nice maneuver, there*. Then his teammates fired up the cigarettes they were offered by Peter and James Genna and they started in on their rookie pitcher once again, but Chicago's young reliever had enough of all of it by now and needed to open a new opportunity to take the pressure off. He'd need to make an unassisted double-play. "You know what guys?" He addressed his mates from the Cubs. "I am through with this — this ill attempt to change who I am. If some smart batter steps up into the box to wave his stick in what I believe is a threatening direction toward my team's lead with the score, I *am* going to take him down. I'll trust *my own* better judgment on how to do that. And I'm doing this for you. So excuse me."

Tad got up and noticed James Genna had been watching him. That man had the look of someone who wanted something. But Taddeo ignored this and started to look for the opportunity to make good on his promise to intervene in any threat against him or those he cared for — exactly where he'd find Angelo, to then separate him from Arlene. Only when he had readied himself to make his move, Taddeo found that he was not the first player to take up that game plan. Michele was there trying to pull his brother's arm off of Arlene's shoulder and then slapped it away when the younger Genna brought his hand back to start to journey below her waist. In a second Mike had thrust his body in between Arlene and Angelo, waiving his finger in his younger sibling's face. "You know what? You *will* learn to be more respectful Little Brother, like Tony, you know."

"Some fellas aren't gonna change Mikey. And you are one to know. You think you're just so charming that you're entitled or something?"

Tad shrugged off the irony of overhearing this discourse from *these brothers* and stepped in to grab Arlene by her arm. "Alright, let's go," he told her in a low tone. With all the money Antonio had saved him, he could dial for the taxis to get all his teammates home.

"Do you speak for everyone, Taddeo? Your friends are all having fun. Aren't you?"

"No. I've been growing rather tired of the company as the night's gone on. Haven't you?"

"Not really. It's been both very entertaining and enlightening," she answered him. "I do want to stay for a little longer to see what happens next. You boys are going to start a fight over me? Aren't ya? That will be quite amusing, you know."

"Really."

"I'm sure of it."

"I'm not."

"Villetti," now Mike Genna was calling him. "Is this *your* girl?"

He nodded to Arlene.

"I don't know."

"You see. He doesn't know. That means she's my girl if I say so," Angelo told his sibling. "It's endemic with those Villettis anyhow. They can't make a decision without taking weeks to think about it. It takes me less than an hour before my enemies are on the ground."

Taddeo felt that old familiar anger warming him, rising up his back — that he had only moments ago wished his own teammates would get the hell off of. It eliminated any sense of caution he should have had when it came to dealing with Angelo Genna. And he should know when he was being set up. Only then Charlie Hollocher crossed the room and naively said, "Hey, how's it going Taddeo? What a great night this is turning out to be. Wouldn't you say?"

That did it. "Angelo." Taddeo called out the Genna brother who bothered him so. "Arlene is my girl. There are plenty more on Taylor Street, so if you want to visit my house, you are more than welcome to do so."

"Oh really," the Genna stepped over and got into Tad's face. "You're not saying I'm not good enough for *this one* though? Are you?" His newsie brim jabbed into Taddeo's face and lifted his hair they were so close. Taddeo had no trouble smelling what the other had too much to drink of.

"Whoa. Whoa. Whoa. He's not saying anything but what a great time you've shown us and that we're very thankful for it," Hoff moved in between them and spread his arms to pat both the Villetti and the Genna on their shoulders nearest him. Arlene's hand disappeared into her purse again. Michele Genna's mouth opened a little when Tad's warily surveilling eyes caught him, and taking note of the woman, the pitcher felt some confusion over his opposition's reaction there.

"That's not what I thought he meant," Angelo said. He shook the catcher's hand off him.

"No. You're distorting what I said, George. You don't speak for me, Hoffman."

"I'm on *your* team, Taddeo. I always have been."

"Okay. You know what? It is time for this to stop. Now I *am* getting tired, Mister Villetti." Arlene decided to jump back into the conversation. She too had been up to something and obviously concerned about this escalation in tension. Taddeo saw her make rather cold eye contact with each of the two youngest Genna Brothers. Michele acknowledged it by swallowing and putting his arm across Angelo's chest, implying his younger brother hold himself — and his tongue — in check.

"So you're back to calling me Mister Villetti again?"

"Fine, *Tad*. But we really don't have to stay out all night," Arlene explained. "Especially not talking about baseball. You and your boys seem to have more than adequately entertained my friends, I mean in spite of all the sports talk. I admit I am *surprised*, but I actually did have some fun. Thank you for that. And thanks to the Gennas. We all appreciated the park, the skating, and the dining — and umm, maybe not all this *whining*. That makes us ladies wonder who the real pussies are. But I understand if you felt the need to demonstrate some sort of good intentions, chivalry I suppose. *How very gentlemanly of you*." Arlene laughed as she spoke louder so more of the Cubs could hear her. "And now that you all can feel satisfied that you at least *pretended* to come from good breeding, your mothers can all be proud of you. And I hate for our good times to head toward a closure for such a wonderful night — but shall we finally get to the boarding rooms? Time's wasting. I have our own special accommodations already arranged to end this evening, Tad."

"Wait. What? You think this whole night just chalks up to foreplay? That the boys and me have only just been waiting for the right time to just take advantage of you girls?"

Arlene laughed. "You boys? Take advantage of *us*?" She looked at him incredulously. Then her expression focused on him, more direct. "Yes. I *know* that for a fact, Ball Jockey. Do you think I'm stupid? You did not just seriously ask me this, Taddeo?" She addressed him by his given name while noting that even Angelo had somewhat relaxed, as from her purse, the young woman extracted only a cigarette and a matchbook.

"Uh-huh. Yeah. I did — I mean I am asking you that."

Arlene's small face frowned. She struck a match to ignite the smoke she placed between her lips and flicked the dying match toward the men who separated to avoid being burnt. "Jesus Christ. How could you be a Villetti and possibly be so naïve?"

"What?"

"I can answer that," Angelo interjected.

"You're right on that one," Mike Genna added.

"He's young. Like me. Like some of you. He's just learning all the rules," Hoff said thinking it would help.

"C'mon. Quit playing a fool's game with these boys — and with me. Now that I've enjoyed playing my little game on you, let's go fuck." The girl pursed her lips to puff on her cigarette. She turned her head slightly to blow her smoke over the bar instead of in her companion's face, while Tad's eyes grew five times their former size as Arlene concluded, "If I *have* to do this for you, I'm ready to get the rest of this night over with. We'll go to The Sisson Hotel. They'll give us your father's usual room."

The athlete was shocked. So were the Genna Brothers and the Cubs who were present. They all backed up to recheck their ears and their memories about what they thought they just heard — from the best-looking, most cosmopolitan of any of the ladies. Now for his part, Taddeo tried to delay directly responding to the girl's latest proclamation. Lowering his voice, he said "Uh, Arlene, if you need a place to flop, we have guest accommodations back at my *home*."

"That would *not at all* be acceptable. Besides, I won't ever feel comfortable there."

"You're kidding, again. Right?" His expression changed. "I didn't mean my papa's place above the lounge. It's not quite Hyde Park, but we have another family home that even has a yard; I keep a dog, and the space there is really generous."

"I'm sure."

"There's plenty of rooms — especially for you, Doll." Tad tried to sound like he heard more confident men talk. "What is the problem?" he asked Arlene. But too late to catch his proclivity for too many extra sentences, his further questioning sounded like pleading as it whined out of him. "And you just arrived back near the South Side of town. Err, Chicago's kind of a big place and it's late. Do you have far to travel to where you regularly stay? Um, I mean of course I'd escort you."

"Where I stay is meant to be lodging for women only. Women taking residence to stand up for a real social justice movement. Evidently needed for your society's enlightenment."

Tad grinned while not concerned he couldn't understand whatever the latest object of his fascination meant. "But by your just-spoken words, I know *that* shield of deceit must get broken."

"It's a rather flimsy silk shield."

"And with you girls in the kind of business you're all dressed for back at the bar seems to suggest you're in, plus *my family* always alleged to be behind it — by your own admission. Well, I mean obviously Hoffy confirmed it — once or twice already tonight."

"That I did do," Tad's backstop said interrupting to not let his buddy drop the ball. Tad's red-headed companion and his teammate's new brunette lady-friend both glared at Hoffman.

"So then quit this innocence act. Covering for your family. And wasting everyone else's time," Arlene said to Taddeo, interrupting him taking his time to tiptoe around his thoughts' only natural conclusion. "My God man, learn to be direct and just say what you mean."

Tad continued. "You oughtta try taking your own advice too, Arlene. But hey, I'm reasoning here. That some men must have gotten in where you lodge — on one or more of you ladies' direct invitations, and certainly for only the *one purpose* I can imagine. That is if what *you're not telling me* reveals the actual truth." Taddeo had gotten annoyed with her. Again. "Yeah? Which is to say that someone, even when she seems as 'special' as you do, is only around for the same reason as the rest of any of my father's other girls. Which yes, I guess my buddy here did already establish to be the right call in the first place." He smiled sheepishly but on the inside, he cursed himself for not knowing when to shut up, though he couldn't help himself from still talking anyway. It seemed wise to collect more information about her. There was something very wrong with this young woman that he just couldn't put his finger on. And he knew there was something definitely not right with The Sisson. But with what he already said, he'd really only been trying to rib her, right? Or did he *need* more information? His instinct was strongly telling him this. And yet he might have completely lost the night he had always and inwardly been pining to have with her.

Arlene did show, but for only a moment, her own irritation with Villetti's last comments. "Well your blathering is not winning you an opportunity to stay in *my* room. Or allowing you to bring a whole baseball team into what is designated a women's boardinghouse." At her own words, she laughed. "The truth is, it'll be a rare occasion when I take a chance with a rookie. You better use it."

"Oh. Really?" He should have shut up right then, if not long before this moment. She was about to agree to what he had wanted from her all night. But Tad just had to press on. "So you've seen a lot of playing time? Have you?" Hoff was shaking his head side to side but his pitcher couldn't be called off. "And what about The Sisson? What did you mean when you said my father has a *usual* suite? There? I didn't even know they were open this week. I thought they had just finished building the place. So I'd also really like to know *for just how long* has he had a bed made for him over there." Tad wished his nature wouldn't be that of one quite so suspicious where it came to his family. But he did have experience when it came to *who* had helped shape his opinion in that area. And there was his secret concern for his late mother that he kept very close to his chest. He wondered for just how long his father might have been occupied with any dalliances.

"Oh I wouldn't know," Arlene answered him. "It *is* my first time on your side of town, remember? Young Irish girls don't ordinarily want to venture to that part of Chicago. Or the Near West Side for that matter," she said glancing around to catch Angelo listening, shaking his head, and switching from a smirk to a frown. "But what did you think I am there at the bar to *do* for your father, Tad? *Really*."

"You mean he actually makes you…?" Tad's voice trailed off. "What? With him? Why? I mean how did you come in to such a life?"

"Oh, it's just what I always wanted," Arlene quipped. "Now let's waste another hour discussing this." The girl sighed, seeing that he needed a real answer, so she asked him, "Remember when your fellas Joe and Donny were killed the other week?"

"Yeah. When my father sent Urso up so far north he was practically in Rogers Park — but with only good intentions. And I heard Hymie Weiss and Bugs Moran then tried to send him home to us in a box? Yes. Unfortunately, I remember that." He glanced around at their hosts. Tad had heard some other rumors.

"Yes, well Urso wasn't very cooperative about getting into that box and O'Banion had to move quickly to make a peace with your father before your house would retaliate further against the Irish families for resisting your brother's intrusion. So maybe it did quite nearly kill Rinaldo Villetti's firstborn son, but the defenders were busy protecting Irish-owned businesses on their *own goddamned streets*." Apparently Arlene had suddenly decided to be more forthcoming. Like a flood. Of red hot volcano lava. Now she did blow her smoke right back at him. Tad coughed on her rhetoric. "So can it just be called the *luck of the Irish* for some of our wives, mothers, daughters and sisters? That some of your father's would-be associates have *other* priorities besides fighting another feckless turf war in Chi-Town right now — and even more horrific priorities, I might add — from my own *personal* experience. And all this on top of it having been only, what? Less than a handful of weeks? Since the previous month's killings of husbands, fathers, sons — and *our brothers*. But the Market Street Gang knows they have been losing heavily ever since your people that Morello had Masseria send out from New York, and maybe even straight from out of your greasy forbearers' Old Country, started reinforcing this Italian intrusion into *our business*. It's not a secret that the North Side can't possibly absorb any more losses in manpower right now. Losses to your hordes of Sicilian boat people. Yet my people will put up a winning fight. Of that you can be sure. The lesson will have to be taught the hard way — that you don't mess with the Irish. But since I was already orphaned in some of my own clan's previous stupid misadventures, along with some territorial concessions, I was traded away as a conciliation prize so no more blood had to be spilled in order forge us at least the current temporary cease-fire. That's life in America."

"That's horrible." Taddeo was shocked. "That they did that to you? And trading in skin like that."

"And your ignorance is astounding."

"Thank you very much. But your people did try to kill my big brother. However, I *will* talk to my father about this. I can't stand one more minute hearing these kinds of things being said about my family."

"This settlement was to your father's pleasure. If you ever get out of your sandlot on Clark Street a little more, you'll know *exactly* what kinds of things your family does so that your father retains this self-proclaimed control over *his* streets. Out in the real world. Visit it sometime. You may try and trick yourself, but your family's *philanthropy* isn't fooling anyone, especially me." Arlene snorted. "But at least now you can appreciate *my* situation, while you take your father's gifts, his money. But just use me already, just as you've been hoping to since you first spotted me at the bar. I really want to be left alone soon. So just do with me what you will. Your most base desires are not at all that difficult to read, Taddeo. But don't waste any more of my time than satisfying them will take, please."

"Um. Alright." Tad's eyes scanned Arlene up and down. She'd removed her coat when she'd danced with Angelo and was she ever a sexy sight to behold. Taddeo shrugged. He wasn't sure he could affect any changes in the present situation. But he thought he might as well enjoy it. Somebody would — and it might as well be him. His teammates didn't hesitate. They had girls at home and many had girls on the road. And this is the life he'd wanted, right? Tad was also not so sure about that anymore. "So. Look," he said, "Uh. Just wait here, Arlene. Treaties or not, I don't want us all staying over on the West Side." He glanced at several of the Gennas. They were laughing. "Umm. So I'm gonna go call us some coaches, taxis, or something."

"If you can arrange it, a couple of pigs pulling a hearse would be perfect," she commented dryly. "That'd go great with my nights I've been having lately."

Chapter 7

Several hours later, Taddeo rolled his naked body off of Arlene's. Burning hot, he used what energy was left in his legs to kick the top sheet and cover-blanket completely off the hotel bed.

"That was amazing," Tad proclaimed between panting and wiping the sweat from his forehead.

She reached for the nightstand to light herself a cigarette. "You're easily impressed."

"Hey, I like to come to my own conclusions. Thank you. Not have my father, my coach, or some other know-it-all make my evaluations for me."

"I'm so glad you didn't feel the need to invite them to join us — and that you were able determine just how I would spend my night all by yourself," Arlene retorted.

"I'm not done yet." Tad hugged her fiercely and then, still loosely holding her in what Arlene worried could actually be affection, he slid down her naked body caressing her nipples in his warm mouth, and sliding lower and lower past her smooth midriff to a place where she was forced to admit she enjoyed his attentions.

When another half an hour had passed, and both she and her young partner were quite through with taking their turns being satisfied, Arlene lay content and able to concede to being receptive to the worst the son of her enemy could do to her: make her his confidant. She didn't want to care, but the girl didn't seem to be able to help herself. For now.

"I see I *can* do some things correctly," Taddeo said. "Only a short while ago I had to listen to way too many other people criticize my performance."

"Well I don't have any pressing complaints," Arlene said, her nether-region still throbbing from the pleasure Taddeo had brought her. She hated to admit it, but her immediate plan was to double-down on that. *Might as well make him useful*. But for the moment, Taddeo wanted a release from *all* his tensions. *But why is it to be my dumb luck that this has to encompass humoring his obsession with baseball?*

"I do — have complaints, I mean. Why do I have to tolerate such disrespect?"

Arlene was caught off guard by that. But of course Taddeo soon went back to referencing his silly game again, amongst every other subject he could ramble on about. But this was his favorite one. Still, she listened carefully, in hopes of gleaning some information that could be useful, like maybe what Tad suspected one of his brothers was up to with that maneuver he pulled by bringing the Genna Family into that dangerous mix of affairs the past night. If he'd even considered it. That move *was* really unexpected. Arlene came upon a frightening thought. *Tad's brother could actually be even* more *dangerous than that narcissistic and homicidal maniac he has for a father*. This discovery would teach her to not underestimate any of the younger Villettis.

"I mean why do I have to put up with this crap even from those allegedly on *my side*?"

Good question.

"Also, whatever that was between you and Angelo."

Now I could be the one who's suspect. Tad was developing some good paranoia here, but then again she knew better than most that everyone really was out to get him.

"And okay. Maybe I did get too smart for my own good and caused our team's loss yesterday, stemming from me plunking that Robin batter. But am I just supposed to stand for being some kind of stooge? Babied with only the *safe* work assignments being called for from me? Alright. I *am* a rookie. But I worked hard to make it to the pros and that required experience with knowing what I am doing. The more I thought about, Coach had me pitch two-thirds of an inning more so that he could pull The Hippo before he succumbed to his ankle pain, sub in the pinch hitter, and try and save Carter for the late inning work rather than because he really wanted to give my arm another chance. Fact is, I'm not even sure even how I got called on to play in that game — and even still left out there to finish the inning after that brawl."

"Hmmn," Arlene purred. "They must have decided to spare your friend Carter from the more immediate after-effects of experiencing *your* special kind of talent. You do fuck the shit out of things." However, she had enjoyed it. *But now it's his coach who's wronged him. Who will be next? I'm still waiting for my second turn. Truthfully*. "Well, maybe some of the time you actually do know what you're up against." *But I doubt it*. "Your role in the service of others' satisfaction instead of your own. But since I guess I'm playing, I'll agree. If some people work really hard for something and they keep working at it, no matter what obstacles stand in their path, I'd personally hope that some of those people would attain the victory they set out to achieve." She considered more than what Taddeo was thinking about when she made that last comment. *Or at least I'll die trying.*

"Getting retired after only one inning was not what I set out to achieve, but thank you for understanding. You are a very special girl, aren't you, Arlene?" He smiled kindly, ignoring his pain, with his body now hovering over hers, braced on his strong arms.

You have no idea. But just how special I am, your whole family is about to find out, Villetti. But in spite of his momentarily swollen face, he *is really attractive, though not for his intelligence.*

Then the pair continued to intimately enjoy one another's company, each trying to consume the other's essence that strengthened what were their own, private resolves. And very ambitious, individually personal resolves.

* * * * *

Back at the Villettis' nightclub and lounge, Greggorio now sat at the bar the baseball players had vacated some while ago. His frustration and ambition had kept him up all night and it was going on three o'clock in the morning. His first cousin Corrado Delasandro had joined him for more than a few drinks. But the serious men remained nearly sober. At twenty-six and two years older, Corrado nevertheless knew to also behave subordinate to a direct heir of The House Villetti, and he'd taken on the kindly advisory role a caring big brother ought to have offered Greg — unlike the bully he knew his actual older brother to be. But the Villetti patriarch had seen to pitting his boys against each other from the earliest age — presumably to strengthen them. And though Greggorio would have run The House differently, he admitted the current approach might be even described as practical for these brutally competitive times in Chicago. But what was done was done. And he'd adapted his own plans.

So Greg considered putting more good use of his training into play as he sat and watched Old Man Lamont rush to bring Urso and the new goombah wet towels where the pair sat in a booth next to his father's favorite one. Everyone else in The House was also still awake. Urso used his towel to rub off some blood that had spattered his hands and then dipped a still clean end of the rag into a glass of water a waitress brought him to dab at small spots on his white shirt that were exposed at the edges of the jacket belonging to his favored dark suit. By contrast, the new man was a mess, and the nearly sixty-year-old Lamont had to hurry the best he could in order to fetch him two more wet rags from the kitchen as the rookie goombah wiped at wounds, and maybe hidden tears, that fell all over his beaten body. A gash in his hairline wouldn't stop dripping a thin red line down the side of his face, running through his still neatly oiled and shaped short dark hair. His hat rested on this table, behind Rinaldo Villetti's, and his bloody plumbing tool lay down by his feet, alongside the partition between the one window booth offering sanctuary to the new help, and the one seating his aging boss who still held command over this neighborhood block. He looked apprehensive about whether this senior Villetti soldier would approve of him. The head of the household's sons both knew the feeling.

But Greg marveled at the purity of the simple social hierarchy that had been established by nature. He imagined how it would feel to sit at the top of that food chain while he plotted his route of ascent he'd take to get there.

"Still, nothing has changed."

"Huh?" his cousin wanted clarity.

"You're two years my senior. You ought to remember. You moved here with me when we dropped out of grammar school. Our people first controlled *several blocks* in the Levee District, right? It was negotiated with the Irish city fathers. Coughlin and Kenna liked the deal D'Andrea proposed to them through Merlo, which also first got us *our* streets. The politicians could profit from the money we helped make Colosimo even when the Irish in charge of Chicago's underworld wouldn't allow prostitution to make its bed on their precious North Side. Little did the public know. Or rather did they admit it. Then under Papa's immediate onsite management, we managed to lose control when O'Banion decided he *didn't* like that deal. And at the same time, The Black Hand thought they could force themselves upon new immigrants in cultural shock upon arriving in America, after leaving the options of a war or a stagnating economy in our homeland, only to see some of us spread out thinner and thinner — and just as poor — ready-made victims, heading south or west looking for new opportunities to etch out a living far away from all that in the first place. So the Irish took the advantage and rolled themselves back across the river. And we hard-rolled those fucking shamrocks back again — in barrels. They thought *they* got smacked by The Black Hand from the eastern seaboard to the Great Lakes. Maybe they did — sometimes. Colosimo's asked for help. But we did a lot of that work ourselves. We had to. Just as we handled the next eastern interlopers who showed up — and from our own kind. It's just that now The Family is only back to where we started. Our generation, I mean. No better than the one which preceded us. Still servile to New York. But look at Papa. He's so proud of himself." Rinaldo Villetti was patting his oldest son on the shoulder, and had actually gotten out of his seat to walk around the table and approach the next booth to reach for a new towel and glass of water the elderly negro Lamont had brought him. And he feigned his concern when he also dabbed at the new goombah's wounds. His middle son and nephew still watched him from across the lounge. "Yup. And tonight we're being treated to seeing this low-level trash actually consider admiring that. I mean right now he's nurturing the thought that my father is someone to respect and that he truly cares. The new punk's loyalty bought over a dirty kitchen rag."

"What are you thinking?"

"Maybe that if they bring him morphine, my father can really have him hooked. Your father over there can always seem to get that. Meanwhile, I never put *my loyalty* up for sale. It was assumed it was just a legacy of my birthright. And it's not much of a legacy with Urso always in my way. Look at *him* over there. Huh. Meanwhile, Taddeo is headed his own way. Stupid young fool is on a crash course with his destiny right now. And my father is only indulging him. But Urso's not any better — or smarter. He's good muscle for Papa. But he can't run this outfit. He's not any brighter than Taddeo. He never needed to be. Everything given to him."

"I should have asked what are you *planning*?"

"We're the best of friends, right? I mean besides cousins."

"We grew up together. I tried to look out for you."

"You got between Urso and me a few times. Prevented him from doing his worst, at least by being around as a witness. If Urso touched *you*, my auntie — your ma I mean — could really lay it into my father. Hell yeah, she could. Then Urso knew that he was next if Papa's oldest sister came down on *him*."

"That your papa loves my mother, like he loves and even lives for all our family members — this brings him back all of their love tenfold in return. They're grateful. No one can say anybody else has done more for our family. He wants his sister to be happy and so he even extends his generosity to bring my father to the *legitimate* work opportunities here in Chicago."

"Legitimate?" Greg laughed. "What, drugs? Yes. Like he helped him start up a pharmacy so he could begin getting supplied with the raw ingredients for cutting and distributing cheap heroin. Very generous of him when he comes up with the financing program for your father's new line of never-expiring-and-self-prescribing-customers — with their ever-expanding gambling and interest debts to come along with them. Trust me, he's not that altruistic toward a family he resents as he is currently pretending to be. He's really running this show for himself. Though still rather ineptly." Greg's tone had become decidedly insolent.

"What do you mean? We're in business with a real doctor. You should be grateful your aunt married well so your family could merge with a house as respectable as ours."

"We let *your family* join *our house*! Get that straight for once. Right now, Corry. Or never mind."

"At least my father is here providing the medical care your papa needs. Did you stop to think about that?"

"There's much more important things to be concerned about. We're also in business with New York. Thanks to Colosimo reaching out on account of this Black Hand business. But I nevertheless do admire Papa for one thing though. He did do so much — all of this — to help our extended family make it — in this new country — in spite of his true feelings about the rest of them. And he *has* earned everyone's love. But maybe not your father's approval of the work he's offered your brothers and you. Only that was *not* a mistake. Your father wouldn't be doing so well if it weren't for us. Look at him over there. Wishing he could join in applauding *our* business practices — and that my father would relent from his ego trip, making it easier for him. But Papa's always been that way, too proud, and my dear Uncle Delasandro won't ever change either. Your father is who he is — and who *he* always will be. Proud as well — a stubborn one *of his own kind*. Over-impressed with himself and his education. But me? Well, your cousin here is both more practical and a bit more ambitious than his father. Now Papa's resolve tires. He's grows sicker, and if I don't do at least *something*, Urso will next lose everything my father ever gained for any of us, 'cause Urso will never be wise enough to know how to truly protect The Family. He's tough and not afraid to seek out a fight, but he doesn't think ahead of his own actions — or inaction. And too much of his time, he's also just plain lazy. We must grow to survive — and accumulate more and more strength and power, or the families that stand as our enemies certainly will. You see we gain by striking — the Irish, even the Gennas — first. So what if we don't realize any new ground that we can keep? The other houses? They retaliate against Colosimo, but they'll think twice about plunging themselves into another war *this far* into our territory on the South Side in Little Italy — which they could never hold."

"I thought you invited the Gennas into our territory?"

"Their stay will only be temporary. While they're useful. They might even unintentionally sacrifice themselves by standing up to Cardinella. Better them than us — losing their manpower. But Merlo and D'Andrea will eventually throw up a wall of resistance to the Gennas overreaching. That's in the latter's nature. But even D'Andrea will see wisdom in keeping the peace within the syndicate. Or he will try. But right now, it's all remarkably comparable to the trench warfare in Europe. I mean the treaties, alliances, and the stalemate. Except Colosimo pays the price for our actions, instead of us."

"Wait. *What have you done*?"

"Let's have another round and we'll discuss it. There's more I have to teach you Cousin, so when the day comes, I may depend on *you* to help me stay the course, keep pursuing my vision. And The House Villetti will be greater than ever."

* * * * *

"So are you done now?" Arlene asked him. She turned away to hide a smile. She hadn't expected the young man to satisfy *her* as well. He was very different from what she'd been prepared for. She'd rather appreciated this unanticipated part of her assignment. Thus far she'd been able to duck from far worse abuse by patronizing Taddeo's father, and what was required of the other girls, hadn't been forced from her. Yet. But she had her own agenda that would avenge her family of the Villettis' crimes. *Maybe too late, but I won't waver from my course again*, Arlene told herself. Going out with Taddeo might have been a big mistake — letting herself enjoy the company of the young athlete could become a liability in her plans that she couldn't afford. She was determined she wouldn't let herself develop even the slightest positive feeling toward him. If she had any control over that. She had managed to maneuver him to take his father's room at The Sisson versus her own place. Arlene had to remain in command. "Alright. I've been waiting for my chance to depart for a while," she stated matter-of-factly, so as to not reveal any temptation to do otherwise. And if Arlene even wanted to re-evaluate anything having to do with her situation, she would rather do it privately anyway. Taddeo was becoming too distracting.

"Back to being a part of my father's *brothel*?" Tad emphasized the last word to emphasize his distaste.

"My lifelong ambition. I'll just have to pursue it again, later," she stated tonelessly. Tad frowned. "It's well into the morning already and light will come in only a few more hours," she continued. "*I* don't have to come in to work until the late afternoon. But you have a pre-game practice. Don't you? I want to rest better, somewhere else, and alone, without *your* constant chatter. I need get my beauty sleep."

"Well, I wouldn't want you to miss out on *that*," Tad said dryly. "But why not just quit? Don't let my father *own* you. How can you tolerate being his — his slave?"

She looked away from him. "It's not like I have a lot of other options, Tad. Besides, my sacrifice here will save lives. At least a few. And maybe only for a short time. But I do what little good I can."

"Arlene, don't worry about the action on the streets. The soldiers are going to fight anyway. This crap goes on and on. I have seen it my whole entire life. I've only chosen not to acknowledge it before since I go to work every day on the wrong side of the river. But I'm not part of that world, and am never going to be, in spite of my own family. And you? You're not saving any of your kin-folk by staying here. Yeah, that's for sure. They're behaving typical for *their kind*, or so that's what I've always been told about the Irish. I haven't seen much to dispel that assessment anyway. Their boxing new immigrant families into the slums and protecting the Gold Coast as if allowing my people even a visit, to let even one ripple of the smooth water of Lake Michigan lap at our tired Latin feet *even on a holiday*, will somehow stain Coughlin and Kenna's sacred grand vision for a segregated city. You've no idea how lucky we are to be staying in a beachfront hotel right now."

I don't feel very lucky, Taddeo. And his father likely preferred this cheaper room with a view over the South Side and his narcissistic territorial ambitions, versus one of Lake Michigan that vacationers actually paid more for, to wake up to that pleasant view out across the water, anyway. *But that's all right. The Villettis* should *see the sun setting on their time in Chicago.*

"Though for plenty of time now I have also seen my *real* family for who *they* really are. And I can honestly say I did not like what I saw there, either. Obviously I know enough to never be as ignorant about this stuff as I actually would like to be. But even if everyone else eventually submits to the latest 'new, great plan for Chi-Town,' I don't see why *you* have to. Run away. Far away from here," Tad urged her.

"With what resources?" Arlene asked.

"Look. I don't know. Well, maybe — maybe I can help? I know I can't do much. I am earning so little, but my friends just pointed out that it's not like I need to work. I'm getting a second job because that's well what normal baseball players do."

Tad's last statement made Arlene giggle for a second. *Normal baseball players?* Surely not understanding her reaction to the humor in what he was relating, Tad continued on. "But my family's not going to watch what I do with my own wage earnings. Uh, I don't think so, anyway. But you know how I'm getting this second job? I'll just say I'm saving whatever I can make from it for a rainy day — or whatever. Papa knows I want a car. But I can probably give you the money — enough so you can at least get yourself out of the city and set up some place better than here."

His sympathy and generosity were really unexpected. *Who was* Taddeo Villetti? He acted genuinely concerned for her. Arlene was truly touched, though she told herself that she knew better than to believe in him. *I do, right?* Nevertheless she said, "Aww. That's so sweet of you, Tad. But then what? After the war in France ends, it will return to there being less and less opportunities for women to work. I mean at regular jobs that I could support myself solely on my wage earnings alone with. Even widows are not really going to get a lot of sympathy. It's just wartime propaganda. They're not even going to win any nationwide right to vote. Then it's back to the way it always was. In this moment, Wilson's government needs soldiers. But the administration's platitudes don't reflect any truth to how it really works out in this cold, cold world. No. All ladies *of a healthy age* will be expected to re-marry, or go back to their own fathers' nests — or worse, survive on charity — or some things even darker."

"Like what we just did? Nice to know how you're feeling about it." Arlene scowled and didn't immediately respond to Taddeo.

After a pause she said, "Without *that* great option *here*, really being for me, I just go back to being dependent on other strange men. Things will be exactly as they are right now, with my waking up in the same situation as I am at present — and definitely worse — in Indianapolis, Detroit, Milwaukee, or St. Louis. Wherever I can make a new bed for myself. Des Moines. Only however far I can get away from my memories here, in Chicago. Unless I actually marry someone. And who? Somebody who doesn't know what I've done to survive. Who I don't even know very well — or haven't even met?"

"You know me," Tad replied.

She couldn't help herself but laugh out loud. "Yeah. For the last half-a-dozen hours," Arlene quipped. She didn't bother to hide the lopsided frown her mouth reflexively repositioned itself into, along with her involuntarily narrowing green eyes. "Besides, don't tell me *you're* going to marry your father's bar-room entertainment?" Her loose long hair and shoulders moved when she laughed. Arlene's face broke into a smile. "Ha! What I wouldn't give to be at your family dinner table when that subject is broached. I can just see your father approving your marriage to *me*." The bed they sat on gently shook. "Then what? How are *we* going to get out of Chicago? Have you even thought this out that far? Or did you just come up with it a second ago? I definitely can't live with your old man, Tad. But let's be real for right now. *Your* whole sweetheart deal is right here. Playing for the Cubs, I mean. Trying to be a hero, like it seems you've always been aspiring to be. Now even to me. But stepping into a better light and out from under your father's shadow. Strange as it is to me, maybe for you, actually playing your stupid game is the right choice — again for you."

"Baseball is not stupid, Arlene. But it also offers no guarantee. That's also why I'm getting other work," Tad protested Arlene's reluctance to be a part of his plan. "I actually am looking for a real job. I don't want to be dependent on *him* — on *that* money. I can't ignore where it comes from any longer. And I don't want to get drafted into the war. But I could have additional income soon. And I mean from baseball. And it will be more than just the league minimum that they offer rookies. I *am* one hell of a pitcher. They'll all see. I just need some more time to prove that.

"Now look, I can't promise you that I'll make you happy. And I'm not such a blind optimist that I think it will even work out. I'm not even saying that I can commit to always supporting you. Forever. I don't expect to earn *that* much," Taddeo laughed. "But I don't have a girlfriend — and anything's gotta be better than staying here in my father's grasp — in my brothers' company. For either of us. You don't know the half of that. But *you're* better than just *anything*. Uh, I mean anyone, Arlene. So how about we *do* move? Together. I could get us a place over in Gary or South Bend if I have to go that far. Just for now. Both are kind of lower rent. But I can take a train and taxi into work, and even have my second job over in Indiana while still being close enough to play for Chicago, but nevertheless out of Papa's reach. Maybe I'll even make enough to get us a car, and even better, get traded to another team. Far away from this city. After I increase my stock."

"Your friends you care about — your teammates you came up with — aren't they all here? Playing for Chicago? I don't pretend to enjoy baseball, but at least I'm able to understand it. You're winning and you're bonding with your brothers — I mean the other loser ones you spend most of your time riding your ball club's bench with anyway. But *right now*, you're sounding more like you really *do* need to stay in another kind of home. And not the domestic kind. Get some help, Tad. I mean are you really that much of an idiot that you'd sacrifice so much for a girl you just met, just because we fucked?" Arlene's eyes searched Taddeo's, and then she paused and suddenly wondered, "Wait. I'm not the first girl you've ever had sex with? Am I?"

Tad looked startled by her question. "No. No! Of course not." His face turned red where it wasn't black and blue, and he blinked, shifting around on the bed, partially turning his body and his face to look away from her. "It's just that somehow, you're special. Don't you feel a connection?"

"You're kidding, right?" *Maybe he never had a girlfriend?* His confidence with socializing wasn't exactly Tad's strong suit. But he must have had his opportunities with his fair share of prostitutes. The guy lived in between one whorehouse and the whole Lords of the Levee District filled with almost all of the rest of them. He actually did make for a memorable lover. So he couldn't have been that inexperienced. Could he?

"No, Arlene. No I'm not kidding about a connection — between *us*. Why? Do you think I'm always this attracted to women so sarcastic, with such winning personalities, like yours? I think you're a bitch."

That label couldn't even sting, as it had actually been quite funny coming from a Villetti. "I really haven't lost any sleep over it,"

Arlene told him. "Yet." She yawned. "And if you don't like who I am, why are you trying so hard to convince even yourself that you do? That you what? You love me? Yeah. Sure you do, Ball Jockey. Nevertheless, your effort is admirable. Oh yes. Aren't you *my* true admirer? But that *would* seem to be the case, or you'd have dropped this, dressed, and got me a taxicab already."

"At this hour, on this side of town, it gets even harder to find one with pigs and whistles. But seriously, Arlene. You're *really* in a lot of trouble. You just can't see it. Now why can't you understand I just want to help you? I've wanted to at least do *something* that matters with my life. Maybe or maybe not I'll become that golden arm in the Big Leagues that they'll all be talking about for years to come. Unfortunately, that's not what anyone's predicting for *me*. My talent is only modest, realistically." Tad looked down, dejected by his facing the truth. "But baseball is *not* the only thing I'm good for. I do love the game though. It's just the only thing I am *already* good at. What comes naturally to me. And I never want to become whoever my father would see me be. Who my brothers will undoubtedly become."

"Huh. I thought your father inadvertently nurtured this. Letting you play baseball. Was *my* guess," Arlene voiced her speculation.

"Nope. You're not even close. It was my dear late mama, actually." Tad looked up at Arlene, his round brown eyes widening, and in motion, searching for some much-needed empathy. "Before she died, my mother had somehow softened the old man. I used to play in the streets and it always embarrassed me around the other kids — knowing Mama watched over me like she did. She — my mother — was always sad." Taddeo looked down again. "But the only time I'd see real happiness light up in her eyes was when she was watching me play. So I decided to just go with that. Yet Mama didn't interfere, and I strove to play harder and better every game, secretly relishing every time I gave her just one more opportunity to be proud of me. I got so good I earned the respect of the other kids. Then my father's told me himself that it used to mesmerize even him — the way my mother doted on me and got excited when she talked to him about my games. He saw a side of her that he could no longer access. But I think he'd loved that side of her the most. Papa had taken both my brothers away from her when they were very young. Then Mother had fallen ill after Greggorio was born and it would be years before she'd conceive another child. But she held on. Willed herself stronger, and gave Papa another son. Me. So I'm more than a few years apart — from when Urso and Greg were born. My mother had me more to herself, since my father already had two older sons to train to one day run The Family. So he let me stay by my mother's side — and my being there comforted her." Arlene had just become aware of Tad's other, worse pain, from a wound almost no one would ever see. Only she really cared, and she hated to admit it.

"Aww. Your mam, *she* taught you about love," the young Irish woman's comment came with a rare, quiet tone, unusually sincere for her.

"Yeah," Taddeo kept looking down again at the bed they were sitting on. "That's right. Then she died when I was still so young." He swallowed. "But maybe she taught my father something about love, too."

I wouldn't bet on it. Arlene looked away so Tad couldn't see her crinkle her nose as an instant reflex to his last highly doubtful speculation. It made her aware of how silly all their discussing dreams and wishful future plans had actually been.

Tad must have realized that as well. "Look. Give my idea some thought and give me some time. *You don't have to say anything now*. I can hear your doubt, unspoken. First, I'm going to approach my father about wanting to get a job. If I have to accept his help once more, I'll do it to speed things along. I can't do anything else without more income. And you'll just have to hang in there for a little bit, Arlene. And I'll try and use up your working time." He turned, and gently pushed the young woman onto her back, as he moved in so they would lay naked, he on top of her.

"I'm sure you'll enjoy that," she replied sardonically.

"You just try and save the money."

"*You're* going to pay *me*? Your brothers and their goons will take away everything that I earn, anyway. They do that to all the girls to pay for their so-called *orphanage* we live in with the blessings of the ignorant elitists who prop up The Hull House and their charities. Washing their filthy money. And all the while, the members of your precious Family are taking their liberties with us like an entitlement they were born into. The reformers call it white slavery. They passed the Mann Act to abolish it but it's always existed and will continue to exist in one form or another. That Republican hypocrite Mayor Thompson hasn't made any difference in Chicago. He's as corrupt as they come. He's got money coming in from Merlo and D'Andrea, in a negotiated alliance with Coughlin, Kenna, and O'Banion, now collaborating with men like your father under Colosimo and from yet another side, with the Genna Brothers to the west. Meanwhile, I'm on my back. It's all only temporarily keeping more coffins out of the ground. And how are *you* ever going to change all that?"

"I can change it for you. I mean personally. I'll say that since I want to work, that I'm also going to train to take over the collecting. At least in your particular profession's case. As even my *third* job. But that's what my father really wants for me anyway — to turn out like the rest of my wonderful relatives. Take my place in The Family's business. You just hide the stash when I return to you what's really going to be both *our* running-away funds. Turn in the rest to cover what The House expects you to earn. Don't worry. I've had lots of examples over the years to learn how to work the skim. And you just admitted that your service here won't keep the peace for long anyway. So you're also not able to make a change in anything either, Arlene."

"And you're going to play with your balls *and* be a pimp?" Arlene laughed. "I gotta love *this* plan. And you're even going to steal, skimming off of what your old man considers *his* money. Okay, Tad. Best of luck with that. I can't wait to see what happens next. But I still don't get why you're helping *me*."

"Because it's not right. What my father's done. What he's doing."

"You'd turn against your own family? That's sheltered you. Provided for you. That's what they're going to ask if they catch you. Before they beat the crap out of you or worse, of course. And they'll even say your beating is for your own good and that it was your family that made possible your stupid baseball opportunities." Arlene didn't believe Tad was prepared to go through with all that. Not surprisingly, he wasn't.

"No," Taddeo admitted. "At least I'd never admit to going *that far* — but that money is my inheritance so it's not a *real betrayal*."

"In your eyes, maybe? Tell me if that's not how Benedict Arnold also reasoned. And while you're at it, quit whining, too. That's what they'll also say."

"Hey, I don't have to stick around here and play the beneficiary of their so-called business, that is until I'm eventually and permanently dragged down into it. I know they're never going to stop. New York's always been giving my father *and his big city boss* all their marching orders — especially now. You probably don't even know the half of *that*. And *they* aren't going to stop. Chicago's never going to gain its independence again. And my brothers? It's just going to go on and on — and they wouldn't know how to do anything else, so they couldn't quit if they wanted to. In fact, for some reason I still can't even figure, Greggorio had to be the one who called the Gennas out with us tonight. Only I don't care *what he's plotting*. I now have this one great chance to be my own man. And I've already worked so hard to gain this *once in a lifetime* opportunity." She knew he referred to his pitching. "And I'm going to create even more with it. Plus, you get this straight: baseball is not stupid, Arlene! It's the dream of a lifetime — an adventure. For the best of the best, a journey toward immortality in the record books. Once they deem them important enough to build a museum for them or something. And I can't possibly know how far and for how long I'll make it as a player. All of us — my teammates I mean — *will* eventually get cut, or injured even earlier than that, maybe traded somewhere else first, and that last possibility maybe well before the rest of the *bad stuff* that can happen — and of course any of those things could happen to me, especially. And worse. At any time. *In my current environment*. But, as I said, maybe my being traded would be good — for both of us. So I need even *the idea* of making plans for something better, something else, with *someone else* — like you Arlene — someone else who can take this journey with me. To inspire me to push on. Take control of my own destiny for once. I'm building up my experience."

Tad was seriously delusional. *But then why am I so reluctant to push him off of me, leave him and get myself out of this damned hotel room?* Arlene thought. "Your experience? With what? Mental illness? Seriously, I don't know, Tad. With this plan of yours, and *my experience*, I can already imagine a lot of *bad stuff* happening." She didn't need him. Though Tad was sweet, and all too idealistic, this young woman especially didn't need *him* in her way. She had her own journey to take. And she would have to take it, even in spite of him and however unexpectedly amusing she might find him. The suggestion was there that he didn't need what befell his other family members to happen to *him*. But just maybe she could make good use of him. She felt his hard pressure against her midriff. Taddeo pointed out to her new options she never could possibly imagine being made available to her before, from which she could now manage her mission. Then she felt Taddeo repositioning to slide down soft and moistened skin, tiny thin hairs tickling both of them. He re-entered her body, thrusting himself forward in the missionary position, while in a dark place in her mind, and from possibly another new position, Arlene began to readapt her own plans, her mission.

Chapter 8

"The next thing you need to do is learn to adapt yourself to be better at managing women. I'm surprised that I am your junior, yet I am the one teaching *you* this," Greg said to his cousin. "But while I have you in mind for far greater things, someone will need to run this bordello when Papa or I cannot supervise it."

"That won't be an especially painful lesson to learn," Corrado commented with a short-lasting smile while looking from the ladies who had recently returned to the lounge with a few of the baseball players, over to the seriously thrashed goombah that Sigñor Villetti still tended to. "There's worse jobs to be had around here." The new man remained still, recovering at Urso's table, Corrado's eldest first cousin also comforting the man with the familiar but empty security of platitudes that he knew were worth less than the bloody rags he could wipe his relief into.

"It might be for the worse — because that also means I need you to deal with Arlene, the latest Market Street forfeiture. You know which one she is."

"Hmmm. The one that did not return back here with your brother's team. With the hair of a hot scarlet? I have *most certainly* noticed *her*."

"Huh. I'm very sure everyone has." Greg studied his cousin for a moment. *Corry* did indeed *notice the girl as well as did Taddeo, and* Corry *might even like this one now. That may also be worth noting.* "It would seem Papa got himself into something interesting in return for bargaining away Urso's honor."

"I've heard that rumor. Did *you* care?"

"About Urso's honor? Are you kidding me?" Greggorio laughed. "My brother doesn't even understand the deal, nor is he sharp enough to even consider it, or how she wound up here. Or wherever my little brother took her down with him tonight. And if Urso had known about it, he'd have just taken the girl away from Taddeo — if *he* knew she were even made available by my father like I suggested. But Urso's easy to satisfy. And it's more than likely that he has also noted Arlene. She's just been kept out of his reach by Papa, and now presumably Taddeo. It's not like he was ever going to get to act on any interest he had for her — not when it would mean his making an effort when other substitutes are more easily available. It was pretty inconvenient for me too, but not the way you'd expect. I planned my initial moves a little differently but I *can* adapt. Urso, not so well. But that's my big brother. And that's exactly why in the bigger picture, I sure as hell wasn't going to risk my own neck on some retaliatory strike north of Lincoln Park for Urso's sake and all over Bugs Moran's mood swings either." Greg deliberately misled his cousin over what had really occurred north of the river last week. It would not be good for him if that ever got out. Not at all.

"Of course you wouldn't risk it. You're next in line to lead The Family — after Urso, anyway."

"Huh. *Really*?" As Corry then paused to more carefully study his cousin, as if the young man was only just realizing something, Greg decided not to comment any further on the topic for the meantime. But he did give his cousin an appreciative sidelong glance, turning up the nearest corner of his mouth, very well aware of how useful someone with Corry's intelligence would be to his own plans. All the Villetti line — even the extended family line — looked somewhat alike. But his cousin Corrado thought like him, too.

"So back to the girl, you obviously know which one is Arlene."

"Yeah. I obviously do."

"I should have bet on that. Well anyway, you will go to her. Tonight. This morning. Well, whatever time it is now. First, find out what she's up to. For this, you may have to follow her, discreetly. Staying back. Invisible. You won't need to venture into the Gennas' territory. Unless I'm on a real lucky streak with *all* my plans, Arlene will have asserted herself even upon Angelo, and sooner than later redirected the alternate course I set up for my little brother this evening. Some of his teammates are already back right now, obviously. Because in not too long of time, I'm sure I'll learn that it was *she* who winds up being the one who gets whoever's left of the rest of them all back from the Near West Side, or most of them anyway, if only to end her night with Taddeo over at that new high-rise hotel by Rainbow's shore. I'd bet my little brother's still keeping her real busy over there by the beach — teaching her how to play ball the way *he* likes to. Even right now. As pathetic as I'd guess that would be. So I want to know, if she leaves after that — ."

"Wait. What was she doing over there? I mean on the West Side with the Genna Brothers?"

"Who are under *my* control, remember? We have some common — *interests*, you could say. You needn't concern yourself with the details. Or whatever happens there. I've figured all the probabilities and made contingency plans in case one particular individual or another does *not* return from their little trip out by Cicero." That comment raised both Corry's eyebrows. "But I doubt I'll get that lucky. Now don't interrupt me again, Corrado. I have a good idea of who I'm dealing with. You'll most likely be tracking the bitch's movements and report back to me what she does next on the South Side. If that's where she remains. I don't expect her to, or that the Gennas would have touched *her*, though even that's not an inconvenience, but the probability is doubtful. Now if she next stays in the hotel with Taddeo, you'll visit her and my little brother — when you're very sure to be disturbing them — and let them know The House is watching over them — perhaps so that *they have everything* they *need* — that sort of thing. For reasons I can't fathom, my father was actually impressed with Tad's pitching. Offer this as an excuse for the interruption anyway. I'm not sensing an arrival by a girl *like that* into our bordello is any coincidence I could see myself living with. Now even my papa is being care-*less*, so you better be *careful*."

* * * * *

Corry heard Greg's last instruction very clearly as he now approached the beaten victor of last evening's street brawl. He smiled and offered the man a gentle pat on his back. "So I hear you've only just started, but you look like you could already use The House's vacation plan."

"Yeah, well I still have enough of my senses about me to tell me that I don't want to be sent on vacation the way new guys who aren't '*Family*' get sent on vacation around here. I've heard some rumors about *that*."

"Huh. Well, I'm Corrado Delasandro. I *am* Family and I think I can help you out."

"How's about that?"

"I'm sure you'd like a nice easy job for your second assignment."

"That's what Villetti said about my first one when I'd just arrived here from New York."

"Yes. And I can see how that went. But you always need to earn more pay, right? And I only want you to visit a girl."

The man smiled. "Done. Now you're talking. You can call me Dulio and I will gladly do *that.* I already have some specialized experience with uh, insight into the activities of certain ladies around here. And I thought I was hired only because they anticipated my prowess in a brawl."

"It was not for your skills as a plumber. That I can tell you for certain. But this time, your discretion will be the best part of your valor."

"Huh?"

"Well, this assignment is not exactly what I can see you're already thinking it is. You know you may very well wind up not having any contact with this girl at all."

"Should've figured it wouldn't be *that* much fun."

Now Corry actually became aware of a growing concern for Arlene's safety once he set this goombah loose on her tail. *Dammit. I don't need this.* So he felt compelled to add, "It doesn't *need* to be *fun.* And while you recover, I think you'll benefit from the kind of work where you'll have just about no contact with anyone at all."

"That sounds boring."

"Oh, I'll bet it won't be."

But Corry had to admit to himself that *he* did find Arlene to be all too tempting. So he just couldn't bear to see her in the arms of Taddeo Villetti, thus he would accomplish what Greg asked of him, but send Dulio to do it for him. He just hoped he wouldn't regret that decision.

* * * * *

After Arlene let Tad believe she had just consented to staying with him, two more hours passed. Now it was close to dawn, and Arlene made to leave the finally resting athlete with barely any time before the sun would actually rise over Lake Michigan.

He lay there so vulnerable to her, but yet so dedicated. So her evaluation returned her to the same conclusion about his worth that she'd made the previous night. Perhaps it was an instinct she felt when they first met in his father's bar — and before the Genna Brothers would intervene. Which was that Taddeo would continue to be weak and vulnerable *to her*, but that he was better off the way he was for right now, at peace, his naked chest slowly rising and falling, and thereby also *useful* — to her. With his heart still quietly beating. Beating for her. *His mistake*.

Then — while she finished dressing in a poor girl's wardrobe, not leaving out once-donated tan-colored ladies' harem pants she kept stuffed inside her older less-decorative, over-sized purse that she'd recovered from the senior Villetti's room — her whole being shook and spasmed when she buttoned up her white blouse. Grabbing her hat, she nearly dove for the door, not caring if she woke Taddeo, but hoping and praying she'd make it down the hallway to the hotel's ladies' restroom. She didn't. So falling against the wall, her heavy purse sliding off her shoulders while she heaved, Arlene decorated the wood paneling with probably everything she had been eating and drinking. Looking around to make sure no one had noticed her — and the corridor *was* deserted at that hour — Arlene proceeded to the bathroom and procured a rather thick towel she dabbed at the corners of her mouth with, and then carried it along with her down the indoor staircase that served as one fire-safety exit, this one emptying into the hotel lobby, and leaving that mess she made behind her on the wall. It wouldn't be the last mess she made, though she hoped the rest of them would be intentional, but she wished she could rinse out her mouth. Only now she had to hurry.

The central front entrance was occupied by only two staff members and one patron at this early hour of the morning. The latter's features were undiscernible, as he held the newspaper he was reading up high, covering her view of his face. But the desk clerk and the nighttime bellhop curiously ignored Arlene as she made her way to the entry-exit and out the stylish glass revolving door. This prickled the tiny hairs on the back of her neck, as ordinarily the help fell all over *her*, trying to be of service to someone they viewed as one extremely attractive girl. But because of this lack of a *re*-action, Arlene realized, she was in danger! So the woman instinctively adapted her plan of action.

Once out on 53rd Street, Arlene angled southbound on Lake Park as if to go around Woodlawn instead of heading toward Kenwood and then the North Side. She'd already walked the streets before, but for the explicit purpose of scouting escape routes she might need should she encounter complications like the one she knew she was experiencing right now. Speeding up her pace, she continued on an obvious course for two blocks — which she hoped would be more than enough to determine if someone followed her by coincidence or predetermination. She started panting, curiously working herself to being out of breath far too early than she was accustomed to. Sweat stung the corners of her eyes — as it couldn't be tears. And she could feel her heart pounding in her chest. It was fear that she felt. Abruptly, she twisted her course and spun to her left into an alley. Entering into a run, Arlene splashed through some collected puddles she didn't quite make out in the early morning gloom and hurried down the narrow passageway, until finally flattening herself against a brick wall, ornamented with piles of uncollected garbage. She smelled something foul was about as she tried to resume her normal breathing.

From her purse she removed an object which she quickly covered with the towel she'd taken from the hotel's ladies' room.

Footsteps resounding in the dark became accented with the splashing of water. The silhouette of some character did indeed follow her. The sounds made her shiver. Light from a fire started in a trash can by a street urchin trying to keep warm through the night lit up the stranger. She held her breath as if continuing even any respiration would render her detectable as she tried to observe her stalker. From the unusual shadow he cast, Arlene could predict his head was bandaged — white wrapping reflected the brightness from the fire even under his dark fedora when she could risk a peek to confirm it. There was some kind of object in his hand. She ducked back under cover and gulped, realizing if her life was in danger already, it'd be a shame if it was so only because she was suffocating herself. That thought brought strength to her anger that let Arlene overcome her fear. Then she imagined her pursuer moving around to his right, then back to his left. He'd lost track of her in all this blackness. More sounds of motion through collected water. Then in her own hands, Arlene locked down her hatred and used it to motivate her courage and one very cold piece of metal. Then she whispered, "Over here. Are you looking for me?"

"Huh?" The figure swerved, angling right back in her direction. Only then the alleyway momentarily lit up with a much stronger but briefer flash of brightness. The flash came with a fairly decently muffled sound from under the young lady's bath towel. And for only a second, the light revealed the man falling face first, toward her, into one more puddle on the soiled ground.

Arlene moved to leave him there, unsure if this man had also been followed — all the while he was following her. It would not have surprised the woman now, having truly reconsidered the clever and dangerous men she had come here to deal with. But as she tried to vacate the scene of the crime, she suddenly began heaving again and threw up once more. It felt like only bile this time, as her supper and her alcoholic beverages had also long since been evacuated. But she attributed it to her agitated nerves. After all, she'd volunteered herself to be in this extremely stressful situation. And she had no prior experience with taking a life from someone. Ending all that they ever were and all they would ever become. But she'd been nearly paralyzed by death before. To gain momentum away from it, she'd chosen to move in a direction that would only return her to its frozen embrace — the day she commanded it well enough so as to fulfill her plan to have a lot of grateful guests at her own funeral. What she would become — they would all remember! Those that she let survive anyway. And now there was no doubt Greggorio Villetti acted by sending that man, because Arlene had surely screwed up the plans he'd arranged with the Gennas the past evening — though that only escalated her eagerness to return to waging her war. Curiously though, this killing had actually made the woman physically hungry. Careful to observe her surroundings and anyone else who might be watching her, she looked left then right, then left again, and back the way she had come. Then the lady of the night cut a new route away from the homeless man so that maybe he wouldn't ever be able to identify her. She decided upon making her way back to the hotel for now, looking forward to the opportunity to think more on her present situation, plot her strategy of attack while getting back to feeling healthy, light a fresh cigarette and then appease her new appetite just as soon as the café opened up for breakfast. Arlene knew she'd lost too much time over everything that had happened during the course of this night to accomplish what else she had planned. She would bet that Taddeo wouldn't wake up until much later though, and then she could be ready to quickly get rid of him.

* * * * *

Greg was still drinking at the bar, early into the start of the next day, having remained way past closing time from the night prior, until it was nearly arriving upon their re-opening time. The morning staff would soon come in. His father had finally gone home to go to bed. He helped himself to The Family's stock while he examined and re-examined all his new creative musings. Sobriety had stayed with him before he'd even emptied a single wine bottle and remained with him through the latest. He was not a drunk like his oldest brother, but now for just one night, he wished he were. *No I don't*. But his always-busy mind wouldn't let him rest and relax. It never did. *It is just who I am.*

Corrado and a policeman entered Villetti's together, and they were encumbered by a body. Already wrapped in bandages, it wasn't hard to recognize Dulio even if Greg hadn't cared to be personally acquainted with the man. They dropped the body across a nearby table and Greggorio hopped off his bar stool and approached the corpse to examine it, and the men who brought it to him.

The Irish copper had his hand out as soon as Greg arrived. The Villetti's mouth bent downward at one corner, but he reached into his suit-coat pocket, produced his money clip and peeled off some greenbacks for the civil servant. The policeman went for them, but Greg drew his hand back. "Ah-nah. Not just yet. Wait here a minute."

Greg was already quite familiar with the cop. He was just a training rookie who opened his mouth and was about to protest.

"I know you'd prefer not to be involved in this Olsen, but you'll have a chance to earn even twice what I was going to pay you. Just be patient." Addressing Corry in a low tone to not be overheard, with a hand on his cousin's shoulder to steer him away for a little privacy, Greg asked, "You sent *this one*?" He nodded toward the carcass. "And then you followed him?" The answer was already obvious and Greg had been correct. His cousin *was* smart.

"That's right."

"The girl?"

"I assume so. I didn't see it happen. I was too far behind. My fault. But we're dealing with something that feels very wrong here. She might be more than what your papa bargained for."

"No shit. That's why I want her followed."

"You suspect — ?"

"Neither of you need to know what I suspect, and this is not a public discussion, Corrado." Greggorio nodded toward the patrolman. He and his cousin might not be sufficiently out of an alert policeman's earshot. And the copper might be on more than several payrolls. Such was the unease new immigrant families had to operate under on what was once only Old Irish dominated territory. Greg also knew this one worked under the trust of Detective Conway. The Family had its frequent dealings with him. And so with additional volume Greggorio said, "So now the two of you are going to dispose of this." He gestured to the dead man.

The policeman looked at Greg skeptically, but the Villetti brother held up his money clip and his eyebrows in an imitation of innocence. "This wasn't my fault but I'm generous enough to take responsibility for it. Twice this amount. Remember?"

"Uh. I guess I know a place," the cop started.

"Oh, I don't care. Instead, what you're going to do is cut him up — and just the way fresh pork chops are prepared to be consumed — and then place him where *I* tell you. You'll use a barrel. Don't weight it. I want this one to be *found* — floating. Tomorrow. Today. Whenever. You'll probably need to use a police wagon to carry this package. But the fog will cover you over by the river. Drop him and then *you* keep as far away from this as you can," the final instruction meant for his cousin specifically.

"Wait a minute," Corry took a long stride toward Greg, grabbed him by his right bicep and pulled him back towards the bar. He then conversed with Greggorio in impassioned whispers that they both hoped were once more out of earshot of Officer Olsen. "This could reignite the war. What the fuck do you think you're doing? Our Family is going to think the butcher's friends retaliated."

"Exactly. But don't worry. I'm about to make sure Urso is the first to learn what's left of this one. As I'll also instruct our copper here to make sure his close buddies pick this meat up, and moreover, keep it quiet, but next bring it to the attention of my dear big brother. He can't think for himself — so he won't. So then he'll take this to Papa. After which they'll then question me. I'm going to point him to *you*, and you'll tell him exactly what really happened. Nothing to worry over getting caught lying about." Greg shrugged. "Just tell them exactly what happened, but leave out Olsen's involvement or anything that would suggest the plumber's body's ever been brought here before. The result is that at the very least, Papa will wake up and realize the implications of trusting that whore — who's undeniably involved and after all, a gift from the Irish. See any irony in that?"

"After all *that* trouble, your father and your brother will never suspect you were involved and they both will want to take upon a course of vengeance — against Arlene, too — if I don't omit anything from my report. But if Uncle Rinny wants vengeance, Taddeo will be in the way."

"Exactly. As *he too* has *always* been in the way. And now *you're* learning."

Chapter 9

Wednesday, May 22, 1918
5:02 pm CST
Weeghman Park, Chicago, Illinois

8th Inning
Brooklyn – 0, Cubs – 0

0 Outs, 0 On

AB: The Brooklyn Robins (11 W – 16 L):
Ivy Olson (SS, Bats: right, Throws: right) AVG .239, OBP .286
Age: 33, Games: 417, Status: veteran player,
5th full season in The Show

On the mound:
Chicago Cubs (17 W – 11 L)
(Fighting to not be in last place in the National League)
P: Claude Hendrix (SP)
(Bats: Right, Throws: Right) 20 W – 7 L, PCT: .741, ERA: 2.78,
SO: 865, HB: 40 x (in 7 years)
Age: 29, Games: 268, Status: 7-year veteran

AND THEN:

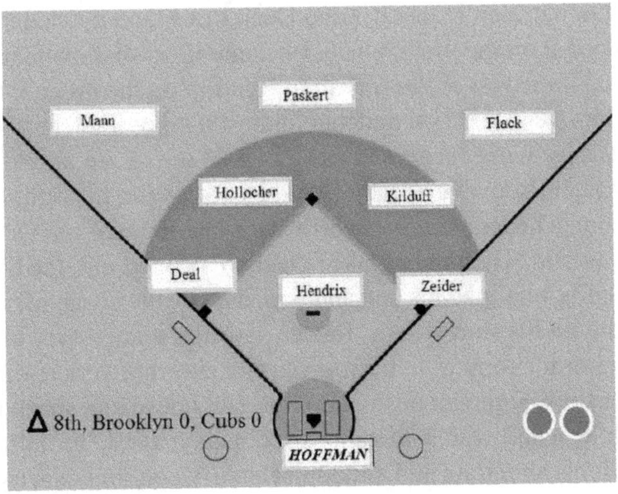

"Alright. Let's go Cubs. Show me you are learning *something* since yesterday. We've dropped two games to the Robins already. And it's way past payback time." Coach Mitchell swatted Claude Hendrix on his backside as he jogged out of the 3rd base dugout to take the mound for the eighth time this Wednesday afternoon. George Hoffman flashed his best friend in the whole wide world his very best smile as he took off to join Hendrix as his battery-mate for only The Hoff's sixth time appearing in a Major League ballgame. Tad slapped his buddy's shoulder to encourage him, as George ran past him, still carrying some of his pads and facemask in his hands, his huge catcher's glove tucked under his arm. Tad couldn't have been happier after his night with Arlene, but in close second was that Coach had brought in George to add a left-handed bat in the bottom of the 7th against Brooklyn's right-handed Lawrence Cheney. It hadn't paid off — *yet*. That determination only according to The Hoff. The rookie backstop just needed a little more time to get used to Major League pitching. So both teams remained tied at Ø runs going into the late innings.

Now Hoffman had to demonstrate he'd carefully studied Will Robinson's bats and was at least capable of making the right pitch calls for Hendrix. The Cubs' starting hurler faced the top of Brooklyn's order, beginning with Ivy Olson. All of Chicago's boys remembered *exactly who* drove the Robins' winning RBI yesterday — and not with any fondness.

It did not start well with Hendrix and Hoffman bringing the Robins' shortstop to a full-count and then walking him. Nor did it help that 3rd baseman Ollie O'Mara drove a single into shallow left-field in between Hollocher and Deal. Les Mann hustled in and stopped it on the first bounce. He came in so shallow that he just tossed it the rest of the way in to Hendrix on the mound. In the dugout over by 3rd on quite an interesting day, Tad could tell Coach was growing concerned as he looked across the infield and saw Ivy Olson take a lead off 2nd base and aim his right foot toward him. The Robin's eyes narrowed as he focused on his next destination and "Gentleman Jake" Daubert stepped into the batter's box. Hendrix removed his cap and wiped away the sweat off his forehead with his shirt sleeve. Taddeo saw him glance over to the Cubs' bench for support in time to see an aide who worked directly with Charlie Weeghman push out of the clubhouse and sprint up to Coach Mitchell with something scribbled on a note for him. His coach became irate and although Hendrix couldn't exactly hear what the Cubs' manager was screaming about over the roar of the Brooklyn fans, he could surely tell by the thrown scrap of paper and all the hand-gesturing that Coach was furious and taking it out on the messenger. Finally after heartily demonstrating his protestations, Mitchell turned to glare at Hendrix out on the mound and nodded to him. Then he turned and said something to the bench and Claude surely saw Taddeo Villetti excitedly jump to his feet. The rookie reliever had heard everything and gave a thumbs up signal to Hoffman, who had been positioned behind the plate and got an enthusiastic mirror response in return. Another smile had lit up behind the catcher's mask, this one huge. Then O'Farrell, who'd been benched after even hitting a double in the middle innings, got up and grabbed his glove to get Villetti warm.

But what undoubtedly burned Hendrix most was Daubert, a lefty who jumped all over Claude's first offering and drove a line-drive out between Rollie Zeider — who'd taken over for Fred Merkle — after he'd been pretty severely wounded by a pitch in the very 1st inning — and Kilduff, who returned to play 2nd base. But instead of easily catching it, Max Flack overran where the ball touched down and kicked it clumsily toward centerfield. But Dode Paskert was on it and scooped it up fast enough that Olson didn't dare to test his arm once the Robins' shortstop arrived at the 3-bag. Now the bases were loaded and that brought up left-fielder Zack Wheat, as well as a very disgusted Coach Mitchell for an awkward trip to the mound.

He took the game ball and with only one finger and a jerk of his head toward his left, he sent Taddeo Villetti off at a run toward him, to take the ball and the hill. Coach didn't even look at the reliever. He knew what Tad would be waiting for. The game would now be in Villetti's hands.

Hoff was on hand with the rest of the infield for their conference at the mound to greet Tad when he answered this challenge. "At last!" He smiled brightly.

"God help us," Mitchell said, glancing between his rookie battery mates. "So whatever it is that *you two* have got planned — don't. *Don't you* dare *fucking do it*. Do you understand me?"

Hank O'Day called out for the two of them to hurry it up as Coach offered his final advice before he'd depart the field. "Now Brooklyn is loaded to end this stalemate. *Weeghman* wants to see what you can do with a chance to run the game for us. Don't kill your best opportunity to prove you have the ability to do what you need to do, Villetti." Then the Cubs' manager crossed the 3rd base line directly in front of Ivy Olson sending him a contemptuous glare on his way to Chicago's dugout. His players knew when their tasked coach was next about to need to sneak his flask out for some bourbon to help calm him.

"Okay, Tad. Now you settle in and we'll show them all what we *can* do." With a smile, George spelled out his plan to the infielders gathered around. "They got one of their big guns coming up to the dish. Zack Wheat thinks he's going to take a rookie for a ride. I'm calling a pitchout." He glanced around at his other teammates in the huddle, who looked surprised at this strategy, given the bases were loaded. Then he looked at Taddeo. "*That* pitchout." Villetti nodded, understanding as Hoff continued. The other Cubs looked confused. "Don't worry fellas. I'm gonna explain. Now he's a left-hander. So Charlie," he addressed the 3rd baseman, "we're going to show you a little trick we used to play in Iowa. As soon as Tad releases, come in — all the way in. There won't be a play at 3rd and I need you to back up your pitcher. Holly, you'll back up Kilduff. Ignore the 3-bag." To his buddy he relayed, "Tad, just bounce it back off the bricks and let me show Killefer that I've got every bit the arm he has. This won't even be a sacrifice play. Buckwheat won't even make contact for the suicide bunt. Deal will back you up so we can cover the ricochet in more directions than one. You've got the 1st base side of the plate. Whoever, gets the ball gets it back to me fast. When Brooklyn runs, I'll clean those bases for you, Buddy." The Hoff smiled. "I'm getting two with an assist, taking Olson at the plate and then throwing down to Pete to take Daubert at 2nd base. Their big guy's not too quick. That's for sure."

"C'mon Hoff. Cheney beaned Merkle in the 1st inning and Hendrix hasn't done anything about it," Tad pointed out with a smile and delighted mischief escaping his black, swollen eyes.

"He probably hit him as payback for you hitting Ernie Krueger yesterday."

"Yeah, but I didn't take him all the way out of the game."

"Only you pitched like you tried to and they all know it."

"Let's go Chicago!" The Reverend commanded.

"Let me take a chance with my own record and prove that now I'm loyal to my teammates."

"What's the matter? The pressure on? You aren't afraid are you, New Fish?" the Robins' left-fielder, Zack Wheat – who was next in the order – was taking practice swings when he called out from alongside the batter's box. He probably thought the veterans were refusing to play ball with the rookie Villetti. Since the fight yesterday, the pitcher looked like one beat-up mess.

"No. He's crazy. And you're stupid. So I'd shut up right now if I were you, Son — that is if you know what's best for you," O'Day warned the Brooklyn batter. Then he called behind the screen to someone tending to security behind home plate. "Better call the medic — just in case."

The Robin's comment was indeed really not very smart of him, considering who the Cubs had just sent out as their relief pitcher. "Aw, George. C'mon. Now we know Wheat's just asking for it. Would you listen to him?" Villetti pleaded. Then he smiled.

"But the bags are crammed. You *walk a run in* if you pull this shit right now, Tad."

"It will be worth it for me to get some teeth subtracted from that asshole's grin. He knew the risk when he opened his big fat New York mouth. Besides, we're home team. We've got at least two more ups and you're hitting in O'Farrell's spot. You going to back me up or what?"

"Yeah. Alright. I always do. I guess you know what you're doing." Then The Hoff addressed all Chicago's players meeting at the mound. "So Guys, reverse that plan on the *next batter*. Once Wheat goes to 1st on a stretcher, Hy Myers is a righty. So Bunions," he addressed Zeider, who was substituting at 1st base and whose face signaled he was not fond of the rookie using his nickname, " — what I told Deal. Same thing goes for you. So there's no play at *1st base*. You'll come all the way in to help Tad when Myers bats. Shooter: now you're on the 3rd base side. Fellas: they won't be expecting Tad to hit Wheat and our play to be on the bat *after* him."

"Are you sure about that?"

"Well, we got you Hoff. We'll trust you this time and you guys will show 'em all what the Cubs' rookies can do," Charlie Hollocher added. "But you two better not fuck this thing up, Marshalltowners. Especially you, Villetti. Giving them a run. Geez. I'm up next inning, and I don't want to get hit by Cheney. But I'll do what I can to help. Only this is for Fred." Kilduff and Deal didn't look too happy about all the rookies making the plan and yet they did have to appreciate the new guys avenging Merkle. But right then, there wasn't time for any further arguing about it. They nodded; they understood the differing strategy for each batter that was now being called for.

"Okay. Let's go. Play ball!" O'Day hollered.

"Boy is Mitchell going to kill us. But this move has worked. So you better settle down and throw for real after you serve 'ol Buck Wheat," Hoff told his pitcher. "Alright then. Let's win some more baseball."

"It'll be just like Iowa — back in the mudfields again. But I bet I'll also win Merkle over on to my side, too — since Hendrix won't answer these New Yorkers back for what happened to our First Man." Tad smiled.

"Yeah, you do that, Marshalltown. Meanwhile, I'll be praying this works," Hollocher told the Cubs' new hurler.

"Now Rookies!" Hank O'Day yelled at them.

"Yeah. Let's go Rookie!" the ass-fan who was always in left field hollered toward the mound.

The Cubs' infielders broke up their huddle and ran to their positions. Olson, O'Mara, and Daubert were all on when left-fielder Zack Wheat came up to the dish. Normally confident batting with an amazing .335 average and on track for plenty of RBIs already this season, the Robin left-hander had gulped when he saw that Taddeo Villetti had actually been allowed to climb the hill to take the ball from the equally apprehensive Chicago Coach Mitchell, to relieve Claude Hendrix — and then narrow his eyes and tighten his jaw when he stared at him, and articulated a single nod of his head. But the Brooklyner had made a point of hiding his fear by making his taunts — to display a fake show of overconfidence. Now actually feeling real confidence, Tad could barely prevent his smile from eclipsing his cut-fastball between the rubber and home plate when he took his last warm-up tosses that fine spring day downtown in The Windy City. His best friend in the whole wide world George Hoffman was finally about to catch for him in their first game as battery mates since they had at long last come up to the Big Leagues! In Tad's mind, this was a historic occasion. This was The Show.

But Brooklyn would be ready to take it all back from him in the extreme. They didn't have the lead yet, but with more thanks to Flacky's *second* error of that game than Ivy Olson's base-running skills, they had the bases crammed. *What was going on with Max Flack?* Tad took only a second to wonder. No sooner than Villetti would take the mound, Daubert could have even got the go-ahead to steal 2nd base. Even though the bases were loaded, the Robins were that aggressive to use a him in a sacrifice. There were no outs and no score by this late-late inning. So Daubert could be used as bait for the inexperienced pitcher to chase him or even O'Mara — and ignore Olson who'd run in to score. The Brooklyn 1st baseman took a huge leadoff, even with O'Mara so obviously in his way. The unconventional Robinson *would* call for a suicide sacrifice squeeze in the 8th — still with no score and no outs, with the bases jammed, and not even a batted ball in play. They wanted to shake up a rookie. That alone was insulting. But Tad wouldn't take the bait. He did not throw over, and everyone held their positions around the horn. A Villetti could also have his own unorthodox plan. However, Wilbert Robinson then gave a different signal. And then the one pitcher hated by fifteen out of sixteen teams, the man, the menace, Burleigh Grimes stepped out onto the 1st base sideline to warm up for Brooklyn. He looked at the Cubs' next hurler as he spat in the opposing pitcher's direction.

Now Wheat, who batted left, was more than likely to punch a hit through 1st and 2nd off right-handed Villetti, and the only southpaw Mitchell had remaining was Lefty Tyler, who was resting since he'd pitched on Sunday. Vaughn still recovered from yesterday. Tad felt doubt probing him for just a second as he wondered why Coach sent *him* into the middle of this. But the Cubs' box score was just one of the threats Chicago faced coming from out of New York that afternoon. All it took was someone being minutely aware of their sixth sense and the wave of barely contained anger became detectable, permeating the entire stadium. Ernie Krueger, Jack Coombs, Mickey Doolin, and Dan Griner, with restless legs, and fists formed, and held back in their second hands, and with more of their teammates behind them, had all gathered right at the bottom of their dugout stairs waiting to enjoy knocking Taddeo Villetti off the mound just as soon as he pulled something — anything — whether they were even on deck for this game or not. The Cubs' pitcher noted their smoldering eyes that matched their personalities with the red, hot tips of their cigarettes they smoked while they zeroed in on him. However, Mitchell wanted to avoid the Cubs repeating the same kind of bench-clearing brawl that had occurred yesterday. Perhaps that was also why Team Captain Bill Killefer sat out this game, but remained stationed at the opposite end of the Cubs' dugout from Coach at all times, so as to at least block in Trip and The Bass-Man from any easy access to the field, as well as any other Cubbies who might be so inclined to get into a fight again because of some stunt pulled by Taddeo. But there were no outs, so Brooklyn's runners returned close to their bases and the plan changed to appear as if they would wait to see if they might first score their hits from the batter's box. Or as if they doubted Tad could even find the strike zone. But

Taddeo's best friend was with him as Villetti soon got the signal he really wanted. He tightened his jaw and returned an angry, hateful stare right back at the Robins' bench. Villetti was going head-hunting no matter what. Only for three tosses in a row, and with a larger grin under his mask every time, Hoff signaled for Taddeo's special cutter, which moved inside on a left-hander. However, it was taking Villetti a few more than a couple of tries to plunk the Robins' leftfielder as Wheat, now extremely conscious of defending his health even more than his batting average, weaved and dodged the first couple of pitches that Taddeo tried to slam into the left-handed batter's exposed side. And when Wheat's knee proved an elusive target, Hoff nodded and motioned upward with his finger.

After the next potential collision, a fastball aimed at his shoulder got dodged by Wheat, who fell over backward and lost his bat in the process of looking alive, Ernie Krueger had now actually ran up to the edge of Brooklyn's sideline as if to make like the Robins needed two 1st base coaches. But the bat had actually been struck when Wheat had held it up in self-defense and strike-one would be awarded on the foul in the dirt. Hank O'Day held up George returning the ball to the mound as he pointed a warning finger at the Robins' catcher, who was now totally out of his dugout and on the actual field. Brooklyn's manager caught sight of that, as well as a rather irritated and tired looking would-be Det. Will Sweeney, who'd swiftly walked down the seating box aisle closest to the visitors' dugout on the 1st base side. The plain clothes peace officer nodded to the baseball manager, then looked at Charlie Ebbets, who had seen to it that he'd be in Chicago to personally attend every game of this series — now from even out in the stands, and even in spite of any danger to his person and the riot his players fought in yesterday. So when his teammates tried to join Krueger, Wilbert Robinson caught Ebbets' non-verbal instruction next, and then took some rather long strides to quickly get out in front of his backstop, force all of his players back into line, and corral them down the stairs. Ebbets watched from the stands but still appeared to not be too disturbed by any goings-on off the diamond. He focused his attention on what was happening to his batter.

Taddeo observed this with satisfaction. He also noticed Burleigh Grimes continuing to turn his head away from his warm-up practice to glare at Tad and spit, which only resulted in getting Villetti madder by all of these goings-on. Hoff seemed a little upset too now, and scowled under his mask. He continued to be so when he returned the ball to Tad and squatted, calling for another one inside. Tad saw that no one from Chicago looked to be critiquing him. Of course, the Brooklyn fans were booing as a chorus in the stands. Hank O'Day kept looking like the umpire wanted to say something, but would glance over to Detective-hopeful Sweeney, in the spectators' seats. The Reverend knew this youngster also wanted to make a name for himself and rise up in the ranks of an all-too-corrupt police force. And now, with some satisfaction, Tad saw that Killefer had moved from his position guarding the steps to go and talk to Coach Mitchell, pointing toward Fred Merkle on the bench being attended to by a sports physician. Mitchell was shaking his head and wouldn't even look at Taddeo again, looking to Merkle then back to Killefer instead, shrugging and slapping his hands against the sides of his legs. This time Hoffman, all smiles behind the plate, jerked his thumb up on high. Villetti knew what that meant. Ivy Olson saw this from his leadoff at 3rd and did something with his tongue hanging so far out of his mouth such that he could lick off his own ear with it. Tad saw that when he looked as if he'd throw to check the runners and thought that if he got the chance to face Olson, he'd love to fix his face for him. His step off the rubber caused all the runners to retreat some more. Then the Cubs pitcher planted his foot back on the rubber and threw a hard and swift head-hunter in his frustration, but Wheat was warned and ready to duck under that one. He still hung in there, waiting for something to line-drive. It was three-and-one when Hoff then signaled Tad to come in low and inside. Then the one who fancied himself The Shooter prepared to launch a new cannonball. And that's when this cutter finally clipped Wheat on his knee, the left-fielder crumpling at the plate.

O'Day appeared to be exasperated and kept making eye-contact with Chicago's "top cop" in the stands, though feeling finally free to act in some minor way, he allowed Mickey Doolin *alone* to come out of the dugout and help his wounded teammate after Taddeo Villetti had completed intentionally walking in one run. Now the whole stadium booed. Risking a side-glance to his own dugout, Tad saw Mitchell turning as red as a Cardinal. Trip and Bass-Man were directing all smiles toward their pitcher, however. Wheat, one arm over Doolin's shoulder, walked off Villetti's sting on his way up the baseline. Mouth clenched, eyes narrowed and his lips puckered, Coach looked like he was trying not to breathe fire as his jowls trembled and he made wild gestures with his arms. Tad hadn't hit Wheat *that* hard — although he had tried. Villetti still reasoned the

Cubs still had at least two at-bats left to catch up and pull ahead. And he had Hoff ready to go to work on that. Nevertheless, Ivy Olson took an exaggerated bow aimed at Taddeo when he'd crossed home plate. Villetti still wanted to hit *him*. But meanwhile Tad very matter-of-factly assessed that he also still had more work to do in controlling his cutter besides his slider. But the booing that continued throughout the stadium by all those visiting from New York attested to no one believing Taddeo had aimed for the strike zone in the first place. Even the asshole in left field had joined the opposition to the unsportsmanlike behavior — and that coming from a rookie. *Really?* — the angry fans must have thought. And now Griner was pacing in the Robins' dugout, while Robinson kept looking to Ebbets in the stand, like he was actually pleading for permission to turn their largest man loose on Villetti. It became undeniable that some of Chicago's fans had joined in heckling *the stinkin' wop*. Then line-officer *Harry* Olsen looked alive as he got recognized from the mound, rushing down the steps to join Sweeney in the stands. Tad knew who these rookie policemen were from some of their more memorable visits to his papa's establishment. But instead of their attention being focused on a Villetti, this time they both turned their heads and nodded toward Charlie Ebbets just in case even the umpire couldn't inspire Robinson to control his boys. O'Day had already gotten furious and aimed warnings at both benches again — instead of Taddeo — while throwing his gear around as soon as Villetti nailed Wheat. But Tad smiled to himself as he made The Reverend curse. The umpire was powerless to do much about anything even in the very house in which he was supposed to act as the final decider. This kind of tension made the game way more exciting anyway. The crowd had grown restless too, while no one was scoring. They were looking forward to another hate-induced fight in The Friendly Confines and adding on to their own hits. At least Villetti had made something exciting happen and the Robins got a number on the board.

However, by this point, Tad recognized that *Officer* Olsen, Sweeney, *and Walsh, and now Detective Conway*, plus it looked like every other Chicago patrolmen on the thin blue line were *all* making their way down the aisles of the stands, just to be prepared or send a non-verbal message by their presence, while the Robbin Henry Harrison Myers stepped up to the plate. Tad wasn't expecting this batter to do anything but tremble after he'd witnessed what Villetti had done to his teammate. However, now that Hoff had let Taddeo bean a Robin for Merkle's sake, and it had caused the Cubs to fall behind a run on the scoreboard, Tad relaxed to follow his buddy's plan. He never minded that Rollie Zeider, Pete Kilduff, Charlie Deal and Hollocher all came in to meet him and George on the mound again before he faced the next Robin batter.

"Okay, this goes just like I ordered before," their current on-field *team captain* called the play as Hoff didn't hesitate to re-brief them on exactly what he'd originally asked from Taddeo one batter prior. And even the Cubs' veteran 3rd baseman admitted that George might've voiced a sound plan. They returned to their positions before O'Day or Lord Byron the field umpire, had to say anything, and Hoffman squatted down and set up for a normal first-pitch delivery. Myers at last could step into the batter's box for whatever would be Brooklyn's next punishment. And that's exactly when Tad threw one way outside for the right-handed center-fielder, the passed-ball looking to run all the way back to the brick wall. It set O'Mara taking off for Home, Myers back-peddling to make sure he was out of his teammate's way. But George knew where the wild pitch was aimed and leapt up and pivoted to snag it on the rebound from the bricks first. Zeider's running in proved unnecessary. Also prepared, Tad ran for the left field side of home plate faster than the Robins' lead runner could get there. But according to plan, Zeider had still run in from 1st. And almost as quickly, all Brooklyn's other men on the diamond were advancing, Deal chasing O'Mara, even though he was empty-handed. Hollocher bolted over to cover 3rd and Kilduff guarded 2nd. In a split-second, Hoff saw that Wheat limped from being hit all while the Cubs' catcher also ran at O'Mara, driving him back beyond Charlie Deal, but Hoffman twisted his own plan and fired to Rollie Zeider who was running back to 1st. He took off to put the tag on Wheat, *then threw to Holly at 3rd.* However, O'Mara was back safely already and Daubert retreated toward 2nd. Only when the baseball got flipped to Kilduff, who had to leave his bag since Hollocher got sloppy with his short-toss, being used to playing much closer to 2nd than he had now found himself, it caused Daubert to see his chance to retreat safely and he dived back head-first for the 2-bag. Only, because he was too busy watching the Cubs' basemen, he dove completely over it! The audience instantly filled the stadium with cruel laughter. But Rollie Zeider, having not ever expected to be playing 1st base, had left it unguarded to come toward 2nd's rescue after he tagged out Wheat. Taddeo was still at home plate, so when Zeider got the ball from Kilduff, recovering from the short-toss,

Daubert had already gotten off the gravel and a safe enough distance away — behind him — and with no other choice and some very unexpected fast running, he could actually return all the way back to 1st base!

This was incredibly irregular. But Coach Mitchell didn't protest it, busy instead with concentrating on not letting his rookies' errors to cause him to have an aneurysm. Meanwhile, Wilbert Robinson preferred there being only 1 out instead of 2. So when the dust settled, O'Mara and Daubert were at the corners as Tad returned to the mound. O'Day and Byron just looked at each other dumbfounded, not sure what the heck they had just seen — except for noting that Chicago's finest were all standing ready in the seats. Shouldn't Daubert have been out by all conventional base-running rules? This was not the time to review that. The best thing the game's officials wished to do was avoid another big brawl. Now Detective Conway held up his hands to freeze O'Day from making any new decree either way. Meanwhile Henry "Hy" Myers resumed standing in the batter's box, acting as though he expected to be pitched to, but likely acting purely reflexively, by raising his bat if only in self-defense against the highly unorthodox Chicago team. He couldn't guess where the next shot the Cubs' pitcher took at him was going to go. His bat deflected Villetti's very next pitch mostly by accident sending that offering as a fast dribbler that looked as if it could jump over the foul line before 3rd base. Charlie Deal couldn't do anything but run up on it and chance it would stay fair until it hit the 3-bag; it did bounce fair, and without further hesitation he grabbed it up and sent it back to Hoffman still in time to cut down O'Mara at home plate! The Robins' runner should have scored on that one but reacted in a manner as to suggest he was still very confused, possibly even afraid, and thanks to Hoff's fast reaction — who rose, snapping the ball back all the way across the diamond to Kilduff, and nailing the slower Jake Daubert at 2nd base — O'Mara was the first out in a crazy 5-2-4 Chicago double-play. But Tad had to duck so he wouldn't get hit by one of the Cubs' own screamers. It was an amazing and great looking pick that George had just made! The crowd roared and the Chicago Cubs held Brooklyn to only one run. Tad ended the top of the 8th with the Robins only claiming that 1 off Olson's scoring by way of Villetti walking the run in when he beaned Zack Wheat. Tad marched off the mound with quite the satisfied smile on his face he directed toward Hoffman who clapped his hand as he ran up to meet him. Fred Merkle stood up from where he was recovering on the bench from being hit by Cheney, and thanked Taddeo for answering the Robins back on his behalf, but a vein in Coach's forehead was visibly pulsating when Chicago's manager finally had to look at Villetti. The Cubs' skipper didn't even bother hiding it when he took a large gulp from his concealed flask of whiskey. Then Mitchell covered his eyes with his hand. He turned away to go light a cigarette.

However, now the Cubs all thanked Hoffman for his semi-effective plan, that did manage to hold Brooklyn to that single run. Only they needed to make up for that run, and quickly. Not much had worked exactly according to the rookies' plan, though Tad had gotten out of a no-outs, bases loaded situation by only throwing seven pitches and without striking a single batter out! That took some teamwork.

Next Taddeo turned to his right to also look behind him and see if Burleigh Grimes was watching, and to enjoy what he imagined the reaction on Brooklyn's bench would be to his throwing — especially when the Chicago Police held them back from answering his arm by the most-likely way they wanted to answer it — with the filthiest of their own.

But that's also when he saw two more patrolmen rush down the steps of the 1st base stands to get Conway and his posse to follow them as if they had intentions to quickly depart the stadium. Tad wondered what could possibly be more important than watching him pitch in a Cubs-Robins game.

Chapter 10

Wednesday, May 22, 1918
5:13 pm CST
Weeghman Park, Chicago, Illinois

8th Inning
Brooklyn - 1, Cubs – 0

0 Outs, 0 On

AB: Chicago Cubs (17 W – 11 L)
(Fighting to not be in last place in the National League)
Max Flack (RF, Bats: left ,Throws: left) AVG .257, OBP .343
Age: 28, Games: 547, Status: veteran player,
4th full season in The Show

On the mound:
The Brooklyn Robins (11 W– 16 L)
P: Larry Cheney (SP) (known for wild pitches)
(Bats: Right, Throws: Right) 8 W – 12 L, PCT: .400, ERA: 2.35, SO: 791,
HB: 46 x (in 9 years)
Age: 32, Games: 255, Status: 9-year veteran

AND THEN:

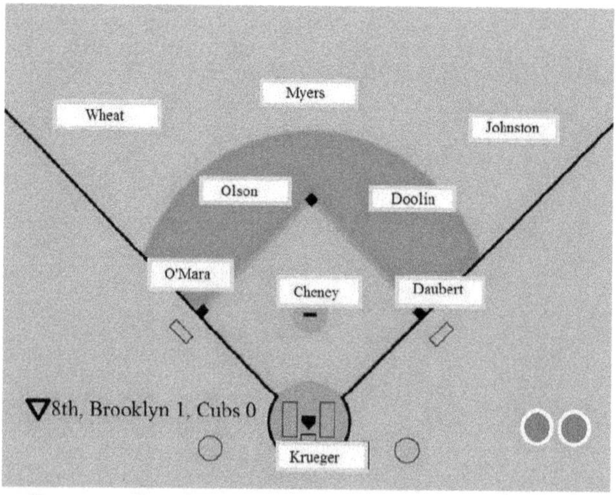

"What's important now is we get that run back. It's the bottom of the eighth, Team. Your all-too-generous pitcher has rested the fate of this series with *your* solid at-bats, Gentlemen. We are all on the line." Fred Mitchell's speech in the Cubs' dugout was more foreboding than inspiring. It would be up to somebody else to be more exciting.

Frank Pieper, popularly known as just "Pat," ran from Chicago's 3rd base dugout, making a speedy return toward home plate, and climbed back over the short brick wall, still sweating in Chicago's warm spring air even though the humidity had given over to the mid-afternoon breeze. His wool suit, vest, and tie didn't help, even when he abandoned the jacket, but the Cubs' thirty-two-year-old sports announcer kept his body in great shape if not his wardrobe. He'd confirmed there were no more new lineup changes made by Mitchell and he now brought his megaphone to bear on the spectators who'd paid for the most expensive seats. "Attention! Attention please! Have your pencils and scorecards ready Chicago fans — *and others*. We're going into the bottom of the eighth and our Cubbies are down by one run. It's going to be close, People. We've just seen some amazing talent displayed in a sizzlingly great defensive inning, but now we've come back to the top of our order and we're going to see Flack, Charlie Hollocher, and Leslie Mann due up for your beloved Chicago Cubs. Now — let's *play ball*!"

Some of Chicago's fans actually heckled him with, "Yeah? A great *defensive* inning?"

"Which game were you watching?"

"He walked in a run. Get rid of the rookie pitcher."

"Yeah. Ditch the dago!"

But the loudmouth in left field was actually encouraging. "C'mon. Let's go Max! Let's *go* Max!" Other fans of the home team bolstered his cheer.

The Cubs' right-fielder advanced to the edge of the gravel surrounding home plate to take his turn once more leading off. He took some practice swings.

Climbing the mound for his eighth outing — and the first time he'd come in with a lead this game — Brooklyn's Larry Cheney didn't appear to have any plans to continue playing beanball and take revenge for Wheat. Even with Ivy Olson hollering from shortstop, "C'mon Larry, skin that Cub!" Dode Paskert and Leslie Mann both stood up and paced around Chicago's dugout, but Killefer and Mitchell had once more posted themselves at opposite ends with no intentions of letting Flack's platoon from the outfield, or Charlie

Deal, who rose to join them, get beyond their leaders' control.

But going after Max Flack didn't seem to be any kind of bright idea to Lawrence Cheney. After all, the Cub batter had been so prone to errors in this game, that the last thing the Robins needed was someone actually competent in Chicago's right field if Brooklyn's pitcher could end up injuring Flack. But his left-handed bat, discipline at the plate, and careful timing took right-handed Cheney's breaking ball and smashed it out between Jake Daubert and Mickey Doolin to be grabbed on the bounce by Jimmy Johnston in the Robins' outfield. Flack was on at 1st base with no outs.

From the bench Tad cheered and actually thought good thoughts for Charlie Hollocher as he stepped up to the dish to see what Cheney served him. But Cheney didn't like having Chicago baserunners and repeatedly threw to Daubert to keep Flacky close to 1st. Hollocher, also batting as a left-hander, worked the tiring Robins pitcher to a full count. Patiently he waited for something he could drive to the opposite field. Charlie finally got his wish and Zack Wheat caught something the Cubs' shortstop smacked deep into left, hooking toward the foul line and making the wounded Robin run far for it. Wheat nevertheless took it on the fly but though the ball had stayed fair, he was far back in Weeghman's left-field corner when he made his throw to Ivy Olson who cut the distance off. But Max Flack had tagged up and came in standing at 2nd base. Tad cheered along with the rest of the Cubs from the bench as their offense advanced them in order to catch up from behind. But both Mitchell and Killefer looked stoic, and just stared out onto the field except for when Coach told Kilduff, "Pete, you're on deck. Get up there. It looks like this game is going to come down to you." Now Mitchell slowly turned to scowl at Taddeo, as if to emphasize that Coach knew exactly *who* had purposely seen that the Cubs fell behind on their runs in the first half of this inning.

Yeah, everybody knows, Tad thought. But Max Flack was making more than his share of errors. However, Fred Merkle seemed grateful for what Taddeo did by pegging Wheat. Now Tad said silent prayers so that all the rest of the Cubs would eventually come to feel that way. Plus Hoff with his pick had gotten to show why he truly deserved to be there.

Now Leslie Mann came up to bat on the right side of the plate, with 1 out and Flack on 2nd in scoring position. Mann was 0-3 this game and he was 0-4 when he sat down. Now there were 2 outs. Cheney wasn't done irritating Chicago's offense yet.

So Pete stepped up into the right-handed batter's box. The pressure was on him. The Cubs had left 5 stranded in previous innings thus far. Kilduff was only batting .204 with an OBP of .267. Tad was nervous, but his 2nd baseman was 1 for 1 so far this game. He'd been penciled in for Merkle in the No. 4-hole very early in this game. Now it all came down on his shoulders. For some reason, Cheney and Krueger just couldn't fool him. Chicago's batter took the first toss for a called strike. Then he held off on a sinker that hit the dirt and kicked up some dust to decorate his cleats. Kilduff took some practice swings as Cheney removed his cap and wiped some sweat on his brow with the back, then front of his pitching hand, running his fingers through his sweaty hair. Krueger must have called a cutter next, but the Robins' arm found too much reserve energy from somewhere, and it broke far away. Pete stayed away from a circle change that got called for a strike and showed his obvious disagreement with Hank O'Day's call on that one with his mouth open and his arms spread wide.

"C'mon. Play ball." The Reverend had enough of the ongoing arguing from both of these teams by now.

Pat Pieper once more announced the count on Kilduff into the stands, not at all forgetting to remind Chicago's audience that there were already 2 outs. Then at 2-and-2 the Robin hung a slider right in Kilduff's wheelhouse and Pete drove a line-drive shot out between Olson and O'Mara that had Wheat chasing it while Max Flack scored the tying run and the audience and Pat Pieper erupted into cheers; the Cubs were back in the game! Flack had this stupid grin on his face when he picked up Kilduff's bat and jogged back to the Cubs' bench, getting a high-five from Dode Paskert who batted next for Chicago. Charlie Deal followed that up as he arrived to the on-deck circle. The rest of the team rose from their seats in the dugout and congratulated Flack as well, who had made up for his poor performance in the field and then they all applauded and waved to Pete, who'd gotten a double out of his hit that drove in the Cubs' first run.

Taddeo let out his breath he didn't know he'd been holding. There was a chance he wouldn't become the losing pitcher now. Hoff patted him on the back, knowing his friend's thoughts. Trip and Bass-Man gave Tad high-fives to pick up his spirits as well. Killefer glared at all of them. He hadn't been amused by how the rookie battery handled the top half of the inning. But Taddeo still hadn't heard anything to make him think he wasn't going to take the hill again for the 9th. Tad could actually be the closer. Through his black eyes, he watched

Cheney walk Dode Paskert, who was batting .286 with a good eye.

Charlie Deal was only batting .239 this season, and there was a force-out at any base now. Kilduff was the runner on 2nd heading to 3, and Paskert was on 1st. But Coach Mitchell was feeling gutsy and wanted to eliminate every base being available for the Robins to make a play. As Charlie took a ball for his first pitch, the Cubs' manager gave Pete the sign. Cheney started to wind up and Kilduff kept light on his feet as he took a bigger and bigger leadoff. Cheney released toward home and Pete was off. Krueger got the ball and jumped up, Charlie leaping out of his way as the Robin catcher threw down the baseline to O'Mara. But Pete had great speed and dove head-first, hands outstretched for the 3-bag. His jersey created a sandstorm beneath him as Lord Byron ran after him on the outfield grass pronouncing him "Safe!" Pat excitedly used his megaphone to repeat the call and the audience roared.

That move took some nerve and now there would no longer be a force-out at 3rd base. On the mound, Brooklyn's pitcher looked rattled. Cheney lost some concentration and paid for it. Right-handed Cub Charlie Deal drove the ball right down the line and over O'Mara's head, getting an RBI while making Zack Wheat go chase another one as Kilduff crossed home plate!

"And the Cubs score!" Pat announced. Weeghman Park exploded in more cheers. Tad clapped his hands from the bench and Kilduff got even more celebrity treatment than Flack did as he returned to Chicago's dugout. Tad was so excited he didn't notice that Trip and Bass had scooted over closer to him.

Where was George?

"Wow! Hoff's going up to bat!" Trip pronounced. "Only this isn't Marshalltown anymore."

Tad's head suddenly on a swivel, he'd lost track of his own team's order in all the excitement from that last play and hadn't noticed his best friend get up to stand on-deck. Rollie Zeider had gotten 4 straight balls for an intentional walk and now George would be batting with the bases loaded. But this wasn't Iowa. No, this was the Big Leagues and Dode Paskert was now on 3rd base, Charlie Deal the runner on 2nd, and Zeider was on 1st. 3 men on and 2 men out.

Now was George's big moment. And then The Hoff struck out, leaving all the Cubs stranded. "I'm so sorry guys. Tad. I guess I still get too nervous," he said as he was sent back to the dugout to get his catching gear back on.

"It's alright, George. You're still in this game and I need you.

Clear your head. I need my best catcher," Tad explained to him. "We're winning now. And I can close this game for a Cubs victory!"

The two youngsters eyed both ends of the dugout as the rest of their teammates who'd take the field for the top of the 9th grabbed their gloves and several practice balls. They quickly and silently deliberated whether they could run with all the others — past Mitchell or Bill Killefer — and figured the latter would be the least likely to stop them from going back out on the field. Chicago's newest call-ups really wanted to end this game. Tad could actually earn his very first win!

Pat Pieper announced that Johnston, Doolin, and Krueger would be up next for Brooklyn.

"Okay, Tad-Man. Can you just close these guys down? No foolin' around, but a 1-2-3 punch-out so we can all go home."

"You bet I can, Boss!"

And just like that, Johnston and Doolin were sat back down with Villetti's teammates' help. Taddeo quickly got 2 outs and was ready to ride to victory.

"On no!" Or at least that was what it looked like Coach mouthed from the home team's baseline when he saw Ernie Krueger step toward the batter's box to face Villetti again.

"Oh no." Or at least that's what Tad imagined Ernie Krueger was thinking when it finally registered that Villetti would still be left in the game and allowed to pitch to him — again.

"Oh shit." That was what Wilbert Robinson said from the 1st base line. He quickly called Krueger back and got up Jimmy Archer who the Robins had acquired from the Pirates and who made sense in this spot, while batting .273. He'd also just played the prior season with the Cubs and might have still had some friends on Weeghman's bench. At least that's what Robinson might be hoping for as it could settle down Chicago's pitcher and even encourage the rebel hurler to behave himself in what could be the Robins' last inning, last at-bat, and last chance. Robinson laid his wager that Villetti wasn't going to nail his teammates' friend. Tad agreed. He struck him out instead.

The Cubs won and all Tad's friends came bursting out of Chicago's dugout and high-fived and patted Villetti on the back as he just earned his very first professional baseball win! Then they raised him up on Hoff's shoulders. But as baseball politics went, it was not ever going to be recognized as any clean win. Not with the way Taddeo had handled Wheat's at-bat and walked a run in. Hank O'Day didn't even need to say anything about that. There was an indisputable rule — that the official box score couldn't be counted on to tell the complete story. But Claude Hendrix barely walked away with a footnote and Villetti nevertheless came out of the game with an official win. Now he could have something to celebrate with his teammates. But celebrating with someone else preoccupied this Cubs pitcher's mind.

George had traded a cigar he must have stolen from somewhere to get Rose's private phone number from Turner Barber, who commended him on the way he'd called the last 7 frames, without including Zachariah Wheat's at-bat of course. And apparently the young lady had means to get her across town to Lakeview and she was bringing with her *several friends*. But Taddeo knew Arlene wouldn't be among them, for he didn't figure her as one caring to be around any of the other girls in the employ of The House. Now he wasn't interested in just any woman, so Tad would see what she was up to instead of actually partying with his teammates. And even after his first win? His emotions in this whole thing presented him with that difficult choice. But completely taking him by surprise, baseball was no longer keeping his thoughts from eventually returning to *her*, and Tad bade his teammates an early farewell and set out heading south, and back to Arlene. *What is it with that girl?* He couldn't believe he was turning down celebrating the successful start to everything he'd ever dreamed of achieving, to split, running after some woman he'd only just met. *Well, actually, since it is Arlene, I* can *believe it.*

Chapter 11

"Taxi? Taxi! Dammit." Taddeo had walked from Weeghman almost to the river by now. *And after he'd just won his first game*. At the Addison / Clark Street station, the conductor had first proclaimed that they were all sold out of "L" tickets. But Tad could see for himself that was bullshit; there was plenty of room on a train that came and went by without him, and somehow he just knew that Charles Weeghman wanted to keep any Italians from boarding trains at "his station stop." *Or Tad's treatment was even more personal than that*. Maybe Mitchell could actually influence this? But next, at least four cars for hire, which he noted were absent of fares, had passed him by, once he started on foot, and even after he'd frantically waved at them. People on the streets would only stop to curiously glance at him, then quickly turn to go back about their business. Like the others, this black model-T just drove on by — until it stopped.

Taddeo now jogged down the one-way street on his left side of the southbound road and hustled along the dusty boardwalk to catch up with this least-costly, common vehicle. He ran behind it, coming up to reach for the passenger door handle. The taxi driver stretched across his cab and held the door from opening for the baseball player.

"No you don't. My car's not in service." The man wearing a gray and white plaid-colored newsie on his crown said with his Irish accent. "And it won't never run over on the South Side neither."

"What are you talking about? You're carrying no fare."

"I said you're not getting a ride across the river. Not from me. Not from anyone. I recognized you and just figured I was being friendly by informing you of the situation."

"But you don't sound very friendly to me," Taddeo said.

"Yeah. Well I didn't stop to argue with you. Look around you." He scratched at one of his long bushy sideburns that stretched down from his cap. "You might think you're some hot shot ballplayer. Which amazes me after I'd have thought by now even you would have woken up to the fact Mitchell is being *forced* to pencil you in on his roster. But you're really on the wrong side of the town, you stupid dago."

Taddeo did indeed look around. He involuntarily gulped after he'd clenched his fists. More people stopped and continued staring at him, now that the driver had halted and they were conversing. This time they didn't quickly look away. Now wasn't the time to start any fight he *could* finish in spite of how angry the driver made him. But of course Tad acted with his gut and not his head. And Taddeo didn't like standing in the middle of the road, so he nodded, acting as if he were surrendering to the inevitable, let go of the passenger door and raised his hands as if in surrender. Then he darted around the front to the other side of the car, quickly stepped up on the running board and pushed his face into the taxi operator's. He grabbed him by both his shirt and jacket collars. "Now say that again."

The heavy-set driver wasn't intimidated by the young man in the least. He pushed the pitcher away from him and kept control over his active vehicle with only a second's interruption of his foot's pressure on the brake. The car barely moved. "Oh there's a lot more that definitely needs to be said, Boy-oh. And there is that some would say I can put it to you as friendly as it's going to get around these parts. Though I'll only be telling you the truth like it is. And believe me Man, I'm already doing you a favor, you stinkin' wop. They're all going to betray you. I mean right now, sure they let you walk here. People know you're on the team. They even like you playing here. What can I say? They're Cubs fans. They want to try anything if it will bring them some wins out here and against one of New York's. Or is it more about the money? "The *guinea's antics* keep filling more seats" the owner is claiming, even if it is from ticket sales to the foreign scum. He has to do what a fella has to do to fill the seats while there's a war on. But it's all good for the local businesses I guess, and at least everybody's wondering what *you're* going to do next."

"Win."

"Yeah? Well they'll take the revenues. And Weeghman? He made the news by letting *Mitchell win* — his begging for your contract. Or is that how it really happened? Or just how you perceived it? In these trying times, when this nation has much larger concerns than the next baseball season — international troubles straight on down to some *private concerns* — we saw the Cubs nevertheless retain an audience because they made so many line-up changes before the start of the new year. And it does look like it's beginning to pay off." He shrugged. "A little bit, anyhow. But they can always replace *you*. Well, a real fan can only hope." He laughed. "Though right now, a lot of people do have bigger priorities than baseball, Man. Crowds are harder to come by when many people have family going over to fight the Kaiser's war machine or they're staying here, left behind and having to fight that fucking Spanish flu. Rationing resources. No doubt the reports are wrong, as it's always worse than what our government tells us. But all of your detractors are definitely right. And Mitchell and Weeghman especially. I'd bet they just didn't want to argue with Coughlin and Kenna when they all have enough to deal with in *this* city. And both agreed they can throw your father just one more teensy scrap to feed his lousy family — and Colosimo's fucking whores. While you're playing attracts the immigrant audience, I s'poze. If they ever have any funds to enjoy a traditional *American* pastime. Goddam pig-Latin speakin' beggars. But I wouldn't really know. I don't sit near the niggers' section. I work to make an honest living and I pay to not have to sit in cheap seats. Now I won't lose my job to boated-in scab labor that don't tip neither. So like I said, this cab won't *ever* service dagos. Weeghman can do what *he* wants to raise money. Just like Sisson's doing." The driver looked directly into Taddeo's eyes and pointed a cautionary finger at him when he said that. "And I bet you like that hotel. Don't cha? Hah." After he laughed in the pitcher's face, the driver next altered his concentration toward unscrewing the lid to a flask, taking a swig, and then lighting up a cigarette.

Taddeo clenched both his fists. "I'd be very careful about being this disrespectful, Mister. There's no call for this. Whatever you're alluding to." But Taddeo's growing inclination to stand up to this mick in a buggy took a rapid change in direction as he gulped when another dark car pulled up behind the taxi. Taddeo stepped down and coughed, his face backing out of the driver's window and the smoke.

"Yeah, well there's no call for *you* to have to do *this*, Young Man. I mean, come here to play across the river — and on top of it, pitch like *you* usually do. Reaping what you did upon Wheat. And Ernie Krueger the other day. Especially when no one likes you. That I'm serious about, Boy-oh. The team just got lucky in spite of you this afternoon. That play in the eighth? And as it always turns out, the Cubs don't need any more agitating than the East already provides them. But you wops like to provoke, don't cha? Word on the streets now is this truce with you bright-eyed migrants will be toast and your family was first *to throw it into the river*, and into jeopardy —, " he laughed, " — again. But what is new? Though now I think some fellows in the car behind me want to *enlighten you* about that.

I'll let them be a lil' more specific." Tad turned his head slightly to glance sidelong at the next vehicle and its four occupants. He bit his lower lip as the driver of the taxi kept talking. "So my *friendly* advice concludes with this: ain't nothing going to happen to you now, Boy-oh. So you just listen to what these fellows have to say. And when Mitchell cuts you from the team — and mark my words that will happen — you go quietly. Then you don't come back here no more. Not ever. You hear me? You won't always be untouchable. And someday someone might get after you to punish your papa for your papa's sins. They won't care what you did, or haven't never done." He waved his hand in a gesture of dismissal. "So, you should choose to live your own life. But do it far away from Chi-Town wherezever you do it. And definitely not on my side of the river. Now that's my friendly advice. You now will please excuse me." The driver put his cigarette back in his mouth and his vehicle in gear. Taddeo pushed back out of its way as the taxi lurched forward and down the street, the wheels narrowly missing his feet.

Immediately, the second car pulled up alongside Taddeo where he turned to stand with his back to the shop windows. He could see the dark silhouette of four figures occupying the vehicle. His legs started and wouldn't stop shaking. His instincts were telling him to run.

"I think *we* might be able to help with offering you a ride somewhere. As it's funny how all the taxis seem to be out of service," said the younger driver of the next vehicle with the slightest *German* accent. The newly arrived car was a Studebaker four-door model. Each door unfolded out to allow the men in the vehicle to disembark and approach Taddeo from the north.

"Thanks. But I've decided to walk."

"Yeah. You *do* have permission to do that. For now. And you've gotten yourself nearly down to the water's edge. Seems appropriate." The man's hat pivoted up and down while he laughed. His associates did as well. "That's a useful landmark. The Chicago River, I mean. This is a big town and it helps you locate where you are, and find some indication of where you are going. And I hear them say anything could turn up under a barrel *here*." The men laughed again. "I guess you're in the right place at the right time to find out about that, huh?"

Tad couldn't stop shaking. His eyes blinked more rapidly, and he didn't want any of the men to notice either affliction. "I have no idea what you mean."

"Oh. That's right. Yeah. Ya know, he hasn't been home yet," one of the other men said.

"Oh yes. I forgot about that. This Villetti was at the game when they found him."

"Found who?"

The coats and ties shook as the men who wore them laughed once more. "He doesn't know," said another man.

"Well, I can't give you exact information. But if I can't give you a ride with the boys here, I will at least have given you more for your consideration while you enjoy your walk today. So here it is, *Boy-oh*: you should watch your step more — around the river I mean. 'Cause when these games end, it's always gets progressively darker and darker. Toward the end of your season — and by this river? It's getting very dark indeed — and well, *you might accidently fall in*."

"Yeah? Well summer's coming and it's actually staying brighter, longer and later — and so's the Cubs' run for the postseason maybe lookin' brighter than ever this year. So, we're nowhere near the end of *this* campaign."

"No." The driver, and perceived leader of the group, acknowledged. He and all his friends came up shorter than the tall Cubs' pitcher. "You are not, Bright-Eyes. Not at the present, anyways. But things have a way of changing in this city's kind of winds. *But we don't have anything to do with the direction they took last night*. You remember that. Now you've been given good advice. You should run along now and go tell it to your papa." Everyone's eyes narrowed. "I hope we are clear." Then the men feigned tipping their hats to the athlete, and one by one re-entered their vehicle, the last man taking the passenger seat next to the driver after he turned the crank to restart the noisy engine. "And I'm sorry that you won't let us help you speed you along your way this afternoon. But maybe next time." The leader of the group winked when he nodded, stretching to stick his head out the vehicle's window. That made him look a bit uncomfortable when he struggled to force a fast smile. Then the car drove off slowly, its pilot very likely to have deliberately dragged out its departure as if to prove he was no less confident about how things would turn out.

Taddeo picked up his own pace with which he walked. As he journeyed over the bridge he switched back and forth between the idea of going directly to his father's saloon, or returning straight to the hotel. He settled on rushing back to The Sisson as fast as possible — to make sure *she* was safe and find shelter in the kind of comfort only Arlene could offer him. Whatever the cabby alluded to about

The Sisson made Tad concerned for her safety, too. But he hoped she was still at the hotel for whatever reason — her beauty rest, he supposed. It was already paid for. He wanted to talk to her alone and he figured a place out in the new spring sun and right on Rainbow Beach like The Sisson, would be far more charming than The Hull House — and so it made sense for him to look to see if Arlene was enjoying her relaxation by the south beach first.

She threw up when she heard how his day had gone.

"Well, I wasn't expecting that kind of reaction."

Arlene, wearing nothing but a cream-color nightgown, held a small aluminum garbage pail on her lap that she looked up from as she sat on the edge of the bed. Her hair was loose in a tousled mess. "I was only getting prepared for you to tell me some *more great details* about another one of your baseball games. You know how much I look forward to that." She moved away from him as Tad tried to sit down on the bed and put his arms around her.

Tad couldn't control not showing his disappointment. He'd imagined Arlene as being so excited for him when he returned to share with her every pitch-by-pitch detail about his first Major League win. But now was definitely not going to be the time. "Right. Well something's up. I think I was right and there will be more fighting sooner than later. And we're obviously in a known location — known to not just my family, but everyone else who comes here for uh, *recreation*. We'll have to move soon. But speaking of which, I am very glad you decided to stay here by the beach for today — as *I'm* definitely now in need of some recreation." He tried to use a clever play on words.

"I don't feel like *recreating* right now, Taddeo."

"Fuck! I just want someone to hold. Someone to hold me." A tear escaped each of his eyes. He threw his fedora across their room, spinning it. Then Tad took off his brown suit jacket and let it fall behind him on the bed as he loosened his bowtie and unbuttoned the top buttons of his handed-down dress shirt.

"Really?" She projected a look of disapproval when she assessed him. "Well, I'm ill, Tad. That's why I couldn't leave. And until now, I enjoyed my day — being left alone. 'Cause maybe I'm sick of your shit."

"That quick? Didn't you just hear how my day had gone? I could have been killed. For the first time I felt really afraid for my existence, Arlene. That's how my life is going."

"No, that's just how living in Chicago is, Hon." But he'd gotten to her. And she was afraid now too, at least a little bit. Now that Taddeo's family had actually turned *her* into a killer. And of course her lover boy just had to vocalize that he was afraid of dying now, right on top of that. Right when she knew she felt something for him. Besides nausea. Though she didn't know exactly what. *How perfect is this?* And Arlene's new existence since she came to the South Side sat quite familiar with feeling scared and suffering constant worry over the future. Her day had been spent being back at it. She also now knew it was a pattern with Taddeo to turn to a feminine source for a feeling of home, shelter, comfort. A substitute for a boy who had lost his mother. So she exhaled and surrendered her standoffish-ness, scooted closer to him, and put her arms around him and lay her head on Tad's shoulder. He looked down as she turned to look up at him, seeing how he was doing. A powerful force drew each of the couple's very essences toward one another. He looked so relieved once he could hold her. She had to admit that she too found comfort in their trading of at least a pretense of affections. It was pretense, right? Their shared experience being at once — and at least more powerful, than Arlene's urge to vomit again. And she needed some affection as she'd nearly started to hate herself for what she'd just done — her killing of some strange man rather than a Villetti that she'd come to hit. And instead, she was actually sleeping with another Villetti. *How ironic and wonderful is that?* But it had been wonderful. Their lips were now so close. They touched. They passionately locked. And their two bodies entwined until they became one.

Taddeo located empathy's rejuvenating embrace in his lover's arms. Though he found the slight flaw with even this, in so much as he wished Arlene had rinsed her mouth out first. But he forgot all about that, and the pain from all his wounds, as the pair twisted around and out of their clothes, writhing for hours instead, in the bindings of their all-consuming and completely satisfying indulgence of passion.

Later that night, or perhaps early the next morning as it could have already become, Taddeo lay on his back. Awake in their bed in the hotel room. Arlene naked on his side and partially covering him. Her thin arm reached out across his muscled chest, and most-likely coming out of her dream for a better life, subconsciously opening a little hand trying to clasp on to his. In turn, the athlete's arm held her on base. It was up to Taddeo to decide whether she would make it home. And he'd already decided that she would. Now, as soon as he possibly could, he would go and see his father about Arlene, a couple of jobs, Irish taxi cab drivers — and then how some things were going to have to change.

Chapter 12

Rinaldo Villetti pushed a spoon around in his morning coffee and watched the steam that rose from the hot beverage change directions in response to his action. Finally he looked up at his visitor who patiently waited for his attention.

"So tell me Detective Conway, *why* am *I* here so early?"

"Well Sigñor — there's no other way to put this." His Irish accent was muted, yet audible. "You're here because someone got sloppy — mistakenly less effective than they thought they'd be. Unless they're sending another message — deliberately? And in that case, I hope you'll be opting to ignore it. My investigation into this has not yet concluded. But *you're here* because I have to be thorough. You wouldn't pay to have it no other way — I'd assume?" said this younger man wearing a bowler hat and a gold badge on the breast of a tailored black suit and a no-nonsense face. While youthful next to Rinaldo Villetti, he still looked serious.

"You assume correctly. Go on."

"The victim was told to have been recently employed here to fix some bad, old plumbing around your place." The detective was also accompanied by a blue-uniform, the second man in the octagonal peaked hat sporting a silver star and keeping silent inside of it. "There's still a lot of that in these older neighborhoods. Regardless, our patrolman Walsh here learned 'bout some of our other alert patrolmen finding the deceased in that barrel that they recently fished out of the water." He nodded at the container they'd delivered — a wine barrel near the center of the lounge floor near the main entertainment stage. "That and other pertinent information got brought to my attention by him and my junior trainee-detective Sweeney while I was across town at Weeghman. Now we're pretty certain what the killer left of this poor bastard resembles your plumber, a fact someone who was here at your establishment recently told us when we discovered the body and called for anyone to identify the corpse — once we had put all its parts back together — along with a compelling incentive. We have some select people that we've learned to ask first you know, for a financial consideration."

The investigator's eyes met Villetti's. "Eventually, you always spring a new leak. Anyway, somebody had cut this feller up real good." He nodded toward the container behind him. "Go take a look for yourself if you want. You might hold some admiration for the handiwork. It seems he has been butchered by a professional you might say — and a professional butcher was beaten within inches of his life outside of your eh, *establishment here*, two days ago."

"What an incredible coincidence," Villetti said rather quietly.

"Yes, that is quite a coincidence," the detective replied in his Celtic accent. "And it's also a really bad coincidence that the elusive Black Hand writes its story in a very physically distinct Italian glyph, using *an example* instead of an alphabet, though the victim here *is* Italian-American, the butcher was Irish, and the body was disposed of in a barrel. While it's contrary to what we've come to expect, some commonalities with other murders paint quite the intriguing mystery, don't they Sigñor?" Conway folded his arms across his chest. "It's like someone knew their handiwork would merit extra special attention if it was personally delivered this way."

Greggorio saw his father nod an affirmative. "Your deductive abilities are just plainly brilliant, Detective," the Villetti patriarch responded.

"Yes. But you should be smart enough to deduce that I don't want another war exploding over this. You pay me to keep the peace and the other side approves of the job I do as well."

Greg had made sure he'd be on hand for this meeting. He'd waited up all through another night for it, as a matter of fact. Having barely slept for going over forty-eight hours, he showed no sign of slowing down as he walked over, withdrew his money clip, and peeled off some greenbacks for the uniform, and then even more for the detective and placing them in the copper's hands, he folded the investigator's fingers over them while his oldest brother watched. "Well I know the clues don't make sense. Yet, I figured that you'll approve the sense of this?" He motioned with his head toward the cash. "It is yet another bad coincidence that some mysteries just cannot be solved."

"Yes it is, Mister Villetti. I do reckon it is." He nodded to the son and smiled.

"Please put *all* of what you found back in the barrel. Later you'll make a discreet delivery, and that will close the lid on this." Greg would have enjoyed his moment to be crafty some more, but for Urso letting go a derisive snort in the background. He glared at his taller, proportionally muscled sibling. A neatly trimmed brown-haired ape in a suit and hat if there ever was one, and the familiar warmth of anger's trappings came over the younger brother, but he folded that over to further ambiguate his ambitions — and make sure he could cultivate new friends. Well-compensated friends. Plus, he'd needed and expected his older brother to be here for this meeting, and Urso didn't disappoint this time. Fortuitous for Greg's plans.

Next the two coppers departed Villetti's, with Walsh lighting a cigarette and noting that he'd come back with his training partner Olsen, and with a vehicle that could transport the barrel. So they would see to it that Dulio was properly set to rest where he wouldn't be disturbing.

"Goddammit! They send my man back to me like this? Who? The merchants? The leprechauns? Now who the fuck is out to get me? And who ratted?" Their patriarch punched his right hand into his other palm. Urso looked down, not having any answers or meeting his father's passing gaze.

"No, Papa," Greg responded. Then he put forward, "The real question is who's making it look like someone's out to get *you*?"

"What? Well I just can't wait to hear your brilliant idea."

Urso approached his two closest relatives at his papa's table all of a sudden interrupting everyone's somber disposition with his laughter. "Wait. Which one of us are you talking to? Not Greg? Him having a brilliant idea? Rrright."

"No. I just happen to have intelligence." At that statement, Urso moved toward his brother and puffed out his chest, clenching his fists. "Wait." Greg held his hands up in a signal to stop him. "I mean that *I* have knowledge that you haven't had shared with you yet, Urso," Greg quickly added. "Geez. Let me explain, will you?"

His brother backed down. "Well then, I just can't wait to hear *your* intelligent explanation."

Greggorio turned to his father. "I told you taking in the Market Street girl was a bad idea, right?"

"Hah! What's she got to do with it? No. You wait. Are you actually saying *she* killed Dulio? Little Arlene? You've gone bugs on me," Urso proclaimed, not waiting to even give his patriarch the opportunity to weigh in. But Rinaldo Villetti looked thoughtful as he placed his chin in his hands and then studied his *second* born.

"Corry, would you please come over here?" Greg called, continuing his performance.

The Delasandro son got up from where he'd sat so he could

recline in a booth across the deserted lounge room, and crossed its space to come upon Sigñor Villetti's table by the window. He yawned and stretched both arms out then brought them to his waist and bent behind himself to crack his back. "I'ze knows what you're going to ask, bud I didn't see anything, Sir." He properly addressed his uncle but spoke with a dialect that made a sharp man even sharper, by purposely sounding ignorant. "Greg asked me'z to follow da girl last night. I thoughts Dulio over there in the barrel could do *that work.* Maybe an easier assignment to test him out on since the butcher was kind of a tough job? But I'ze thought to follow them both anyway. You know? Make sure stuff gets done right. But the broad. She's real smart Uncle, you know? Takes off real fast. Knew she was being followed. She was out of sight for less than a minute, the same time Dulio disappears ahead of me. Alls I see is some bright flash when I turn the bend, but the girl is gone. 'Stead I find *this guy.*" He nodded toward the barrel sitting in the middle of the lounge. "What *she probably* left of him anyway. So you know, I figure this is all my fault. If I'ze was following him, I shoulda backed him up. I know. But look, I'ze was stupid. Or slow at any rate. But I didn't want to get blamed for this fiasco. It was a rookie mistake — not one I should make. So there was this barrel — ."

"So *you* cut him up into tiny pieces and pushed him into the river? Yourself?"

"I know, Uncle. There was so much blood. And I also didn't have anything with me to weigh down the barrel."

"You're a really sick man. Do you know that?" The young Delasandro shrugged and looked sheepish. "Your father didn't raise you to be that way. As I've come to know him, it's not very hard to see *that.*" Villetti said. "Unless you're sampling some of his product?" But Corry shook his head to indicate the negative by his gesture. " 'Cause you certainly didn't get to be this way from your mother — because of *my* big sister. That kind of sadism doesn't run on my side of the family."

Greg coughed, but made as if he cleared his throat, then re-entered the conversation. "Uh, look Papa. That's not the issue here-nor-there right now. We have to keep this quiet. Corry didn't know what he was doing but if this news spreads across the streets, people are going to start to think the Irish killed him in the Black Hand style to *mock us* — as after all Dulio was pretty close to being one of our own."

"Yeah. Kind of."

"So I'll take care of the newspapers again. Urso, do you think you can take care of the girl?" Greg asked of him.

Corrado stepped forward, eyes tightening, and looked to both brothers concerned, but he remained silent.

"Arlene, right? Why do you want me to do that? Dally may have messed up. But you're the one who sent him, so it's your problem. At least one of you two should fix it," Urso said.

Urso had *noticed her*, Greggorio observed with satisfaction. He knew her name. A good place to begin this from. "Well, it started as my problem, but if this is not taken care of quickly, it's *all* The House's problem. S'poze that's what she wanted. *She* came here to start something. Didn't she, Papa? But I can't be in two places at once Urso, and I have my way of handling the papers. Don't be so lazy."

"Lazy?" Urso started advancing upon his brother again. "I'll show you how to move."

"Wait a minute. You two can't decide anything here. I'm in charge of my own house, all right?" Rinaldo Villetti grew impatient with his sons. "Let's get that straight right now."

"Well, you *did* bring her here Papa. I'm sure my brother and I would both welcome you taking charge when it was your original decision that caused this problem."

"Don't you get smart with me and twist this. Now here's what we're going to do: Greg, handle the newspapers and pay what we need to buy us rumor control; Urso, go pick up the girl from Taddeo and bring her to me. They're at the new Lake Park Avenue high-rise and I *will* find out where she got a gun from."

"That's what I *just said*, Papa. Is there an echo in here?"

Greg felt his father's eyes bore into him. "Well, congratulations. You're a genius Greg. But you got that from your Papa." He waved a finger at his son and stifled an involuntary smile. His eyes still revealed pride in his son, because it couldn't have been affection. But along with his father's humor came a more disconcerting feeling. His papa was smart. Possibly wise enough to not allow his offspring learn just how smart he truly was. He did not seem the least bit surprised about the girl. "Now I'm going to get to the bottom of this, my sons." Then, finally, after a long pause while the patriarch studied Greggorio with some more awful scrutiny, he said out loud, "But hmmm. *You* were having her followed." Then he turned back to his oldest son. "Urso, this situation might not even have gotten this far out of hand and people wouldn't even suspect the takedown of the butcher could connect our house with this, if you could have waited for him in the foyer or lured him into the alley instead of turning Tuesday into a whole *day* of street brawls on both sides of the river after Taddeo went and also set one off over at the stadium. I guess our overly ornery family has to learn to accept paying for the consequences of our actions if we deliberately choose not to be more discreet. So some among us still have a lot to learn. That's how we get smarter."

Hypocrite. But Greg did his best to not voice his thoughts out loud like his big brother often did.

"Ah, and here *your genius* thought Chicago would be this great move for us to advance some profitable and peaceful business opportunities."

"Shut up, Urso."

"I'm just saying, Greg's paying out all our earnings over the containment of information about this, and everything else that's recently gone sideways, and is now — at this very moment — *also* spreading out onto the streets, and it's getting even more expensive."

"That's exactly what I mean by paying the consequences for our actions."

"It's like the news just got *you* over a barrel."

"Clever. That's real clever Greg. So Urso, show your papa that you've got some real brains and just manage to get the girl back over here. Find out if she has a gun, first. And don't get shot."

"Well now, that would be wise. And oh — Urso," Greg put his hand on his brother's large arm. "Taddeo might also give you some trouble."

"Well fuck him. Little shit. Always spending his time playing. That fucking Tadpole doesn't give a damn about anything that goes on over here anyway. Maybe *I* shouldn't, also. I could have *not* stopped the butcher from getting this close to you, or not agreed to go run another stupid errand for you either, Papa. I kinda want to live my own life, at least some of it, for *me*. Not die on the wrong side of the river."

"You just do what I tell you to, Urso."

"Yes, Sir."

Greg smiled. Turning to his father he said, "But you know *I am* right about something else, too. If your intention is to do away with Taddeo's newest little plaything, which I think you'd be stupid not to if Dally's theory on what happened proves conclusive," he nodded behind him toward his cousin, "then your super boy over there at the comfort inn is going to really go bugs over this one. I think he's already gone and gotten himself obsessed with Arlene. They've stayed more than one night in Hyde Park together already. And I've got information that says he's sneaking around with her, using your own room permitted you by Old Man Sisson." He paused for a moment to let that sink in before continuing. "But a fella who's his own man can get over just another whore. However, your little baseball star is nothing but a boy, still making his first trip around the horn, and he has yet to slide home."

His papa finally showed what he'd really been thinking when he decided to reveal his hand. "You're enjoying this too much, Greggorio. I can see you're too pleased by all of these recent events. Playing me against your brothers, and them against each other. I didn't forget Corrado is *your man*." He glanced at his nephew. "Your friendship with your cousin goes all the way back to Brooklyn. So he was following your orders in spite of his own ill interpretation of how to follow them." The Delasandro brother looked down at his feet.

"Papa, I didn't know this would happen."

Urso laughed as he caught that from the doorway. He'd started on his way out. "That's right. You never know shit, Greg." He made to vacate the room, waving them all off behind him.

"And I don't believe you, Greggorio. That is a serious problem," the senior Villetti said.

"Well, Arlene and your sentimental fondness for her, Taddeo, and that ape you call your first-born that just trooped out of here, are only a starting point on a pretty long read-through of the list of your problems, Papa. Now I do need him right now." Greg nodded in the direction Urso had departed. "But you need to spend more effort communicating your wisdom to your first-born over there. And maybe the last idiot Mama bore you, as well."

Taddeo had arrived earlier and had been prevented from entering by his father's other help, Vico and Ignacio, while the police were there discussing business. Urso went out of his way to shove the athlete as Greg viewed him through the glass that divided the foyer from the lounge/restaurant while the oldest passed the youngest of his siblings and made his exit. Tad spun around and made a fist, but then thought better about the danger of going after his oldest brother. "Perhaps you could still teach the both of them much. Especially if you can't believe *I'm* trustworthy? Is that it? Well can you believe *that one* is reliable?" Greggorio nodded toward the door. "You know,

I can't do everything myself. Everything that will help this house. But I'm trying here. And you would suggest I am acting *against* our better interests? Huh. We both better hope Urso doesn't also screw this up any further. This gets out of hand, and that copper Conway could be right. There could be another war. This could be the first signal there'll be more bad business with the Irish."

Rinaldo Villetti nodded, tightened his jaw, and looked down at the table. He couldn't see Greg's eyes smile over his father's impotence, or his nephew Corrado's concern. Now Greggorio had planted and watered the seeds of doubt in his father regarding all his closest relatives and associates. It was even easier when Urso wasn't there to defend himself and neither the lumbering enforcer nor Taddeo would hold a claim to the title of favorite son for very much longer. But now they'd both be the favorite brother as Greg was free to make sure that Urso *did* screw this up, and Taddeo and Arlene would unwittingly help him — and his father would finally see his middle son's worth. *And Arlene must have protected Taddeo from the trap I set for him with the Gennas, and I bet she now so obviously means to use* him *to get to the rest of our family. Or he'd be dead already. Stupid fool. Ha. I'd already predicted this and planned for the contingency, too. I'm sure I know why she's really here. But if Urso will take Arlene out of the picture, her own alleged actions nullifying the treaty with the Irish, and our having* my *manufactured* proof *in a barrel, well after it's all accounted for, it will also have the effect of rendering New York's support worthless. Even Colosimo and D'Andrea would see that. And with the plumber's death, I can arrange that incident to manifest retaliation, and control it so that instead of our home-grown people, any Latin blood spilled will belong to the next enforcers New York will undoubtedly send us — or even the Gennas. And then our fledgling outfit could have real grievances with which to rally around to win our independence from the weakened East Coast with, once* I *take over, probably before Masseria asserts himself over D'Andrea too, as he will need our family's help because Morello falls in New York, and that fool Colosimo unwittingly laid a faster track from Manhattan to Chicago for the Big Apple's newest boss. At the same time Arlene will no doubt be maneuvering Taddeo into a fight with Urso, whether she's alive or dead, as a conflict between my brothers and that girl is exactly what I could use to get rid of* at least *one of my problems with that bunch. Hopefully even* two *of them. And I will have used her* as *she must be now planning to use my little brother. What irony. And there's so many angles I can play to accomplish this.*

If only D'Andrea and maybe even Masseria and Morello would even learn just how good I am at what I do — or maybe, if I actually knew them, they *wouldn't impress me any more than my father? It might just be that my business instincts have evolved beyond any of them? Nope. I don't need New York and I certainly won't need Colosimo. If only I could make some more money from out of all this business, I would certainly not need D'Andrea. And meanwhile the Genna Brothers* could *feel the same way. With the cops coming to* me *for their payoff money, I'm destroying and reinforcing all the right alliances.* Greggorio was most impressed with himself.

But considering the less-than-impressive, his youngest brother finally gained access to the lounge and more importantly, their father, only the next moment after Urso departed. And Greg's delinquent fourth cousin Pepe escorted him — *or no, it actually looks like he is trying hard to keep up the chase just to chaperone Taddeo.* Lighter-haired and even more lightly working Cousin Pepe was always such a non-contributing sycophant, but Greg's little brother was sparking energy like he was a live wire. He had been pestering everyone by phoning them from his father's favored new hotel that morning, and then coming down to the lounge early enough to be just one more disturbance in what was already an unpleasant morning for his father. Greg couldn't suppress his new grin.

Papa had kicked him out once already so he could conduct his meeting with the investigator, and Greg imagined his least-mature brother had stalked around in circles in the foyer until he saw that both the cops and Urso had concluded business with their patriarch. Meanwhile, he'd finally left Arlene alone, and maybe his eldest brother would actually do what he was supposed to do, and assist with eliminating another threat to The Family's operation. Though due to his experience with his brother, Greggorio still had some doubt about it. But he was prepared for any contingency, like usual.

Now Taddeo made his move. And some other young punk, though a large man — Greg guessed some friend of Pepe's looking for work — stepped into view and cautiously looked around dumbfounded while he held back in the doorframe. Then Pepe made some frantic motions with his right arm, and this timid fellow awkwardly hustled over to sit with Pepe at the bar. Greg watched him kind of shake. He appeared really uncomfortable as he and Pepe were the only individuals who were not immediate family or allegedly staff of some of the more dubious sort The House usually employed who could sometimes be found in Villetti's even at this hour. But several of the entertainers, still in their colorful nightgowns, had come downstairs for coffee and upon noticing the newcomers, went directly over to them and started their practice to make any visitors feel that much more comfortable. Such was their job. But Greg signaled the girls to leave himself alone and returned the focus of his attention to his father and his little brother. He forgot how tired he was while his whole world he had created, kept up its motion most assuredly just to entertain him.

Chapter 13

"So what's this about you wanting a job?"

"The other guys work. It is time I did, Father."

"Father? What happened to *Papa*? And what other guys? Your brothers? They work for *me*. If *you* want to learn the family business, I'll give you a job," Rinaldo Villetti told his son. "I'll fucking give you a job," the old soldier muttered under his breath.

Tad had already predicted his elder's reply when he'd rehearsed this meeting over and over before in his mind. He'd had to continuously emphasize how important this conference was to him, just to get a sit-down with his father, and even do *some* of the speaking. He'd been both anxious and dreadful of this time that would come to see him sitting across the table from the patriarch at his old man's favorite booth by the front window of their family's "entertainment house." Taddeo was used to being treated like a pet, happy to be greeted by his papa but only when his father called for him, instead of being able to call for a meeting himself. Now he had to capitalize on his first small victory in order to negotiate to win some more *very specific* concessions from his old man, who unfortunately, just had to already be in a really bad mood. Taddeo had just learned that the latest "jobs" offered by The Family, hadn't gone his father's way. And the cops had been there. And he wasn't on his father's good side this week any more either, not after his outburst of only a couple of days ago. But he had that win he'd earned last night still going for him. Didn't he?

"I meant that the other guys on my team all work, Papa." Tad clarified who he'd referenced, though he was already sure his old man knew exactly who he spoke about. "Please. I could use your reference." Taddeo adding what he hoped was an effective pleading tone to his voice's inflection.

"Hey! Don't you ever sound like you're whining in front of me," the senior Villetti ominously cautioned, jabbing a finger at his youngest offspring. "Or anyone else for that matter. Ever! It is no longer cute. What it *is*, is time for you to grow up some more, Tato." Taddeo remembered that was exactly what Arlene told him his father would say, while Rinaldo Villetti continued. "And this is ridiculous. I know exactly what you really meant to convey. But no son of mine is going to have to go off to work with coal, in the industrial mills or the assembly lines, or whatever other bright idea you have for where you might contribute your efforts. And these Americans? They even have the gall to act like *that's* some kind of privileged position for immigrants — from *our homeland.* Birthplace of the modern cultural renaissance. The catalysts of entrepreneurial progress. Those bloody limeys just don't want their wives and daughters gaining their independence by working their way into the bourgeoisie. Or *our men* being able to compete with them. And who can blame them? There's a real battle for control of our women going on around here right now." He sighed. "I know better than some. But the industrialists have learned to love their profits from more and more war materiál, no matter who's building it. So they publicly scorn *us*, but privately welcome more immigrants by the boatload. See, I've known for a long while, ever since our family had arrived here, that lots and lots of the so-called Nativists would publicly hate on us *guineas* — with a passion — until Orlando decided to rethink Bismark's alliances, and had done gone and went and changed our country's side, having a now unified Italy become America's provisional ally in this foolish European war. Banking on Trento and Trieste, but effectively turning the tide. That *our* contribution did. Opened a new front against Austria-Hungary. And new cash flows. But 'Employ the dagos?' All of the sudden it's shouted as a rallying cry, like it's some sort of great philanthropic thing that a Rockefeller does to show appreciation to us. *For his own profit, obviously*. Not to acknowledge our contribution. Now war *is* good for business, but especially so if you have the capital to get into that business in the first place. We don't — as of yet. But Son, I've worked *very hard* so that you and your brothers will never have to labor for someone else's benefit like *that*. That kind of exploitation. Can't you only see what I'm building for you here? *Give you a job?* One day I'm going to give you all of Chicago! One day…" his voice trailed off for a second. "You're special. You're *my* Tato and you're a Villetti. Learn what that means. Go with your brothers on collections. That's *their* job — for the meanwhile, anyway. My loans that are building business and expanding prosperity on the South Side is *my kind* of philanthropy. Learn about our own family's philanthropic *empire* that one day you'll have to administrate."

Taddeo didn't bother to argue the obvious contradiction in his father's point but saw his own opportunity and quickly volunteered to take over collection duties in the bordello. "I'm ready to start even today," Taddeo informed his elated patriarch. His brother Greg who'd been standing there all along looked like he'd been suddenly stung, and stepped forward.

"I'll bet you are. Ready to work for me *there*," Rinaldo Villetti eagerly agreed upon hearing his son had an interest in studying and expanding The Family's profits they reaped in from prostitution with being part of Colosimo's organization. He finally sensed that he was getting somewhere with his most stubborn son, but stressed that a real Villetti needed experience on the cold, hard streets of their great city and "shoving around a few bitches and slapping them up a bit if they aren't forthcoming with their earnings" did not prepare him to handle Chicago. But he shared a conspiratorial smile with his youngest boy when he stated, "Well, it is indeed a start. And yes, I've noticed you like one of those girls in particular, young Taddeo. Good for you, Son. She is a special one. Certainly attractive. A rare prize. But don't let that become a distraction for you though. It's important to me that you're happy. But what makes me really happy about this latest development is that it turns out that it's actually *this new scarlet whore* who is working out to be useful after all. She may yet prove to be worth what she cost me and Urso. Victoria, err I meant Madame Moresco, didn't seem to care. But now Arlene's motivating you to not only want to learn how to stay happy, but also how to do the work that will help you stay alive. Glad I didn't get rid of *her* already."

"What do you mean, Papa?" Tad grew concerned and started to get angry while he prepared to throw down his other demand of his father — to leave Arlene's fate up to him. And that's when Greggorio, who had started pacing behind him, something obviously on his mind, abruptly stopped and stepped up directly beside him.

His father glanced at his other progeny, then focused back on Taddeo and shrugged, speaking before Taddeo recovered from his surprise at Greg's suddenly intense interest. "I mean it's nothing you need be concerned with. I'd just been worried she'd become nothing but trouble. Something to foul the water. And then she went and surprised even me — I mean that she would be the one to finally and inadvertently encourage you to undertake your training. She's bought herself some time." He nodded toward Horatio across the room so it became obvious that he had been positioned watching them from the bar since before the cops had come in and waited for a signal. There was some motion and the young man nodded toward Gervasio, then moved to go to a phone booth placed into a poorly-simulated alcove on the far wall. To Tad's right, he saw Greg distinctly scowl. The youngest brother dismissed it while his family patriarch continued his monologue to Taddeo. "But, oh. I also know what *you're* up to, Taddeo. That I do," his father said pointing a finger at his offspring. Tad gulped and wondered to himself *just what did his father know*. "I'll let you slide safely for now. It's good for you to have some goals. And like the conqueror Augustus to his son Tiberius, I will eventually pass on to *you* all that I have learned. That is what will really help you achieve your full potential. You're the one offspring I have who might actually understand *the right values* that could be worthy of a true Villetti's ambition. Your mother, God bless her, did better with you than I could with your brothers." Taddeo next saw Greg trying to crowd even closer, looking really confused. "Love for life, being a willing team-player, and love for your family is what really matters. And though right now you haven't one good clue as to how you should express your love to see to the continuation of this family, rather than its destruction," he glanced at Greg, "my baby Tato *will* finally start to grow up into the man that I would *want* to be my heir." Villetti's eyes returned to Taddeo and he smiled. Greggorio's face turned white and his mouth hung open. Glancing behind him, Tad saw seated in a booth close by, his cousin "Dally" stiffen. Corrado had been observing Greg's reactions.

"But I don't want — ."

Only then Tad's ability to speak with his father was interrupted by an old, semi-trusted friend of his papa's who Ignacio allowed into the lounge as the newcomer announced, "Excuse me Rinaldo? You asked me to find out where O'Rourke was hiding. I found out where O'Banion had him moved from County after he was fixed up in the Jackson Park Center. His people *would* transfer an Irishman twice of course. I figured I'd just wait back and track *the flowers*. Well, they led me right to him, but I was spotted. Should have figured they'd know me and that I hadn't *stayed* retired. So I used one of my guys from Racine to follow him, being relocated again — of course. And at night. They brought him once — and then back across the water again. He *was* just southeast of Grand Crossing. Yup. They must've thought we wouldn't look for the butcher here, right under our noses. But he is back on the South Side again. Bet he can't wait to heal up and get back to his business just to smart us."

"Us?"

The associate ignored the slight offered as a question and continued his report. "Yeah, well they must have paid off Doc Fishbein pretty well to treat him in the back of our Chinese laundry."

"No kidding. Kean's here? In Little Italy?"

"Uh-huh. They moved him over by The Maxwell Street Market. That's where *he wanted to go*. Must have wanted a Polish. That, and Fishbein will actually practice medicine when he's offered the right motivation, of course. And guess what else? Some poor goombah from New York, New Jersey or somewheres — might have even been local — winds up being fished out of the river in bits and pieces they dumped out of a barrel. *My cops* even questioned *me*, so I was real friendly with the greenbacks — which by the way, now you owe me — and also because I questioned *them* back. Bet you didn't know anything about this? I'd figured you'd want to."

"Your information is already late as I already know." Villetti nodded toward a barrel that Tad now noticed had been left in the center of what was the small wood-laid dancing floor. The stranger saw it and gulped. "What's more, I'm not paying. You just offered it up and never asked. So I'm not even going to be sorry about that."

"God you're a hard man to do business with, Rinny."

"No I'm not, Old Buddy. You're just not good business. That's not just my opinion. That's actually why they said they kicked you off the force. But I'll tell you what. The butcher's recovering with the Chinaman? I'm about done with *him*, so I'll give you something for that. And with me, it probably even clears your latest numbers debt. So don't go reselling this information, now."

" 'Course not. With you being so generous and everything."

"I meant that." Villetti pointed his finger at someone who was also apparently a seasoned confidence man, among other things. "Alright. Now get out of here." He slapped some money on the table and his old friend gladly scooped it up. "Since that's more than you deserve, you'll pay me back what you owe me out of this later. It should ensure that I see you again real soon. My free information that I'm giving *you* is that I'd advise you not to gamble this paper away again. Your debt's still accruing interest and you're rather lousy at the numbers game. But I'm not done talking with my boy here. We need a little father-son time. So go on and scram."

As Rinaldo Villetti's old "friend" made to leave the lounge, Tad's father afforded the young Cub some attention again. "You see that?

Those Irish cops. You can pay 'em. But you can't trust them. They take my money and then sell me out. They sell out their own kind, too. There's no loyalty. That's why *we* are different." He glanced at Greg and reflexively clenched his fist.

Then he noticed the information broker hadn't quite made it to the first door yet. "Thank you for the new knowledge. I'll be looking into this," he said to his buddy who hadn't yet completely made it to the door. "You can go now." The man in the dark suit and dark hat had deliberately dawdled. As he nodded and finally left the lounge, Tad's papa glanced over at the barrel, strangely left in the center of the venue, which the athlete now noticed to be dripping some dark fluid out of the container. Disgusting. His father nodded to the same barrel and next spoke to Greg. "I will be trying out that one's possible replacement when the next new guy arrives. Giovanni somebody. New York is sending us but another. Interestingly, he's Colosimo's nephew by marriage to Lady Moresco, a few years senior than your big brother I think — yet someone rumored to be much more skilled than Dulio. Real smart supposedly. Cosmopolitan type the politicians will love. Has his own small outfit Back East. Wants to move on up in the world. Sees Chicago as an opportunity. Hah. I will test his loyalty. His talent might be useful for something special I want to do next weekend. And I just learned where I'll want to do it — and by the hand of that someone *my brother* asked me to extend some extra special courtesy to. You and Urso will meet him Saturday and pay our house's respect. We'll evaluate how good he is. Meanwhile, Taddeo here has a baseball game I may have to personally attend." Tad's eyes brightened at that pronouncement. He'd love it if his papa took more interest in his games. "I'll be meeting with some other very important people," his father continued. "There will be time before the evening line arrives at Union Depot, so you may join me if you'd like to Greggorio. You can behave yourself. Urso may be preoccupied. And I'm sure you'd also like to watch your little brother pitch, anyway." He paused and stroked his chin hairs. "Hmm. Well moving along, they call this new one The Fox. And I guess we'll soon know if *he* works out."

"At wasting more of our money?" Greg added over his shoulder, now drifting back a ways from his father's table, as his impatience started leading him to pace once more, and become critical. Tad's papa suddenly turned red, then started coughing. He signaled for an empty glass to be brought over to him immediately. He spit up some gooey fluid into it.

"Ha. Why? Didn't you search down to the bottom of that barrel for every last cent of value a good plumber could be worth? Or did you? I'd at least figure your cousin did." Greggorio crinkled his nose and looked back toward Corrado. His cousin was yawning. But then ignoring his middle son as well as his nephew, and turning back to his youngest boy, Rinaldo Villetti continued. "Now just learn from *my* example, Taddeo. Do what I tell you, don't question my orders — especially when we're in public, and let me play this out here in The Windy City my way, without *you* causing me any trouble. No more temper tantrums and 'specially timing your little scenes. I know *you know* exactly what I mean. I don't need the rest of The Family telling me how I should raise my own sons right now. They would *all* not survive, living as well as they do, were it not for me and several of my smarter brothers supporting them. My parents, your grandparents, could not do anything to help them in the Old Country. So the most enterprising of my generation resettled our family here in these United States. Therefore I must never appear to be weak by being challenged, especially by my own son, and thus unworthy to administer *my leadership* over our family here. Word travels fast. Now some secrets *do* manage to still be kept in our immediate house, but information about many a certain game, I still prefer to keep even more private. Played close to my chest. I am not the eldest of my brothers, you know. And this is the reason why I originally moved your siblings and your mother out to Chicago. Away from The Family in Brooklyn and its criticism about how I choose to live my life, with the costs of living it *there*. And look now — I'm managing *their* business affairs *for them* — and even my own aunts and uncles — which I can now conduct more efficiently from my own newly adopted town anyway. Meanwhile they still criticize, yet hypocritically reap the benefits as it were. Yup. I see that all the time." He glanced at his other son. "But usually from far away and from all the rest of our extended, meddling Family back in New York. *I* am the only one who speaks for our house on the shores of Lake Michigan."

"Yeah, we're really on *the beachfront property* here, Papa," Tad said, rolling his eyes. He didn't need the esteem his father held him in lowered any more when he wanted to use it to help him protect Arlene. But his father's ways irritated him like they always did. "And so now we moved away from perhaps all the better doctors in New York City who could have helped us more — by saving Mama's life?"

"Don't ever speak to me like that or question my decisions about how I cared for your mother, Taddeo!" he thundered. The older man was quick to return to being severely agitated once more. "Don't ever do that again. And now, just like I did — and am still doing — your brothers are receiving instruction on how to provide for the future security of our family here in Chicago." He glanced at Greggorio. "And *I* am coaching *those* particular skills clinics. And that's still called good parenting, even in America. So I am doing the best I know how to without your mother to help me. You, me, your brothers — we are all in this together, and I have never given up on still establishing a record of success here, myself." Taddeo thought that maybe his father was trying to off-handedly reference support for his goals he'd set for himself in baseball with that last comment. His papa continued, "But we have real opportunities here we'd never have had in Brooklyn. And you shouldn't be afraid of Urso like it appears to me that you always seem to be, nor disrespect Greggorio like you do. They're your brothers. And your family loves you, Taddeo. So much more than you seem to know. My older boys are just trying to help me toughen you up. You'll need to be.

"But I can see that's really going to be up to *me*. Now I've let you play baseball. You've got talent. Oh I'm going to give you *that*, too, Son. So to a fault, I've humored your inclination to be so irresponsible and play a child's street game all these years. And wouldn't you know it? All the way up to a professional level. My boy. Breaking the barrier open further for us Italians in this new country. And oh are your brothers ever jealous! Of that, I'm sure you're aware. So I've always said, 'Let him play for as long as it can last. He'll get too old to do this forever. He's only what? About twenty years old? And very lucky.' If you were this age and our family was all still over in Europe, your generation is now seeing *the* most horrible war. Boys younger than you are having their guts ripped out and left to die, on that blood-stained earth with barbed wire entanglements ensnaring their friends, messing their trousers and crying for *their* mothers. Lice and rats eating away what's left of them in trenches that become disease-ridden cesspools with the ever frequent rain. Or freezing in the ice and falling off The Alps. I can imagine it all. But no one should ever have to see the things that your stupid-stupid younger uncle and some of your idiot cousins *are* actually seeing of that — right now. I pray they are even still alive. Hunkered down, having found some shelter somewhere. But they were all idealistic fools — the whole lot of them — to go back there and volunteer for it, or let Orlando's goons pressure them into it."

"And you exploit their sacrifice to tell everyone else how selfless and patriotic our family is at no sacrifice of your own," Taddeo interrupted his father to remind him of that.

"You are the one who spoke to me about providing you with a car just the other night. Now it would suddenly appear that today you agree with me — that you don't deserve it? For no sacrifice made *on your part*. Your relatives are dealing with having a lot less. Some days they are just praying they get food. So don't ever tell me that *you* feel underprivileged, Taddeo! Like I'm really spoiling you *that much*, either. There are just things in this world that I have strong hopes my children would never have to witness. Every day I strive to shelter you from that kind of ugly fate and premature death. And I've made it so that *you* have a better life — than even Urso or Greggorio here." Rinaldo Villetti was becoming quite mad. "And you *still* can't appreciate it. *But now you want to work a job?* Huh. I should cut your allowance." Greg was openly smiling.

"I just want to be like everybody else on my team, Sir," Tad replied, using the honorific his older brothers often used to address their commanding father, especially when they knew they were in trouble.

Rinaldo Villetti exhaled, knowing he still hadn't completely gotten through to his impudent offspring. "Then I'll make you feel like everybody else," Villetti's tone turned threatening toward his son. Next he shouted, "Pepe, get over here!"

Villetti's lackey left his drink with the two bar-fly girls he'd been trying to impress and double-timed it to quickly arrive at attention before his Godfather. His eyes, relenting to just one involuntary shift back toward the bar, was enough to convey his fretting over the inconvenience at having actually been interrupted by his boss. Tad didn't think his slightly older cousin's showing *any* lack of enthusiasm for obeying a command by his father was at all any kind of bright idea, and especially not with the current mood he'd been turning his father toward. Pepe was definitely one who had gotten way too comfortable accepting a false expectation of entitlement to the free benefits that came with being part of the Villetti House. But in reality, nothing was truly free.

The senior Villetti scrunched his mouth up as he stared angrily into Pepe's young face. Tad knew his great aunt's unloading her grandson onto the mentoring of Rinaldo Villetti had annoyed the aspiring street capo. But Taddeo's old man actually needed someone else who was lacking in discipline himself, if only to further the training of another just like any of his own sons and his nephews, the Delasandros. So Villetti often used Pepe to make an example of for Family members not completely complying with his orders. Now the elder gangster would demonstrate he was fair, not playing favorites with his sons, and make an example of Taddeo to prove it. "Junior here wants a job. Take your cousin into the back and give him over to Old Lamont. Let him learn to do the dishes with the niggers. And let him think long and hard about how he likes that. I don't want to see him for a couple of hours."

"Yes, Sir." Pepe motioned for another member of the goon squad, just another new hanger-on and definitely from outside The Family, but who looked like he was a fraction older than the athlete but more physically capable of controlling Taddeo. "Thorello." This fella only got a second's attention by way of Pepe's introduction. The fresh meat had hurried over to stand with the tall athlete's cousin. When the novice enforcer motioned toward Taddeo and his father had nodded, granting his permission to touch his son, they grabbed the young pitcher and rather forcefully pushed him along toward the back of the establishment to the place's kitchen and cleaning areas.

Villetti watched them go and snorted. "I hope you enjoy your *new job*, Tad."

Pepe and his pal he'd called Thorello escorted Taddeo into the back of the restaurant. Plates, bowels, and utensils were piled high and covered with refuse comprised of vegetable matter, tomato sauce, bits of bread slices, soggy pasta, liquefying egg waste, and shreds of meat fats along a molded aluminum counter that stood next to large steel water basins on long legs, so they lined up at the average man's waist height on those long legs that stuck out beneath them. It all smelled pretty bad and some of the stench was erroneously thought to be covered up by having piles of dirty cloth napkins laid out on top of the mess — not to leave out a thick curtain of cigarette smoke.

Instead of working, three dark-skinned men with short hair and wearing stained white aprons were enjoying that smoke and chatting over to the side of the back room. Half of a double-door out to the alley behind the establishment was propped open for ventilation. Their voices were invigorated with joy and each tried to raise its volume above the next until they suddenly noticed The House personnel enter their room and they snapped to attention. But then upon recognizing it was only Pepe and his friend, they slouched back to their previous posture but clapped their hands upon distinguishing it was Taddeo that the newcomers pushed along with them. The ballplayer smiled and took a bow, while he choked on the assault to his breathing sensitivity.

The skinniest and eldest among them, and the one with noticeably lighter skin, showed no reservation about breaking ranks with the other two and extinguishing his current vice, stepping forward to clasp Tad's hands. "Oui! Mon homme," he said in his French accent. "My man, Monsieur Taddeo. The Golden Arm. North Star of the South Side."

Tad smiled. "Hello Old Lamont," and warmly accepted the other's dirty hands in his own.

Pepe looked confused. He probably expected this was supposed to be the Villetti patriarch's way of making his son miserable. To him, the friendly reunion that unfolded surely didn't resemble anything like punishment. "Uh, hi Old Man," he said. "The pitcher here is supposed to clean up the dishes and the rest of the mess around here. It kinda stinks so uh I guess you'll be in charge of him. We're going to take a smoke break out back." He nodded toward his friend.

"Yeah. Be sure to take that break because you work so hard, Pepe," Tad called after his cousin and the other man who accompanied him.

"You in troubles, Homme? Why your papa make you wash the vaisselle with us?"

"That'd be easy," one of the other black men, this one an American, offered. "We be hidin' back here, so dah great white mastah runs out of us niggahs tah boss 'round so now he be whippin' on his own son. Gotta always have someone under his boot or he not keep bein' da mastah."

"Ah. Travail, Homme. Travail. Now you two get back to work," Lamont encouraged his other cohorts. "My seniority makes me the mastah back here in my own domain." He raised his hands to run them through his white hair, then noticed how dirty his fingers were and moved over to wash his hands and then his lined face at the clean water sink. He'd now taken a good look at the athlete's bruises from the fight the other day as well. Over his shoulder he spoke with Taddeo. "So?"

"So. The Man's been in a pretty bad mood. There's been another barrel murder. I am having trouble with the Irish cab drivers. Nobody can tell if it's even the work of The Black Hand. Shit's been happening. And I guess I just chose a bad time to approach my papa. But I think I'm in love." He decided to spill his guts. And why not? As far as he knew, only his family and not their associates socialized with the black men. His father and Greg had surmised everything going on between him and his new woman already. And for some reason, Old Lamont always proved himself a wise sounding board for Taddeo. That and for another reason he could not explain, he knew the old man was worthy of his trust. "You see, I'm trying to help this girl. Arlene." His elder companion straightened when he regarded him most curiously. Tad went on. "She's the new redhead? My papa forces her to work here. So I just met with my father in hopes I'd make him understand I needed a job. An income. More than what's typically paid to play baseball. As I think I'm going to do what I can to help her pay for her boarding on my own. But my father's not going to humor me about this one. Actually, I only managed to make him so mad I didn't even get to talk to him about everything that I had hoped to — like what The House's plan is for Arlene. I know I shouldn't have popped off on him about my ma, but he often makes me really mad."

"Oh, Oui. I see. That *is* fathers and sons. But you play ball so well. I've liked what I got to see and also what I hear my great-grandson tell. He's your *plus grand admirateur*." Lamont smiled.

"Alright. Stop with the French. Maybe you can help me figure some things out, but it won't help if *I* can't figure out what you're saying to me in the first place."

"Oui."

Tad rolled his eyes, as the other kitchen workers laughed as they listened in while they started cleaning up the mess still left over from the previous night. After all, it did not seem like Villetti's son was going to do it. Instead he stated, "You used to offer me good advice with my game. It always was a great help to talk things out with you. This time, well, as I mentioned — her name's Arlene. And I can't stand her while at the same time I can't stop thinking about her. But you especially can appreciate this: my father's got her under his thumb, too."

"I'm a free man, Taddeo. I'm not under your papa's thumb, as you put it." But the elder man did look deeply thoughtful about something his young friend had brought up.

"That's why I've never been able to figure out why you choose to work *here*. Oh — and hey, I better get started helping you men. Papa wasn't kidding about me working. So let him get mad at Pepe when they come to check up on what's been happening and find him shirking off his duties, smoking out back. I'm *not* afraid of hard work. And I mean to show Papa that I'm serious."

"Yes, well don't the Cubs have practice before the game? You're playing later."

"Yeah. I hope. I guess you know I earned my first win. Man I did great yesterday. As a matter of fact, my experience in Iowa was what saved the whole game. But that's also why I can't stay the whole two hours he wants me working back here," Tad said. "I have to walk a lot of my way but use the train where I can. The taxi drivers just won't relent over on the North Side. And Weeghman's not offering a rail pass. Not him. Not to an Italian," he continued to explain as he collected up all the cloth napkins out of the disgusting pile and took them over to another wash basin and began soaking them in the soapy water. "He's even got pot-lickers guarding the North Clark Station. Decided not to make it easy for me, I guess. I've just now began hearing *he got coerced* into calling me up from Iowa."

"I believe I understand," said Lamont softly. He looked at his hands.

Taddeo was reaching for the wash board when the front door that led out into the dining area swung open. Greg stood there with his arms folded. Apparently he wanted to watch. Tad's father joined him in another moment. He'd also decided he wanted to see his son work after all. The baseball player ignored them and continued to mind his task so he could then begin cleaning up at the plates.

"Your son is a good worker, Monsieur Villetti. He is too mindful of his duty to his father to speak out, but I will remind you for him, that he will have to leave to cross the river not too soon. The Chicago baseball team will have practice for him."

Rinaldo Villetti nodded. "Tell me again about *your son*, Lamont."

"My son is French. As am I. But I am an old man now. He saw it as his duty to fight in the war and defend our motherland from the Huns. He is very brave. My son, and now my grandson — he joined Guy to now fight at his father's side. I received a letter."

"You can read?" Greg asked, rather surprised.

"Yes, I can read and write," Lamont told him. The other black employees looked at their elder cohort and involuntarily expressed their curiosity, which then morphed into frowns.

Sigñor Villetti only smiled and glanced at his older son who had spoken. Then he also looked back at Taddeo. "You hear? Lamont's son and grandson fights for his family. They're educated and smart, too."

The old laborer continued his story. "They fight for France. That's different. But it was I who taught them that lé France gave my family great opportunity. Anyways, I eagerly await more news, as I fear for the both of them. I think the last I heard, they were near Reims, that's northeast of Paris, and the combat will be getting even heavier, as on the other side of the Kaiser's great war machine, the Russians, they have changed over their government, made a separate treaty for their peace, and exited from their front in the war. It might signal "the begging" for the end of tyranny by those born so much more fortunate than the common man. But we will see."

"You know an awful lot to just be the kitchen help," Greg replied.

"I know how to work my job with European style, Mister Villetti." Lamont had addressed Greggorio with the appropriate respect.

"That's true," the Italian patriarch informed his son. "That's why I have him here. Do you think Pepe could cook?"

Everyone laughed. "Well, then we could advertise we're serving *real* Italian crap. Though I shouldn't have to break this to you Papa, but people really don't come here for the food anyway," Greg added. He had to smile.

"No. But our family is off to a fine start at recruiting a lot of new people choosing to undertake new adventures *here*, because we're making the whole South Side of Chicago *work*. Isn't that right Taddeo? And you see? Already two generations of poor Old Lamont's family has been swept up by the war, working to just stay alive. How do you like laboring when all you have to do is just clean napkins and tablecloths?"

"I'm sure I'm finding it wonderful. But Lamont's right, Papa. I have baseball practice in another hour." *But I also have new information. Papa* does *talk with Old Lamont. A lot. And I best remember that.*

"How I wish I was young again. I'd love to leave and throw around some baseballs," the eldest man put in.

"Rumor is that they are developing that league for niggers — ," Greg started.

"Negroes," Lamont corrected him. Tad liked the old black man because he was still strong and proud and stood up to his father and his brothers. The other black employees, eyes widening, their nervously taking a glimpse of the one among them who dared to have spoken, then turned back to their work, looking scared by their old cohort's audacity. But Tad knew Lamont had the leverage to speak like that because his papa and his oldest brother absolutely loved the old man's cooking. Villetti's signature dishes topped with some cigarette smoke at no additional charge. They might have bad taste, but Lamont sure benefitted from their opinion that he wouldn't be so easy to replace. And additionally, Tad just had now figured that it made sense that his father also probably appreciated an elder and educated European to interact with on a different and more relaxed level than that with which he had to deal with Family or rivals who approached any kind of similar description. Even if Lamont was a Negro. The pitcher appreciated him for his intelligence too, and Taddeo was surely thankful that Lamont was also a baseball fan. That was most important. "Anyway, I'm too old to play," his elderly friend concluded.

"Well, you keep working hard for me and maybe things will change and your great-grandson will be able to," Rinaldo Villetti softly commented to him. "What's his name? Parnell? He really enjoys it when I send him to the games. In the meantime, if you think you got even a quarter of an hour's good work out of my son here, you can determine yourself if he's ready to move on to his baseball practice. He'll still have to have enough time to get across town to remind Chicagoans that the Italians know how to play this game, too. However, since Taddeo likes his work here so much, he is going to return to help you tomorrow, bright and early, well before any Friday game. Okay? Is that understood?" Villetti looked directly at Taddeo.

"Yes, Sir," he replied with little enthusiasm. He already had knowledge of a forecast that told him there'd be no Friday practice, or game, just plenty more dishes to wash and trash left over from his father's business that he would have to deal with. He decided not to mention his trial with the Irish on his commute the other day, nor whatever message about the body in the barrel the thugs in the car had been trying to communicate. Tad's apprehensiveness had been relaxed by Arlene; he trusted that he wasn't in any immediate danger and he didn't want to be involved any more in that part of his father's business. The leaky barrel in the other room on the dancing floor seemed to suggest his father had already gotten a message anyway.

Once his father and Greg left them alone, and Pepe and his buddy came back in through the kitchen and were called back out into the lounge so the senior Villetti could yell at Pepe for shirking off his work once again, Tad took Old Lamont by the arm. "Can I talk to you for a minute — out back?"

"Oui, Monsieur Taddeo."

"Look, I'm not trying to get you in trouble by telling you any of this. So you can deny you ever knew anything if I'm caught," he said as the athlete and his old friend moved outside, into the cooler fresh air, and away from anyone overhearing them. "But I'm also to start work taking over the ledger for the bordello and I plan on robbing my *dear* father blind." Lamont's mouth moved, but he maintained a lack of any expression. He found a cigarette pack in his apron pocket, and a match book, then lit one as Tad went on. "Well, I can't rob him blind, but what I mean is that I'll skim off the top. I'm only really taking my own money — my inheritance, as it is anyway. And well, you see, I'm not even actually taking it anywhere, either. I have to return it to the pot. So I get a little of what each of the other girls are making, and I return it back to cover what Arlene alone should have made. This way at least she's not being abused, and the other ladies are still covered."

"I see."

"Do you see it — as a *good* idea I mean? 'Cause what you don't see is my papa paying anyone fair wages for doing any of these so-called *quality* jobs. Or there'd be a lot more pride taken in the work allotted out." He nodded toward the kitchen to suggest he meant the hired help. "So if you can keep quiet about this — about everything I'm doing — I'll make sure that something's in it for you, too. My *Homme.*" *Now I* have to *make sure Old Lamont stays quiet about this when he talks to my father. I shouldn't have opened my mouth in the first place. But he's always here late and could witness what I'm about doing. Plus I just needed some damn support and sought to get it somewhere. And who knows? Maybe Lamont will turn out to be useful? He kind of has in the past.*

"I see. You want me to keep what you just told me just between us. Have no fear. The way I am looking at it, young Taddeo, is I am getting a lot more out of this than I am putting into it. And for a black man in *this country*, this is the way it's going to be unless someone discovers a way to change things. Your contribution is more than welcome. I still have other very personal priorities in my heart. I hope I will not become too old to fulfill accomplishing them, and one day return to France. To my wife and the family that I love. But if this plan of yours is what's in your heart, then you help your young lady friend. There is a good in you that makes you so unique. Not just because you can play baseball, but because of who you are, and where you came to rise up from, so much that now you *could* become the most successful man I have ever known. There are several quite exclusive pathways open to you that in time, I'm sure you're going to discover. You'll have choices. Some could pay off. That is what I see."

Chapter 14

"Are we even seeing any real pay for all the work we're putting into this?" Trip asked as they stretched out on the field at Weeghman Park early that afternoon.

"We're getting a chance to play in the Big Leagues. And for the best team," Hoff said. "It'll pay off later. Have more pride in what we're achieving here."

"What Charlie Deal is achieving here. I'm not seeing any playing time. Besides, you can't take pride to the bank."

"Not even the veterans can with what the league is paying almost any ballplayer now that the union's gone," Trevor added. "We should be getting some more of the box-office's revenue shares at least."

"Yeah. And at least laundered uniforms. I hate playing in my filthy sweat-stains," Trip said.

"Well there's grumblings about a strike. Now if we keep winning we can gain more clout with which to bargain with," Hoff contributed.

The conversation struck a chord with Taddeo, not just because it reminded him of his conversation with Old Lamont less than two hours ago — and Arlene before him — but because he'd finally surrendered the illusion his own pride hadn't allowed him to let go of until now. And though Taddeo had already worried that maybe the taxi driver he encountered the other day was right, he'd continued to deny it if only to harden his resolve at least for appearance's sake when standing before his father and Greggorio. But the same conclusion just kept resurfacing as he listened to his teammates. The only pitching time *he* would probably get used to seeing was when he'd face the bottom of the opposing team's order. Then Mitchell might need to send in a stronger hitter for the Cubs' next turn at the plate than Hendrix, and/or switch out Vaughn or Tyler, when Coach needed a right-hander in a setup or easy close situation at the start of the next defensive outing. So Tad would just face one or two batters usually. Most starters were expected to pitch complete games. Babe Ruth was being trained to. But Taddeo had been lucky they'd even served him up Wheat the other day when Claude's arm started giving way. *Or was it luck?* But it did make him some new friends on the bench, or so he could hope. Though even after Tad's great win they could always forget about him again. He didn't pitch that many baseballs. It wasn't his skill that saved him. He was very fortunate indeed that he got what might have been his one and only win, on only his third outing in the Major League. But that came from strong teamwork, his friends' contribution. Chicago still didn't really trust him to protect his squad's work on the field almost two full months into the season. *I'm only being used, when Coach has no one else to use, just like Hoffman and Bass-Man are being, even* if *Hoff* can *remain patient and positive about it. But he's just better at setting the right example than the rest of us. Trip's seen even one less game than any of the other rookies on the roster this season. Well fuck Mister Optimism over there*. He glanced at his best friend. *I could piss on this situation!* But Taddeo had been told that even after they brought him out of his trials in the mud fields, he still had dues to pay in order to play with the pros. *Just like the plumber did. It's still my tryout time here — and now, even with my father's organization. Like I want to worry about controlling whores when I need to worry about control over my cut fastball. But now I also have to take care of Arlene. And* I *volunteered for all this shit*. Tad had noted that tryouts hadn't gone so well for the plumber. But to the 3rd baseman who was still complaining he said, "Hey Trip, why don't you just shut up and stop whining so we can take our run?" His friends he came up with had so much less to deal with than he did right now. Tad was not sympathetic. To his knowledge, Charlie Hollocher was the only rookie who was married already, or he was engaged to be married to his girlfriend Jane anyway. Thus he even had a domestic situation to worry over like Tad did. And as annoying as it was to his other struggling teammates, that rookie shortstop would be great at adding to the Cubs' winning record — since he was already almost as successful at their sport in reality, as he was in his own overactive imagination. *Holly* had something to prove as the Cubs had been disappointed they'd gotten *him* instead of Roger Hornsby. But the rest of the new guys actually had even further to go to demonstrate their worth, earn their keep, and then pray it paid them something. At least the Cubs hoped that in summation of all their effort going into this season, they'd each get out of it more than any one player singularly put into it. Because it was hard to imagine *winning* being overrated. Though as Lamont had hinted, Tad just might have other games at which he could be better at winning in. He needed to see all the options he could have for his future. His papa had even said he had good instincts, right?

"Okay. Well, if you're all finished running backward, we gotta stay positive moving forward guys," Hoff told his friends. They began their warm-up jog around the field.

"You get to be. For sure *today*, Boss. 'Positive,' I mean. Coach is resting Killefer — or making sure he uses him to hold together the bench — so you may see some playing time if O'Farrell doesn't go a full game."

"Why wouldn't he?" But Hoff glanced over at the empty visitors' dugout to which the Robins would soon arrive. "Well, never mind. Have you seen the lineup already?"

"No. I came out from the clubhouse when you did. But Killefer had some days off coming anyway. I think he has been feeling a little sick."

"Of you, probably," Trevor teased Tad. "Wake up. Coach will keep using him as additional security as long as we're playing Brooklyn."

"That's why I was dreading sitting on the bench next to him. But oh. Mitchell wasn't there yet. Probably drinking." Taddeo winked at his best friend.

"Yeah, and having you on the team is what would drive him to drink, Taddeo," Trip joked.

"So maybe I get to catch for you once again — after our first pro game in which we were both victorious on the field together," Hoff said, not hiding any hope that came through his voice.

"Not likely," Tad told him. "It's the last game in this series versus the Robins. And it's Weaver's turn in the rotation. Coach isn't going to need me. Harry's a righty, so Mitchell's got plenty of other potential right-handed relievers and I don't think he wants to see me play against *Brooklyn* any more this entire season."

"More like in his entire lifetime," Trevor added, smiling and smacking Tad across the butt with his glove as he jogged past them, crossing the 3rd base side foul line and onto the outfield warning track ahead of his friends.

"Yeah, it's only about as much as Coach wants to see you bat against the Robins' pitching," Trip told him as he passed.

"Who's on for them today?" Tad asked.

"Dan Griner. Right-hander as well," Hoff told him.

Tad reflexively rubbed his chin. He already knew that detail very well from his previous encounter. "Oh. Great." The swelling of the wounds to his face had only just began to relent.

"He struggled his last year with Saint Louis in 'Sixteen' and didn't play pro ball until his big comeback with Brooklyn now."

"Well, we'll make him wish he didn't come back." Overhearing them was Charlie Hollocher who had just come running across half the field to join them.

"That worked out so well the last time we tried it," The Bass-Man told him. He glanced at Taddeo, who mistook the irritation the outfielder showed Holly, for an entirely different reason.

"Hey, who said you could run with us?" Tad asked Charlie. "And you're cheating yourself out of a good warm-up run if you cut across Taylor-Dee's grass like that."

"Why break a good habit? I'm saving some energy for the game. Some of us expect to play you know? And I've advanced a lot of distance rapidly. All the time. That's what I do," Hollocher told him. "And I'm going to be a success with it, too. Ask yourselves *who's* building a record here? It's you guys who need to keep up with me this season, so we show them all what good rookies can do. Especially on this team."

Tad didn't respond to him. Instead he called to Hoffman, "George. Stop a minute? I gotta talk to you."

"Yeah. Sure. What's up Taddeo?"

They stopped. Breathing slightly faster than normal, but healthy considering the athletes' pre-practice run. Their teammates jogged on ahead as they conversed. "Look. I'm sorry I didn't celebrate with the rest of you guys after our great plan worked and we won yesterday."

"Good. I was waiting for an apology. And you need to tell that to the rest of them." Hoff nodded toward Bass and Trip's backs. "And not just our family from the Ansons, but the rest of your infield, which includes Hollocher, too. They all got you out of your jam. I'm sure glad Merkle appreciates it."

"They really seemed to appreciate you. You lent your voice to setting up our play. The fellas — they went along with it because of you, not me. You're a leader, George. You're going to appear to have potential." Tad smiled at his pal.

"Yeah? Maybe. Well I was wondering where you'd disappeared to when we all went out to party as a winning team — and the guy who was recorded as having saved the entire game in the first place — was missing. What the hell was that? It had better have been for a woman. I'd understand if it was for a woman."

"It was. And I know *you* would, Hoff." Tad laughed. "But

seriously, say I do get a chance at them again," he nodded toward the still-empty visitors' dugout and smiled. "You good with me having another go at my enemies?" He winked at his friend.

"I'm good with it. Teach them Easterners that they gotta respect Chicago. So you think you still owe Olson? Or it's Griner now? It is, isn't it? Or are you moving on up to the heart of their order? Inventing more new enemies for yourself now? What's the matter? Your father doesn't provide you with enough of them already?"

"Funny. But I want my shot at that spit-baller. If you think they'll let him bat?" Tad thought of a fun and healthy relief to his stress he was feeling — healthy for him as long as he was the one throwing the baseball.

"At who? The man and the menace, Burleigh Grimes? Ha! That guy really does deserve something else. But Wil Robinson would also really have to hate him to put him out over the dish and serve him up to *you.*" Hoff laughed. "We'd all have to really knock Griner off the hill today anyway — to even see Brooklyn turn to their pen."

"True."

"Though you're absolutely right about *that one*. Grimes. I've seen his stuff like it were pure evil and coming at me from exactly sixty feet away. But dream on. Reluctantly, I have to agree with what you first said. Weaver's a right-hander and so is almost everyone but two of our arms. I'm really sorry, Tad. I want to team up with you and have us a go at these guys again, but I guess it doesn't look like anyone's going to need you today."

Arlene does. I'll concentrate on that. And then I'm at least worth something to somebody, Tad thought. But he wished he could have done better even in that area, as had he found a way to not aggravate his father so much, he might have also gotten the old patriarch to have exerted his influence in the community to get him a better job already. Or to recognize that Arlene meant something to him, and release her from any plans he had to force her service to him in The Family's wonderful way they employed women. *Yeah, now I* am *dreaming*.

Chapter 15

Tad's father hollered into his phone, "Am I dreaming, or did you just tell me you won't disturb *my son*, for *me*?"

["Um. Sir. He asked that he not be disturbed. He — he was quite explicit about that. When he grabbed me by my shirt collar and spit his instructions into my face, I don't think I could have misheard him."]

The signor sounded most angry, but he probably had to raise his voice anyway. A new music ensemble, some negro group conveying the latest popular tunes making their way around the underground club scene in Chicago, was auditioning on Villetti's small stage. Colosimo had been promoting their style. Rinaldo had no idea who'd suggested that *he* would also do that. Aside from the noise which was difficult to ignore, the old soldier didn't care and they were paid no attention to by all who could be concerned. It wouldn't matter if they could play. People didn't come to Villetti's for the food, or the music, either.

"If I have to come over there to speak to Urso in person, then I will do more to *you* than spit in your face!" Rinaldo Villetti thundered. "No. Hmmm. Well you know what? I am beyond tired of waiting to ever get any results out of him. But this time it might actually even be my fault since I was the one who sidetracked my boy." He thought about Arlene. He wasn't going to handle her the way Greg wanted him to — with Urso — and play into his scheming other son's hands. She wouldn't die. Not this week anyway. Not when he found her useful with Taddeo — a surprise to be sure. But if the young lady thought she was going to circumvent his control over her and get away with murder, he would have to teach her a hard lesson. Thoroughly. "So, what *I am* actually going to do is come down there and have *everyone* answer to me in person! Teach you all *why* you're earning something else in addition to what you're paid by Harry Sisson. Make sure my room is ready for me. I'll be staying for a bit. And have the new girl prepared for my arrival."

["Well Sir, uh, about that. Well, you see, your *other* son has that room reserved right now."]

"Who? Taddeo? *Still?* Jesus Christ! Is he living there now?"

["Uh. Yes, Sigñor. For about half of this week, so far. At least it would seem that way."]

"Well, it would seem he's not there now. The Cubs have a game. So I'm coming over. Have that bitch in *his room* waiting for *me* when I get there!" Villetti didn't wait for the hotel clerk to acknowledge him before he hung up the phone with force, slamming the earpiece onto its hanger on the microphone stand he had to steady with a tight grip, Rinaldo's knuckles white. His blood was boiling, and his face and neck turning red. So either Taddeo was playing games with him and the new responsibility his boy had just bargained for, and that was definitely why Tad wanted to take over managing the bordello — to protect Arlene — or that smartass scarlet whore was manipulating him. It was surely the latter. He hated to admit it, but his youngest son just wasn't that bright. And worse, Villetti knew she had the motivation — and his son had enough naivety — to make him susceptible to her particular charms. *And she could be just* so *charming*. But he also knew she could be potentially very, very dangerous. That's why he thought she'd make one impressive trophy in his harem. Only she had already managed to use his son to escape his harem or she'd have returned to The House already. And therefore this was why he also was going to redirect her smart ass and put it to use the way the boy's seasoned patriarch preferred it. And that was when he became aware of his other offspring Greggorio smirking at him from his seat at the bar on the other side of the room. His middle son did his best to cover his mouth to hide his smugness. Too late. Villetti's head snapped in place to bore his eyes into his attitude-challenged second-born. *Speaking of smart asses.*

Well I know what. *That is, I'm not walking into this blind — whatever these maneuvers everyone seems to be jockeying around me are — for all they* won't *ever amount to anyway. But they're all conspiring against me now. That's what this really is. Arlene is Arlene. But my boys are growing up and they think they can betray me? They think I'm getting senile? That their old man is losing his grip? Then they are all going to learn their father still has a thing or two to teach them. And I'm going to teach Arlene.* He'd reset the phone down where it was supposed to be after untwisting the cord, walked away from its station at an alcove in the back wall and then surveyed some gentlemen already all too eager to enter his business establishment on this early afternoon, even though Villetti's was opening opportunities for newcomers later than was usual — due to all the goings-on with the cops, his stupid nephew and Taddeo that morning. Villetti looked his customers over through the glass door. Crowding into the foyer, when their wives probably thought they were working or watching baseball, these men were definitely not there for the food, or at this hour, not really the drinks either, and no one had called Rinaldo to get in on any action over the Cubs–Robins' final game in Chicago. No, these were his establishment's real customers. Or he liked to think they were his and not those of Colosimo and his wife, Madame Moresco. He was sure they were already over-eager and confused why Greg or somebody else had let the niggers from that band in ahead of them, while the nightclub's owner had been dealing with his youngest son. And he wished there'd been time to get that barrel moved already. But if the cops didn't come back to get it soon, he could just throw a tablecloth, a candle holder, and some dinner settings on top of it, Rinaldo figured.

Villetti would admit only to himself that he was tired. There were a lot of moving parts to his operation. It certainly didn't feel small-time. That was for sure. And he knew he was still very sick. He needed to see his brother-in-law for more medication, and very soon. Now with what was nearly his last thought he mulled over before taking his subsequent action, Rinaldo also knew it was the last game of Chicago's home series with Brooklyn, and it already looked as though the teams would split it. The Cubs had dropped the first two, won the third by his son's very first Major League save the other night, and already played their 1st inning today where Chicago had scored off Griner to jump to a very early lead. Lamont's great-grandson Parnell had looked a little shy when he'd been sent off to the game this time, along with Rinaldo Villetti's youngest nephews, the twelve-year-old PeeDee and his youngest brother Bennie Delasandro. They'd been begging to go to some games, too. But though a "more-than official" segregated seating rule kept the black youth from sitting with the other boys at Weeghman's ballpark, he got to enjoy himself as long as he phoned in to give Villetti updates on the game. Rinaldo had a few reasons to want this information, ahead of his meeting on Saturday, and to see if he could start training his youngest nephews as well. It was never too early to become a productive member of The Family. *Hmmm. If his ball team wins tonight, Tad will return late — probably first stay out on the North Side celebrating with his friends immediately following the 9th. No one was betting because it looked like the cops were going to help the Cubs to close this series on a new victory streak. However, if I could have motivated Urso in time, I bet* he *could have scared up some gamblers who would try to win, maybe play the spread, so as to retire their debts they still owed me. But I'll just have to suck it up and take responsibility for diverting him today. Fortunately for me, Salvatore Cardinella wanted to continue trading favors, so I'd owe him more maybe, but* my place *hasn't been bombed, Colosimo's none-the-wiser about my arrangement — possibly — and "Il Diavolo" had other interests with that young East Chicago woman he'd sent Villetti. And so I gather, Urso found* her *very interesting. But now I have to watch that conniving broad, too.*

Then the senior Villetti moved to act on his new idea. He retraced his steps, made another quick phone call, and then picked one out the lot from his establishment's eager visitors that afternoon who appeared to be especially meek and easily receptive to orders. He'd grind this one under his thumb while he promised him the deal of a lifetime with *a really special girl*, and then send *this loser* over to The Sisson. Yes, he would put Arlene's smart ass to good use. Public use. And perhaps sooner than he would have liked, but neither she nor his son were going to plot to undermine his control over his own business' domination. Rinaldo Villetti had to be at his best to manage this *other* new business opportunity, and he would drive his point home that he'd wanted to impress into the girl a different way — and test her next reaction. It would at least allow him to evaluate her as a security risk and provide him with a clue toward her abilities and resolution. And it might wake up Taddeo from his newest delusion concerning the Irish woman. Rinaldo had now been delivered one message in blood — from the North Side — even if perhaps the order for sending it didn't originate there. But he'd send *her* a message back — likewise, painted in blood. Now he'd force Arlene to spell it out, where she'd be found out — and in doing so, separate her from *one* of his more difficult children, and hopefully to render at least this son into something less of burden — now that his youngest boy had finally started working for The Family. If Taddeo's eyes were open even a sliver, he should be able to discern the lesson. Then being around all the other ladies, he'd lose his obsession with any singular one. And she? She was becoming as much of or perhaps more of a burden than his middle child had suggested, after all. At least his most thoughtful son had called that one right. Now maybe she'd be willing to offer up a better attitude toward working with him once he demonstrated exactly just what he could do to her, whether she was residing at The Hull House, the bordello or somewhere else. Arlene was indentured to him or the treaty with her people was forfeited. She would be reminded of that. Rinaldo Villetti could always manage his property. He'd show all of them.

At this time, Greggorio still sat with one of Villetti's sycophantic nephews from his sister's brood while the pair observed everything unfold *exactly* as he bet his equally smartass offspring would probably have expected it to. They were both clearly amused as they'd watched him pace around in circles, order or make a couple phone calls to the hotel, holler at people, and keep changing his mind and his plans. This aggravated Rinaldo even more. *My boy really thinks that I'm becoming indecisive, old and senile. They all can see I'm sick. And he's been watching me, looking for weaknesses. Weaknesses that I will* never *allow him to find.* Rinaldo Villetti was not getting benched by the flu, his little affiliation with the Cubs, or the rookie pitcher's conniving whore, and neither was he going to play as another pawn in his middle son's chess game against *his* other brothers. No doubt Greggorio was encouraging more confrontations between him and the other boys. But Rinaldo was the game master. First he'd remind Arlene, for she was actually the most dangerous — and then soon enough, Taddeo — of this fact. After that, he'd figure out what to do with Greg and Urso. His sons would not be allowed to grow too smart for their own good on his watch. Or too irresponsible in Urso's case. Nope. But in order to be a good parent, he had to leave at least one of them sitting in a strong and *stable enough* position to run this always changing outfit and build upon the power he had already established for his family. But even to Rinaldo, it was unclear which boy that would be. He did not enjoy the uncertainty.

Greg sat in his stool turned so his back rested up against the bar. He and Corry quietly drank and smoked their cigars with admittedly stupid smiles on their faces that they just could not avoid. And they did watch Rinaldo Villetti order or make one phone call after another. Then pace around his establishment. Then much later, make another call. But first feign some interest in some out-of-town tenderfoot loser that *he* actually put money into the hands of, and next called a taxi for. *This was good business?* No. *What was this?* Then it occurred to Greg without any doubt it was to send this horny and thus easily malleable man off to Arlene, as pretty much only she, Urso or Taddeo could frustrate Greg's father *that* much that he would pay for even some idiot to relieve him of whatever ailment one of his other sons or the whore had caused him now. But that was his father's weakness. Underneath his callous persona, he really cared too much about how his family was doing, and by letting his feelings control him from his gut — no, actually from what his heart told him — he stopped listening to much of what his head told him. He didn't want to cause them pain in person, so he farmed out the work and could claim he was innocent later. Though he never had gone far enough to be effective yet. What Greg's papa really needed to do was recruit and use more capable help. But another guy *was* coming from Brooklyn. Though with this fella's credentials that Greg had heard about, this newcomer would *not* be under his papa's control. Greg would do something about that, though he had yet to even meet the man. But the senior Villetti still doted on Urso and Taddeo — even his nephews — too much in Greg's opinion. All the while the old man was losing it. He would only weaken if he counted on these incapables. Or was he playing the game at even a higher level than Greggorio comprehended for the moment? Arranging something else Greg had not yet anticipated. An alarming prospect to be sure. *Am I witness to my father thwarting* me *now? Well, that is not going to happen*. The young man could be quite adaptable, and he would never allow himself to have such vulnerabilities.

"Go over to the hotel again, later tonight. After the game," Greg told Corry. "Wait until my little brother shows up there. Could be a while if the Cubs win. And it won't matter if Urso is there or not. We both already know *he's too busy*. The irresponsible — well never mind. You'll be easily able to stay out of his way. It's not hard to figure how my father distracted him intentionally, but it seems for longer than even *he* found convenient. But it sure screwed up my original plan. So do not make contact with your dear old cousin. And I doubt Urso would have thought to send anyone else to Arlene in his place, either. *But my father* is *sending someone*. This fool won't even pay you a second thought, the idea of having that fire-crotch has him all so worked up." Greg nodded at his elder, who was now putting his arm across the shoulder of their visitor, passing him even more cash while the new man used his other hand to continuously push his glasses up on his nose and stare between the money in his first hand, and Rinaldo Villetti as his ocular assist slipped each time he excitedly nodded his head. His father then even gave him a complimentary drink. Tad didn't have to even be here to serve as the straw that stirred it. Greg just had to keep smiling. He knew the next move his father was making. "Let that guy arrive before you do. Don't disturb Arlene until she's accompanied with my brother. Besides, it would be healthier for everyone if more Family didn't come around until later, when she might possibly have run out of bullets."

"Sound advice. But if it's all the same to you, I'm still not going to be the one who handles this personally, Cousin," Corrado said, speaking normally again as he watched the other men across the room. "And now I have more than one good reason."

I don't blame him. I couldn't stomach watching how this wimp handles himself with Arlene, nor allow myself to wind up in the next barrel they find in the Chicago River, either. She's not going to lay down quietly for this. Somebody's probably getting shot or at least worked over good if my little brother has inherited any Villetti *in him.* "Hmmm. Then why don't you send Pepe's friend in first? Make some use of *that* guy. What's his name? Thorello. He's lazy, not Family, and he got to manhandle my little brother. No one gets to do that to one of us — even if it is the Tadpole — and then walk around to talk about it. Plus, I just don't like him. That bruiser isn't hanging around here *only* to be our pitiful little worm of a relation's *friend*, at any rate. And I don't think he's very qualified, but nevertheless, he is looking for a job. Give him one. I want to see what Arlene does. I can already predict how she'll handle *that one* that Papa's sending over right now. And the same instructions that I gave to you, will now also apply to Thorello."

"Great. Well, I'm certainly glad you don't want to see what she tries doing to *me*."

"Unfortunately, I've already imagined what I think you'd like her to do with you. But back to the real world, if the new guy lives long enough, tell him that he's to relate to Taddeo that we expect him to wash dishes tomorrow. He's on the schedule. Not Weeghman's, but *our schedule*. I want my brother to also know he's on The Family's active sonar. If he wants any real responsibility in The House, he's to be tested to see if he can handle it. The truth is, today when he got his sit-down with Papa, he went after *your job*. That should motivate you to explain to him that this is now The Big Leagues for him. Just like the Cubs. More so even. Someone needs to teach him this is not about his inventing some imaginary family situation with Arlene and getting caught up in his domestic fantasy. This is for real." Greg swept his arms out in a way that indicated he spoke of the lounge they were in, the business. "It's still not much. Not enough right now, that's for sure. But *this* is going to be his future. With his true family. This is going to be what he has to reckon with. This house is going to be either Tad's life or the end of him."

"Well, I'm just glad it doesn't have to be my end."

"It's still early. So later, after all of this foreplay — if and when Arlene leaves — and it'd be wise to bet she will, you will also use Pepe's suck-up Thorello over there, to follow her. Then I want you to go back and bring my brother *a gun* — when he's alone. One of the .38s. Doesn't matter which model. Actually, here. Take him this one." Greg opened his suitcoat and withdrew his piece from his under-the-shoulder holster and spun it before he flipped it so his cousin could take it by its handle.

"And if she doesn't leave?"

"See that you know who comes and goes first — starting with that guy." Greg nodded toward his father's new companion. "If she stays, do not send our new fool in. But hang back. Both of you must wait for Taddeo to arrive first, and don't be seen by anyone until your new man can follow her without being spotted, and you yourself can meet with our pitcher. Or at some late point, I actually don't care if *he's* alone or not. Even better if he's not — if *no one's* left that room. You first might have to wait up all night, another night, to make sure *she* doesn't go anywhere. I mean stay until you see the sun rise. And know that I haven't rested either. But this plan is worth losing a little sleep over. Also, see what you can learn about Thorello over there. I don't trust him, either. Then you're to bring Tad the gun anyway — and personally. I don't want the new goombah handling *that*. Instead, my brother had better have more respect for his older first-cousin. And then be sure to see if my dear Taddeo learns where *this guy* ends up." Greg nodded toward his father's newly prepared sacrifice and sneered. Rinaldo Villetti's fool was re-stuffing his shirt in his pants and re-arranging his bow-tie under his suit jacket, flattening down his hair, while trying to see his reflection in the glass door, preparing to unwittingly depart for the unfortunate fate that the senior Villetti had prepared for him.

Corry watched as he reminded Greg, "I already said I don't really want to see Taddeo with Arlene, Cousin."

"I don't care what you want to see, Dally. And I'm not giving Pepe's lumber-jerk over there a loaded weapon. *You* need to give it to my brother."

"But she'll — ."

"She'll know he has been delivered the gun whether she's still there or not. *'Cause he'll tell her*. I can see it happening. Tad doesn't know what to do with a firearm yet, nor when to shut up. But you deliver it to him. And also reinforce that message for him that I relayed to you. Or actually make sure Thorello delivers that part of this *before* she leaves. Let her know *we will* have control over Taddeo. And hopefully Arlene having seen Thorello, will provide new motivation for that one to be extremely careful she never spots him following her later — if he knows what's good for him. I could make plenty of use of the information concerning where she goes and who she contacts, but if he doesn't survive, I'm not going to shed a tear over that guy either. And maybe we ought to keep her out of contact with her shamrock allies. But when you've both seen Taddeo, or at least you've delivered that gun, that's when you'll get out of there and go home to get some sleep."

"Well, I will definitely send the sycophant in first, if there's the opportunity." *I really don't need to get hit in the crossfire*, Corry thought. "I just sure hope you know what you're doing, Cousin."

"Hey, I'm a genius. Remember?" Greg said.

Chapter 16

Thursday, May 23, 1918
2:26 pm, CST
Weeghman Park, Chicago, Illinois

1st Inning
Brooklyn – 0, Cubs – 0

0 Outs, 0 On

AB: The Brooklyn Robins (11 W – 17 L)
Ivy Olson (SS, Bats: right, Throws: right) AVG .239, OBP .286
Age: 33, Games: 328, Status: veteran player,
5th full season in The Show

On the mound:
Chicago Cubs (18 W – 11 L)
(Fighting to advance their ranking in the National League)
P: Harry Weaver (SP)
(Bats: right, Throws: right) 1 W – 1 L, PCT: .500, ERA: 2.20,
SO: 20, HB: 1 x (in 4 years)
Age: 26, Games: 9, Status: 4-year veteran

AND THEN:

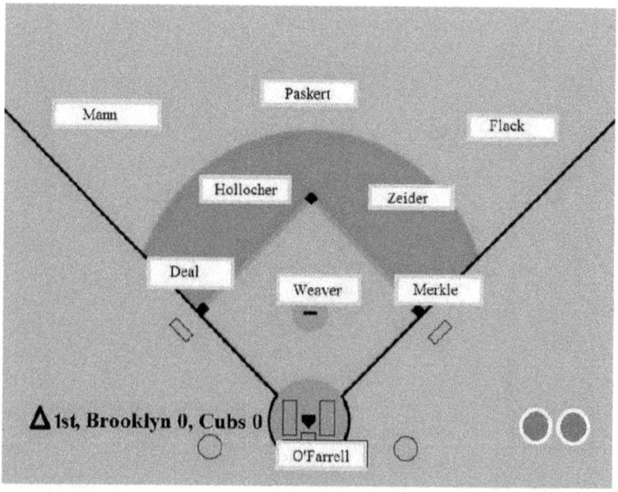

"Okay team, you've seen the Robins three times already this week — at our house. And for most of you, you also saw them on the road before that. You should now know what you're doing with them at this point." Fred Mitchell addressed his ballclub. "I want you to go out there and play sharp on defense." He looked at Max Flack. "Very sharp. And then our bats must look alive when you get back here — and mostly in one piece. That would be nice for a change."

"Alright. Let's do it Cubs!" Bob O'Farrell led the team out of the dugout to take their positions for the first inning. Flack, Dode Paskert, and Leslie Mann followed right behind their catcher for this game and then launched themselves out deep in the grass, flipping a warm-up ball between them. Fred Merkle, Rollie Zeider, Charlie Hollocher, and Charlie Deal manned their stations around the horn and began their own 1st inning warm-up. It was next twenty-six-year-old Harry Weaver's turn in Chicago's rotation. He started taking practice pitches.

"Go on now and give 'dem Robins hell — Chicago-style!" The cheer came off the Cubs' bench.

"Shut the hell up, Villetti," Coach told him, suddenly dampening down his youngest pitcher's enthusiasm.

Only now Tad was almost *not* going to stop himself from whining about how his manager had hurt his feelings, and even after he won the game yesterday, but something else distracted him from somewhere left and set-back behind the dugout that Thursday afternoon.

"Tad!"

"Tad!"

"Cousin Tad!" it registered like children's voices in the stands. He got off the bench where he'd been watching his team warm up and walked through the dugout in the direction he'd heard the noise — peeking his head out toward the 3rd base seats.

"Hey! I said 'No niggers!' Did you hear me Boy?"

"You. Yeah *you*, sit where you belong, Darkie!"

"D'you kids even have tickets for these seats? I don't think so. You gotta get on outta here. Now."

"Security. Security? Does anybody see security? There's a nigger down here."

"If you'z feelin' dat strongly about it, why don't you'z toss 'em out yourself? They're all just a stinking bunch of guinea kids anyway. *All* the rest of 'dem."

Taddeo used his ears to find where all the commotion was

coming from and finally spotted three very short figures, one with a small brown face, pushing their way under the arms of all the suits and dodging lit cigarettes and cigars or the spillage from just-refilled beers. It was his most junior cousins, Elpido and Benedito Delasandro, along with little Parnell Lamont. That last one and one of his uncle's kids couldn't be older than ten, and his brother they called Pee-Dee, Tad thought to be about twelve. And Tad knew his papa didn't purchase them baseline seats and he didn't know what had gotten into Old Lamont's great-grandson to think it was wise for a colored kid to push his way through the business class' 3rd base field-box seats. But all smiles, the athlete bade them all hello by their first names and reached out over the brick wall to high-five and clasp each one of their miniature hands. Taddeo was immensely warmed and flattered that they liked to come and watch his games. He also knew the crowd was watching this. However, the baseball player ignored the ire he stirred in the seats by his encouraging the youths. The children reminded him of himself not that long ago. He always fancied himself a rebel. But he gently warned 'lil Nelly that he'd rest easier feeling the boy was safe if he'd next turn back and go sit in the coloreds' section. "If you get injured, how am I gonna explain it back home? It'll crush your great-grandpa's heart." He also tried pleading with his little cousins to get back to their real seats and escort their friend out of there.

"Oh. We're not with the nigger, Cousin Tad," Elpido explained. "He was just following us."

As if that made it okay.

"Will you pitch again today, Cousin Tad?" Bennie asked.

"Yeah. We want to see you hit somebody again," Parnell smiled with a glance behind at all the racists still yelling names behind his back.

"Hey, you think you can knock one of those Robins out?" Pee-Dee asked him, not hiding any enthusiasm.

Tad had to laugh even though he knew that he really ought to be settling in and showing more skill versus attitude on the mound. He needed to prove that he could be a professional. But today wouldn't give him that opportunity. "No. I pitched relief two days straight now. Plus I'm a righty like Harry Weaver. He'll probably go the whole game or my coach will put in Paul Carter."

"Hey Villetti. Get your nose out of the stands before I put you out of the dugout! The game's 'bout to start," Mitchell yelled at him. "You don't go interacting with the crowd right now and leave those boys alone."

"They're family, Coach."

"Good. Then you can just go visit with them when it's time for you to go home and you better hope I don't call for that to happen sooner than later." He tried to turn into the wall in the back of the dugout so the rest of the team didn't notice him take a nip from that flask he'd always keep hidden in his uniform pocket – not like the outline wasn't clearly visible and everyone didn't know what he was doing anyway. Tad also saw Killefer look at the dugout ceiling and light up a cigarette, turning his head from side to side.

But to the children Taddeo said, "Now go on and get your butts back in your assigned seats if you even have any. I'm not the one allowed to break the rules around here. You're getting me in trouble." But it was great practice for them anyway, because they were Family, and that's all his family ever did — get him in more and more trouble.

"Sorry Cousin Tad."

"Yeah. We're sorry Cousin Tad."

Taddeo watched the boys climb the steps back toward the lowest deck and Parnell separate from his relations among the Delasandros.

"Eyes on the field for the last time, Villetti." Coach shook *his* head from side to side as *he* lit a cigarette and took a puff to calm his nerves while he got set to meet with Lord Byron before game play would start. He'd explained before that he was the Cubs' manager and could do anything he wanted. But Taddeo didn't think the umpire would agree. He looked behind him once more to make certain that the youths were now actually leaving to sit where they were supposed to.

When Tad stopped watching the boys and relaxed, telling himself that they'd be safe, the relief pitcher returned to his seat on the bench as he knew he'd best comply with Mr. Mitchell.

Then Ivy Olson had hit a leadoff double, way back deep in the outfield and made Dode Paskert and Les Mann go chase it. But Harry Weaver settled in to sit down Ollie O'Mara, Jake Daubert, and Zack Wheat with assists from the defense and ended the inning with Ivy stranded in scoring position no less. Fitting with his great personality, Olson even saw fit to argue with Lord Byron over some of the calls that the *other* Brooklyn bats received. Wilbert Robinson had to leave his dugout to go and deliver Olson's mitt to him by shoving it into his chest and forcing him to take his station at shortstop, lest he got thrown out of the game in the 1st inning for arguing balls and strikes, even from that of a runner's position out at 2nd base. Preaching from the outfield for today's game, Olson would now find The Reverend watching *him*.

Better that he's watching the Robins rather than us, Taddeo thought on the bench. Then he recollected what the taxicab driver had insinuated the previous day and fear about his fledgling professional career gripped *him* — followed by fear for his future plans with Arlene and her safety. While he didn't have to concentrate on the game as much as he would were he on the mound today, he had too much time on his hands to focus on whomever might be concentrating on him — possibly even every game this series. Tad had really started wondering about that. He knew that on Saturday, his papa was meeting with Colosimo and some very particular New Yorkers at the stadium. Those out-of-towners might already be here, right now, watching him. So his instincts told him he'd best use his time on the bench to think of any approach that would see him more prepared in case that was situation. He'd wanted to think it was some promise he'd shown that saw him being used by Coach for relief in two back-to-back games. But he was at least smart enough, that he couldn't fool himself. He might ride the bench today, but he'd seen an unusual increase in playing time for someone of his rookie stature. Did it have something to do with not only his father, but with this kind of timing, also the East Coast?

Meanwhile, Dan Griner took the mound for Brooklyn and the huge man tried to look as intimidating as possible and threw all he had to the inside on each and every Chicago batter. But left-hander Max Flack launched one right back at him so that Griner had to duck, and the Cubs were on at 1st base. However, Hollocher was too much of a rookie still to not let fear get the better of him while facing " 'ol Rusty." Or maybe that still had to do with getting beat up by these guys on Tuesday? Another out served on the dish to Leslie Mann, and it was a freshly recovered Fred Merkle who knocked a double between Hy Myers and Jimmy Johnston so Flack-Jack could put the Cubs up by a run as he crossed home plate. The Cubs' right-fielder's teammates welcomed him home and forgave him his latest errors on the field he'd been guilty of committing yesterday. But Griner got Paskert out and the 2nd inning began.

Then the Robins' Henry Harrison or "Hy" Myers tried to instruct the Cubs' Weaver that he was *not* going to crown himself Chicago's ace that game. A single by Brooklyn's leadoff batter that inning was recorded. But Johnston and Doolin went down, not even getting

Myers to 2nd base until Ernie Krueger drew a walk. But it wasn't awarded as any kind of Chicago apology. Weaver just knew he'd have an easier time getting Griner out batting — and Taddeo felt suddenly paranoid that his teammate wanted to demonstrate to him that you could award Krueger a free base without beaning him. And after that, the Robins were retired.

Deal, Zeider, and O'Farrel couldn't get on base in the Cubs' half of the 2nd.

The same could be said for the Robins' Olson, O'Mara, and Daubert in the top of the 3rd.

But Harry Weaver hit a leadoff single off a very frustrated Griner as the Cubs started their half of the inning. Adding insult to injury, Chicago's pitcher took it upon himself to steal 2nd base while Flack was batting. The Robins' server notably struggled in his extra-focused effort he put to making sure Max went back to rest in his seat after having sampled all of the Brooklyner's specials, unlike in his last time up at the plate. He ignored his other customer and at least Weaver came in standing, as were all the rest of the Cubs and their fans — all except for Fred Mitchell, who had *not* sent his pitcher. He had to sit down and wish he had something stronger to drink on that bench to help him swallow today's menu, Chicago's last game to split the bread with these New Yorkers, and especially the bill for any remaining gamblers. But Holly and Mann left Harry out on 2nd base even after all the Cubs' hurler had done to personally help his cause from up at the plate. Much of the crowd grumbled its disappointment. Mitchell lit up another cigarette and offered one to Killefer.

So next from the mound, Weaver offered the same treatment to the Robins' Johnston after he too, hit for two, but the Cubs' fielders had sat down Wheat and Myers first, and then took care of Mickey Doolin, seeing no more action than Brooklyn's outfielder's 2-bagger.

After Merkle became the first out, Chicago restarted keeping up their pressure that they could put Dan Griner under. Dode Paskert hit for a base and then stole 2nd, proving that even at thirty-seven, the Cubs' outfielder was not showing any signs of slowing down. Being good at his job helped him beat the draft, and to play centerfield he had to be able to move like Chicago's wind. That and because Charlie Deal wasn't doing anything at his next at-bat to help Paskert get home. But when there was 1 out, and having felt inspired somewhere between Weaver's strong pitching and not wasting a runner in scoring position, Coach Mitchell had sent Dode. Krueger popped up from his crouch on a fastball that bounced to him and he whipped it to Doolin, but the streaking Paskert slid under the tag, his cleats scattering gravel faster than the laces spun. That's when Charlie Deal, frustrated with his offerings for glory thus far, reached for the fences and aimed to put one out where the porch of the old Lutheran Seminary was under demolition behind Weeghman's centerfield wall.

Young Parnell Lamont had gone outside the stadium but peeked through the left-field fence at gaps created by the work on additional improvements to the ballpark, as the neighborhood rising in the redevelopment of what would become Waveland Avenue's new addresses continued. The boy was easily distracted from any of his other concerns that Thursday afternoon as he excitedly saw Deal's rocket reaching for him, but then he watched Hy Myers go into action, jumping high and slamming his back against the outfield barrier while he put a raw-hide leash on Deal's plan to wander outside of the park. Nelly felt the whole fence shake. But the hit ball's distance was great enough that Paskert could still tag up and then orchestrate his advance from 2nd to 3rd base. Deal's contribution was almost ruled a sacrifice. But Myer's arm had its moment and the ball got back to Krueger from even that deep in The Friendly Confines — friendly to the Robins for that play. But Dode spun on the toes of his cleats and with a run and dive back to 3rd, Brooklyn prevented him from advancing further, but didn't manage to get Paskert out, either. This brought up Rollie Zeider who singled and got an RBI as Paskert completed his own staggered tour of the bases and beat Jimmy Johnston's throw to Doolin, which was relayed to Krueger after Paskert slid around a hook, his hand reaching for home as Ernie tried to spin around only to find Dode had gotten through the side door! Holding superior court this game, Lord Byron called him safe and when the dust cleared, little Parnell was cheering in back of the field and now the Cubs were up by 2 before Zeider was stranded while O'Farrell was retired from his second turn at batting. This ended the 4th inning.

Parnell also retired his attention he lent to the game. There were other things just as important going on in Chicago. He didn't need any attention drawn to himself were he to try and snag a homerun ball and keep it away from any white kids either. He wished things were different, but little Lamont was in his place for other reasons. And those reasons might really change something one day.

The Cubs next busied themselves with stopping Jimmy Johnston from putting in any more work for the Brooklyn organization. Doolin got out and shortly after that Krueger was sent back out on the field only to catch — as he'd made no more contributions to the Robins' *offense* from home plate in the 5th inning.

The Cubs were almost back to the top of their order coming up in the middle of the game. Harry Weaver was out, but Max Flack forced seven pitches from Dan Griner before he got something he liked to get on base with. This lit the Cubs' lineup on fire once more. The rookie Charlie Hollocher got his confidence back and even a ribeye he sent Flacky all the way home with. He lit Griner's fastball up and sent it radiating out to left field. But even with his speed, Holly could only get to 1st even on a hit to his opposite field; Max had to hold up long enough at second, where he'd advanced on a passed ball from Griner, but he still had to tag up after Charlie sent Zack Wheat all the way into the corner of The Friendly Confines — forcing him to throw to Ivy Olson as the cutoff. But Max got around 3rd as the ball bounced to Brooklyn's shortstop who spun and threw it as hard as he could to Krueger. But there was no force-out at home. O'Mara ran after the Cubs' right-fielder while Olson raced to cover the No. 3 bag and Griner hustled to back up his catcher. Flack's eyes narrowed, also protecting him from his sweat as he focused on his destination and his determination to get there. His cleats dug in hard and scattered Taylor-Davis' dirt around the hot corner stabbing a track of loosened gravel all the way to home plate. There, Krueger squared off and blocked the rest of the path. Max put his head down, squared *his* shoulders, then turned the right one in and found all the reserved strength he had. At top speed Flack collided with Krueger landing right on top of the Robin catcher after forcing him to fly backward underneath Chicago's right-fielder and into another hard impact onto his rear — the collision knocking him into spinning three-hundred-and-sixty degrees around! That also knocked the ball right out of the Brooklyn catcher's mitt. Flack's left foot connected with home plate. "Safe!" Lord Byron issued his decree.

"And your Cubs score!" announced Pat Pieper through his megaphone to the seats that had the best view of the play already. The audience cheered with enthusiasm.

But Hollocher wasn't content to just watch the action. He raced towards 2nd against Dan Griner, who sped after Krueger's lost ball and fired it to Mickey Doolin as Charlie dove under it and Hank

O'Day also yelled, "Safe!" The Cubs' rookie shortstop called time-out and rose up to dust off his jersey he'd just mopped up the infield with and flash a triumphant thumbs-up back to Chicago's bench. Everyone there high-fived Flacky, his second time he scored for the Cubs in the same game, and they waved back at Hollocher, clapping and cheering. The audience that rooted for Chicago roared its approval even louder and Weeghman Park was alive with the sound of baseball. To the most optimistic, the Cubs might have just begun their ascent to the league title.

Only no sooner than that had happened, Hank O'Day was alive with irritation from the infield, where Ivy Olson was arguing his call!

* * * * *

The next call was clearly audible, coming from the other side of the door, and accompanied by knocking. "Excuse me, Miss? Uh, Miss Arlene?" It was the hotel porter's voice.

Arlene didn't feel like getting up from her chair. She sat nearly naked — and perfectly still — her cigarette burning down, unsmoked, while staring out the open sixth floor window, the sunlight feeling good warming her emotionless face. Nothing else felt that good. It was only her stomach that was in motion. She worried as to why. So the young woman had even less interest in mustering an expression that wouldn't serve any useful purpose that early afternoon anyway. The rest of her frozen, she only realized she was being called to at the same time she realized she hadn't blinked. Her eyes fluttered and lost control of a couple tears that were in reaction to her thoughts, while her mouth moved in reaction to the voice. She breathed in and out deeply, then trembled. "Yes?"

"A gentleman is downstairs to see you. And I — uh — I mean we the staff — thought you might want to know, it's uh *not* Sigñor Villetti."

No. He *would have marched right on up here*. Curious but nevertheless alarmed, Arlene got up and walked across the room in her front-opening soft white nightshirt. It fit purposely too short on her, exposing what Tad had reassured her were some very sexy legs. More important to Arlene, she could stand pretty strong on them. Taking double puffs, she extinguished what was left of her smoke in an ashtray on the nightstand, turned and passed the bed and picked up a pillow to hold to her breasts, embracing it in both arms while she thought. "Alright. Thank you."

"Should I send him upstairs to you?"

She opened the armoire across the room opposite the foot of her bed and reached into a pile of her once-neatly folded clothing. She'd only recently been able to once again undress and relax, her sickness seeing her having to make frequent runs out of her room, to the ladies' restroom down the hall, and attempt to relieve herself. Arlene felt a hard, smooth object in her hands that she gathered up from underneath her stored garments there. "You could do that," she called outside her private room, her place of tentative safety — if for only another moment anyway. Her place where she'd been reflecting on how now she'd become a murderer, among other things. They could already be after her for that. But that was *exactly* what she was supposed to have prepared herself to become. Wasn't it? It was about time she got better with practice. That's what Tad always said he was doing in his game.

Not long after, another knock came at her door. Arlene, still barely clothed, knocked back a shot of whiskey straight from a bottle she'd co-opted from Villetti's, wiped her mouth on her sleeve staining it with crimson lipstick, and then unlocked the entrance to her private accommodations. The man outside wasn't any cop. Not that she thought there was ever a high probability that even *if* anyone from The House figured her for a suspect after that barrel murder — that it would be their style to turn her in. No. Not the Villettis. They didn't do things that way. Now she didn't know for certain *who*, but someone from The House obviously followed the goombah that they'd sent to follow Arlene, and then mutilated the body that she'd left cooling behind her. Rose had told her about the gruesome corpse when she called in sick from The Sisson. The girls always gossiped. Then Taddeo confirmed the casualty, when a note passed to her from the hotel staff had forced her to dress another time before, and in spite of her illness, phone him back at the baseball stadium. He'd only just learned about the killing when he went to meet with his father prior to his game. Now this was to be followed up with her waiting outside her room, by the 6th floor telephone, rather uncomfortably when what she needed was to lie back down, until someone from Weeghman's security located Tad on the baseball field before his stupid game. He'd been worried about her. *How touching.*

However, Arlene didn't appreciate him making her feel worse while wasting her time. This was not her "handling Taddeo well." And she really didn't need to be observed by any of the other hotel guests. Fortunately she wasn't. But the dead guy hadn't been found anywhere in Hyde Park's vicinity, Tad informed her. Those factors should dilute some suspicion of his killer being none other than she. And in addition, when Arlene called back to reach one of the very few she'd attempt to trust in The House, Jasmine told her that Rinaldo and all his usual lackeys weren't able to learn much — whether or not they had their suspicions. But her visitor she was forced to receive now, would seem to confirm that at least one of them disagreed. So someone, and that someone likely being Greggorio Villetti, was testing her.

Now the new guy, warmed to the point where he sweated with nervousness at the sight of Arlene when she opened the door, wore one very ill attempt to dress respectably, with a mismatched coat and slacks, a bowtie topping his soup-stained shirt, a dark brown shaggy beard and mustache — and glasses over his eyes that widened as they absorbed his first full view of her. They moved up and down her body and he had trouble looking her in the eyes. His pants grew tighter on him as he spoke, while he loosened that bowtie, not quite clear what was restricting his breath once he saw her. "I'm — uh — err I'm Herbert."

"Good. I'm so very happy for you." Arlene forced herself to smile at him and wink. Her faking her expression of the bare-minimum of a flirty sort of hospitality came with a delay following her toneless unenthusiastic words. And she held her pillow from the inside, pressed close against her chest. Her nightshirt's neck was loosened all the way down, and she knew the man was trying to glimpse her naked breasts she hid underneath the pillow as she licked her left index finger and motioned with it suggestively, beckoning him into her room. The smile she managed was less than half-hearted, but the nightgown she wore *was* extremely short and Herbert concentrated on looking beneath the pillow she held, at her bare pink legs, which drew his gaze with their motion when she repeatedly alternated her weight on them. He was imagining what his seeing of the full length of them, beneath that pillow, would lead his eyes up to — between them, at about that level but just below where they'd meet her hips. Only now, far up her frame above them, Arlene's mouth moved again. *Those* glistening red lips parting. "Well, come in, Darling. And Herbert? Would you be so kind as to please shut the door? And then you may get even closer to *just* what you came here looking for."

"Yes. And oh, yes. Oh my. Villetti was right." Herbert used one hand to grab at his bowtie and loosen it some more, along with the top buttonhole of his shirt. He'd started to visibly sweat even more from his rising excitement. He breathed faster, and heavier — and quickly closed the hotel room door to No. 66, nearly jumping to turn around, as if he were afraid that if he let Arlene out of his sight, the girl of his most-private dreams would disappear. She definitely wanted to.

Arlene wished she was left with any other choice as to what to do with *this one*, but any other alternative than the one she hardened herself enough to decide upon, would have been way too problematic. She'd not be trapped or show any weakness in what she'd demonstrate was her steely resolve even though she knew by this move, probably Greggorio, was forcing her hand.

"When Villetti's right, he's really right." Herbert could not stop himself from involuntarily reaching for crotch of his pants and grabbing and pulling on what he found under there. "He said I'd come to him just in time to find his *most special philly*."

"No. This is a Colt." Arlene pulled on what *she'd* been grabbing on under her pillow. The sound of the gun was muffled, another hole was loosened under Herbert's shirt's collar, and a new stain added to the color it had been already tainted with by his last meal. His breathing changed again, too. It stopped — about the same time his body hit the floor. Arlene coughed on a single puff of smoke. "And the young *Sigñor* Villetti is wrong. He's now established quite a strong history of being wrong. Everything about him is so very wrong. So please excuse me if my benefactor requires me to collect payment for services rendered. I suppose no one warned you? I'm very expensive, Herb."

In her short nightgown, Arlene *did* bend over for Herbert. She bent over and picked the dead man's pockets for his money clip and kept everything of value that she found on his corpse. The kill and the immediate profit that came from it arrived much easier the second time. She had changed. She now could really be able to do her job.

* * * * *

Next, even *before* the Cubs had been retired, Ivy Olson was out for the count at 2nd — during the Robins' *defensive* half of the 5th inning. The Reverend called Lord Byron down on him after he was through bearing witness to Brooklyn's shortstop's mouth moving any more. The umpires were not *ever* going to allow these New Yorkers to argue over *their* "perceived as 'blown calls' " in The Windy City. Not in *their domain*. And Conway's people certainly did not care about what happened to the Robins. The bias was obvious, a blight on Weeghman Park — maybe in fourteen other cities — but not in Chicago. Wilbert Robinson was also warned when he tried defending Olson, but the Brooklyn infielder was taken out of the game, ending that particular problem. Ray Schmandt replaced him in the lineup but moved to play 2nd base and Mickey Doolin was assigned to shortstop. As live-ball playing resumed, it was still the bottom of the 5th and the Cubs continued to screw with Dan Griner, forgetting any intimidation they felt from him during their fight on Tuesday. Chicago learned to find his punches far more effective than his pitches, though maybe Taddeo hadn't yet. But he wasn't likely going to get many chances at-bat as a relief pitcher anyway. He sat with Hoff, Trip, and Trevor, watching, excited for their fellow rookie as Hollocher took a bigger and bigger lead off 2nd base.

Griner was clearly rattled now and Krueger saw a lot of daylight between the runner and the bag. Popping up, he used a pitchout to make a play himself with Schmandt's help; together, they recorded one such rare time when Holly actually did get himself caught off base. Well, it couldn't be called rare in this early stage of his rookie season, but Hollocher was right. He did keep getting better at his game. But Tad thought his teammate's ego probably landed harder than his body did from that late dive back to the bag, just before Charlie's butt landed back on Chicago's bench.

Now Les Mann had to hang on in the batter's box and help the Cubs expand their lead. If Bill Killefer, "The Reindeer" was also called Captain, Leslie Mann could be called Major. He'd been earning his place as trusted counsel on the team this season, mentoring the rookies much more than their impatient veteran catcher had. He now would show Charlie that he should never be afraid of getting caught and keep encouraging him to accelerate the rate at which Hollocher *did* successfully steal bases. With Griner flustered, Mann put a bunt down the 3rd base line right where Holly could see it closely from the Cubs' bench, and Les used it to get on base, keeping Chicago alive that inning. Then even with 2 outs he stole 2nd, risking Coach's displeasure, while after a few more pitches Griner walked Fred Merkle, but not by intention.

The Cubs had runners on 1st and 2nd when Dode Paskert entered the batter's box. But as Charlie Deal started up the steps, Mitchell waved him off. The veteran hadn't hit for two at-bats as of then.

"Everston, get your bat and get into the on-deck circle." Trip was caught totally off-guard with this surprise. His smile came with his fast reaction to orders and he raced up the steps and onto the field, passing Deal, who just stood in the middle of the dugout with his hands spread out to either side as if he were trying to ask the Cubs' skipper "Why?"

Chicago's manager saw this and decided his starter was worth an explanation. He explained, "We've got a solid lead and there's already 2 outs. Now while your bats are excited, and you are also so impatient with *me* — or outright ignoring my calls — the probabilities are saying it's almost as safe of time as any to see what the new kid Everston can or can't do. At least you all shouldn't think you can blame *me* for this call. I'm actually listening to most of you. *Most* of you. For right now, anyway. But me making this call is the result *you* achieved. And as you're not driving in all my runs I want — congratulations: here's your big chance at collective management. Ha."

As perplexed as Deal might have been, and even with Bill Killefer moving his head from side to side, Tad, Hoff, and Trevor were delighted to see Trip assured he'd get to play. But the pressure reached the boiling point for the young rookie just off the 1917 Ansons' roster when Griner walked Dode Paskert as well. The bases were loaded with 2 outs when fresh-off-the-Iowa-farm "Michael Everrrrr-stawwn" was announced by Pat Pieper, who might have ran almost as fast as Charlie Hollocher to get around the field that afternoon. He was really excited, too.

Now Trip didn't quite pull off trying to look as confident as he wanted to. He bounced his bat handle on the ground to try and catch it off a spin like some famous sports star somewhere would. But it did spin — right into his shin, and Mikey tripped on his own stick while stepping up to the table to see what this game would serve *him* on the dish. It certainly wasn't stardom. At least not yet. There was muffled laughter in the Cubs dugout at their own teammate's expense. But the bases were loaded.

Now Trip's legs were shaking in the batter's box as busy as his mind was trying to get over any doubts he had after having also decided to switch-hit. Griner was a right-hander and by batting as a lefty, Mike hoped to keep any live ball behind Paskert so even on a base hit, the Robins would have better luck trying to cut down the centerfielder or the Cubs' 1st baseman heading to the 3-bag, instead of going for the long throw to try and prevent The Major from scoring. Not that there was much hope with 2 down and force-outs in play. But suddenly, it had actually worked!

Though in reality what happened was the ball bounced off his timid bat in what Trip would explain afterward was really his brilliantly strategical, intentional soft-swing — on which everyone was just too nice to call him on his bullshit — and Everston outran the dribbler towards 1st, his lean athletic form faster than the plus-size Griner could move to field it, even when Trip hesitated at the contact. "Run!" the rest of the Cubs shouted from the bench. "Run Dummy! Run!" And in that second, Everston remembered where 1st base was, and took off at his best speed while his accidental impact he'd made tripped up Dan Griner, clumsily trying to field it.

"I got an arbee-eye! I got an arbee-eye!" Trip was silently mouthing across the infield and pumping his fist in case he needed to make any more certain that his friends were aware of this fact. But Tad, Hoff, and Trevor were already on their feet with the rest of the Chicago fans in Weeghman Park as they cheered when Mann crossed home plate. Especially loud was the fan in left field. But the overthrown ball was instantly caught on one bounce and the return came in from Johnston, and all the way to Doolin, bypassing Schmandt and trying to get out Paskert at 2nd base. Only the Robins were still too slow. But then came a quick toss to Daubert while Trip was dancing off the bag celebrating and waving — and a blatant idiot became both the celebrity of the moment and the 3rd out, too. Openly drinking in the dugout now, Coach Mitchell must have decided it was in bad form to also cry — especially while he was winning. But he probably needed to.

And on the teams played on into the 6th inning with Griner trying to take his turn to profit off Weaver the second time he faced Chicago's pitcher. His own domestic battery-mate hadn't faired so well already that last "too-long-of-an-inning." Krueger had made the final out from the Robins' brief chance at taking the offensive the last time, but Griner now connected and got to 1st base with no one out and Olson batting next as Brooklyn returned to sending up the top of their order for the start of this next opportunity.

* * * * *

It was also Arlene's turn to connect with some alleged major hitter from New York. Things were definitely escalating. No doubt a Villetti had seen to that and that now the young woman would have to make *her* next move to control the score. One of them — the father — or more than likely the middle son, was testing her again. Pushing her to blow her game before she was even ready to continue playing. But exactly which one was it *this time*? She needed to be sure.

["I'm a Jew. That's why I can afford to do this."]

"Well, do it quickly," Arlene said over the phone downstairs in The Sisson.

["Do not give me orders, Young Miss. I'm not Irish, and I certainly wouldn't be Italian — ."]

"I don't care if you're a God-damned heathen Indian! You don't need to be charming. If you want to come over here and get a scalp, just do it already." The red-head struggled to keep her voice down and lit a new cigarette to calm her nerves. The hotel staff was watching her and probably trying to listen in while she made a call from their front lobby. If someone else would be on her phone lines, it would likely be on a wire to the floor her room was on — she hoped. The newly built Sisson actually had lines to individual floors and its own switchboard operator. The lobby dialed outside. But what Arlene now really hoped for, was that no one had listened to the last if not only firearms lesson that'd ever be offered to poor ol' Herbert upstairs. And that she'd muffled it well enough to not arouse suspicion. There was still a lot she needed to get away with — and she'd barely accomplished anything by staying in this hotel with Taddeo.

Arlene had quickly changed into her simplest day clothing and headed downstairs as fast as she could before Herbert's body had even started to cool. Now she needed to move to cover up the rest of *this killing*. It was one more for the record. Another notch on her most-special gun. "Hey there smart Fella, I mean that I truly don't care. So whatever enables you to do what you obviously get off doing, you'll get over here and do it for me before my boyfriend gets back to my room."

A woman passer-bye, another guest at the allegedly upscale establishment, did overhear *that* and raised her eyebrows in shock by her quite reasonable mistake she'd make with any assumption she'd come to by way of her extrapolating on the details she could have gathered from Arlene's side of the phone conversation. Arlene's green eyes glared into her, and she blew the smoke from her cigarette the woman's way, and then the busy-body hurried to get far away from something about the brilliant red-haired lady-caller that just about emanated every sign of severe danger.

But the voice on the other end of her conversation was not intimidated by her. [“What I’m not, young lass, is available at your beck-and-call. And so what I was trying to communicate was that what I do, requires discretion. And I’m very good at what I do. That’s why The Big Man recommended me to your family and I’m visiting Chicago. But that’s also why I can’t work with you while you’re being watched.”]

Arlene looked around the lobby. There were a few people, couples, some businessmen coming and going in their own little hurries, and the hotel staff of course. Some other man she couldn’t see all of sat behind his newspaper. She realized he’d been there since before she’d come downstairs and he didn’t look like he was in a hurry to go anywhere. Maybe she’d have to invite him to another funeral, perhaps sometime sooner than later? She reflected that they were becoming easier and easier to arrange. “That’s convenient.” But her present sarcasm was offered mainly for herself. “But you’ll have to take care of it by tomorrow. That I can probably still manage to work with. This was unscheduled. It wasn’t something I’d planned for anyway.”

[“That seemed to happen to you once before already. Are you able to do your job?”]

“That’s my family’s concern, not yours. I’m sure you’re getting paid well to do what you do, so just keep doing that. I will be thorough.”

[“Then you should also try being a little faster about your own work. Though I don’t really care that much, as I am well-compensated for every day I spend in this town of yours, but my mission being one-hundred percent effective depends on yours being likewise. So get the information you were sent after. And may I suggest that you are not going to find it there on your back in the hotel room. Go and return to Villetti’s and stop fooling around with his son.”]

“How do you know what I’m supposed to be doing here?”

[“My people were in on the planning of everything since our mutual great undertaking was first conceived of. And it was supposed to make money and save lives. Instead, I’m watching you destroy more and more of them.”]

“Who’s counting? And are you also the one who’s going to see that I’m *not the one* who’s destroyed?” Arlene turned her head about, watching the man behind the newspaper. He didn’t move, but he shouldn’t be able to hear her. However, she’d bet this phone line would be listened in to and reported on just as soon as someone made it so that her enemies could. That was as troubling as the fact that so far she'd killed twice, but still hadn't managed to hit any of her intended targets. And she started feeling nauseous again.

["It's not really my concern after I take care of this job. Then I'm gone. I can't be tied to this or I could have shown up already and shown you how a professional takes care of these kinds of situations. Like I said, I'm good at what I do. But they told me there's someone else — around Villetti's — who's been in place to protect you anyway.]

"There's information I could use."

["It's not mine to provide. I have to go now. And you're drawing attention to yourself. Suggesting you could be up to something. And that you're not working alone. What other reason would anyone else think a girl like you has for being on the phone all the time? Oh, right. Never mind."] The other side of the conversation cut off and Arlene hung up her end of the line.

A girl like me? he said. *Well, who am I now? And just what have I become?* In her mind, she challenged her own hope she'd at least gotten more help and that she was not facing her end alone. The young woman turned and felt herself being watched as she made to retrace her steps upstairs and confront the cold hard consequence of just what she had just done — where she'd left the latest evidence of it motionless on the floor of her current residence. *Well, at least I have Taddeo? Boy I sure wish I could say that was comforting.* She already predicted the Cubs' relief pitcher wasn't going to be very reliable. Charming maybe, but ignorant and unstable were also the adjectives she'd use to best describe him.

* * * * *

Ivy Olson and Ollie O'Mara weren't very reliable either and Jake Daubert wasn't any kind of gentleman to leave Dan Griner with no run support while Chicago dominated the New Yorker's pitching and had already enjoyed their success in taking advantage of him for 4 earned runs. That brought the Cubs back up to strike offensively, once more.

Chapter 17

Thursday, May 23, 1918
4:33 pm, CST
Weeghman Park, Chicago, Illinois

6th Inning
Brooklyn – 0, Cubs – 4

0 Outs, 1 On

AB: Chicago Cubs (18 W – 11 L)
(Fighting to advance their ranking in the National League)
Robert O'Farrell (C, Bats: right, Throws: right) AVG .283, OBP .347
Age: 22, Games: 24, Status: junior year rookie,
1st full season in The Show

On the mound:
Brooklyn Robins (11 W – 17 L)
P: Donald (Dan) Griner (SP)
(Bats: Left, Throws: Right) 5 W – 11 L, PCT: .313, ERA: 2.81,
SO: 222, HB: 25 (in 6 years)
Age: 30, Games: 124, Status: 6-year veteran

AND THEN:

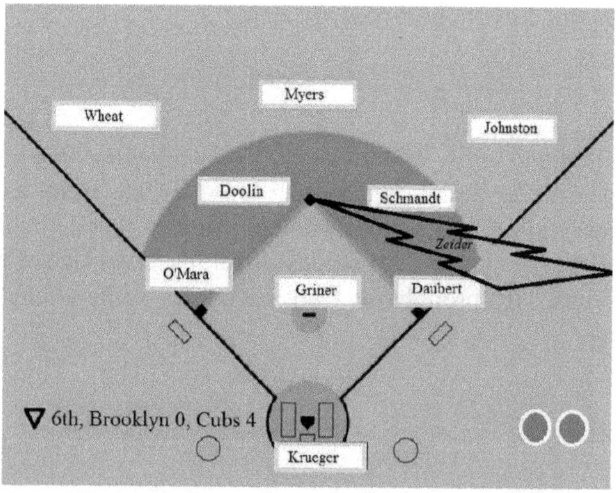

"Attention! Attention please! Have your pencil and scorecards ready, Chicago fans," Pat broadcast through his megaphone. "We're now into the bottom of the sixth with no outs — and our Cubbies are staying the course with a man on First, and well on the path to yet another victory, holding the lead by four runs already, for one great game on this fine afternoon in The Windy City.

"We've just seen another incredible inning pitched by the home team's one-and-only Harry Weaver. But now back at the dish, *and to take the offense one more time*, and batting eighth, is your Chicago Cubs catcher, Robert Ohh'Farrrrel!" Trip had just made the 3-out last inning since after knocking in Paskert, he'd been caught off-base dancing with there already being 2-outs. It hadn't put Coach Mitchell in a good mood. That was for sure. Chicago's manager needed his club to be following orders and playing smart so they could at least split this series with Brooklyn. To come to that end, Mitchell had felt it best that he commenced screaming before the Cubs even took the field at the top of the inning. But when Chicago got to bat again, Rollie Zeider demonstrated he understood his orders and exemplified discipline in the batter's box. Now it was Pieper's turn to continue hollering. "This inning will still see Weaver, Max Flack, and we will all hope, Charrr-lie Hollocher, due up for Chi-Town's finest. Now let's play ball!"

And before anyone barely registered it, Flack was back on 1st base after Zeider had hit a liner and gotten on, and before O'Farrell and Weaver each grounded out, the latter on a weak hopper to Doolin. But O'Farrell had advanced Zeider into scoring position. Now Max wasn't known for his speed and could have been insulted by Mitchell signaling for him to steal in tandem with Zeider. At bat, Charlie Hollocher definitely was the overly eager and active participant in the Cubs' offense. He wanted his chance to hit in a run. But the ground ball outs with the steal had already seen Zeider advance all the way to 3rd base and Mitchell figured correctly that with 2 outs, the Robins would just let Flack run. Chicago led by a safe score as it were. It was alright to take crazy risks. Holly didn't trust that assessment, so like the Cubs' shortstop had never heard of playing small-ball, he actually walked out of the batters' box presumably to change out bats. Coach met him on the field as Tad imagined the egotistical rookie infielder whining to the manager. He would argue the play his coach signed him.

Really? Tad was glad to see someone else getting in trouble with Mitchell instead of himself for a change. But he couldn't believe

Lord Byron was tolerating this. O'Day was in the field this game shaking his head, having already getting Ivy Olson ejected for the other side. So now Byron then decided he didn't tolerate anything after all, and yelled at Coach Mitchell to get the hell off the field or he'd be the one ejected next. They all had to respect him, *but not Holly*, who the Robins expected to get out at the plate, and thus pitched to, ignoring the Cubs' runners.

Trip had also been complaining per usual that he hadn't had even as many chances to play as Tad, Hoff, and Trevor Bass, so Coach predictably would use that to threaten Holly that he'd move Mike over to shortstop and give somebody else a chance to play 3rd base. But the Cubs' middle-infielder knew Trip wasn't on Mitchell's reward recipient list after his stupid base-running error the previous inning, so now Charlie would *still* refuse to bunt with 2 outs. This secret strategy — not so secret any longer while the two argued over it — was supposed to be Mitchell's own unconventionality he wanted to use to surprise Wilbert Robinson and Charlie Ebbets with. But then demonstrating exactly how much he erroneously thought he was worth, Hollocher bounced his bat off the dirt and caught the handle on its up-spin and took a bow. He was showing off especially to Trip — and showing the team he'd won his argument. That little victory demonstration would come at a cost later, if Tad knew Mitchell. Lord Byron's frame seemed to expand and contract while he must have just swallowed a double-breath to calm himself.

Then, when Charlie Hollocher came back up to the plate, he swung away at the next couple of pitches. However, he did connect and hit it so far out to right field that when Schmandt cut Johnston off and got the ball back to Daubert, Charlie had himself a base hit and Zeider went all the way home. Next, Holly took a huge leadoff and held his chin up to smirk at Mitchell from across the diamond while Les Mann batted. The shortstop probably saw Coach start drinking again but Hollocher should have been watching Griner and Krueger. The Robins caught the base-thief on his run for infamy when Schmandt tagged him at 2nd only three seconds after Krueger threw down. But diving through a cloud of dust, Hollocher was called "safe" in that previous second!

Only Charlie stumbled when he tried to stand up, and clutched his rib cage. Ray Schmandt might have kicked or punched him during all the excitement of that last play, when visibility was limited. Tad could observe Bill Killefer changing colors as he watched from his post as security for the Cubs' own bench, where Coach had to place the captain on guard over his overly ornery Chicago team. Maybe Killefer was losing any sympathy he might have had for Brooklyn at long-last? He could be readying himself to turn Chicago's bench loose. None of the other Cubs could be accused of having any mercy for the birds. But that play was going to be contested for sure. Only Killefer was preventing his teammates from once more trying to literally kick the crap out of the Robins because Schmandt might have really been asking for it by arguing the call at 2nd with The Reverend. Even Tad thought Charlie was tagged out. But there was no excuse for any sucker punches. And any further action in excess of regular game play by the Cubs' bench wasn't necessary in the 6th, because Mann got a base-hit and then with 2 outs, Griner and Krueger ignored loaded bases to concentrate on the batter. The result was their failure as Merkle's next hit sent Max Flack home. But Dan Griner and Ernie Krueger would not be fooled again as they picked off Merkle who dived back to first from his big leadoff, but too late before Daubert put the leather on him.

"And the Cubs have two more runs going into the late innings here in The Windy City!" Pieper announced. The score was now 0-6. Chicago was winning. But apparently Trip still had issues he wanted to whine about, no doubt because he was jealous of Holly's successful rebellion.

"Everston, shut your God-damned mouth and go out there and show me that you're not gonna screw up our lead," Mitchell told an elated Trip, who grabbed his glove and jogged out to 3rd base — his natural position. Coach was right on the sideline by way of the Cubs' dugout's location and also reminded the bruised infielder of that fact. "I am right here where I can keep my eyes on you and so help me if you get in any more fights this series, Rookie. It won't be the Robins you'll have to look out for."

But he should have looked out for Wil Robinson backing up Ray Schmandt, who made a successful case to cancel Hollocher's reaching base safely from counting — thereby cancelling Flack's scoring on Merkle's RBI, between the innings. There were grumbles on the home team's bench, but not a huge fuss made over Charlie — probably or only because the veterans did not care for the rookie's arrogance. Mitchell tried to argue the counter-point, and that the call should not be reviewed *after an inning had ended*, but if this series versus the Robins was anything, it was irregular and neither The Reverend nor Lord Byron had any more patience for these teams this series. Mitchell's case about the rules did not appear to have support from Chicago's law enforcement this time. But why should it if the Cubs had this kind of a lead? And Merkle could re-do his at-bat, but get no RBI.

Now Tad watched Charlie Deal shake his head and throw his glove onto the bench before he sat down where he'd hurled it. *Well Deal hasn't done anything this game anyway. Obviously he wanted to play and was plenty resentful over being taken out for another rookie. C'mon,* Tad thought about it, *let Trip have a chance.* His friend took every grounder Fred Merkle bounced toward him for warm-up with great enthusiasm, his smile lighting up the late afternoon shadows that fell on Weeghman's field as they headed into the top of the 7th. The Cubs still had plenty of men who were ready to fight, to make a difference for their team, with or without the authorities on their side. These were the rookies. And they were winning. They were going to do it without anybody else's help or cheating. This was the young's revolution. Now was *their* time.

But the pall of Bill Killefer's disapproval fell on Taddeo for some reason as Brooklyn's seventh at-bat got underway. "Hey, Villetti. Congratulations. You manage to screw up a game you're not even in." Tad returned to him a perplexed look. Responding to the question on his face, Killefer said, "Get down to the locker room. Maintenance called up. They were fixing our shower finally. But dey said some kids are here to see you. More of your family? Well you'll make it clear to them *right now* that they are *never* to come back here during a game. Never. And I mean it."

Tad's cousins Pee-Dee and Bennie didn't like that order when they came there by evading the guards and hoping Tad would introduce them to Michael Everston, who they knew to be their cousin's good friend, after his past inning of Major League heroism back in the 5th. "Well, Trip's playing third now. We don't want to distract him. Where's Parnell?"

"We don't know," said Bennie.

"We don't care," corrected his barely older brother. "Not our job to keep track of niggers," the twelve-year-old only repeated what he had learned. "Because I *know* where I could see myself growing up to work for The Family." The Delasandro boy smiled brightly and Tad knew he was now at that age where he'd take an interest in his uncle's lounge girls. *That was just perfect.*

"Well what we are going to do is see that you two boys get back to your seats and I'll talk to you later," their cousin Tad told them through a quarter-open door out of the Cubs' locker room. He heard running footsteps and opened the door slightly further and as the young boys tried to look in, their slightly elder family member looked *out* and saw a security guard huffing to catch his breath while finally running up to grab both boys by the back of their shirt collars. They could no longer evade him.

"Okay. Let's go you two."

"You're not supposed to ever come down here," Tad told them, obviously not moving to help the boys.

"You better let go of me," Elpido was saying as the park employee was dragging them away. "All I'm supposed to do is anything I want. I'm from The House Villetti," he was proclaiming as Taddeo shut the door behind him to turn around and get through his locker room and back out of the tunnel to Weeghman's ballfield. He could still hear his little cousin's high pitched voice coming through the door. "Don't you know what that means?" Tad shook his head from side to side, disappointed with the youth's behavior — and possibly, slightly, that the security guard probably wasn't even aware any House Villetti existed. Ironically, it didn't take any effort on Taddeo's part to discern how disappointed Bill Killefer continued to be *with him.*

But everyone else was elated with the Cubs' performance, as during the Robins' final three at-bats, Chicago went for the kill. They had beaten Dan Griner and the audience roared as Harry Weaver closed his own shutout, 5 – 0.

All the team went out to one of their favorite post-game hangouts on the corners of Addison and Clark and reveled with the fans for a while, as Tad, Hoff, and Bass drank to Trip's success. He'd gotten his first RBI he reminded them about every three or four minutes just in case they forgot.

Chapter 18

Tad returned late to Hyde Park and The Sisson as he finally remembered that he'd been worried about Arlene and the warning he'd received from the cab driver. She seemed to have been all right when he'd phoned earlier. But now he had Hoff drop him off via his friend's Ford flatbed that George's grandfather had given him as a hand-me-down off their farm. They'd sandwiched the third-string backstop's latest "girlfriend" Rose, between both the boys in the front seat when they picked her up at the players' first stop in Little Italy. The young lady announced that she was thrilled the bordello now saw Taddeo taking charge, as it meant Roslyn felt free to do anything she wanted. And the rookie catcher had already caught a lot of free kisses on Addison Street while the team had partied, but George had a taste for catching his best companionship specifically from Villetti's — for at least this week. Tad wondered what, and how soon would it be, when The Hoff caught something else from one of these girls.

"So what did you do all day while I was gone?" Tad asked his own presumed woman upon returning to the hotel — and late. He had changed into his only suit but he could have still been wearing his uniform anyway. He smelled of sweat and beer when the tall, lanky athlete entered their room.

"Gee. I'll have to try very hard to remember," Arlene replied. "My days couldn't possibly be as exciting as a couple of late inning frames straight out of your life. I guess I've spent my time realizing that I'd be just *so lost* without you, Taddeo."

Tad took her literally of course. "Well I wished you were there with me today. We won again! And remember I recorded my first win?"

"Last night."

"Well, can't you bring a fella down."

"You have no idea."

"Well, yeah. My last moment of glory *was* last night."

"In our world, you never know how accurate that statement's

gonna be."

"But, actually, I uh — I didn't get to play today." He blurted out, looking down to the floor instead of meeting her eyes. Until he did — reinitiate contact. "So I want to play tonight — 'cause raising glory in my world is what it's all about for me, Doll." Tad offered a full-toothed smile.

"Oh believe me. I *couldn't* be happier if your own world was *all* you focused on, Hero." She crinkled her nose to involuntarily react to her senses alerting her of being in the presence of one more giant Villetti ego. "But while you were away *in your world*, nothing so fascinating that I could tell you about happened around here."

He began to strip off his clothing. "Well *I know* how I could get you real fascinated and you'll be even happier once I get started. I'm glad you're well-rested. Are you ready for *this*?"

Overheating for another reason — her fever — Arlene sat on top of only the fitted sheet, having pushed down the flat sheet and comforter. She closed her legs together since she wasn't wearing any bottoms. "Oh, well since we were out the whole night celebrating that *special time* we shared with the Genna Brothers not less than forty-eight hours ago, I decided to stay around the bed." She would have liked to have left for her other arranged lodging already, but Rinaldo had reordered her calendar. Arlene kicked Herb's arm back beneath the box spring's elevated frame where the corpse's hand had possibly still been visible. But Tad didn't notice. He was very busy looking over *her*. "So I got some time to meditate on my situation, and found I was ready for a lot more than I ever expected I'd be." She'd also first kicked the bedsheets off her naked body to distract him. She was after all, positioned over her kill, in a manner of speaking. Her distraction seemed to easily work. *Big surprise*. "But boy oh boy, *you* seem to be alive with plenty of energy, while some other people are just dying to get a long rest. However I was actually not feeling well again today. Now you wouldn't mind getting yourself a shower *before* you soil my bedding? This is not a ballfield or a brewery here, Taddeo. Though your family does raise its men to play hard. If I have to give them something, I'll give them that." Her eyes risked a glance lower for a moment.

Herbert was turning harder as rigor mortis set in beneath this most charming couple as they frolicked on the bed above him later that evening. His last wish, joining with Arlene for a night full of the expression of joyous sexuality being unleashed in triumphant victory, happened, just not as he'd hoped. He probably never expected the game saving pitcher to arrive at Arlene's side. *But the athlete's brother had.*

The young woman was now getting sick to her stomach with each new time there came a knocking on her hotel room door. But Arlene was getting sick to her stomach from this whole business anyway. She'd tossed and turned in spite of having more time lying in the bed she'd made than Taddeo had experienced as of yet, but she still did not feel good enough to get the door. She pushed on his back and shoulders while her partner groaned until at last, when she didn't let up, he was finally roused out of bed to answer the late night caller.

It was his cousin Corrado Delasandro that The House had all too curiously sent. As if there was a great need to tell them at three o'clock in the morning that it was raining and the change in the weather suggested the field would still be too wet to play on by the time the overcast skies burned away to let in the sun. It had actually been forecast to be very hot that day, but the Cubs would neither practice nor play that afternoon, their scheduled game versus the New York Giants. The next east coast team the Cubs faced would take their time coming into Chicago from St. Louis instead, and Taddeo's team would have the day off for spring showers. And as his alternative, to his visitor's pleasure Arlene was sure, the Delasandro brother informed Tad that he should plan to get to do the dishes for his father again. And this time, all day long. That did not go without making an impression upon the young woman that Tad had done something — perhaps truly stand up for her — that led to what sounded like punishment being handed down by his father. She made a note of that — but also that whatever Tad had set out to accomplish, his punitive reward was a clear reflection of how ineffective he'd been at it.

Meanwhile, Corrado spent a good time of his visit leering at Arlene, who had only the bed sheets to cover herself up, but then he also had a gift for Taddeo. In lieu of payment for the kitchen work he had already done, but had not yet been compensated for, Corry gave Tad a cheap model .38 caliber handgun. *Just what he needs.* But predictably, Taddeo wasn't interested.

"Don't think of the gift of this weapon as The House depriving you of payment for your work. Think of it as your family investing in a good tool. All Family members carry one, Cousin. I heard that you wanted to step in and manage our main entertainment enterprises.

Well, do you?"

"I don't need any firearms but only to treat the ladies *right* to handle The Family whorehouse, Cuz. 'Spose you haven't figured that out. But I guess I am taking away *your* job? What else could *you* be so worried about?"

"Worried?"

"You came here even before the crack of dawn? Couldn't sleep?"

"Well, uh you never know what kind of trouble you'll find when one enmeshes their fate with such talented women," his uncle's son informed him with another glance at Arlene. "And I see that The Family needs to train you better. The gun would be a tool that from time to time we might have to use for *customer* service. But I heard you've got a lot more troubles than just your learning curves, Taddeo. Your papa's not too happy with ya. You best get yourself worked up to be fast enough to handle this next Friday night's shift in the kitchen. It's already been related that you're about as bad at doing dishes as you are at playing professional baseball."

"I just won my first game. I backed Hendrix up on Wednesday night and I've proved that I can save everything."

"Maybe. They say you have got quite an arm on ya. Though I guess *you* would know better if you can throw a punch as well as you can throw a curve, and back *yourself* up. But, you'll need to carry a gun on you for when your *regular teammates*, that is *your real family*, needs you to back *us* up. And that just might happen — sooner than you'd think."

"Whatever." Wearing only his knickers, Tad had sat back down at the foot of their bed. "I'm sure you'll do what you gotta do. Another one of my father's bitches." Arlene cringed with that statement.

I'm no one's bitch. *Not Rinaldo's. Not my family's either*. She needed to have a talk with *her* real family. Forced to kill twice already, and with one dead body hidden under her bed this very minute, and The Family now bringing Taddeo a weapon, her mission was not going as she planned and got even further and further twisted sideways as every hour passed. The senior Villettis had surely made her and now they were toying with her, increasing the pressure to see how much she could handle. She hoped Rinaldo and Greggorio had enjoyed themselves. But now Arlene knew of one place where her own family said to have already sent someone in case she needed to make contact, get help. She imagined whoever had first brought her weapon — to hide it in The House for her — its journey had originated there. She'd only received a note saying where her gun had been stashed, but hadn't yet made any effort to make personal contact with anyone else who wanted to help her — except with Taddeo Villetti. Of course this was because she had gone off the preordained path, on her own personal hunt for vengeance. That had always been her plan. But events were progressing. Her adversaries were now pushing her, testing her. And these visitors sent by The Family, not to mention her not feeling well, had too long delayed her already. Only now she had another victim to remove from her latest *re*action. And as soon as that was taken care of, Arlene had to become more *pro*active with her personal mission.

"You will not call *me* your bitch, Rookie!" Corrado lost his control for only a second. Tad jumped to his feet, squaring off with his smaller relative. "I help our family — and not by sticking around to argue with you, Cousin. I've got my orders to leave it here and I did my part in relaying *your orders* to you. So I'm leaving the gun. Take it." Delasandro thrust the weapon out in his open palm. Taddeo glared at him but didn't take it.

"Fine. If you won't reach for it, I'm placing it here on your nightstand." Corrado had lost his patience and barged his way into their room pushing Tad out of his way. "Hah. Wasn't it only two nights ago that *you* needed some more backup yourself with the Genna Brothers? Yeah. I thought so."

He doesn't want to be here in the first place, Arlene deciphered from his body language. He would speak to Taddeo but Arlene felt Corrado's eyes keep shifting to her. The Delasandro brother was interested. *In her!* While dispassionate about it, she noted *that*, and would determine what it meant for her efforts later. That the newcomer desired her was already obvious — but it might also be useful. However, Tad had not even seemed to figure out Corrado's clue into the larger picture — that his charming cousin had just slipped up. *For just how does Corrado know about their night with the Genna Brothers anyway? Rinaldo doesn't like them. They trouble Colosimo. So Corry is working with Greggorio*, she reasoned, as he continued degrading Taddeo. *Greg has always been the immediate threat more so than his father. Salvatore Genna had said Tad's* brother *had arranged their evening for them on Tuesday, and no one would figure that to be Urso.*

"Well, you better grow up if you think you can do my job. Yup. I did hear all about that. So I'm moving on. My instructions were just to deliver the message — and the gun," Delasandro stated. "And I did what I was supposed to." He turned to leave their room. Arlene thought on the topic of instructions, and how she too had her own, and like Corrado, more than likely, a separate agenda in addition to what they'd each been *told* to serve. But he'd nevertheless inadvertently armed her newly sworn ally. At least that's how Arlene could imagine Taddeo. The irony of a Villetti now protecting *her*, if Tad could be remade into being worth something. Arlene would never bet on him being reliable — a matter of Tad's competence, not his good intentions — but she decided she could have some fun with this. She'd been waiting to find the rest of his siblings and his father *together*, so she could take them all at once and not lose the element of surprise. But the corpse beneath her feet suggested she'd been sent the message that *she* wasn't surprising anyone.

And now actually feeling like the woman had caught up enough on her sleep, Arlene was also strangely experiencing real security and possibly even hope, something which she hadn't felt for the first time since she'd arrived on the wrong shore of the river, what with this particular young man by her side — even in spite of her low opinion of his ability to handle matters of life and death. But she'd secured Taddeo's devotion to her. That was something. And the pair had even turned in early. She'd get more rest, recuperate over whatever afflicted her, and had some time to resettle herself over what she'd been forced to do already. Right now might be the only time she could even allow herself the fantasy that she was going to chance relying on Taddeo. But that could never happen. As her pragmatism returned, Arlene knew that Tad was just a means to achieving her true end. But she must have felt secure enough with him, as she even returned to further slumber, and slept well, in spite of the now customary — and frequent — interruptions by the newest flunky sent by The House. And now finally able to think clearly after getting a much needed respite, Arlene postulated that she might even be able to turn Corrado against Greggorio. *I have* some *effect on men*. Then she wouldn't need to put Taddeo in danger that she might really want to spare him from — a new development she could not explain, and tried to deny. But her influence as well as her self-confidence was growing stronger and that was a fact — with proof of it established via Herbert's cold body now lying under her bed. But reassured she was handling things better and better, Arlene nodded off for a couple more hours of quality rest and further replenished her strength.

In the morning, Taddeo decided to broach the subject of Arlene's strength to be all on her own while they shared coffee and a hearty breakfast in the hotel's connected café. He noted that Arlene already had a more-than-sturdy appetite. "That's good. Eat up. I need my girl to be strong. Strong enough to make some tough decisions."

"Your girl?"

"Well, uh — yeah. I mean if that's who you want to be. I mean you could be. 'Cause uh, I like you and stuff."

"And stuff? Lucky me."

"Look, don't make this difficult, Arlene. In about a week, I'm leaving." She squinted her eyes and tightened her lips, asserting control over her features so she didn't reveal the first expression she'd been inclined to reflexively make. It was easy for her to fake-out Taddeo.

But her thoughts rested on his last words. *He's leaving?*

"Road trip. It's the start of a new month, and the Cubs are gone most of it. We head to Boston first. Then Philadelphia. And after, we play the other East Coast teams. But you could — I mean I want you to — you know, come *with* me."

"Yeah. That's not going to happen."

Now Tad frowned. "I don't think it's a good idea. I mean, you staying here when I'm gone."

"I know. How do you think I will even be able to survive if I won't have a chance to keep up with Chicago baseball?"

"C'mon. Be serious for a minute."

"I always am. Now don't you have a serious mess to clean up in your father's kitchen?"

"Unfortunately. I'm *sure* it's quite a mess."

"I have no doubt it is. So, go."

"Alright. And I'll think about what we're going to do to keep you safe while I'm gone."

"Yes. You do that, Taddeo." She would think about all her options as well — while he was gone.

Old Lamont was rather impressed with the effort the youngest Villetti put into cleaning up the place that Friday. The other black men on the kitchen staff got a kick out of seeing the young man put some sweat into the place that bore his surname.

"Well, I suppose I really need to work if I want to get paid with any real money."

"Dat ya do, Mistah Villetti."

"Your efficiency is improving, Monsieur Taddeo. Keep it up and maybe I'll consider putting your name in for closing duties."

Chapter 19

Tad had been gone awhile already, no doubt honing his skills at cleaning up after his father's business when the next visitor came to knock on Arlene's front door. She would answer clutching her revolver even though she was expecting a guest. He would clean up after her mess.

"You requested room service, Madam?" he said from outside her secured room.

"Will it cost me?" she called through the door.

"I've been prepaid."

"So it's all *kosher*?" That was the challenge question.

"Yes. I'm the Jew. Open the door."

"I asked if it's all kosher?" Arlene's eyes went immediately over to the nightstand in which Taddeo had left the .38 that his cousin had brought him, which of course he'd refused to carry even in spite of the trouble he'd had coming home from baseball over on the North Side on Wednesday evening.

"I'm not even going out of my father's territory today. Why the hell do I need to start packing, Arlene?" he'd asked her.

"Well it's not going to stay fresh when you spill milk over the meat. Not to worry though. I found you some flower on *this* side of the river. It will help soak up all the stench."

At least part of his cynical answer contained the right response from the voice in the hallway. Arlene had then moved toward where she would return her own gun to its hiding place but stopped, opting to unlock the door instead. She shouldn't need a weapon in this moment after all, but it still was best to be prepared. If this Jew took his contract from the Bernstein brothers' operation in Detroit, she sensed she could be in real trouble. She opened her door. "That's not the meat that smells bad. That was my boyfriend."

"My condolences. You spent the night with him?" he asked as he entered her suite.

"Yes. But my man's not the one who's been temporarily fixed in his place for you, here and now. Mister Sweatbox is off playing the dishwasher for the moment. So *you're* going to substitute in the cleanup slot." Arlene thought he was handsome. She didn't expect that of someone in his line of work. But also surprisingly, he was a lot younger than she expected. He might've been younger than her. Didn't her family take her seriously? *I thought my mission was of the highest importance to them?*

A tall man with light brown hair showing under a hat, his nose was slightly bent, but it lent him the character of a man with competent strength who had successfully weathered his experiences at a still young age, rather than detracting from a rather dapper look. But with every observation she made of him, with her close scrutiny, Arlene reminded herself that this guy might stand high, but he was younger than she was. He was just a teenager, she realized. Her jaw clenched and teeth ground as she thought her family would've taken her need for competent backup as important or something. But it was his eyes, beautiful and blue, but nevertheless appearing so old which captivated Arlene. Her visitor had seen even more than she had, no doubt. Maybe this *boy* was qualified, after all. He wore a brown fedora with a black band around it. And Arlene did feel a curious attraction toward him. They shared the physical chemistry between them for he too offered her an appreciative look. To meet him she'd put on a more conservative dark blue dress, tied with a red sash, to create her appearance as being another professional. *Is that what this guy is?* He then progressed beyond that to their business together.

"So where's the mess I'm supposed to wipe out?"

"Under the bed."

"Does your man know?"

"No."

"And you two —? You and he —? With *that* under your bed?"

"That's Herbert. And don't judge. I couldn't let my real man suspect anything was out of the ordinary. And I thought you said there was a flower?"

"I am *a real man*. From Brooklyn. But you don't expect."

"You're right. I should know better." Arlene felt relieved he wasn't from the Detroit Jewish organization but then also decided he was too condescending toward her, and probably toward women in general. That *was* more typical of a man in his line of work. No, still a boy, she had to remind herself. It helped her when she needed to be more assertive with him.

"I'm glad you realize that." This overgrown child, dressed to create a good impression of being a real man in a black suit and long coat, bent down on one knee and found his grip on a stiff arm. Then as he stood, used the appendage to pull the rest of its owner out from under Arlene and Taddeo's bed. The body was cumbersome and leaking fluids. "Darn it. He's heavier than he looks. The cumulation of idiocy. There's a lot of that here."

"Nice. I could make do without a lot more commentary."

The man in the room who was still breathing had to stand up and remove his coat and used a handkerchief to wipe at some sweat under the brim of his hat. He then removed that as well. There was more tousled light brown hair he'd hid underneath. But he wouldn't comb it right now, with blood on his hands. He glanced at them. "You'll wait here. I'm going to get a laundry carrier from the hotel to stuff him into."

"You have a truck or wagon to get rid of him in?"

"Hey, I'm telling you I'm a professional. I hope you don't judge me by my age. I know all too well how to take care of this."

"You got a name?"

"You'll never see me again. So you don't need to know it." Arlene rolled her eyes as he looked her over, once more seemingly liking what the rather attractive-looking youth saw of her, but he continued on with his work anyway. "Once I do a job, I'm gone. If you mess up again, they'll send somebody else. We know *your name*. Now my advice to you? Don't mess up again. It gets expensive."

Once the carcass was removed, Arlene's high-priced cleaning service went over the room inch-by-inch moving forward from where she indicated she'd shot Herbert, to where he fell, and where she eventually had dragged him. The hired help loosened his clothing to allow himself the full range of motion he needed to move the bed and crawl around on the floor to do his work.

Finally, he finished erasing any evidence of the murder just as Taddeo returned from his own cleanup job and eyeballed the Jewish fellow who passed him in the doorway and made to leave the floor. Arlene's help was slightly younger, but still a little more distinguished in appearance, definitely more experienced, and just seemed that much more stronger and capable than Taddeo. Unless he was a completely overconfident fool, the pitcher would immediately recognize that. But Arlene should know better about who she was sleeping with. Tad's brilliance wasn't really one of his cultivated qualities.

Oh no. Why did he have to show up here, and now? This is not going to look good. His presence often annoyed her. *His timing right now could make things worse*. "You're home earlier than I expected," Arlene said, her voice flat.

Tad glared after the new fella, who possibly younger than the pitcher was, nevertheless gave him a smug look as he left, as if judging the athlete to be his inferior. "Yeah? Well I am able to get myself out of a bad inning." Tad was a baseball star. He resented some better-dressed teenager carrying himself around like he was actually a more important man in Chicago. "So who was that guy?"

"A business associate — of your father's," she lied, turning her head, the young woman's eyes not willing to meet his own. She had to practice adapting to the constantly changing circumstances of her mission anyway, and Arlene would make use of her lover's bad timing toward her own ends. But though she was correctly predicting the response she'd get from Taddeo and exactly how he would interpret the situation, it gave her no pleasure to hurt him.

"Business associate?" Taddeo asked, his head turning to once more watch the back of the guy who'd just departed, while the stranger still occupied himself with readjusting the way his shirt tucked into his pants. She saw he'd seen that, too.

Arlene sighed and shook her head from side to side, still avoiding a meeting with his accusatory stare. "Tad, once more, explain this infatuation you have with me. You know, it's really going to turn out to be uh…very unhealthy — for both of us."

Tad didn't even bother to come up with a way to try and hide his feelings. He was not an idiot, although everyone always underestimated him. At the moment he cared more about how *he* felt than if his next words hurt Arlene. Among all the constant euphemisms, outright omissions, and then the total lies, deception, and manipulation from his woman and even from his own family, it was best to just get to the truth anyway, from his point of view. He wished things could be simpler. "I was supposed to meet you. Remember? It's Friday night. We have a date. And I've been doing the dishes all day, in actuality, working for you. And while you were having just what kind of meeting with that guy?" he demanded.

"That kind of meeting," Arlene said, as though she thought it would be a complete enough answer. She could tell by the incredulous look Taddeo couldn't help but direct toward her, that this wasn't going to be an adequate answer. She'd tell him what he wanted to hear. Or what he didn't want to hear. But what he would believe. Arlene had enough already and didn't really care. "I was fucking him. Okay? What is it that you think I do for your father? I don't really have any other alternative skill sets at the moment. But I bet I am a lot better at fucking than you are screwing around with kitchen appliances. So tell me who you think 'probly earned more money today, Tad?"

"You would either way. Because you're going to take whatever I make, as if my father is even going to pay me with any real cash anyways. Jesus. It's like we *are* already married." Tad shook his head. "Whatever. I'm trying to help here."

"And I'm trying to help myself. To not get beat up. Or used up — by your wonderful brothers. So are you now running your family's comfort services? Or are your brothers purposely sending me more losers while you play at it in Weeghman's sandlot?" *I'll purposely channel his anger toward his siblings as I can handle Rinaldo more easily myself. I think. And I want to.* But she had no doubt that one or more of Taddeo's relatives had sent her the man who was fated to become her second victim. And that at least maybe one of them was trying to drive a wedge between her and the youngest son. Someone was making an awful effort to tear her and Tad apart one way or another: dead bodies and hidden firearms. It was only going to get worse. She would show them all that she was the wrong woman to mess with. But she was still sick and might need more help. "I'm better off spending my time making customers pay me their real money, Taddeo. As your relatives don't give me anything but shit for doing tricks for them, at any rate," Arlene said, her last statement actually being truthful. "And after which, I will then get punished for not earning enough bread for my upkeep. They enjoy that sort of thing, too. Abusing an Irish. It's what I'm here for. That is the ugly truth you've yet to face. But I live in that shit now. And it's going to only get worse. So since I can't count on you — . Well, I'm sure you didn't bring any money home, right? 'Cause now I bet they're all just having you pay off that gun you won't ever use. They're making you buy it. Aren't they? Of course, of *that* I'm also sure. But now I'm getting pretty good at taking care of myself and this is the only way I know how to." She gestured around the hotel suite. "Because you didn't even start managing our comfort services this morning like you promised to. Get us some real income that way instead of washing dishes. So I'm not even earning my quota. But I'm really glad you got to feel at least half as fucked by this situation as I do. And there are just some things you will have to learn to accept about me Tad — if you're going to persist in some pretense that we have some kind of a relationship going on here." She lit up a cigarette.

Tad started coughing from her smoke and moved to open the hotel window. "Well, the way you're taking care of things yourself, you are only going to wind up, fucked up, used up. Just another filthy, putrid, and eventually worthless saloon girl." Taddeo shrugged, stating it plainly. "Even if you happen to be the one with the prettiest face, nicest body — uh wait. Okay I'm digressing here. *But that's just fine. Face it Tad,*" he said to himself out loud. *"You found yourself a real prize bitch."* And then to Arlene, "Only all you are is just another fucking prostitute. That's the sad truth, Arlene. And I imagined you were special. Once a whore, always a whore, I guess." Tad's stomach and his heart were in turmoil and he had really wanted to let Arlene hear him call her every insulting name that reminded him of her occupation — and for quite some while now. Like it was her fault. A strong part of him held the opinion that Arlene actually liked what she said his father forced her to do. He'd already witnessed her best efforts to behave so scandalously flirtatious with the Gennas — and Tad thought that if *he* was required to sleep with different *women* all the time, he might really enjoy that. Hoff did. Of course, Tad then reminded himself, that all the women he could picture himself with looked like the girls in his father's brothel. But then why had he started to get so mad about Arlene's situation? *Face the facts. Oh no. I* am *in love with her, dammit! That's where this whole double-standard is coming from.* And in Taddeo's jealous and confused state of mind, he could lash out at anyone — and did — the list of recipients of his outbursts already including the young woman he thought he cared for the most, his teammates the other day, and even his own and ever increasingly dangerous father — who was the one who most rightfully deserved it. And before he knew it, Tad was already getting paid back for that one, in full — and then some. He looked at his water-cracked hands, left in a condition reflective of the work he did today. His father had said there would be retribution for his outburst right in front of Uncle Dally and his Great-Uncle Vollero. Was this all there was to it? Or was there something still worse yet to come?

But Taddeo couldn't let his so-far-ineffective steps to undermine the Villetti patriarch's plans for Arlene impede his success with achieving what he had set out to do here in the first place: defy his father and save his girl. Even if he was rightfully good and mad at her right now — living in her world of vice — versus his father's. But he hated to fail. He'd never given up. Ever. And therefore, he couldn't afford the time he would waste letting the anger he felt continue to fall on this beautiful face, framed by that soft red hair, which now reflected a color so very close to his own current complexion, where he felt the warmth spreading around the sting on his cheek — right in the spot that Arlene had smacked him on. Hard. But that made Taddeo aware he'd lost touch with the actual reality of their circumstances. In his fantasy, having stated the truth, Arlene would then all-of-a-sudden repent for her sins that Taddeo also took so much upon himself, personally — and because of his old man. But then she'd feel free from being so crushed down by the guilt of ever being forced to be associated with his family in *this way*. And finally, his loving woman would volunteer her never-ending dedication to being only with him, as Arlene's soiled past as a saloon girl would somehow be washed away — or could at least forgiven by him — for all of time — and then they'd live happily ever after. If she was convincingly sorrowful.

But Arlene favored a different story. "My preference is to think of myself as a highly qualified entertainer," she retorted, recovering her arm from the extension it required to reach up and punch the tall athlete. "Don't spoil that for me, Ball Jockey. The one thing I have going for me is a good reputation for being *a very bad girl*. But c'mon, Sporty. Think about the situation. I get this. You want to be a hero and have me think of you as just so charming — as if every day I just can't wait to see you, rushing home to save me. Like my life would just never be complete if you didn't walk through my door scratching your balls and farting peanuts after every home game. Wrrriiight. I just live for that." She took a hit off her cigarette while she set him straight. "But you know the first night? Your father set that shit up for you. Effectively giving you — me. His little reward for liking the way you pitched your silly baseball, I suppose. That's the reality *I* live in. And they *will* start actually rewarding you if you keep improving your stock. Your family I mean, with regard to their business. You could have done the accounting for the bordello instead of forgotten the work that accumulated any real value, having washed away all the effort you could muster with the dirty dining ware. Think about the choices you make. And if I were you, I'd start carrying that gun your cousin left you. Consolidating clean control. That power is your future and the Villettis have shown their potential to become a powerful family. So tell me if you still think what we're having here is so special now, Little Boy? Get with the program. Grow up. There was one night. One trick. That was all it was ever meant to be. Now it's half a week of *whatever*. And I am an entertainer. So entertaining you? It's just a job I do — which your family assigned me."

He'd finally and really made her mad. Yes she could and would use him. Put him at risk. He was a Villetti. Their sole remaining purpose was to be victims — of her vengeance.

Taddeo just wouldn't see this. "Well, I can't believe that. You felt our connection. Just like I did. And we've both been liking our nightly get-togethers regularly ever since." But Tad also seemed to feel more comfortable quickly changing the subject, probably so Arlene wouldn't have a chance to argue his last point.

Which Arlene did anyway. "Yeah, New Fish. Half a quarter of one month is always the measuring stick for calling it true devotion by my calendar, Baby."

"Don't call me 'new fish' or 'little boy,' or any of your other insulting pet names you have for me. And also, we're about the same I age, Arlene. And finally, there's nothing little about me. Uh, I hope. I don't want to get into *that* right now. Though please do tell, just how long have you enjoyed working for my old man's gratification?"

"I told you that truth already. 'Member? If you're so dedicated to me, why don't you ever listen to me? I'd gone and asked if you recollected that beef they had with the North Side over your family's rude intrusions into Irish territory?"

"Yeah. I remember. Trouble is that I'm having a hard time believing anything you say right around now. And that incident, you should very well know, is going on over week behind us already. People die every night in Chicago. And *you* should be able to believe *me*, that it was the Genna Brothers, not the Villettis, who were responsible for the original shit that went down."

And Greg is working with the Gennas.

"But Colosimo asked my father, and he asked Urso, to take some men and go up there and maybe talk to Vincent Drucci to learn their side to the story about what went down with this big cigar company my house was working, such that maybe our people could settle 'Bloody A' the fuck down if we had the facts to take to D'Andrea. We'd explain it wasn't our fault at any rate. There was a big misunderstanding that got out of hand and led to the trading of shots. We had a problem with a client not paying their taxes. The micks were never supposed to be involved. Our theory is the Gennas shot up the micks, then The North Side Gang shot at *us*. But Drucci's not Irish and not our ally either, so it was hoped for that he would understand and be an impartial third party that Weiss and O'Banion could agree on. Impartial my ass. Your people and their friends think of all of us dagos as the same. But I guess those shamrocks sure fool Drucci. So when Moran opens fire, Urso lost an enforcer and one of his friends. And for my family's peace effort at that."

"Right. It just breaks my heart, too. Blame the Genna Brothers if it makes you feel better. We both know from experience what charmers they are. But I'll tell you why all of this shit doesn't really matter. A lot of blood had been traded already, and more before that. You think my people just forget about it? The killings had been going on for quite some time, fueled by the desire for vengeance from both sides for, as a matter of fact, right up to about the time your father first saw *me*. And that was when someone higher up the food chain than him and that fellow's counterpart in my extended clan — all sat down together with other interested parties like the Unione Sissy-Liars, whose leaders must have had their own reasons for brokering our current and fragile little peace."

However, she really didn't want to get Tad working too hard to analyze all this. That would not be good. She'd already picked up the idea that the Genna Brothers had other reasons for being uptown than most of the Villetti House or especially Colosimo would know of. Mistrust between rival nationalities could be known *not* to always supersede a good financial opportunity. It helped explain why Ang would back down before her, once he discovered her identity back at the cemetery. And it also seemed reasonable to consider The Villetti House was not unified, but rather fractured quite well, as it appeared Tad's brother Greggorio might have plenty of ambition that was not aligning with his father's.

"As I said before, being around this shit, I've learned too much," Tad said, his statement more ironic than he would possibly ever know. But his reasoning did surprise her. "Any big meeting like that must have also included the Jews. The bankers from Manhattan. Wise up, Arlene. You can't know everything." He laughed. "And to think my father believes that I barely know anything. But the Jews have these ties with the Italian families back in New York. They also have some complicated relationship with Annenberg at the *Chicago Examiner,* and in exchange for favors for them, the papers can start printing all the scandalous charges they can associate Mayor Thompson with, and create vulnerability in who could be this city's last Republican. Who knows what for? To get Thompson back under control? I've just been overhearing talk about that, the rising expense that paying the police cost us, but I definitely know the Annenberg connection's used when Greg fixes the sports page. But no matter how corrupted Thompson keeps getting, he must have betrayed somebody good because just about everyone in the city I know of — Italian and I guess Irish — may want to see a Democrat win the next election now — *if they can buy him*. They want to use the reformers for something — and I wouldn't believe it would be to reform anything. But maybe that's why they're all so enthusiastically pretending to support Wilson's war that some of my teammates like 'Old Pete' Alexander could even get called up to fight in. The Chicago bosses' reasons are not rooted in patriotism, I can assure you. See I wish I didn't know any of this stuff. But it affects my friends and I hear my father whining about the house over all this shit — and way too often.

"So great for them. The Jews, I mean. I'm real happy they're enjoying themselves. I don't think they would have singled out you personally, though. I can't figure that one. One whore or another would have done. Oh. I'm sorry. *Entertainer*." He was clearly still mad at her and wouldn't pay her any more compliments if he could help himself. "But at the same time, Merlo mediates our territorial dispute in exchange for the gangs on both sides of the river coughing up all their evidence that Thompson has dirty funds coming out of every orifice because his hands are into grabbing at anything and everything going on which is filthy in this town. Just like his puppeteers, Coughlin and Kenna. Maybe O'Banion's even trying to gain more leverage with them? I'm *not* sure which leprechaun owns which other ones. It's always reversing. But it would seem like it was the Jews that first saw themselves an opening in this business with their ties to the newspaper and the political clout that can yield. Which can even influence who's on the list of a war draft. I guess New York's not big enough for them. And they have other shit going on in Chi-Town, you can be sure. This is only the beginning. And the Irish decided to go along with this program for once, *Coughling* up one of their own — if only because Thomspon's actually English descended and falling out of favor with some, and the Jews will help to threaten the limey to repeat his lesson on obedience, again."

Arlene thought, *Oh, I already knew about the Jews*. "Well, all these gangs must have something big planned because all of them need this cease-fire to hold. And exactly as I explained it to you, I was just a throw-in — part of the deal for your dear-dear Family's temporary truce with my people. And don't call us leprechauns, or micks, or shamrocks. Whether they even acted duplicitous or not, and made the latest killing of your father's man happen or not — ."

"I hope you're not throwing around unfounded suggestions. I first heard, and then next *told you*, about my father's man Dulio's untimely end, *while you haven't even left this hotel room*. This new guy nearly beat to death Kean O'Rourke, who is Irish. And our house doesn't kill one of its own. And so it's obvious which side had motive for retaliation. The police are still investigating. So no one really knows specifically why that new man was killed or *who* did the deed yet. But I can accurately guess what the evidence is going to show. Only I don't see where you get personally involved or how you'd go around thinking you could even know anything about it."

Well I sure do.

"But it doesn't change the fact that your people shot at Urso."

"Tad, just shut up. And learn that in the end, the results are all the same for *me*. Some territorial concessions, Thompson's future a convenient excuse, and D'Andrea and Colosimo's promise not to let their people retaliate — but a truce nevertheless negotiated for just a long enough a period of time to give them respite in order to call in some bigger guns from New York and Jersey. I'd guessed your father needed some help. And that probably concurs with a clinical opinion. But anyway, Bloody Ang surely has all the manpower he needs from the West Side already. We've seen some of it. Though I'm sure he'd love to let the North and South deplete their own manpower by swift attrition. Maybe even *he* produced that body in the barrel you told me of, to make it look like my people did it to mock your family?" Arlene suggested this with no hesitation about lying to Taddeo. He was a Villetti. "But somebody's hoping for a great fight to thin out the herds on both sides of the river. Then maybe the Gennas *will* make their big move? All his older brothers seem afraid of Angelo. He's dangerous. We both felt it. So the rest of his house will go along with wherever that psychopath leads them. And that is downright scary."

"Only did he even once impress you that he was smart enough to be plotting this all on his own? He's the one who's got to be getting help."

"Well, the Jews could be after something, too." *They sure are.* "Though I don't know what. So I can roll with your conclusion there: about the fighting continuing. What, with a family like the Gennas just waiting on the bench until it's their time to play, peace will be impossible to attain. And Colosimo has to build his own force up. While he also has to maintain a reputation as a joyful easy-going guy with little ambition but to promote new wines, jazz and blues music, and his own *special* kind of appreciation for women. He has your father working for him behind the scenes providing more skin and more muscle, which requires every scheme of Rinaldo's that's imaginable to make more money so that the South Side can afford this — the security required for their wonderful operations." She was hoping Taddeo might know enough to fill her in on what else his father was marketing. "But everyone knows what Diamond Jim and Madame Moresco are truly selling. And with Colosimo's innocent act a popular one, as it's the only one that's always staying in a positive spotlight, this only helps Merlo and D'Andrea to stall for more time while they fix an election to keep control over City Hall and the police force — without the public ever gaining any evidence. Legitimate evidence anyway — with the newspapers also under control. After everything, all those two's and Colosimo's little political business, is really the greater Unione Siciliana's business. And that's all just a front. More lies covering up something else." *But what? What else are they working on?* "And in the end, you *are* probably exactly right when you said it all will mean nothing for us. Just like my life, now that my parents are dead. Killed by this endless violence." *I guess the cleanup man the Jews sent was also right. I better get back to Villetti's and find out everything that's been happening. My sacrifice here has to not wind up being for nothing. And now Herbert even had to pay that price. Plus if he had a wife or child somewhere?* Arlene quickly banished the thought of how she'd been orphaned and might now have done the same thing to some other child, as had been done to her. But Herbert had gone where he never should have been. That was on him. Arlene now had to complete her mission without any more interference by her emotions. She'd killed twice already, but having never come close to even hitting her primary targets, and had to just not let herself continue dwelling on it. This was no place for emotions, especially guilt. She had a job to do. "So the streets *will* never see a lasting peace, Taddeo. That's just life trying to make it in America. Or anywhere in this godforsaken world where human nature is concerned. It's not easy. It's not fair. The pain is always returning. And your enemies will never stop opening old wounds. So I might as well just die."

"You don't really mean that, Arlene. And I'm so sorry about your parents. Because of my own mother, I really should have realized how much that affects you. You don't open up about yourself a whole lot."

She shook her head. "I'm not quite done writing my autobiography. And this isn't group therapy, Tad."

"But you can't tell me that after what my family has done to yours, that you don't hate Italians. That you wouldn't enjoy seeing us all killed."

"Well I don't know, Loverboy. Is my other option a good dinner and a movie?"

Taddeo ignored her quip. "So the desire for Italian blood burns within you too, Arlene."

She worried it might burn within her a lot more than either of them knew as Tad continued. But she wasn't letting herself be maneuvered into killing recklessly — again — and possibly by the Jews *or even by her own side*. Was she? *Was she?* No. She was her own mistress. However, there were already two less bullets in her gun. The Villettis were clearly the ones who had seen to her need to fire them. Rinaldo or Greggorio? Or one time per each of them? And now there was this prevailing sense that Taddeo Villetti had inadvertently maneuvered himself into being somehow important to her. Damn irritating though he might be. What was that all about? It all made her want to throw up.

"Don't pretend like you're above all this either," he said. "You'd be right to feel exactly as I imagine you do. Though it's not getting us anywhere. We are supposed to be becoming partners. But my guess is that now I'll have to sleep with one eye open. I can't say that leaves me all too enthusiastic about living with you in The Sisson."

"As if you think that's what I'm agreeing to do? On the brighter side, this is Chicago. Room service is already trained to handle bloodstains on the carpeting if you pay them well enough."

"Ha-ha. That's really comforting — you insane evil bitch. *Jesus*." His words were strong, and he probably meant it, but his tone was jocular. "I can't be sure about what you've done, or what you're capable of doing, can I? Still, I also can't believe my father's all-invested in this scandalous trading of skins." Tad had quickly reverted to sounding serious again. "Colosimo…" his voice trailed off. "Well, he and his wife basically set my papa's business up."

Arlene frowned. "Don't you know what sort of businesses they're all in? What *your dear Papa's* capable of? Are you really still that naïve? Your father works for Colosimo. You know what Diamond Jim and his bitch wife are all about. And you're living in a fucking whorehouse, Tad. Apparently with your head buried under the pillows. 'Cause it sure seems like before we met, you were never getting anything. And now I know that includes not getting any smarter."

"I know my father and my brothers are shaking people down. The restaurant doesn't make that much. Hah. The food is terrible. I've been in the kitchen. And there's nothing I can do about any part of a bad taste my family leaves in this town."

"That's true. But if at least only one of my prayers is answered, they won't ever start you cooking."

"Thanks. I just keep my head down and play baseball, Arlene. That's all I ever wanted to do. And it's not stupid. Okay? It's important to me. So, no. I don't really know all of what's going on at my Papa's table or out on the streets. I actually have to try not to know. I've already heard much more stuff than I'd have liked to," Tad informed her. "Colosimo and Lady Moresco originally found all the whores — er, entertainers. And they'd gotten the building which they could run as an inn with onsite dining. We added the bar and created a nightclub scene. My papa and also Greg had originally worked to manage it. Urso doesn't really do much of anything. But Papa got our name placed over the front door and a great way to clean our money. Then I've also learned Papa offers to settle some disputes in the neighborhood. People come to him. He creates more stability, he makes some loans, collects some interest, trades some services, and a little gambling goes on. And sometimes bad stuff happens."

"Like a monkey in a barrel shows up."

"Yeah. Really. Well, meanwhile, my family makes a little more money but they never cease to try and drag me deeper and deeper into all their shit. Whatever it has to do with New York. That sort of thing. So let me be clear, just like I was very clear to my old man. Only the other day. And yeah, I really did stand up to him by the way, *for you.* I said it and I meant it — that I just want to make my fortune happen on my own. Not get involved in anymore of the rest of their crap. Except that I stepped up to begin managing the bordello only so that I could protect *you.* And I just did dishes all day to prove that I otherwise just want to be *left alone* — to become the kind of man that I want to be. There's nothing I — or you — can do to change anything around here. But the bottom line is: I'm getting out. I am earning my going on my own way. That's what I'm now going to work towards. No matter what, I'm leaving this life all behind me."

"You're very lucky you have that luxury."

Just the mere mention of luxury or privilege jostled Tad. He remembered all of the last conversation he had with his father. "No. I really meant what I said."

"Oh. I get it. You really meant it. Okay. Go on Tad. Really." Arlene rolled her eyes and didn't make much effort to hide her smirk.

Tad's face flushed and he scrunched it up, controlling another urge to verbally strike back at the woman's insolence she wore like permanent armor. This time he was successful, partly because of her half-hidden smile she couldn't control whenever she affectionately teased him — only served to encourage him. He almost laughed. *Frustrating little bitch. But I can't keep my thoughts off of her!* He continued explaining, "You know — Fuck you, Arlene." But the harsh words were laughed out. "I can't choose what family I was born into, but I can choose what kind of human being that I become. And for not one minute do I like what I'm learning is going on here. What my family — nor what your paddy-whackers have done, either. But I've come to realize that there really is nothing I can do about changing it. Really. At least not in any significant way. But I can make some kinds of small amends — and one thing I will do is get *you* away from this place. As soon as possible. But I wouldn't mind a little appreciation here and there. I'm offering to take you with me."

The young woman's piercing green eyes softened and a sympathetic expression came across her countenance. And what was that? He might have also spotted a glimmer of hope. Apparently, his words got through to her, or she'd already been thinking the same thing. But she countered him anyway. "Tad, face facts, there really is nothing you can do. About any of it — *even for me*. The money they pay the average ballplayer — you can't survive on that. Plus, your run in sports won't last forever; and you already know this and that you don't have a real job either. Sports might even cripple you. Then what? Forget the Italian one. What you guys need is a players' union or something. Plus there's going to be a lot less of any kinds of jobs once production slows down to levels it was at before the war. So I survive by doing what I'm doing. At least I got quickly established at it. And my line of work is always recession-proof." Arlene sighed and looked toward the ceiling. "And neither one of us can pay for even this standard of living by washing dishes, or being in manufacturing or vending." She gestured around their so-called posh hotel suite. "All you have to do is just think about where you'd be if your papa cut you off."

"He almost did. The last time I opened my mouth. Again, all for you. But my teammates somehow make it. And many of them have families — and jobs in the mills, processing coal even so then still others can work with steel, as well as be waiters, cooks. They're even concierges waiting at the train station. Breaking their backs for slave wages while catering to supposedly rich vultures like my morally bankrupted father. Now Arlene, if you'll leave with me, I swear I can make an honest living. I've got prospects. I mean, do you know Mister Li who runs the cleaners?"

Arlene nodded. "I've seen him before."

Tad paused, slightly disturbed by what that response could have meant. "Well, he's always been kind to me — and he's followed my baseball career since back when I was a boy, only just starting to play. He liked to watch us when we were kids practicing over by Polk and Canal Streets in this sort of wide alley outside the back exit from his laundry. My family had to live over that way, before Colosimo helped us out of the slums — as we had no better place to go when we first arrived. Well, occasionally Mister Li would wave to my ma. She liked that — when someone was friendly to her and shared in the accomplishments of her favorite boy. *That was me*. So naturally I think he's a good man. And he tolerated a few broken windows when I was younger. But now I have some new information to trade him that might very well become of some *value* to him and another friend of his. Unfortunate information, I guess. But still useful. He will need to hear this immediately actually — and then he may very well help *me* out."

"You hope. And so now your goal in life is to work for a Chinese laundry? Okay, Taddeo. That's just the fresh kind of wonderful."

"I'm not done. So shut up and listen to me, Arlene. Mister Li's at least been able to carve out a niche and make a living for himself in Chicago, even outside of Chinatown, north of it and where separated from his kind, he's a member of one of the smallest minorities. You have to respect courage like that. And I think he might have a place coming up for rent. Kind of uh, soon. Like as of maybe tomorrow — following another funeral. So yeah, I'll work for *him*. Then I can at least move out of my papa's place and you can stop living in hotels being visited by strange men."

"You're by far the strangest man, Taddeo."

Used to her ongoing commentary, Tad went on, "Don't ignore what was supposed to be the goal here, and while I see 'Pants' leaving your room when I came to find you for our date tonight. But our new flop will only have to be temporary — I mean in Chicago. But it will be safer for you. Hidden from my family while I travel with the Cubs and play in our away games. It'll be all right if you insist on staying in town after I'm gone then. No one will know where you disappear to if we're careful. And soon after this temporary move, we can leave this city. Disappear for good. Let me make this happen for you, Doll. I can just tell Papa that you died or something."

"Oh, I bet you won't find any shortage of help for making that actually happen," Arlene responded. *If he only knew*, she thought to herself. *This was originally supposed to be my suicide mission. Plus I may have gotten seriously sick from it already*. Her stomach churned if she thought about it. "And *you* know, I've been wondering if my death ever came to be, whether your father would go all out and throw a block party?" she asked. "And in the spirit of the way everyone's getting along so well now, I also wonder if my own family would accept that as an invitation to come on over to Maxwell Street and make it a rager. We're really headed for heaven now, Taddeo. Oh what promise the future could hold."

"Well it's not going to hold anything funny for you if you don't stop cracking jokes and seriously reconsider coming with me on my away game tour."

"I'm trying to keep my sense of humor. Involving me in more dead-ball games than I'm already forced to deal with now? That's not very funny at all, Taddeo." She saw him frown and she took a drag off another new cigarette. He reached for it and tried a puff and coughed twice, unused to the experience. "And what are you going to do in light of your new responsibilities at your papa's *establishment*?" Arlene had an idea, but it would sound better if it came from him. "You'll lose any control you think you can gain by taking over for Greg, just as soon as your team leaves town. Your cousin Corry will be here — and I've noticed how he really wants to contribute his part to certain jobs. You might be able to hide where I'm sleeping, but you can't work for your father in the capacity you or he wants, still playing baseball, and what? Protect me while I can't leave Chicago with you."

He looked at the smoking tobacco stick, coughed violently this time, and then handed it back to her. "Why Arlene? Why can't you leave and — ?"

She cut him off. "Because you will you be hiding *all* the rest of the ladies as well? So no one punishes them? For the whole fucking month you're away? There is constant abuse resulting from the whole of all womankind's situation."

"Huh?"

"Never mind. You couldn't possibly understand. But in theory, at least the ladies on Taylor Street are all *your girls* now, Taddeo. But if your brothers and your cousins — ."

"If they use up their every working hour, The House doesn't make any money and we lose the main source of income we're trying to syphon for our escape fund," Tad acknowledged. He swept the air with both his arms out, conveying his surrender of that point.

"Of course. That's exactly what I was just thinking of," Arlene responded, her sarcasm not registering with him.

Then Taddeo snapped his fingers and pointed at her as if he'd just thought about something. "But they might deliberately lose a significant amount of money, too. Just because they'd enjoy making sure they see me fail. But my father won't like it — not one bit. He needs that income for payments to Colosimo and the drug purchases he runs through my uncle."

I figured Rinaldo had a lot going for himself on the side. Drugs. Probably heroin — newly outlawed. It fits his profile. "Right," she said. "But I agree that your brothers would like to see you fail. Plus the first full day on that new job of yours has come and gone, with another having nearly passed, and you're back here with me when you said you'd be collecting from the other ladies — *for me* — but presumably to next turn in for your papa. For use as his precious drug money I'm now to presume. And after you skim from the proceeds I guess. But you still are here, not at Villetti's and I need to turn in some money at the end of my 'recreation hostess time,' or I'm going to pay a much higher price than you will for shirking your other new duties. I can guarantee you that. And I've been with you for four nights now. I have no such thing offerable like a *free* date. I was supposed to have at least been working out of this hotel room while you were away."

"It sure looked like you were."

"Things aren't always what they look like, Taddeo." And as much as Arlene would have liked to have brought into question the entire injustice of this sickening skin trade, Tad coming to his inevitable conclusion was no inconvenience for her. The filth coming out of the sex trading slime those crawling serpents called the Villettis left behind them was useful as the new raw material that gilded her wings — wings that Arlene might yet use to escape with. Though it could already be why she felt so sick. However, so far, it sure beat dying. But it also meant keeping the other girls working as rigorously as possible. That would be the only way to enable Arlene, once thinking she'd taken on a suicide mission, to see a new way to seize a victory and then even finance herself taking flight. If she could stomach the hypocrisy while also adapting some familiar assistance — Taddeo and now maybe even better, his cousin who was also so very interested in her — into being more effective for achieving her primary cause. But finally bringing down vengeance upon her enemies wouldn't end the plight of the other girls anyway, and hardly impacted the institutionalized sexual slavery in America. So she could rationalize using them — like she would use everyone else — especially Taddeo, who was susceptible to her influence by any affection — or further extent of her own skin — that *she* showed him. But the laundry, once it was cleared out of its current refugee that Taddeo suggested it harbored, could serve as a very nice hideout in which she could find some spare moments with which to catch her breath until at least the young woman could at long last, breathe in her own freedom. So *there* could be one very clean getaway that she could even survive, she mused. But she would have to accept that it would come at many others' expense — or damnation — if she wanted to be truly honest about it. *Now I can give Taddeo the weekend to see if he can pull this plan of his off, but in the meanwhile, I'll put into motion my own contingency plans. I've seen I can't count on him before. And I need to get my money I'll need in case this doesn't work. I'm thinking if I can get at more money, plus Rinaldo's drugs, I can smoke out or buy out even more among others willing to help. And I can probably get this done faster than Tad could deliver anyway. But I* can *always use a vehicle to bring in additional funds so that I may be certain I will be able to afford to go it my own way, just when I'll probably need to*. Plus Arlene had to admit that executing her plan while Tad was out of town could even save his life — and her own inner voice was telling her *that* was far more important to her than in her wildest dreams she'd have ever expected it to be. But why? That still didn't make any sense. Or it did? And she might already know why — but now her greatest fear could overtake her if she admitted that. *So I'll take over running the prostitution just like Madame Moresco, and I will survive. And my favorite stupid idiot here will, too. If I can help it anyway. Just make the offer Tad*, she thought. So out loud she said, "But wow. The Villetti prodigal son is still interested in doing something to help me?" Arlene blinked, taking one more fresh look at Taddeo. "That is rich." Then she blushed and quickly looked away, hiding a smile she couldn't help herself from displaying, and obviously hoping Taddeo wouldn't see. He truly wanted to be someone's hero and acted such the gentleman, always so very chivalrous toward her. Arlene couldn't suppress showing some feeling of her affection for the youngest son. But she wouldn't allow herself to put a lot of stock in any future his well-meaning intentions could distract her from her own priorities with. And she couldn't afford to take any more personal risks while she surrendered any more of her time to him. Thus far, he was neither wise, experienced, or even the least bit competent. These feelings she still tried to deny that she held for Taddeo, were becoming a continuous temptation that had been leading her astray. She needed to discontinue them, if she ever could. They were now going to be why she would try and give him the weekend to see what he could do.

"Then let me at least have a week, Arlene. I'll get a job and get you relocated."

A whole week? But that's way more time than I'm comfortable offering him.

"Trust me. I have a good plan about what we're doing for money," he pleaded. "And I have to act — and fast. My team *is* leaving for almost a month of more stadium tours on the East Coast and I need to make sure you're protected and safe while I'm away. It doesn't have to be like this." Tad gestured around the hotel room.

"And I'm going to be happier doing Mister Li's laundry?"

"You'll be happier not having to suck Mister Li's dick — or anyone else's, Arlene."

There's a point.

"Geez. God knows I'm trying to help here. And I know my brothers won't treat you right — and I can't stand thinking about what they'll do if I have to leave you behind in Greg's, and Corry's tender care. Or worse — Urso's. You could come with me. Or I could give you the money or a train ticket to meet me over there."

Arlene shook her head no. "If you're really so concerned about me suffering, sitting through almost a month of your baseball games could almost qualify as being just that, Sporto."

Tad ignored that last barb. "Hey. Wait. I got another idea!" Taddeo suddenly jumped up from his seat in the chair he'd turned to face Arlene where she sat on her sex-soiled bedding. "That is if you really won't come east with me — for who knows what reason. Or maybe now I *did* figure why. Because my family knows you've been with me all this time. And my father expects you to show up around the lounge if you're freely keeping up your own family's side of their cease-fire agreement. Right? So we just keep it a secret where you're flopping at next — and say you're working out of the hotel. Maybe from some other room? It's more comfortable here. You're good at lying anyway. And then you take a different Italian taxi over to the saloon when everyone else is all tired and exhausted at the end of each night and say that you're there to do the books and pay out The House's share. Tell them I ordered you to do it while I have to pitch in our away games, and for this *I've been training you.* You can insert the money you were supposed to make from some of the skim. Along with the rest of it we'd deposit anyway. They see only the final count and The Family shouldn't question you as long as they're happy with the consistency in the numbers. Just be careful you believably represent the receipts of the other girls — we don't want them complaining — but don't forget to stash some for yourself."

Well it took him long enough. Her favorite dumb jock finally came to the conclusion she'd been waiting for him to get to. "Wow. I'm really moving up in this world by sticking around you, Taddeo." *I'd been right to wait him out.* "In less than one week I've gone from being a human sacrifice to a whore until I'm actually becoming the madam. Oh my! Do you think at this rate you should also teach me how to throw? 'Cause in a few days maybe I *will* follow you to Boston and see if while I'm there, I can try out for the Cubs. I've heard they've long been thinking about replacing at least one of their terrible relief pitchers they've been fielding this season."

"Very funny." Tad scrunched up his face to attempt to scowl at Arlene. "Yeah, you're just such the funny cunt now, aren't ya?" He was evaluating her, but not too secretive about not being able to help himself to *not* show that he liked what he saw. She only had to look below his waist to know that. She wasn't even dressed seductively at this moment. And his harsh language Tad now tested out with her as they leaned back into their bed, would only be delivered using playful tones. *But he was changing.* He was experimenting to see if he could become the kind of man around women that he saw his brothers were. Sadly, he didn't really have another example of how else to be. Arlene saw this, even if she wanted to deny it. And she pondered if who he changed into could indeed actually be someone she could control, or even want to still have standing by her side. He didn't really love her. He was lying to himself if he believed that. Taddeo Villetti loved baseball and what he truly desired was to think of very little other than becoming a star for his own glory. To her this should signal that she was only his passing fancy and that he would become more of a danger than someone she should count on — if he ever was, or even could become.

"Well, I'm still probably better at playing with balls than you are —."

"Then let's get this game on because your call could be construed as a compliment — if I'd said it, anyway. Though I don't think either of us appreciates that statement in the larger context."

"You've curiously phrased that. I'll have to think about that one," she said.

Then he climbed on the bed and got on top of her, mounting her. She felt her body gain more and more excited energy, immediately, from right upon his very first touch.

"And I'm thinking about *you*."

"Yeah, *you* do that — But so now your goal is to also become some kind of pro at doing laundry?" she retorted, trying to change the subject and keep a straight head. She'd made a little progress with him and wanted to continue the momentum. "But it doesn't say much for your own evaluation of your pitching performance, does it? That this is a move *up* in the world for you — maybe from washing dirty dishes I'd suppose. Bet it's all part of your great plan that will one day see us becoming the sort of reeeally interesting domestic couple they'd feature in *The Post*, right? A regular Norman Rockwell painting. That'll surely be us. Me depicted on my back while you're bent over another sink. You know, I'm starting to just love all your ideas, Taddeo. We should take our comedy act out on Vaudeville."

"Cute."

Chapter 20

Tad was sort of cute — and annoying — in his deep slumber after his full work shift and play night on Friday. They'd made love, or did what felt best while faking it, and then retired to rest in each other's arms.

When a demanding and repetitive knocking came on their hotel room door early Saturday morning and woke Arlene, she decided she would have to handle this, as her tired partner couldn't be roused by all the racket in Chicago. Getting up from the bed, wrapping herself in a discarded towel, and quietly extracting her gun out of its place in the armoire, the young woman had yet to decide whether or not she was going to physically answer the door. "Who's there?" she didn't take too much time to call out. But Arlene got no answer, though she could hear the sound leather shoes make when they're bent by someone shifting their weight inside them, so close to her that this was even audible from outside the door. She detected the slightest change in the light coming through from the hall as there was motion in the shadow coming in from under that door. However, Arlene did not feel any change in her confidence. She figured it to be one or another of the Delasandro brothers who the Villettis decided to send to scare her, right on time. Or was it one of Tad's wonderful siblings who finally decided to show up themselves? Maybe they had at last chosen to risk starting what would be one pretty ugly fight with their younger brother. That might work to her advantage, though she dismissed the idea of encouraging that right now, since she didn't trust Taddeo would be very competent even if he had very wisely become suspicious of Greg. The two of them needed to talk about that in the near future. Although in this moment, she'd be happy to shoot any other Villetti herself. She didn't require Tad's approval. Though the Delasandro, the cousin, might still be useful to make to do it for her. But the thought that this could also still be about her first killing — of one of Rinaldo's men, last Tuesday night, troubled Arlene. But only slightly. She immediately hoped the cops hadn't decided to ignore their payoff, and reopen any old investigation. Or worse — The House was back on it. She did not know what fate would call of her from just outside that door. But it could signal an opportunity for another kill — and this time of someone who was really owed her fiery vengeance. One third of one half of the real work she did indeed come to the South Side to execute. But then she'd wished she were dressed as she might then have to move quickly to follow through — if she killed Greg. His brother Urso wouldn't be troubled to see her with Taddeo at this hour, and neither would Rinaldo. But any one of them might have hired out. So Arlene glanced back at the nightstand where Taddeo had left his gun. It *hadn't* been fired. If they even thought to implicate her, all that any low-level agent of The Family — that she could not risk lighting up right now with Tad there — would have to do is a search of her room to find any weapon that had been recently used, but the actual firearm they were really looking for was now already in her hand. Ready to shoot — again. Only if she was lucky, they'd come to face the other one. The .38 — if Taddeo would finally take it up to defend her. *He* wouldn't let anyone from The House manhandle her in a search. Would he? Thus they should only be able to turn up *his* weapon so long as she needed to conceal her own. And it wasn't likely to be the cops waiting for her on the other side. The Family had already paid them to discontinue their investigation and just leave their man Dulio's murder be. Rose had found out that much because her father was consulted regarding the body. And Arlene's own family had enlisted the Jew to take care of Herbert's remains, so betraying her now would serve no logical purpose. But she wasn't going to be able to figure out *who* or *why* right then. So Arlene reasoned she should just open the door and get whatever this was, over with. But in error she thought she had to switch the hand she held her .45 behind her back with so that she could unlock the latch. She didn't really, *and needed to remind herself that she could defend her life with both hands*, but Arlene tried to reason whoever The House sent, was not going to touch her right in front of Taddeo. She was very sure that *he'd* take her side, plus he could quickly arm himself if this encounter went south — though he'd never hit anyone besides a Brooklyn batter. *Maybe they ought to have left him a Spalding instead of a Smith & Wesson?* She felt sick again, but repressed her nausea. How she wanted this to end already. Taddeo could be more useful if she gave up her emotional ties to him. And his self-entitled attitude, his language, and the general decline in his chivalry he'd now been demonstrating toward her had started making her new conclusion become easier and easier to arrive at. So in that moment, she reconciled it with herself — that she could accept a very dangerous new idea. Her mission, but next her suddenly *even-possible* chance at survival, needed to both matter — a lot more than he did.

And at last, Arlene opened the door — but only partially so she could see who it was, though then she retreated back when she didn't recognize *anyone* similar to the big man who stood waiting for her. He was not at all overweight. Quite the opposite, having a height and athleticism about him. He might have been one of Taddeo's teammates. But one she had never met before.

"Is Taddeo here?" His voice was youthful and lacking in confidence. The opposite of what Arlene had expected from such a large, tall and intimidating young fellow, with such a commanding knock.

"He might be."

The new light brown-haired man cut her off. "Wake him. Uh. I mean please wake him. Miss? Ma'am?"

Arlene regained her composure and saw it would not be a problem asserting herself over this one. *Not quite confident after all, is he?* "I never said he was here. I said he might be." The man shifted in his shoes making that leather stretch under his size. "Is this about something private, or can I pass a message along to him when I see next see him? I was sleeping, you know."

"Oh. I'm sorry. I thought you'd be working, Miss."

"This is The Sisson. You could have phoned a message to my room first. Before you marched over here. I don't take too kindly to being disturbed, you know. My clients surely don't like it either."

"Uh, well uh anyway this came down from Greg, I mean Mister Villetti, and through his father I'm told. It's just that they don't need Taddeo to come back to the kitchen any more. Uh, said he's not fast enough for the weekend shift 'cause he's as bad at cleaning dishes as he is at pitching a baseball."

"Yeah. We heard that joke before. Thank you very much for telling me at who-knows-what-hour in the morning."

"Ma'am. I mean, Miss. I said I was sorry. I mean I just do what they tell me. Um, please. Uh. Good night." He bowed and departed. Arlene slammed the door behind him. Tad never even stirred.

So Greggorio is definitely the one sending these guys over here. With or without his father's blessing. Could be either. It wouldn't be Urso's style to send a proxy. That's for sure. I've been fortunate I haven't had to deal with that one until I can be sure I am ready.

And I can now also be sure Rinaldo's quite annoyed that I got out of his bordello no sooner than I arrived. Though still not fast enough. *But Tad's resistance to his family could really be useful. It would seem I've already stirred him into rebelling. He's willing to wash the dishes. So I could even bet that I can sic Taddeo on either one of those two — or even Corrado or who knows? Possibly even Urso — if I really needed to. I haven't yet had any chance to evaluate* him. *So far I've been planning to use the youngest brother only to play* defense. *Maybe to aid an escape. But if I could turn Taddeo to go on the offense?* And apparently, by having already tried that once — on his own and on her behalf no less — he'd been sentenced to doing those dishes. So why wouldn't he be motivated to further his rebellion in retribution? Though it hadn't yet proved to be very effective. And there was no way he'd commit patricide or even be ready to take out one of his own brothers. *Yet.* But then there was Corrado Delasandro. Up until now, he and his patron, Greggorio ran the comfort girl services. However, Rinaldo's favoritism he'd always shown his youngest son threatens to take that away from the middle brother and his cousin the great sycophant. So Greg *would* cling to anything that's cause for his significance, since Urso is the eldest, and supposedly predestined to inherit it all, while Taddeo's star was rising. And Corrado followed in Greg's footsteps. Arlene knew she had to very carefully figure out what to do about this one. Greggorio was too far along on his way to unexpectedly becoming the most dangerous adversary she now faced. More so than Rinaldo. So Corrado might also still be an alternate option. Using both *his* apparent interest in her, and likely frustration with holding a lowly position in The Family, might keep Taddeo out of danger as well. There was some part of Arlene which told her that over all the other options, she still really wanted to do that. However, she sensed somebody had really started working hard to split her and the youngest son apart. A dead body recently under her bed told Arlene that. So then why supply Tad with a gun? She couldn't visualize any scenario where he'd use it on her. Who was planning what? There was much tension in The Family. Rinaldo and Greggorio could very well be working to achieve opposite ends. But she would enjoy escalating the competition. First, she had to take inventory of all her promised resources. To do that she needed to make a business trip.

Arlene actually feeling like she'd at last caught up on her sleep, was strangely clear-headed, experiencing real insight, security, and possibly even hope, something which she hadn't felt since she'd first arrived on the wrong shore of the river, what with this particular young man by her side, now. The irony of a Villetti protecting her. And the real possibility of also turning *him* into her weapon. If she had to.

Now reinvigorated by all her ideas, and having woke still hours before the new day dawned, Arlene shed her dreams about escape in the future and arrived back in the reality of the present. She reminded herself that she was only enjoying a fantasy, and not any *real* peace. She needed to get to work to accomplish that. Even after temporarily settling for the false self-assurance that it would be all right with The House if she spent the rest of Friday night with Taddeo, not to mention her entire first week on the South Side of Chicago, and that her safety would not be an issue, her serenity actually then became her new cause for concern. *I know better than this*. Everything in her new life was a lie. But now she was inspired to nurture another lie: making The House turn onto a new route that could see her having actual power over her destiny and create yet *another* new life for herself. They did not know what they'd brought unto themselves by indenturing her. Arlene's latest fantasy thoughts preoccupied her until suddenly, she was up and running down the hallway to their floor's shared bathroom again. This was occurring all too frequently. And she felt like she needed to urinate, but often experienced pain and burning when she tried instead. And any other manner in which she could clear out her system, was also problematic and did not need to be her focus in the present. But Arlene was now acutely worried because of the widespread scare of the spreading influenza epidemic and knowing that in her occupation, she could be especially susceptible to it, and obviously a lot of other uncomfortable things — the worst of which she wouldn't let herself think on. But as long as she was awake, Arlene realized, she could get dressed and use this time to finish her heaving and then steal away in the last hours of the darkness that cloaked her true intentions. Unobserved, and keeping this other new development with her health a secret — as well as the more familiar aspects of her situation — she would finally achieve her errand she'd attempted to complete on Tuesday night. It would be most beneficial to her new change of plans if she did.

Now Arlene had been needing to make a private phone call, but not have it on any record such that it could be tracked down, even lending to a suspicion that it was *she* who made the connection with these specific operatives — who were busying themselves with the ongoing endeavor that was being staged in Louisiana.

When Arlene returned to her room she put on her striped harem pants again and tied them with a ribbon. They were only slightly more common attire for ladies now that they had jobs in the weapons factories, where flowing dresses could be caught on the industrial machinery. Fortunately, from a distance, they allowed her to portray the silhouette of a man, in ill-fitting clothing anyway. She picked out the right hat for her outfit — what had once been Herbert's — from its hiding spot in her clothing stash that she'd been allowed to keep in what used to be Rinaldo's room, and hoped that the disguise might help her attract less attention. Then she collected her hair up and pinned it in underneath, also grabbing a second and very sharp hairpin she might have another need of sooner than later, plus one other very important tool. Then Arlene donned her brown, trench-style overcoat adding a black purse to carry the necessary equipment before she took the elevator down to the ground floor of The Sisson and made her way through the lobby to exit the hotel building.

The central front entrance was deserted at this early hour of the morning, the latest fool The House sent to disturb her probably having gone back to Villetti's to report. Probably. However, Arlene could never be too cautious. But this left both the desk clerk and the nighttime bellhop none too busy and this time they were more than eager to rush to the attractive girl's assistance; Arlene being even much more noticeable than she usually was — in the otherwise emptied lobby. They'd already seen her a few times before and now her unusual dress was a cause for even increased attention. She knew she held all the temptation of some sexy mystery to them. But she waved them off, dismissing both of them, after each had individually offered to escort her, were she intending to leave the premises and venture out onto the streets alone at this hour. *Delasandro or his lackey likely paid them to inform on me. That's what I would have done*. But in the short time since she'd maneuvered it so that she'd been boarded there, Arlene learned her residence at this specific hotel might be very valuable in leading all the necessary people to exactly the assumptions she wanted them to make about her. Especially since they would have by now figured that these immediately neighboring streets no longer belonged to nearly anyone of *her kind*, not even on the *Near* South Side, and considering it would be helpful to her if they'd all recognize exactly who she'd been indentured to. The Italians and the Jews had been moving in.

But the hotel she stayed in was representative of resistance to that situation changing, gentrifying hopefully back to what the Irish would find at least *almost* favorable — and with Jewish money, ironically. At the very least, it kept the niggers out. But Arlene grimaced, remembering how Taddeo had described as *her* real kind —meaning what *else* she'd been forced to become now. What people really did see her as. But for that same reason, her carrying her marked room keys, not to mention a "slave's" necklace ornamented with The Family's crest, could actually prove useful in her defense, since the senior Villetti's name alone would protect her. For the moment anyway. No usual type of random interloper wanted to tangle with the kind of trouble that upsetting Little Italy's local, newly returned, and growing-ever-stronger neighborhood boss would cause them — even this far away from Taylor Street. The guineas presumably paid for this privilege, or the Irish let them have it as part of their larger plan, Old Man Sisson being up to something himself. The Jews could have arranged it, too. All were likely and suspect. But Villetti's goombahs had a long reach. Arlene didn't have complete information — yet. In reality, Villetti was only a soldier — much less important than he thought he was. Her people were almost going to let him destroy himself as it were — and by way of his very own ego — with just a little Luck of the Irish. Their egos would seem to be every Villettis' Achilles' heel, to put it in Greek terms. And Arlene wasn't privy to the whole plan yet — just that she'd receive instructions once she had infiltrated the wops' house. But she just couldn't be patient, obedient or *not* become the catalyst who saw to this happening a lot quicker.

She used the opportunity her family afforded her, to strike out with plans of her own. Rinaldo Villetti and his family were far more important to her — to see planted six feet under — rather than to spy on. She'd make sure she never lost her thoughts about the present over her fantasies about the future, so Arlene stayed vigilant. Hyde Park and Rainbow Shores were seeing serious investing by some prominent Jewish and another, newer Irish interest, that wouldn't tolerate any mischief within their borders — until maybe only after things got settled a little more? Then it'd be back to business-as-usual, she could reasonably predict. Meanwhile, these guineas were still getting away with murder. Or they were only because *she* was now "owned" by one of their houses. What she had to endure to be in position to handle what came next — came at the most-difficult-to-pay of a price. And it was a far more difficult task for her, than anybody else from the North Side Gang had. However, it was one that only she could accomplish. But the feeling in Arlene's purse of a polished extra-smooth grip, a heavy iron cylinder, and short but deadly barrel extending out from its front, also reassured her. The plan — her plan, not her so-called-clan's design — was going almost exactly as she'd planned it, when Arlene first took advantage of this golden opportunity. But there existed nothing golden with how torturous and long seeing the Irish scheme through was. The time it already took was *not* part of what she'd considered, when she volunteered for this job. The young woman hoped that in her heart, she wasn't just imagining the Villettis were running out of time and would not be getting away with everything for very much longer — because she would see to that.

Though her weapon was now a couple of bullets lighter, that fact also let her know she could take care of herself. And that was exactly why she was approved for undertaking this very important mission.

Only now she had a great shot of using her experience to turn the tables even further and use the Villettis to her own end through their naïve and idealistic son, and even possibly Corrado Delasandro. And due to her recent change of fate — that is getting involved with Taddeo — she'd incredibly been even visualizing some scenario where she could become like Madame Moresco. Then Arlene would have real reason to have all of her confidence, for she'd have real power. It would nicely suffice, since real redemption was never going to be within reach. And now, in this rare moment, she would also take advantage of this opportunity to make contact with her real family, and turn the tables even again, so she could use *them* — and through this other assistant they had in place to help themselves, by helping her. The Jew who'd arrived to be the cleanup man had probably already known of this guy's identity. Probably. But he had told her of another *on the South Side*. She didn't yet know who *that* was. Some flower? She couldn't figure. Still Arlene could now make good use of this known man she currently went to see at his safe house, a lot further *to the north* of Little Italy, and alongside of whomever the Jew had referred to. Though she did really need to find out who the South Side plant actually was and meet with *him*, as well. But her main objective had always been singularly more important than her true family's one. And that she still needed to accomplish on her own. She just finally felt ready to do all of it now. And it was time to collect from all her provided resources as well as use her newly developed ones. She didn't really have any other choice since she felt certain Greggorio, and likely his father, had discovered who she really was, and had begun probing her, testing her for weaknesses and measuring her resolve. Obviously they were willing to sacrifice two men's lives already to accomplish that. She couldn't blame them really. It was their lives that were on the line if she caught all of Rinaldo and his older sons together at the same time, somewhere private where she could give them all of her most intimate attention in what was Arlene's true signature style — one and only one final time.

But the timing of her real family's plan was not turning out to be such that it was anything but very inconcenient for her, and now she couldn't wait for the execution of it to begin. Everything that had started happening had left her anxious, angry, impatient — now sick — and if she would only be honest with herself at least, frightened.

So in her present state of mind, and the still of the night in which she walked, Arlene found her immediate circumstance conducive to giving her greater situation, and that very personal mission she was actually on, plenty of uninterrupted thought. It was not for the first time she explored the conclusion that she might no longer have to sacrifice her own life for her clan and especially her private vengeance. She actually could have cared less about what her real family's objectives were but had used the opportunity presented by undertaking this mission, to achieve her own ends. Now in her hands she turned the Villetti Family shield — a simulated jeweled "v-crest" — on her prisoner's chain. Unfortunately, and as now possibly painful as it would be, she could even sacrifice Taddeo for the sake of her mission. That had been part of the original plan anyway — before she'd gotten to know him better. She'd hesitated because the young man had somehow managed to engender very real feelings for him on Arlene's part. But she could not allow herself to be locked deeper in his father's prison on account of that. The Family knew where she stayed — they thought they'd been the ones to arrange it after all — and delaying making her move against the Villetti House *even for this long* wasn't at all part of the original instructions she'd received anyway. Or at least not part of her original expectations going into the operation. She had other tasks she still hadn't completed, too. Their successful completion would probably be required if she wanted her money she was owed from her relatives. And she still didn't know exactly what all this particular job entailed. The payoff had originally never been a part of her personal consideration. She wouldn't need it since she thought she'd be dead. However, she'd been forced to take her position in this plot far earlier than was convenient for her. And there had not yet come the opportunity that she really pined for, only one inconvenience after another for four nights now. Though Taddeo was a nice diversion, so at least she found some pleasure in the acceptance of her fate. She'd reflexively played defense. Arlene needed to take the offense. Only now, and for that first time, Arlene sensed there could also be a very real chance at survival. She'd gained greater inside help than she'd ever thought possible *through Tad* ironically, and potentially had a new safe house in which to stay at the laundry, since she'd make use of her new lover's total devotion to protecting her.

Though sadly, Taddeo *would* quite likely have to die for that, after all. His family — though most likely Greggorio acting on his own — would be suspect to setting *that* up. After he received a really good beat-down. Arlene was now aware she moved against one very keen operator in Tad's middle brother. He was adept at manipulating things from the other side, from the shadows — and he had great cause for motivation: himself, his rise to power. So she had to be really cautious now, but she did have other agents, already in place who would definitely help her deal with her new offense, much more so than Greg's inept little brother. They should have been instructed to obey her. And the best part? Greggorio didn't suspect *that* part of it. She made her way to contact in-person, one of those allies now.

Along the journey, Arlene tried to rationalize this conclusion she'd come to. Her mind was as sharply focused as were the jolts that vibrated up her calves to her kneecaps as her heels impacted with the new cement upon every step on the path. Arlene could not wait until she was far enough along that she could hail a taxi — if any were operating at this hour. *I should not have worn these shoes*. But her thoughts kept on more important matters. There was no denial that Tad was changing — the blunt, cursive language he used now in the new way in which he spoke to her; his own rising confidence; the methodical processes his mind had now begun plotting and scheming with — and against *his own family*, of all people. They'd begun to stress him as well as her. The irony was that Taddeo was becoming a true Villetti and he didn't even know it. It was in his nature, she reminded herself. He journeyed toward a predetermined destination. The young man could eventually become very dangerous. And nothing would change that, but Arlene could use it, before eventually she could hate being forced to put a permanent end to it. And that was something she sensed she'd strongly regret doing for some reason — which for the moment, still alluded her. She pressed on, but had begun really feeling sick to her stomach again.

Now the streets near Grand Boulevard were almost deserted save for a lone police officer she observed, sliding his hand up and down the length of his nightstick. A man in a heavy, long blue coat and peaked hat walked along the opposite side of East 43rd Street and nodded as he saw Arlene through the drifting fog when she passed by a streetlight. But an Irish copper in this part of the city would not interfere with *her*, unless *he also* cared to proposition her. But he'd be safest having gained permission first. Not that it was even heard of Villetti girls being bargained for on the boulevards, outside of and far from the control of The House. That wasn't Rinaldo's or Colosimo's style of operation. Madame Moresco wouldn't allow it. But this patrol route's personnel were recently paid all too well to not interfere with Villetti business however it manifested itself, and Arlene was relieved that this copper just assumed her relationship with The House, given her location, likely occupation, and thus he did not interfere. If he even recognized her gender, considering how she had dressed. No matter the case, as they were paid to also be enforcers for the Italians, the Irish coppers on the South Side sold out their loyalty to their own race. There was still just too many of their numbers for all of them to make a good living. So their true blue allegiance was to a green shade in their wallets. However, as a gesture of chivalry, and were she unfortunately of need of it, they just might offer Arlene some unintended but hopefully effective protection. As did her gun, a different kind of family crest marking its polished handle. But there should still exist some ways that Irish helped fellow Irish people because they always had to in order to make it in this new land that was being built up as these United States of America. Because the ways of the Old World always applied as usual. And since the Irish were no longer the newcomers, they had to defend what little was now their own. So Arlene was truly learning how to use *what* — and when. But she couldn't wait until she'd walked far enough so that she could use a cab once she got to Pine Street. That trip proved short and sweet, as she only risked anyone being able to identify her as last being seen just south of Wacker, and she thought she'd disappeared with no trace of her even getting this far from Hyde Park. Arlene hoped.

She ditched her cab when she got close to the North Branch of the Chicago River. Nevertheless, certain she was being a smooth operator, she lit a smoke as a creature comfort her pride told her she'd be entitled to, but Arlene didn't have time but to take barely a few puffs before she hurried to discard it. She suddenly realized the lit ember would mark her. The calming buzz might've helped her stress level. Only it didn't. She needed to fully disappear in the darkness again. Only now it could be too late.

Arlene had to immediately make good time and cross many more darkened blocks, making an inconvenient detour to avoid anyone following her. She couldn't be certain that her cab trip had even conclusively eliminated that possibility. Her adversaries were good and these streets were owned by Little Italy or *their* kike allies. Longing for another cigarette, the young woman wouldn't dare light the next one only to reveal her location. But just as she had that thought, her perceptiveness let her become aware of a shadow that did indeed follow her. She wasn't safe. A glance behind her and a flutter in her backlighting from the new street lamps. *How is it I am* still *being followed?* So she even crossed the waterway on the Rush Street Bridge, then went back and over it once again — and through the ongoing construction of the Marquette-Jolliet crossing, to use no less than two different bridges spanning the Chicago River — and too much time. She was really feeling ill, and furious on top of it. And her remaining level of patience was not good. Twice, her foot and even her whole lower leg fell through temporarily placed boards, ineffectively secured, only meant for the use by the workers in the daylight. Each time she lost her breath and felt her heart skip a beat as she'd see a dangerously closer view of the black river come up beneath her. Yet her small hands would clutch at anything that could stop her fall. Successful, though cut and bruised, she refused to cry out and once more mark her position. Only wearing pants rather than a dress, helped to somewhat protect her. But with visibility on the streets at its poorest, and encumbered by more mist floating in quite an impressive distance from the Great Lake, she appeared and disappeared like a wraith. So too did her stalker. But in her hand, manifested Arlene's gun.

Shapes moved in and out of the mist, between the steel construction pylons. They darted back and forth, their motion but a flicker, though inconveniently accompanied by the rapid click of some heels. So it quickly occurred to Arlene to remove her shoes. Regretfully, she tossed them away. They didn't go with her pants anyway. Then her shadow's *target* having grown suddenly silent, caused it to move erratically, hurriedly stepping up its pursuit. Fearful it lost her trail. It would appear then disappear and reappear. So quickly that Arlene grew frightened there might have been more than one. Then once more, back and across over the river, another bridge, Columbus this time, and then suddenly a shape manifested itself much closer. The clearest a target might get. Then there was another flash in the middle of the night. And with the bright light, came the sound of thunder. Only Arlene missed! Her quarry she'd turned the tables on, the hunter that became the hunted, now became the defensive.

The shot was so loud and the night so silent that it echoed back to and fro off the buildings on either side of the river. Another flutter of the backlighting, of the kind that could have been made by a long coat. Then one or more pursuers were suddenly all too close upon her and a new shot rang out! Arlene heard a whizzing noise as the bullet strafed past her ear. Someone determined *they* were going to kill her! She had fired on her enemies first — several times now — with most deadly results in the recent past. Somebody had now decided they were done tolerating her, indeed. So she instinctively dropped low into a crouch and fired back where she'd seen her opponent's muzzle flash through the drifting haze. This was followed by another gun discharging, probably as a reflex, and then succeeded by a muffled squelch — and then a splash!

It was all over in seconds. Maybe. Somewhere in the darkness of the sleeping city, a dog started barking, and others of its kind answered it. And with the night awakening to this symphony of disharmony, Arlene had finally just about reached the end of her disconcerting journey. She countered and triumphed in one more contest and then instantly disappeared like a ghost into the black once again, only to soon reappear in The Loop, get another cab, and then finally cross into the Irish-controlled part of town belonging to the Near North Side, where she started heading west, all now on bare feet. But her journey was taking too long — and too much ammunition. She worried Taddeo could discover her missing. *It must already be past 4 o'clock in the morning*. He should have gotten up and headed over to the lounge to start the accounting before the new day's reopening. And it could only be less than a couple hours before someone discovered the latest body left in Chicago's bloody waters, absent even a barrel to carry this one to Hades. Yet she assured herself there was little Tad would want to say or do about that if he even noticed she'd been gone anyway. They'd been through enough fighting with each other already the previous day. And he was supposed to have only taken a nap and then left to close out the earnings of the comfort girls over at the bordello. If Taddeo woke to find her gone, he'd know that she knew he'd neglected fulfilling his half of their partnership. He'd be right in assuming he'd want to avoid any confrontation with her, over *who* was supposed to be doing *what*. He *really did* want to avoid any confrontation with her. But he might even assume that's where she went — to the lounge to start her new work in his place, perhaps so he could focus on baseball. Like that was ever a challenge for him. But her absence might at least motivate him to try and track her down over there — where he was supposed to be in the first place. Like she cared to do anything that way. Arlene could get more money in her own way that she pursued right now. And with it, she wouldn't need to rely on the skim off those dagos. And she actually doubted *hers* would wake up, as she was getting to know Taddeo pretty well by now. But she knew she'd better go over there soon. Tad *was* offering her a good opportunity. And at that point, she might be able to learn to use and employ poison as an alternative. Though that wasn't in her skill set. But Arlene really had enough of gun battles, having been involved in three new shootings already, when it was her assignment over there that was supposed to be keeping the peace in the first place. At least until Arlene could actually manage to kill who she went there to bring her vengeance down upon from the very start. This mission was becoming ridiculously complicated.

Now even as cold as it was being out in the dark, her blouse stuck to her back as Arlene sweated from her state of increasing hurry. She also felt more fatigued and even winded, compared to her accustomed state of youthful fitness. Or was all of this the after-effect of having survived her first gunfight with an actual exchange of fire? Was it too soon to feel some form of post-traumatic stress? Her head was throbbing. At least she found she had decent aim with her weapon. She wasn't out of practice. But Arlene really wished she could've now affected her situation by finding herself a bicycle and made use of that instead. She could have even stolen one from a child in a single heartbeat. It might have saved her nearly two hours, at this point. But at long last, after another taxi ride and some more walking, Arlene finally turned on West Armitage Street to head up North Larrabee, which *was* actually lit around a park by the new Westinghouse electric lamps, even though now the sky had lightened anyway as the predawn hour arrived. And the housing had turned to the single-family, detached styles, inclusive of even small yards and gardens now, each separated by narrow alleys. Arlene proceeded along until arriving in Lincolnwood upon the street number where over a week ago she'd been told her contact was being offered his temporary boarding by a mutual friend of theirs. She waited impatiently after having softly knocked on the front door. There was no answer. Frustrated, overheated, and short of breath, Arlene knocked once more. Louder. She was going to recheck the address when suddenly she felt nauseous and was throwing up over the stair railing before she even knew it. That's when through the corner of her eye and a triad of glass panes arranged toward the top of the door, she viewed an oil-burning lantern being turned up and then proceeding to sink lower in her view as it would if someone was carrying it down a flight of stairs. The lantern all but disappeared, but the lighting behind the windows intensified as the one bearing the lantern drew closer and the release of a latch allowed the door to open to admit her.

"Be quiet. You'll wake my wife and you're the last person for whom I want to answer a cross-examination about — especially from her." Before Arlene stood William J. Fallon esq., in his nightshirt. He had brown hair he kept short, yet long enough for some waves in it that framed his youthful face, with the further appearance of sharp edges to it by his squared eyebrows. His ears were positioned so they began beneath his eyes, and were more parallel with the frown he wore upon seeing it was her. Arlene did not let herself look either surprised, or happy to see him. But she was — surprised, though not happy.

"Well hello Bill, you smart man, you. You brought your wife here?" Arlene said pretending that's what factored in her disbelief.

"To protect her, My Lady," this particular lawyer who she had in truth, really not expected to find there, said with his old and familiar East Coast-altered Celtic accent. "I guess. Actually, an associate from New York collected her and escorted her all the way out to meet me here shortly after I arrived. I had no idea that when I agreed to this job, that she'd be coming along, too. They said they preferred doing business with *a family man*, but it's no secret that I'm not to be trusted. I'm Irish after all." He laughed, then came clean. "They have pictures of me in a compromising position."

Arlene's eyes narrowed. *That's really* not *a surprise*.

Fallon went on. "And they actually told the wife that *I* sent for her — to come to Chicago. Incredible. Since I would certainly never do that. Not to come here. But like I said, I wanted — ."

"No questions from the misses," Arlene interrupted. "So who were *they*?"

"They are not people who you need to wonder about, Lass. But now the new and latest mystery asks what the bloody hell are *you* doing here? And throwing up on my porch, on top of it all?"

"Well, maybe 'cause it's that I think that scum like you *deserve to live in a toilet*? But oh — uh — never mind. I'm sorry about your porch. Actually, no. I'm not. However though, as I have no longer any need of your ass-can Bill, I do need to use your telephone. And quickly."

"Right now? And you came here all the way from Grand Crossing or somewhere south of hell for that? To make a bloody phone call?"

"I have a better reason than that."

"God, what if the dagos know where I live now? Where my wife is?"

"Look. I had to deal with a lot just to get here. But I even took two different taxis once I was back on the North Side."

"Sorry, they didn't tell me where you were living. Just *not* in Little Italy everyone imagined. It's you, after all. Yeah, I am sorry about that, but you usually like to do things *your way*."

"Well, I am staying on Rainbow Beach for now, actually."

"So by the damned Queen. What the frack *did* you come all the way here for?"

"I missed you. Or not that either. Maybe I need to call Louisiana, you dumb shit," Arlene revealed. "Did you hear me just explain that? And no, *I don't need to be compromised. This*, is no one else's business."

"Oh? *You* really did cross this whole damned town to make a single phone call? And who are you calling 'the dummy?' What do you really want from me? Or you just wanted to meet your handler and threaten to drag him down with you when you make more demands our people might not find reasonable to meet. Good luck with that. And you're going to need to be lucky if someone's awake at the switchboard at either end. I mean at this hour."

"You are an idiot. Someone has to answer emergencies."

"And calling *him* from here is dangerous. Don't *you* think, Lass? Or don't you think? Must be too difficult for a woman, huh?"

"Well maybe you would stop to think that maybe this could be an emergency?"

"Yeah? Well the guineas will instantly suspect *me* once I introduce myself. You know they're not too fond of the Irish, my precious. And they, *would be awake*. And following you here I imagine? Now thanks to you, my role might be discovered even before I have the opportunity to sit down with Villetti, Colosimo's other representatives, and their new Jewish bosses to play my part. I don't need anyone looking into *my business*."

"You're too funny, Darling," Arlene said, though her serious expression indicated she was not the least bit amused. "I'm not that sloppy. No one followed me. No one still living to breath a word about *where I went* anyway. And I've not gotten stupid. Just sick. Probably from all this crap our people have me dealing with. But I purposely didn't hire transportation until I crossed the bridge and I doubled back on my route just to make sure I was always alone. Plus I am not even sure these goombahs are smart enough to investigate *you* that thoroughly — even when they do make your acquaintance. To play your part in exactly what? They don't really tell me everything. But the dagos checking with the switchboard operators over your telephone activity? I don't think so. Especially not this early. They have yet to even meet or hear of you, don't know where you're staying, probably don't have the means or yet the cause to pay folks working for the phone company over here on the North Side, and finally they haven't even discovered you to be as big of a dick as I know you really are. You haven't even offered me a cigarette. But I guess *I* am making sure that you'll back my play if you've actually got as much at stake in this game as I do, Bill. Now I know where exactly *who* lives."

"Did you just threaten me?"

"You know, I'll come clean. I did not know for sure who I was meeting with — I just had an address for an ally — but I should have suspected that *you* would be the help our family sent to assist me."

"I volunteered."

"You saw an opportunity. So do you still like your wife? Or how about a kiss? For old time's sake. You have no idea what it takes out of me to play my part in the clan's *big operation* here. Now your *latest* arm trophy will be just another one of us who are among the all too many at risk in this business — unfortunately for her, I suppose. But I don't really care."

"I love my wife."

"I'm sure. I'd bet she really has no clue about you Bill, but she must have had *some* dowry. You got married after all. Still honor that old tradition? Well, never mind. Like I said, I could care less anyway. But just get the hell out of my way so I can make that call," Arlene growled at him. "Please," she added to be polite, but came off thoroughly sounding insincere anyway. Then, not waiting for an answer. She pushed past the attorney and forced her entry into

Fallon's fashionably upscale, furnished, and cozy abode.

In close to pitch black, Arlene still found the telephone on a stand against the wall near the staircase up to the family resting level of the attorney's temporary lodging place. Not everyone was asleep in the dark. "Operator: connect me with the Rectory. Saint Alphonsus, Lafayette, down by New Orleans."

("Connecting.")

["Saint Alphonsus?"]

("I apologize for the time, Sir. I have a call here from —?")

"Information about the red velvet you ordered," Arlene offered.

["Go ahead,"] one of the voices on the other end of the line said.

"Hello, Cousin."

["Arlene."]

She waited listening intently for a click indicating the operator was no longer on the line. "I'm in. Most things are going as planned. I've had to take care of a few surprises though."

["Take care of them quietly until you get me all my information I need from the wops."]

"Easy for you to order when it's not your ass that's left unprotected."

["Our family needs to monitor this new deal we're progressing and Fallon can't do this by himself. He won't have the kind of access you do with the Villetti Family. Living day-to-day with them."]

"You mean access to pillow talk."

["I can't help that Arlene. And you volunteered for this mission. You can achieve what no other Irish there can."]

"Gathering more secrets for this collection of my own wonderful family's?"

["I can see where you're going with that. Why do you want to rehash this again and again? We were children. Isolated, alienated, and inexperienced — ."]

"And brutal. On my ass again. Just like another family I'm spying on. Or don't you and Cousin Bill here get the comparison? Such irony that I'm reaching you in a church while we're talking about *this*. You *can* see all the reminders that you're still on a path straight to hell — and right in front of you? Huh?"

["I see an opportunity for an orphan girl *in this day and age* to achieve all she ever wanted. And that's rare. The road to fulfillment's not without its sacrifices, but it's a lot faster of path than the one the suffragettes will take. And to a dream that's more real and more meaningful to you and your family, which we must advance forward before any kind of other multicultural collective community, or some other such idealistic new concept-of-America-crap. Freedom to make that choice, is the difference between being born in America instead of say somewhere like Russia. But we *are* born here and never agreed to give our livelihood, nor our blood and hard-won soil away to these guinea immigrants. That's on the politicians, and the shylocks bankrolling them. So this *collection* we are gathering, is one for the repayment of *new* debts. A lot of new debts."]

"And some very old ones. But I'm just so sure we are *all* really pursuing the American dream now — and that all of your multiculturalists are, too. But the new arrivals aren't content to wait for their time. The Italians brought their war here instead. And our people accommodated them with their itch for a good fight. But how come I don't see the Russians turning on their own relatives when parents are no longer alive to protect their children?"

["Arlene, let it go already. And you'd be surprised what the stirrings of revolution have caused to have happened over there. You wouldn't believe the changes."]

"Well, I've actually been surprised just by what's happening with our people in Chicago. I don't have the kind of time you obviously do to follow every current event, but I'm inclined to believe something even more alarming is about to happen. I've learned firsthand — and by a few more hands — which tried to run all over *me* by the way, that it's the Jews who are now the ones most likely plotting to arrange a new, bigger, and better managed *peace* between *all* the families. Including ours. And our fellow Irishmen are selling out. For exactly what purpose I haven't determined."

["That's not your concern."]

"It has to be money of course." Arlene found herself a clear path to twist this conversation on to her first priority. "Except for a few minor incidents, that the Villettis could blame *me* for — if they only knew — I've witnessed the Jews willing to help cover up and smooth over anything that might disrupt their goals — whatever they are — and shatter the fragile peace. The Villetti boy, the baseball player, even confirmed it."

["I'm aware of what's happening."]

"I know you are. That must have been expensive. I mean even Henry Ford's writing a whole anthology to ponder. But we're selling out to the hymies, now?"

["There's about to be quite a financial consideration in it for us, too. If we play this game right. It is your mission to help make sure our family gains more than just knowledge to ponder over. So you won't make your big and final move that I know you want to make until you can tell me everything that needs be known so that Irish interests come out ahead on that deal. For being loyal to your people is something that I know you are also not."]

"Really? For me, being loyal to my true family is what this is all about. But I really don't care what you think about me. Only what deal? What are you talking about? Though I'm willing to bet who you really mean by *our people* is O'Sullivan? Right? Aren't you working with him? That would explain what you need Bill for. So is this about gambling again?"

The voice on the other end of the line ignored her question. ["Because I'm sure that it's a safe bet that anything that's to *our* benefit is *not* what the dagos want out of this. Betrayal is planned if not for one season, than another. The Jew, Rothstein, is manipulating them, to his ends of course. It's a double-cross most likely. Counting us, a triple-cross. We just have to be smart enough so that we can cross them first, and then cross everyone again — last. Meanwhile, yes Mister Big and Sporting Joe *are* at it again, to simply answer your question. But we need to beat those shylocks and their wop allies at their own game. *And Sullivan*. He's Irish, but he's not *our* family's concern. He's out for himself. Though I know what you're really after, too. Have known all along. You and Joe have much in common. But you're too obvious and you cannot control your anger. So again I stress patience."]

"Why can't Bill — ?"

["Your cousin Fallon is there to be a facilitator. An important player at the table who will be less disruptive and garner a lot less animosity than Dean O'Banion, Hymie Weiss, or a heavy hand like his pet Moran, who has to be kept on a short leash for this Jewish part of the plan to even work. We actually need it to. We need the money I suspect it's gonna yield."] On the other end of the line Arlene could hear her cousin sigh. ["You know? All right. If it helps any, I'll explain the plan to you. It's all this money. We don't need it anywhere near Chicago — or New York — or Sullivan, if that isn't obvious. We don't give a damn about Sullivan like he doesn't really care about us. And the dagos will be the ones moving this load — one huge ton of cash, too. Yes, from gambling proceeds."]

"How original."

["Fallon is there to promote the appeal of our *neutral*

philanthropy in Louisiana. Our cousin understands the intricate legal aspects in the mechanics of this. And he works with Rothstein, who will never be privy to our angle in this, but we need him to goad Sullivan. He brings in our other Irish friends because O'Banion wants Sully investing with him — as does Kenna and Coughlin, not to mention Thompson, who is by now feeling the pressure to need it — and that's also the pressure the Jews can supply through Annenberg. This is simply the elites wanting to protect their bookies, information about who they are and what vices the members of that social club are guilty of, keeping up their public image, and also — of course — laundering their money. But no one with an Irish name will be fronting any of this — as the face for this plan — to stave off natural suspicions."]

"Because we're still suspect in our own fucking country. So who then will be collecting it?" Arlene was curious. "The Jews?" She was also suspicious.

["The Italians. But they won't be keeping it. We only agreed to that bullshit for very specific reasons. It brought them aboard, eliminated competition, and even further and greatly expanded the pot. But you don't need to know everything. You'll pick up most of the details on your reconnaissance mission as it is if you'll just play your role. I just need to know exactly how they'll move it."]

"Yes. I'm sure you do. And while I've had no say in the matter you've already factored in on just how I can earn a little for my subsistence — and not the easy way. So maybe I'll also pick up my own financial share of this, too. And first. Didn't it ever occur to you that I might need more resources? Where and when will I find *my* money?"

["The most important part of your assignment is to find out if the Italians honestly go for the greater plan. You can't rob a bank before it actually exists. But the important part to all of this is the guineas go bankrupt and we even take the shylocks' money and actually with many thanks to you, we make it look like the wops did it. Then our family should have plenty to pay you with."]

Arlene swallowed as she concluded her conversation with her cousin in New Orleans by reminding him that few people went for anything *honestly* anyway, and then got off the phone. This really wasn't her business. Her family's objectives were only a means to her own. But she was nervous that their resources would not be there to support her when she needed them the most — namely when Arlene moved to achieve *her* objective — *if* she didn't fulfill the mission her clan originally sent her there on first. Actually, she now suspected — no feared — they didn't have any money. That's why they were so desperate for Rothstein's and even Sullivan's. Her own blood even plotted to also betray the Irish Mob. She quickly regained her composure by reminding herself that she'd attained some new options via the weaknesses she'd uncovered in the Villettis so that she might not have to either die for her vengeance, or even make a hasty escape under fire. She could still get money and she just might be able to stand her ground. But Arlene was very afraid that now something quite life-changing might've happened, which limited some other options she once could have taken. This once was a suicide mission. But she'd reconsidered. Fortunately, Fallon didn't notice her reservation. She ordered him to call her a taxi. "I'll just have him take me near the bridge by Wabash. I'll cross by foot myself. No witnesses. No shoes either." She pointed at her bare feet, only now realizing her skin was torn and probably bled under her heels — and they hurt. "But the taxi will help me make up for some lost time." She put out her hand.

Bill laughed. "What do you expect me to give you?"

"Cab fare. Enough for at least two rides. Now. And without any shit."

"As if I carry that in my nightshirt."

"Smells like it."

"Wait a minute."

"And I need I need to change my appearance again. Give me one of your coats, hats, and a scarf. And how about some shoes?"

"Why don't you just take my heart?"

"As if you had one. But as you did just make a point of it, you're not wearing your coat, hat, and scarf right now, so I've concluded you obviously don't need them. Bring them to me, also. Immediately."

"I said, 'wait here.' " He disappeared for a moment and then returned with everything Arlene required. "Rob me. Why don't you? A thief in the night. Looks like you've become the perfect South Side girl. That fits right in for your cover."

"That's right. I want my money. And you're the one to lecture about morals when it comes to regarding burglary? While you plot your heist? I'm actually disappointed your grand scheme all boils down to common robbery. Seriously. That's lame. That's just — very lame."

"It's the motherlode. Besides, no one asked for your approval."

"Just my cooperation. But aren't you the motherlode of crap? And lameness. And anyway, my currently evolving nurture beats out my old nature. So do you like the new me?"

"No. Not at all. And you had something of a bad nature in you to begin with already. Burn this stuff when you get close enough." William Fallon nodded at the expensive clothes he presented to her. "I don't want anyone catching you with it. So don't sell these threads, either. Now get out of here. I'll be across the river in an official capacity soon. Remember, you don't know me. But then I can be of more help. Now please don't come here and disturb me in my home. I can't take the chance of who might follow you."

Arlene reached into her purse and pulled on an object inside just high enough to expose the gun handle. "Then they'd be following me right into my fire. You better hope you don't find yourself there as well. I've gotten quite good at my game. I'm so ready to bring the hammer down on all of this. You better never *ever* test *me*."

Chapter 21

The third taxi Arlene had to take to return her from her forte on the North Side pulled up to a new cement curb that was built before the front entrance to The Sisson. It was almost at daybreak but still dark enough for the young woman's disguise to work so she did not stand out a lot as she disembarked the vehicle. She'd be extra relieved if only she would find she'd returned before Taddeo's customary late-to-rise routine that she'd quickly become acquainted with. Less questions that way. Of course, that would mean he hadn't accomplished anything by way of managing the bordello. Keeping up his consistency. But the whole reason she went to contact Louisiana from Fallon's was to test her own family's reliability. Arlene didn't expect Taddeo to change. She only hoped her own family's participatory cooperation, would rate better. It also was not off to a good start. But for now, she'd keep their secrets. So as a precaution, she'd changed out of Fallon's clothes in an alleyway between cab rides, burning the most obvious among the rich clothes inside a trash barrel as he suggested. They'd be too easily seen and suggest that because *she* had them, she was someone else. And then Arlene re-dressed in her former clothing, became the poor orphan girl living the brutal life of an entertainer, once again.

However, she groaned when she spotted Corrado Delasandro leaning against the building just beyond the door, probably entertaining all the ideas he'd come up with for how he'd like to be entertained by her. He immediately recognized her. And now he was stalking her? It hadn't been even a week and she was sick of all of them from The House already, so she didn't waste any time hitting him *first* — with a full frontal assault. He'd earned it with this maneuver. As had the others who'd stalked her, earned worse. She'd killed them for even trying it. She had to.

Presently, and while low on ammunition to deal with the Villettis, Arlene opted to just insult their cousin but maintain his interest in her, since that still could be very useful. "Well hello there, 'Daddy.' Or my big Daddy-wannabe. Aww. You aren't still waiting up all night for your little girl to come home, are you? Or are they *making* you do this? Poor thing. They never let you sleep. And I know it gets pretty chilly out here. Maybe you'd have more fun if next time I invite you in — *to my room* — if you'd like to *watch* — me — and Taddeo — *you-know*." Arlene offered a fake smile which she over-exaggerated on purpose.

"What you were about wasn't just with Taddeo, Lady. Instead, what you *are* is something else. But whoops. Nah. Actually, I'm sorry. I was wrong about that. My mistake. One thing you ain't ever are, is a lady."

"Is that what you are hoping for?" Arlene kept up with a counterattack. "Oh, I didn't know *this* about you. Or are you just jealous, Nancy?"

"That's real funny. It's Corry. And no way, Sister. I ain't jealous — of *this* fucking nightlife."

"Oh no, Dear. I meant jealous of me? Of my body." She ran her hands down from high up on her chest over her breasts and down her tight midriff over which she pulled her shirt tight upon, displaying her fit form with all its curves and tempting Corrado so that she might be able to manipulate him for her own use later. She'd already discarded her cousin's menswear. A hobo who may have succeeded in rescuing it from her fire might wear it now. If he could put out her fire. Good luck with that. No one could put out her fire. But Corry was in her *line of fire*, in this very moment. "You're jealous of what *you'll* never have. But you know, maybe that's not true. I do have some hair trimming shears in my room upstairs. I'll go and get you so excited, it will warm you up and then I can more easily and permanently fix this problem for you — so you'll enjoy life on the receiving side, *just* like I do — if you'd only give a little girl the opportunity."

He snorted. "All you need to give me is an address of where you just were," he said. "And that's all you're gonna do."

"I'm sure you're keenly aware that thus far, I've never given *you* anything, Corrado Delasandro. And I'm not about to start. I'd just guess you must rank pretty low on The Family's most-entitled roster. Else you wouldn't be *here*. And I would ask you to wipe that scowl off your poor sullen face, but you have to ask *a Villetti* for permission before you even do that. Don't you, Darling?" She blew him a kiss.

Just then Arlene heard a laugh come from somewhere in the building's shadows. "Well, fortunately Corrado knows the Villettis are his *true* family, and I'm always around, backing him up and making sure that Family members *are* well-looked-after. And I can't wait to learn if that's what will really make *you* happy, Arlene. After all, now *you belong* to this family, too." She shuddered as she recognized a voice reaching out to her from the dark. "But it really does chill one to the bones out here. Looking after you properly indeed has its challenges. Why don't we curb that tendency of yours to offer a cold shoulder and let's go inside the hotel and discuss it.

"I can feel the humidity's disappeared for the moment after that rain we got Friday. There's no water in the air about to piss on us again, for the time being — so what I've sensed — must be blood. I wish I could say I was happy about that, but there's an unexpected coldness coming down upon Chicago now. Cold-bloodedness. We need to discuss it while we warm things up maybe in a way that will make Mister Delasandro here very happy, as well?" Greggorio Villetti stepped into the front entranceway's light.

The young woman hoped she'd suppressed that involuntary gulp she couldn't control herself from taking. No such luck. "Yes, well Taddeo *Villetti* should be along to *look after me*, shortly," she noted aloud for the other men's consideration. "Perhaps we will get his opinion on the weather, too. How much the highlight of everyone's night would that be? Though I hope he was performing for the success of the local girls' show for a while longer. You know, for all the girls that are working for The Family. But neither of us knew we still had to check in with you, Greggorio. Or I'm sure *I* would have been looking forward to that *all night*. But we were both otherwise occupied as it were."

"I bet."

The three walked into the hotel lobby and the sneering middle brother motioned to Arlene to take a seat on a cushioned recliner. He and Corry walked around a coffee table to take seats next to each other on another couch, positioned facing hers. But the next voice in the conversation came at them sideways. "Yes, in fact all the Villetti brothers are here to look after The Family's best interests." The elevator doors were open and Urso Villetti, having also overheard the conversation with Arlene, stepped out of the carriage — with another one of the working girls he had just been playing with. She wore a black dress. She appeared to be drunk. And she was unfamiliar. Or was she?

"My. I could carve a turkey," Arlene said. "Everyone's here gathering for the roast."

"Ha." Greggorio found the young woman's comment amusing. "Is that what's going on? I mean I'm just trying to figure out the plan for a future myself."

"Don't try and figure too hard, Greg. You'll be disappointed when you can't reach up to even your own limited expectations."

"Well now, hasn't our girl been busy? Both talking and walking — a bit too much, I might add." Corrado remarked. "And expecting *something* to come of it. Isn't that right?"

"And not yet saying anything that *I* want to hear. But I wish *you* could share more of your wonderful insight with us Corry, yet you actually lost touch with Arlene earlier tonight. You did, didn't you?" Greg narrowed his eyes and continued. "Yes, you failed at such a basic duty as to keep a lady of our Family *safe*, and escort her through this still most dangerous city."

"Aww. Such missed opportunities to do so much good. But why would it be dangerous at all if you have gentlemen out there at all hours of the night ensuring your family's street's security, Greg? There wouldn't be a *new threat* or something? You *have* achieved control, haven't you, Darling?"

"Wait. Shut up a minute, Woman. Were *you* following *me*?" Corry asked his patron.

Greggorio sniffed and then completely ignored him.

Haha, thought Arlene. *My little game of switchback I played on the bridges lost* both *of them, plus the guy I sent down the river. It is an exercise in futility to try and follow me.*

"Well *you,* Arlene — you should know better than to go running around, especially at night, unescorted by a gentleman from our house."

"It sounds like I'm to be kept as a shut-in. A prisoner. That was never part of the deal. But how could *I* ever be sure? The only thing I can really guarantee you is that your father didn't welcome me in for my intelligence."

"Yes, well unfortunately, I'm growing concerned that he should not have overlooked *that* wonderful feature about you, Arlene."

"So will you be inviting the old man to our little reunion here? The Sisson has just the right facilities to prepare a feast." Indeed, this hotel being Irish-owned, with Jewish financing, there might be a good chance the staff could be ordered to assist with burying all the Villettis here. "It being early enough, I'll have time to carve the meat," Arlene forced a smile upon Greg. That would be a fitting way to do it to also reap revenge on behalf of the Irish butcher that Urso beat up — not that she really cared. However, Greg still wouldn't even blink when he regarded her. *He's pretty confident*. But he did unbutton his jacket and rested his hand inside of it, his eyes narrowing as Arlene brought hers to rest on top of her open purse. *But I know I only have two bullets left. Does he? Now I could take Greggorio and Urso, but what would Corrado do? And exactly what role was being played by the new woman in the black dress? I now think I can recollect* her *from a meeting about a week ago, in East Chicago — which was actually out-of-state and really in western Indiana. Definitely out of The Outfit's territory. Rinaldo had dragged me there on an unscheduled stop on his return to Chicago from New York City. He was secretly meeting with Sam Cardinelli, away from any chance of Colosimo's learning of it, and before I'd ever met any of Villetti's charming offspring. I had been witness to the eldest of my enemies deciding to curb his interest in me for only the briefest respite, and take up with this new lady of the night. That's where I've seen her. He surprised me too, after Villetti was so interested in acquiring me Back East. He had an unexpectedly strong libido. But then it was at the stopover in Indiana when I was passed a note to give to Rinaldo. It had been from his son, Greggorio. He was supposed to call him in Chicago. I hadn't met Greg at that point, and it made no impression on me.*

In fact, despite that I had not met any *of the Villetti brothers at that time, I'd already discerned there was tension in The Family. I could hear Greg raise his voice through the earpiece Rinaldo held as he attempted to force me close to him, later when he'd finished with this other woman. Over the telephone, the son had asserted in one of his frequent "advisory" conversations with Rinaldo, that* I *might be fancied by Urso. However, his wonderful father didn't want to give up his prize — that being me. But that's also when I think Rinaldo started showing signs his business trips east had made him ill, and the conference ended abruptly. When I finally got to Little Italy, the eldest was already caught up in that bad business with O'Rourke. And the ill-fated Dulio — an Easterner — had been pressed into action. However, maybe nothing of this was coincidental, nor was my being placed where Taddeo would surely notice me — and dressed the way the Villettis preferred for their working women to appear in The House. So my decision to connect with what the Cubs' young pitcher offered might have been influenced by machinations I had not ever considered. Only Greg had never foreseen that the latest to be abused by the Villettis, me, was only to be handed down to* another *of the "most evil one's" sons. Only that wasn't such a good way for Rinaldo to reap his desserts, was it? Not where I am concerned. Or did Greg also arrange* that *on purpose? But he wanted to send me to Urso, not Taddeo. So exactly why is this bitch here, now?*

Only now, she pondered if another operation could have been started cutting counter to Arlene's — and probably Rinaldo's offspring's? The new dark-haired young woman, though maybe five years or so older than she was, represented some new trouble cooking in the kitchen.

"Huh? You're gonna carve up *what*? Are you seriously hosting a hotel convention right now? Do you know what time in the morning it is?" Taddeo said, in turn just emerging from another ride in the elevator. He yawned and was wearing his bed clothes. Apparently he *had* just gotten out of bed. "And what are you *all* doing *here*?"

Speaking of Rinaldo's offspring.

"It's almost eight o'clock in the morning, Tadpole. Think you should be up already by now? Stretching your legs, your arm, maybe your little mind over your balls you're going to put into play today?" Greg asked him. "I mean, there's a game pretty soon, isn't there? And that is what you do professionally? Right?"

Tad yawned. "Yeah. I need to get over to the field in a short while. Hey, Papa said he might finally come and watch me!"

"Watch you what? Ride the bench? I've heard that I may even have to endure watching that no-show as well. Best of luck. You'll need it," Greg muttered out under his breath.

"Well thank you for your overwhelming brotherly support, Greg. For your information, I've already earned my first win in a professional baseball game."

"What did you win? And what did that finally get you? A train pass?"

"Fuck you, Greg."

"Uh-huh. That's my brothers," Urso said to his new woman. To the pitcher he said, "Well we Villettis always need to be on our best game, Tadpole," Urso advised him. "So you *do* know what you're doing?"

"Yes." Taddeo seemed to quickly feel annoyed by his oldest brother's question, that no doubt did not refer to baseball, and to which Urso purposely had made his allusion apply toward Arlene, probably, just to needle his youngest brother. Or he was implying that Tad never showed up for his new job he'd wanted so badly over at the bordello? But did Urso know about that? Or even care? Or was he trying *to warn Taddeo* about his new woman? Now Tad paused possibly when he remembered Arlene's awkward behavior with the Genna Brothers when he had first met her. Who was there left to trust?

The pitcher looked over how Arlene was dressed on deck — like she could be ready to do a man's job. Next, Tad glanced at the new woman with his oldest sibling. With straight long dark hair, she was very attractive. And familiar in some way that Taddeo couldn't place. He gave her repeated glances. She wasn't any typical lounge girl, but a barely older woman in a skinny black tight-fitting evening gown. Well, she might be slightly older than Urso. Or maybe not. It was hard to tell. But very sensual. Very classy. *So what is she doing with my big brother?* At first glance, she looked like she should have some taste. Women could really confuse Tad. "But now we obviously know what some others of us are doing. Don't we, Brother?"

"Yup. We do, and we have yet to have a talk about that," Greg said to the oldest brother.

"This is Sega," Urso introduced the dark-haired woman.

"Hello," she said, maybe with an uncommon accent.

"Her parents are Greek," Urso proclaimed.

Tad nodded, "Congratulations." He wanted to make a show of it that he barely acknowledged her. But he found he couldn't quite forget *all* about the new woman who had stirred his interest, while he asked Arlene, "Now why did you leave our room? To come down here?"

"Because I'm sure your brothers didn't want to wake you," Tad's lady friend answered him. "Again. Because they know you must have to get up in the middle of your sleep to do The Family's accounting on your own. Prove you've become responsible. Right? You did that *here* I guess? I sure didn't see *you* leave. I don't know. Maybe you got on the phone. Called Jasmine or Rosyln? Someone responsible. Delilah might have a brain. And you found yours? Took your work seriously. Maybe had someone read you the numbers. *Started actually working?*"

"Who? Not Taddeo?"

"But of course a star pitcher needs his rest." Arlene knew that not one among the other men would refute that, her sarcasm aside. Nobody wanted to arouse Tad's suspicion about any of their own nocturnal activities early that Saturday morning. So everyone else would contribute to misleading him versus criticizing him. Either wouldn't be very hard — because it was Taddeo, after all. But his arrival couldn't have been timed better. She'd use the baseball player's appearance now to cut a surgical slice out between these fellas who had taken up good defensive positions. The timing just did not feel right to start firing up that roast by way of Arlene's signature recipe. There were too many new ingredients — what with the Greek woman and Corrado also there, Tad's new gun being out of reach, upstairs, not to mention the complete naivety of her paramour — and his father notably *not* there, yet informants buzzing around The Sisson like it was the hornets' nest. It was a recipe only for a cataclysmic disaster. "But now I should escort you back upstairs and help you get ready for your game today," she said to her lover, loud enough for all to hear.

"No. He doesn't need *you*. My brother needs practice at becoming more and more capable of looking out for himself. It's best he cultivate some independence. Now that he's a big baseball player, there will be times on the road where he's going to need to be more and more self-reliant. But Arlene, why don't you stay a little longer and chat with us?" Urso asked her. She could feel his eyes running over her body and noted that Sega caught that, too. And she didn't look happy — about any part of this.

Greggorio remained silent and noted his oldest brother trying to grope at Arlene with only his eyes as she stood up to join Taddeo. For his oldest brother, his eyes were all that were available to run up and down the young woman's harem pants, as his hands were already engaged in molesting Sega. Once more, Greg smiled. Another new plan began to warm him, since his first one that used Urso had so obviously failed. But that must have been due to their father interfering and knowing to send Sega. What was it? Two days ago now? And she looked like a young approximation of their mother. That might not be a coincidence. Greg kept smiling to himself. The boys' papa must have known Urso would be attracted to her on some subconscious level. But Greg had been reading psychology. He thought gaining more insight could bring him even more advantages. And he'd already initiated his back-up plan in case of any complications he experienced with his initial strategy.

So their patriarch had ordered up this young lady to waylay his eldest brother once their father had decided upon his own course of using Arlene to manipulate Taddeo. *Well, my first plan's failure wasn't* my *fault*, Greg thought. But now he would use Sega, too. He secretly thanked his father for providing her. He shouldn't let his ego be bruised but rather stroked because of his amazing adaptability. His goals would require him to now cause tension between Arlene and Taddeo as soon as possible — and break up that particular and unfortunate pairing. But he knew his baby brother and how to use that one's immature emotions against him. He hated to admit it, but his father had beaten him at arriving at this strategy, probably when he'd sent out his sacrifice as a message to Arlene on Thursday. But obviously the little bitch could also adapt fast. She rose up to the challenge of defending the continuation of her relationship with the youngest Villetti brother. So since therefore it was to her advantage, it would have to be unceremoniously ended as The Family had to move quickly to deprive her of any allies, especially within The House.

Greggorio's agents had failed to learn who else Arlene was working with. So he'd begin by eroding her one obvious alliance. But he'd still be careful to preserve a situation where each of his siblings would still be protective over their hand-picked provider of their "entertainment" — just enough to set them off on a course of conflict between the both of them. Greg now had to alter his approach from what he'd originally been scheming — though not too much. But Cain versus Able was documented thoroughly enough to act as a recipe that a man as cunning as he was, could easily and successfully cook from. He just added more spicy ingredients.

"No. I don't think I'm going for that plan. But thank you anyway, Boys." *she* interrupted his thoughts with her usual charm. "I can hardly imagine an offer more appealing than the kind of mind-stimulating conversation I'd have with Brother Urso. And is it *Sega*? But anyway, as long as I'm here, it's a safe bet that I can be of more than undying assistance to your other sibling. Come along, Taddeo."

Greg squinted his eyes again. He was beyond just starting to severely hate that scarlet whore. He might have first been amused how taken his youngest brother had been with her, but he'd also questioned his papa about just how smart their progenitor was being when the elder Villetti took the girl into their bordello in the first place, presumably as part of the arrangement in their latest municipal armistice. And then he still let her live — even after evidence that Greg had arranged relating to that barrel murder, had pointed toward her. And that had cost him good money. Now Simone, possibly just another one of the tails *Corry* put on her, since Dulio and then Thorello proved ineffective, had not returned either. And shots had been fired in the night. They'd all heard it for certain. Simone was likely dead, and Thorello was missing. Had he lost her, possibly been afraid to fess up to it, but experienced such convenient incompetence that might have actually seen him live? The luck of the stupid was just wonderful. Though he hadn't yet questioned his cousin over Simone or Thorello, as of yet. Corry had been sent off to work this, and Greg was giving him a second chance to tail the North Side cunt, but Greggorio had failed to follow her as well. And he didn't want to admit that. So for this reason, he'd refrained from criticizing his cousin too severely. Only now one or more additional dead bodies would probably turn up. They always did unless you could afford a professional. But for now, one other thing Greg did not need, was his father being disturbed by whatever stunts Arlene planned to pull next as more retaliation for *his* seemingly ordering continued surveillance of her. And then their papa asserting absolute control over everyone — which Rinaldo Villetti was characteristically liable to do as a security precaution — just as soon as this little scheming vengeful wench's plans would be revealed to turn everything sideways *again*. There was no longer any doubt that she was more than capable of ruining everything. Greg needed some good leeway so that he could make his own moves and get rid of her — breaking the vicious cycle and hopefully in some manner in which he could still set Taddeo and Urso upon each other to get rid of at least one of them finally. It just would not be even close to as easy as he thought it would be. But this new woman Sega could help.

"Well, hold the elevator. I'll make another stop on my floor. I think Sega can be of more *assistance* to me," Urso said. It came off as though he were trying too hard to sound as clever as everyone else thought they were being. But in Urso's case, it was hard for Greg to take anything he said as intelligent, though he couldn't pinpoint exactly why he had this perception of his big brother, but it had started in their childhood and persisted to this day. He'd kept a list of reasons he could refer to in any case. Maybe it came to be a defense mechanism to dodge any opportunity Urso could use to pick on him? Greggorio had to become the smarter of the two. But as he watched both his brothers and their women disappear with them, he motioned Corrado over to him. His cousin had gotten up and started pacing during the course of the exchanges between the Villetti brothers. Finally they could talk alone.

"I want you to take your designs off Arlene," Greg told him.

"What?"

"Don't argue with me. I'm a lot smarter than all of them — and you. But you will do this now. That's an order. I've seen the way you look at her. But I definitely *do not* mean for you to take your eyes off of her; just don't let her lose you again. Learn how to follow her, use more competent people than Simone and Thorello, and cancel any plans that *you* are currently considering making for *her*. I need that to stop. Immediately," Greg ordered his cousin. "I mean did you just see that?"

"What now?"

"Urso. He had his eyes on Arlene while his arms were around Sega. I'm pretty sure I can use that to get the two of them together."

"The two of who?"

"Are you stupid? *Urso*. I'm going to entice Urso to act on *his* interest in Arlene."

"Why? She's with our little pitcher. And sending him after *her* didn't work out before."

"That's because my father interfered once he figured he could use Arlene to hook Taddeo into actually working for the family. For his own twisted reasons you could count on him owning, my papa's protecting her. One of his phone calls we watched him make? — Or the one he had Horatio make. He sent what's-her-name? — Sega — over here to reset Urso's priorities — my big brother being so easily predictable and manipulated. And that move cost you both the Irish girl and your job almost directly."

"Damn. Seems your father can also match the talent you figure that you have with running both of your brothers around. Though I guess it doesn't take too much."

"Exactly. Wait. Did you just insult me? Never mind. Though I'll have you know I first came by information about that other one before my father even met her. But Urso can neither seem to take an interest in effectively recruiting any more competent help who could follow the leprechaun whore, or take her to Papa, or even end her himself. He's been here messing around with *that other one* for going past forty-eight hours after our father originally asked him to only deliver Arlene. And although it's with no thanks to you that I have any evidence, I am positive that she is up to no good. Filthy Irish. Sleazing her way into our house. Then dropping a trail of bodies. But it also couldn't be too hard to get past the guard of my dear father as he gentrifies on his throne, just dreaming of usurping Colosimo's. And you've noticed that he's sick? I think that's why we've seen your father over to the lounge so frequently. He's treating Papa with his drugs. I'm suspecting Rinaldo brought that flu home with him from his trip Back East. Who knows? Somethings from New York might be fatal. But my father's time has passed anyway. He's expanding by a few streets, but in truth his real opportunity was squandered. He should have taken full credit for everything that went right on the South Side when he was right there — I mean before Morello's representatives. Colosimo's slipping too, if he couldn't be bothered to attend. We all have blood on the Eastern Seaboard. That's the only reason we're respectful of Mafia they create — well, at least to their face. But your uncle missed a great opportunity to get some help with our greenie problem, when he had to deal with New York personally. He was alone so he could have played a better hand than the absent Colosimo. He could have recruited low-level Sicilians. We already have the Camorra. Now to his credit, he tried to accomplish something that helps us deal with Cardinella. Only actually *I* did that. But now too much time has probably passed, and he has to deal with New York again, anyway. Only now when Masseria consolidates his power, and you can trust that he will usurp Peter the Clutz, and *he* — Masseria — won't know enough about anything out here in Chi-Town to care one bit about any contribution by my father. And he'll have no clue how useful and instrumental the Villettis have been in making business gains in Chicago — the actual origin of our protection money this house has to contribute for the security of our family in Brooklyn.

"Look, all Joe the Boss has been the boss of for the past several years may only amount to the caretaking of Morello's prison block. D'Aquila's been making some pretty bold maneuvers from Brooklyn out to Manhattan. Another of our uncles told me Morano had to report to prison so the new captain established complete control over his ship. Our Family? We're good there now, I am presuming. But it won't last. Watch: Masseria will rise to take full charge. And right quickly expand his power. This experience, covering for Peter Morello, has now made Masseria even stronger, and more resolved, eager and ambitious, with that many more unknown outside allies. He is rumored to be arrogant and predicted to act boldly. Grow his organization, since Morello will have to acknowledge what he's maintained and improved upon with the Terranova empire, and take a subservient position from that which he once mastered. Joe The Boss has been frustrated for far too long. Trust me. He'll make his big move. And then D'Aquila's time will fade out as well, or be put out, and Papa's not getting any farther along up the ladder, and neither is Chicago either — I mean in terms of not being subservient to our

Sicilian masters in New York."

"Yet," Corry smiled at his patron. "Someone may still introduce and get passed a prohibition act and we should do everything we can to get a chance to support violating it." He smiled. "You know this is coming. And whereas we're well positioned and near enough Canada to benefit from this, independent of *any* interference from New York. In fact, we're in a *better* position than New York. At last. Smuggling mostly overland, instead of in more easily spotted ships isolated out on the water. Then we may not even have to deal with the Bernsteins in Michigan, we'll earn so much. We could pay them off — or extort their rum runners. But I'm not the next to catch any wind to sail very far myself. There's that and Urso's *your* oldest brother…" Greg's lackey paused. "He has seniority over you. Now — hey — wait a minute." He must have realized what Greg was thinking.

"Let's not wait any more minutes. I know what your small mind just thought of. You finally get it. But I can *not* be *caught* getting my own brother out of the way. And Urso is Papa's firstborn son. That and we all still need Papa functioning as best as he can manage, to control this whole thing, while I'm in the same place as you are. The second son. Stefano is *your* papa's firstborn son. But beyond doing the full extent of our accounting, and functioning as the bagman who makes our drops for Colosimo where our full house's operation is concerned, he's really clueless, too. About Chicago politics. I think so anyway. Maybe Stefan's been my brother's friend, but Urso doesn't ask him to be his backup even when tonight, when shadowing Arlene could have — should have, if you'd done *your job* — led us right into another potentially dangerous situation — on the Near North Side of all the great places. But even a run-in with the Gusenbergs would have also proved she's still working for the leprechauns. But *your* brother could have at least got us some damned information. Stefano knows both skill and discretion. Only now I have no clue and no proof of what the Irish are up to, I mean beyond what Arlene probably thinks she can get away with doing. And Urso never even bothered to help us out. So I'm sure he never asked for backup from your big brother anyway. And now it's obvious that as soon as he came over here, he found the wrong girl, what's-her-name — ."

"Sega."

"Yeah, Sega. By what my father thinks is his own design. But meanwhile I can't operate blind. Do I need to find better help than you? I shouldn't. Because if anything did go wrong, it would have affected your brother instead of either of us, if only *he* would also put more work in to also help his family. *I feel so blessed I have* two *brothers like that*. But instead, my best help *I* have, namely you, kept too far back, and then you lost Arlene. What a great tail you made."

"She killed Simone and at least lost Thorello, too."

"Yeah. What's-his-face, Thorello, wasn't of any assistance. Idiot. Now, I have no information about what Arlene and the paddy-whackers are up to, nor did either of us benefit by the attrition of any rivals. Instead we lost another enforcer or two, and *your brother* is off who-knows-where? Minding the blissful married life I suppose? Until he too will probably provide your papa with the first heir of your immediate family's next generation."

"Greg, you also need to know that I didn't send Simone. Thorello delivered his message and then left. But I didn't want to fail you. So to follow her, I used Vitale *and* Tancredo. The former really was itching to volunteer."

"And the latter is the young ex-cop that lost his badge his second year on the job?"

"Yeah. He's good at what he does for our house."

"He doesn't seem to be good for nothing."

"The city fathers used him to say they practiced fair-hiring and employed Italians to patrol the neighborhoods of Italians."

"Yeah. Then they used any excuse to fire him and said 'He didn't work out.' So we got him. The other one came over to us from Back East. Friend of Gervasio's I think. He should be a little more experienced."

"Well the fellas — they were under orders to not engage the girl. And they never did. That gunfight? Your papa could have ordered her dead or he didn't instruct Simone properly. I can assure you, my men didn't fire."

The Villetti brother paused for a moment. His mind raced quickly to a natural conclusion. *His father would have then definitely sent the other ones. The ones that died. But only if he saw through Greg's plan and wanted to eliminate any options for his second son. Rinaldo was hiding something*. But Greggorio didn't want to show Corry that anything surprised him. "Okay, I believe you," he said and offered a tight smile he hoped didn't look as fake as he feared. So he continued lecturing his cousin. "And don't I think I don't know exactly what you're doing. What *you* yearn for. But understand me: a wife and children right now, before this whole thing settles, is a huge liability. Events this past week should be telling you that mixing family and business can give you a lot to worry about. Best to retire young and wealthy. Make the money quick and then set up proxies to run your businesses. Just lay with whoever. Then worry about finding your right woman after you make it. And Arlene is definitely not the right woman. But if I were to just give up my plans now, we — you and I — won't be able to securely retire, and life will not be good at all. Not when the Gennas eventually run all Chicago — if they can kill off Cardinella. The Outfit needs to be on top of things, dominating territory. Making sure everyone else serves *us*. So meanwhile, I need you to closely follow my plan."

"I *am* following you, unwisely perhaps, but I will not raise my hand against another Delasandro, against my own big brother. My own closest flesh and blood. I see *you* wanting to create the scenario which sees *that* happening. So that you and I then become the heads of the households. But if my brother has a son, he'd actually want to see him become a doctor like our father, anyway. Not wind up in this kind of life. That, and Stefano was never a bully toward me, as I've seen for myself, that Urso is toward you and Taddeo."

"But who are *you* to stop Taddeo, or raise your hand against one in *our house* who carries the Villetti name?"

"What do you mean? I wasn't planning on it."

"I mean, just suppose my irresponsible and irrational little brother flies off the handle because this Irish cunt's got him so twisted around her finger that he comes after Urso as well as your big brother because Tad feels *they've* wronged *Arlene*? Then Papa will have to make the little clown answer for that and — ."

"And that hasn't happened yet. And Stefan's not interested in messing with Arlene. He barely knows of her, keeping his eyes either on his books or else, only on his wife. But you're going to bait Tad against Urso, with my big brother potentially caught in the crossfire, your great plan ending with you being left as your papa's sole heir," Corry finished Greg's words and showed that he could predict the rest of what the Villetti brother was not saying. "I figured it."

"And you figured this leaves you, the senior heir of yours. Reconsider that. The best part is neither one of us are ever caught raising one finger against our family, but you will remain my consigliere, just as your father and the House Delasandro has been for my papa. Though your father barely does anything."

"He can legally order and serve prescriptions for morphine. He gets to import raw opium mash — supplies The House with all our ingredients for processing heroin — and a lot of our customers."

"Which is a small-time operation right now. I doubt Colosimo even knows — or knows of Papa's source anyway. He doesn't want to get involved with this kind of stuff. Probably doesn't even care if it can't come back to burn him. And I wouldn't trust *him* to take advantage of any prohibition on alcohol neither. I bet New York will become concerned about that. They're backing Volstead — even working with the Christian Women's Temperance Movement and the Suffragettes. Though I don't know if the ladies even know who they are in bed with. I think that's probably why all the outfits really only pretend to want Thompson gone. At least temporarily. They just need the teetotalers to supply them with an acceptable challenger. They'll get both Madden and even Mann on board. Trust me. The Democrats will only hold temporary municipal power in Chicago for the sake of their support for the Women's Movement — especially if Thompson won't get back under control and it really becomes necessary to permanently replace him. But it won't change anything in what short time the Democrats will have control of the city government. To think Thompson still needs to be taught about politics — . But the Dems will only be able to celebrate their *perceived* control of the city. Except *we* will be the truly oldest and strongest power in town once we can disable the Irish and dominate the unions, because through sex, drugs, and gambling, we will always own the bureaucracy. From there we can expand into the commercial matériel industries, with limited opposition. Maybe shut Henry Ford the fuck up. But meanwhile, you could advance to being the oldest son by then. *You* can affect changes. For The House, I mean. More profitable ones. We're both smarter and better suited for this life than Colosimo, or even our elders in either of our own immediate families, adding in all our brothers while we're at it. But hear me on this: you will still never touch a Villetti."

"But *my* brother — ."

"Stefan's fate will not be the result of any direct action of your own. Your conscience can be clear of that. I just need you to let go of your misplaced loyalty to him, and your increasing obsession with Arlene — and since you have five younger brothers, think of them instead while you help me to manage Taddeo. Then that is all — and enough — that you'll need to be concerned with."

"But you obviously suspect the pot-licker broad is up to something."

"You're just on top of everything, aren't you? Well, we probably won't have to worry about her. Urso will see to correcting *that*. If I can ever get him out of his hotel room. Unless she's really so capable that Arlene can take care of *Urso* for us. I originally thought to let this thing go that direction, but the bitch has proved to be smarter, more capable than I'd first imagined. She's been pretty careful while the green cunt made each and every one of her little moves. In some ways, I'm fortunate that it hasn't gotten her very far. I've come to have to respect ever so slightly, that she's dangerously capable of things. So we're first going to get back to work on *him*. Urso. That's the way I had wanted to play this, when I made my initial plan. Now it will have more amore than mortalità to it. Either which way, they all begin to fall like dominoes, after Arlene succumbs to her fate, then Tad will take care of Urso, or my father will finally step in and order someone more competent to end that bitch if she actually costs him his firstborn. In which case I think I'll still have another way to handle Taddeo — with Angelo Genna." Greg smiled to himself once more. "But, in the end, we'll be the last ones standing. We win. No matter how this all goes down."

"Well, dizzying as the journey has been already, I think I'm finally going to like the direction of this road trip you're taking me on."

Chapter 22

From the lobby, the only direction the elevator car took the ill-comprised and unwisely compressed group from The House Villetti was onward and upward — towards higher and ever more uncomfortable temperatures with a stop on "awkward" at every floor.

Arlene was acutely aware of all the bad vibes she detected from each and every one of her companions. Urso's eyes were thoroughly checking her out while his hands weren't waiting for discretion's virtue while his fingers entered down beneath the top of the dark-haired Greek woman's skinny black dress, felt around for her nipples and then sought more distance from one another for a better position with which to apply some great squeezes of her breasts. He took a deep breath that came upon him with a bulge at the front of his suit pants. And they rose past the second floor.

The new girl Sega, was not aroused by any of this, but maintained a good poker face while she tolerated it. But the skin around her eyes trembled, as if she were almost successful at not letting them flinch. Almost successful. What she was not the least bit accomplished with though, hiding what else she wanted to keep secret, was through no fault of her own. She'd allowed herself only a moment to glare at the Irish gal, but Arlene caught her, and suspected that she knew exactly who this young woman was. And now she thought she was certain as to why this one would have been sent there. She knew who Arlene was. That wasn't good. They passed the third floor.

The two women had never formally met before, but Sega just might have either been sent in now as Arlene's backup, only more likely — her replacement. Could she represent the flower on the South Side? Then why didn't the Greek woman also leave East Chicago along with Arlene and Rinaldo? Or did she represent something else? The Irish had probably nothing to do with her arrival — or any knowledge of it. Arlene could have almost ruled out that any of the Villettis were behind Sega *in particular*, arriving as a new hostess-girl now. Greg might be, but it didn't make sense because Sega neutralized Urso from making any attempt to contact *her*. Why delay a confrontation where Tad would lock horns with his eldest sibling and the outcome would only serve to benefit the middle brother? Arlene had pondered that the inevitable fight was what Greggorio might be trying to arrange now. It hadn't worked out that way with the Gennas beforehand. Colosimo or his conniving wife would not have been involved, considering who Arlene just *knew* that Sega actually was truly connected to, being aware that this Greek woman was based out of East Chicago.

So the Irish woman suspected Cardinelli of course, though she didn't know what *he* would have to gain by this maneuver. Rinaldo was paying him off. Arlene's people had already maneuvered it so the senior Villetti picked her up from New York, so why would the Irish or especially the Jews — who rushed to support Arlene in that body disposal matter midweek — lay down the tracks to send in another agent while she and "The Sigñor" had to stop in Indiana? Maybe even her own kind didn't trust her immediate family? From what Fallon had told her, with even going so far as to relocate his wife, it sure didn't sound like it. However, Arlene also knew that Greg was aware "Il Diavalo" had been tempting his father with the pleasures of the flesh, back during their negotiations in Indiana. Obviously, Urso Villetti had temporarily fallen for the same trick his father did, and possibly twice. No. Definitely. Only Rinaldo *or Greg* could've brought a new girl into The House, and not Urso. But infiltration through seduction seemed an approach most acclimated to the Villettis' particular vulnerabilities. She got in that way herself — and the people who could have sent the new woman might know that method worked by way of previous experience. Though it just couldn't be Greggorio. That made no sense. But it was all just too convenient for his father. So had all the conspirators lost confidence in Arlene this soon? Or was nearly a week gone by, too long? It wasn't Arlene's fault that The Outfit was not yet organized to make its move. But it couldn't have been her fault for pressing Fallon and then Louisiana either. Could it? Sega had already been there at The Sisson with Urso *before* she'd taken her threat north, and then aimed it at the South. The thought came to her that it might have been the fucking Jews who would be the next ones to find the motivation to make any kind of deal with Cardinelli. The shylocks had a lot of new real estate to be mindful of protecting from The Black Hand Bomber, themselves. *He* — Cardinelli — had been the one to originally and specifically pick out Sega to send off to Little Italy. Though through that phone call Arlene had once dismissed, Greg might have helped Il Diavalo make the choice of the agent to use. And there were plenty of rumors that the shylocks had the ears of The Mafia via goombahs, under Masseria — and that hymie bastard that visited Arlene in her hotel room might have made a report that had painted *her* as incompetent. This had seemed to be that teenage punk's opinion all along. Had the kikes decided this even *before* they sent their representative to meet her to clean up after Herbert? That meant that by what she'd learned from her visit to Fallon's, that her people had possibly placed her in Villetti's with the expectation that whatever this plan of theirs was, it would take a lot longer than the only five or six days that the Jews were allowing. They had lied just to placate her. Then "Il Diavalo" obliged and provided them with Sega, taking advantage of Rinaldo and Greggorio both underestimating that whore. She heard Cardinelli took his orders from Cosa Nostra, and they were in business with the Jews. Now all of the ten-percenters could no doubt be arriving today, among the New Yorkers that Rinaldo would be meeting at Tad's baseball game. Sega might be the way some of them were secretly hedging their bets.

So the group in the elevator passed the fourth floor while she was doubting Greggorio would've picked this woman since it would be within his character to be a little more thorough in checking out someone new's background — and he already suspected Arlene. That was evident. But what was also apparent was that Sega could represent a new and very dangerous threat to Arlene, and it was less and less likely originating from The Villetti House. The Jews could even be planning to replace her — and then they and the Mafia could double-cross the Irish. No, she didn't like this new woman being there. Not one bit.

The group wasn't stopping on the fifth level either while she noted that Sega didn't seem to like *her* as well. There was now really strong reasons to suspect she was there to move against Arlene and had also either grown annoyed that Urso was checking out Arlene, or that Taddeo was now checking out Sega. His woman had also grown annoyed with Taddeo for the same reason by the time Urso and his new lady-friend finally watched them exit on *the seventh floor*.

Though obviously through Rinaldo, and Harry Sisson for that matter, anyone who wanted to find Arlene and Taddeo's room could get that information, the couple had waited and listened to the sounds made by the elevator until they figured Urso and his friend were delivered to their own stop, to call for the carriage for them to now descend again and get them to the actual floor Arlene and Tad were staying on. Neither one of them thought Urso was smart enough to figure it out. That's when they told the old man who operated the elevator to which floor they were really headed. He'd looked like he had really wanted to be left alone while he was subjected to having to pretend he didn't notice Urso and Sega's presentation of some show of the former's dominant-male chauvinist sexuality. But nevertheless, in an elevator car, how could he avoid not being nearly forced to watch? Then to get the pair that had re-boarded the carriage to their truly desired level, he had to come back a floor when they could have gotten off already at the sixth, except for *that pair* was deliberately trying to be deceitful. Every little thing helped. Though Arlene thought it peculiar that this guy was an old *white* man. But then again, she shouldn't be surprised that Harry Sisson wouldn't allow for the hiring of any black man, even for *a Negro's job*. She knew in exactly *whose* hotel she resided. And now they finally arrived on the correct floor where their room was.

"I'm definitely not going with you out to the East Coast, Tad. And that fact's final," Arlene soon found herself telling her dedicated courtier. But his concern for her had touched her, in addition to his pawing hands, and the love he finally professed to her, in not so many words, had begun to matter even in spite of her never having wanted to let that happen. But in that moment, Arlene struggled to remind herself of all the doubts she had about it.

"What's a fact is that both my brothers have their eyes on you. Apparently so does my cousin. I'm not blind. I saw. And that's not good. I don't like how any of them handle our women. And I can't help you if I'm gone. And I have to go, Arlene."

Well you haven't been of much help even while you're here, so what's the difference? she thought next. But out loud she said, "Your team has a road trip, Taddeo. It's not like you're going off to fight in France or something."

"Better give Mister Li time to evaluate my arm with a laundry bundle before you can proclaim that with finality."

"Huh? Oh, right. And when will you find time to go and see if you can get this new job?"

"Yeah. That's right. I haven't gone to ask for it yet. I guess I will have to go and make that happen today. Though he *will* hire me. I think I can assure myself of that."

"And so then I presume that you haven't inquired of him whether I may stay there either?"

"Please refresh *my* memory, Arlene. Why do you have to stay *here?* In Chicago I mean."

"You made me madam, remember? I have a business to run." *And you're still not effective. In fact, I may be allied with the greatest under-achiever that I've ever known.*

"What? You're actually taking that role seriously?"

"You've yet to work at it seriously, so somebody will have to. You've let two nights pass already without collecting. You think the girls are just going to report their earnings honestly? I have to produce an income from that income. And I'd rather not do it any other way. And *you* worked so hard to convince me that the skim from *that income* facilitates our running-away money. Or was *that* just a lie, Taddeo? But you insisted we needed that. It would fit with your paranoia that we're living surrounded by *them* — that is everyone who's out to get us."

"No. Well, yes. Look who just greeted us downstairs. Everyone *is* out to get us. The gun. Remember the gun? I was just tired and I forgot to tell my favorite brother *exactly* what I thought of him sending me a loaded gun. What the hell is he trying to instigate? I can guess and I'm sure Urso doesn't know anything about it. This has Greg's brilliant designer signature all over it. But I wouldn't compare which one of us tells more lies if I were you, Arlene. But I — ."

"But you need someone here to collect our cash. And what? You think your brothers don't steal from your father? Wake up, Tad. Rinaldo knows that they do. *He lets them*. He's teaching them all how to become better criminals. And that way they all don't come whining to him about getting a car — or whatever you whine about getting, Little Man. I'm already sure the list is extensive."

"So's something else. But they're both more extensive than my patience I have left for *your* attitude. I'm trying to help, Arlene."

"Then get a pitching coach."

"Very funny. You know, you're impossible. If you insist on staying, I have to go and see Mister Li right away before my practice and bring him this new information I got concerning a mutual friend — the butcher — Kean O'Rourke. Remember him? This is kind of time sensitive — and time might have just ran out. Greggorio and Urso both being here at the *same* time? That's not good. Trust me. They don't like to stay in one place together for very long. I think that at any time now, they were assigned to go and *together* extend my father's welcome to a new fellow from Back East who's expected to come in by train today or tonight. I'm not sure. He's rumored to be important. At least to Colosimo, who's extending the full red carpet for him. And that'll also be all the full extent to which my siblings can stand one another — unless they're doing another job *with* the newest help to which they'll then have to continue to show a united family front. And if they are, I think I know exactly where they'll be doing this. But maybe if Mister Li's house guest can suddenly and safely *depart*, with no trouble for Mister Li, before my brothers get their act together, I can then at least deliver to you a more secure place to flop while you run *your new business*, via Mister Li's, in exchange for that favor I'm doing him."

"Well, that might work. Mister Li hasn't had to listen to you bemoan all your woes — yet. Which believe me, is no favor to anyone. And he doesn't need your family's kind of trouble. So I guess you *will* be doing him a favor he will owe you for. You sure learned well from your father about just how that kind of deal works."

"I'll be doing *you* a favor."

"'Cause *you* owe *me*, and I haven't seen any money, just that filthy hand cannon your family bequeathed you. So then it'd be best to get yourself going so you aren't late if you want to run your new *laundry list* of errands before your other pre-game practice. And also, I'd see if you can't make use of a fire escape. And I mean that. Greg and your cousin Corry are probably still in the lobby waiting for Urso to stop fucking around, quite literally. The longer they think you're still here, the more chance I'll have for them to just leave me alone."

"It can wait a few more minutes. 'Cause maybe *I* don't feel like leaving you alone right now." Tad sat down on the bed by Arlene's side, smiled and leaned in for a kiss.

Wrapping his arms around her, he gently eased her back on the mattress, and started removing his pajamas — and she even enthusiastically began removing her own clothing. *At least he's competent in one area*, she thought as she let Tad climb on top of her.

"So let's exchange a few more favors. I can make all our plans and dreams come true, Arlene. I know I can. I promise you."

For one more time, Arlene let herself be seduced by Taddeo's passion — his passion he presented toward caring about her. Or at least thoroughly enjoying her. And she him. The young woman would unapologetically make use of him now, in the short term. Especially in the most recent moment in which she could remember that her stomach didn't hurt. But in the long term, her evaluation of his unreliability did not let her forget she couldn't trust him — that was both due to his incompetency — and with who he was, or who she feared she saw him transforming into. But at the conclusion of the affair, Arlene knew the true power of her own seduction lay in how she would use it to manipulate even him, to her best ends. Now Taddeo had changed positions if only momentarily to let that sweet tongue of his work on one of those ends. So in the present she had to admit, there were many a scenario where she thought it would be very important to her, that Taddeo survived what Arlene considered her own plan's best outcomes. They were definitely coming. What was it with this young man?

Chapter 23

"This man is going to die. My family is going to kill him — if he dares to go through with what he's now probably planning. And who knows what my family is going to do to you Mister Li, to teach you a lesson, once they learn you've been hiding him."

Still wrapped in some bandaging and with one arm in a sling and the opposite leg fitted into a blue brace, Mr. O'Rourke appeared as if he was sweating and shivering at the same time as he lay there on some old pillows that topped the stained mattress that had been placed in some annex room Mr. Li apparently used for storage. O'Rourke's dark hair obviously storing plenty of moisture.

Mr. Li didn't have much hair on top any more, but he had obviously stored up some ill feelings toward the Villettis that had gotten into what he had left. At first glance he looked like all Chinamen did to Tad, with a large sloping forehead and tiny slanted eyes, and straight, neatly swept black hair at the sides, except in the back where Mr. Li wore a long braided ponytail. But he was not unfamiliar to Taddeo, who'd grown up knowing him for about half his lifetime, though Mr. Li had more hair on top back then, less wrinkles too, and a much warmer disposition about him every time he would see the young athlete. That wasn't the case now.

"What happened to Mister Li little baseball friend? You once be your mother's boy. Now what Mister Li sees is all of your papa's influence." The businessman scrutinized Tad and his bruises, shrinking lip and black eyes, all. On the floor, Kean O'Rourke might have even seemed frightened of the tall and strong young man. He nervously lit a cigarette, struggling to hold onto the match. An open flask stood on the floor next to where he reclined.

Taddeo hadn't relaxed much himself. He'd woken early when he became aware of Arlene's absence, and then found her with his brothers. After that situation had eclipsed, he'd stayed awake via his arguments with his woman, then they'd kissed and made up. But just after that he'd walked many a few city blocks over toward the Maxwell Street Market neighborhood, where the older apartment housing served the lower income residents. He'd first gone down the fire escape at The Sisson that Saturday morning like Arlene suggested, to then discreetly go and visit his elderly friend from his childhood. But the trip took him back to a place of nostalgia during which he really didn't want any present reevaluation of himself to ruin. But a change was coming and Taddeo couldn't see any way to avoid it. "Relax. I won't let anyone kill him. Or let anyone touch you. We're old pals. But I'm going to teach you both a new lesson about gratitude," he said to the individuals he'd come to see.

"Yes? And you believe Mister Li not grateful? Or now so does Taddeo papa? So now Mister Li pay him good money out of what Mister Li business earns to show Sigñor Villetti that Mister Li grateful? Is that right?"

"Wait. Is that what you think I am doing here? Collecting money — no, stealing it from you?"

"That is what Taddeo family do, young Villetti Son."

"We don't really make you pay anything at all, personally. And that's not why I'm here. I came *here* to make both of your lives easier."

"Oh, great. Villetti doesn't make *you* pay," scoffed O'Rourke, angrily flashing what teeth he had left toward Taddeo, but his comment meant for Mr. Li. Then to his nemesis' son, he said, "I can't wait for this to make my life any easier."

Taddeo and Li ignored him. "See, I am not my father. One, my first favor that explains what I'm doing here right now, today — and I've got to get moving on because I have baseball practice — is important. I am saving both you and Mister O'Rourke here *from* my father." The defiant butcher looked up from his position of refuge down on the mattress. Taddeo finally refocused his attention on him. "Mister O'Rourke, you can leave with me under my protection. If I can use your phone Mister Li, I can call up one of my teammates who has a truck that can secretly drive over here and pick us both up, then drop you wherever you want to go on the North Side, Mister O'Rourke, seeing as we're heading that way anyway." Kean O'Rourke grunted and only offered Taddeo a palpably angry wide-eyed stare. "And oh. I'd advise you to not let your pride be your downfall this time. Instead let down your skepticism, and take me up on my offer."

"You don't even have your own car. How do you expect your *protection* to have any credibility?"

"I have knowledge and a plan, of which you look to have neither. The reason I know where you are is that I found out at the same time that my father did. The House is sending someone else for you — traveling help from out of Brooklyn I hear. Not the good kind 'neither. He's arriving tonight and *he* will not be offering you a ride across the river to a place of your choosing. We all can be sure about that."

"But if he gone, what will then be the trouble for Mister Li?"

"They don't trust you. My family. At least Papa got the report on a certain defiance of yours — something about you rebelling and harboring fugitives, *from him*. So my brothers and the new guy are going to turn this place upside-down and when they don't find anything — which they won't — they'll shake you down for *more gratitude* — which they'll demand as payment to justify their time. Especially the new guy. He's Colosimo's nephew-in-law or something. Real slick like a fox is the rumor. Supposed to be some Back East big shot it would seem."

"Oh, so this to make Mister Li life easier?"

"No. Of course not. *This* is." Taddeo removed a wad of bills from his coat pocket and reached out to hand them to Mister Li. It was the money he'd collected in the skim when he stopped first at Villetti's after he left Arlene at The Sisson — while his brothers remained at the hotel, thinking he had too. "So this is my second point worth a favor: here's your fee for services that my brothers with the new guy are probably going to attempt to charge you. Keep the extra."

"You give Mister Li money? Are you crazy?"

"You wouldn't be the first to think so."

"Mister Li *do* think so. You pay Mister Li so Mister Li can pay your brother what he says Mister Li owe Taddeo father? The same man who family who money you first pay Mister Li from. That definitely crazy."

"That's right."

"You no good for Taddeo family business, Young Villetti."

"Ha. That trait runs in most of my family. Which is good since Urso can be easily bought off. Especially since he's lazy. When they go and *increase* the contribution — which would be all that Papa would ask for — and which amounts to still nothing right now — you'll have that something extra. Just give it to them out of this." Tad nodded at all the stacks of paper he'd placed in Mr. Li's hands and closed his old friend's fingers around the bills. "Then Urso — being that lazy — won't let anyone else look into this any further. He couldn't let them waste any more of his time that might be better spent drinking and gambling, right?"

"That still crazy."

"That's my generosity."

"Wait. What you want from Mister Li?"

"My number three. Mister Villetti — uh, this Mister Villetti — wants a job from Mister Li. And a place to sleep."

"Now Taddeo really crazy. No you bananas."

"I'm serious. Now you Mister Li will show you really grateful." *Wait. Am I starting to talk like him now? What is that? Mandarin English?*

What Mr. Li was, was less than half as grateful as Tad hoped he would be. When Tad was done asking for his return favors, it had been determined that Arlene could at least interview with him to then determine if *she* could be a tenant on the floor of the large closet in his laundry, and Tad would then regularly supply Mr. Li with the insurance payment money he was required to pay out to Taddeo's family, as Arlene's rent. He was neither welcome to stay there, nor to be provided with a job working there because he was Rinaldo Villetti's son and Li was risking a lot just by operating behind the local street boss' back helping the others who he had, and who he was about to. He didn't need whatever path of rebellion against his father that Taddeo was going to blaze a trail on, causing the fire to blowback on the old Chinaman. Tad hated still being treated like a child, but tried to tell himself that it wasn't his negotiating tactics, but rather that *as a child*, is how Mr. Li always knew him, and it could reasonably be how he'd always see him.

He gave up trying to push for any more concessions out of the old man at this moment and the Cubs' young pitcher had to call Hoffman for a ride to baseball practice so he wouldn't be late. But at least Mr. O'Rourke did not have it in himself to resist being taken out for the ballgame. Taddeo's family had left the Irishman in pretty bad shape. The youngest Villetti tried to not let the tough butcher see when he turned his head in order to wipe away a tear before it could fall while they waited for their ride. He was well aware he was actually turning into his father — and right before his very own watering eyes. Tad felt ashamed that Mr. Li had recognized it. Did his well-intentioned ends justify these means? The way he negotiated to get what he wanted? Or failed at it? But times were changing with each day's passing, and Tad feared there was nothing that he would be able to do to stop it now — or stop his own changing with it. Was this the adjustment required when one came up to play in the Big Leagues?

Chapter 24

The intersection of West Addison and North Clark Streets,
Chicago, Illinois, May 25, 1918:
2:05 pm CST

"Big Jim. Mister Weeghman."

"Welcome back to my house," the ballclub owner said with a seemingly forced smile as he greeted them at the exit from the tunnel, their party growing to almost a dozen. Then they all walked down to settle next to the red brick partition and take their field level seats near the New York Giant's visiting team dugout. The stadium's most special guests that afternoon had requested these particular seats on the 1st base side. They were almost exclusively occupied by white Anglican or Irish men. "I'm always interested in another opportunity to entertain you."

"Rinaldo. It's always very good to see you."

"And you, Patron. Behind me, you know my son, Greggorio." But with a glance of annoyance, he noted his middle son to be paying more attention to a blonde-haired young lady who others in their gathering had brought along to accompany them.

He elbowed Greg, who quickly nodded and brought out a smile and a hand to shake. "Big Jim. Mister Weeghman."

"And of course, this is Vincenzo and Ciro Terranova, brothers to Don Morello," Colosimo introduced several members of the company they'd be keeping that day at the ballgame.

Villetti suppressed the urge to gulp, and then bowed his head before forcing himself to smile and stiffly extend his hand. "Mister Terranova. *And* Mister Terranova. It is an honor, once again."

The older of the two New Yorkers responded with a tight smile. "Yes, of course."

Rinaldo thought they both had puffy fat faces under their fedora hats, no doubt from the living high on the hog afforded them by the Morello Family criminal empire's profits. "What brings you both to Chicago?"

"We're following the Giants. Though the Yankees would be my

favorite team," Ciro Terranova added.

"They have tough competition from the Red Sox this year."

"So I've also seen. You're a baseball fan, too?" Vincenzo asked of him.

"No. Not really. My businesses keep me quite busy. Not a lot of time to be a fan and pursue any of the activities of leisure." The bright sun and the Midwest's humidity had started to irritate Rinaldo as soon as he sought his seats in the stands. He was one who tried hard not to have to be outdoors — especially wearing a three-piece suit and tie.

"That's right. You and your boys run the comfort services offered by Colosimo, here. His wife's been busy with — other concerns." Villetti kept his expression flat as Terranova continued. Big Jim's eyes flickered at the New Yorker, perhaps with a little anger in them. "But one of your sons plays. Your youngest?" Vincenzo asked.

"Yes. Taddeo."

"Taddeo. Will we see him perform tonight? He's a pitcher among the Cubs' reserves, is he not?" Ciro asked.

"You are also correct. But we probably won't get to see what he can pitch right now. I understand this Lefty Tyler the Cubs are putting out there today is pretty good." Rinaldo nodded toward a player now crossing the field from the opposite side, to start warming up on the mound. The sound of the baseball smacking into the catcher's mitt accented his point.

Another of Weeghman's guests laughed. "That's what I love about competitive sports, Sigñor Villetti. There are so many variables. You never know what surprises might happen."

"Rinny, this is Abraham Attell, former lightweight boxer. They nicknamed him The Little Hebrew because he's a Jew. He's here representing Mister Arnold Rothstein, a necessary Back East financial partner for some." Charles Weeghman made the introduction with an explanation. "He's quite the sports enthusiast, among other things."

"Well Mister Attell, it's my pleasure." He did not let on to Weeghman that the two men were already acquainted when he'd visited Brooklyn last week — and that he knew one of the other guests in attendance was actually Mr. Rothstein himself. In fact and instead, he slighted the Cubs' bigoted team owner, but very carefully. It should score him points with most of the others. "It will be interesting to watch the game with someone else so knowledgeable about sports the way you are, Mister Attell. Oh, and my son duly informed me that this Lefty Tyler's ERA is less than 2.5 right now. I suppose that means he can handle your Giants." Villetti smiled a rueful smile at the Sicilian New Yorkers, hopeful that Greggorio now paid more attention to his tactics he utilized with Weeghman, the Mafia and the shylocks, rather than that blonde woman his son was suddenly so fascinated with. But Rinaldo was very eager to continue his conversation with The Morello Family.

"My brother's team," Ciro Terranova said. "But I don't know. It's true his *National League* club that *he's really been betting on*, has had some pretty active bats recently. So I guess we'll all see about that. As I understand it, your personal *business* has promoted some rather active batters. Lately. Or actually a rather active plumbing repair worker. Then he came to try the new Irish drink. Now I've heard he wasn't working for you so well *underground*. Because then your network of pipelines that got serviced just sprung *another* leak via the reserve barrel?"

"True. That is one way of phrasing it. And it's likely the same leak I've been having trouble with thrice now. There's a problem with the gutters from Little Italy reaching all the way to run off in the Chicago River. Probably with shit that floats toward the North Side. The old Irish families originally created it. Or so some of the police have informed me they've come to suspect. But a second leak in the system might be just a case of a mistakenly missing person who never returned back to New York." He tried to change the subject from Simone or Dulio. "There's no hard evidence of any foul play yet. Plus he's nobody. No one you'd care about anyway. It's just his family has already been looking for him since Thursday. They talked to the cops. Only I have that under control." Rinaldo nodded behind him somewhere. "But then maybe this guy doesn't want to be found? Especially if he has a wife. Ya know? You never know with the kind of clients my business attracts. Disappearing, what, only two days ago? That means very little in Chicago. However, I'm handling it. All of it. In fact I'm really glad you're here this weekend. You may be witness to how well this old hand does at personally plugging any leaks in the local organization around here. I think you're already passingly familiar with my patron's nephew, this Giovanni Torrio?"

Rinaldo Villetti could feel Colosimo turning his head slightly, watching him as intently as he could with his peripheral vision, while his underling interacted with Peter The Clutch's relatives. Good, Colosimo was smiling. Villetti confirmed that while he was busy covering all the bases at this game. He just hoped Urso would correctly accomplish *one* errand he sent his son on today. But since that was almost too much to hope for, Rinaldo actually had to rest his faith in that his newest assistant, this fella that one of Rinaldo's own brothers Back East had sent his blessings with, would arrive soon and get to work on helping *him*, besides that man's uncle. This guy was in fact Colosimo's wife's nephew or something. Though Rinaldo didn't even trust any of his own brothers. And he should know better than to trust Victoria's agenda. Nor did he even trust his own son. Being realistic about Urso, he'd have to send along his firstborn's next-oldest brother as well, though Greggorio should feel better about his role since his papa had brought him along here, to enjoy the baseball game first. Greg wanted to prove he had grown into taking on greater responsibilities in The Family. His papa thought he could reinvigorate Greggorio's loyalty to him by giving him this opportunity to represent The House and he watched his son introduce himself and start building relationships with people he would need to know. Urso by contrast, wanted to spend his whole afternoon with some whore before he'd have put himself together to go to Union Depot. Typical. Rinaldo had probably himself to blame because it was seemingly the same working-girl he'd sent to intercept his son when he was about to make his move on Arlene on Thursday. Though now it was Saturday. But it was more embarrassing to have the butcher back on his side of the river, just waiting to recover enough so that their old nemesis Kean O'Rourke could rebel against him once more and reopen his business just to defy Villetti — right when he knew New York evaluated the stability of his part in the syndicate's operation. And on top of that, evidence pointed to Arlene having come to represent another Irish-aligned danger to which Rinaldo himself was responsible for subjecting their fledgling Chicago Outfit to. She too, had to be gotten under control or it was possible that the body count wouldn't be, according to his middle son's theory. Not that he was trustworthy, either. Now, Greggorio still appeared too distracted with the young blonde lady. *Great.*

"Well I don't want to talk about some customer the business misplaced. Don't ramble on trying to change the subject when by my count you've actually lost *four associates*, with two turning up floating down the river in broad daylight, and the others falling in a shootout that nearly felled your other son for a total of probably five dead in just over two weeks. In Chicago, that's easily as overlooked as it is in New York — by the cops we all have to pay and with the specifics quickly forgotten by the public. Only we don't need *any* bad press to print any written record. Not now. There must be nothing that could even be rumored to be linked to *us*. Crimes — or what we'd call mistakes — logged in *their* archives. So I'm not inclined to just forget about it, but I'm going to be hopeful that things are getting back to working out for you finally. That would always be good news to hear," Vincenzo Terranova said. He nodded to a group of four men in the stands a few rows and to the right behind him. They all wore business suits to the ballpark without one uniform among them today, but Rinaldo figured the Terranovas were good enough at this that they had immediately identified Conway's police strike team Chief Alcock had let him assemble. Villetti had nodded toward them to make that abundantly clear anyway, in case these Back East fellas knew more about The Black Hand letters and bombings than they let on — as well as Chicago's cops. Nothing about what The Mafia could do would surprise him. But it would be Colosimo's place to discuss that with The Morello Family, not Rinaldo's. Handling Cardinella was supposed to be above his station, or so he needed them all to believe. But Villetti took precautions.

The senior Terranova was going on, "Because now I've brought some other friends — or fans of New York, here with me." He nodded to Attell with some other gentlemen seated along the baseline to his left, and thus closer to home. Rinaldo didn't plan to ever let on that he was already acquainted with them. "Doing some patchwork myself you could say. Now we've noticed some good things about *your* borgata, Villetti. And it's just your luck that some business associates of me and my brother's might be interested in further investing in Chicago. And so some really great things could be just about to start happening here."

Great for who? Villetti wondered. But he'd been tipped off weeks ago to prepare for this.

Meanwhile, the Chicago Cubs with Lefty Tyler taking command of the hill, prepared to meet their visitors from New York as well.

Chapter 25

"George, you feeling all right today?" Fred Merkle asked. He met up with Lefty Tyler when all the Cubs all ran it back in from their warm-up stretching and calisthenics on the field. The players now gathered into their dugout to hear out Coach Mitchell's customary motivational speech before the starters would take their positions at the center of the stadium. As some lit their smokes, the team breathed its concern the Giants would call up a lot of right-handed bats to answer Chicago's left-handed pitcher. And that could keep right field really busy that afternoon — an issue with Max Flack's defense also progressing on as a new, but yet *unvoiced* concern for the Cubs' bench. Most had some feeling about that. None put theirs into words. For the team's morale, this couldn't be good. But the problem would persist, untended to.

Hoff turned around to curiously take in Chicago's 1st baseman, as if he had other thoughts about this game he had yet to reconcile. But Tad then ran up and punched him in the shoulder. "Not *you*, George. He was asking Tyler. The *other George*."

"I know that Pooper."

"It's 'Shooter.' My nickname is 'Shooter.' I told you to stop calling me by that other name. The other guys will start using it and —."

"And no. Your nickname is now 'Pooper.' Because you stink." Hoffman grabbed Taddeo's ballcap in his right hand so he could mess up Tad's hair with his left. "This isn't Iowa. Oh geez."

"Now what?"

"Not 'what.' But 'yuck.' Too much grease."

"Funny."

"Oh, you know I am."

"Yeah. Okay. You know I straighten my hair. I don't want to look 'so Italian.' It just sees me get bullied. And you also know a pitcher is at his best when he's playing with a great catcher, supporting him."

"And that explains the wonderful relationship you have with Bill Killefer."

"Yeah. But all right, already. You know I earned my first win on

Wednesday — saving all of us from losing the series against the Robins."

"No you didn't. We fought the series to a draw and it was *my plan* that saved *your ass*."

"All riiight. You know I'll concede you that point Hoff, if you'll just shut up right now. I wanna hear what the vets are saying."

"That's what I was doing before you interrupted me, Pooper."

The pair then overheard Lefty Tyler. "Hey my arm's been feeling great, Fred. I'm confident I can throw the good shit. My confidence in our umpire? Not so much," Tyler answered the starting infielder. "Now I think I can handle this, but it's true that New York's going to play a majority of guys who can hit a southpaw. So I haven't been so sure that Coach should pitch *me*."

Tyler lacking any confidence was not good. "It's your turn in the rotation Buddy, and you'd have to face the Giants this series anyway. Best to get it over with."

"Hey Bonehead, you have history with that guy, Bob Emslie."

"Yup. And it's not the memories I'm most fond of. Now Emslie didn't make the infamous call. Our good friend Hank O'Day did. But Emslie didn't stick up for me either. He said he wasn't watching. An umpire? Not watching? Yeah. Well, that entire outing was supposed to be over and my team won, but I swear they didn't even tag me with the legitimate game ball. I believe that one had already left with the Cubs' winning pitcher."

"I guess it didn't make a difference. Just touch 'em all when you get on. But the situation's reversed now. You're not on the Giants any longer. You're playing against them — for us Cubbies."

"And you're going to be the Cubs' winning pitcher now, *Lefty*. So just relax. You'll come off with the game ball and O'Day's not even going to appear behind the plate — or even in this stadium today. And that's a fact. Bill Klem is calling balls and strikes on this one. Rumor is the Giants won't ever trust The Reverend again. Not that I can say I blame them. But Emslie's in the field this matchup anyway.

"Klem? What? Did the Giants request him? That's really not any better news."

"They shouldn't be allowed to do that. But maybe — ."

"Well, maybe we're exactly 4 games behind the trolls. Win this *series*, and then we, versus New York, will quickly rise to leading our entire division."

"Tie up our division. Until we can get ahead. But that's the dream," Bob O'Farrell touched Ty on his shoulder. "But it's only

May. We still have a long season ahead of us. C'mon George. Let's get you out on the rubber so we can get a few more extra tosses in before it's time to start actual game play."

As they departed with the rest of the veteran starters, plus the addition of Charlie Hollocher, who always had to remind everyone that he was also there, Tad followed them up the steps. Trevor Bass, who watched them run out to take the field for the start of the game with only the sincerest admiration, noticed Taddeo. "Hey, what are you doing, Tad?"

"Huh? Oh. Just lookin' for my papa. He said he'd be here. I think this time he is actually coming to one of my games. I'm trying to see if I can spot him in the stands." Tad looked behind the Cubs' dugout. He didn't see anyone he recognized, much to his disappointment.

"Hey, Villetti. Where are you going? Get back where you're supposed to be. Grab some bench," Coach Mitchell ordered. "What is it with you? Are we starting some kind of new tradition now? Do I always need to show you where your seat is? I swear I'll have Killefer sit you down. And I know you won't like that."

"C'mon." Trevor pulled him by his arm. No one cared that Hoffman was already flirting with some woman in the stands. That was *his* tradition.

Then Pat Pieper told the audience to get their pencils and scorecards ready and he announced the first three batters for the Giants would be Ross Youngs, Benny Kauff, and George Burns. Lefty Tyler fired his last warm-up shot to O'Farrell, and Pieper waited until Klem called for the game to begin — then hollered into his megaphone, "And now the action starts with the New York Giants versus yooourrr Chicago Cubs! Play ball!"

Chapter 26

Saturday, May 25, 1918
2:30 pm CST
Weeghman Park, Chicago, Illinois

1st Inning
New York - 0, Cubs - 0

0 Outs, 0 On

AB: The New York Giants (23 W – 7 L)
(Commanding a 1st place ranking in the National League!)
Royce Middlebrook (Ross) Youngs (RF, Bats: Left, Throws: Right)
AVG .302, OBP .368
Age: 21, Games: < 70, Status: sophomoric rookie,
1st full season in The Show

On the mound:
Chicago Cubs (19 W – 11 L)
(Climbing up the ranks in the National League)
P: George "Lefty" Tyler (SP)
(Bats: Left, Throws: Left) 14 W – 8 L, PCT: .704, ERA: 2.00,
SO: 102, HB: 64 x (in 9 years)*
Age: 29, Games: 247, Status: 9-year veteran
*1917 stats

AND THEN:

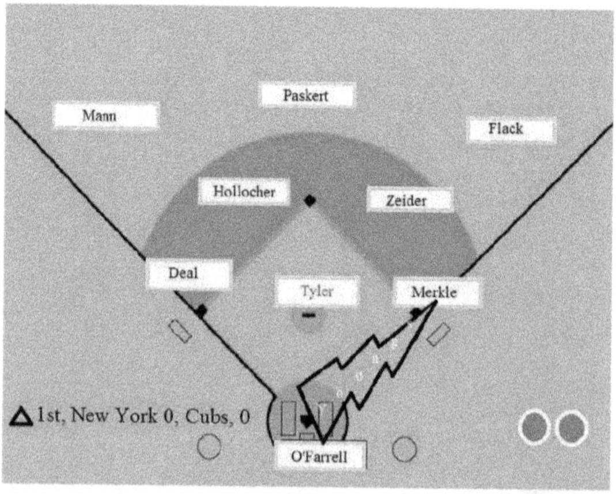

And then Ross Youngs finished working Lefty Tyler to a full count. Youngs showed he would not be replaced as New York's leadoff man and settled in to be patient in this lefty-against-lefty contest at the plate. He sped up his timing so that he was early, and he finally and accidentally hit weakly to the opposite field. Though not really his opposite field considering who was pitching for Chicago. But Charlie Deal hadn't come awake yet, and in error, didn't expect to have any work supporting Tyler with a left-handed batter, so it got between the 3rd baseman and shortstop and Les Mann picked it up shallow and bypassed the cutoff to send the ball back to the mound. Youngs was on 1st by that time. George Tyler stood on his self-assigned shame.

Next up was Benny Kauff, also known as "the Ty Cobb of the Federal League." A double off Tyler that scored Youngs all the way from 1st base was not the way the Cubs' starting pitcher wanted to begin this game. It was "One – Nothing," Giants. Then Burns got his RBI with only a base hit that Max Flack didn't appear to want to strain himself getting, but Kauff started from scoring position and might've crossed home plate anyway. It was hard to lay the blame on Flacky, but Tad had been watching him and what fielders backed up their pitchers. The man in the right field gap had Taddeo's suspicions up, though as a rookie, the pitcher kept that mostly to himself. But Hoff had suspected as much, too. So Tad wasn't the only one.

While the next three batters for New York went down in order with the only excitement being a thwarted sacrifice by Zimmerman to wind up leaving Burns stranded on 2nd base, the Cubs returned dejected to the home team's bench. Tyler immediately lit up a cigarette. Only Tad sat there in brighter spirits because he hadn't held much hope until now that his papa would even get to see him play — if he actually was at this game — because Tyler had a very sharp ERA. Only it didn't look good for the left-hander after the way the top of the 1st had started out. Things were changing and now Tad had already thought up a plan to plead and beg his coach, but it would seem he'd already put Mitchell in another bad mood just by arriving at the stadium. Coach had started drinking early — in only the 1st inning. However, if the Cubs' starter were somehow "off" today, then Taddeo might get to take the mound in front of his father after all. He knew he shouldn't root against George Tyler, his own teammate. That wasn't supposed to be right. But taking control of the game was what Tad honestly valued.

And this was New York that his ballclub was facing. The Cubs were only 4 games out of 1st place now and this was an important matchup with the team currently ranked as holding the best scorecard in the National League — after Brooklyn found the Cubs could give them "some trouble" in that very last series. But when he'd overheard O'Farrell voice his opinion, he agreed with the pro catcher's assessment. This *was* not even the last week of May. The standings would be constantly in flux and far from close to being settled.

In the stands, Rinaldo Villetti valued another chance to strike up conversation with Vincenzo Terranova while New York's athletic squad spread out around Chicago's diamond. Meanwhile, Charlie Weeghman seemed very busy talking to some ballpark lackey who security let approach him in the stands. Greggorio had distracted Colosimo as his father had secretly hoped. But out of the corner of his eye, Rinaldo watched the man who'd spoken with Weeghman take off across the seats to approach and then lean over the edge of New York's bench once he and his boss had exchanged only a few words. Rinaldo concluded he needed to take some extra interest in this. Something had upset the Giants' coach, John McGraw, who threw his clipboard spinning across the dugout and smashed his fist into his other hand.

As the bottom half of the 1st inning had begun to commence, the senior Villetti did indeed find more to converse about with the acting-leader of The Morello Family. Something very interesting had indeed just happened. "Although you can say what you will in denigration of Chicago's starting pitching today, nothing good can be said about your Giants' Jesse Barnes either. Am I right?"

"Good point. But I see he only likes to pitch just like *your son*," the older Terranova brother said.

Upon having started the second half of the very 1st inning by walking Max Flack after not even bothering to hide his aiming his very first pitch straight at him — Barnes got himself immediately kicked right out of the game. It made no sense to bring on a beanball war now. Especially for the Giants who were winning. *Very interesting*, Villetti thought. But he wasn't surprised.

"What'd he do that for?" Tad asked, very much afraid that the first conclusion he'd draw, would definitely lead him to the correct answer. *No one will let me play not one fair game*. And now he figured for certain his papa *was* in the crowd — and that he would be called on shortly to pitch for the Cubs. New York's Jesse Barnes had just hit Max Flack.

"Watch this," Les Mann had said, pointing toward home plate from the bench. "Hey Everston. You've got the rep as being the new hothead. Pay attention at the plate. Here it comes," the Cubs' left-fielder announced. Tad reached around Bass and put his hand on Trip's shoulder just when he'd started to stand up to talk back to Mann as would be predictable for him by now. "Watch Rookie," The Major ordered. "Klem's going to draw his famous line in the sand."

"Don't cross my line! Do *not* cross my line," Dode Paskert imitated the plate umpire in a deliberately comical voice, while they all saw that Barnes had run in from the mound to complain and probably even suggest Flack let himself be hit deliberately and that Bill Klem was tolerating nonsense by letting the Cub walk. But Tad suspected the call on the whole play came down from a higher authority. Barnes was following orders with his act *and acting*.

"New York thinks they're so entitled," Rollie Zeider commented. "That never changes."

"We should be out there kicking the shit out of Jesse Barnes," Trip said. "That's what I think." Killefer glared at him until Trip noticed and saw their true captain shaking his head from side to side.

"Hey Bright-Eyes. Yeah, *you* Everston. Shhh. And just wait for it. *Just wait for it*. And here it comes. Watch," Bob O'Farrell was best described as giddy with excitement. "And you all know I have to work next to this guy for 8 more innings of this shit. What a day today is going to be, eh Cubbies? Ha-hah."

"Ready now," Les Mann said.

"One. Two. And three. Yoouuu'rror outta here!" all the Cubs bench yelled at once, making enough noise with the words so they could only see Bill Klem mouth them and pump his arm, finger extended, telling Barnes in no uncertain terms to get the hell out of his sight. Chicago's whole stadium roared with the local fans' delight.

Then Coach Mitchell spoke up, glad to enjoy a continuing show of solidarity he witnessed with his young team. "Looks like they're going to send out Al Demaree." The Cubs watched the next New Yorker jog out to take the hill and start his warm-up from the mound. Lew McCarty would still remain out there to catch for him. "Hollocher, Mann: both of you hold on to your bats, stay up on the grass and work on timing him. He's fast. I also want the rest of you boys to study him. Demaree used to play *here*, back 'bout just three years ago."

"Then he's an ancient, old-timer now, Coach. He's like thirty-three I think," Charlie Hollocher looked back into the dugout as he added his comment with a snarky smile and nodding head, declaring, "I'm the new big deal."

"Hollocher, shut up, grow up, and do your thing so we can move Flack around the horn and catch up, 'Big Deal.' We're two runs behind possibly thanks to you *and the real Deal* sleeping out there. Talk about who's taking 'grandpa naps.' But enough with the age cracks, all right? You're the new big asshole. That's who you are." Dode Paskert called out.

"Yes, well I don't want any of you all underestimating Al, Fellas," Coach warned his squad. "Having the lead will energize him and his hardball shots keep on picking up more and more steam. Then you all should be on the lookout for a changeup. He's nasty. I'm going to need the whole bunch of you figuring out what you're going to do when you get up there. So work on *that* now. And I'm already considering sending all our left-handers in against Demaree. Hoffman, maybe for this occasion even you can run the bases instead of your mouth." George's eyes lit up with too much excitement to realize that his yearned-for call-up also included any insult.

Once Demaree was warm and ready to go, Charlie Hollocher used his call to the plate to also put in work for his team. A left-handed batter against Demaree's well-known swift, right-handed pitching, Charlie also had his attitude to assist him gaining another advantage. He knew Demaree wouldn't start him out with a changeup and his timing the Giant's hurler could help him right now. But he also wanted revenge. Hopefully, Tyler would answer for Barnes hitting Flack, but Charlie would answer for New York, making his team look stupid — especially he and Charlie Deal, who'd fallen victim to Youngs' hitting to his opposite field. Holly had a hidden talent for doing that on his own. He hammered one between Zimmeran at 3rd and Fletcher, playing for the Giants at shortstop. New York's left-fielder George Burns returned it fast to the latter from deep in The Friendly Confines but Max was almost to 3rd.

Holly should have had a double out of that, but he stopped in between 2nd and 1st and whistled. Fletcher only realized what he did and looked just as stupid — throwing the ball *before* he realized it. So sending it to Rodriguez, playing 2nd for New York, Fletcher tried to stop Charlie from advancing. He ran in to cover the 2-bag while Demaree got behind Holke, the Giants' 1st baseman, so they could run down Charlie. The Cubs' shortstop pivoted and sprinted back for the safety of 1st. But the ball reached Holke ahead of him and he took off gunning for Holly. So Charlie pivoted again and passed Rodriguez, but the ball was flipped to Fletcher and Charlie's cleats exploded up and out, scattering plenty of the infield dirt, as he spun around to retreat again. Only Rodriguez was tossed the ball and was the closest to the wild Hollocher, running like a crazy-man. The Giants had *all* taken the bait and caught Chicago's smart-ass shortstop between the bases. However, his antics worked and made fools out of all New York when Max Flack scored the first run for the Chicago Cubs standing up!

Al Demaree looked incensed when he returned to the mound as Flack and Hollocher both returned to all high-fives in the Cubs' dugout. Then Les Mann took his very next pitch for a ride to the outfield and was on base before New York knew it. Not content to let the Giants' pitcher recover for even an instant from his embarrassing inning, and already replacing the embarrassed Jesse Barnes, "The Major," took control of the field and bolted for 2nd base. Behind home plate for the Giants, Lew McCarty got the snap and fired to "El Hombre" but Mann dove under his glove and a cloud of dust. Emslie shouted "Safe!"

Fred Merkle's single got Mann to 3rd base. Dode Paskert's base hit brought Mann home and the Cubs had tied the score! But Youngs got it back to Rodriguez fast and he relayed it ahead of Merkle and took Chicago's 1st baseman for the 2nd out. Charlie Deal grounded one and got on, but it was down the 3rd baseline so Dode Paskert couldn't go anywhere. Then Rollie Zeider popped one up when Demaree offered his breaking ball, Fletcher running in to catch it, and that was 3. It would be New York's turn to bat again.

But in the 2nd inning, Lefty Tyler did answer for Barnes beaning Flack.

"Don't do it. Don't you even *do* it," Bill Killefer warned Tyler before he could sprint off to take the hill for the second time. But Chicago's pitcher looked determined. Because he got encouragement from a very surprising source. Both ballplayers saw Coach Mitchell quickly speaking with someone from park security and then swiftly cross the dugout and grab the Cubs' catcher for *this game* and relay some instruction to O'Farrell that wasn't audible to the others, aside from probably Tyler and Killefer. And Coach Mitchell did not look like a happy skipper. Taddeo had slid down the bench just so he could listen in.

Mitchell nodded to George Tyler. "Don't think I approve for one minute. But unfortunately it's not my call. You know what *we* have to do. Obey Bobby's call."

Interjecting into the conference of course just had to be Bill Killefer, learning for himself exactly what had upset Coach and triggered the Cubs' current "acting team captain" — on the field at least. Bob O'Farrell already responding for the starting pitcher, agreeing they'd follow Mitchell's plan; and he'd seemed insulted that the first-string catcher joined them and he addressed Killefer next to complain even before the senior backstop articulated one word. "Oh, c'mon Bill. *You* — don't do this. I already know what you're going to say. But this is my game to captain. New York wants a bean-ball game? Well Chicago's always ready to give them one."

Killefer ignored the backup catcher who got chosen to play this afternoon. He spoke to Lefty Tyler instead. "George, you're twenty-eight years old and a star. You gotta set an example for these youngsters. We don't need *you* thrown out of the game." He looked at Mitchell, his eyes revealing how much he hoped the Cubs' manager would change his mind. "Really, Coach?"

"Billy, it was deliberate. That first pitch. Barnes hitting Max? I *am* setting an example for the rookies. Besides, that's even Coach's orders." Lefty Tyler also looked to the Cubs' manager to support him standing up to Killefer. Getting caught between these two was not a good position to play. Mitchell didn't speak a word, opting to drink from his flask instead, eyes moving around to look at anything other than the three ballplayers he stood with. His command had been effectively stripped from him, no doubt by the team's owner, Charlie Weeghman.. He appeared like he thought he should no longer care about anything in this game.

"Klem will throw you out. I wouldn't mess with him."

But Lefty Tyler declared he'd ignore Killefer's final objection after relating, "You know, I'm just an employee. It sure looks like I don't get to vote."

"Apparently, neither do I. But I am going to have a long talk with Mister Weeghman later," the Cubs' manager finally said. "To pull this shit in the second inning — . Fuck!" Mitchell shook his head from side to side and looked down at the dugout's peanut shell-littered floor.

Next, sooner than later, and with a great big grin, O'Farrell totally called for the Cubs' pitcher to send one out to clip the Giants' 7-year veteran catcher, Lew McCarty. And Bill Klem did award Chicago's Tyler with the next free ticket for the exit to the stadium. On the bench, Taddeo Villetti pumped his arm and mouthed "Yes!" while he squeezed Trevor Bass' shoulder. He hoped that here was his opportunity to impress his papa if he was in fact in the stands — and maybe even throw for 7 and 2/3rds innings for the Cubs — and show *everyone* what he could really do.

But his very best friend looked over at him and shook his head side to side in disapproval. "Tad. No. And I hope you're really listening to me for once. Because you really want some sound advice?" The Hoff continued leaning over to speak softly in Tad's ear from the pitcher's other side. He was going to offer his opinion anyway, so the young Villetti just went with it and nodded. "If you do get the opportunity, pitch an honest game Tad. And right now. If Coach does call on you instead of Carter, don't escalate this and get any more of our guys injured. Show them why you were called up from Iowa. I wish I'd be going out there with you again, but you can work with O'Farrell. He's not Bill Killefer."

In the seats, sitting behind most of the other more important men, this gathering of sharp business instincts, Greggorio Villetti saw Charlie Weeghman responded to the top of the 2nd inning with inspiration. The game was paused while Bill Klem called both team managers out to home plate to try and put a stop to any bean-ball war before it escalated. But New York's 16-year manager John McGraw was not going to forgo any chance to fight if he could. Chicago's Coach Mitchell was going to love *this*. However, Umpire Bill Klem had one most intimidating reputation. And he was probably about to demonstrate his artistic talent again by drawing another line in the sand. So in plenty of time to allow for another performance by the maestro, and after he extinguished his cigar, then a glance toward Abraham Attell, and a nod to several of his other distinguished guests, in addition to Charlie Weeghman's eyes lingering on Greg's father for some reason, the Chicago team owner asked if everyone would please excuse him for a moment. Then he moved out of the first row to the aisle so he could approach the field and signal for a member of the security team to pass another message for him.

Darn. And I was just going to ask him for some game pointers about how a guinea like me could apply to join the Klu Klux Klan. Greg mused over that missed opportunity — which was not really missed at all. Why was the largely Italian Chicago Outfit *sitting with this racist bigot* who held one of the largest keys to the city? *Oh. That's why.*

Now Weeghman next sent off this next lackey to cut across the entire field to personally guide his team's game play to make sure his club would win — especially while Chicago entertained such important visitors. That *was* what he was doing? And why? *Wasn't it what he was doing?* Greg pondered these questions, not sure what he had just witnessed. He was sure things had started changing again, rapidly. Every Villetti had to be constantly ready to move so as to keep control over their destiny. Greggorio understood that game.

So still in the stands, and thinking he would not ever let himself be too intimidated — even by the present company — to *not* take advantage of a situation, this other Villetti got to make *his* play. He'd been adapting his strategy again. He always was. And a fascinating opportunity had wandered into his sphere of influence. Everyone else that really were important to Greggorio's more immediate plans just weren't here. So they didn't know it yet. "Well now, who is *that*?" Greg wondered, leaning forward in his seat, and inquiring out loud, hoping he'd get a response out of just the right man whose help he'd need.

"Who?" Colosimo's eyes ran over the replacement Cubs' battery from the plate to the youth running toward the hill, and then proceeded to re-examine the playing field before glancing back at Greggorio to see where he'd been staring. But the young Villetti's eyes focused a lot closer. In the stands, one row in front of him and to their left. Colosimo's gaze followed Greg's to another member of the visiting Morello Family party. "My mistake. They'd just called on your little brother to be put in. So I thought you were talking about the game. But you were talking about *the game*, weren't you, My Boy? Haha. I forget how now you're not as young as you were when I first met you. Not anymore. But then every man at every age appreciates such an attractive woman. I attribute my success in business to understanding that." He turned to his right far enough to allow him to smile behind his position. His thick, dark mustache moved when he aimed the expression at Greg, then nodded his fat head toward a woman now behind Big Jim's head who he didn't even need to look at to know where *she* sat. Her long straight dyed-blonde hair glistened with a bright sheen in contrast to all the dark hats that surrounded her shiny aura of radiating color. Colosimo turned back around to that enticing view to his left before looking back at Greggorio again to answer him. "This one's calling herself

Lumia now. She's one of Morello's girls. Word is she got out of running around with Brooklyn's circle, Frankie Yale's crowd, to reinvent herself in Manhattan. Great ass. So *everyone's* already now been told. Dyes the hair. Used to be called Lena Gallucio. Since then she earned the nickname Lucky LuLu. Something had happened back in New York. And she's been very lucky she's been able to run away from it. So far anyway. But unfortunate for you, you have a keen eye for beauty — and complications."

Greg took measure of the blonde girl in the white summer dress and started thinking about Colosimo's words, suggesting he "attributes his success in business to understanding exactly how far men can be motivated by women." His new plan about how to motivate Taddeo — and Urso especially — into finally doing exactly what Greg wanted, began to sharpen into an ordered process that he'd proceed from out of the darkest corners of that *complicated*, calculating mind that he could call upon. And just maybe use to succeed with, even more than Colosimo.

Now *Sega* looked kind of like the Villetti boys' mother. He could make use of *her* with Taddeo. Studying his little brother with contempt, who was just now ordered out on the field with the Cubs' catcher as they would warm up his pitching arm to finish the second inning, Greg knew what he had to do was cool things off between the Tadpole and Arlene. That team of two just begged for an ending to their happy cooperation. She'd thwarted Greg and his papa's intentions toward her more than several times now. For all everyone's alleged concern about an increase in Chicago's shootings, *she'd been the one dropping the most bodies* — and of that he had no doubt. He just couldn't prove it. And then Greg's own father had then stuck by his original conclusion that it was in his best interest to protect her but only *subject her* to show the bitch who was boss, *because* of her inconvenient relationship with Taddeo. Or had he witnessed his papa's change of mind when he sent her that wimp that had never returned since last Thursday? Greg only wished. But he did not know. Then there was that firefight the witch survived her crucible in, early this very same morning — that Simone and probably Thorello did not. His papa allegedly sent *one* of those goombahs too, but one of her bullets found its mark real quick. Greg had been better at choosing his own support men, though he still had no proof that Arlene was the shooter — or information about who else she might be working with. Yet. Though while the middle Villetti sibling watched Taddeo struggling to just locate the strike zone while still only practice pitching for the moment in an all-tied-up Giants game, Greg figured his kid brother wouldn't find any evidence of Arlene committing murder either, even if he'd tripped over the dead bodies as frequently as the rest of The Family did. *You only sent a message that was apparently never received and registered by one, and completely ignored by the other, Papa. You failed. But* I *won't.* And Tadpole would never want to wake up and blame Arlene. That idiot might even think he was in love. But much more so than his papa, Greggorio needed this new couple to split up and take a break — from their cooperation, but not their emotions.

Only for his plan to work, he saw he'd have to help Arlene arrive at that conclusion, but leave Tad still passionate enough about protecting her, no matter how far he was led to stray from her deadly green flytrap. Greg would make *her* dump the Tadpole and then his imbecile of a little brother would run right after her trying to change her mind, only to wind up charging straight into Urso. First he'd separate the oldest brother from Sega with Lumia, Greg's own plant in his papa's brothel, while he tempted Tad with Sega instead, and then "disappear" a no-longer-so-lucky LuLu, leaving Arlene with Urso's undivided attention until Taddeo would confront the eldest brother over that. And he'd keep an eye on Sega, to evaluate *her*, either as continuing to be more useful, or ultimately too dangerous to keep around. So the plan was still almost the same. But it was most inconvenient that Arlene was a lot smarter than even he'd expect to ever have to give a shamrock credit for. This little operation was going to take some really careful scheming just to maneuver around the murderous cunt. She'd become wise to this scheme almost immediately, even if Tadpole never did. Though it would be complicated, it would also be so worth it. *But I could have to use almost all of my favors and my own money.* This kind of payoff for Greg's sacrifice would come at a very high price. *Yet I* will *make it worth the cost to* me. *The opportunity of my lifetime is here in Chicago. Arlene and* her scheme *is the only thing standing in my way — only she still could* be *my way. But this Lumia should get Urso's attention.* Meanwhile, she was paying her full attention to the game as Greg thought, *Additionally, her usefulness might be multiplied if while I'm watching her, I learn this dumb little lily-flower-in-the-wind might actually like baseball. That could be quite useful to me again, later — with handling the Tadpole. If* he's *still alive and the shamrock witch is not. Huh. How lucky could* I *get? But first my little brother will have to discover a new agapé. One that realizes the injury done him by the loss of our mother. And to think Arlene first thought a woman would be my house's undoing. She just won't get to be that woman. So I'm going to have to deal with her and at least one other would-be alpha bitch no matter what, to make sure that I succeed with all my nice plans I have for my brothers.* But Greg thought he now knew how he might be able to neutralize all of them. And even without all the information he knew he should have had about Sega, the plotting middle brother prepared to initiate his new plan, having accepted that he would be involving himself in over his head with the most powerful and dangerous companion he now sat with.

Big Jim continued on about one of those relevant subjects for Greg's interest now. "So this acquaintance of Frankie Yale's — from Brooklyn originally I think — she'll probably belong to Masseria sooner than later. He takes what he pleases from Morello's outfit while their boss is in prison. Well, that Don's only been locked away for many seasons, and he's furious, but there wasn't a whole lot of hope that he could do anything about it until now. If he ever will be able to do anything. Some people are very concerned things are changing."

Yeah. No shit. But Greg kept that thought to himself.

"Well, in any case, the girl is destined to be Joe's property very soon. By the way, be most mindful that the cops you can *buy* can always *already* be bought by someone else. However, no matter what's happening in New York, I'm making sure that nothing will so drastically change — at least for the worst — in Chicago."

Greg had long since noted Detective Conway had gotten seats for his men this time, a little ways further back in the stands, here on the 1st base side. *Who set up the pig trough so close? Colosimo?* Or that still could possibly have been his papa, further stretching what The House could afford. The Villetti son knew Chicago's Finest did real fine looking out for themselves and *Weeghman* might surely be sympathetic to their cause, as well. *He* would need all the swine in uniform, too. The men in blue who regularly met with the ballclub owner *knew* who he truly was.

And Colosimo continued, but keeping his voice from reaching any further than Greggorio behind and to the right of him. "Meanwhile, Joe the Boss is both an effective asset for The Clutch, and has grown with their Back East organization to become very powerful. Too powerful. I cannot trust that he is not running The Black Hand — and even dealing with our dear blasting friend

Cardinella, personally — to mean giving *Il Diavolo* himself his support — and his orders. So The Boss takes what he wants and Masseria has had his eyes on this one, I'm sure. Or he soon will." Big Jim motioned with his eyes only, toward the blonde-haired trophy at the ballgame. "I heard all the gossip while I personally poured the Terranovas drinks at my place on Wabash."

Meaning you'd already been asking about her.

"Okay. So now here's the real skinny about the girl. Ya better listen up, Son. The Sicilians got her in a trade with D'Aquila, who'd been hiding her from Morano in Yale's bar as it were. She's the sister of some small-time heavy who occasionally looks for work and thinks he's a lot more important than he is. Meanwhile, Brooklyn and Manhattan have attempted to cool things off and try and forge some kind of common agreement. Like The Outfit and O'Banion's leprechauns did here in Chi-Town. Lumia was just one conciliation prize the two factions of Morello's house exchanged. I think you understand how that works. But Morano loses her out of Brooklyn before he even knew he had her. Irrelevant story. He's a fool and he too has currently got more bars than I think he could handle keeping track of in prison anyway. Not that I care. But now the Terranovas only brought Lumia here to flaunt her in front of Arnold Rothstein's people. He's one of Weeghman's other new guests over there." Colosimo nodded in the stands to their left. A largely built man in a white suit and hat was watching the game from the best seat on their side. Lighter-complexed, he might have been a German. A young Villetti would know better. And that shylock had remained quiet and instead let Abraham Attell speak for him while the fat but sharp Jewish crime boss watched and listened, gathering information. Very clever — a master at his work. "So the Terranova side of the Morello Family thinks the girl makes them look good, sophisticated, and in control, so they can shine one last time, and win as much confidence as it is possible *for them* — to gain the head Jew's favor, before they fall under Masseria's and their half-brother's shadows again. Word is Morello's getting released in only days and *this game* might be truthfully changing, significantly, and real soon. So everyone needs allies, right? Now women *are* nice things, M' Boy. But remember, they can be of many great uses, not only as breeders to grow our houses, but as these political trophies, too. And they can definitely serve to a great capacity in underhanded negotiation tactics." He winked at the son of the Villetti House behind him.

"You don't say?" *I'm way ahead of you on that Diamond Jim.*

Don't lose your polish. He knew Colosimo had earned several other nicknames including that one, which had floated around town in The Windy City. Then Greg looked out to the other side of the field again and at his younger brother on the practice pitcher's mound. Tad fired away another one *the Cubs' catcher* ruled a strike. There was that obvious bias. But his sibling's performance was improving, though it was still only the second inning — and this was still only his warm-up. Tad had yet to climb the hill and face any real guns New York brought out to bear on him. But Greg saw LuLu intently watch his performance — which had been preceded only by Taddeo's dumbest antics yet — with her most sincere and admiring interest. "Hmmm. Just for once, I'd like to win the trophy too." He knew Colosimo might not resist such a simple opportunity to encourage more loyalty from one the most likely on the rise among all his own soldiers' houses. Maybe he could procure himself a bargain? It would be a bargain if Greg didn't have to again reach for his thinning money holder and this time Colosimo paid his bill instead. "Do you think *she* has a stake in this game, or might she be persuaded to cheer for Chicago?"

"I think the Terranovas must be aware that whatever is theirs now, will be their new patron Masseria's in only moments from now. The balance of power shifts in The Borgata. That'd be where I'd place my bet. I'd also predict that if Vincenzo and Ciro have any *capital*, they will want to invest it before even *his* patron collects his long overdue taxes. They know Morello's coming home. So they are using the girl to play for the Jews."

"Sorry. I was trying to be clever. My apologies. What I meant was do you think you can make a deal for her to come *here*, to stay with me?" Greggorio asked as innocently as possible.

"I'll ask Victoria, but why not?" Big Jim smiled at the youth from his organization. "Vincenzo and Ciro will see it as an opportunity to forge an alliance *in Chicago* before Joe the Boss asserts himself over Morello. They might be persuaded to trade the girl. I think their current plan *is* to win them favors from the Jews, but they might see the wisdom in taking an easy opportunity to make gains way over here in Chi-Town. The Mafia is fractured. Through our organization in Chicago, the Terranovas have another way to gain a stronger alliance with the shylocks. There are strategic patterns you must learn to recognize in Cosa Nostra. But Peter should never think that when he leaves prison, he may just walk right back in to New York and everything will be the way it was when they forced him to leave his city for Atlanta. So now the Terranovas will see it as having invested in *me* owing their half-brother a favor from The Outfit. *If* there ever came the day when I could be assured I'd be dealing with the weakened Peter Morello instead of a hard-case like Giuseppe Joe Masseria. Huh. I only wish. But it's a great deal for me to make because it's the nearly free kind-of-cheap, plus it keeps a channel of information about New York open for me that my business certainly needs. What I need to always have is my own ear on the grapevine and people who might come to me with things they won't bring to D'Andrea, and because they are afraid of Sal Cardinella. I am not afraid of *him* — and because of your papa, I actually don't have to be. I know a lot more than Rinaldo thinks I do. I have my ways. *But I can be friendly*. Oh, yes. I'm not unaware of the cease-fire he took part in that saw negotiations try to assure that Taylor Street would become a neutral zone. And *other* friendly men who are trying too hard to impress their lady escorts also talk — too much. About too many things. A good girl can be trained to listen for what's best for her patron to hear." Colosimo laughed. "So way to keep your eye on the ball for me, Young Villetti. I have a place for a beauty like that one over on Wabash Street."

"No."

"What?"

"I mean, no she can't just be treated like that. A lady like *her?* Lena, or Lumia, whatever she calls herself now. She must be allowed to go home first. And I mean *not* to Manhattan, but to Brooklyn. Now I figured her to be Neapolitan. Isn't she?" He relaxed Colosimo's guard for a moment by bringing up trivialities. Those that centered on talking about women were always fun.

"Yes. No. Swiss-Italian probably. I think by her looks at least."

"That's right. Didn't you say she dyes her hair? But anyway, she must have family. Among blood, maybe refugees. You mentioned a brother. And like a lot of people, her real family probably fled tragedy in the Old Country — brought about by the earthquake, the war. Or one of the wars at least. Or economics. Something that shapes the heart. That *is* everyone's story isn't it?" Greg looked over the rise and fall of the young lady's chest. She had a nice chest, too. "And now she has certainly, definitely *developed* some *wares* that she can use to survive over here. But let her pack and say goodbye. I'd like her to look forward to coming to Chicago — as a better place. A positive move to change her otherwise predestined life, maybe for the better. And I mean for her to be offered a position in The Villetti House. So she's still to be *yours*, in so much as that aspect. But look at it as being a reward for my father — or really me — who sees to it that your favorite soldier gets his work done."

"Oh, I see. I see that you've got some nerve asking this of *me*. I see that you're manipulative, and that you're cruel, Greggorio. You'd give her hope. What shaped *your* heart?"

"Well, I — ."

"Yes. You needn't say it. That's what I like about you. I know what you're really up to, My Boy." That startled Greg. But his tension quickly ebbed when Colosimo said, "You want her to be grateful to you because you're coming to like her. Ha. That didn't take very long. *You're not married, are you?* And you're still so young. But you're also becoming a smart businessman and a gentleman like your father." Greg laughed to himself while the man also called Diamond Jim continued. "Want to appear respectable, eh? You give *me* hope — that my businesses are in good hands over on Taylor Street. I suppose there *is* a reward for that. The work your people did to keep Cardinella in check. But do not forget that *you* will then still owe *me* an extra inning. Indeed, I understand why Morello sees much he likes learning about in 'The House Villetti.' " Colosimo turned his head back toward the game, smiling because he likely enjoyed predicting his underlings fancied themselves their own "sub-level house" in The Outfit, as obviously, so did Greg's papa. Then Big Jim grimaced and had to rub his neck where he must have cramped it from turning it for so long behind him. He glanced over his other shoulder to take account of Rinaldo, who was watching his other son prepare to pitch to his first batter. Colosimo looked like he'd just grown acutely concerned about something else. But Villetti was seated closer to the Terranovas upon *their* request.

My father knows more about what's going on than Big Jim does.

So finally — on Morello — Colosimo offered, "Peter has had plenty of time in his cage to muse over the word he receives about all kinds of operations that could interest him. And he feels the respect in the tribute we pay him — for our family members in New York's behalf — and in how our outfit and D'Andrea have managed to get along in Chicago right down to the local level, in a manner of speaking. And it's not only those who follow Cosa Nostra that are admiring us. But know that the Jews also see plenty of opportunities in dealings with Chi-Town as well." His head was now turned in such a way that he was most likely focused on Taddeo, while tasting his beer, his eyes narrowing, but then also nodding to the men seated in the stands toward his left at the same time. Greg made some more observations. As Colosimo's eyes moved to his cigar he brought up to take a puff from, another man's eyes kept dipping downward to one of the seams in the young lady's stylish dress, which exposed the intoxicating shape of Lumia's trim tan legs. She'd crossed the nearest one over her lap and wiggled it with toned muscles while she watched the game and the boys on the field, with youthful excitement and smiles. And in short order, *many a man* watched her. Meanwhile, the many wheels that operated in the middle brother's mind worked overtime as he noted exactly who else was taking interest in the girl.

Greg raised his arm to rest his chin in his hand while he tried to consider *what Colosimo was considering*, and what the associates that came out from New York with the Terranovas might represent, and what they wanted in Chicago. Did it also have something to do with his brother? Why have their meeting in a ballpark? How could Taddeo *possibly* be important to these men from out of town? He dismissed that idea. Maybe this was all just to make their work introductions fun? But Greggorio could also use more information about these New York *Jews* — of which group Big Jim revealed the gentlemen to the left belonged to. He might have considered them useful friends to have in light of The Chicago Outfit's proximity to the Bernstein brothers and their Purple Gang in Detroit — the most dangerous kind of kikes to have on Chi-Town's back doorstep. However, until he gathered more intelligence, Greg couldn't even consider being really informed enough to be capable of further manipulating everything else to his own advantage. He wasn't that well-traveled. It sure felt like things *were* growing more inter-statuary and more complicated. *There were so many players*. And then only a second had passed when he felt shocked by himself — by his sudden unplanned-for self-reflection on just how much his own ambition had grown. What he'd started thinking. What game he just stepped up to playing. What without hesitation he had just accomplished regarding the girl — stepping up right before Big Jim Colosimo. And that he would be so quick to act and set into motion in his next new and unique approach to making more gains on his own behalf. And one more very fine pair of legs that would help him along his journey there.

"Then you know what, Mister Colosimo? I think I can really help you make it worth your while if you'll introduce me to well — to everyone." Greg smiled.

"Oh, don't worry about that. I already know who you want to

meet first."

But then, a short few seconds later his and Lumia's arms were locked as he escorted the young lady for a walk up from the field level seats and back out the tunnel nearest the 1st base side. They were arm and arm, laughing while he intended to parade her around the concession stands on the main concourse to buy her a refreshing, cold *Coca-Cola* on this hot day, plus peanuts or some cotton candy, making a presentation out of it. The Terranovas *and* Arnold Rothstein's party turned their heads to watch them and neither looked amused. *Good. It's about time for them all to notice* me. *My little brother's not that entertaining*. Big Jim might have been chuckling to himself, but Greg's father's eyes were caught somewhere between revealing he was incensed — and really afraid. All at the same time. To say the senior Villetti was also not amused would be understating it. And at the same time while, with their last sighting of Greg's little brother, he had been making an absolute moron out of himself trying to emulate ballet with a baseball or something. Greggorio didn't know what Tadpole was thinking or doing in front of the whole goddamned stadium. But "LuLu" laughed and giggled. Greg being sure the youngest Villetti thought he was just such the highlight of the afternoon for everyone. As all the while this girl, who was shockingly pretty, in a cute sort of way, put Greggorio in the best personal position to see that it only took one idiot to entertain another. With his best plan now adapted to deal with the evolving circumstances, and now improved upon — and still only involving the singular addition of Lumia, with Urso, Taddeo, and Sega — this was going to be easy. That is, he'd be mostly working to manipulate incredibly stupid people. And their own idiocy would then serve to thwart Arlene and his father, the most dangerous customers at his store of intrigue. Even Colosimo was being accommodating. And LuLu, as she had announced Greg should call her, smiled, pressing close against his body, so close he could feel her so glad to be there, trying to warm him, his cold misshapen heart, her blue eyes looking up into his — with hope and possibly affection. It surprised him how anyone could be that naïve and trusting. But he could be quite charming, along with also being extremely dangerous.

So next the pair stopped to play a baseball-themed beanbag tossing game set up on the main concourse and they held hands for a brief moment while Greg guided her arm. And in his carefully guarded coldness, Greg thought the only ones he really had to worry about guiding their going his way now, were Arlene, and his apparently more-clever-than-he-had-estimated, papa. Everyone else couldn't be that smart. But he was gifted so Greggorio *should be* disappointed with the majority of humanity, or impressed with himself. He preferred the latter, and just like the bean-bag and bean-ball players, all the lesser-people just lined up to play their sacrificial role.

Chapter 27

Saturday, May 25, 1918
2:59 pm CST
Weeghman Park, Chicago, Illinois

2nd Inning
New York – 2, Cubs – 2

0 Outs, 1 On – (NY Lew McCarty, 1st base, HBP)

AB: The New York Giants (23 W – 7 L):
Jose "El Hombre Goma" Rodriguez (2B, Bats: right, Throws: right)
AVG .160, OBP .239
Age: 24, Games: < 40, Status: junior year rookie,
1st real full season in The Show

On the mound:
Chicago Cubs (19 W– 11 L)
(Fighting the 1st place NY team, CHC now ranking 2nd in the NL)
P: Taddeo "The Shooter" Villetti (R)
(Bats: Right, Throws: Right) 1 W – 2 L, PCT: .333, ERA: 3.0, SO: 4,
HB: 3 x (in 3 games!)
Age: 19, Games: 3, Status: freshman rookie
[in trouble again, of course]

AND THEN:

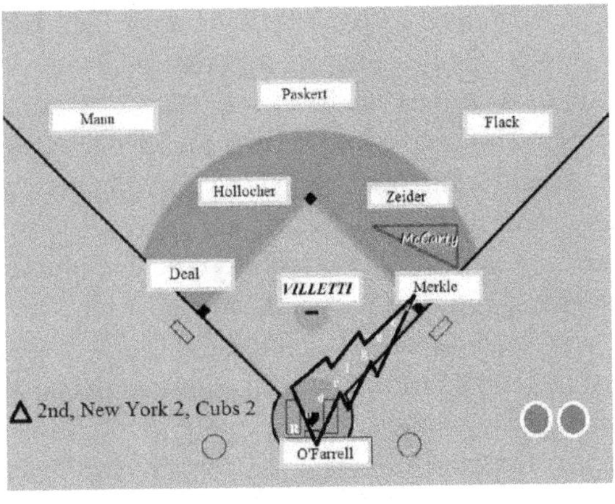

As his manager's signal guided him to now run out to the mound to complete his warm-up tosses with Bob O'Farrell behind the dish, grateful that at least it wasn't Bill Killefer, Tad couldn't help but think of how he could be so much more comfortable if Coach Mitchell would just keep putting him out there with The Hoff. Now Taddeo had to worry about coming in with a runner already on and no outs to boot. But he wanted to show them all what he could really do if he would be allowed to pitch for more innings than just getting the quick assignments in which he'd so far opted to just use tricks and an attitude to help him make the outs that the Cubs needed to get from his work. But first things were first, and he'd settle in to pitch one hell of game even after he'd deliberately danced in towards the infield grass doing all manner of moves not to exclude gymnastics, tossing up his hat, and then juggling it with his glove and a baseball while running backwards — and all the objects weighing in differently, and thus only making him appear like a clumsy idiot as Tad waved and smiled at the crowd. The youth had a pretty good idea about how a lot of Chicagoans felt about him already, and he, even when *he definitely did not*, displayed for all, that he had a sense of humor about it — plus the black eye and swollen face which Dan Griner gave him on Tuesday. So thereby he demonstrated that nothing more anyone said or did now, could get under his skin. And Taddeo Villetti lit up the stadium with his boyish smile, reassured by the knowledge he'd start from a safe spot by facing the bottom of the Giants' order. At least the rest of his very first inning in this game couldn't possibly go *that* wrong, Tad thought.

Previously, he'd sent George on a mission for him just to ensure it. Hoff had already gotten in trouble with Coach for flirting with a woman in the stands once already this game. *Wasn't that every game?* But that woman was Roslyn and young Villetti knew something about Rose's true identity that George hadn't learned yet. And what Tad knew would now be of use to him. The reliever was even thankful that Hoffman could at least manage to get his woman to The Show. Arlene would never relent to being bothered to offer up any enthusiasm, and support Taddeo's pitches. But Tad wasn't about to stand for *anyone*, especially from the syndicate, interfering in the way he played his game. The real truth was the pitcher was plenty angry, only he'd just gotten better at hiding it. Subterfuge being a new skill he'd developed for his arsenal, along with his slider and his cutter he continuously worked on.

So he started stretching out his arm some more with extra practice throws to O'Farrell from the mound this time, his mind continued evaluate everything. His partial success with Mr. Li that morning increased his self-confidence. Taddeo's effort might've yielded weak results, but they should at least *and finally* keep Arlene safe while he left for the Cubs' away games. He continued to toss his warm-up pitches while he also figured Mr. Li would come around to the right decision about the whole deal in the very near future. Greg and Urso would be visiting him after this game. Then Mr. Li might also be inclined to change his mind about Tad working and also living there — either because of Tad's generosity, and that Mr. Li thought Taddeo would be a buffer to shield the Chinaman from the rest of the Villettis and especially any low-level goombahs, or because Arlene would charm the Chinaman. He sure hoped something would work. But then he reminded himself he needed to stay focused on *his work* in the immediate present. For Tad that would be what was happening in this hour, in Weeghman Park, his work *there*, rather than on what the closely following days were going to require of him. Only one thing that wouldn't happen, Tad swore, is anybody from New York, or his papa, seeing him as anything less than accomplished by his turn as the reliever that afternoon. Taddeo had his first win under his belt versus the Brooklyn Robins. He thought he might no longer fear facing *them*, and now he'd let all the Giants and their fans know he was just as unafraid. They were only 3½ games ahead of the Cubs. It was May and he and his team had little to worry about. Tad hoped. But Hoff was right. Now was the time to show his worth on the 1918 roster. Tyler had answered Barnes and Tad should feel no need to hit any Giants batters. If the Cubs could only sweep New York this series, the two baseball teams would nearly tie within that half-game. With this in mind, still in the top of the 2nd inning of the first game of this series, Taddeo hoped to make his contribution to that sweep.

He had flashed that bright smile and waved to the crowd, turning around and running backwards around the infield grass, tossing the baseball up and catching it behind his back, and then took his cap off and waved it as he spun around and then caught the ball inside of it. After that, Tad had taken a bow toward the visiting team's stands, hoping his papa watched him from somewhere. It really bothered him that because New York visited there, some spectators were likely guests of The Outfit, and therefore his father might not even be able to sit in the home team's stands — the very first time his papa came to see him play professionally. Tad would resent any knowledge that reached him about his family having to once again cater to The

Empire State. There were small waves of anger beginning to form in the calm lake of tranquility Taddeo tried to imagine himself relaxed on. He then decided not to particularly try and spot anyone in the stands during his "first performance." He had just finally danced back up and onto the hill and taken another bow he aimed at Charlie Hollocher. Now he needed to relax and settle in to do his duty for his ballclub. So Tad also didn't bother investigating the possibility the audience was booing him and Taddeo ignored whatever the big-mouth in the left-field box was hollering at him. Screw that guy, anyway.

So he pretended he didn't mind them all thinking of him as some precocious fool. He was going to be the pitcher of record for this game, not *fool around* once the action really got started, and he'd show them all that he was really an ace hurler, indeed. Yet he was still angry and nothing seemed to work very long to help him find peace. Instead he'd take his fury head on — and use it. There'd be no backing down now. This was who he was.

But the situation was not that grim as the Cuban, Jose Rodriguez stepped out of his side's dugout. Hitting right-handed with only a .160 batting average and a .239 OBP, Tad wasn't afraid of "El Hombre" — or John McGraw's strategies. With no outs and McCarty already on 1st where Tyler had put him, the Giant's coach would order up a textbook sacrifice bunt. It was predictable. A no-brainer. Tad waved his infield in.

"Tell me you're not going to order a hit on anyone with one of your cannon balls, Villetti."

"Just listen up guys." Without Killefer trying to dominate the diamond, Tad felt better about his relationship with his infield. In the huddle, Villetti took control and asserted himself before O'Farrell even got to speak one word. "Zeider, cover 2nd base. Charlie, get behind him. I've got 1st. I'll spin off my follow-through. Merkle, charge all the way in. You'll have your balance to react faster. Deal, be ready to come in as well and we'll take 2 of them Coogan trolls."

"That's good leadership skill you're showing, Pooper — er, I mean Shooter," O'Farrell complimented him and patted his pitcher on the back while using the nickname Hoffman had circulated around for Taddeo. But he wouldn't let Tad feel too good about himself, although he seemed to have an easy time brushing off any insult he might have taken by the rookie pitcher calling the play. "Just remember, when I'm on the field, I'm the captain and Merk here is The First Officer. You're the pitching peon. But I am still impressed you're not planning on hitting anyone."

"We're only in the top of the second inning."

"Of course."

"Alright. You're done, Chicago!" Bill Klem hollered at them. The conference split up.

"That's right. You're done, Boquita Hermano. Finita." Rodriguez was trying to goad Tad into hitting him so maybe the pitcher with the bad rep for a bad temper would just load the bases for New York and they wouldn't have to sacrifice anyone except for a few bruises until they could move more men around the horn. Tad had never really hit anyone hard. Yet. But Taddeo Villetti was changing.

The Cubs had just lost one of their ace pitchers in only the 2nd inning. The Giants had a runner on 1st. And for some reason the Cubs' skipper could not have fathomed, the orders came from the top to send Tad in following Lefty Tyler getting himself intentionally ejected from the game. But Taddeo had acted like he didn't have a care in the world and was just out there to enjoy himself, showing off. He needed to in order to feel like his old self — the self he knew *before* the leprechaun behind the wheel of a taxicab had dumped on him the reality of his Big League career thus far. So the young Villetti had vowed to make all the changes that he could to improve his circumstances. But something in him had really changed. After his meeting with Misters Li and O'Rourke that morning, he almost wanted to deny his own reflection in the mirror. He had scared himself. He was getting tougher and stronger, but more calloused as time went along since he'd gotten home from learning his craft better in the minors, while with the Cubs' farm team. Instead, he was finally learning to really command a new game, and started this inning on a new approach — one Tad knew would change him into the same kind of men who eyed the challenge he represented to *this particular visiting team*, from up on his position at the top of Chicago's hill. Taddeo Villetti had just then spotted some of them and knew who the real men would be in this crowd. A shiny white suit reflecting the sunlight stood out — this revealing exactly *who* would come to The Friendly Confines, to not be very nice at all, but root for New York. And it would be with those fellas that Tad would likely find his papa. He glanced in the stands but couldn't spare any real time to look for the old man. He just felt angry that it would be The Family's interference that saw him assigned to the hill and to relieve Lefty Tyler before only the second batter in only the 2nd inning. He wasn't naïve, it was just that Taddeo needed to become known for his skills to get him called upon — that presumably got him called *up*. Not as who — with his papa's insane influence he held over Mitchell — *but surely not also over Weeghman* — got his son to see more playing time. That was insulting. So it would be his skill, not his lack of self-discipline that Tad would put on display next, this outing.

Instead of continuing the bean-ball war, he started working against Rodriguez by throwing him an off-speed pitch that broke toward the outside. *And El Hombre Goma thought he'd throw off Taddeo with his bunt move...*

It was just like the play would be described in one of McGraw's books — and just as predictable. Fred Merkle raced right in after the ball, which stayed fair by traveling close enough to the infield grass. But it was slow enough that *O'Farrell* barehanded the ball, stooping low to grab it with his fingers and then pivoted as *the backstop* rose up and threw it down to Zeider. Merkle ducked out of the way. Simultaneously, Taddeo ran for 1st base with his cleats chewing up the grass, green blades flying off behind him in contrast to his dirty gray uniform, which was supposed to look white. The Giants' Les McCarty started his slide early, realizing he wasn't going to make it in time to beat the throw to 2nd and with one leg crossed over the other, his heel he had down to the dirt sprayed the gravel as he aimed it to connect with Rollie Zeider's shin. Now tagging 2nd and jumping over McCarty, untouched after making one force-out, he was mid-air when he fired a bullet at Taddeo, who got the ricochet to put Rodriguez out at 1st.

"Double-Play Chicago!" Pat Pieper announced. "It's a two-four-one by your Cubs!" That was true in at least a couple of different ways.

Now the Giants had just scored 2 in the 1st inning and the Cubs had come back and made it an even game. So O'Farrell was catching for Tad since Mitchell gave Killefer even one more day off to rest. *Or was he guarding the restraint of my teammates again since Coach doesn't trust me pitching? Was my outing even deliberately planned upon? Before we even began this game? Later I'll have to see if I can remember to get a look at the scorecard and if Bill's name was ever on it, now scratched out. Well it's all good. I'll get to win in front of Papa, and show everyone else from New York City to Chicago's taxicab drivers just what I can do. I mean besides becoming paranoid.* Tad looked for his papa in the stands once more. *He must be here. And while Coach thinks I'll fight Bill and he doesn't trust that putting me on with Hoff won't encourage us both to act up again, there's still no one out here that has the wherewithal to stifle my playing the way I want to play this game. O'Farrell is afraid of my family as maybe Killefer should be.* However, with Demaree on the mound for the Giants, Mitchell still might need to bring George off the bench to send in another left-handed bat. Tad could hope. As the Giants' reliever approached the plate for his turn to bat, Taddeo knew he wanted to keep that guy in the game. But Taddeo had just shot for a pitcher's best friend — the double play. And speaking of pitchers, Demaree wasn't very hard to retire with a strike-out on straight fastballs — just like he preferred to throw, but obviously couldn't hit. That was 3 gone. New York would have to return to the field. It was Chicago's turn to unleash punishment with their bats now.

So Tad didn't know why he instead of someone like Paul Carter or even Phil Douglas wasn't called out there to relieve the ejected Tyler. It just *had to do* with Tad's family. But he finally felt he was showing them all he deserved to be out there. Because in truth, interference in his baseball career was one of the very last things Tad wanted to see come out of his family. Though this one time, it might not be so bad. So before he would next take the mound in the 3rd as he hoped, Chicago's rookie pitcher went over all New York's lineup in his mind, determining who he still might want to plunk, and the various other, better ways he could handle the batters he faced. Ross Youngs would be up again, the first batter next inning. His attitude was that he did not need O'Farrell's calls on that. And seizing the opportunity to take the hill for only his fourth-ever official Major League appearance, Taddeo had almost relaxed.

But then he became a lot less comfortable when he stepped into the on-deck circle. Charlie Deal was now on the record as having become the last out in the 1st inning. McGraw had surprisingly — and successfully — contested the play at 1st base that had been called by Bob Emslie. But the Giants manager would regret that soon enough. After Zeider got another opportunity, succeeded with it, as did then O'Farrell, Taddeo would be called up to the plate for his very first turn to bat — not only in this game, but it was also his first turn to bat *ever*, at the Major League level. And it felt like the entire stadium booed him. It wasn't just the New Yorkers. The so-called Chicago heckler in the left-field seats even took to bad-mouthing *him*, and the "new nativists" in the stands took to chanting "Whop the wop! Whop the wop!" Taddeo gulped. He just knew Al Demaree was going to try to hit him with one of his fastballs, not only because

Tyler had thrown a blow to McCarty in the top of the inning, but because Villetti, with only his 3 games on the books behind him, already had forged the kind of reputation that screamed he really deserved to get hit. But Bob was already on 1st with a single now. Zeider had gotten on before him. Was it worth it to Demaree to put a third runner on base by beaning Villetti? That would put O'Farrell *also* in scoring position for the Cubs while Zeider would be on 3rd and New York had gotten ø outs.

Tad stepped into the right-handed batter's box and felt his knees shaking. He looked at Coach Mitchell for direction and received the signal for a sacrifice. *Yeah, it looks like I'll be making a sacrifice one way or another.* Demaree glowered at him, clenching his jaw and narrowing his eyes the way a sniper might before he took his shot for the kill. Making sure Tad kept at least one eye on him, he tried to look to his left so he could also receive Hoff's reassurance from the Cubs' bench. But Hoff was distracted by trying to talk to some girl in the stands. Naturally. And perfectly predictable. The relief pitcher wasted a second hoping that it would be Rose he was speaking with again. This could be almost as comforting to Taddeo as it would obviously be to Hoff. He'd hoped she'd accomplished a certain errand for him. But Tad had to keep his eye on the ball. He was ready to come around and square off his bat so he could at least defend himself against Demaree. That would hopefully at least get Bob O'Farrell into scoring position, and in a less painful way. But in the corner of his eye, he saw extremely quick motion in the stands and if he weren't mistaken, Harold Olsen had burst out of his seat and was running down the stairs towards the brick wall.

That's when O'Farrell wound up becoming the Cubs' runner on 2nd base anyway as the Giants' Al Demaree really wound one up and struck his hit right into the young Villetti's face! The impact of the 85-mph baseball felt like it smashed Tad's left eye socket. His body followed his head as he reflexively spun 360 degrees and he fell over the dish. He had been served. And was it ever painful. Then, even over the ringing noise in his head, he could hear the unmistakable voice of his father screaming "He hit my son! *My* son!"

I guess it was *worth putting a third runner on base just to come at me,* Tad thought. *Hell, I've even intentionally walked a run in before. And a third of the time I pitch.* Now, through his undamaged right eye, whose vision was half-filled by a close-up examination of the infield dirt, he raised his head up just enough so that he could look back underneath his awkward position, for a desperate, hopeful view of Chicago's bench. There he saw Trip and Bass-Man push Killefer aside and back against the dugout wall as George took off running onto the infield. He ran alone and went straight for Tad, as Bill Klem hustled to put himself between The Hoff and Al Demaree, while the Cubs' manager ordered the rest of the team back off their feet while he began running out to meet with Klem and John McGraw to settle this himself. Young Officer Olsen had actually thrown his legs over the short brick barrier on the visiting team's line to hustle over and insert himself as a weak obstruction to any attempt by the Giants to clear their bench, should Chi-Town decide to take up that tactic first. Out of uniform, everybody there could easily be oblivious to the rookie officer's position. He looked exactly like a kid. Only stadium security knew who he was and rushed to support him. One drifted around home plate's gravel to go stand near the boys in the Cubs' lineup. But New York and Chicago already had *their men* stationed all around the ballfield — different kinds of men. Though the strongest irony that hit the *second* hardest in this moment, was that the wounded pitcher sought out his teammates for support, over that of his father.

Taddeo, picking himself up, off-balance, incensed by Demaree, and stumbling as it were, still managed to tumble around the umpire who was then distracted by the Cubs' and Giants' coaches as Tad tripped over himself trying to pay back what was New York's latest shot they took at him. Was he ever ready for a fight — his father's anger encouraging him on — even if his best pal made known he disagreed with that move in the extreme. But Hoff's first concern when he caught up to him, was his pitcher's safety.

Caught in all the restlessness out in the stands up on the right field viewing deck level where Greggorio Villetti had walked Lumia to as they explored the park, Tad's brother decided upon caution first. "C'mon. Maybe we'll go explore *outside* the stadium a bit. I'll introduce you to a baseball player I know a little later. This is your first time in Chicago?"

The petite blonde haired girl looked up into his face and beamed her smile, lit with her large, bright blue eyes. She nodded. Greg put his arm around her. He could see that he could take her just about anywhere right now. And he thought that *out of proximity to any further ensuing trouble on the field* might be a good location to start with. His plan to really hurt his competition took priority over how much he'd have enjoyed watching his little brother stumble around in pain after getting hit.

"Tad! You all right?" Hoffman had quickly reached the wounded batter.

"I'll live. That guy Al doesn't hit too hard. Not while he's scared to play in Chicago." Tad tried to show some bravado, responding loudly, as George helped him to stand up. "I'll have to reaffirm that he should be. So you better let me go, Hoff. Right now."

George looked his buddy over. "I don't think you are seeing the situation clearly, Pooper. Demaree let you have yourself one hell of a shiner. In any event, it will go well with your other one. Either way, you're in no shape to fight right now. What I had better do is make sure you stay in this game. And playing bean-ball won't help you there."

A one-eyed glimpse at McCarty behind the plate for the Giants showed him turning away to hide his smile. After receiving the ball, Al Demaree was looking away into the outfield, his back towards Taddeo and the umpire, who could now be heard in a screaming match with Fred Mitchell and John McGraw.

"Really? Well did you speak with Rose?" Tad asked his best friend.

"Yeah. Your message is being delivered. You could still have a chance to handle this your own way, without any interference from your father. So I wouldn't implicate yourself as an accomplice to any more trouble your family might create. I hope you're right and that they'll listen to her and heed your wishes. I guess you know something about my new girl that I don't. But I also guess you could have blurry vision *and still foreseen that pitch coming*. So listen to me: do not continue something that'll just get worse and worse. Uh-oh," Hoff said and helped Taddeo turn to see Klem drawing his line in the sand right in-between the opposing managers.

"What now?"

But McGraw and Mitchell backed down from the blue, though the umpire called out Demaree by name and made him turn around and see Bill Klem issue him a message by way of one more official warning. Then he issued Tad a free pass to 1st base and he let the Cubs' George Hoffman walk Tad down to take the bag. That's when the young Villetti did finally connect eyes with his father in the stands. It was once a universal truth that he would have been overjoyed to see his papa there, watching him play, save for the fact that his father's companions occupied almost a whole two rows in the 1st base box seating over *on the Giants' baseline,* and Taddeo recognized Diamond Jim Colosimo — who was busy actually cow-towing to someone else which had started while his father was screaming at Bill Klem and John McGraw as the latter turned to head back to the 1st base dugout. Not one part of this could ever be considered good, especially considering who the Cubs were playing and exactly *which fans* from out of town they might attract. Tad was now both afraid of his family — and for his family. He always imagined his papa standing to cheer his son's performance at his game. However, Taddeo didn't want to remember seeing his father at his first professional game like this — nor deal with and accept what had happened to orchestrate these crazy pitching changes by both teams, either. And on top of that, have to worry about how his papa might see to another one — in the most brutal manner.

His papa was still standing up, on top of his seat, and reverted to hollering at Klem once more for him to throw Demaree out of the game. "He hit my son! So he's going to be taken out of here! Your way or my way. And right the fuck now!" And Rinaldo Villetti was instantly recognized, causing extreme alarm to reverberate all around the surrounding spectators. They grew nervous that they were next going to witness some more extreme violence — and very close up at that. A small number of spectators sitting in various areas around this dangerous group began vacating their seats, perhaps even forfeiting their chance to see any more of this game — their regard for their own safety registering as more important. Glancing to his left as he walked the baseline, Tad saw Al Demaree regarding what now went on, while turning whiter than his jersey — though that wasn't saying too much since the athletes from so many clubs weren't often receiving even half-way decent services — inclusive of clean uniforms — now that the players' union was history.

Hoff saw it all, too. "Don't worry. Rose delivered your message. She found your papa even before what Al fired, found you. I imagine he's only posturing right now. Your father knows that's what would be expected of him. Though I'd love it if you let me in on what good her speaking to Rinaldo Villetti will do."

"Maybe one day I'll have to. But that's nothing to be hopeful for." All of this wasn't anything surprising to Taddeo. "Just hope it works, and that my father will understand his son values him not interfering with what happens in this stadium right now. This is *my game* to lose — *or win.*" But what was curious, was that Mr. Weeghman also sat with Colosimo's party as well — on the 1st base side. Tad had heard

Weeghman coincidentally rose to his success the same day his former mentor and potential lunch-counter competitor Charlie King died. Now he used the ticket revenues Tad and his teammates earned for him — ironically from even their black spectators like little Parnell — to fund Weeghman's position with the Klan. Such an upstanding patriotic and Christian fellow, that Weeghman. Tad didn't relish any prospect of his friends like Old Lamont being put into danger as he recollected his own treatment by the bigoted Irish almost every day he'd left this ballpark. It was ironic that he slept with and now loved a woman born from among them — though satisfying in more ways than one. But it was furthering a tragic irony that doing what he always loved to do profited a man like Charlie Weeghman even more than Taddeo assisted the profiting of his own corrupted flesh and blood, what with his father's small-time gambling racket. That had been suggested before, however Taddeo was just a rookie and no one wanted to wager anything on him, except maybe the possibility that he'd bean another batter. But anybody Colosimo's family could be showing preference to, especially at this game versus the Giants, obviously did call out the presence of New York's higher-ups in the East Coast's underworld. In addition to the usual outfit's crew, now there was The Mafia and likely their Jew allies — and sitting with a rumored leader for Illinois' conKlave of the Klu Klux Klan? At least the team's owner fancied himself a competitor for the position versus Harry Sisson. So this was all wrong. The leaders of these respective organizations were all hypocrites — keeping company with one another when they allegedly hated each other. It didn't add up. Except the money surely did.

But the youngest Villetti planned on giving them all something new to figure. He had beyond enough of everyone trying to control his career already. But he worried that was what they were all here to do.

Taddeo also worried that he didn't have any reason to feel like he'd be any competent baserunner. It wasn't something he'd recently been practicing as he'd been brought up as a relief pitcher, at a time when the role was barely used in Major League Baseball — unless of course the young arm had a doting father like Sigñor Rinaldo Villetti. But that was also why he thought he could help himself by being a team player and show his papa and Colosimo's *friends* that they could never coerce or pay him to turn against his teammates and only serve himself. Yet to demonstrate his worth, Tad still wanted to show them all that he was valuable enough to be considered in any plot like that. And Tad also knew Bill Killefer would be watching what he did next as well, once he was on 1st base. The crowd had settled down and the presumption appeared to now be that this contest with New York might actually be settled only according to the written rules of the game. Well, maybe it would be.

Because with the bases crammed, Demaree caught a break and forced Max Flack to pop one up. The ball launched so high into the clear blue sky with enough height that Lew McCarty could toss of his catcher's mask, call off the Giants' pitcher, and count the birds in the sky while he took his time getting under it — and Flack was the 1st out.

So Tad remembered how Wil Robertson tried to taunt him when he was on the mound for his first great save by running Jake Daubert from 1st when the bases were loaded, to squeeze in the Robins' 1st run of that game last Wednesday. So Villetti wanted to see if Demaree could be likewise motivated so New York would chase him while Rollie dove through the back door. Tad knew his win-loss record for his pitching was far more important for his positive stats, besides his teammates,' versus chancing getting further injured running the bases. He took a giant lead off of 1st and forced Demaree to step off the rubber and repeatedly look him back to the bag. Villetti could tell he just wanted to take another shot at him and peg him on the bases as well as at his turn at the dish. Only Al was smart enough to know he didn't want to play that way with Taylor Street's boss' son while his menacing father was in the stands. The Cubs had themselves an effective nuisance to use against New York's position in the ranks, but other dangerous men could even have been assisting this player's big step up. Word had gotten around the Major League clubs fast about The Windy City's wild storm Fred Mitchell had gathered, to now threaten to come sweeping down on the other ball clubs. The Giant's arm wasn't ready to tackle that new twister yet.

But Tad didn't get the chance to continue trying to provoke New York – in the bottom of the 2nd at least. Hollocher was up next and batting left-handed shot a line-drive towards left, but Rodriquez was fast. Catching it in flight he flipped it to Fletcher who jumped behind O'Farrell and put the tag on Bob when he'd reflexively started from his lead-off towards 3rd expecting the roper launched off Charlie's bat to land in right field. Instead it landed into a 4-6 double-play and Chicago left two stranded on the bags as the 3rd inning got set to begin. Taddeo ran across the infield grass towards his dugout where Trevor was already prepared to toss him his glove and a warm-up ball while he waited for Bob to get his catcher's gear back on to start their pitching duties together for the Giants' next at-bat.

As Tad jogged out on the diamond to return to the hill he glanced into the visiting team side's stands and continued his musing, wondering why all those particular individuals he'd identified could all be there, meeting together, on the North Side. He had to turn his back to them as a right-handed hurler when he climbed the pitcher's mound to start the 3rd. But he couldn't forget them. *And if they're scouting me, for whatever they might have planned, I'll show them who controls the way I play this game.*

Now the Cubs had tied it up in the 1st. He intended to see that Chicago held New York back and hoped the Cubs would advance upon their next turn at bat. And then Taddeo realized he was still too distracted as he started firing away to O'Farrell, with that much more of his attention going towards the stands than where it was supposed to be, on the field. *Crap!* His next warm-up toss traveled up high and tipped right off Bob's glove to break through all the way back into the home plate seats. Some Anglican fat cat that paid to be almost on the field — probably so he could fulfill his emotional need to yell racial slurs at the Cubs' young pitcher — then got to also feel as if he participated in one of Villetti's bean-ball games. His fedora knocked right off his crown, the man's friends laughed as a darker-complected security guard took back the ball and returned him his hat, along with a warning not to respond. A new and darker side to Tad let himself enjoy the moment, but he also knew that he needed to settle down and command control over his anger, right away. Then Holly ran up to the mound. *Great. Just what I need. What the fuck does he want now?*

"Hey. The game's over here, Villetti. Do your job. I don't want to see you looking distracted. You can believe that we're really going to try and help you out this time. I mean that. And I hope your eye is feeling all right. But where are you? I can tell ya that if you'll help our squad out again — like you did for Merkle on Wednesday night — then I'm with you Taddeo. One hundred percent." The shortstop actually smiled at him, winked, and touched his arm when he said, "Now let's go get them!" before he ran back to his position. This time Tad didn't regard him with the customary annoyance Charlie would usually stir in him. It sort of felt good to imagine they were actually on the same team. But now he had to also return to busying himself with worrying what his family was up to, and who even they could actually be worried about. He didn't have a choice.

Unfortunately, that's also who Mitchell may have worried enough about — which would explain what Taddeo was doing on the mound in the first place. Well, he hardened his resolve. *I'll keep showing them all who's in charge out here.*

But he hadn't settled down when Ross Youngs came up to the plate to face The Shooter as he came back to the mound in the Top of the 3rd with a tied game. A left-handed bat, Youngs was a danger to a right-handed pitcher like Taddeo. However, Tad wanted to unequivocally demonstrate to them all he was a professional and he worked Youngs to a full-count, even making him foul off one of Tad's best Rembrandts to defend his chance to remain up at the plate. Finally, Youngs knocked Villetti's slider — which Tad meant to offer him up at the top of the zone, so the lefty would chase the purposely high pitch — which O'Farrell had called for, chop down on it to avoid a called strike, and bounce it back straight across the middle infield and out toward right. But Tad moved fast and hustled to 1st base while Merkle dove into the dirt and stopped the ball from even penetrating the outfield. Rolling in the dust cloud, Fred flipped an underhand toss to the bag, trusting Tad would be there — and Youngs was called out by Bob Emslie refereeing the field. Thus the fellas didn't even need to worry about how Max Flack would handle that play.

"Way to go, Villetti!" Rollie Zeider called over to him. Tad saw Hoff, Trip, and Bass-Man clapping from the bench. Mitchell might have even looked happy, or he'd taken an extra sip from his flask.

"And the Cubs see one away in the top of the third," Pat Pieper announced through his megaphone.

"That's my son!" Rinaldo Villetti smiled as he proudly stated the fact to Vincenzo and Ciro Terranova. The latter leaned over and offered a light to the new cigar he'd noticed the senior Villetti had just cut to enjoy with his youngest son's defensive success this inning.

But every hitter wasn't going to be that easy. New York's very next bat, center-fielder Benny Kauf with a .315 average and an even higher OBP took Tad's fastball out to right field from the left-handed batter's box. The young Cubs' rookie was in the habit of now being nervous whenever the ball went out to Max Flack. Sure enough, it was taken on the bounce so Flack didn't have to work too hard and he got it back to Rollie Zeider as his cutoff, but Kauf was on 1st.

Tad thought about throwing to Merkle to keep Kauf close to the base, but there was already 1 out. George Burns, the left-fielder, would bat right-handed for the Giants next. Taddeo wanted to get him to ground into a double-play. Zeider, Hollocher, and Deal came in for a second and agreed with him. George Burns did not and he got one between Deal and Hollocher that first bounced behind them and Les Mann picked up in the outfield and then the Giants had runners on 1st and 2nd. There was still 1 out.

Heine or "The Great Zim" was up next. There was an audible cheering from even the home-team fans who actually sounded more enthusiastic about the Giants' infielder than they did about Taddeo Villetti, because Henry Zimmerman had been a long-term installation at 3rd base for Chi-Town for many, many years before he was traded to New York and Charlie Deal inherited his position. The cigar smoke broke around the field level seats from all the motion through the air as the fans applauded Zim.

Fuck that guy, Tad thought as he offered him a fastball for his first pitch. Zim fucked him as he showed no respect and swung on the rookie's first pitch, the right-hander taking the ball into center field on a bounce and picking up a single out of it. Paskert whipped it back to O'Farrell so fast that Kauf didn't dare run in. But now the Giants had the bases loaded. The Cubs fans were even booing Tad, led by that loudmouth in the left-field box, with many making their anti-immigrant sentiments known in the stands across the entire ballpark. Weeghman was probably loving that.

Taddeo felt the fire. They wanted to mess with him. Called him a dago and a wop. Demaree had hit him, and the bean-ball game was still on as far as Villetti was concerned. *But maybe it'd be better for my team if i hit someone else in the stands instead?* Art Fletcher, the Giants' shortstop, was up next with an OBS of .311. He was a right-handed batter and though the "Union Man" Walt Holke, starting for New York at 1st base was a switch hitter, batting after Fletcher, his OBP was only .276 — only. So Tad kept shaking off O'Farrell's signs until the Cubs' catcher relented and gave up. Bob likely still didn't expect what was coming next, as Tad was playing a very professional game up until then, but Villetti shot Fletcher in the hip with his straight fastball, even with the bases loaded, thus walking Benny Kauf in for the Giants to take the lead.

Of course the audience booed Taddeo, and O'Farrell, Merkle, Hollocher, and Deal all ran in to the mound. Zeider stayed by his base shaking his head from side to side. "What the hell do you think you're doing, Villetti?" Deal started on him first only because the others didn't, though O'Farrell probably should have. "Thank you very much, Pooper. Now New York has the lead again. Are you going to walk in a run every game Coach lets you out here? You fucking fuck-up!"

"Yeah, and you also just messed up my assisting your tying it up out here by my sacrifice in the 1st, Pooper," Hollocher just had to pile on.

"Well fuck you, Charlie. Both you Charlies. Demaree hit *me*. And I'm 'The Shooter,' not the pooper."

"Not if you keep throwing shit. And now you've got a stink eye anyway. Are you even seeing this game clearly? But because you got hit doesn't mean you need to lose this match for the rest of us," O'Farrell commented. "Now we still need to gain some more runs but you need to gain some maturity. Right now. We need a clean sweep. And we can also take First Place right now. But you can take a seat on the bench if you want to. Or pitch *what I call for*. I'm the acting-captain here. Got it?"

Although now with his anger towards New York calmed a little by his own seizing the initiative and his satisfaction with watching the Giants' shortstop limping to take his free base with the assistance of a teammate, Villetti felt settled down again so that he could play professional baseball. He saw no further need to keep angering his teammates with his performance. Bill Klem had thrown off his umpire's mask and was going to come out to the mound to also yell at him, but Chicago's Finest officer-in-training Charles Walsh and some security guy of Weeghman's wanted to speak with the umpire again and had him lining up by the home plate bricks before he drew any more lines in the sand.

Behind those bricks, and even though Chicago had fallen behind by a run again due to his son's last toss, Signor Villetti enjoyed receiving nods of approval from his patron, Colosimo; both Terranovas; and even the Jewish Mob boss, Arnold Rothstein — after his lieutenant the boxer gave his signal of approval. *And so, the shylocks notice me again*, Villetti thought. Now Taddeo was indeed his son thst might actually turn out to be the most useful. *And maybe I will see some financial benefits after all, from this latest meeting with the ten-percenters*. However, Weeghman watched on silently, not even acknowledging Rinaldo Villetti, but instead, observing some entirely different movement around his stadium.

With the bases still loaded and only 1 out, Taddeo Villetti had to figure out how to take over full control of this ballpark for himself — and right now.

Chapter 28

Saturday, May 25, 1918
3:25 pm CST
Weeghman Park, Chicago, Illinois

3rd Inning
New York - 3, Cubs - 2

1 Out, 3 On!

AB: The New York Giants (23 W – 7 L)
(Commanding a 1st place ranking in the National League!)
Walt "Union Man" Holke (1st Base, Bats: Switch, Throws: Left)
AVG .252, OBP .276
Age: 26, Games: 245, Status: 3-year veteran in The Show

On the mound:
Chicago Cubs (19 W – 11 L)
(Fighting the 1st place NY team, CH now ranking 2nd in the NL)
P: Taddeo ~~"The Shooter" Villetti~~ (R)
"The Pooper" Villetti – antd by The Hoff!
(Bats: Right, Throws: Right) 1 W – 2 L, PCT: .333, ERA: 3.0, SO: 4,
HB: 4 x (in 4 games!)
Age: 19 , Games: 4, Status: freshman rookie
[in even more trouble than last time, of course]
Yeah, the bases are fuckin' loaded now, Wise Guy! – Trip

AND THEN:

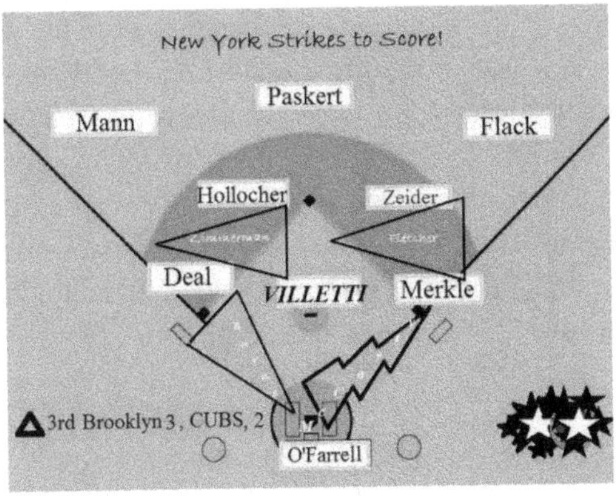

After Tad got the Union Man, who switched-hit from his left against the Cubs' right-handed pitcher only to ground out to Rollie Zeider, Taddeo faced the Giants' catcher Lew McCarty, up to bat once more. With 2 outs and the bases still crammed, which should have still definitely shook young Villetti's rapidly returning over-confidence, this right-handed at-bat sent a looper over Charlie's head at short, and Les Mann had to chase it down all the way into the corner of The Friendly Confines after it nearly went out of Weeghman Park. But Zimmerman wasn't willing to test his arm and held up at 3rd while Burns scored the Giants' 4th run on the board.

Then came another meeting on the mound, as O'Farrell checked on Tad's mental health. *Everyone seems to think they need to do that these days*, the youngest Villetti son thought to himself.

In the meantime, his brother was confident with his plan, buying his newest lady friend and himself drinks and fresh hotdogs on soft, warm buns. The pair helped themselves to relish, ketchup, and mustard, and then took a walk around Weeghman's first-level concourse to check out the view from around the stands once again. The probability of a fight still existed, but lessened with the non-response the audience paid to Taddeo hitting that Giants batter. The two of them hadn't found it necessary to leave the stadium after all.

LuLu laughed and smiled at Greg, especially when both of them bit into their dogs and got a little red decorating their faces, too. She was frequently touching his hand and they were the definition of joviality as the pair even tried feeding each other to see which way made more of a mess.

Greg felt very happy to note that his little brother was in bad shape out on the mound and had given up two runs and was still dealing with New York having all the bases loaded against him. He would be the type to enjoy his brother failing. By then, the new pair of friends had completed their walk inside of the concourse and now ventured back out into to sunlight through another tunnel to watch the next at-bat. But with a resounding crack of the bat, the Cuban Jose Rodriguez flew out deep in center field where Dode Paskert retired the side for Chicago. However, Greg still felt confident his little brother would find a new way to embarrass himself some more.

Chapter 29

Saturday, May 25, 1918
3:28 pm CST
Weeghman Park, Chicago, Illinois

3rd Inning
New York - 4, Cubs - 2

1 Out, Ø On!

AB: Chicago Cubs (19 W – 11 L)
(Fighting the 1st place NY team, CH now ranking 2nd in the NL)
Fred "Bonehead" Merkle (1st Base, Bats: R, Throws: R) – yes a righty 1B!
AVG .297, OBP .349
Age: 30, Games: 1,276! Status: 12-year veteran in The Show!

On the mound:
The New York Giants (23 W – 7 L)
(Commanding a 1st place ranking in the National League!)
But not for long!
P: Albert Wentworth Demaree
(Bats: Left, Throws: Right) 8 W – 5 L, 5 SV PCT: .571, ERA: 2.47,
SO: 441, HB:26 (in 181games)
Age: 34 , Games: 181, Status: 7-year veteran

AND THEN:

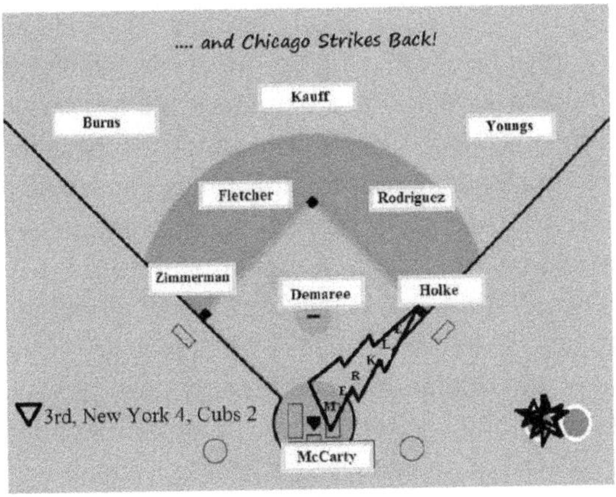

Trask K. Finnegan reported the exhilarating outcome of one incredible rally by The Windy City's favorite ball team for William Randolph Hearst's *Chicago Examiner* — Annenberg's top competitor.

Les Mann flew out, but beginning with Fred Merkle's base hit, the Cubs started a 3rd inning rally that took them completely through their entire order! Dode Paskert singled deep after Merkle got on and the hit saw Bonehead get completely around the horn. 1 run was in.

Then Charlie Deal tripled! Paskert scored for a tied ballgame.

With only 1 out, Coach tried to get Deal home by ordering up a sacrifice from Zeider. But Rollie's bunt fell too close to home plate and McCarty sent it racing ahead of the Cubs' 2nd baseman, remaining where he could easy guard the dish if Charlie tried to move home.

The Cubs' manager wanted to try that again, and even with 2 outs — and faced without a choice — Mitchell having been ordered to keep his rebellious *and insulated* pitcher on the mound, Taddeo Villetti appeared on deck for only his second time in the game, and his entire Major League career. Mitchell appeared inspired by his bourbon, to try everything that was unholy, unorthodox by McGraw's books.

Al Demaree had probably already decided it wasn't potentially worth his life to keep beaning a well-connected player like Villetti and thought that maybe the Cubs' pitcher was actually trying to make amends by purposely giving up that hit that saw McCarty safely on base in the top of the inning. Tad intended no such thing. He just couldn't fan the Giants' catcher. But Demaree must have figured he wouldn't have to worry about facing Villetti again this inning until he unintentionally walked O'Farrell right in front of Taddeo, leaving Cub runners at the corners. He likely thought he would end the Chicago-New York bean-ball *war* for this game, but that would be up to Villetti. Tad didn't want to make up his mind too early in during The Show, but waved to his papa as he actually connected with Al's offer and took an earned trip, albeit this one a much less painful one, to 1st base! He now had quite the OBP for a relief pitcher in this game. Tad would bet his was even higher than even Babe Ruth's. But he figured he wouldn't mention that back in the clubhouse because one of his smart-ass teammates with who he usually warmed the Cubs' bench, would remind him that he only *ever* had 2 ABs. So of course it was recording at 1.000. But the hopper that bounced off El Hombre's glove got picked up by Fletcher running behind 2nd to keep the Giants' middle infield under control, and Charlie Deal still could not leave 3rd base for home on what was barely a shallow infield hit.

But it kept the Cubs alive with 2 outs. And the next play was interesting as Max Flack came to the plate with the bases loaded. The Cubs already destroyed the Giants' lead by getting back 2. So Flack then followed his manager's unorthodox coaching and bunted for a real suicide squeeze play. With those 2 outs, McGraw's squad should have never been prepared for this — as Mitchell never should have called for it. But the result from the contact looked good heading down the 1st base line, only Holke fielded it fast and sent it back to McCarty for the force-out that cut down Chicago's *lead* runner. Charlie dove, but the Giants' catcher applied the tag, Deal was called out *by Emslie in the field*, even after he'd hit a triple, and now there would have been 3 away. New York's players started running in to start the 4th inning.

But Training Officer Harold Olsen made a seat available for himself behind home plate as he sent the former seat's occupant off to avail himself of a beer, compliments of Chicago's Finest. And now Klem turned the color of a beet and must have felt his duty *was to function as a vegetable* while his head turned up to listen to what the cop had to say and observe Olsen making eye contact with Detectives Sweeney and Conway in the 1st base stands and only *the* Charles Weeghman with *distinguished guests* sitting a few rows in front of him. That call at the plate had always been his to make. But then the home plate umpire reversed Emslie's call from the field, and Charlie Deal was pronounced safe! The Cubs had *one more* run and took the lead. New York's fans were outraged as were the voices that hurled their protests from the Giants' bench. Within seconds, Weeghman Park collected more shouted profanities in one inning, than box office sales for the entire game.

Meanwhile Tad was on 2nd — with O'Farrell on 3rd and Flack on 1st — after that ridiculous play, reversed call, and the game being back to there still being 2 away. The Giants' fans still kept up booing and hollering expletives at Klem continuously. Security had to run around the foul lines and the warning track to locate which spectators were throwing their garbage onto the playing field. That's when Villetti took in a clear view of his *former* on-team nemesis and Hollocher gave him the most subtle nod from the dish. It was a force-out situation at any base and a left-handed batter versus a right-handed pitcher. It didn't matter whether Charlie could hit for the opposite field or where he placed the ball, as long as he kept it on the ground. He did. And he gave the Cubs another chance. Slicing a single between Rodriguez and Holke he got on, O'Farrell scored and Hollocher had loaded up the bases again for Chicago. Youngs had come up with the ball in shallow right-center and threw it all the way in to McCarty, who Demaree backed up in a perfect McGraw textbook play — and Taddeo couldn't run any further. But he would have liked to. He would have liked to have advanced all the way home as he was sure his run would show everyone especially *everyone-who-was-anyone from New York* how he and Chicago would command the score.

Then Lester Mann smashed a double that went over Giant centerfielder Benny Kauff's head but didn't quite make it to the wall. New York's outfielder had to chase it back but slammed into the fence, the impact knocking the baseball just off the tip of his mitt. Taddeo ran home and scored standing up — for the first time he ever crossed home plate to add another crooked number for Chicago!

The Cubs had the lead by 3 runs now. And that's when Demaree showed his fatigue with this seesaw match and threw a wild pitch to Merkle. Flack charged home at his top speed but the ball ricocheted off the bricks and back to McCarty, who dove on top of the Cubs' right-fielder before he ever reached the dish. When the dust cleared, Bill Klem shouted "You're out!" And that was the end of an amazing 3rd for Chicago. But Tad thought there was suspect irony in how closely the play resembled what the former Ansons had used against the Brooklyn Robins three nights ago. *Someone* had been studying Villetti and his pals on at least some of the New Yorkers' behalf.

However, Chi-Town's 1918 prodigies were not done for this game, even after retaking the lead. Demaree was, though. John McGraw called out Red Causey to try and hold the Cubs until New York could strike back. But they never could and Chicago took to running the bases on him twice more — in the 5th and the 6th. Though no more were they allowed to score. However, Taddeo Villetti ascended to his second game winning victory right in front of both cities' leading families — and more importantly, The Shooter's proud father!

While Trip and Bass-Man had nothing better to do during the game in which they got to ride the bench again, the mischievous pals of the winning pitcher did have time to slip away into the clubhouse and fill Taddeo's locker with dominoes. The friends prepared for this and had been waiting for just the right occasion. And after he was paraded up high on Hoff's shoulders around the infield grass, he was buried down under the flood of the playing pieces that emptied out of his locker when he was subject to just how prepared his best buddies from the Ansons were — to prank him. Everyone had a good laugh and poured out their water cups to bring another river down on Villetti.

The Chicago team had beaten New York 7 – 4.

The Giants didn't know what to make of this. The Cubs had risen out of being nowhere last season to be 2 ½ games behind and threaten their domination of the league.

Picking himself up to leave his seat, in that exclusive business meet-and-greet, Arnold Rothstein — Mr. Big himself — with his lieutenant Abraham Attell at his side, had said very little to Rinaldo, until now. "Mister Villetti, I am very impressed with your son. I am sure you are aware I've been watching him. He is doing quite well with learning to achieve his control."

"For the most part." Rinaldo agreed. He appreciated the compliment, but at the same time wished he could further discussion about some important things to come in the near future with the king of the Jews, and he also wished that he knew where his other son Greggorio had vanished to. He reassured Mr. Colosimo that his boys must *both* be already on their way to pick up his patron's nephew-in-law, Johnny Torrio. They had better be or there would be hell to pay for all the Villettis. How he wanted to scream at both Urso and Greggorio now. His usually reliable middle son did not at all need to pick *this time* to take his leave — and with the Terranovas' woman, by way of whatever Colosimo had to do with that. It kept the old soldier from being in any kind of patient mood to head down to the Cubs' locker room, where security would allow *him* to go visit Taddeo. Instead, he showed no concern with disappointing his youngest offspring, and stuck with Big Jim, making sure he could offer his patron excuses as he made them up to suit the circumstances. But this was his boss' own fault — Greg's disappearance. Villetti would remind Colosimo of that if the man even once got angry with him that Greggorio was not on hand to bid farewell to Rothstein's people, and especially the Terranovas. He didn't want to blame his own lack of good parenting skills to seeing that his sons couldn't tell the difference about when it was time for business, and when it was time for pleasure. When New York visited, it was time for business.

Chapter 30

Greg didn't know what he would make of all this. He and Urso — who fortunately did show up — had both been somehow sent *with the blessings of the Irish* — but with the knowledge that they should feel very privileged to be allowed to go and meet Colosimo's nephew-in-law at Union Depot, north of the river. No doubt this was Bath House Johnny's legacy at work. The little leprechaun politicians always liked their cut no matter where it came from, as long as the Italians respected some boundaries. And the Irish bosses "knew the wops were good for making a buck or two for them." So for the time, it was suggested they would tolerate such "a gentleman" from among "all those fuckin' guinea people they were constantly having to put up with."

Greg knew a lot of the shamrocks' money went around in the sports gambling circles. That could be the baseball connection to this. *Why else might this extra extension of professional courtesy be even happening in the first place?* O'Banion might want a share of cleaning even the Italians' winnings for them, and it suggested that there could be a big fix coming on, and Greggorio's people were even in on it. Vincent Drucci now worked for The Northside Gang, yet he was Italian. The players were now all mixed around. However, the most professional amongst the whole pot of them, O'Sullivan, would want everything about any such operation to stay underground and be kept low-key. The less who knew about it — like the kikes and their boss, Sullivan's big rival Arnold Rothstein, or the pigs that comprised Alcock's force — the more profit they could keep. And they'd also keep it away from any "public morals squad" like Conway's little outfit, but make the Villettis indebted to them instead.

Most of the bosses who were smart enough bosses that they could remain in power, like they now resided on Easy Street, lived very humble, simple lives. O'Banion ran a flower shop. They didn't draw attention to themselves. Living lavish lives was not the goal here. Survival was. And the leaders of the criminal underworld were not in that world originally because of choice, but rather because of necessity. It was just that anyone who was smart, wanted to learn to be like them, because making an income — surviving — wasn't very easy in the first place. So while Greg dropped out of formal schooling, he was constantly tasking himself with learning.

But he had also learned that when one was really successful, they had to expand ever larger to ensure that survival, for their business family. Anyone else who learned of them, would constantly be coming at them. But anytime they could save by not having to pay off the cops — like for instance to ensure there wasn't an incident at the train station that the police would have to respond to — that was a good thing. Only Greg wasn't sure his family was really doing anything to help themselves survive. He was going to have to take care of himself — and he was more than gifted enough with the cunning that would help him succeed at that. But the thought had come to him at the game: *what if there is some kind of a connection with the Irish gambling, Charlie Weeghman's interest in it, the Cubs' win-ratio,* and Taddeo? *Is that why the Jews were also there? Why they brought Attell to watch my little brother? Were they preparing to bait O'Sullivan because he'd have more money than the Cubs' owner, or O'Banion? And Weeghman wanted desperately to get his hands on a good share of it.* The ballclub owner's cash reserves were way overextended. Greg had heard those rumors as he'd been thinking, *Isn't it really irregular for Taddeo to get so many appearances on the mound, in only* one week, *and right after they just called him up? And after he threw all Lakeview into one hell of a riot?* Maybe his papa's business acumen wasn't failing, but neither Greg nor Urso was the son he needed involved in his latest money-making scheme? Or one his father had been forced into. This could even be why his papa was keeping Taddeo happy with Arlene. But he had cut Greggorio out.

An hour and then some minutes after the game, Greg had arrived by rail into the station to first meet up with Urso. He'd departed directly from Weeghman Park — as the gentlemanly escort for Lumia. Colosimo even suggested he do this small favor for the Terranovas while his father's boss said he'd apologize for Greggorio's early exit from their meeting at the stadium. But this was really only a favor for Greg that he would do for himself, Colosimo coached him. And it was all to get Lulu on the train back to Brooklyn after a phone call and arrangements were made to pick her up at the station there. Back East, Masseria had Vincenzo and Ciro's backs against the wall and that added to their incentive to deal amicably with The Windy City where the warmest breeze they might feel, could still carry them along. Besides, before they could say anything, Lumia was gone.

The smallest skin trade was really no sacrifice against the larger picture. But the girl was grateful to have been offered a chance at carrying on a new life for herself at least temporarily in Chicago versus what she appeared glad to leave behind in Brooklyn. So LuLu just could not hide her enthusiasm which manifested itself in the affection she now showed Greggorio. He'd already been told she wanted to run from her past and something terrible that she wanted to leave behind her in New York. However, her return after an extremely short leave she'd take from Chi-Town, was only supposed to be an extension of her temporary visit to Chicago. But she was apparently very excited to take care of all her arrangements Back East, and return to The Windy City and this handsome man that had taken an interest in her, just as quickly as possible. She definitely looked forward to her own definition of what was an extended stay on the Great Lakes. Greg also enjoyed seeing that his older brother was jealous when he purposely let his departing and arriving companions make each other's quick acquaintance, hurried along on a schedule that still ensured LuLu made her train. But before that, she jumped into his arms, her tiny feet off the ground and the pair passionately locking lips as Greggorio spun Lumia around in his arms. There was a tear in each of her eyes elicited by having to part ways with this smart, gentle, and debonair young man before the train conductor pronounced the final boarding call and she had to catch her ride Back East. Curiously, Urso might have caught a cold or something. Greg's brother looked away and coughed. Urso wasn't entirely acting like himself and it wasn't at all the girl who threw him off. That was strange though what he caught wasn't any priority concern of his brother's. Greggorio could even hope it was a bullet as his glowing kind eyes he used to make one final contact with Lumia's, narrowed into something dark and cynical as soon as she could no longer see them.

But Greg's eyes also saw reason to fear — fear that he had real and immediate competition as soon as he first focused their view on their new guest, one Johnny Torrio. "The Fox" was a quite the charmer — slightly older, with his refined suit, skinny dark tie, neatly slicked and parted hair, equally manicured short moustache, and his designer matched luggage. He traveled alone so confidently, the middle Villetti brother was sure he concealed a gun, and a backup weapon, and a backup for his backup weapon. But his white-toothed smile was even more dangerous. Everybody was going to like this guy. Colosimo had brought in somebody sharp who was probably just as acute at being effective. Torrio already had a great reputation as the fella who made the money come in Back East. But he was Victoria Moresco's nephew and should therefore be a hand that held the ace which was all Colosimo's to play. It would be a better hand than the Villetti boys' father's.

Apparently The Outfit's new man had already been informed of the O'Rourke problem and was going to finish what The Villetti House had messed up so that there would not be another public rebellion in Little Italy that might embarrass Colosimo. But Torrio was going to be really hard to dislike. Magnanimous from the get-go, he invited Greg with Urso to accompany him along with another young gentleman by the name of Frank Nitti, who arrived and had presented himself as some first cousin of a favorite protégé of Torrio's he'd had to leave behind, back in Brooklyn. They made an appointment for all of them to work together later, but they'd first enjoy some relaxation as the Villetti brothers tried to assist their new visitor with his luggage and bring it up to Urso's blue car, sporting a gaudy red-blaze — which he'd insisted on driving to the train station against his brother's better advice. Model-Ts came in all colors so long as they were black. But Urso took The House's money along with his alleged gambling winnings to have *this* custom job done. So next it didn't surprise Greggorio at all that a slick operator like The Fox preferred to ride in Nitti's less-conspicuous vehicle. But their new friends would first follow them to relax on a Saturday night and only discuss Colosimo's plans over a couple of drinks and cigars, flanked by more of Chicago's most alluring women at Johnny's uncle's already quite successful place over on Wabash. It was more than a few steps up the scale in sophistication from Villettis,' that was for sure. Nothing The Family had established under The Outfit could even, ever compare.

Yes, Johnny Torrio was going to be trouble for Greg. Colosimo had relied on those like his papa, he and his brother along with the Delasandros to control things for him. That was a key to Greg's plan since he could betray Colosimo on behalf of himself, or his father if Greg needed to keep the senior Villetti relevant, only once he had eliminated Urso, and he and his cousin Corrado actually ran The House, with Taddeo alive or not alive, but under control, one way or another. With the Genna Brothers placing their trust in Greg, he could take advantage of their naivety and collapse D'Andrea, probably using those men this gangster had kept a close, unsuspicious relationship with over on the West Side, until they were eliminated by attrition while getting rid of the Irish — or Cardinella. And Greggorio was already the source of funding that cops like Conway, Walsh, and Olsen knew to come to for. But their kind were going to just fall *in love* — with Johnny Torrio. Greg needed to still be able to persuade the pigs to sow some certain grounds with more fertilizer, that his scheming would result in him seeing all of his competition become. Arlene by herself was nowhere near making Chicago's murder quota for the year. Yet Greggorio couldn't stay too mad at the new fellow's uncle Colosimo even while he plotted the boss' downfall. In only a little over another day, Diamond Jim had promised Greg could return to the station here and pick up "Lucky LuLu." That would be very lucky for Greggorio indeed.

But however gifted he might be, he admitted that he also might have still been the slightest bit jealous of Taddeo. All his baby brother had to worry about was playing baseball over those next couple of days.

Chapter 31

On Sunday the 26th of May, Chicago defeated New York again, this time 5-1. Almost only the regulars started and went on to play the whole game with Flack, Paskert, and Bill Killefer being the heroes of the game, each with doubles and the last being the favorite catcher for Hippo Vaughn who pitched the complete game for another win for the ace hurler. Yet Deal wasn't hitting against New York's wicked left-hander Slim Sallee and his 2.25 ERA. So Trip got a chance to go in there and play the hot corner, but he didn't have too much to do defensively since the Giants only got 4 punches in on The Hippo who dominated their lineup, Ross Youngs getting their single hit to become a baserunner that had any chance to actually score. This happening only way back in the 1st inning.

Tad told Mike that he was still lucky to get some more experience playing his natural position and facing pro pitching in the Big Leagues. He wasn't sure that placated his frustrated friend and fellow rookie. In fact, this coming from Taddeo might've sounded really hypocritical. When he reminded Trip that he only had 4 outings himself, his friend countered that Tad was a relief pitcher. The comment was meant as a degradation even if Trip didn't bear the pitcher any actual hostility. He was just still prone to impatience and anger. And that didn't appear like it would change any time soon.

If Trevor Bass was feeling as disgruntled too, he kept it to himself.

But Hoffman would probably still be smiling if a grand piano dropped on him. Here was a young man truly grateful for his every new opportunity.

Chapter 32

Now Greggorio Villetti continued with having *his* share of good fortune. Quite unsure of what they might find waiting for them at the Chinese laundry, he'd encouraged Johnny Torrio to visit the site in force on Sunday morning. "Just in case the chinks are allying with the micks," he told The Fox, presenting himself as the one who could show Colosimo's new fella all the particulars about working in The Windy City. Anyone and everyone turned up in the Maxwell Street Market's multicultural commercial zone. It offered all kinds of the predominantly legal types of goods and services, and those otherwise, plus the best Polish hotdogs in all of Chicago. Greg made sure to colorfully describe all of the area's denizens that came to do business there. If anyone wanted to arrange a deal for perhaps something a little more personal, and privately, they could make a contact who could escort them to the right place two blocks south over on Taylor Street. There The Villetti House could accommodate them.

But the Maxwell Street Market is where Mr. Li chose to locate his business and not even in Chinatown, where one would think he'd enjoy some protection by his own kind. Greg hadn't turned up any information suggesting the slants could develop into any sort of standing opposition that would need to be reckoned with in any part of Little Italy. And the Chinaman was allowed to provide his services to all the small businesses and tenement housing residents in the proximity of Polk and Canal Streets — never being hassled. In fact, the chinks seemed to curiously leave him alone. Their kind were the least likely to be found among Mr. Li's customers. So for over a dozen years, the Chinaman enjoyed Villetti-provided protection. So he was around to see all the Villetti boys grow up to become young men. And so he even had extra personal protection. That was the popular rumor. Any one of the Villetti brothers would look out for him if they could, but loyalty had to run both ways. However, Greg was sure *this situation* would indicate it no longer did. And it would therefore be as easy to manipulate as the one with the ladies — easier for him actually. He could just exaggerate information damning to

Mr. Li at his leisure, and his brother didn't have the attention span to scare up an effort to verify anything or realize what was happening. The time when Mr. Li enjoyed Villetti protection was over. But in truth, after all these years, and the privileges extended to him, Mr. Li had betrayed The Family.

The Chinaman was about to learn he was no longer granted a free pass by The House. He would be dealing with The Outfit now. Even better, the ever-so-slick Johnny brought along a teenage wannabe-lightweight-boxer he introduced as Vinny Gibaldi, as well as Nitti, who already had a bad reputation. *They were both acting as Torrio's backup*. With Urso also there, peacocking instead of providing any real, useful intelligence, Greg was sure the situation would get out of hand. Anything could go wrong. And it would no doubt benefit him, by causing Big Jim to immediately lose confidence in his nephew-in-law and irrefutably win any argument with his wife over why The Villetti House should remain in charge of his street-level operations. Greg would bet Moresco was pulling her husband's arm on behalf of her nephew anyway, but Torrio would miss a soft toss, now O'Rourke and possibly Li would wind up dead in that laundry, and Greggorio could clean up. Blood being blood, Urso would have to back his play. Only then Greg could spin a cover-up — for any outcome which he might find convenient. A Villetti knew when he would see an opportunity to close a game.

However, once again it could not have even gone better than it did for the middle son. The Irishman was completely gone. Tipped off by someone no doubt — and someone who the middle Villetti child could almost kiss. This made Johnny Torrio look like a complete failure right on his first at-bat — as the boy with the golden reputation couldn't get his man.

And on top of that, neither he nor the enforcers he recruited — Nitti and young Gibaldi, also known to Greg by his local false tradecraft boxing name, Jack McGurn — got to demonstrate any of their particular skills at anything. When Urso responded to Mr. Li's denial of ever helping O'Rourke by then demanding payment of the Chinaman's South Side insurance dues, he eventually collected the sum without much resistance offered at all. Li back-talked Greg's older brother a little, but his complaining and weak arguing seemed a little too contrived to Greg. Mr. Li knew all the boys since back when even Urso was a teenager and they didn't frighten him. Their papa was always nice to him as well — for as nice as their father could be to any mark — because their mother had liked the Chinaman and spoke well of the way he treated her with much kindness — especially when Tad and his friends broke the windows with their baseball games ever so often. Greg couldn't remember for sure, but maybe Mr. Li even helped his mama out when she was ill and could no longer do all the household chores, like much of the cleaning, on her own. The result was that the brothers, and quite honestly no one in The House, was ever really enthusiastic about forcing any collections out of him and Greg always wondered why in the heck did Li pay them anything in the first place now. He never had before. And new goombahs weren't ever assigned to visit the laundry — only Family ever really called on him — as it was understood they were especially friendly since Mr. Li knew all of them since the old days. The Chinaman alone could have probably gotten away with what O'Rourke would never be allowed, and possibly then some more. So there was something very much on the sly happening at this place and Mr. Li didn't want to attract any special attention. The middle Villetti brother wanted to figure this out but Torrio's schedule forced them all to move along. The Fox had probably been out-foxed but saw no reason to press the laundryman since he appeared clean and unspotted by anything that wouldn't wear well with his outfit.

And these new guys were supposed to be what? Effective hit-men? Effective bag-men? Effective they weren't. How Greg wanted to be there when Colosimo heard about that.

But as it turned out, Colosimo had plans for Greg to soon be somewhere even better than that. Very early on the morning of Monday the 27th, as the Terranovas would be assumed to be preparing to depart Chicago at the conclusion of the New York Giants versus the Cubs series, upon the turn of the very next day, it turned out that they also helped make good on Diamond Jim's favor he promised to Greg. Obviously, Lumia had never been offered to the Jews but sent unmolested all the way back to Brooklyn that Saturday night, to see her family and get to explain to that family, including her hard-case brother Frank, that she'd been offered this wonderful chance to visit Chi-Town for a little longer at the personal invite of the uncle of Johnny "The Fox" Torrio. This carried a good-enough feel to it for her over-protective older sibling who might have actually admired Johnny Torrio, and no doubt should have heard of Colosimo, so that she was conveniently allowed to travel out to The Windy City alone, as long as her brother got to threaten all her train conductors and the engineers, not once, but twice — about seeing to it that his little sister had a safe and secure journey. Frank Gallucio might have been under the delusion that any good grace from The Outfit that his sister fell under, could possibly extend to mean new opportunities for him, too. And there could be something that trading his own sister would be worth to these good fellows.

LuLu was one blonde bundle of excitement when she leapt off the train before it even came to a complete stop at Union Depot and even before the dawn of that Monday's morning. She recognized Greg immediately as her new paramour from the baseball game and jumped into his arms. He spun her around twice when he caught her up in the long reach of those arms. She was so full of such young and enthusiastic joy that Villetti had to recheck his priorities. Lumia really did seem to like him.

He didn't have to work very hard to encourage *that* continuing. Colosimo had negotiated a place for Lu at The Lexington. It was temporarily available, as it was meant to be gotten ready for use for some meeting in the near future actually called for by Greg's papa. Or so the Villetti son's father thought. Greggorio had put in work on *that*. He risked a lot now getting caught lying. But in his playing the role of "Diamond Jim," a caricature of himself that Colosimo invented to facilitate his winning what he needed out of others, he often demonstrated that he was just magnanimous, which really supported his earning this nickname. *Naïve* was another way Greggorio would actually describe him. However, Tad's adopted *second* Godfather certainly wanted to make gains in the loyalty he'd get from Greg — who was in charge of finalizing arrangements for The Family. Perhaps the Villetti brothers' father had spoken with the boss? About him? Helping this to be so easy. Or more likely Colosimo brought him up because Greggorio had impressed him. He was very impressive. And Greg had also been trying to feel out Big Jim's attitude about keeping his papa at the table were they to arrange some new sitdown with O'Banion. Probably the very meeting that was going to occur at The Lexington. It was only a ruse by Greg's own creation, though he'd been curious why it had still been only all too easy to have actually suggested it be arranged himself, as irregular as this kind of meeting would be. But he knew that he could manipulate his father by tempting his papa's need to be recognized as important, especially now that Torrio was in town. That hotel was way too expensive and public in which to be having this kind of a convention. But Dean O'Banion would never waste his time having a sit-down with his papa — who had so little of a relationship with reality concerning such a matter. At best Hymie

Weiss might show up if they wanted something from Annenberg and Greg's family could secure it for them. They'd moved on the newspapers with real foresight — and even before the micks could start up with that racket. Or so they imagined. Only now, instead of the Irish, what all the Villettis had to immediately watch out for, was that Torrio hadn't arrived there to replace all of them.

But with what luck Greg had never even imagined, Johnny had embarrassed himself almost immediately upon his arrival, by The Maxwell Street Market failure. So Colosimo wasn't given any reason to *not* look upon The Villetti Family with his customary favor — even awarding the middle son *this* favor. Only Greggorio now had to watch that his own short-term temptations didn't distract *himself*. Here was just one more girl who was really supposed to represent something else — quite the missing weapon of temptation Greg needed to set up his brothers. But altogether too tempting to Greggorio, she also was.

Now LuLu was beside herself at the luxurious first-class treatment she'd been offered in Chicago and she wanted to do something to show her appreciation — beyond what she did with Greg in her hotel room in the wee hours of that weekday morning almost immediately upon her arrival off the midnight train. *I'm sure glad her brother didn't insist on coming with her, but I had an uncle pull a favor for me to see* he *ensured that.* Lena was really able to start enjoying her new freedom that came with her new persona, Lumia, also to become quickly and affectionately known as "Lucky LuLu." It started out far better than her old life in Brooklyn, or how it would have been if she had even elected to stay in Manhattan, she told Greg.

So after enjoying her company the rest of that Monday and all the way into the evening, as Tad had presumably taken his place running — or attempting to run — the bordello, Greggorio suggested she join him when he visited his family's restaurant/nightclub. He expected he'd have to do a little work to supervise how its management was faring under his little brother. Taddeo could always be away and out of Greg's hair for a while as he probably planned to party all night after his team won yet again, sweeping New York. The rest of the baseball squad had already no doubt started celebrating which could go on for the entire night, after yet another Cubs win — and another opportunity to expose the Tadpole shirking his other responsibilities. Greg doubted their papa would allow his youngest son's failures to get out of hand, just like he bet on Colosimo not letting his nephew's go on. Sooner than later, the bosses would have to put their feet down, and looking for a better solution, agree that Greggorio was the right choice to run the Taylor Street operations.

Meanwhile, if LuLu liked The Family's place, he could see she got to cocktail there a little, as he had this other business to attend to. By necessity, it would really eat into Greg's time, but then he'd take her out shopping and show her more of Chicago on Tuesday. He told her that whatever she earned, she could just use for her convenience and to tip the staff at The Lexington.

He explained to Lumia that the other girls at Villetti's provided more than drink services, but this would not be expected of her, of course. Used to how similar things were back in New York, LuLu wasn't surprised by The House's business model. She was enjoying herself so much that she was already looking to see if Greg would take her to be his regular woman. She did have a great ass and he used that desire of hers to please him, to thank him. That had been a very satisfying part of his plan. He then complimented Lu for her humility and generosity and asked her if she would consider donating one of the beautiful dresses she showed him to a more unfortunate girl he was trying to help, when she inquired of him what he'd like her to wear when they went out in Chicago. She brought it with her when they first crossed over to Little Italy early Monday evening.

Since she wasn't quite sure what all she wanted to see and do there during her stay, he also recommended she talk to the other girls and become friends with the one named Arlene, who was sort of the new assistant manager of the place. Greg said he could use a little behind-the-scenes knowledge of how the family's lounge was operating as a favor to him and explained that employees openly discussed things that they didn't relate to the owners. To Greg's chagrin, his unexpected leprechaun princess of an adversary had convinced his weak brother to let her control their family's lounge and "recreational facility." And if he were honest with himself, as he didn't like to be angry with himself, he should have foreseen that coming. The Tadpole's priority would be to party with his baseball team.

Now what was witnessed and didn't have to be pointed out to anyone when they got there, was the scene Sega made running half-naked out of one of the rooms above the lounge with Urso's verbal assault chasing after her. This happened just as Greg foresaw it would, and right as he brought LuLu upstairs to The Family's office — actually this was his papa's private office — though he didn't mention this and that he wasn't supposed to have a copy of the key or be using the room without his father telling him to do so. But *Taddeo* had already been allowed all-hours access, which irked Greg to no end. He'd never been openly trusted like that.

Only what made an impression on Lumia was that as Sega fled by them, she was bleeding from her mouth and kept one of her eyes shut. Urso's abuse wasn't usually just limited to verbal assaults. His brother had counted on that. But Greggorio, demonstrating embarrassment, which was not hard to fake, explained to her that his oldest brother was "going through some difficulties because things were changing around there" and that he was really a great guy — only that Lu might want to stay lucky a bit longer by avoiding Urso for a while. Greg was a little more than suspicious now that his older brother was sampling their uncle's drugs. The sons had been watching their Uncle Abramo trying to cure whatever ailed their papa. That it seemed to be working, was evidenced by the strength he showed before The Morello Family and the Jewish gangsters at the ballpark, Saturday. However, Urso with his shirt off, his muscles seemingly always flexing as the natural away about him, was also working — even while he was unaware of it — to capture the new girl's fascination — *with him* — as he emerged from the room he'd taken up with Sega. The ladies' timeless fascination with the bad boy, the tough guy. But this was actually indeed very convenient, and not just because Urso could actually work at something. But because Greg saw these fights going on regularly for the past two nights, ever since the arrival of the new "Greek" woman, and *this show* was also exactly what Greg was hoping he'd be able to present for his new Italian lady friend.

Because Urso then noticed Lu. "And now who is this?" Of course he'd already forgotten he'd seen her once before at the train station just last Saturday evening. And for *that* to have happened, Greg's brother was definitely busy disabling his own brain with one chemical influence or another. Lumia's beauty would have otherwise struck him as mind-altering.

So Greggorio played it perfectly to make his older brother angry with him and just itching to bully one of his younger siblings. "She is a friend of mine and no I'm not going to introduce you to her while you're treating the ladies like *that*." He nodded in the direction Sega had run.

"Well who the fuck are you to judge? You are obviously so busy, that you don't even know what just happened."

"This time?"

"Any of the times."

A perfect answer. Urso's so predictable. It's like I'm writing the script for him. "That's true. I wasn't here to see everything that happened. But never mind that. This is Lumia since you insist on asking, and I've plans to continue showing her the nicer parts of Chicago. For some reason, we left your room off our list."

"Yeah? Well why don't you both show up in my office right now? And you better not have a copied key, Greggorio." Rinaldo Villetti had come upstairs and walked past his sons with his own key out to unlock his private office on site at The Family-owned watering hole. He'd pointed a finger at his middle son, and then turned to greet Lu. "Hello," he said to Lumia and grinned as he maneuvered around her. "You must be the young lady who became friends with my boy Saturday — at the baseball game." He nodded toward Greg, but his smile turned upside down for a second when he looked at his offspring. "I remember you from there. See what you missed, Urso?" He didn't even look at his oldest, returning his face to Lumia, onto which his new smile beamed. "But please Darling, go downstairs and make yourself comfortable. I would like to show my hospitality and cover whatever you would like. After all, you're a guest of my boy's."

"Oh, I am a friend of Greg's, but I came here to work."

"Indeed? Well isn't that interesting. Serving drinks, I assume."

"That's right. And that's all." Greggorio clarified the situation for his father.

"Well, go on then. I'm sure my son here has a plan for how we can use you. Check in downstairs with the *interim manager*. She's quite conspicuous with her scarlet hair." Rinaldo related that last bit of information with a tone of contempt he couldn't quite cover. He turned to his boys. "Greg, you and your brother will come with me. Now."

Arlene retreated from where she'd been spying on all of them. She'd had plenty of experience now to realize that she had better always know whatever Greg was up to, and at all times. She had also witnessed what had went down between Sega and Urso and the timing of the introduction of this new girl, Lumia, with growing concern. She wished she now could both confirm *the Greek woman's* true identity and learn what Rinaldo needed to discuss with his sons, as that could not be good for her. There was that and her own family ordering her mission be completed before Arlene killed them all, which *would* be very good for her. But the Villettis went into their patriarch's private office and she had to disappear quickly before she got caught by the new girl, eavesdropping on them. She also had one target more than bullets as things stood. She needed to do something about that or just move on to her strategy to use proxies to kill the Villettis for her. But that just wouldn't feel as satisfying. Nor would it achieve anything at all in terms of alleviating her guilt over having shot the others who had to die so as to not be any kind of impediment to her carrying out her assignment here. But one had been a thug, the next a perverted adulterer, and the last had actually returned fire on her. No. She didn't feel sorry about ending any of them after all. However, Arlene did have too many misgivings about what it would do to Taddeo if she manipulated him into killing his own family for her.

Arlene also lamented that she'd barely had much time to spend out with Tad — when she knew he'd rather be celebrating his team's wins with *her* than getting drunk with Hoffman — a positive change in his maturing amidst all the regression she'd seen in his character to date. But Arlene would counter any challenges he could offer from the mound now, by reminding him of the change *he* made in the lineup, which saw her pinch-hitting as a late change in *managers* — for the bordello's roster. This served her well for both her empowerment and for her excuse. It at least sounded kinder than while wanting to keep him around, to protect her, also having to tell Tad at point blank that she didn't want to roll with him all over the floor of Mr. Li's laundry service store. Arlene felt stressed, plus she was still sick and fighting *that*.

Now this new girl LuLu was just sent off to look for her to play that new managerial role she'd won — it having been confirmed that this was her role, by Rinaldo himself — because the past five nights of logistics and accounting since Taddeo was awarded control, had to get done by someone. To run a profitable whore house, there could be no fucking around. So she would handle the other role that Taddeo had in mind for Arlene, which was exactly what would be needed in the present — for now both his family's interests and her own agenda. He couldn't be bothered with the night-by-night minutia of the bordello and achieve what he really worked for in baseball. And so Arlene could use this position to afford her the time she'd need to figure out how to deal with these next new developments — and what they meant.

Greggorio Villetti would definitely never be underestimated again. But she had started to suspect that Sega's introduction might have even caught *him* off guard. And she'd clearly witnessed that Rinaldo didn't trust his son and could very easily act to thwart him should the old man see it necessary. Everything was constantly in motion. But though Sega had appeared to have lost all control over her situation — considering her wonderful connection she made by playing her way into The House through Urso — Arlene didn't think Rinaldo could be too comfortable with *any* of the new recruits who came to work in the bordello, either. The current situation would become untenable and rather soon, she was sure of it. It had sure begun to become maybe even more than she could cope with.

Unfortunately and no longer unexpectedly for Greggorio, Rinaldo's current strategy for his children had the potential to once more derail his middle son's plans for what he'd like for his near future. And after all that risk Greg had decided to take with manipulating Colosimo and The Morello Family to attain the very specific concession he wanted out of them.

"When was the last time you three brothers did something as a family? For fun? I want you to collect Taddeo and take him fishing. Or on a hunting trip. Whatever my kids would like." In his office he addressed Greggorio and Urso.

"You think that's what I would like?"

"Really Papa?"

"Well I really wouldn't like to."

"And I am really your father. I really don't care what you'd like. And I can really insist." His sons sighed and slumped their shoulders as Villetti continued. "Now I want you to bond with your little brother. And strengthen the relationship between the two of you. I've noticed this house is strained. There's been a void ever since your mother — . Well, let's just say this house has seen happier times. And the *three* of you will need to hold it together so it remains a family long after I have also passed. So while I am still here with you, will you please try on my suggestions?"

"Tonight?"

"Yes. Taddeo now has a couple days off per the Cubs' schedule. You can get on the road while it is still a little light out, *tonight*. And maybe you could ponder how you will shed some light on the subject of how Kean O'Rourke got away from Johnny Torrio. You could do *that* on your trip as well. That he did, *was to my advantage*, but it is also in my best interest to know the details."

Shortly after the meeting with his father — who had been very pleased The Fox had failed — Greg explained to a disappointed Lumia that he would have to go away for a couple nights to help out the morale of his *oldest* brother who was having some personal issues that Lu had even witnessed that very evening — the incident with the dark-haired woman, Sega. He'd be going along with his youngest brother, the baseball player that they watched on Saturday. It was a family support kind of thing. Taddeo could meet her at a later time, but perhaps he too would benefit from both his big brother and Greggorio's help adjusting to his new role in The *Big* Leagues. But that is what good brothers are supposed to do for each other, he explained to her.

Lumia impressed him with her positive attitude, even more so after she'd said that she'd even decided to give her dress she brought to Sega "because I think what I saw, might have been that poor woman getting beaten earlier. It's not much but maybe it will help her feel just a little better." But Greg explained that had been an isolated incident and that they didn't beat girls at Villetti's but rather that it was a safe haven for poor immigrants who otherwise wouldn't have any other opportunity but to make their way on the streets. Nevertheless, he privately knew that it all couldn't have gone down any better for him because he'd planned on needing Lu's fancy clothing to supply it to Sega in the first place, coinciding with what else he was initiating by "*easing Urso's suffering* through their camping trip" by explaining to his oldest brother that it'd be just fine if he brought his woman along.

After his game on Monday, which clinched the Cubs sweep of New York, and now made 5 wins in a row for Chicago, Tad had wanted Arlene to come uptown to meet him. But she was refusing, saying she felt sick again, had work to do at the bar anyway, and that since they had won again that afternoon, it would be too crazy hanging out with all of his teammates — most of whom were all too over-excited to go drinking instead of heading to their second jobs to be sure. The privileges going to the victors once more. Tad thought he'd heard Hoffman supposedly brag he had a new woman lined up for this evening, but he did his best to only act reluctant when agreeing to take an extra turn driving Tad down to the South Side because Trip had to work and Trevor also had to get on his second job, neither of them getting to celebrate the Cubs sweeping the Giants. But Hoff almost sounded like he complained that he never got a break from being Taddeo's personal street car driver. However, he'd overheard Tad asking around the dugout for help that afternoon. The pitcher had been contemplating a different approach from the hill, even before New York's last chance was put out. So Taddeo's other friends' objections were pre-prepared. And Hoffman would only be faking his reluctance. Tad was sure his buddy wanted to see *someone* at Villetti's, but just get out of the work that might be involved with the pitcher's extra assignment he called for.

Meanwhile, most of the starters' bosses were kind enough to let those Cubs party. Their newest rookie pitcher admitted to himself that he envied his teammates, who all had gotten both cars and decent jobs *through their families' help*, and Tad felt he didn't have much to brag about in those arenas. But he was grateful that his fellow rookie teammates were his true friends and they did help him. Most of them, most of the time, and even Charlie Hollocher was sort of coming around. But he wanted desperately to bond more with the veterans and maybe even have Arlene coerce some of her girls to go along and further ingratiate Taddeo with the starting players to help him establish himself as at least some kind of leader on Chicago's team. Though that actually wasn't his plan in this particular moment. It sincerely wasn't at all about benefitting himself.

What he wanted to do now, was only for her. *Except when Hoff wants to see Rose, she comes around as soon as she is requested.* Of course, that was her job. However, Roslyn must have been preoccupied too this time, Tad supposed in the moment — if Hoff had been seriously trying to get *a different* "date." Though he had to ponder whether The Hoff could actually be falling for her, and The House's girl was manipulating things to make George now pick her up? His friend could be hiding it so as to not diminish his reputation, even while Tad spent time wondering why Arlene couldn't be more like Roslyn.

However, he needed to get in front of his own woman in person. Over the phone, his girlfriend wasn't planning to be of any kind of support at all. ["I don't have time for this Tad."]

"It's not what you think. Not tonight. I've done everything for you. Planned all of this. A great surprise *gift*. And all for your behalf."

["What did you do for me now? Get arrested?"]

"Jesus. No. I got you something you desperately want. I just thought you'd slip out so no one from my family can waylay me. And right now I've got George and likely Rose, to help us both."

["That's your surprise gift? And just my favorite people in the entire universe. Thanks, Taddeo. But I think I'll skip having a foursome."]

"Well fuck you. That's not what I meant."

["What did you mean?"]

"Well, it won't be totally unexpected, but I still want at least one of my successes to be a surprise."

"Well, almost none of them are ever really good enough," Arlene said. "And any *success you have*, is always a surprise." She needed to get back to being successful with learning what Greggorio was up to. Taddeo's games were not amusing to her.

Arlene didn't even have time to be on the phone. She was supposed to be guiding and evaluating this Lumia who was just brought in. She regretted her choice of the harsh words toward Taddeo for a moment, yet wouldn't bring herself to apologize. Her newest injury she caused Tad's ego might wind up motivating him into doing something that actually impressed her after all.

["Well would you be good enough to surprise someone and at least treat Rose, who works for you, and The Hoff who goes out of his way to drive me back to the South Side most evenings — so *your clan* doesn't beat the tar out of me — with some God-damned respect for once, Woman? Geez."]

She answered that last question with her hanging up on him. And she rolled her eyes, not that he could see the gesture. But in not too long of while later, Arlene surrendered her opposition when the two ballplayers — Hoff having at once "just decided" to gather up *Rose* to come with the now "three-of-them" anyway — congregated at the lounge. It was apparently as Tad had thought and now confirmed — that his friend George always had planned to head to the South Side anyway. He just didn't want anybody to know that Rose had turned his old team captain into *her new chauffer*. But Arlene was proud of Roslyn for that. So the boys both showed up at Villetti's, in George's Ford flatbed. Then Tad had pleaded and even begged Arlene to go for a ride with them. She finally relented. She couldn't make any further progress with learning what Greg was up to and now he had busied himself with returning to entertain their newest lady-visitor from Manhattan — or Brooklyn, judging by this Lumia's accent. So the charming pair of *ballplayer couples* left pretty much unnoticed, and as if they were on some kind of a double-date. But it would in fact be a pretty quick roll through the sheets at the Chinese laundry as they were really there so Tad could introduce Arlene to Mr. Li before the Oriental business proprietor locked up for the night. But they were also there instead of going out to have fun only for the explicit reason that the pitcher wanted a place his gal could slide in safe now, as he'd already heard from Urso when he'd come into the bar that his papa was sending them all camping — possibly that very evening. Taddeo had really insisted he needed to run a quick errand with his friends when his father had glimpsed and tried to stop him before the sun would disappear around South Chicago that Monday night. But Tad still had that one fast pitchout ready for the occasion. And he gave his old man the slip — momentarily. Something had seemed to have suddenly elevated him to an obviously new and uncustomary state of nervousness.

But Arlene couldn't hide her concern from herself. This his new plan of Rinaldo's would leave *Corrado* in town, with unhindered access to her, and no supervision. However, Greg would also be gone. That was a plus. But this wasn't the time Arlene would want to decide whether she would be making use of the Delasandro son. She had failed to get together any extra money. If she took down Rinaldo while all his boys were gone, there was the reaction to consider of more than only one of his nephews. She'd need to bribe all his associates, and she did not have the funds.

Now, though Tad did have a couple of weekdays off from baseball coming to him, he didn't have much of a choice for what he could do with them. His papa insisted. However, at the minimum — and achieving the minimum did seem to be his specialty — her man would leave Arlene with the one choice he'd successfully created for her — namely that to escape his cousin Corry if she decided she needed to, and even his papa if the senior Villetti came on to her again. Mr. Li finally demonstrated he would go along with this favor for Taddeo, perhaps persuaded by Hoff and Rose's help — the second girl sworn to secrecy. Although Arlene privately expressed she thought she almost *could* trust Rose as it were. And Mr. Li wasn't very good at hiding his genuine enthusiasm for meeting up with Hoffman again — who he also knew as a boy and through several broken windows before the kids got signed into the minors and were relocated to Iowa. It was a nice meeting, so far as meetings about all this sort of business went.

But Tad later expressed that he felt Mr. Li was still plenty unenthusiastic — just very reluctant about Arlene moving in there, and also and especially giving her a key. Instead, Taddeo related that he thought for sure that Li was hiding something else. And Arlene continued thinking that she sensed her man getting unusually and extremely nervous about this camping trip. There was something else that Tad was thinking — and that he wasn't sharing with her.

Now Taddeo would make one final try to be as persuasive as he ever could with his papa after he got back to the lounge, alone and on foot. He had wanted to walk back alone because he needed way more than a moment to think, undistracted, about just exactly what he could say to win over his papa's changing his mind regarding that camping trip. He really feared his life could depend on it. Taddeo's heart was racing. He was in danger. His mother had always warned him this day would come. But Tad always wanted to do "the right thing" — the fair thing — right now for Mr. O'Rourke and definitely for his friend, Mr. Li. But did his father know what he'd done? Did he understand his son's motivations? Or had Taddeo gone way past the point of just taking advantage of the limit of exactly how much his papa would tolerate of what he'd see as some sort of adolescent rebellion, that now crossed over the line into the impenitent realm of perfidy beyond any forgiveness? The only thing he knew right now, was The Hoff had left with Rose ahead of him, and were probably waiting for Tad to cause a distraction so they could slide in unseen, in one room or another, upstairs at the bordello. His backstop was catching something on the cheap Tad suspected, and Roslyn was blowing her commission. But it was his best friend, so Taddeo didn't really care about that business. And meanwhile, Arlene remained behind on Maxwell Street, changing Mr. Li's mind, about a few things. Only very soon, the Sigñor's attention was intentionally sidetracked by his youngest son who followed him around their family's business. Urso was probably with Sega for better or worse, and Greg had disappeared to take care of something personal, before the time all the brothers had been ordered to collect together, so they could make their group departure. The pitcher allowed himself some pride over getting better and better at being deceptive so that he could make sure that hopefully, at least no one there would notice the next play his catcher was framing by his arrival. His best friend had said he "might agree to lay down a sacrifice" and stick around the bordello to keep an eye on Arlene when she showed up to work there — on behalf of the rookie reliever, of course. *Though it was some sacrifice. George staying in a whore house? Who was he doing a favor for again?* But with Jasmine's help, Rose thought she could help The Hoff somehow survive, hidden, *on those premises*, for the next three nights. The ballplayer was sure she could.

But Tad's papa wasn't granting any requests when the pitcher tried to reschedule his next outing. "You wanted more authority and you've begun exercising greater leverage with this new position in The House that you so passionately auditioned for. Then you made Arlene the assistant manager. That was never what I had intended by granting you the promotion. So consider this a business trip you are going on with your brothers, for your required job training. Your minding your responsibilities around here. And if you get going now, you and your brothers might still make it safely up to the Wisconsin state line before it gets completely dark outside. Now I've heard enough from you. I'm your papa, but now I am also your boss.

"And I have a special assignment for you. You'll recall Mister Kean O'Rourke? And how when we had that previous meeting, I was visited by that old friend from my past? Not long after, well Mister O'Rourke that meat-head, failed to be around when your brothers took *a family member of Mister Colosimo's* to meet the butcher, after your Saturday game. I know you couldn't know anything about that. You were out on the pitcher's mound and then partying with your team after your victory over New York. Now I want you to find something interesting about the family business that will to be of great importance to me. Something useful. Your brothers should be of help. I need to know if I should suspect a betrayal, Taddeo. I already have a feeling."

Tad felt something he'd never felt before. Panic started to gather in the pit of his stomach as he finally, truly thought about what he did. For Arlene, and with good intentions toward Mr. Li, he had interfered with his father's business. He had helped Kean O'Rourke escape and in doing so opened a fissure in The Family. However well-intended his acts, this fault-line was one there wasn't any doubt would be labeled as a betrayal — of his own papa. Arlene told him that they'd see it that way. And she wouldn't be the only one among the Irish who would learn about it. O'Rourke always had a big mouth. Maybe less teeth in there now, but the same stubborn attitude still governing it. His father could always suspect that other fella, the ex-cop, resold the information, maybe because he was mad about his numbers debt. Or because he was also a leprechaun. But now the youngest of the Villetti siblings was about to be escorted out for a ride with his brothers. Taddeo had seen people being escorted away for a ride with Greggorio and Urso. He couldn't recollect when he'd seen their previous guests return. He suddenly found himself shaking with an inability to otherwise move once he'd left the study. What was this? Was this his turn to be taught another lesson? What did his old man know?

Still outside his papa's office, Tad turned his head to stare a thousand miles down that dimly lit hallway to where he'd heard Hoff had taken a room. He willed his feet to drag him there, pausing before he knocked on the door. He hoped his friends still had their clothes on. George had one of the fastest throw-down times and Tad hoped they would soon all bear witness to his success with it in the Major Leagues. But Hoff had also earned a bad reputation because he'd been rumored to practice it in bedrooms all across America. Tad knew it wasn't just a rumor.

Now his friends were witness to just how fast Taddeo's other life, the one he kept hidden at home, brought him down. By way of his Uncle Delasandro's help, Tad's father kept the brothel's hospitality suites above the lounge, well-stocked. George and Rose did not indulge in the party-favors beyond drinks and their occasionally smoking with Mary-Jane. Hoff said that "other stuff" looked like the vaccination medicines they injected their animals with on his family's farm, and incredibly, Roslyn was the daughter of a real physician. The young lady had picked up plenty of knowledge about the effects of drugs for herself. But she preferred the honest underground socialite scene rather than the fake and stuffy high-society one — but with the young woman being way too wise to have ever buried herself very deeply in it. She was only *alleged* to be a sex-addict. No wonder she was perfect for George. However, the sporting couple was quite surprised that the usually confident athlete had come back to interrupt their game by demanding they forfeit up the standard bestowment by way of The House.

With no real reason or position from with which to object to Taddeo dosing himself, his friends surrendered the vial and needles in the small silver tin case trademarked "Sears." And as Rose watched, The Shooter noted her holding her breath when the protrusions of her breasts through the thin bedsheet she'd covered her naked form with, rose with his level of pain from the sharp prick. Then everything was quickly released along with his hurt and anxiety when Taddeo felt the heroin enter in as the relief for this game. He truly felt he needed this to get through his next inning and how much he could really wind up hurting — and not just from his being separated from Arlene.

Chapter 33

Now Tad was quite perplexed about just *how* he should feel. He didn't require even all his fingers and toes to count how many experiences with *just* his brothers he had partaken in. The Villettis were about the epitome of the twentieth century dysfunctional family — but with the exception that had to be made to accommodate their own special kind of extreme. The well-outfitted and equally well-armed siblings were rather quiet during the second day of a serene stay up north that had seen them drive up to and into the secluded and forested area just over the Wisconsin border. Their father still hoped that his offspring might create a little stronger bond with each other by spending time enjoying this road trip; hence this hunting expedition.

But it was *not* just the three of them. For reasons that eluded Taddeo, they weren't entirely alone. Greg had counseled Urso that it'd be all right if he didn't have to abandon his attachment to Sega for their big game-chasing excursion after all, and the eldest brother had brought his latest comfort girl along to camp out with them. Naturally, she'd stay in Urso's tent, but Tad would sleep apart from his other brother, since Greggorio was expected to keep his lantern on and maintain watch, as he was known to stay up brooding many a night anyway. This was fine, as it afforded Taddeo some privacy with which he could utilize his last "medicinal dose" of sanity he'd been rationing for himself along this new trail they were on. Inexplicably, while the Villetti brothers wore their outdoor sporting accoutrements, no one had bothered to tell "Venus" here not to wear an expensive-looking evening gown that was slit up the sides, exposing some alluring skin the color of silky cream on her long legs. The brunette with a straight length of strong hair which curled only at the ends looked nevertheless especially sexy while they sat her next to Taddeo in Urso's flashy but small buggy of a car. She might have been wearing the nicest dress she owned. At least Tad couldn't recollect her ever dressing that nice before, though she had barely been exposed to him. However, along with being cramped in there with all the camping gear, she appeared saddened by more than just that, as if something dark troubled her. But every once in a while she flashed a bright smile *at him*. It would not be the first time he'd noticed how alluring she appeared.

Though Taddeo quickly had other things to focus on now that they had arrived at their next stop, and the four of them left their vehicle and preceded on foot until they could all circle each other, as they stalked their prey. The brothers' previous attempts at making their kills hadn't yielded them any trophies yet, but now Urso claimed to be all excited because he'd seen something. But he just usually liked any excuse to shoot his gun and Greg had responded in good nature to humor him. So they'd jumped out of the car and stalked off deeper into the lush green woods even before they ever set up camp for what would be their last full day of this field trip away from Chicago. But this wasn't terribly safe since they could all have easily gotten lost if they ever became separated and were unable to depend upon Greggorio's steady sense of direction — and their only compass. It was still on the edge of morning that Wednesday and Taddeo had an early game the following day after. The Cubs faced the Reds in a double-header. If his brothers respected Tad's professional responsibilities, they'd have to get going and leave Wisconsin pretty soon.

So now as the brothers closed in on their target, Tad broke the ever necessary silence with his ever more frequently recurring and reliable attitude problem with whatever The Family was doing. "No. I'm not going to shoot the mother, Urso. Her offspring are depending upon her to nourish and protect them from harm, from other predators," Taddeo explained. His words elicited quite some loud growls coming from the foliage ahead of them. They'd also already heard the gurgled answering sounds that must have come from smaller animals, hidden somewhere close by. The brothers had discovered impressive prey. Sega covered her mouth with her hands, but her eyes were opened wide with shock, then clenched reacting to her sadness. By now she should have learned to expect the play that was coming from the eldest brother. After all, she may have spent more time with Urso in the past few days than Taddeo had in his entire lifetime.

The furry form of a huge black bear took shape, emerging from the underbrush which broke from its forward thrust through the crackling branches and crunching of dead leaves. Taddeo fell back shaking. The thing was enormous! Greg and Urso held their ground.

"Now you got her upset Tadpole, we'll have to stand our ground, and I'm not going to stalk all over the backwoods, looking for something else to shoot. We gotta go pretty soon and I'm not going to start any habit of leaving any of my ventures, empty-handed." Urso even took his eyes off the bear for a moment to look at his pocket watch. "I've done too much of that already."

Greg thought, *He's worried only that "there goes precious time of mine that could have been better spent drinking and gambling."* But Greggorio also remembered this particular watch and how it was once shown to him by his father. It had been his grandfather's before that. And his papa had been given it when their family was first leaving Europe with wishes he'd invest his time in his new life in the United States wisely, and make it a productive one. Well, Greg was so young he didn't really remember that, just the stories his papa had told his two older sons. Now, apparently, their father had chosen to pass it along to Urso. Greg envied the bear for a moment. At least she didn't have to hide her anger at the intrusion of others upon the ground that she'd counted on being her own.

"Hey. Look, Taddeo. I'm trying to teach you something. There is easy prey right here. Right in front of you," Urso went on. The mother bear exclaimed her point of view and priorities differed, and displayed gigantic claws and fangs to illustrate her points. "But we're in her territory and this mother is about to charge, answering our challenge, especially now since you've made it very clear we've come into her backyard with harmful intentions." Urso had returned to observing the bear, surprisingly demonstrating he actually had a cautious side. The animal roared and looked like it was about to charge. "Nope. I don't think this bitch is taking prisoners. Neither do I. So this bear is going to die, Little Brother. Better her than you. And that's life. Things are tough by nature and those that can adapt, will be the ones who sustain and expand their territory. So these cubs will just have to learn to survive on their own."

Greggorio smirked as he turned his face so his siblings couldn't see him enjoying all the great irony radiating from this latest exchange.

Then the monstrosity of the dark-furred beast stood on her hind legs, towering over ten feet tall and let out one hell of a roar. But Taddeo turned his attention away from her, so he didn't have to look when he heard the thunder crash from his oldest brother's hunting rifle. The sound echoed with enough strength such that he couldn't be sure if he heard the animal vocalize any last sound of her own, but the ground seemed to offer up a thud from a large body dropping in the soil. In his peripheral vision, his eye caught Sega collapsing to her knees and putting her head in her hands. Taddeo had flinched when the gunshot rang out and his thoughts were on the injustice of what was only nature. But all *his* instincts were in play and another drove him to turn a little so he could study this young woman — yet older than he was no less. Taddeo had no idea why his brother had brought Sega along on what his papa had been encouraging as being his boys' bonding time — this pointless hunting trip. She definitely didn't belong there. And Urso wasn't ever that co-dependent that his little brother could recall. So were his siblings trying to embarrass Tad in front of the woman? He couldn't fathom. Nor could he reconcile with whatever was the reason Sega dolled up so brilliantly, beautiful and dressed in such a seductive costume such as to reveal long, slim but succulent legs inside fashionable openings that ran nearly the entire seam of her dress. Not to neglect the skin showing a fair amount of her breasts, glistening with the tiniest bit of sweat, drawing more attention to her obviously endowed chest, exposed in the early morning light by her low-cut blouse which bared her arms as well. The young athlete couldn't stop looking at her. Or her side-boob she displayed. Intentionally? She was a great distraction for Tad who did not want to think about what just happened to the bear. Instead, this exotic young lady's long dark hair reminded Taddeo of his mother, and how soft her locks felt to the touch when she'd learned in to kiss her youngest child and put him at ease. But Tad was not at ease. As the echo of the gunshot faded in his ears, he found he'd started shaking once surprise gave way to fear in the silence of the forest, that now settled down upon their little group. What had just happened, felt so wrong — and it all looked so wrong, too.

What possessed *who* to have Sega dress like some high-roller hotel escort on a backwoods hunting trip? And where did she get *that* outfit? She seemed to exude more class than the last time Taddeo recalled seeing her — when his brother first introduced her at The Sisson. He hadn't been able to stop thinking about her all the previous night, while in the nearly silent woods, he was forced to listen to Urso frolicking with her in his tent and Tad had really missed spending his nights with Arlene. He really missed that. The peace brought by his uncle's heroin was an illusion he didn't have a dosage strong enough to sustain.

But his thoughts were interrupted when he saw that Greg caught him looking at her, and smiled. "Now it's your turn, brother." He rested his right hand on Tad's shoulder and detached a long knife in a leather sheave from his utility belt and handed both to Taddeo. "I offer you a gift and consolation. You can relax around me, learn to trust your big brother. I understand why you didn't want to shoot. But it's all over now. So *this job* must be yours. Every member of the family has to play their part. Some part. Let me teach you how to skin a kill."

Taddeo first glanced back at his oldest brother's girl, then got pushed by his other sibling along and toward the bear who he'd just became aware was still breathing, panting out some awful sound, perhaps her regretful farewell to her young offspring who could be heard now baying back toward her, but hidden somewhere in the undergrowth. And then Taddeo couldn't help himself. Approaching the animal he got even more scared. Then he threw up. As he fell over dropping the knife and heaving, while tears escaped his eyes, Sega rushed over to him and wrapped her arms over his shoulders and across his chest to hold him. Tad brought his hands up to gently rest them on top of Sega's and nodded his gratitude toward her.

Urso crinkled his face and started toward the pair immediately, but Greg put his arm out in front of his brother and gently blocked him off.

"You want your arm broken, Greggorio?"

"I want you to let our little brother be. It's Tad's first real hunting trip. This is different from taking him fishing as a kid. Remember, he didn't like to see *anything* get hurt? He used to try and unhook and toss back as many as he thought he could get away with freeing, right behind our backs. We used to catch him and then ride him into the ground or toss him out of our boat for doing that. What we didn't learn then was Tad will need to make the adjustment on his own, as much as possible anyway, in order to prepare himself to one day take down larger prey."

"All right. Fine. But that doesn't mean he also needs to take my girl. Little shit."

"She's trying to help him. Tad's used to responding to women. After all, he had Mama mostly to himself during his formative years. He should draw on his own strength to demonstrate it to Sega any minute now. And appearing like he presently is, and in front of *her?* He'll realize just how much he's embarrassing himself in just a little moment longer. So just give him his time. Papa had so busied himself with raising us, he must feel he did his part. Now we are to help with our little brother. Isn't that what family is for? Let him have what he needs to grow up. It's his right, Urso.

"And speaking of doing just that," Greg felt himself grow warmer with such a great pride that he needed to keep it in the tightest check, at least for the present, "we also need to help him steer away from that little Irish bitch. Now I saw *you* notice Arlene. Take her. Don't worry about this." Greg nodded behind him to Taddeo, still embraced by Sega, crinkling up his face and twisted his head from side to side with his hands up. Greg just shrugged. "Little Red? She's *your* right. Not to forget your mission that Papa gave you, but which you neglected. Who said you can't be the big, bad wolf, doing what you're supposed to do, and enjoying your work, too? They're just whores, Urso."

"Taddeo's made *her* into kind of our bordello business manager. She told Papa he's been training her. Can you believe that?"

"Yeah. I know. That was kind of *my* job. And I was going to pass it off to our cousin Corry in short time."

"You were?"

"Never mind. But I guess I wouldn't suggest hurting the girl. *Can't you — without?* Gaghh. No? Well, it's no wonder you're not married. I *know* you never fail to reap what you sew. But you are his big brother." Greg nodded toward Taddeo, still on his knees with Sega. "You need to step in and at least make Tad take a couple smart steps back from this little leprechaun bitch *before Arlene ruins him.* You know how this already looks to Papa, though he still won't act. But she's a killer. And the Tadpole will have to get over her. Faster than he'd think." The pair watched their youngest brother curl up on the ground before the dying bear and shake, wrapped in the new woman's arms. "But since I know you'll let Sega go sooner than later anyway — as it fits with your well-established pattern, Urso — let Taddeo take this one. It's a fair trade. A girl for a girl. Besides, nothing helps you forget a woman better than another woman. And you are long overdue to deal with Arlene. Though when you're through with her, what you were always supposed to do with her, is bring her before Papa."

"That's all true. About Tadpole as well. But I can't figure why. You're saying our little brother is really *in love?* With her? And out of all the whores he could choose from? And the trouble *that* could cost him? Has already cost him. I mean you also told me that was why he was washing dishes with the niggers, right?"

A gunshot rang out. Then another sound. Tad had fired his rifled long weapon and ended the mother bear's suffering; her last pained but continuing moan she sounded toward her children. And then she expired.

"Right. But love dies. Just like everything else," Greg told his brother.

And now Greg had "Lucky LuLu" to substitute on the team for Arlene, after his brother had *her*, so Urso could feel completely indifferent about eliminating that troublesome red-headed wench, once he separated the Irish woman from Taddeo, who in turn Greg had been tempting with Sega. And when she learned of that — as Greggorio would see to it that she did — Arlene would turn on the Tadpole, losing her ally, while he would run headlong into Urso, even as he tried to figure out why. Everything was going as Greggorio had planned while Urso moved past the youngest brother, shoving him, and un-sheathed his own knife to set about separating the bear from its fur coat along with her body from her head. But given Taddeo's nature, evidenced by the way he'd just reacted over a bear — Greg wasn't sure Tad's constitution would be strong enough to face down the eldest brother in that fateful confrontation he so much wanted to set up. Though with Tad's sense of what he felt was right and wrong that Greg saw by this testing of his brother with the mother bear, he expected "The Shooter" to aim for some kind of justice for Arlene, even after he was no longer with her. Only not certain he could count on that, Greg was suddenly inspired by another opportunity to set one more thing up, as Urso lost his watch. It fell out of his pocket while he was in motion, working at the skinning and taking of his trophy, as all the motions he went through suddenly made the chain break. Urso didn't notice he'd missed his papa's gift. But the flash of silver reflecting sunlight stood in pretty clean contrast to that whole mountain of dark fur, red blood and blue veiny meat. However, Greg smiled to himself and didn't hesitate to move in to retrieve it for his oldest brother, only first making sure it had soaked well in some of the dead animal's blood. Then he made as if he were cleaning the pocket watch for his sibling just prior to returning his "precious" item to him. Only he deliberately didn't do a good job. The watch could become very useful to the middle brother when the time was right, later.

But if Taddeo were so truly in love with his precious scarlet treasure, he'd *still* come after Urso over over what Greggorio would instigate his oldest brother inflicted upon Arlene, and relentlessly even if cautiously — and *if* Urso even survived his own encounter with the murdering little Irish wench. Currently though, there was little evidence Tad had the stomach for that sort of thing. The bear had been a great test. But Greg could only hope that his father's actions the other week, by sending that fool from the bar to his former room on South Shore Drive to harass Arlene — who she had to have offed herself — would indeed become known of by Taddeo, and at least shake his blind loyalty to her. That man — or human sacrifice — was never to be seen again. Greg himself didn't know where *she* buried all the bodies. Or how she could. He needed a bullet count on his old gun he had Corrado leave his little brother. And the cunt needed to be searched. And if nothing turned up from that, something else could shake out the trust his little brother must hold for Arlene, so that Tad might now be turned on to Sega. At least casually if not intimately, so thus he would still care just enough for Arlene to be motivated to avenge her if a new red scar on his family could be bled savagely enough to enrage her rookie boyfriend. But the pair's smooth cooperation would be over.

He'd once thought his father's sending the john to his death at The Sisson was an impediment to his own plan. Greg had since reevaluated that in light of obtaining the opportunities that using both Sega and Lumia allowed him. Opportunities to cause Tadpole to reassess his own pledge of fidelity to Arlene. Then it would also reinforce Greggorio's plans if Arlene could be caused to lose her own affection for using Taddeo — like if she could be made to perceive he was cheating on her — whether it was true or not. Then Greg could attain the advantage from destroying their united front. But he would not risk completely counting on Urso being reliable either, not after Greg was asking Big Jim Colosimo for the privilege of gaining Lumia for his plans and then competing with Colosimo's nephew Johnny Torrio for the head Chicago boss' favor. Greg had to succeed with all his plans, now. And this could be very dangerous, even with as nice as everyone from The Outfit seemed to be playing. But he did not have to be curious as to how the hell did Sega show up through his father's order — and be so perfectly suited to what were Greggorio's new plans. Greg was almost ten steps ahead of everyone. Only he had to split up his little brother Romeo from *his* Irish Juliet. Now. Yet it needed to be civil if Tad would hold onto any motivation to defend Arlene, if at a later date he could be convinced he needed to. So if at least enough instability could be created in The House, Greg's takeover of a controlling position would be both necessary and legitimate in everyone's eyes. After all, he still had the chance to convince Colosimo that Greg's papa had been the first to falter by bringing Arlene there. Meanwhile, Torrio couldn't have done any better at proving his little crew was ineffective — however conveniently that had occurred. *But in their own less than convenient ways, all my inept pawns actually* will *be turning out to be reliable in some way or another. Tad obviously doesn't have the stomach for killing that I bet Arlene would wish he had. Only* after *it's too late for her, he might be able to find it. Just when I'm the last one left standing to control it* — and *my aging father. I've only had to learn to play to each of their individual natures. Just like the Genna Brothers and the cops.*

But he did have to wonder if Arlene had already killed his father while they were away on this trip. It was neither Greg's first wish, nor would the timing be convenient. But that would also be well within her expected nature.

* * * * *

Three nights of restlessness that came with sleeping on an old mattress laid on the floor of a storage closet was not natural for Arlene. She'd known rough times, but not necessarily physically uncomfortable ones — at least when she was alone. But her back, neck, and shoulders ached, and when she could convince herself she laid her bones down where she was comfortable with them, she'd wake up heaving and vomit into a small wastecan Mr. Li had provided for her once he'd seen *that* would be necessary. He was very concerned, bothered by her presence. Arlene quickly discovered that it was not because he feared she carried some communicable disease as a secret, but because of probably the most important thing of value to him that the old Chinaman wanted to keep hidden: someone else lived with him.

When she woke sweating in the middle of the night, Arlene heard voices. His, and one softer, surely feminine and perhaps quite youthful. Mr. Li could have kept a slave girl. She'd heard of such things, and by less of a strict definition, wasn't that what Villetti did? Almost two dozen times over? But Arlene never heard what sounded like sex, or abuse of any kind for that matter. One of the only other natural conclusions she could reasonably arrive at, was that Mr. Li was hiding *his daughter*.

And as long as Arlene stayed there, the girl was unfairly being confined to live in the family quarters upstairs, at least when the Oriental's houseguest was around. *However, a child could easily use the fire escape, and I'm gone, working at Villetti's all the time anyway*. At first Arlene wasn't sympathetic toward the unseen girl. She was asked to bathe at Villetti's while Mr. Li tried to prevent her from accessing the live-work building's upstairs. A few older places in the Maxwell Street Market area still had outhouses, even after indoor plumbing had been installed. Only this wasn't any comfort to someone sick with her conditions. But perhaps for the better of everyone, she then caught the girl's small brown face and flutter of lengthy straight and strong locks of dark hair, spying on her. The girl had snuck downstairs a little while later, naturally curious to look over the mysterious, but probably — in her child's eyes — "glamorously fashionable" lady-visitor. Yet it really was for the best that there was one less house forced to live shrouded in so much deception and lies. So she assured Mr. Li that she intended to let no harm come to his innocent child. Mr. Li was clearly displeased his only daughter had been discovered. But Arlene remembered her own life at that age — which she learned to be was thirteen, in the Li girl's case. She thought she should at least try to make it better than what Arlene had endured. William Fallon wouldn't understand that. Nor would her other cousin in Louisiana. But Mr. Li seemed to show some gratitude where it concerned Arlene's decision there. An increment of success — if she really wanted to say she desired to maintain her new accommodations. But the Irish woman's presence in his home remained clearly on his nerves. And on her own too, of course.

Chapter 34

Taddeo's little hunting excursion with his brothers had worked out to be his rather successful fact-hunting expedition with them. Even if what he found was discouraging. Though *they* had learned nothing about the fate of Mr. O'Rourke, they didn't seem to care to, either. The subject was actually never brought up. Though the boys' papa would not be pleased at all by this. Meanwhile, Tad thought it all through several times while he walked onto the sidewalk and reached the same conclusion when he reached Mr. Li's laundry — *having driven himself* because he just could not wait any longer to see Arlene. But he parked down and across the street. He wasn't sure, but recent events made him paranoid that someone would be having him followed — especially since he had just borrowed a vehicle without its owner's permission. But Hoff would have agreed to lending him his old flatbed anyway, and this way he didn't disturb his catcher who was possibly still with Roslyn, and *their ballgame*, in its something-dozenth extra inning. So Tad thought that by adding speed to appease his impatience on his next outing, he also added the necessary taking of extra precaution. But his conclusions he came to had a lot more to do with The House surely knowing all about Hoffman staying up in one of the rooms there, probably as protection for Arlene, and the other women covering for him. Except any of those girls could sell-out for her own ends. And Taddeo now strongly suspecting Greggorio of working towards some very different ends than the boys' father, as well as being Tad's one family member that would take the keenest interest in him. The Genna Brothers had, per Greg's influence, as had nearly everyone in the underworld who'd surfaced at his ballgame. Though Taddeo hadn't seen Greg there; just his papa, from The Family. But he still drove around a few extra blocks checking for any tails before he arrived on Maxwell Street just to make absolutely sure he'd taken off from their place on Taylor Street, before Greg could arrange to send any spies after him, in the event — the hope — that The Family still didn't know where he was going.

Only next when he entered the Chinaman's place of business,

as Arlene was supposed to leave it unlocked for his return, Tad kept very quiet, preferring to imagine he really did arrive there unobserved for certain. But at the time in the morning at which he got back from the trip to Wisconsin, he also did not want to disturb his new benefactor. In that moment, he only wanted to see his woman. Then he too caught a clue that someone else was there with the elder proprietor. He got the impression of two voices, one lighter pitched, and the fast flight of a smaller person — maybe a young child who'd been interacting with — their father? He'd always wondered if Mr. Li had any family. He'd never seen the man *not* alone in all the years he'd known him. But it was not Arlene's voice that reached him. Tragically from Taddeo's point of view, he'd only managed to spend part of last Monday night with her in the laundry — and only while she helped him — or he helped her, Hoff and Rose move in some of her stuff that they picked up from The Sisson. So Taddeo was now very eager to see his woman again after three nights apart from her and as soon as he, his brothers, and Sega got back from their trip. Only he never stayed long enough at the business before to wonder if anyone else lived there. But someone already inside the place had been watching his arrival, early that Thursday morning — and it wasn't Arlene.

Taddeo and his brothers had shot the bear around mid-morning the previous day. Skinning and butchering the beast's meat had taken quite some time. And before leaving, they cooked and consumed some of their kill. Mostly continuing in silence beyond the meal, it made for a long drive back from Wisconsin in a closely cramped, nearly-stock Model-T. Longer, because Urso insisted on stopping at several road houses so he could order drinks. There were never three more different brothers from one another, and they — and Sega — had very little else to say to each other. The conflict that had occurred already among each of the young men was enough for most of them. For *most* of them.

Now, Tad definitely didn't want to disturb anyone else while they were likely sleeping at the Li's live-work residence. Well, except for one person he'd been hoping to find there. Only then Tad couldn't find *her* at all.

So, on extremely limited rest, Taddeo had to take his leave of the place again, only with plans to return, coming back a second and then a third time only after completing another couple of short errands — and hopefully with permission to be driving his papa's prized touring car. Unfortunately, now there wouldn't really be any time for him to lay with Arlene if he did find her anyway, because eventually as the time flew by, he'd have to go to be at the ballpark, also earlier than would be normally required of him. He had to warm up for the Cubs' games versus Cincinnati that afternoon. A double-header was scheduled — of all good things to come — with such excellent timing — as the pitcher was seriously overtired. And tired of it being too hard for him to try and find the time to be alone with the woman that he'd been longing for — after a road trip with Urso *and his woman*.

But first, any sound of voices finishing their conversing he'd overheard for only the second time, must have abruptly fallen silent, just after the ringing of the two bells that hung on ribbons over the laundry's front door when Taddeo re-entered the establishment, still so early on that Thursday morning. His woman had muted them by stuffing them with paper for Tad's return, but he removed any muffling of the sound upon his return in order for the bells to once more continue their protection they offered the Li family.

Now Arlene's special man had to first take care of business with the bordello operation to acquire some money he'd need, only Tad couldn't find the object of his affections in The Family's business either. He'd actually reunited with his father though, who'd decided to stay Wednesday night in a room *there*, and waited up for the expected return of his children. Luckily, Tad skipped any debriefing over his hunting trip, promising answers would be forthcoming later. He knew his papa wanted information about O'Rourke. But in this moment, he needed to make an urgent request of his papa. To his relief, his father found his favor he'd asked for amusing, or he was too tired to argue with his son at that time in the morning, or even better yet — he was more than pleased his boys had done what he asked for once. Tad was awarded with the positive answer to his request. He then raced back to Mr. Li *in his father's automobile*, to fortunately find the old Chinaman had decided to reveal he was awake.

That was all for the better. With the money he first had gathered together at Villetti's, Taddeo had no difficulty making a new deal with the laundryman concerning Mr. Li's true purported line of work, and then the relief pitcher moved fast to strike out across town to Weeghman Park. And then he launched into a new workload closer to home. In only several hours, he'd have to make a second round-trip between the North and South Sides on top of *that one*. There'd be no rest for the weary. And the Cubs had that double header versus the Reds beginning early — which meant late that same morning. With no time for even a short nap, he and Hoff were going to have to warm up to show themselves continuing to take the initiative — and just in case Tad would get called on again to play. Hopefully, Killefer would be getting out on the field, and not on the rookie's back. Then Taddeo might just fall asleep on the bench. Today, everything he wanted to succeed with his pitching, was *off the field*.

George was quite well-rested, though. As was predictable, Tad found the catcher with Roslyn. Hoff's only concern was that his pitcher still had at least a little gas left in his tank, after all the motions Tad had already gone through since he'd been brought back for his next round with Chicago. But the former farmhand tool wasn't letting them down. The engine in that old truck was burning fuel at a well-balanced rate.

And in that moment, something else that was warm, was Mr. Li's reception for Taddeo. Though George Hoffman had to wait in the customer service area, while the proprietor walked with Taddeo into the rear of the laundry where they could converse with more privacy. His friend from childhood, quite pleased with Tad this time, informed him that his money had worked and held off his brothers, especially in front of Johnny Torrio and his pack, and if Taddeo kept up being able to fund him, Mr. Li said he could meet with the other merchants and convince them that Colosimo, through dealing with Tad's father as their intermediary, was the best deal they were going to get. Other Italians — the majority in their community on the South Side — should much prefer to work with The House rather than be subject to paying tribute to those who lorded over Chicago's Chinatown, for example. *Why did Li bring them up?* Tad wondered. And there was that Mr. Torrio was an unknown factor at this early juncture. But Mr. Li said he could reassure the shopkeepers of all the good parts to that. They certainly would feel protection from The Black Hand were no more barrel murders to occur. That might have been a hint for Taddeo to pass along the comment to his papa. Thus there would be no merchant rebellion against Rinaldo Villetti — and the two of them, Mr. Li and Tad, would keep it to themselves as for the reason why. The bombings would end, too. *And how come Li is so confident about that?* Well, maybe because they already had, for the short time being. But the old Chinaman also mentioned something else — that Taddeo had been waiting for — would now finally be gotten ready for him. Mr. Li had labored — he meant by way of his other workers' assistance, all requested to report to the laundry at this ridiculous hour — to get all of some other job done, and just in the nick of time.

In this moment, he said he wanted to introduce Taddeo to someone to demonstrate his trust and faith in the young athlete. He called out to the upstairs of his live-work place. "Zhen Li? Zhen Li."

* * * * *

"It's not like I'm not predicting your answer — ."

About three hours later, Tad met up with Arlene. He finally found her at the bar as they prepared to open up the restaurant for Old Lamont's breakfast orders in the kitchen. She'd started the cleaning work while Tad ran around to tend to the washing of his special dirty laundry. She'd already suggested they must have just missed each other in passing when Taddeo had first gone to Mr. Li's. His reactions to her suggested he'd nurtured some doubts about her while their responsibilities in their respective lives apart, saw them separated far too much.

"Yeah, that's the way to predicate your next question," she said.

"Will it change your response?"

"No. And for the millionth time. Don't even try, Taddeo."

"But I still have to ask you to come with me." He thought about how Urso even took his girl along with them on the brothers' hunting trip. "We're done with this doubleheader with the Reds, and then I'm gone. For three weeks, Arlene."

"So let me count. That's got to be like five-hundred hours that I'll have to live without having to listen to you whine about *something* and then next talk about baseball? Pitch by pitch. Let me give small thanks for small miracles."

"That's not funny. Aren't you afraid of what will happen if I'm not here to protect you?"

"You can't stand up to your brothers and your father to protect me when you are here, Taddeo. But yes. I am afraid. Of Urso. His brutality. Of Greg. Whatever he's plotting. He and his friend, your creepy cousin Corrado — they are up in my business far too much already — for my taste. And your father. I *know* what he's capable of doing. I've already had a taste of that. That's for sure. But so far I've been the only one who's really taken care of myself."

"No, Arlene. I'd like at least some teensy amount of credit for having helped you *take care of yourself.* I found you this place to stay in and an ally in Mister Li, who will let you attempt to hide out there now, once we get ourselves all out of the hotel."

"So we can trade in a bed and breakfast for sleeping on some old mattress on the floor of a laundry and — ."

"And I also got you into a position controlling the bordello that's not one my father can afford to let Colosimo see suffer — by way of making any more rash changes with his business model. *His* nephew-in-law is in town — though I think he's going to start up his own place even up-town, with permission or some kind of compromise they made with the Irish. And on my camping trip I also heard from my brother that Victoria Moresco likes you. And the girls seem happier with the changes we've made — the way they're being treated now."

"The way I'm treating the girls now — and insisting Family members pay for services since they are all getting paid out of revenues collected *for* services. So less of those thugs are hanging out abusing the ladies, unless they pay me first. And you already know Rose is running around proclaiming she can do whatever she wants. Except that we're behind quota and making up for money that went missing last weekend when you didn't mind to the accounting or even bother coming around after your stupid baseball games. If only I could say the same about Urso."

"He better not touch you. But I took some of that money to pay off Mister Li for our rent and also passed on some to Old Lamont for his silence about it."

"Swell. But so far, you've been lucky. Only Sega has any real complaints. Though she has never seemed to really work *here*, as opposed to having arrived to only work *for Urso*. She disappeared for three nights, too. But since you're never around unless I am, it also seems like you don't really work here either Taddeo." She lowered her voice. "While Urso's always getting worse, I can't say I blame her. But in the meantime, *I've been cutting the skim for our departure funds.*"

"See. That's good. That was all part of my plan to teach you the business."

"Really Taddeo? Yeah. Alright. Whatever helps you sleep." She shook her head from side to side to show that she doubted his sincerity, while making a clicking sound with her pursed lips.

Why? He thought of himself sincerely clever for having just come up with that explanation less than heartbeat ago. *And when do I get to sleep?* Tad looked down at his coffee she'd brought him. *But this stuff is really working this morning. Boy am I quick. I'd even bet that*

I can *have some great games today.*

"Well, whatever we should attribute it to, the girls are in a better mood than they have been in for a long time and they're treating our clients in a way they're paying more for. Just ask Juicy Lucy," he told her.

"An authority if there ever was one."

"Arlene, look, The Family won't interfere with you so long as you keep even exceeding their every historic experience with profits. That's starting to happen with the cops starting to show up here more frequently for legitimate business reasons. You know; *like to take girls upstairs with them*. Madame Moresco obviously likes that, and she also often takes the pulse of the girls' morale and *knows* how it affects business. Colosimo listens to *her*. And there's also that she's never been a fan of my brother's."

"My, there's a great voice for the fairer sex's independence, and a good judge of character, too. And I thought Rinaldo had more say in how he runs The House with his name above the door as long as he pays *his* tribute — but this business is now more or less left up to his boys? That *in*effectively means you for the time-being, Tad. For however long the situation can last."

"Uh, you are the business manager now, Arlene."

"But what *they-all* or *we* do here is not that important now. Thanks to your exemplary negotiating skills, much of the money we skim, we now lose to pay rent to Mister Li. Don't we? For those so-much-improved living conditions I'm trading up from The Sisson for." Arlene raised her hands parallel to the bar's wooden floor, each holding a dirty dish towel she was about to send back to Old Lamont as one more expense of the cleaning up of their place, only then she let them fall to her sides in exasperation.

"Well, Mister Li also provides noodles."

"Riiight. Of course and he likes his free ride he also got for his new insurance arrangement. But I was a lot more comfortable in that hotel. In spite of — well whatever I had to keep hidden under my bed I made there. But your Papa will have three weeks while you're away to contemplate and execute any changes that *he does want to implement with the bordello*, Tad. By way of Greg's influence, or whomever's. Corrado's? Remember that. Because so too will your brothers and your most-chivalrous cousin. So I'd bet you that this 'great' situation will not even last as long as your next losing streak."

"Nice I have your confidence. The Cubs are winning by the way. But my house has all gone bugs over me for putting them in this position — with you — at any rate. I'll acknowledge that."

"I'm so happy for you. You acknowledge it. Yeah. I really ought to thank you for that one. I could have wanted to abandon prostitution, you know. Even empathized with the girls who likewise wanted to escape its harsh realities and that of the human trafficking and skin trading that flows like the dirty river through this town. Sanctioned by the private nods of all our city leaders and their paid-by-the-play police force. But instead of an escape from it, now you've made it so that my survival depends upon me actually running it. Great job, Taddeo. You've really improved the situation." She faked a smile toward him so badly that Arlene didn't even need any more words to convey her true feelings. She lit a cigarette just so she could blow smoke in his face.

"I used what I had to work with." Tad coughed from her smoke.

"So now I — ." Arlene moved quickly to cover her mouth. She coughed, too. Her midriff contorted inward and her body shook. She leapt up, dropping her cigarette, and bolted out of the bar and out though the light, hung collection of his clean baseball uniforms Tad got Mr. Li to see were washed only a little while ago, which he'd then set up on the lip of the doorframe. Now Arlene was out through the kitchen, and out the double-door to the back alley where she vomited. Tad stamped out her smoke before she lit Villetti's on fire and then ran after her and tried to reach for her shoulders in order to hold her and offer her comfort as Sega had done for him. But Tad hesitated, and feared that Arlene might even bite his hand should he even attempt to touch her. Then the thought that this relationship with Arlene *was more than complicated to say the least*, approached him like it was suddenly new insight. *Maybe Arlene and I are not really destined to be a happy couple?* Or had he thought that before? But Taddeo recalled how he could be notoriously slow for admitting any condition he'd rather wish he didn't have to acknowledge, as *if he pretended for long and well enough*, it would never have to be the truth. Just like the truth regarding his on-field playing time. But this thing with Arlene had nevertheless been there — all along. He'd just cultivated an involuntary refusal to recognize it. She'd never go all-in with him. She didn't trust him like he really didn't trust her. That's why she wouldn't tag along with him when he had to leave town. Tad felt sick himself and was glad he hadn't sampled Lamont's cooking while he watched his woman finish vomiting. This relationship was going nowhere.

Arlene did seem to feel his presence was there *for her*, however.

"Thanks. Your thoughts for me do count. But you see. I'm ill, Tad. I haven't been feeling quite like myself for a couple weeks now. I can't go to Massachusetts, then on to Pennsylvania. I don't think it's a great idea for me to travel anywhere — even to go to hell, and that's always felt like it's a lot closer to *here* than New York, from my perspective. Besides that, people — your people — specifically your father — need to see me *at Villetti's*. Else he reneges on his promise to forego revenge for my clan's alleged attack on Urso, the latest mess-in-a-barrel, and all the killings that only continue. You told me yourself that New York came here. You saw them at the Giants games. I've seen them in the bar. And they've surely only come to back Colosimo and your father's play. Or assess what they'll need to do to assert their further control over it now that their hitman came up empty when you secretly moved O'Rourke on them. So I don't even need you to corroborate that. I've seen strangers visiting The House at all hours, myself. And I think I spotted this Johnny The Fox and his creepy bodyguards. And were they ever mad. It has been keeping all the girls quite busy distracting them — and because I made sure that their ears are up as well as those pussies — and their earnings. I meant the girls, too. But by way of my position, you've seen to it that I *do* know — a lot. I've been uh, well, *making a killing in my part*, while you were on your silly hunting trip."

"Which I'm hoping might have helped us. I don't know, but maybe if my brothers liked spending time with their kid brother, I guess they could want to see me happy." He'd kept the knife Greg had given him in his suit pocket and took it out to examine it then. Was his brother trying to give him something with more permanence than Arlene had offered him? Greg was his flesh and blood. Arlene just offered him another source of trouble. He figured that maybe he should leave and not feel like he owed her anything. The awkward but kind of amicable camping trip sort of did offer him a little assurance that his brothers wouldn't harm her — that they wanted him to be happy, were proud of him — and that Taddeo was only imagining the worst possibility. He had *only imagined* that they'd harm Arlene, right? "So then, I guess that maybe if you do stay like you insist, then maybe they won't trouble you. But let you be — for the sake of — of *me?*"

"Hah. Aren't you suffering from delusions of grandeur. But if thinking that will help you sleep while you're out of town — ."

She just had to mention sleep again. "I can always stay here. I mean I guess I would if there is real evidence that you are in any real danger. Though it would mean quitting the team."

"Everything you worked so hard to achieve? No, you must keep playing your stupid game. What you're finally learning, is to take command from that hill."

"Yeah. And realizing it's lonely at the top."

Then once Arlene could stop her seizures brought on by her being nauseous, they made their way back past Lamont and his co-workers, and into the bar. That's when Taddeo noticed Greg had been sitting in a dark booth along the far east wall, watching them.

Greggorio Villetti did indeed sit there, sometimes glancing at his newspaper, surviving on coffee and very few hours of sleep as well. But how could he rest while he was thoroughly enjoying his front row seat to his little brother and his woman airing out their dirty laundry?

Tad reflected on what else had already gone on that busy day. His papa had showed up at the establishment way earlier than he usually liked to. *Once again.* No. He said that he'd stayed very late long past Wednesday night, seeing as none of his sons were there to trouble him while they were away in Wisconsin. And he wasn't shy about expressing *he* had gotten tired of this babysitting his adult children, though to his son's chagrin he too did seem to get a moment of amusement from also watching what he could witness of Arlene and his youngest boy's little lovers' quarrel. But next, when he caught almost all his offspring together, he was yelling at Greg about how when they had gone to all the extra trouble to receive Johnny Torrio, and take him on an assessment tour of his uncle-in-law's outfit, Mr. O'Rourke had managed to slip out of the South Side and right under their noses, and their old friend the slant laundryman was ever-ready with a payout. So he thought that he'd meet all his boys when they'd return from their brief hunting trip and they'd have produced the information that he'd wanted — namely of just how that happened. Of course that was suspicious, but Taddeo laughed to himself supposing he deserved to enjoy his father's frustration if his papa was going to enjoy observing Tad's domestic problems with Arlene. Luckily, no one suspected *he* could be that crafty, betraying his own papa, having helped O'Rourke escape. He overheard that his paranoid father had already started musing on whether Detective Conway had circumnavigated him and got the Irish butcher out of there if only for the sake of more damage control. This theory did have some merit of course. Almost the whole police department was on the take — from every source that outbid the next one. And there was his old partner-turned-informant — who easily could have resold the information. But neither Tad nor his brothers had brought their father any useful knowledge about O'Rourke if they were supposed to have been collaborating on what they knew about it during that stupid hunting trip. All Tad got out of it was a new knife to add to his collection of the little things that kill, which he supposed he would start to be accumulating, courtesy of his brother.

Meanwhile, Detective Conway had previously arranged to finally spend another early morning meeting with Rinaldo Villetti *again*, and once more in the lounge over steaming cups of fresh brew. Tad just missed seeing the cop while he ran around with his papa's car, washing his own dirty laundry. But the Chicago Police Department had fished another body out of the river last weekend over by the Marquette-Joliet Bridge construction project. And apparently Greg decided he had to be there to stick around for that meeting as well, because the boys' father had sworn he had nothing to do with what was Simone's killing this time, and he wasn't paying Conway or Chief Alcock one dime over it. The two Family members had already been in an even earlier meeting over that before as well, and now Villetti practiced reinforcing his position, exactly as his nearly equally tired son and he had rehearsed it, while he met with the opportunistic detective. So Tad guessed that since his father had then been expecting it, he decided to stay at their place of business and take some girl to a room with him since he'd already stated that he'd prefer to decompress there while he remained for the evening musical act that apparently Arlene had decided that she herself could hire, and *that* probably influenced by Old Lamont's recommendation. All of which his papa rather appreciated, rather than would mind. All of it except the police investigation that had started off his morning while Arlene threw up. Taddeo felt lucky his father had actually relented his unyielding hard disposition for *him*, and approved his small request.

The senior Villetti was nevertheless pleased enough that Taddeo had gone on the hunting trip with his siblings and their nights of brotherly bonding, that he'd actually been willing to loan Tad his personal car still in the early hours of that Thursday morning. He'd first used Hoff's farm truck that had probably stayed parked down the street from the bordello for all three nights Taddeo had been away, he'd presume. He'd taken that back and forth from the laundry, but driven his papa's car to Weeghman, secretly hoping he'd impress someone. The little gas he borrowed from Hoff he would take off the catcher's bill for the Rose-laden service on the Villetti's dish. Then next, after he and Hoff departed together, in his papa's vehicle, and before his spat with Arlene, he took his father's 1914 Cole "Big 6-60" he'd borrowed which he used to go and pick up the cleaned uniforms he was returning to his friends on the Cubs, driving it back to Weeghman Park in this cleaner transport where Tad saw his effort was even gladly appreciated by Charlie Deal and Hippo Vaughn, though Killefer didn't say anything and only grunted when he reported to the stadium and received his clean uniform. And then Trip had been a good friend to accompany Tad after those deliveries and on his way back south again to return his father's car, only to then drive Tad back to the ballfield in his own vehicle for that doubleheader. Hoff might have now finally left the whorehouse for a seven-hour-stretch, which would be truly a new wonder of the world.

So Trip waited for Taddeo in the bar now and nibbled on some sausage, eggs, and toast Lamont had fixed him. *How is it that my friends who are only baseball players can all have their own cars?* Most families in this day and age were fortunate if they had only one vehicle. Well, Tad's friends did have second jobs that all paid more than Taddeo's would, especially with his side expenses. *Here I am, effectively playing a pimp with the greatest looking girls in America's greatest city, and I can't even make any money in this game.* And while he thought about his life and those of his friends, he noted that while it was still early, he didn't see Rose anywhere in the bordello. *Great. I also missed seeing Hoffman at the ballpark and don't want to guess if he's back here, now, or she's hiding in the Cubs' locker room.* He didn't look to see if George's truck was back where he'd parked it on Miller when he returned it and then used his papa's vehicle. Why would he? But his pal Michael and he were surely going to be late now. What else did they need to do to aggravate Coach Mitchell today? And Trip's dad was a top electrician and tool engineer for Commonwealth Edison. Bass' father was interestingly enough becoming a mildly successful salesman of sporting goods amongst his other dry goods. The fellas had comfortable second jobs or opportunities to work positions alongside their families which they could fall back on — and ones that they probably would not get hospitalized, killed or at least arrested for. Tad only had to watch Faith move past him to be reminded of what his father sold. But now the fellas would have fresh jerseys and pants to take with them when they left for Boston because Tad was finally going to become an apprentice laundryman.

It was still cool that early in the morning from being near enough Lake Michigan that the sun hadn't triggered the oppressive humidity they'd have to play ball in a little while later. But both young men felt themselves get warm all over when the new pitcher returned his papa's car's ignition coil, and he and Michael took in just what Sega was wearing that morning. Apparently she'd stayed the entire night there — with Urso most likely, but the athlete's oldest brother was predictably still sleeping. Taddeo had heard they'd already been having problems again from a couple of the other girls, but he guessed that this pair had also patched things all up — again. To him they seemed to get along on that road trip. Only that was already now ten hours ago. But it'd been quiet this morning when he'd been around.

Tad was now supposed to be controlling the bordello and easing the life for *all* the girls, but he was glad Arlene had begun taking care of that and he didn't personally have to deal with Urso. Or he hoped she could, as it was not one of his even slightly developing talents. And she wouldn't leave — though it did appear that Arlene was handling everything quite well. There was money there for Tad to collect some skim from so he could pay Mr. Li. And then Sega was getting *some tantalizing* new clothes. *She* looked to be the one who was red hot while Chastity told Tad that she had just reappeared on the scene to also talk to his papa about something, when the detective the pitcher just missed, was done meeting with the Sigñor. But every time Tad looked at Sega it made him start to sweat. She probably did the same thing to Trip too, for Mikey grabbed the pitcher's arm, causing him to want to quickly shake loose of his friend's grip on him and wish he didn't notice his friend's tightening pants. Mike had then started to inquire of him that if Hoff could stay over in the bordello, maybe he could, too? Tad didn't answer that and excused himself and said he had to go and say goodbye to Arlene.

She was also observing Sega when he returned to her and told her he had to leave to practice for his games.

"Fine. You do that."

She seemed to have suddenly turned so cold to him. Maybe it was just that she was preoccupied with something else. But the chill he felt bit him — deep. "Doll, don't you know you're driving me crazy? I just want love — and a rest from all of this. With what all we've got planned — for once I just want to finally make it."

"But you can't keep it. In this world, any happiness we might ever feel can't last forever, Tad. Just like the relief that Roslyn said you helped yourself to when you were leaving with your brothers. That was smart of you. Don't you feel the burn yet? The desire for what you also want, or will want, soon enough?"

"My desire only burns for you." But now that Tad thought about it, 'that juice up' was great.

"And do you believe all the lies you tell yourself?"

"Oh fuck it. *Whatever*." Leaving all *that positivity* behind him, Taddeo planned to continue getting warm — for playing baseball — by next working out his arm with Hoff — late, upon his and Trip's tardy return to Weeghman.

Grover Cleveland Alexander had other plans when Tad arrived at the stadium. He had not put on his newly cleaned uniform and stood there before the Cubs' new young pitcher, wearing a different uniform: that of one in the United States Army. He did look impressive. "I'd have a word with you, Rookie."

Taddeo looked over the seasoned pitcher who was thirteen years his senior. He'd always admired the man as a celebrated athlete and one who Tad wished would have become his mentor. There was so much technique he could have learned. Killefer and O'Farrell were even training Hoffman. But Taddeo might have only been regarded as a joke just like Greg said he was. The Cubs' guinea gravedigger because he would always give up a run now and bury Chicago's players deeper when he took the hill. No one else but his friends like Hoff took him seriously enough to really train with him, obviously due to his juvenile antics on the mound he hadn't been able to help himself from committing — as of yet. But Alexander had obviously committed to a far nobler, more challenging cause. His patriotism would be put on display in front of the crowd before the first game. Well, he was born to be an American, so what else would Tad expect? "Geeze Pete. You're a soldier."

"That's right. I'm thirty-one years old Villetti. It's about time I take up some responsibility and serve a higher cause I guess."

"You got drafted."

"I got drafted."

"Yeah, well about that. You see there could have been a mistake made in the paper and my papa — ."

"I'm going to France. That's settled and I don't want to owe *your family* any special favors. I've been in and out of training. Artillery.

And I guess I'm ready for deployment. That's why you've barely seen me around and I've only played three games this season. But I come about this way — to the ballpark I mean — cause I get some furloughs to go see my family in Nebraska. And the government wants to use me in their propaganda to raise more money from war bonds. Plus I am a patriot for my country. But *my family* is also in the Major League."

"Still is. We need your artillery here, Ol' Pete."

"The Cubs are going to do just fine on their own." To Tad he started sounding like an older brother could — though Alexander was even older than Urso, who he couldn't recollect ever really trying to encourage him like big brothers should. Grover continued. "You've got aces like Vaughn, Hendrix, and Tyler. They're strong young arms. You won't need my services."

"*I* could use your help. So I could contribute."

"What I would tell you that *could* help you is that you've got the talent. A cannonball of your own. And the dedication to your practice. But like everyone keeps telling you — though you keep ignoring them — you need to work on your maturity. Study your batters — you and Hoffman since you obviously like throwing with him. Find their weaknesses — other than their fondness for not getting hit in the head — and develop your pitches. Listen to Bill Killefer. The Reindeer is the best catcher in the whole league. He calls the rain down on every other team's hit parade. So do what he tells you. He knows this game. Your obedience to his orders will show him that you want him to help you."

"But — ."

"But nothing. Who the hell do you think you are?"

"Nobody." Tad looked at his shoes.

"Well I don't think I can believe you. Check your ego. Baseball is like my going off to war, Brother. I have to trust my fellow firemen in my platoon I'm on the line with. Just like you need to just trust the twenty-four to twenty-five other guys that you are in the dugout with — and they, you. In the heat of things, there's no room for veterans with attitudes, let alone rookies. You're very lucky you won't have to deal with any situation further from home than your East Coast tour you guys embark on tomorrow."

"That's what my papa said. I've got an uncle and a few cousins serving. Uh, in Italy's corps. They uh, changed sides. So they won't be shooting at *you*, Pete."

"No. I suppose maybe some of your family won't be. But the

Germans or the Austrians and Turks will be. And I'd just as soon rather take it from Burleigh Grimes or our friend Dan Griner who you're so fond of. But the world's not giving me a choice. Well, actually I did have a choice. But I want to and will stand up *proud* to serve my country. So if I'm assigned in your family's home country, what's their name over there, Villetti? I could say hello if per chance I meet any of them or I get the time to look them up."

"Vollero," Tad divulged. "Their real name is Vollero. Names got messed up at Ellis Island."

"I figured. That's common."

"Yeah. Well Pete, I hope you don't get into any more trouble than you're possibly in now, and —."

"I was totally going to say the same thing to you, Tad."

"I'll keep my head down and practice my drills. I haven't any doubt you'll do the same. I've trusted you to always know the right thing to do. And you're already so successful at it."

"You will be, too."

"That's what my friend Old Lamont says. Hey — he's got a son and a grandson in that shit over there. They're actually black troops. Well, they were black before all this, but I'm sure they became good troops. French Army. Now I'm just guessing, but you probably won't serve with them."

Grover Cleveland Alexander looked at his pitching hand as he turned it over, perhaps also contemplating what it might look like with a gun in its grip, instead of another baseball. "No. I probably won't serve with the frogs' black corps, Taddeo. But I've never been to war. I can't predict what I'll see over there. But I'll keep a lookout for them. The Negroes are usually used for supply runners or cooks, and in construction of the fortified positions for the gunners over there. At least in Pershing's units. The French actually do let them fight. Though it's a big country. Lot of ground to defend. But you really never know."

"Yeah, well I guess it would be swell for them to hear from a friend of a guy who's friends with their father or grandfather. Him living so far away and across a whole ocean from them." Suddenly, Tad found inspiration to contribute to the good cheer of several of his associates he also held fondness for. "Oh. I just remembered another good idea. Can you do me a favor and take a walk with me for a minute, Pete?"

Alexander agreed. It took them several minutes to move around Weeghman Park out to the "unofficially" segregated seating where the colored fans were already all there and ready for the double-header against Cincinnati. And Taddeo was right. Little Parnell Lamont was ecstatic with joy to get to personally shake hands with Grover Alexander who lifted the small boy up in his arms and held him up high so he could get a great view of the whole ballfield — on the shoulders of a white man who held no qualms about coming to share one rather memorable moment in the coloreds' section. And Alexander promised him that he'd say hello to Parnell's father and grandfather — if he came across them in France. The kid even borrowed a pencil from one of Ol' Pete's very generous autograph-seekers to draw his father a picture and print his name beneath it. "It's for my family in France," the boy explained. Grover patiently waited for him to finish and greeted other colored fans, then put the folded napkin in one of his uniform pockets to take it with him to Europe. And after that, it was time to say goodbye to one very happy youth.

And to Alexander as well. "Take care of yourself Pete." The acclaimed star pitcher turned to go and say his farewells to his other teammates on the Cubs and said he'd even been around long enough to know some of the Reds he needed to say his parting words to, while Taddeo's parting words followed the pitch out onto the field that fine Thursday morning at Weeghman Park. "And I'll do what you said. I'm going to go practice with Hoff right now."

However, the downtime spent talking about his attitude, further distracted Taddeo. That, plus the lack of sufficient practice was what he attributed to why he might have performed badly in that first game, besides having no sleep. The Cubs dumped it to the Reds, Tad giving up a run that went on Harry Weaver's record when he tried to actually play clean baseball. However, the clean jerseys added numbers to his personal score with his teammates. That they did well. Even Killefer wouldn't ride him and only softly voiced his critique with a useful lesson concerning Tad's latest performance.

Then the home team won the second game, but Taddeo didn't have anything he wanted to celebrate with his fellow Cubs right then. He'd be spending almost three weeks with no break from their company in a few more hours when they'd depart for their away games tour. So he got back to Little Italy by convincing Trevor Bass to drive him next, to show his gratitude for the clean uniform since Weeghman didn't seem to be paying for the Cubs' clothing service. Rumor had it their ballclub owner was hoarding all his money for some other great plan. But once Taddeo already had The

Bass-Man stepping up to the plate, Tad and his "*lady* coach" called a new play. The couple did their best to covertly leave Villetti's and Trevor helped Arlene with Tad, clear out the rest of her things from The Sisson that they hadn't gotten with Hoff, and relocate them to Mr. Li's laundry. Though Trevor insisted that Lucy help them — or helped him. But she had to be sworn to secrecy regarding Arlene's change of location, as had Rose. Then after thanking Mr. Li, they all went back to Villetti's to let Taddeo say his goodbyes to his papa — and unfortunately Greg who just happened to still be there. Tad did not want to reemphasize the fact that he was leaving to his older sibling. But that proved unavoidable, so the couple with Bass — of who this was none of his business — had no objection to Greggorio's volunteering to drive Arlene back to Villetti's after she said goodbye to Taddeo at Union Depot when he'd board the team's railcar with the rest of the Cubs.

So early that evening and after the double-header, circumstances saw Greg following Bass' vehicle back to the North Side and then once it was parked at the home he was boarding at, Greggorio drove Trevor as well as his brother and his brother's girlfriend to the station.

The middle brother waited in his car as he afforded Tad some privacy he and Arlene thought they could steal for themselves at the depot. "I don't want to leave you."

"Yeah, well I'm never totally sure you *are* with me," she said.

"I could say the same thing about you. Remember your *friend* I found you with at the hotel the other day."

"Your father got me into a position that afforded me *that* wonderful opportunity." Her stare was off, distant, like Tad imagined a soldier's. Her face was void of affection and her voice toneless.

"But I was the one who got you settled in secret over at Mister Li's so you have somewhere to hide that you'll be safe. I got you control of operations at Villetti's — and a secret source of income you can draw on from it. But I get no appreciation here? In fact, I could still get you a train ticket and you could come with me to Boston right now." His voice had taken the tone of whining again.

"Honey, you can *not* miss your train. You're not even allowed to buy your own boarding pass so far as I've come to understand. But I've got a rewarding business in Chicago, as you just pointed out."

"And I'm worried about the part of that business who's waiting for you in the car outside this train depot right now. There's another way that your future can leave the station."

"Thanks. I secured my own ticket for that."

"So we're departing from each other like *this?"*

"Yeah. And are we really together? You are the one who just suggested the question."

"No you did. I thought we were partners."

"Huh. Well, partners in crime. That's for sure," she said.

"Um okay. Uh, well then I guess we'll work on being *more*, once again, when I get back." Tad opened his arms and moved to get closer to Arlene but she very subtly moved back. So he did not even get a hug, and when he tried to offer his handshake repeating, "Partner," she folded her arms across her chest. "It's going to be a long three weeks," he said, then exhaled a deep breath.

"All aboard the train leaving for Boston. Our next major stop will be Gary, arriving in Indiana through East Chicago," a station conductor said. A new thought might have just been seen to flicker in Arlene's eyes.

Then a new voice commanded attention. "Villetti, get on board. Kiss her goodnight and let's go!" Fred Mitchell had stepped down from his train car to corral any more of his straying players. Steam blew back from the engine all around Coach, sort of emphasizing his hot temper he had with the rookies.

"I have to go," Tad stated the obvious. The pain of loneliness and his current inability to really control his own future was overtaking him. He was not looking forward to riding for hours alongside of Hoffman, the guy bragging about all the girls he bedded once his teammates broke through the weakness to his bare existence of *any* humility, or Hollocher's reacquainting everyone with his performance stats in case they'd forgotten about them over the past two and a half hours. This to be followed with his friends Trevor and Mike complaining about still not seeing enough playing time. At least half the starting roster complaining about their paychecks. And then Les Mann and Turner Barber's predictable lecture about professional etiquette for the rookies while on a road trip. This to be repeated by Fred Mitchell's same lecture on the same subject in his position of manager and Bill Killefer's threat of "cracking some skulls" if his young teammates didn't do what they were told. Yes, Tad would find everyone else too busy on their own trails this road trip, to assist by at least listening to the problems with his, while Taddeo rode solitaire dealing with the dangerous uncertainty of not being able to more effectively help Arlene and deal with The Family situation.

Arlene nodded as they looked at each other one last time before he departed. She alone understood. But she charted her own course and through no amount of persuasion would she be going down the same tracks as Taddeo.

Having stepped out of his car and situated himself leaning against a huge support column characteristic of the grand architecture of Union Depot, Greggorio Villetti watched with approval this non-display of affection. He sneered then walked away toward his stock Model-T with no need to alert the unhappy couple that he'd been watching. Arlene would be riding alongside Greg with him in the driver's seat shortly. And she'd be more unhappy about what followed after that, but the cracks in the enthusiasm for the affair going on between his little brother and this harlot of a woman were finally showing even before Greg had to do almost anything at all. It was perfect. And now the breakages in their relationship were something the ambitious sibling could use in aiming to drive a wedge further in between them — just so long as Taddeo still wanted her. Any affection need not be reciprocated, and it sure looked like the pair, working together all on their own, had already established that much. Unwittingly, she'd given Greggorio a gift he would use against her and now Greg would see the wench alone, with no one around to run interference for her any longer. She might've been able to take care of herself before, but he would succeed with her where Dulio, Simone, Thorello, Corrado, and even his own father had not.

As Taddeo boarded the train, Arlene turned around and did not even consider looking back at him as she stepped off on her way to exit the station. Instead she opened her purse and examined her .45. She recollected that she now had only two bullets left. Her true family had never furnished the assassin with more, as two weeks ago she'd left the North Side with enough ammunition to shoot down all of her intended targets and then some, to first meet Rinaldo Villetti in New York — but not get into running gun fights and start serial killing. That wasn't ever part of her original mission. Only Arlene could make herself capable of anything.

Now Greggorio waited for her in the car. However, in fact when she was delayed by her condition, it would be Greggorio who had to finally help her into his private transportation when he found Arlene keeled over and vomiting into a trash receptacle in the train station. It was embarrassing, not to say at least inconvenient that this particular pairing had no privacy to settle their unspoken-of personal business, that was so obviously going on between them. There were too many witnesses around who were also trying to help the young woman.

A strikingly severe but regal looking woman in her middle ages, very well-dressed in a fur-collared coat, a fancy hat with flowers, and accompanied by a group of also fairly well-dressed lady followers of hers, who might have even been her children, was the first to help Arlene. She'd started walking back from the tracks through the seating area when she felt light-headed and collapsed on the floor. "Miss, are you all right? Let me help you. Do you have a handkerchief in your purse?"

Arlene could only cough for a moment instead of answer. She was trying so hard not to cause more of a spectacle by vomiting all over Union Depot so she could not object to the oldest woman looking into her purse for a napkin to relieve the emergency. She must have seen the gun but said nothing, and did remove a handkerchief for Arlene like she said she would. The other ladies gathered around to help her up. "I'm Nancy," said one younger woman, closer to Arlene's age.

"Virginia. Pleased to be able to be of assistance," said another very well-dressed girl. And she was a girl. Arlene was surprised as her eyes and ears evaluated this young lady. She might have been only been twelve!

The lady who led them spoke once more. "And I'm Katherine, — um Dexter."

It was a nice try to go incognito, but Arlene already knew who Katherine Dexter *McCormick* was. Who in Chicago wouldn't? She offered her first name only, trying to not admit to herself that even she was impressed with who you could meet at the train station.

"Do you need more assistance? Where are you headed?"

"It looks like I'm headed nowhere for the moment. I was just seeing someone off. I'm not too far from home. I live over on the South Side."

"With a strong Chicago-Irish accent?"

"My mother left me with not much more of an inheritance."

"I'm sure it's impolite to pry, but might you reside at The Hull House? At the very least I can call a ride home for you."

Home? When did the South Side become my home? And since when did I my make my real home on a filthy, stained mattress on the floor of a Chinese laundry?

"That won't be necessary. I'm the lady's escort." Greggorio had come into Union Depot to find out what had delayed her. Arlene threw up again, barely reaching a trash receptacle when a reaction of nature had forced her to bolt free of her new assistants. Well, she gave an honest display of her disposition. Greg shook his head from side-to-side. "I was just giving the lady some privacy when she must have taken ill. She was here to exchange goodbyes with my brother," she could hear him explaining.

Arlene pretended she looked in her purse for a second, clean handkerchief while she checked her weapon. *And you have no idea how badly I want to say goodbye to you, Greg.*

"Oh my. Will he be off to war? To fight with our forces in France under General Pershing?" McCormick asked.

Arlene laughed when she thought about Taddeo being tough enough to succeed fighting for much of anything but to be let off the bench in a ballgame. Then she choked on some bile that had come up in her throat. Well, he did get his little victories.

And Greg used that opportunity to answer McCormick's question for Arlene, himself equally amused. "No. I know his heart and my little brother can't face off with any real enemy — or anything actually dangerous. He's not much of a fighter. He's a thinker. And he thinks he's a baseball player. I think the worst he's facing in the next few days will be the Boston Braves. If his manager even lets him take the hill."

"Oh. Because he's your brother, I take him to be one of the new Italian players who are raising their stock in the game?"

"Yeah."

"What's his name? He's playing for the Cubs, right? I would assume this because he was leaving when the White Sox just arrived back in town along with the visiting Yankees. I see much while waiting at the train station. And I don't have to be a fan to guess which series will be played in Chicago."

"Uh, he's called Villetti. Taddeo Villetti." Arlene could see the would-be game master did not like to surrender any information. "My brother's a relief pitcher they're trying to train," Greg explained. Then he laughed. "So far it's not been a relief to my family, who thus far have been unable to train my youngest sibling to be of any use *anywhere*. I have hope maybe he'll learn something while he's back east." Suddenly Arlene worried what that could mean.

"Villetti," McCormick said. "I've heard that name before."

"My father is in the restaurant-entertainment business. We have a small place in Little Italy. But it couldn't be that well known, Ma'am."

"Well, as a matter of fact, I actually do know of a place called 'Villetti's.' " She glanced at Arlene. She didn't look happy about the information she was gathering from her conversation with Greggorio. Neither she nor the other ladies offered up to Greg anything about themselves either. Instead, they exchanged wary glances. But he would be a fool if he were not knowledgeable about what this woman represented, a threat to his plans for certain, even if he didn't get her name. But Greggorio Villetti was not a fool. "I *have* heard of your family indeed." The high society lady who had married quite well into her own famed family leaned closer to Arlene, who Nancy and Virginia had gone to fetch back from the waste can and now held up before her. So Greg couldn't hear, she said, "And I just had to determine I *will* stay in Chicago with my associates here for a short while longer. I've much other business to attend to but I recognized a few familiar details about your particular *situations*. I will send a car for you in the morning, Arlene. I now know exactly where to expect to find *you* at. We'll probably need to talk sooner than later. It's important, as I am in a position to see to it that my fellow woman wins all the victories that she is after. I think we can be of help to each other."

My particular situations? What does McCormick know about me? Is she an ally? She did just save me. I'm not in good health to kill Greg right this moment, and be able to reach or deal with Urso and at long last, Rinaldo, if I could even make it that far after I take out Villetti's second son in such a public place. I've no reason yet to believe the police will not *arrest me, let alone see me back on the South Side at least before Rinaldo doubles his security and becomes impossible to reach even if I take Greg's gun off him. My priorities are to my personal mission. But I don't have money to pay off all the cops and of course I don't know who already has. I also no longer have enough ammunition, and the police will search me for what they'll think I might have.* She thought about the Jewish hitman. What he'd advised she learned. *Plus now I had better learn what the hell is wrong with me.* This would be the time she had to be really careful of how she went about attaining what she hungered for. Arlene wiped the corners of her mouth with her second napkin.

"Well then, on the life of my family, I will swear to you that I am very capable of seeing Arlene down to rest on the South Side. To our place over there. If you ladies will relinquish her care to me. She and my brother are very close, which means that I will treat her as I would treat any members of my own house." As he signaled the pair would take their leave of the other ladies, Greg smiled nice and brightly. He took Arlene by the arm and applied just the necessary force to get her moving along.

Chapter 35

Now Arlene had to get to a doctor. Upon their return to Villetti's, Greg revealed that revelation to his father immediately after refusing to keep her health a private matter. There were rumors about a highly contagious influenza and because of the status of Chicago being a destination city — for more reasons than just Cubs baseball, though Taddeo would argue otherwise — Rinaldo needed to protect against any bad health reports originating from at least his part in Colosimo's operation. He had a lot of pussies working for him. *And maybe Greg is hoping he won't actually need to give someone an order to kill me — or even do it himself if he finds his mettle. That way I even die under* no *suspicious conditions. But I've at least made* him *sick — of me*. But he could have driven her into the woods on their way back from the station and shot her already if he were going to do that while she was too ill to fight. She really worried that he suspected what *she* was also actually worried about — and she was also beginning to gather more evidence that supported her other theory — that Greg wanted her alive to use her for his own ends, just like he figured she was using his little brother. He wanted to start a civil war within The Family — and over her no less. Then he could eliminate his brothers as rivals for his father's tiny little mantle. Though she knew that even this would never satisfy Greggorio's tremendous ego, and his ambitious plan for ascension that came with it. It also irritated her to no end that Greg's plan so much resembled her own — the obvious greatest difference only being that who survived the great schism each would see created in The Villetti House.

When she was finally pushed into a meeting with him, Arlene ambitiously tried to assert herself over its patriarch, though that just would not work. Rinaldo was one of the strongest-willed persons she'd ever encountered, let alone gone up against. Not that the list was long. But it was getting longer — and she had just found herself deprived of some certain and very important resources. She looked at Greg. There was a lot more that was going to play out here. Though now his father needed to talk to her about something else too, in the meanwhile, the Villetti son *just needed to insist* that she would go and see his uncle-by-marriage, the "Doctor" Abramo Delasandro, the very next day. *Great. That's just what I need. Now all the Villettis are looking out for me.*

Arlene knew the man was not any real physician type of practicing clinician but a pharmacist in violation of the Harrison Act since she had discovered him to be cutting the heroin for The House to supply as party favors for the men taking girls to "relax with them upstairs" — at Villetti's. Of course. What else would he be doing with a medical education? Only because Arlene hadn't "worked the rooms" was she almost the last person to find out about this. Unfortunately, not before Villetti's youngest son could start abusing that. Rose told her. But *Delasandro's* eldest son Stefano was usually busy adjusting their books and import papers with every other business the Villettis terrorized, like some cigar company she'd overheard them speaking about as of late. She heard a lot once she started working at The House — only just not what her real family supposedly needed her to hear. Yet, anyway. But she had to report the bordello's accounting to him. And of course The Villetti Family was always busy dodging regulations and taxes. *Wasn't Delasandro Senior so lucky as to marry Rinaldo's sister so "the doctor" could raise up such wonderful sons like Stefan and especially Corrado?* However, Arlene needed to further consider making use of that latter one, what with Tad's cousin's seeming interest in her. Only another Villetti son had already foreseen this so as to attempt to deny that option to her, as well. Or so he was trying.

But before Arlene's meeting in Villetti's office and when Greg hadn't far to go to reacquire her after his initial private meeting with Rinaldo during which she had to wait outside his office door, they were descending the stairs *the first time* presumably to wait for the old patriarch "to not be busy" while they watched the rhythm & blues band Old Lamont's friends had recommended she hire. That's when Jasmine had approached her alone and let Arlene know about another and more unusual new visitor. At night, unaccompanied and unafraid, came a middle-aged woman of whose reputation Arlene was already well aware of. It would figure that probably not even Rinaldo with most of his charming offspring and nephews, plus their sycophants, would recognize Katherine Dexter McCormick in their lounge. Other ladies who didn't work there also frequented the place, as the whorehouse presented itself as a restaurant and nightclub. Plus it occasionally saw lady customers who favored an alternative lifestyle that they were motivated to pay for. But speaking of being discreet, McCormick had also dressed down and did not wear her expensive, rich furs or any of her fancy hats. She obviously must have been looking out to purposely avoid Greggorio. And she knew what *he* looked like. So she did her best to avoid attracting attention to herself, playing the simple Katherine Dexter.

But she came there to meet Arlene specifically, even more informed about her by none other than Bill Fallon of all people, who said that *Arlene* could arrange a favor for the women's suffrage movement's Midwestern leader. What did her family's scheming have to do with the suffragettes? Their patriarchs shouldn't ever be in favor of a women's victory. Regardless, Bill making any more promises for Arlene was exactly what she also didn't need. And McCormick, of course, was not amused to learn that Arlene now actually ran the bordello in theory anyway, and was making girls suck penises. Amused was something *she* wouldn't be. But in an unexpected particular case, important to *her*, The Lady Katherine decided she would be requiring that service. It was time the Italians who owned the pussy employed there, rose up their small statures even further, and the top men of the United States Congress would be prepared for some new things to arise from "gathering their members" at Villetti's.

While Arlene had no gripe with McCormick's reasoning behind that, nor McCormick herself, having figured her intentions on only being congruent with her reputed aspirations, the two women would never be comfortable enough to say they liked each other — just that they needed each other. Besides, whatever would the Women's Rights movement and the Christian Women's organizations do — without making sure that prostitutes enjoyed full-employment?

Then McCormick had offered again — no insisted upon — sending a private car for Arlene the following day and drive her over to Cicero where there was a real physician, Dr. Warner, who could examine her to find out what afflicted her health condition. That was all well-and-good, because she didn't trust Delasandro even though she hadn't even met "the doctor." But Arlene had wondered and soon found out why McCormick would travel over to Little Italy to tell her again, and in person — again, what she already told her at the train station. It was to do an on-the-site inspection of exactly the kind of place the woman could use to get favors from men, as well as Arlene, of which McCormick was also an expert at trading in. And Arlene was getting out of it medical attention, monetary benefits — indirectly from the new, more affluent customers Villetti's should be expecting, and information. McCormick had declared as much. So the young madam decided to just go along with it for the time being.

Then on Friday, May 31, 1918, and only ten days after she first met Taddeo Villetti, Arlene learned that what she was afflicted with, besides the Spanish flu, was *pregnancy*. Dr. Warner performed a rather invasive and uncomfortable examine between her legs, confirmed this while her bare bottom perched on an icy cold examination table in his patient care room, and then double-checked to make sure he made a good accounting of himself — in his mind perhaps.

Just as Arlene feared — and Greggorio probably had suspected. Arlene was expecting. Plus she had the Spanish Flu on top of it. And she really couldn't have ever discerned when she'd gotten sick to her stomach from either situation. She now had to really consider her options. Yet she felt so ashamed. Pregnant, not married, not even in love — probably — but full of anger and hate, and guilty of multiple murders. And now bringing a child into her wholesome life. Arlene thought, *What would my father think?* Her real father. But she'd never been old enough to even know him. It only mattered that she knew the Italians had killed him. So what *would* he think if she failed him now? But while having first planned on her assignment to the South Side to be a suicide mission, she didn't mind adapting from having to take that course, but she had never planned on having a baby. Dr. Warner was actually the only known medical practitioner near her location in Chicago who could alleviate her of this new and unplanned for responsibility. No wonder McCormick knew which doctor to send Arlene to. However, Arlene's plan could be adapted again and there was *no way she was going to have an abortion*, even if that might be what her new lady benefactor was suggesting she'd approve of. Arlene was *definitely not* the entertainer who would entertain Katherine Dexter McCormick — in this matter for sure anyway. And the socialite was even such a huge hypocrite for even trying to subtly suggest it.

No matter how ridiculously inadept and immature Taddeo might be, she knew the father of her unborn child loved her. That's why he would continue to be so frustrated with her when Arlene had never showed him any true appreciation for the sacrifices he made for her, from the abuse he took in the kitchen to enduring his family's continuous interference in his private life. His departing words at the train station were never so true. She was the liar and she'd been so mean to him when he'd secured for her shelter and power, and was making progress — very slow progress of course — at securing an income to provide for her. That's actually what she was supposed to want in a man she could partner with in order to have a child, wasn't it? And it was only going to probably be about three more weeks when he returned, and his brothers and father could really get back to working on it — until they'd succeed in making sure of it themselves — that Tad wouldn't mind helping her *assassinate all of those mother-fuckers.* Would he? Motivated to protect his own child? His *new* family? Or he could give up on her long before then. Three weeks apart was far longer than the time they'd even ever had together. He might no longer value it unless she could straighten things out with him, now. But she couldn't leave Chicago. However, she could always work on getting Corrado to do the killings for her. That was still one of her best and newly realized options that Arlene hadn't fully gotten the chance to put to a trial — ever since she'd first thought of it. And then if she was very careful, Taddeo might never learn of her involvement. It would be safest for him if he weren't in town at all when this went down, and Tad would never discover her role in the murders of all his former family. But without knowing much of anything about Corry Delasandro, tempting and then seducing him might be very dangerous. How dangerous, Arlene didn't know. There was that and it would be very satisfying for her to pull the trigger herself on those responsible for the deaths of her father, brother, and mother even, as far as Arlene had come to establish as her explanation of how she'd wound up being orphaned. But her thoughts carried her in a full circle since she had to consider that perhaps now it would be too risky for the baby to be there — caught in the crossfire. The fire she had ignited. Now that she had a chance for real survival since she'd gotten prescribed medication for her influenza affliction.

But she regretted the harsh way she'd used her words and especially her body language on Taddeo when they last saw one another. She was trying to motivate him — and maybe unconsciously, she was trying to distance him so he would eventually be able to just get over her if she died fighting his family while he was away. She didn't want him involved if it could be avoided. Only now he was going to be a new parent with her. Yet maybe it was better he didn't know she was pregnant? For less than twenty-four hours ago on the station platform, she was good with him hating her forever if she could accomplish her mission, kill his family, and spare his life if she did it all while he was on the East Coast playing his stupid baseball games. Now she reconsidered, and Greg's brief conversation with Katherine McCormick had even made her wonder if her love was in danger Back East and whether she could make a better life with Taddeo Villetti — if they could both actually just escape their present situations, and run away, far away. Surviving this. *Wait. Am I in love with him? When did it become love? Is that real even? That's not something I ever grew up believing could exist for myself, let alone anything I'd actually ever have the luxury of time for*. But even by this point in time, she'd created a young new life — with him — and a life through which her true family could actually live on though these dark times with. Only she might have to finally make her move, and as soon as possible, if Greg had inadvertently implied to Katherine McCormick that he had arranged to call down something tragic to befall Taddeo while he was on the Atlantic Seaboard, trying to close those dumb games again. She wanted desperately to warn him. Bring him back to her. To protect Taddeo from his own ignorance and incompetence — two separate challenges in and of themselves. She would like her baby to know her — and its father. Arlene never had that opportunity. Therefore, she already knew that she'd made her final decision about this — that she would have to live to be its mother. But now it seemed that Mrs. McCormick also had her own plans that didn't make Arlene's life any easier. And that wasn't even half of everything that the young woman saw in her life turned upside-down. All Taddeo had to ever do was throw a baseball.

Chapter 36

As he re-entered through the tall archways on the 1st base side of The Wigwam, the infamous James Gaffney-designed home field for the Boston Braves, Taddeo wished that he'd get the chance to pitch here. He wanted desperately to learn what his skill set would really let him do, especially in a ballpark like this. The team had come in through the large receiving service area out by right field, that boasted nothing less than train tracks running up directly into the ballpark! But no sooner than the rookies had clambered out of the Cubs' team transport cars, than he, Hoff, Trip, Bass-Man, and even Holly had let loose with their laughter while failing to be secretly giving Coach the slip, and jumping off the tracks for their own personal walking tour around the whole entire stadium, it being all of the first time for most of them, to see Braves Field. It was impressive. The almost brand-new field had been built only three years ago to showcase what Gaffney enjoyed as the "small-ball" game that forced teams to hit the ball and run the bases to score versus relying on the long bomb. It had a reputation for being pitcher-friendly, as it was deliberately constructed to not allow many hit-outs for home runs — with nearly 400 feet outfield fences, up to 500 feet in dead center — but yet the ball could bounce on the ground into The Wigwam's deep pockets and prevent long throws for the out from even the strongest professional arms in the field. The original idea was that fans would enjoy high-scoring, intense-action games with lots of base-stealing versus only the rubber matches that resulted when ace guns were brought out on the mound, or especially easy turn-arounds when those long bombers devastated them.

As it were, Claude Hendrix would be Chicago's right-handed gun, so the Villetti "Shooter" didn't seem to have a role for his cannonballs in Boston. Turner Barber tried to explain it to Tad by reminding him that his family probably brought nothing to the plate in Beantown. So there was no one with the clout who could orchestrate *him* being sent in to take the hill. But Taddeo could enjoy being a righteous supporter of Chicago's first on-the-road victory this June. And from where they took the field, they were only one mile away from where Babe Ruth would be playing for the Red Sox, the almost inevitable championship-pursuing team of the American League. It was the job of the Chicago club to let all of Boston know that the Cubs were there, and a force to be reckoned with in the National League. Tad's team had to win.

The infield was kept cool in the hot summer sun under the giant canopy that was constructed around the stands from home plate all the way out to the extents of right and left fields. From a position of comfort, Taddeo could relax and watch Chicago hit first — to take the early lead.

Grantland Rice would later write the article for the afternoon edition for his sports report and *The New York Times* could then be plagiarized by *The Boston Globe* and maybe even Arlene could then read about Tad's team in *The Chicago Herald*. Yes, Tad was sure that was what *she* would be anxiously waiting to do. *Riiight*.

Pat Ragan with a 3.23 ERA started out for the Braves, giving up a single to Holly with 1 out. He tore up the infield gravel by immediately stealing 2nd base and Les Mann hit off the right-hander to his opposite field in a sacrifice that moved Charlie to 3rd. Fred Merkle brought him home for an RBI for The Merk as he danced off between 1st and 2nd the way Mitchell taught the Cubs to distract the opposing defense while their lead runners scored. But there were still only 2 outs while the Braves failed to scalp him. Only Dode Paskert flew out in that deep center field, where he would wind up offering the Cubs his defensive protection in only a couple more minutes as the inning ended with Chicago up by 1.

Claude had some trouble with Boston early on. After taking an assist with getting out their shortstop Johnny Rawlings, he gave away too much freedom in the city that was known to the nation as The Heart of American Liberty. Herzog and Powell were walked, but the Cubs' hurler was saved by the double-play as Charlie picked up Wickland's grounder to Chicago's shortstop and sent it to Zeider as Powell tried to spike him on his slide into 2nd, but Rollie leaped into the air and slammed the ball into Merkle's open mitt. The Braves were retired four batters deep into their lineup with no score.

But by the 3rd inning, Claude was in another jam. Tad, Hoff, Trip, and Bass watched nervously from the bench, with nothing they could do about the situation but pray. Buck Herzog got a single past Charlie Deal and Mann had to find it in the outfield. Herzog stole 2nd and from scoring position, went home on Ray Powell's visit to the outfield from home plate. Now it was a tie game. Wickland and

Red Smith went down in order after that — and Killefer's visit to the mound to check on Hendrix.

Nothing happened in the 4th inning for either team, but nothing had happened in this game for Charlie Deal either — offensively or with regard to a performance in the field — that was pleasing to Fred Mitchell. But he had plenty of reasons to be pleased anyway. Taddeo watched his manager presumably going over strategies in his mind about how to win this contest against the Braves. It was an interesting and exciting game.

Claude Hendrix belted one out deep into The Wigwam to help his own cause. He was on 1st and before the Braves knew it, Max Flack got him over to 2nd base. Then a fielder's choice helped Boston's Ragan when Charlie Hollocher batting left-handed, was on again with another single out to right field, but Flack was cut down at 2nd by an easy relay for Boston. Only then Les Mann loaded the bases for the Cubs!

Chapter 37

Saturday, June 1, 1918
4:02 pm EST
Braves Field a.k.a. "The Wigwam," Boston, Massachusetts

5th Inning
Chicago –1, Braves –1, as in *TIE GAME!*

1 Out, 3 On! (as in *BASES LOADED!*)

AB: Chicago Cubs (23 W – 12 L)
(Fighting to capture the 1st place ranking in the National League)
Fred Merkle (1st Base, Bats: right, Throws: right (yes, really)
AVG .297, OBP .349
Age: 30, Games: 1,276, Status: veteran player,
11th full season in The Show

On the mound:
The Boston Braves (18 W – 20 L)
P: Don Carlos Patrick "Pat" Ragan (SP)
(Bats: Right, Throws: Right) 8 W – 16 L, PCT: .320, ERA: 3.23, SO: 602,
HB: 25 x (in 10 years)
Age: 33, Games: 240, Status: 10-year veteran

AND THEN:

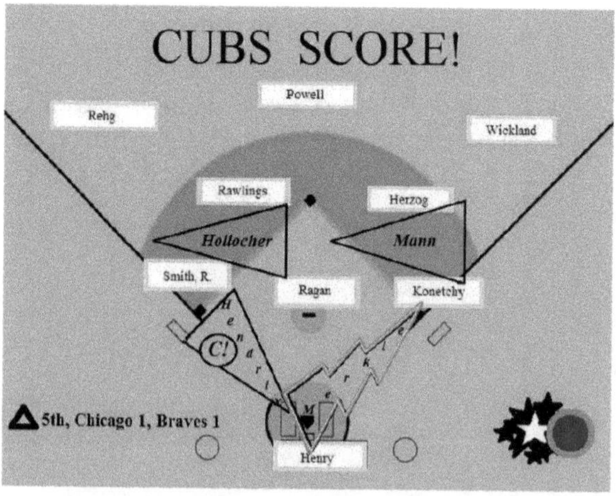

Tad watched with excitement from his seat on the visitors' bench in The Wigwam as the audience roared, cheering on their pitcher Pat Ragan, hoping his infield would gift him a double-play to get him out of this mess. But Taddeo and the rest of The Bonehead's teammates on the Cubs yelled out their encouragement and followed up with elation as Fred Merkle singled and drove in Claude Hendrix from 3rd to break up the tie game in the top of the 5th. Mitchell winced as he watched his starting pitcher dive headfirst under Ray Powell's throw from shallow centerfield all the way to the Braves' backstop John Henry to put the tag on Chicago's lead runner and prevent him from scoring. Weighing one-hundred eighty pounds and twenty years old, Henry would have loved to block the dish and force a collision with Hendrix that might prevent the starter from finishing the game. But Claude could beat the throw from Braves Field's pasture that was deep enough, even at what the sports writers called "shallow," to assist him with helping to get Lord Byron to pronounce him safe.

Not getting the out at home, John Henry whipped the ball back to Red Smith manning 3rd, but Charlie Hollocher was possibly even faster than he bragged he was. Though he wasn't fast enough that Hank O'Day hadn't followed him out to Boston to be called on to serve as the field umpire for this game. Then The Reverend served a "Safe!" decree in the hot corner, as Holly's foot leading from in front of a hurtling dust storm slammed into the 3-bag!

The bases were still loaded as Tad felt overjoyed that his team had retaken the lead. Henry should have thrown to "Big Ed" Konetchy at 1st to get a chance at Merkle, but either way, each Cub would have most likely been safe after Boston had lost time by going after Hendrix.

Dode Paskert earned Chicago's second RBI that inning by getting Charlie Hollocher the rest of the way home after hitting a sacrifice that sent Wally Rehg backpedaling and then twisting to run all-out toward the distant wall in The Wigwam's spacious yard. He caught it in the air for the 2nd out, but far enough back that Holly had time to tag up, and then score — and there was nothing the Braves could do about it. During this time, Charlie Deal had gotten up to walk out into the on-deck circle but Coach Mitchell said, "Ah-nah."

"What?" Chicago's 3rd baseman queried in shock.

And then the most exciting thing in that entire game happened — at least according to one particular ballplayer. Mitchell commanded, "Everston. Get your ass off that bench and get out there. I'm sending you up for Deal after Paskert." And then the worst thing that could have happened in that entire game happened. Trip found his self-doubt. But Coach wasn't hearing any of it. "Son, I know you can do it. Just don't get out like the last time. That was embarrassing. *Cubs*," he now raised his voice to address the bench, "give your teammate your warmest thoughts. He needs your support now." Mitchell coughed. "Not to be a stupid idiot. And uh, also so as to at least try and find his maturity, if that isn't too much to ask."

"Thanks, Coach. That was — uh, very encouraging."

"No need to mention it. Just doing my job. There's 2 outs and we have runners at 2nd and 3rd. We've picked up 2 this inning, but I know you boys can give me more. And I want more."

Then Coach called timeout and signaled for Lord Byron to inform him and the infamous Braves' manager George Stallings that he was making a substitution. Now no one had ever heard of Trip, but nevertheless he was still so excited, "Wolfie Jacobs is going to say my name! *Fellas*. Wolfie Jacobs is going to say my name!" The Cubs' rookie called back to the bench from the on-deck circle.

"Please say that you're locating reality along with your sharp eye. He's only saying your name because Babe Ruth is out of town, Trip. The Red Sox are playing away in Detroit," Bass said.

"Really, get over yourself Michael, and just get a hit to keep this inning alive," Turner Barber told him.

Coach overheard that on his way back to the visitors' dugout and frowned. "No infighting on my bench. That goes for you rookies and you, Barber. You too, Kilduff. And you Charlie. You can at least set the right example for Hollocher. All of you are uh, a *little* older, and ought to know better.

"Mikey," he then spoke to Trip using his most familiar nickname, to soothe any perceived slight on the Cubs' manager's next chance to get a hit with 2 on and 2 outs. "Shake them off. They're just ignorant. And Charlie Deal's just not having the kind of bats we need this game against Ragan, so I need to shake things up. You can do this."

Then Wolfie Jacobs' voice blared at them as he brought his megaphone over to the left field side, where it was much less common to locate the visiting team's dugout — although in The Wigwam, that placed it far out in the center of nowhere. "And now batting for your visiting Chicago Cubs, Mitchell Everrrrston!"

The crowd was less than impressed and you could almost hear a pin drop except for the single voice of Trip piping up. "It's Michael. *Michael* Everston!"

Tad couldn't help himself. "Hey 'Mitchell,' notice how nobody cares?"

But their coach, Fred Mitchell, overheard that. "Villetti, shut up. Everston, get up there and make them care!"

Cloaking his fear of letting everyone down and never becoming even a "remember him?" as a footnote in Chicago baseball's history, Trip resorted to a display of arrogance as he approached the dish to see what Don Carlos Patrick Ragan was going to serve him. And the switch hitter chose to take his order of pitches from the left-handed batters' box. Mikey took his bat and copied Charlie Hollocher's move that originally he stole from Trip. Grabbing it by the barrel, he slammed it onto home plate at an angle so it spun and he could catch it by the grip. This finally done successfully, and without any major personal injury *this time*, he flashed Pat Ragan a hell of a bright grin.

The right-hander sent the arrogant rookie a brush-back. "Ball one!" Byron officiated.

Trip knew that the Brave's arm would like to claim a free strike against him now and did not back out of the box but actually crowded the dish, daring Ragan to hit him. A zipping slider from a right-hander would come inside on Everston, batting left-handed, and he fouled it off into the right-field stands. It might have been ruled a strike anyway. Maybe. Then there was an odd pause to the dead-ball play as park security went to retrieve the game ball. James Gaffney didn't supply his customers with free baseballs, but instead was rumored to concentrate on syphoning Boston's city Elevated's income for any ticket sales he could claim originated from out of The Wigwam. Every club owner's biggest consideration was revenue, after all.

Trip syphoned pitches out of Pat Ragan until he could take the Brave to a full count. With a careful eye on the ball, he used the extra-spacious field to his advantage and finally got a solid piece of one from the mound. His hit bounced all the way to Al Wickman in right field, who returned it back to Herzog fast enough to hold all the runners in place. But they did not have time to go after even Everston. In fact, Trip took off with such speed that he probably hoped that Charlie Hollocher was watching the baseline's gravel combust into flame behind him while he sped as fast as he could to 1st, literally diving onto the bag, head-first, in case Wickman threw at him.

"Safe!" The Reverend decreed. Tad thought his friend Trip might be the only Cub happy the man who refereed the field had appeared that night in Boston. One early rumored verdict from the pulpit, was that he wasn't very fond of Chicago's 1918 team. Many others thought he was *paid* by them.

But now the bases were loaded against Ragan again. Tad's good friend from their Iowa team had not let the Cubs down. Rollie Zeider did instead. And that was the end of The Windy City's storm of contacts for their rally in the 5th. Chicago finished the inning up on the Braves, 3-1.

Miraculously to the rookies, Coach let Trip stay in, playing 3rd for Charlie Deal. Once more, Mikey was thrilled he was playing his natural position. Not everyone was. But Tad was happy for his good friend — as he was happy for the Cubs when they expanded their lead when Charlie Hollocher scored again in the 7th, and after Killefer had got on in the 6th, only to have Claude Hendrix hit into a Braves double-play and Ragan force Max Flack to fly out.

Yet something special was also going to happen in the top of the next inning. After Charlie hung in until Ragan sent him on a walk, Coach gave Trevor Bass a chance at bat. Though Les Mann probably thought Mitchell had become upset with him over his mouth — which had been loose like most of the veterans' after their long train trip — most could see that the Cubs' manager wanted to use a potentially big left-handed bat against the tiring Ragan while Chi-Town had the lead and Hollocher would steal 2nd to get into scoring position of course. The Bass-Man, as he was known in the minor leagues, came up to the plate.

Ragan held a conference on the mound with Henry, Rawlings, and Red Smith until Bryon was going to charge them rent for a room. Tad and Hoff conversed on the bench and Bob O'Farrell overheard them and agreed with the rookies that they were definitely going to try and force Trevor to hit into a double play. And that would force Hollocher to have to attempt to steal. It was inevitable and so Bob even got up and walked toward Coach Mitchell. But Chicago's manager had seen it and with his kind of experience, had already figured it, then given Bass "the sign."

It was a beautiful bunt. John Henry, "The Bull," only saw red for just enough time for The Bass-Man to drop the ball at the plate when he squared off on a changeup from Ragan and the slow ball barely moved onto the infield grass. The Braves reacting late, scrambled when they located the ball so close to the dish, where no one had expected it, that with a wild over-throw to Konetchy, saw Trevor get on base. Holly was on 3rd before Boston realized what had happened. And he was a runner who came in sliding so hard and fast, that his teammates weren't sure if he shot dirt all the way into their dugout even though the slide was so unnecessary since there was no play. An alert Wickland scooped the overthrow on one bounce and shot the ball back to Henry to hold Charlie at 3rd and not dare attempt to go home.

Bass waved as he came to the realization that his fast running through the bag, and the overthrow by Henry, saw him safe at 1st. Tad and Hoff, all smiles, waved back, joined by Charlie Hollocher who saluted Bass, and even Bob O'Farrell nodded at the youngster and gave him a thumbs-up. Coach half raised his hand to encourage Trevor, but likely thought he'd rather keep his character consistent with maintaining that his Cubs live on the edge. Yet Tad knew Mitchell would like it if at least one of his rookies actually listened to him. He grinned, feeling a warmness coming over him. His friends from the Ansons were playing one heck of a great ballgame — and under the pressure of a see-saw game to boot.

Then Trevor stole. He actually stole 2nd base off Ragan who bounced his next pitch and The Bass-Man came in standing up! O'Day pronounced him safe as Henry's throw down was too late. "I could have picked him," Bill Killefer muttered from the Cubs bench. "Rookie got lucky. He's still too timid. We need him to get over his fear of taking a larger leadoff."

Coach nodded, appearing to listen and agree with his team captain. "We'll be doing some base-running drills at the next practice."

Then right-handed Merkle flew out to Wally Rehg for the 1st out. Across the field, George Stallings gave a signal and Hugh Canavan got out on the 1st base sideline with one of the Braves' backup catchers to start warming up. Boston was changing pitchers. Tad saw Coach taking note of it, and Bill Killefer joining him to point that out, in case Mitchell actually missed anything that happened on a baseball diamond. That's when he saw Dode Paskert come to the plate only to make the next out.

Coach and all the rest of the Cubs looked to their right. They had 2 men on, there were 2 outs, and they had only a close 3-run lead over the Braves. Mitchell rubbed his eyes, checking them twice. Rookie Michael Everston was coming up to bat for the Chicago Cubs again!

Chapter 38

Saturday, June 1, 1918
4:59 pm EST
Braves Field a.k.a. "The Wigwam," Boston, Massachusetts

7th Inning
Chicago – 4, Braves –1

2 Out, 2 On

AB: Chicago Cubs (23 W – 12 L)
(Fighting to capture the 1st place ranking in the National League)
Michael or Mikey "Trip" Everston (3rd Base, Bats: switch, Throws: right)
AVG .650, OBP .650
Age: 19, Games: 4, Status: probationary rookie,
1st season even let near a professional baseball diamond

On the mound:
The Boston Braves (18 W, 20 L)
P: Don Carlos Patrick "Pat" Ragan (SP)
(Bats: Right, Throws: Right) 8W – 16L, PCT: .320, ERA: 3.23,
SO: 602, HB: 25 x (in 9 years)
Age: 33, Games: 240, Status: 10-year veteran

AND THEN:

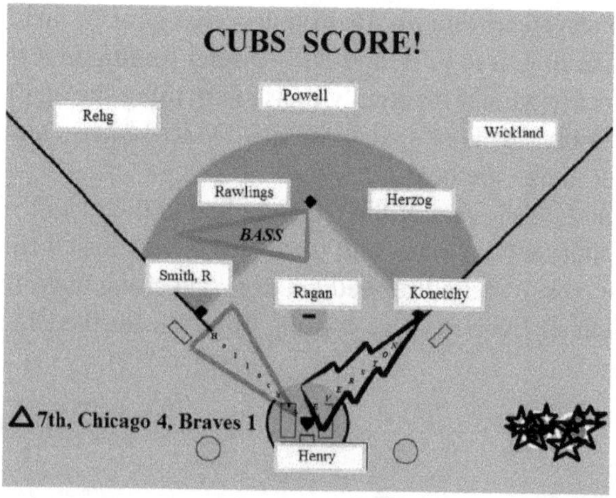

Michael Everston returned to the plate for his second at-bat in this match — and his first game on a road trip. With a little less apprehension this time, Trip bounced his bat in what he hoped would become forever known as *his* signature spin and caught it effortlessly by its grip. He stepped into the right-handed batter's box this time and looked out over Gaffney's Great Plains the man built on the Eastern Seaboard. His hope was to make Wally Rehg chase the ball in the weeds, or what passed as grass struggling to grow, but was better described as Braves Field's poorly nurtured green blades, haphazardly appearing in a whole lot more dirt. But that meant there was less friction against a speeding baseball sent out that way, and it could really roll once hit on the ground. The further it got, the further Rehg would have to throw to get it to Rawlings, and the more impossible it would be for him to get it all the way in to Henry, so Hollocher and Chicago would feast at the dish.

Trip held off on a slider that Byron called a ball. The "one-and-oh" was a sinker that Mikey took for a strike. "Plate discipline. Plate discipline." That's what Taddeo imagined his friend was thinking right then. Coach had been drilling it into the especially over-eager rookies. It still failed to take. But right-handed Ragan hung his slider, and Trip hitting from his own right took the "one-and-one" offering and battered it right out to left field in The Wigwam where it landed and took off rolling with Rehg in pursuit, exactly as Mike had pre-visioned it.

His cleats doing a great job of rapidly weeding the 3rd base line, Charlie Hollocher scored, crossing home plate for the third time in this game, accounting for 3 of the Cubs' 5 runs. Bass arrived on 3rd and Trip had an RBI double! He pumped his arm in triumph and signed to his buddy from the Ansons, Trevor – who pumped his own arm back in triumph and then looked to his right to wave to Taddeo and Hoff on Chicago's bench. Out of the corner of his eye, Tad thought he saw Coach Mitchell and even Bill Killefer kind-of-sort-of give the kids a nod. But finally there had been silence and discipline enforced in Mitchell's dugout.

Then Coach had a change of heart. "Hey Chicago — what do you say? Everston got another RBI today. Now all of you morons applaud or give him the thumbs up. Acknowledge it so that now the dumb rookie doesn't get himself tagged out acting like an idiot trying to walk over here and describe it for us."

"I can't believe we're both on base together, Trip. And you're following me around the horn while I'm about to score. And we're playing in Braves Field, pro baseball!" Bass announced to his left toward his pal who would be running from 2nd base.

Between them, Johnny Rawlings whistled and Pat Ragan stepped off the mound and tossed the ball to the Braves' shortstop. "Hey Rookie," he directed his voice to Trip. "Why don't you take a bigger leadoff? You need to come just a little closer so you can also tell me about you and all your friends' wonderful adventures in Iowa."

"No thanks."

"Aww, why not?" He tossed the ball back to his pitcher. "I know exactly how to help you out with your nostalgia for the mudfields." Ragan and his infield support grinned at the young Cubs as if they looked over what was going to be served for dinner.

"It's really not necessary. The upkeep they did in Marshalltown was just about the same quality Gaffney does for you here in Boston," Trip informed the Braves' pitcher.

That must have also irritated the Braves' shortstop as he shut up and squatted down, coiling the muscles in his legs so he'd be ready to spring to either side to not let the Cubs' next batter Rollie Zeider continue their run-fest in the 7th inning. And Bunions just had to hit right to him, though it was easier to reach for Red Smith, who made the play and threw Zeider out at 1st so The Bass-Man couldn't score. But Trip had gotten his digs in and Rawlings had learned just how irritating all the Cubs already knew *he* was.

The bottom of the 8th inning was not as much fun — for Chicago. After Killefer, Hendrix and Flack went down in order when George Stallings put in Hugh Canavan to control the Cubs' offense, it would be the Braves' turn to get a new chance at making up for being 4 runs down as they approached the end of the game. On the mound, Claude Hendrix was tiring but he would complete this game.

However Coach Mitchell, who usually didn't like his team to ever feel too comfortable, decided *not* to make a move and replace Trevor Bass with Turner Barber now that Les Mann was out of the game. Satisfied with the lead, and especially Trip's performance, he'd leave the rookies in to give them some more experience and see if they could also finish this game.

And this experience out on the road would be one scary one. After an assist by a late-inning bloom out of Rollie Zeider, Hendrix retired Big Ed Konetchy. Then Roy Massey served as a left-handed substitution for John Henry. Claude made him out number 2, and was poised to end the inning. But Johnny Rawlings got a single to keep the Braves' attack alive. It might have shook up Hendrix from where *he* could have slipped into complacency, comfortable with the Cubs' lead. He couldn't find the strike zone and Buck Herzog successfully challenged the Chicago pitcher's patience and took a walk to 1st. There were 2 outs already and it should have been over, but — .

Chapter 39

Saturday, June 1, 1918
5:09 pm EST
Braves Field, a.k.a "The Wigwam," Boston, Massachusetts

8th Inning
Chicago – 5, Braves – 1

2 Outs, 2 On

AB: Boston Braves (18 W – 20 L):
Raymond Reath "The Rabbit" Powell (CF, Bats: left, Throws: right)
AVG .213, OBP .321
Age: 30, Games: >90, Status: 1 year veteran,
2nd full season in The Show

On the mound:
Chicago Cubs (23 W – 12 L)
(Fighting to capture the 1st place ranking in the National League)
P: Claude Hendrix (SP)
(Bats: Right, Throws: Right) 20 W – 7 L, PCT: .741, ERA: 2.78, SO: 865,
HB: 32 x (in 7 years)
Age: 29, Games: 268, Status: 7-year veteran

AND THEN:

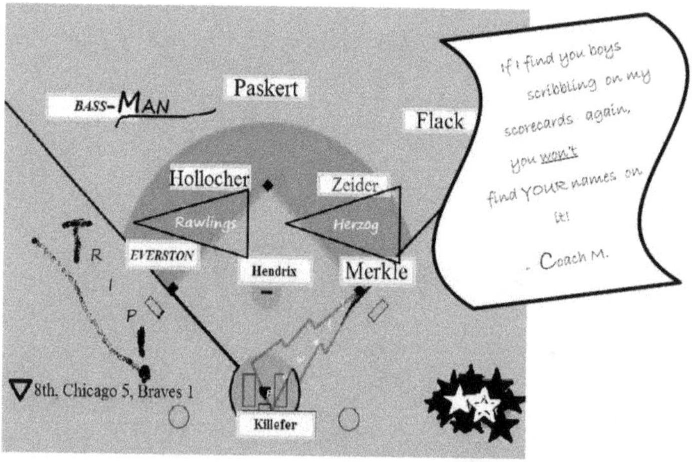

Ray Powell just had to get the Cubs' hearts beating fast. Sending one of Claude's fastballs, that had at last declined in speed in the late innings, rocketing out over Zeider's head, everybody on the Chicago side prayed Max Flack wouldn't screw this one up. He managed not to strain anything executing a textbook play for a ball on the bounce and whipped it back to Rollie Zeider, but Braves Field was deep and Johnny Rawlings used that opportunity to score! Herzog made it all the way over to 3rd to disrupt Trip's enjoyment of commanding the hot corner. Now he tried not to forget everything he learned about playing the 3-bag with a runner on base and an arm like Killefer's behind the plate. Trip prayed he wouldn't screw up any play and especially that he wouldn't let his captain down. Killefer wasn't fond of the rookies as it were.

Nobody on Chicago's bench was fond of Boston narrowing the score. But the Cubs still led 5 – 2. Only the attack of the Braves wasn't over yet. Old Al Wickland wasn't too mature to play tricks and Stallings ordered up a surprise — a 2-out suicide squeeze. It accomplished what he desperately intended and Herzog snuck in and scored when Killefer and Hendrix were made to look like fools by the Braves' manager when they collided in the infield grass — or what was supposed to approximate it — and lost the bunt in a tangle of arms and legs. They came up with it in time for Killefer to get it to Rollie at 2nd base and prevent Wickland from taking any more ground. Instead, Hendrix got Red Smith and the Cubs backed down the Braves before they eviscerated Chicago's narrow lead.

Taddeo watched from the bench as Claude found something within himself to carry on.

Chapter 40

And then it was Saturday night, after the Cubs barely got away with their first victory on this road series here at Braves Field in Boston, Massachusetts. There were no Sunday games allowed or yet scheduled for Major League Baseball *there*, to afford the public observance of the Christian Sabbath. Chicago team manager Fred Mitchell was terrified of what that meant.

His heathen rookies took off on unsanctioned raids from every direction out of The Wigwam and chose to ignore every point their coach had tried to make about being professional on away-game tours. He'd caught George Hoffman with two ladies — likely prostitutes — on his arms before the third-string catcher had even left the stadium. He was concurrently trying to be a bad influence on his friend Villetti, who was curiously reserved — of all the ironies — when Bass and Everston told him there was something "even better than the girls" going on in Boston. That was just great. Mitchell had better find out what they were going to be up to now.

The fact that the Boston Municipal Police Department was threatening to strike against Commissioner O'Meara and Mayor Peters over their working and housing conditions meant that either there was less chances of his young players getting arrested — or that they'd wind up getting themselves killed — with no responsible supervision. Lester Mann had informed Coach in no uncertain terms that he was tired of babysitting rookies, more than likely because his manager had substituted for *him* in the later innings, to give the new guys some more road game experience.

So now everyone on the Cubs took off everywhere at once. However, Mitchell knew to follow the rookies. They could be counted on to act up the worst. And Weeghman had of course been too cheap to pay an effective security team to act like MPs and corral the youngsters. *That means this could take all night*, a very unenthusiastic Mitchell thought.

At first his angst found some relief as he discovered Charlie Hollocher after traveling all the way down Commonwealth Avenue, much of the time on his feet, so he could search venues in which he suspected he'd find the young team members. But while initially he didn't find his players, he noted places he wanted to return to himself. In spite of the current circumstances, he always liked Boston. However, to his great surprise, he did find his star shortstop — who would be a most valuable piece of the Cubs' arsenal to protect — in the First Baptist Church. Holly was stretched out, looking as if he were in deep meditation with his arms hanging over the back of his wooden pew. The shortstop never noticed his manager entering the sanctuary behind him, so Mitchell decided he'd just leave him be, the young man surely pondering his place in the heavens, giving himself over to spirituality. Chicago's manager felt so relieved that at least this was such a surprisingly respectable position to find the versatile rookie infielder to be taking.

Once again seemingly alone in the old church, Charlie called out to God — with his pants around his ankles by his half-emptied whiskey bottle as the two ladies played with him from the floor beneath his pew — and out of the sight of anyone entering this house of heavenly experiences.

Mitchell hurried down Commonwealth as if he were practicing his base-running drills when he heard the roar of extremely loud, likely customized super-engines coming to life. He was losing his breath, panting and sweating in his suit, constantly having to hold on to his hat and work on loosening his tie simultaneously. Then in a crowd that hadn't been there when he'd passed those particular blocks less than three quarters of an hour ago, he at last found Hoffman again, of course, celebrating with Bass and Everston. Finally Coach had located the rest of the rookies. But there was no way to reach them nor could they hear him as the engines started to scream and the crowd — no mob — of young people matched the noise with their own enthusiasm.

"What is this? What the hell is going on?"

"It's an underground rematch! Ralph DePalma is outlaw-racing 'Barn-storming Barney Oldfield' so long as the police are threatening a prolonged strike. This is going to be so bugs!" shouted out a young lady dressed in pants and a leather jacket. Mitchell first wondered why she was dressed that way, then why she wasn't having her father escort her, and then finally found himself wondering how much she charged. This was Boston. "Oh baby! He's brought me his Golden Submarine!" The gal sounded elated and her smile lit up the night. Glimpses of his ballplayers lost in the exhilarated crowd and thrusting their fists in the air revealed Bass and Everston to have the comfort women they'd found for the evening hanging all over them of course, and now Hoffman had *four* ladies.

Mitchell thought, *It's going to be one long road trip with these kids*. He had just lost Grover Cleveland Alexander off to Europe, so the star pitcher could serve his country in the war. But he couldn't deny that the Cubs were winning and he didn't have to rely on just the rookies, but at least Charlie Hollocher was behaving himself and had only gone to church. This season was balanced on a hope and a prayer. For now, Fred Mitchell was fighting his own holy war to control the rest of his unit while they all too, operated outside familiar territory.

* * * * *

Tad thought that at least for one more moment, Coach would be pleased with him. It was true that he wished he could be out celebrating their first victory this road trip with his teammates, especially since he was genuinely happy for Trip and Trevor Bass, both of them having gotten another chance to successfully play professional baseball. But Taddeo could not even leave their hotel once he returned from Braves Field. He'd skipped dinner when he'd received many messages waiting for him at the front desk — that Arlene had been repeatedly calling in. They'd been together for eleven days and this was the first forty-eight hours that had ever passed since then in which they had not spoken. He'd even phoned her from a gas station while he was away on his camping trip to Wisconsin, making his easily irritated brothers stop and wait for him. But for having been so indifferent — even cold-shouldered regarding his departure for the away-game tour — Arlene was sure responding with plenty of emotion over his absence now. Multiple messages being left for him sure sounded like that to Taddeo. If she were in trouble, which Tad felt to be surely the case, then he'd already begun to feel furious about leaving her behind for the Cubs' road trip, even though Arlene was the one who wanted to stay in Chicago. But he'd predicted everything he expected he was about to hear — and dreaded hearing it all the same. He sat down on one of the beds as he waited to talk to her. The upgraded Buckminster Hotel the team miraculously got to stay at, had telephones installed in each of the rooms and employed an onsite operator, just like at The Sisson. No, this was even better. The Boston city operator connected him with Chicago.

The time was earlier in the Midwest and Tad's barely older cousin Baldavino Delasandro took the phone away from Faith, who'd first answered his call to The Family's business. What was *he* doing at Villetti's? He'd thought Arlene had been successful at cutting all his cousins off from the girls. And though it would never be organized in tandem, she had the support of his aunt in so far as keeping all her yet-unwed boys out of a bordello — well except for Corrado. He'd proven far too independent and unpredictable an actor. Now Tad demanded Corry's younger brother put Arlene on the phone.

But once he was eventually speaking to her, it was first revealed that the infamous pariah to men's last rights, Katherine McCormick, had his woman talking to a psychiatrist. Some famous German guy even — Emil Kraep-something. Arlene said it got really necessary for her to talk to *someone* since he was not there for her and this guy was alright, though when Tad returned, he'd have to pay the bill. *Jesus, I've only been gone for forty-eight hours!* And there was something else in her voice over the line. Taddeo detected what he heard as a severe loss of her usually strong self-confidence. She then came clean and related the events that had befallen her since he'd left — without any of the customary sarcasm she'd normally use with her obnoxious posturing.

She related most of the events anyway. Arlene had decided *against* telling Taddeo the single most important piece of news that would affect him. And she omitted a few other details that she didn't need to concern him with. Instead of that, what Tad listened to was a tale of terror and misery.

Greg did offer her a ride away from the train station Thursday evening when Tad left. She'd been very ill and nearly fainted. She could detect Taddeo holding his breath on the other end of the line when she'd only related that much.

But she did *not* tell him that someone followed the pair as they drove south on Canal Street and her boyfriend's brother was even so careful as to turn off on Harrison Street so as to go off the edge of the *electrically* lighted street grid — to check for any tails — only to confirm they had one. Arlene later learned it was McCormick's friends Nancy and Virginia, of whom which she also learned quite unexpectedly that *both* could drive, and to who the wealthy McCormick supplied most-discreet automobiles, like a

Cadillac V-8 to, so they could act as her agents. Greg never learned who they were, but had obsessed with insisting that he would find out. But he didn't even suspect their suspicious tails' gender. He had no clue. There were so many more likely suspects considering who might want to spy on the Villettis. But after their encounter at the train station, Greggorio Villetti should have been able to guess. His mistake. Meanwhile, the ladies had first ensured Arlene arrived safely back at Villetti's without incident and then called their fearless leader using some nearby neighborhood storekeeper's phone. But nothing about McCormick's people needed to be revealed to Taddeo. However, once she and Greg had disappeared inside the busy nightclub, the women didn't immediately follow, as unescorted ladies, especially at their age, would draw undesired attention in a place like Villetti's.

Now, she did disclose that Corrado was onsite to inquire from Arlene about her availability upon the instant he got his chance with Taddeo being out of town. However, Arlene also did not relate to Taddeo that she saw this as an opportunity to take him upstairs with her in order to seduce her own agent. It also was intended to help her hide from Greg as soon as they'd returned to Villetti's. She needed to completely understand why he didn't just kill her as soon as she'd faltered. She had to figure Greggorio's *whole* plan out. And she did not tell Tad that she'd planned on using Corrado as backup once she'd make her move to kill Rinaldo and both of his oldest sons now that she finally had found them gathered all in one place. Arlene did go into detail on how she had been dodging Corry's advances upstairs in a room once he had pushed her to where they had some privacy and some scented candlelight. Though she didn't tell Tad she had seduced his cousin there. However, it was all only for long enough to get him to admit as much that *Greg* did mean for a lot of harm to come her way and that he had sent Dulio. However, *he'd had nothing to do with the appearances of Simone or Herbert.* But *the main subject* of she and Corry's discussion had almost immediately noticed her being absent from her duties running the party and encouraging guests to partake of the services upstairs that provided as the real source of revenue for any of Colosimo's lounges — that which Villetti's was best known for. However, this time Corrado, whose libido she had so purposely wounded before, had refused to allow himself to be too easily aroused by *her* when Arlene had first returned to the bar from the train station dressed in her day clothes. She must have depressed him so, during their last encounter at

The Sisson. So she had disrobed down to her lacy white lingerie, complete with straps connecting her transparent leggings to her tiny panties which matched her mini-bra with tassels, when Greggorio entered their room without even knocking, found them like that, made the obvious assumption, and strongly motivated Corry to go back downstairs.

Greg said that seeing as how she now appeared healthy enough to work, Urso had been asking for her, and in the event he was already busy, she had money to sort so that Stefan could re-check and make official recordings for all the accountings that would be reported back to Madame Moresco — in the case she preferred working with the Delasandros that much. There was this and he also made her very aware that Rinaldo Villetti eagerly anticipated speaking with her. He had just tried to meet with his patriarch and would now go see if his father was finally available and ordered Arlene to locate and work with Stefan in the meanwhile, to resolve some new financial mysteries for Greggorio. That would be a priority over what Urso obviously wanted with her. His older brother had apparently been fighting with his latest woman Sega again and had been looking for a change of scenery, so to speak. But Greg thought Arlene might prefer other less-strenuous duties in light of her illness.

So Arlene had been able to escape downstairs for only a few minutes, presumably to find Stefano, while Greg went to see if he could at last talk to his father *before* her first reunion with Rinaldo. She'd actually been hoping to reunite with Corrado now that she'd tempted him again, but that was also when Katherine McCormick actually had found her while Greg was occupying himself with trying to convince his father that his old man was finished with the bordello's offering of Faith.

Meanwhile, the New Age Suffragette supplied Arlene new hope by way of important written information, contact numbers for her, and then asked to clandestinely place them in the young madam's purse before they were noticed together, hiding in plain sight, amid a full crowd. Baldavino, Carlo, and Tito Delasandro were all at Villetti's, enjoying their uncle's entertainment venue and adding to the Villetti House's security that evening, along with other non-blood associates. Arlene had previously deluded herself into thinking she could ban them if they weren't paying for the girls' services, but they were reported to be allegedly *working* as ordered by Corrado, as he explained when *he* first found her. This was all his idea, again allegedly. He apparently held other misgivings about the capabilities of a different Villetti brother. But he was shy about coming forward with them at present. Arlene would still endeavor to at least explore working with that. In the meanwhile, Corry wanted more of a Family presence about the place, as representatives from New York were actually still there — since the Yankees were scheduled to finish up their series versus the White Sox.

But for that part of the phone conversation with Taddeo, Arlene decided to skip over the ladies' meeting. She only related to him how rough his oldest brother had been when he grabbed her by her arm and dragged her upstairs for some personal time — only to be forced to stay the night in one of the rooms with Urso. The lumbering Family thug pretended to be furious with her over the late proclamation that the bordello was Colosimo's and his wife's business and only paying customers and not even Villettis could take up the other working girls' time. In truth, Urso just had used that as an excuse for why he put Arlene to work to please him, since he said "that was what all the girls were brought to The House to do," and he was going to provide her with the most explicit example of how that went. Greg must have made Urso memorize that speech, as Arlene also observed a few things going on that night. The two Villetti brothers met previously — unusual in itself since they didn't ever seem to get along with one another, plus they'd just spent three nights cooped up in a car with each other. And that meeting happened only moments *before* Greg had forced a second private meeting with his father and removed Faith from that picture while Urso went looking for Arlene to entertain him. This was accompanied by Sega fuming that she was losing Urso's attention, which Arlene assumed conflicted with *her* customary *lack of enthusiasm* for being with him in the first place — except that it kept her unavailable for having to entertain any other man. Now Sega had to worry that Arlene would assign her to do just that. But there was something else always underlying why those two women erected guarded caution between them. Conspiracies and ulterior motives surrounded and permeated The Villetti House. And Arlene had been wondering all week why Sega was really there. Since every part of working in the business going on there could be less than desirable, Arlene had done as much to avoid it as Sega may have been trying to — only with Urso. Just like Arlene's original reason for using Taddeo. Only she hadn't meant to become the mother of a child with the young baseball star — or wannabe — whichever he actually was. Or even fall in love with him. But now Sega glared at her, trying to direct venom from her eyes for Arlene's usurping of Urso's attentions, yet she only succeeded in delaying the eldest Villetti brother a short while longer by actually fighting for those attentions. And that's when Corry Delasandro had gone to sit down with his own oldest brother in a booth in the lounge, brooding over his change of fortunes since Greg sidelined him, and he now watched Urso Villetti finally depart with Arlene. She did not mention to Taddeo that she had been taken to meet with Tad's father *first*, and then Urso got her alone with him when she'd tried to escape downstairs and get started talking business with Stefano.

That didn't matter. Taddeo was furious now. Even from Boston, and over the phone, Arlene could tell from his harsh and quickened breathing that blood had filled his eyes and all they could see now was a path of revenge blazed in the direction of Urso and Greggorio. Too bad he was out of town. She felt the hatred, too — and that she'd been mistaken. She did need him and wished he were back in Chicago protecting her this very instant. She bet her story now — the truth or most of it as it were — would motivate him to return as quickly as possible though. Greg had blocked her from recruiting Corrado and she so she felt nearly as impotent as he did. Her night would have been a lot different and she could have handled herself very independently, if when Katherine McCormick went into her purse — *that manipulative rich minx, hadn't gone and stolen Arlene's gun!*

Of course what would happen next, and after she spent the night upstairs at Villetti's, she did *not* describe for Taddeo. True to her word, Mrs. McCormick did send a car for her — that tan Cadillac again — driven by Nancy, one of the ladies she had met the night before. Arlene rose to meet her after Lucy knocked on the door to the room she and Tad's brother had taken above the lounge and said there was a visitor for her, and so very early on that Friday morning. Naturally Urso was sleeping off all his drinking and couldn't be awakened by the disturbance. Arlene hoped that no one had witnessed her leave the place on Taylor Street. She only wished she could have cleaned up for her examination before she was seeing Dr. Warren. Though things were not going to stay nice and clean when she met with Katherine McCormick again. That was for sure. After all, her gun was missing. And so would be her civility.

What Arlene did tell Taddeo was that when she returned from Dr. Warren's — Dr. Kraepelin, the psychiatrist in the version she related to Tad — during that late Friday morning, Greg was there and finally made good on *his* promise to get her medically attended. Though privately she supposed that Greggorio and Taddeo both would wonder why she let herself provide sex for Urso versus spent weapon cartridge cases. They each knew Tad's .38 had been left behind in Mr. Li's after all, she had access to it — but Arlene had perhaps been sorely mistaken when she had decided not to carry it as backup to her primary weapon. Only Katherine McCormick might have then confiscated that gun as well. However, the Irish-woman assassin hadn't had another chance to retrieve it from the laundry yet, and only saw Sega and a couple other girls who didn't have tricks at that moment, besides Greggorio of the Villettis, up and around at the bar. The latter not knowing she'd been disarmed, and in line with continuing to keep Corrado away from her, Greg decided to then order Baldavino to drive her over to Abramo Delasandro's pharmacy and have Davino's father check her out. They both could have walked, but just to make her day go all too perfect, "The Baller" decided to make the trip double as driving practice for their brother Carlo, the Delasandro sibling the same age as Arlene and Taddeo. Her boyfriend could barely drive a pitch into the strike zone, so she heard, and his first cousin was barely better behind the wheel of Corry's Chevrolet V-6 Roadster that Greggorio had insisted this cousin lend to his own younger brothers. Of course Corrado wasn't there in the morning and she presumed he caught a ride with Stefano. Fortunately, Carlo's driving skills rapidly improved and his father's place for the public practice of his haphazard apothecary arts was not a long way to travel up Halstead Street. But the boys probably both wanted to delay their trip as much as they could to procure for themselves more time with "the fascinating little Irish damsel," squeezed in between the brothers in the front seat. It was obvious that they wanted her. They were both struggling to keep their hands to themselves and not reach too far up her summer dress that the not-quite-fully-emboldened young men had been working as a team to push up. Their fingers now testing her response to their touching, tickling her inner thighs, as if there was some way of being sly while exposing her only cover, nearly all the way up to the dame's *private operation*. But obedient to the letter of a Villetti's orders, she wasn't further molested by the younger brothers whose courage to rebel too much had not yet matured — *but give that less than a week*, Arlene thought — and she received their father's more invasive attentions semi-discretely. Of course it didn't take him long to determine she was pregnant. However, Arlene had begged

Dr. Delasandro — his doctorate in chemistry or drug dealing, she wasn't sure — to keep her condition to himself, and she had a means to providing him with a motive. The woman had begun mulling over an even newer plan to achieve her personal goal through her assigned mission, and she knew that Greg would phone his uncle and demand a report. However, she promised Delasandro that the information could be of extreme importance to his own progeny. He looked upon her with both suspicion and curiosity, but said he'd entertain the idea of protecting her secret. He could honestly report that he had to treat her for the flu and recommend she didn't entertain The House's customers any more for fear she could spread an epidemic. He fulfilled the prescription she required and Tad had told her that his uncle by marriage seemed honorable and also appeared always cautious where it came to involving himself in the affairs of the Villettis. *Smart man.* To combat her Spanish flu symptoms, he truly did prepare the right medicine. But now Arlene had started formulating the smartest plan.

However, what she told Taddeo was that she was found to be only temporarily sick and that his Uncle Abe was extremely helpful and just prescribed the medication that would get her better quickly — after she got a few more necessary shots. Of course he wouldn't know she meant gunshots — once she got her old Colt back from Katherine McCormick or that .38, and turned either loose on Tad's family. The rest of the Villettis really had those shots coming.

By this point, Arlene had already grown very weary after not one, but two doctor examinations since Friday morning began, and passed on into her afternoon. So that's when she'd started to get to work on the accounting privately. She'd figured the paperwork would require less energy being further drained from her, than actively participating in any more homicides for one day. But Stefan Delasandro had already arrived while she was out, gotten pretty deep into it, and wanted to go over some discrepancies he'd found in The House's books. The numbers weren't matching up even after Arlene had been so careful to hide the embezzlement from him. She'd planned on looking for a way to do a better job at covering that up, but it was too late. He'd probably been provided a key to Rinaldo's private office by Greg, and he took her there now. They were sitting on opposite sides of the desk when Urso heard them arguing about the figures. The lazy brother must have finally woken up as it was nearly 3 o'clock in the afternoon and he'd started wondering around the upstairs hall with his shirt half coming out of his pants and his suspenders hanging off his hips. He'd found a green bottle of something and was drinking it when she told Taddeo how he had decided to intrude on the business discussion.

"This is your business," he told Arlene and hauled her to her feet from the chair and slammed her face first over his father's desk, then withdrew a butterfly knife and sliced through the back of her dress and cut it from the waist down to where her legs separated. He ripped much of the material the rest of the way apart, where he needed to. And wasting no time, Urso cut through her panties as well, and then undid his own belt and fly, and pushed a meaty part of himself into her. He drew Arlene away from the desk to collide with him, and then slammed her back into it with every thrust of his powerful body while he spoke to his cousin. "You need to get into this. Oh. *This* is way more satisfying than any of those numbers." He nodded toward the open ledger books. "Do you have any idea how many numbers of times I'm going to do this with *her?"*

Stefan was getting aroused from watching, especially when Urso ripped apart Arlene's shirt and bra, and then pushed her naked breasts toward his face. "Come on, Cousin. You know I'm married. I'm no longer like that," he weakly protested.

"I said get around here and get in on this. Oh!" There was a knocking on the office door but Urso continued thrusting. The sound outside the room persisted, steady but sharply concentrated in a single area, as if a small hand made it. "I mean when *I* finish of course. And do not answer that."

Inspiration answered Arlene. She surprised both of the men when she announced, "Yes. Stefan. Do it to me. You know that I'm a very bad girl. And you know how much I want my punishment that I so deserve." He'd started sweating while watching her being taken by Urso, the voluptuous parts of her chest bouncing in response to his cousin's motion behind her, and Stefan following every bit of it with his now intense, involuntary, and undivided concentration. What remained of her knifed-open dress had fallen down her long legs to her ankles by way of being ripped to pieces and shaken by all the motions between the two bodies that were being pressed together, separated, and then smashed back against one another all right in front of Dally. When the Villetti brother fell out of her, spraying the back of Arlene's legs, the married man approached this altar of domestic bliss. But no one had thought to lock the door to Rinaldo's office and it opened to reveal Sega in the hallway, catching Urso with his pants down. That didn't go well and she stormed out of there to go complain to who? Greg, Arlene supposed. He would be the only logical choice left. Because now Stefan got behind her and didn't permit the woman to move around a lot to watch. However, she did see that Urso was trying to get dressed while he followed Sega, and Arlene was left entertaining Stefano Delasandro. But she had herself a very good reason for why she enjoyed doing that. She didn't mention it or her feelings about that part of it in her report to Taddeo. But though the phone she heard Tad stomping his feet and one thing slam against another hard object while he listened to her go on with her tale. She imagined him destroying one of the Boston hotel rooms in the Buckminster where the Cubs had been put up in for the series. Maybe when he realizes what he's doing, he'll want to get out of there anyway — before anyone else finds out — like management, either the baseball organization's or especially the hotel's. He had enough financial problems that came with the compensation he already had to pay out, to cover her, along with Mr. Li, and Old Lamont. But his girlfriend had already decided she had got him back for choosing his baseball team over her by giving herself to Stefan.

However, there were several things wrong with that assessment: she had been the one who encouraged him to leave her, she certainly did not enjoy being abused by Urso in his customary manner, and poor Stefano wanted most to be a good husband and had not even initially desired her. Or he'd tried his best to only work with her, but once every inch of her had been exposed — and put to use — by Urso, he could no longer resist the urges that his firsthand voyeurism had led to. Arlene chastised herself for being so selfish; she corrupted more men, sometimes otherwise good men. And though Tad didn't know it yet, he was the father of her unborn baby. While as unreliable as he was, she'd always seen his feelings towards her to be true, and well-intentioned. However, being used herself, only taught her to use everyone.

But then Arlene decided that she knew she could also set Taddeo to really go off — and get so mad he'd immediately return to her. The baby changed everything for her. Now she needed him. She needed that support back, more money that she had not been successful at acquiring — and his weapon left behind at Mr. Li's laundry. But even more so, she needed Taddeo, who she could also make herself capable of using — as a weapon, to help her escape. But still she swore, only after she claimed her revenge against the rest of the Villettis.

Now word of what had went on between her and Urso and

Stefano would be spreading around like fire with everyone there at the lounge on a Friday night. And the other girls would get jealous since both she and Sega appeared to never be "put into the rotation." Their existence amounted to exclusively pleasing one or another of the admittedly handsome Villetti brothers and their cousins. But if she still could, Arlene would confirm this rumor about Sega sooner than later *with Corrado*, request his help, and then call the number that she had been given, find Katherine McCormick and get her gun back, and then find herself and her true Irish family its revenge. Corrado could go to hell after she made use of him, for all Arlene cared. She just hoped that maybe some of the money she requested would finally be sent from Louisiana, fund-raised somehow, and through Fallon she would pick this cash up. She was going to need every penny. Or she'd certainly try and get it off McCormick, because the woman was surely scheming something she wanted to get Arlene's help for. There too, was another option. But the young madam's assistance would only be acquired at a very steep price. Because even though he'd tried, Taddeo was not supplying the green in the amount the Irish woman needed. And McCormick now owed her a lot, the way she saw it.

But then, Arlene just knew by his intensely distracting desire for her, she could turn Corry away from the course Greg was counting on him taking. And use *him* for her backup. If she could just get to him. Corrado had been sent somewhere, Thursday night or Friday morning, and she had not yet seen his return. His younger brother Baldavino continued to make use of his absence, to drive his car. But away in Massachusetts, and only if she were able to move fast, Tad wouldn't be able to catch a ride back in time to interfere with whatever happened now, even as she asked him to leave his baseball team immediately, on this Saturday. And with not a single delay.

But this was for the best after all, because what's more, he wouldn't know anything was happening until it was too late and Arlene might even be able to pin her own causing Greg's death on Corrado. Greggorio was the most dangerous, so she would have to eliminate him first, once she'd found out where he disappeared to Friday night. Then Urso would avenge his own brother, killing Corry without likely ever searching for any motive or explanation — but Arlene could say he wanted revenge for Greggorio Villetti losing him his own opportunity to run the bordello. And then it would finally be demanded that Stefano turn on Urso for killing the younger Delasandro. She could influence to see that happening too, as Arlene was gaining a tight grip on Stefan as it were. That was definitely true since she had the inside squeeze on him in this moment, while he busied himself with fucking her. It wouldn't matter if that continued — and she preferred it did not. Because now he was susceptible to blackmail to protect the eldest Delasandro brother's marriage. But Stefano's own father might be more interested in protecting the first child conceived from their family's next generation, than his oldest son's childless marriage. Rinaldo Villetti though, would destroy his nephew for the death of his son, turn on all the Delasandros as he learned of the cumulative deaths of two of his boys — at their hands. Then Arlene would gladly take care of Rinaldo. She'd only miss getting to kill Urso, personally, unless she re-worked something out. *There's no doubt I'd like to*, she thought as she had to listen to him attempt to make things up to Sega once he'd left his cousin, to have his turn with Arlene. And once she'd turned promiscuous, quite the inviting temptress to Stefano, Urso lost interest almost immediately — as soon as he realized he was never going to dominate her. *And* she also controlled the entire payroll now, since Stefan was becoming impotent in a way he could not yet detect, so the old soldier's goombahs wouldn't make a move against her while she controlled their payouts and had the funds to keep the corrupt police from arresting the whole lot of them over their entire stack of cold cases on Chicago's Finest detectives' desks that Villetti's men were more-than-likely guilty of anyway. Though it wasn't like everyone didn't already know that.

But it would all be done and over before her lover could ever make the journey back from the East Coast. But he would arrive — just in time. Then Tad could stand up to his other cousins. And he'd have the legitimacy to command as the last heir of The Villetti House. If they actually did wed, by her Irish blood and a mixed child, they would realign their status of cooperation with The North Side Gang, and catch Colosimo's Outfit, The Black Hand, and the Gennas, all outnumbered and outgunned, and directly in their crosshairs. And her shots she'd fire? They just might smoke out her other ally, the plant or *flower* on the South Side that the Jew had mentioned, and not in reference to Fallon, who still was waiting for orders from Louisiana while comfortably residing in Lincolnwood, on the North Side, with his law shingle and his wife's dowry, as far as Arlene knew. Not that she wanted Bill involved anyway. He was useless and she just wanted her money. Instead, her flower might just bloom into her beautiful ticket out of there — and out of Chicago. Or it might even see her daughter eventually becoming in charge of it — more powerful than Victoria Moresco or Katherine McCormick would ever dream of being.

But her boyfriend was another problem for her altogether. He instantly began to crush that dream. Taddeo was to become a father — her baby's father. But once out of her immediate presence, Arlene found she was losing influence over him. He'd been most malleable when all she needed to do was show him a little skin and give his pining desires a release when he was cooperating. Only now when it was most important she do so, and even with Tad's emotional state resting in the palm of her hand, Arlene found that she could not control the direction of his pitch over the telephone when he could no longer see the call her body language was signaling. Taddeo was very out-of-character while he was pointing out every objection: they'd lose money if he left baseball and abandoned the plan to hide out until he got traded to another team; what he earned from Mr. Li went right back to this proprietor and ally, to pay his rent money for her mattress on the floor and keep the laundry's new insurance payments to The House in such good order as to avoid any scrutiny by his brothers. Plus he was paying off Lamont.

So as he pointed out, they were moderately safe if not otherwise broke unless *she* could get back to work on the books *versus Stefano doing it*, though by way of Urso forcing himself and his cousin upon her, she could keep them from examining her records too closely. Because when they liked her as much as they surely seemed to, they tended to trust her too much. And Urso did not like math very much anyway. Not when he definitely liked Sega more. Plus she could always threaten to contact Delasandro's wife, so she had something on him now, in case Stefano figured out what he had *against her.* Thus she'd outwitted Dally, and he might still not even be aware of it. And Arlene might once more chance collecting her skim, because she and Tad didn't have anywhere near the resources they could have, and could need, to fall back on yet, to relocate outside of Chicago. *So I will need Bill to get me even more funds after all, plus I will have to somehow get Stefano out of my hair. Literally.* With a brush of her hand Arlene found some of her locks were crusty and some strands were still sticky when she touched her ginger hair. And some part of that was even from last night. Disgusting — and motivation for her to be furious with Delasandro as much as Urso, though she would have to play nice with both of them for just a little longer if she couldn't count on Taddeo to help her — as was usual.

He'd be late, but she would get him back to Chicago. *"Moderately safe," he says? My ass.* Except it actually was her ass, and Arlene didn't call getting raped being moderately safe. Only now — and by Urso's doing — she realized she had Stefano in place of his brother Corry — to be the one possibly motivated to help her stand up against Greg. Though she would have preferred Corrado since he was motivated by the strength of lust's passion, not the weakness in an adulterer's guilt. But Tad reasoned that even though he hated it that Urso and Stefan had taken her, if they did this at the lounge, at least in the short run, they should have no reason to trace Arlene whenever she disappeared somewhere safer, like the laundry, since other girls like Chastity, Jezebel, May, and Daphne were all more easily available. And Tad also knew that Stefan preferred to be faithful to his wife anyway. Then he stated that Urso wouldn't go out of his way to acquire her so long as he knew she'd consistently arrive to handle all of what he deemed to be her duties at Villetti's. So meanwhile, Arlene could continue to do her best to effectively hide right under Tad's family's noses.

Well, she had things she needed to take care of. She kept it to herself that she didn't feel threatened by Greggorio searching for her. He didn't need to. She now had figured that without a doubt, his strategy was to use her to start a lethal contest between Urso and the youngest Villetti brother, thereby eliminating likely both she and the eldest sibling, or forcing the young men's father to end *her* if she could take Urso, and still wind up destroying the relationship between the pitcher and his patriarch. It was the obvious reason why Greg didn't personally kill her when they left the train station for that drive alone together on Thursday night. If this all went his way, things could only wind up with Greg being the only one able to succeed in taking the reins of The Villetti Family. And he'd look so innocent. Tad might even live through one of the middle brother's deluded scenarios. However, though Greg might suspect she was pregnant, he did not know for sure. The official report from his uncle said that she had the flu. His father had obviously been sick with it, and everyone knew she and Rinaldo shared a bed when he first brought her back to Chicago.

Only that Urso did not know anything about her being with child, might prove to her advantage. He had fucked her. *How would Urso react if she could make him believe the baby was his?* For her great personal humiliation and suffering, another new and unanticipated option could have just been gained. But Arlene would also not allow the middle brother to stop her from gaining control of his lackey Corrado, either. Because she still wouldn't have to risk the baby or Taddeo if she manipulated *him* just right. *And let's not forget that Corry's* brother *has been with me, too*. The next eldest Delasandro brother would absolutely hate learning this truth. Only *his own father* could always confirm she was pregnant, and all *their house* would surely have reason to believe the baby was Stefano's. Unless The Family suddenly developed the kind of communication skills necessary to piece it together that the eldest and most educated Delasandro had discovered her to be with child before his son ever had any sexual contact with her. But Stefan wanted to cover up his indiscretions, so it wasn't likely he'd admit his sins to his father, and then Arlene thought she'd done well to convince his old man it could be advantageous to keep her pregnancy a secret. She definitely wouldn't trouble herself waiting for the day she didn't have to be deceitful. Honesty wasn't a luxury she had any familiarity with. It was a great plan to almost use Greggorio's own strategy against him, only she certainly could not tell Taddeo she was pregnant now, even though she nevertheless still demanded that Tad come back to her — and immediately. She didn't need *him* claiming to be the true father of the baby when she just decided to make everyone else think it was them. But something was telling her she had to hold all knowledge of this back — from everyone, for the moment. Only Dr. Delasandro knew for certain. Would Stefan and Corrado's father keep her secret? She tried to have him believe it would benefit one of his sons if he did. Maybe he'd think it would protect his eldest boy's marriage, at the very least. But surely the pharmacist was thinking she'd implied he was to have a grandson.

That was amusing, but unexpectedly, Arlene's emotional state grew irate with Villetti's youngest son's protestations — the accumulation of all the stress the rest of the Villettis had put her through in the last forty-eight hours no doubt making her lose control of her temper. But she tried her very best not to lose control of her tongue with Taddeo. Only something was wrong with him and he wouldn't share with her what it was. Imagining what she knew the penchant baseball players had for getting into trouble when they were out of town, away from their wives and sweethearts — as if Arlene *wouldn't know* after only a week of being the madam of a brothel — her anger did get the better of her and she roared at him when he suggested he could get Mr. Li to help her quicker because he said there was something else he had to do in Boston, that only he could do, and that it could not wait.

She warned him that changeup he was throwing did little to help him get ahead in the count against his brothers. Both his siblings were suspicious of Li since their visiting him with Johnny Torrio when they'd expected to find Kean O'Rourke hiding at the laundry. She warned him that yes, she finally knew *she* wasn't safe, and she attempted to convince him that she'd overheard that *he wasn't either*. She finally even professed to being grateful to him for his previous tries at protecting Arlene following that with her insistence Taddeo abandon his faith in Mr. Li and return to Chicago and relocate her once more. And to her utter disbelief, Tad wanted to next place his faith with his father. He intended to have his papa, with whom the youngest son figured himself to be back in good graces, order his other sons and his nephews as well — specifically emphasizing Stefano and Corrado — out of the lounge and to permanently stay out. He said he could pitch this to his father because The Family had become disruptive to good business and they had quotas to make to fulfill their role for Madame Moresco and Sigñor Colosimo. Her skimming the earnings could lend credit to that argument. Arlene screamed at Tad that he was blind if he thought his brothers could ever be made to obey their patriarch, let alone the fact that Corrado wasn't the *only* Delasandro who'd become a problem now, and she would handle things by herself from here on if he would not return to Chicago. "Goodbye!" Slamming the earpiece down into the receiver, Arlene cut the connection. She was on her own now. Almost. Except she reminded herself that due to her recent and unfortunate experiences with the Delasandros, she actually had gained a few *new* agents she could now begin to turn. She couldn't have planned for that, *but Greg hadn't either*. But she could not believe that Taddeo would not drop everything at once and race back to Chicago.

Now it having been way too noisy in the lounge, even when Arlene had stretched the cord to the mic stand as far out of the phone alcove in the back wall as she could take it away from Louis Armstrong, she could not have her ear on everything. Her own age, the young and popular performer was visiting Chi-Town for a few weeks that summer. A friend of Joe Oliver's, he was a friend of Old Lamont's, who had somehow convinced Arlene to pay House money for the black Creole Jazz musicians to offer Villetti's an exotic taste of New Orleans in The Windy City. To her, they were noisy and most of the customers preferred Juicy Lucy and what they could sense with their penises versus what they could sense with their ears. And the only thing that mattered to Arlene was the money. Now at least Tad could pay less of theirs to Lamont. A favor for a favor. But if wet pussies were what really soaked up their share of saturation in her coin purse, that was the priority. It was a universal truth that one thing everyone loved more than music, was sex. So she'd spend a little for the band, but she'd work the girls even more to make the cash jingle back to her. Arlene knew she was as guilty of humoring Lamont as was Taddeo. But the visiting Jews who came with the Yankees fans to now go to the White Sox games seemed to like the music at Villetti's, too. So did the visiting leaders of The Mafia, who had also not left Chicago. And now she recognized the cops, working nights — and always out of uniform — who'd begun to really enjoy keeping their eyes on the out-of-towners *and especially* the women, surely hoping the payoffs from the former, would be a source of funds to really enjoy the latter. *Lamont said all this would be important when he cornered me, also asking for favors — and always of a different sort of nature.* Meanwhile, she observed Armstrong seemed to have a lot to discuss with the much older Jews for just a black kid only nineteen years old. But Arlene had to limit her observation of the entertainment scene where it wasn't immediately important to her survival scene — until the Cubs returned on the baseball scene — to think about the whole damned situation using Taddeo's stupid vocabulary terms. *God it is strange that he can be so far away and yet have so much influence upon me. Just get out of my head you stupid imbecile!* She was angry at Tad for disrupting her train of thought like this — along with everything else. And that he could do that from hundreds of miles away. Or had what he'd done already inadvertently made it better? She might yet take charge.

Chapter 41

However, with all the other distractions, she could not detect the click of the earpiece into the receiver stand for the jointly connected line upstairs in Rinaldo's office that his other, most-dangerous son used to listen in to Arlene's conversation with. Greg pondered what he would say to his father, who had already headed home and was probably on Racine by now. Tad would certainly place a phone call to him there. His brother figured he already knew the most basic details of what would keep the pitcher down in Boston's ballpark. So Greg could not wait until morning and then reach out to New York at a more reasonable hour — and on a Sunday morning. Because he had already recruited a couple of The Family members there who would help assist him on Saturday night. And he'd called in that favor through a connection to another connection, this one in Boston, while Arlene spent her nights with Urso now, keeping her from causing any more trouble than she usually did. At the same time, he used that call to help further set his little brother up for trouble — and really well. Though that was suspiciously easy. It made him wonder. But Greg could assume his designs were starting to work beautifully by way of his listening in on the conversations between Tad and Arlene. Now his help he got from Back East had surely succeeded with their role as pinch hitters in the game — and next Boston would refer Tad to The Family in New York. Then Greg could continue with his inspired plan to cause his little brother to fall into his trap to undermine Arlene and further indenture Taddeo to his family, as well as see what information Greg could get about his father's plans from out of his uncles in Brooklyn. He'd anticipated that it would be to them that his papa would steer Taddeo to look for guidance to in the first place. And while his little boy was frustrated, angry with this situation, that the idiot would never guess his own brother could have put him into, as the Tadpole would find himself stuck all alone, and so far away from Chi-Town. Then Greg would be confident he had a way to also quietly inquire into what his father was really up to — and how it could possibly involve not just the Mafia, but the Jews, and even the Klu Klux Klan. The Villettis had relatives on the East Coast and these were insider Family problems that his baby brother now stressed over — and Rinaldo Villetti would surely not want the Chicago baseball organization tied up with *The Klan* coaching clinics on what Taddeo could do next about settling them. He still couldn't figure what his father was doing working with Weeghman. But Greggorio left the lounge with Arlene returning to Stefano's hands and Urso once again fighting off Sega's. That too, was becoming predictable. So Greg located his personal car where he'd parked the basic Model-T over on Miller, and then headed away on a twisting path and into the residential neighborhoods not too far behind his father.

* * * * *

Tad paced back and forth in his hotel room, trying to take in what Trevor had just told him after he'd entered the room as Taddeo was on the phone with Arlene. He wanted so badly to leave the East Coast and run back to Chicago and help his woman. She could feel so very wrong for him and yet he freely admitted to himself that he loved her, so inescapably too much. And it was all too wrong. But, almost every fiber in his being wanted to rush home without resting all night, and all the whole next day, to get to her and help defend her, just as soon as possible. Almost every fiber. Only now it was also only the Cubs' second night out on this road trip — and George Hoffman had gotten himself arrested — and of all things, *for outlaw street racing*. And somehow, without any hearing or trial, he landed himself locked in with the worst of the worst hardened criminals — lifers — all the way across Boston Harbor in Charlestown State Prison. Tad couldn't just abandon his best friend.

"How does this *just happen?"*

"I know. It's like how can you be sent straight to do hard time right in the middle of the night without so much as a hearing and a trial, Taddeo?" Trevor asked of him.

Tad had already intuited the answer. Without any more of an explanation offered to The Bass-Man he said, "Well, trust me. This really can and did just happen. It's not uncommon even back in Chicago. So I think I'd better call my papa."

"Meanwhile, what about The Hoff? There's no women in prison. How is he going to survive?" For a moment they each shared a laugh. Tad needed it in light of how he hated what had happened to Arlene. "But seriously, this is bullshit, Tad. The cops were supposed to be on strike."

"So Trevor: that makes it smart to start something like illegal street racing? In clear view of all Boston Harbor? Well nice going there, George," Taddeo said out loud though Hoffman wasn't there to hear him. "This is just perfect."

"Hey, he had a valid point. Who gets to race formula-one cars down Commonwealth Avenue?"

"Not most people. Or didn't George think there was a reason for that? He always lives not reasoning things out and just blazing through life at record speeds. Now we have to move fast to get him back safely and cover this all up before Coach finds out."

"And meanwhile, Hoff's in danger. There's gangs in prison. Riots. The guards beat the prisoners regularly. This could still get a lot worse."

"Yup. You don't think *I* know this? And meanwhile, who's with him?"

"Trip went down there to stay with him and see if he couldn't get The Hoff out."

"Not at 3rd base, he can't. We have to make sure Hoff doesn't come home — in a box."

"Well in the event Mike messes up *that play*, he thought he could at least get him into protective custody — he being a celebrity and all."

"A celebrity? A third-string catcher? Killefer and O'Farrell are both before Hoff's place in line — which he needs to keep, to improve his defensive rating and his batting average. And this — this really doesn't help his record."

"He's got power."

"Not the kind he'll need tonight. That's why I'm going to have to call my father."

* * * * *

Taddeo reached Sigñor Villetti at their family's domestic residence. His father told him that he'd have to make several phone calls and he took down the information about where he might reach his youngest son at The Buckminster. Greg was on hand to observe all of this go down exactly as he planned it to, but wondered what the hell was so important about that baseball team that his dear elderly papa would even bother. Why does Tadpole always rate the extra privileged treatment? He overheard his father at least pretend to show some skepticism about his brother's idiot friend as being any kind of special priority.

"And who the fuck is this Joe Halstead?

"Oh, *Hoffman*? I see.

"Well, he's not Family, Taddeo. Why can't you associate with a better class of people?

"Yeah? Well, a lot of *gentlemen* are the business' repeat *paying* customers. You don't see me bailing them out, do you?

"Yes, I'm sure being in prison isn't pleasant.

"No. I'm really sure of it.

"Well, that's why I make payments to the cops all the time.

"All right. Fine. You'll have to go across the water in person to pick him up.

"That's the way these things are done, Taddeo. And I'm too tired to count how many favors you'll owe — and your friend Henry as well.

"Right. Hoffman. George *Hoffman*. The catcher. Okay. I got it."

Rinaldo hung up the phone, checked the time, and then took up the receiver off the stand again and spoke into the microphone to the operator who responded. Meanwhile, Greg listened to him call exactly The Family members who he expected his father would reach out to, or leave them a message. He realized he'd been nearly holding his breath, hoping for things to go this well. Then they got even better.

Urso came home and started pacing in circles. Greg learned he'd just had another fight with Sega. He'd had to leave things with her going badly as Greg had phoned and sent a message to his oldest brother that their papa wanted to see them at their immediate family residence right away. Of course it had taken him a while as he first fought with Sega again before he'd even been bothered to leave and obey his father's orders. Their latest tussle was pretty much the only thing on his mind when Urso arrived, and just as Greg predicted, his oldest brother forgot why he came there in the first place. That was fine. He'd lied. Their father had never asked to see Urso.

In the meanwhile, they got a visitor. The taxi Greg had sent for Lumia to fetch her from The Lexington arrived. *Right on time*. Greg introduced her to Urso and they all sat down in the living room. Greggorio said that she was his new girlfriend and they had a late-night evening planned. LuLu just radiated that new and fresh, innocent kind of beauty with all her such welcoming smiles, golden hair and form-fitting little pink evening gown. Greg knew better than to be, but Urso was entranced — just as *he* was supposed to be. Greg loved every part of this interaction as he watched his new girl and Urso communicate. He kept rather quiet, mostly so he could listen in on his papa, and attempt to hear who he contacted from the kitchen phone. When his father finally returned a call to Boston to reconnect with Taddeo, Greggorio was able to ascertain that his little brother would be kept quite busy over there on the East Coast and he wouldn't be able to run back to rescue Arlene anytime soon. With what fate he had designed to befall *her*, any outcome Greg would see result from it, would then drive Taddeo to come back with all the complete fury necessary to attack Urso, and now Stefan as well. Or his father would avenge his first-born if *she* got really lucky, but Greg had curiously seen no evidence that she was ready to take out any of the Villettis, though he could not fathom what she was waiting for. Perhaps the meetings with The Family Back East that he had indirectly forced Taddeo to attend — now that his buddy on his baseball team would require their help, with thanks to a little luck and Greggorio's superb information highway — *I can't believe it was Formula-One Racing* — would also reveal more than just a clue as to what his father was up to in his own schemes with the Easterners that might or might not involve Taddeo and that stupid baseball team. Could Arlene and the Irish also be involved in that? He already suspected he'd observed good evidence that the Jews were.

So after his father made several phone calls and then bid hello to Lumia, perhaps more interested to see if his son had met a future wife to give him grandchildren versus bringing home a saloon girl to the family's private residence, which was a big no-no for Rinaldo Villetti, he announced he was retiring upstairs. *Old man.* Greg sneered after him. *You go on and retire. I could almost care less if your sickness kills you.* And while Greg could hear his father's footfalls and Urso had his full attention on Lumia, the middle brother pretended as if he was answering *another* phone call. No one downstairs was mindful that it had *not* rung again, distracted like he knew this pair would be. After disappearing into the household kitchen for a moment, Greg returned with three glasses and a bottle of wine he'd opened and poured Urso and LuLu drinks. He announced that there was a situation over at the lounge and he needed to leave for a few minutes and take care of it, but suggested "his girl" and Urso enjoy each other's company and in only a short while, he'd be right back. They should save a drink for him. The truth was that he had no intention of coming back. But Urso's next intentions would be easily predictable.

At the bar, Greg found Corrado, who had returned and resumed deciding he could charm Arlene, and he immediately steered his cousin away to come and sit with him so he could began updating Corry on how all his plans were working. He needed his cousin's report on how another part of their plan was going anyway. And Greggorio couldn't help himself, but to also fulfill his need to brag to someone about how smart he thought he'd proved he was. It took a while, but Urso and Lumia finally arrived. Drunk. And just as he planned. Greg was pretty sure that his brother had found more wine at home, to ply LuLu with enough alcohol to the point where they'd no doubt have to come to Villetti's to lift something a little stronger, like his uncle's heroin, and take that with them upstairs. Their papa wouldn't allow them to even experiment with their product, but he wasn't there at this hour, was he? He sent Baldavino over to set his own brother up by giving him the idea and the means in the first place. Greg made sure a room he'd saved specifically for Urso and LuLu, would receive extra stock, which he'd been sending Corrado away for more than twenty-four hours to see to it being prepared at the senior Delasandro's pharmacy, and then delivered to Villetti's. And Arlene had not been needed to get involved with the arrangements for that. Jezebel could be very cooperative when he knew what her price was. But Greg also knew his older brother already dabbled in drugs. Urso was never content or even temporarily very satisfied with his life. He always wandered around with no direction, no vision. Meanwhile, Greg explained to Corry just how predictable Urso's behavior regarding that was. But before his brother could disappear with Lumia upstairs, Greggorio sent Corry on another errand to keep him away from Arlene that Sunday morning — should Corrado get any ideas when Urso wasn't there to make him afraid of trying something — and to rid himself of any witnesses who might have an ulterior motive to resent and then undermine Greg for what he planned on doing. Corry's duty was just to obey orders. He didn't need to understand everything that was happening.

Then Greg followed his older brother and made sure he got into a fight with Urso over the new girl. To her credit that Greggorio had no intention to repay little LuLu for, she *did* protest going to a room with Urso and said she was *the middle brother's* consort. That was sort of flattering, but Greg didn't let himself consider any feeling he could have had about that. Just as predicted, Urso told them both that he was the eldest brother and because of his age, he had done the most for The Family and hence he had a right to take what he wanted. It was Greg's duty to yield to him. Of course Greg really didn't care in the present situation, but he needed to convince everyone else still there that he did, so he put up a good verbal argument and with a little shoving between the brothers for a hopefully convincing display at the very least. He didn't want to take the risk of Urso really hurting him, but his big brother was drunk. And Lumia was also way too inebriated to make any sort of effective protest. She looked to even have arrived barely conscious. Greggorio also noted that Arlene — at the bar, *and Sega*, who had come out of a room upstairs he presumed the latter had been off pouting in — watched his inspired act with great interest. Then Sega took it upon herself to argue with Urso that she was *his* girl, not Lumia nor Arlene, but Lu was not so drunk as to forget to remind her that she'd given the dark-haired woman nearly all the brand-new clothes and jewelry that Sega owned, and that she was her friend, someone who she ought to be grateful to. Greg didn't bother hiding his smile. The dark-haired one almost discovered her foot in her mouth, but Sega knew that if Urso no longer kept *her*, Arlene would force her to work for The House and see all the random gentlemen like May and Sindie and the rest of the girls did. So Sega would not acknowledge her foot or her gratitude, and instead found her fury. But Urso pushed her off just like he had Greg, raising his hand as if threatening to hit her if she persisted to interfere. Sega fell to the floor and looked terrified of the eldest Villetti brother, who had beaten her before, and started crying. Then Urso announced that he and LuLu were off for a great night of pleasures and all of the others should quit being such the buzz-kills and leave them both alone.

Arlene looked wary of all of the goings-on as she observed what she could by then faking some need to leave this night's position for her at the bar, to also go upstairs into Rinaldo's office and record the receipts. She called for Jasmine to take over and inquired if Greg would open that room for her — as if she didn't already have Taddeo's key. However Vitale had somehow gotten it into him that Arlene was now available to The House and acted very insistent that she be his escort to another room upstairs. Greg thought he'd also noticed the associate getting chummy with Thorello and Pepe earlier, but he now made a noticeable effort to distance himself from them. In fact, the former had suspiciously made it back to The House after he'd disappeared the night Simone was killed. Greg had been away on his hunting trip when Thorello had probably returned, but he never had the time, or even remembered to follow-up on getting any information about that. He'd been too distracted with Lumia. Meanwhile, Arlene distracted Vitale from his inconvenient interest in her, by temporarily letting him attempt to earn as the acting bartender in Jasmine's place. Something about that one had more than bothered *her*, but there just wasn't any time for Greg to even think about that. Next she said Jasmine could assist her with the office work and reappeared in front of Greg with this one. As if maybe he wouldn't say 'no' to two of them. *What was that all about?*

Arlene was secretly sympathizing with the slightly older Greek woman, but just so she wouldn't reveal it, she then coldly told Sega to get herself into an unoccupied room and out of the lounge or the stairwell lest she spoil the mood of all the paying customers.

"I *am* paying!" the siren straight out of Hellenistic mythology's reply came back, to haunt the position she had occupied.

Ignoring her, Arlene planned to send Delilah in short order, to bring the hysterical woman "something that would better stabilize her emotions." Jasmine was supposed to assist her good friend with that. This would prevent Vitale from being able to abandon the bar. Never mind what game Taddeo's brother was pitching, she was going to get all the players in this game under her control. Meanwhile, Arlene's ultimate feelings about Sega hadn't changed, though Arlene couldn't *always* bring herself to be merciless. Yet. And this slight insertion of kindness, might slip in through some weak spot in the Greek woman's armor. That too might even carve out an additional advantage for Arlene, in this house of intrigue, maybe later.

But Greg was so sure he had things under his control, that he even lent Arlene his office key. He already intuited exactly how the Greek gal would interpret the situation developing here. And he wanted to test how the leprechaun whore would react. Sega didn't know that he already knew who she really was. In the world they operated in, you could not trust anyone. But with his newest "mistake," now Arlene would have two office keys. And it was important she'd use her access all so perfectly, and exactly like he'd predicted.

So now it was Arlene's turn to put on a performance. She *could* now lock *him* out. But Greggorio had probably made a copy of *his copy* of the copied key that he held in the first place. He was careful, and calculated like that. Meanwhile Sega had picked herself up to storm off, slam the door to her new hermitage, furious as Urso attempted to slam the door to one of the other rooms upstairs, even more loudly, and after he had to test his own patience by carefully leading Lumia by the hand inside the particular resting place he'd chosen — *or Greg had chosen for him* — perhaps as opposed to just picking her up and throwing her in there, which might be more frequently his style. Of course it wasn't time for them to lay to rest yet. He had also brought the drug paraphernalia Greg had sent Baldavino to insist upon the virtues of. No doubt, Urso wouldn't be hard to convince as he clearly wanted any virtues, that might be left inside Lumia. But the middle Villetti son had a lot of balls in the air at once, and yet he found everyone playing their roles in helping him, only to make his juggling act all too easy. Arlene had vowed, and more importantly, strategized, to see that it wasn't.

Concurrently, Greg never forgot that Arlene didn't need to work with the evening totals *in a private room* and shooed her out of his father's office before she could find a way into his papa's gun lockers. He knew she'd been eyeing them as Urso and Stefan had both informed him. For Greggorio, this confirmed it: she was either unarmed, or very low on ammunition. But he would not be making any mistakes the leprechauns' little princess could capitalize on. Deprived of sleep for forty-eight hours, he'd let her make them instead. So Greg took back his own key, and pretended that *he* had something to do in there, as it would keep Arlene from re-entering for the moment with the absent Taddeo's key, he already knew she had. Then he waited until everyone had seen everybody else's business that night until he was finally alone and the hallway was deserted.

Creeping outside the office and listening in at Urso's door, he was admittedly turned on by what he could hear of Lucky LuLu's soft voice calling out "Oh God! Oh God! Fuck me!" in ecstasy after she and Urso likely had enough time to get into the needles and cook some "H." To supply them with enough self-destructive entertainment fast, the room had to be stocked with mash, since there weren't enough already distilled vials for their syringes. Not that it mattered. It sounded like a great way to keep Corrado busy and away from Arlene while he was running supply errands back and forth from his father's pharmacy. And Greg had also thought he'd heard the snap of what was most likely a tourniquet, or probably what he imagined was Urso's big meaty hands on the naked skin of Lumia's perspiring little ass. It did come highly rated. Then the creaking of mattress springs followed. He felt himself grow hard in his pants and yearn for a release from his arousal. It was time to go find Sega. *A girl for a girl, Urso.* But Greg planned to take away far more from both of his brothers than just each of their women.

So next, he did find Sega, crying in one of the other rooms. She certainly seemed genuinely sad, which even enhanced her resemblance to the Villetti boys' mother. Their weak mother who'd made Taddeo the way he was. Greg resented his mama for that, even while he appreciated that her manner in which she raised his youngest brother did make it easier for Greggorio to execute his own plans to dominate The Family. An unintended gift to be sure. He mused on that while he offered Sega a nice shoulder to cry on, the illusion of comfort in a warm embracing hug. And then "an okay" to take from The House's supply of party-favors for their comfort service clients so she could numb away her pain with a little more heroin herself. A relief she would now be desperate enough to try. Only he found that Arlene had sent Jasmine and Delilah to supply her with one initial trial already. The green cunt had fucked him by trying to get one step ahead of him, and make her move to acquire Sega's gratitude and hope for reciprocity, first. *But I can win at this game.*

Days earlier, and for a few extra dollars in Officer Walsh's greedy hands, Greg had confirmed for certain that Sega was potentially a lot of trouble and exactly who's interests she'd originally represented when she arrived at Villetti's. One of his father's competitors had been most ready for whenever the senior Villetti would need a new girl and perhaps give East Chicago, in Indiana, a call. Somebody, probably Detective Conway, even suggested that to Greggorio — and he helped Il Diavalo set that up. Why would the devil not make that deal? He could collect tips as well as increased protection money thinking he got a leg up on Rinaldo — through his own son's betrayal in an exchange for being set up in some better position. Salvatore Cardinella otherwise known as Sam Cardinelli, was the perfect example of an enemy that his papa wanted to keep close anyway — as in a close eye on. Except that the old patriarch hadn't suspected the Mafia-allied enforcer would come at him by offering the hospitality of one of his own women. With his foresight, Greggorio thought it might be otherwise. The Black Hand Bomber who terrorized Little Italy and a lot of Chicago probably followed

Giuseppe Masseria's orders, but even he only played along with New York in order for *that one* to succeed with his own plans to dominate the racketeering industry in The Windy City. To do that, he'd hire Sega first. Then this would-be local mastermind would insert her in The Outfit's Little Italy operations. Only Cardinella didn't own the cops or the politicians. He didn't have close to the amount of money the senior Villetti kept available just for bribes — or the information and material for blackmail, either. However, Greg knew everyone's price and all the information he needed to know — *enough to even set his father up* — several weeks ago while the old man was first returning from New York. Except Greg had now learned from training officer Walsh that the twenty-eight-year-old Sega was a single mother with a son that she kept hidden away in Indiana but did her best to support. So she'd taken Cardinella's job opportunity. She never had much of a choice.

At first it hadn't worked out so well for Greggorio, when his papa called for her to come down from East Chicago, to join The House. Though the middle-son too found it an annoyance that it diverted Urso from an earlier conflict with Tad over his red-haired, homicidal harlot, but Greg had originally plotted to make use of one of The Black Hand's ways of digging a few claws into the backs of certain Family members, before he knew that Arlene would be arriving on the scene. The Irish woman came as much a surprise to him, as his acute awareness and adaptability came as a surprise to her. And Greg knew Sega had grown very angry with Arlene, nine years her junior, who she then blamed for taking Urso away from her *first*, which had started at least some of the new troubles between the Greek woman and his oldest brother — as if there hadn't been enough already. It would only be made worse when as the madam, Arlene ordered her to work more johns once Sega knew Arlene was stealing from the other girls' earnings to keep herself out of "the rotation." It wasn't hard for anyone to figure *this* when Taddeo and his woman moved in to take over control of The Family's bordello business. It was turning into a real cathouse now. When Greg offered her the heroin on the house, Sega even noted that she was grateful because she didn't steal "like someone else around here does." So she *already* knew about Arlene. Truthfully, the other girls might be scared of stealing because Arlene could bust them herself as the drugs cost The House money. The wonderful result being, any of the ladies with an addiction already, paid The Family for their "medicinal supply" out of their own earnings, thereby prolonging their indentured service to repay for their immigration assistance and any costs the Villettis or Colosimo donated on their behalf to The Hull House. The Family always made such generous donations, enhancing both his father's and Colosimo's philanthropic reputations by any praise they could reluctantly get out of Jane Addams' benevolent society.

But Greg knew that now Arlene had to operate on such a narrow budget within which she could commit her larceny while Stefan was double-checking the new madam's record sheets, that she couldn't allow the other women to get away with anything. Greg also knew that his own stepping up could cause Arlene to be thrown into a panic, or she was already feeling one and might *also* be medicating herself. She was certainly smoking more and caught drinking more here and there — but he would wait to really threaten her, until when the time was right. He knew The House's enforcers could especially enjoy it if punishment would be ordered down upon the women. His father offered them kitchen rags. "Pussy" was a slightly stronger motivation. At this moment, and for the rewards she could bestow upon them, the goombahs were ready to serve Arlene's every beck and call should she need them for anything. Greg noted with displeasure, the new madam's being very quick to begin acquiring more power by the favors young men like Pepe and Thorello imagined she could grant them. But now the ladies who were addicted to his uncle Delasandro's chemical brews were already in over their heads. So Greg figured to let Sega bury herself just like all the rest. Then by manipulating the desperately addicted women, he could once more assert control over The House's men as well as Cardinella's agent. *Il Diavolo* could patiently wait to reign hell down upon his papa while money to pay The Black Hand off could still be procured. However, Greggorio would see that The House Villetti would stop hell's fire cold. And this would be accomplished well before Tad returned to Chicago and in perfect synchronicity with Greg's even larger plan of attack. In fact, he could possibly even convince Johnny Torrio to inadvertently sacrifice himself doing just that, and make sure any more blood The Outfit would have to let from itself to accomplish this, wouldn't come from The Villetti House. In the meanwhile, he preferred the young *allegedly* Greek lady drugged for what he needed to do with her next, anyway.

Over an hour later, as Greg had been letting Sega self-medicate even more while he accomplished other work as best he could, distracted by the temptation of sex himself, he emerged from his father's office amongst the rooms over the restaurant. Not all-together unsurprised, he observed Sega quietly shutting one of the other doors, trying to make sure she didn't wake another room's probable occupant — or occupants if all was going well. She now wore only one of Urso's button-down shirts and was reaching under it with a towel she brought up between her legs — probably heading towards the bathroom. The House also had second-story plumbing installed, even while the building was years older than recent architecture like that which was used in The Sisson. He laughed without smiling, noting that even Dulio could have actually made a living in an always-growing city like Chicago. But he was dead now. Only the strongest, most cunning would survive. Not everybody makes it. One fire-crotch with a very nice pair of sexy pink legs had illustrated that.

Now the middle Villetti son could appreciate what Sega exposed of her sexy, darker yet still white-in-tone legs. He felt something in his pants — and his resolve — harden for what good works he had yet to do that Sunday morning. This development didn't really surprise him even for a fine *pair* of reasons. He'd let Sega clean up for a bit while he had to make an effort to check up on his missing backup. The one who was supposed to be his own surprise sort of backup out of Brooklyn. For now, he had been patient and held his own sexual arousal in check. Lumia had satisfied him, though not recently enough. His brothers would be more lucky and have all the fun. For now. Or until now — when it was about time to feel out how lucky it really was to have brought out little LuLu.

* * * * *

With no game on Sunday by way of one of the funny laws they had in Massachusetts, Fred Mitchell wouldn't rise very early to go around and corral his Cubs. He seemed to have all about given up during the course of the night after the fellas thought they'd spotted him at the race and then neatly outmaneuvered him. This afforded Taddeo, along with Trevor and Michael, most of the night — which they'd need — to get George out of prison before their papa bear found out about what had gone down the past evening. The fellas suspected the coach also managed to get himself a girl to play with on the road and wouldn't come around to bother them until at least Sunday afternoon. They were grateful they could sleep in too, but not much later that observance of the Holy Sabbath, since it took so God-damned long to get someone out of the hell that was

Charlestown State Prison.

Getting in there made an impression. He and Trevor didn't get to see even Mikey upon their arrival. Tad thought the huge gray brick fortress with its six-story main house and the surrounding four-story expansion wings behind a solid brick wall perimeter, plus the heavy iron-barred gates that swung away just enough to let the Cubs squeeze through, were probably especially intimidating at night. Any flash of random light, like from when their taxi drove off after leaving them standing at the entry to the prison, or some fearsome lightning that sparked into a startling strike across the black skies, couldn't help but remind Taddeo of the executions in the electric chair that he heard went on in this place. He wished he could be anywhere else at that moment, especially back home, in Chicago, finding comfort with — and trying to find comfort for, Arlene — and proving he could help her through her problems. But he had to rescue his best friend, who might be in the most immediate danger, first. Yes, Taddeo also had his problems.

The teammates were each searched and interviewed before they were reunited with Michael Everston in a bleak, colorless visitors' waiting room. He'd been yet unable to get through to Hoffman and see that the captured catcher was okay. It would be up to Taddeo to record another save. Then three guards appeared to escort the three teammates through more steel doors in more brick walls — the men's keys rattling and making noise as they were bounced about into the prison authorities' nightsticks through dark corridors. One dragged his nightstick across the bricks creating an annoying pinging sound as it bounced into the mortared crevices as they walked to one more guard station. Tad felt as if the walls were closing in on them and this black hole had not only swallowed George up, but might do the same to them as well.

Only Hoff was *certainly* there. He might never even have been placed in a cell, but was seated with several more guards and appearing to entertain them with baseball stories, anecdotes from his minor league career or some of his many adventures with the many random women he'd encountered. Tad might have predicted this — and how angry at his friend it instantly made him. Also seated in the well-lit employee mess room were two other men in handcuffs and prisoner chains that the guards were flicking their cigarette embers at. They were introduced as Sacco and Vanzetti who were suspected anti-government activists and also being held there illegally, Tad was sure, and also never having been even arraigned, of course. The guards said the Boston police had put them all in there on the island 'just for safekeeping.' They'd draw too much of a crowd if they took them down to the city jail. He was supposed to believe that excuse also explained the detention of a Major League Baseball player, too? So Hoff had only just driven a car real fast and then been summarily branded an anarchist? Taddeo thought that then he'd next better make haste to reevaluate his pitching while he was in Beantown. Only now the large, tough, and armed guards — and a lot more of them — surrounded the young athletes. And they were also closing in.

Ignoring any of this, George was so glad to see his teammates, he gave each a bear hug and then invited them to also sit down and pull up a chair to the guards' lunch table so he could finish the latest story he was telling them. Tad was furious and clenched his fists as he endured The Hoff prattle on. But he didn't get to say anything to his best, as well as most-annoying friend. The captain of the guards, a tall and bulky, plus intimidating blonde-haired man, had wanted to have a private word with him, immediately, upon his arrival there.

Tad was going to get to take Hoff home from prison but one thing he could definitely not do, would be to next return to Chicago. He'd have another appointment to keep this road trip, once the team played in New York. Some calls had been made and the young pitcher would be called upon. Taddeo was already anxious about facing the Robins again — and this time on their home turf. This just made him even less enthusiastic about visiting Brooklyn than he already was. But now he owed some important men a favor for them doing George, and thereby him, a favor. That's how this was going to work.

So finally the four friends departed Lynde's Point, Massachusetts that morning, very weary and tired, all except for Hoff. He had to be stopped before he would probably next attempt to build Offenhauser and Miller's engine for The Golden Submarine after he had requested some paper and a pencil with which he could specifically illustrate for the prison guards exactly what the dual intake ports for every one of the car's four-cylindered engine looked like. He'd explained how those would work with dual sparkplugs to make the speed machine run faster and generate some two thousand and nine hundred revolutions per minute so the car could go over one-hundred miles per hour. Hoff stressed that this was both more efficient than a V-8 as well as faster than Hippo Vaughn could pitch. He related what it was like to feel the wind rush through his hair at that speed, and the smell of gasoline, and the blur of the city lights reflected off Boston

Harbor's water. The Hoff suggested he'd now dream of becoming an engineer when he got too old to play baseball. But he was first going to become a legend he proclaimed, stars in his eyes. His friends felt almost annoyed enough to blacken those eyes. Taddeo specifically, felt stressed enough that his impatience generated enough energy to now power that electric chair that he joked to himself, that he'd become tempted to throw The Hoff into, after all. What George was really going to become — was dead — because Taddeo was ready to kill him.

But when they finally got out of there, what Tad really wanted was some quiet time to spend with his private thoughts concerning New York and what would happen next. Although first the team would travel to Philadelphia. And he also really worried about Arlene, though she didn't even know. She'd hung up the phone mad at him the last time he connected a call to her in Chicago. But the Cubs weren't even done hanging it up with the Braves yet. He hoped she would take his call just as soon as there was another opportunity to reach her. However, right now it was apparent that George wasn't done being The Hoff, since as soon as they were leaving, he proclaimed that he wasn't tired and wanted to know what had happened to the girls that the police had forced him to abandon. How Tad longed for an opportunity to reach *him* — when he'd punch George in the face.

The catcher was now going on about how he'd traded two of his girls away to Oldfield for the car ride. And the Boston Police were initially going to charge *him* with auto theft as well as racing, since Oldfield also didn't own the vehicle himself and wasn't supposed to have access to it, let alone be outlaw racing that thing. But he said they had a better deal for him. Of course that was since he also attempted to bribe the cops with some skin — *the other ladies*, he specified.

However, Taddeo figured *his* "better deal" would be to wait for the Villettis to come to his rescue so who — Tad's papa now? — could use this incident to manipulate him. Only why? He wondered if this had anything to do with his father meeting with Colosimo, and maybe even The Mafia, at his game last Saturday in Chicago. But now all this didn't really interest George. He was way too busy wondering if at least two of those girls returned and were waiting for him at the next red brick tower that he'd stay in, which was called The Buckminster, versus prison. *Really Hoff?* Only Tad now had the new problem that freeing his buddy had left him, in what he guessed, was actually Hoffman's true and better deal — because it had left Taddeo in a possibly far, far worse deal.

* * * * *

Arlene had a few girls left from which to choose from as to whom she'd send with the young and rather timid man who showed up to the Villetti establishment next. He was however, still around the age of Tad's oldest brother. She double-checked what her eyes told her as she thought McCormick's little friend Virginia — *Hall was it?* — had actually driven this particular fellow to the lounge, and obviously for its comfort services. Because this young lady was only around the age of one of the youngest of the Delasandros brothers, the leader of the Suffragettes she'd met with was making *some statement* about ladies' independence if she let *that child* drive a Cadillac with wooden boxes strapped to her feet so she could even reach the pedals — and bring this new customer around to a whorehouse of all places. And at Virginia's age? However, Arlene had been that young when Bill Fallon had taught her a thing or two about driving. Only now, through the large front windows, she was sure she had just observed the girl, only a child actually, drive their new customer to Villetti's door. *What was this?*

Upon entering, the new fellow approached the bar and took a little prodding to get to the point that he was interested in meeting another youngster, little Miss Juicy Lucy. However, she was already booked entertaining another gentleman from New York for the evening, being as how the Yankees were still in town for their series against the White Sox. Sega was now preoccupied with Greg, as Urso was with that new woman, *Lumia*, she recollected the bleach-blonde lady was to be called. So Arlene chose Delilah to be a good fit to work with this fellow, as she was a bit younger than her customer. And he wasn't really that young — probably the same age as Urso — however this fella was younger than Villetti's average client. And he came very early on a Sunday morning. *So he could relieve himself before he relieved his guilt at church?*

As if that wasn't interesting enough, Virginia Hall had parked McCormick's car and came into the bar and ordered a shot of whiskey, then double-downed her drink. A twelve year old? Really? That was not cute. But she had the right coins. Then as Arlene turned around for only a second, the child was gone. Though her money she left on the bar proved the young madam had not only imagined her. And there was a little extra in the change, that Arlene would afterwards figure was presumably so she would tolerate the girl's presence, as she kept reappearing every once in a while, on through the night. Arlene thought that she herself could enjoy something or another to medicate herself since she too had to work in that place.

So Arlene was cleaning some glasses behind the bar, having relieved Gino, who'd been procured by Vitale allegedly to help the former learn how to tend the bar. *Why was that necessary? Was The Family planning to replace the ladies who the customers preferred to see across the bar top from them?* And it was when she asked herself this question, that the alarming reason found her as to why all the other seemingly random events of this night were so important. It was fortunately after other rather embarrassing events occurred that could have harmed the lounge's reputation and impacted Arlene's income by way of different actions that she could have taken. The new madam had been kept quite busy for a good duration first, constantly adapting on the run, unable to sort it all out until later. Fortunately, she was extremely successful at handling what she'd had to handle — as she was forced to work absent of any rest, while under these circumstances, agreeable to making what she deemed careful use of a little cocaine. Lucy managed to be able to procure a lot of things when she put her back into it. But this also demonstrated she might be entrusted with keeping other secrets from The House if Arlene needed her to.

Sega had already gotten into a fight with this new girl Lumia who Urso — instead of Greg — had brought in Saturday night and taken upstairs with him. There were plenty of witnesses. They were all there when that one, *next overdosed on "H,"* causing one hell of a lot of screaming. Arlene wouldn't have minded Urso relinquishing any of the attention he'd paid *her*, but the young madam would have even preferred to trouble herself with entertaining the currently-present, senior Villetti bastard, over what she had to trouble herself with handling next.

When Arlene had moved to find out what the hell was going on, and at once started controlling the situation for the benefit of the other guests of The House, she'd next gotten into a fight with Greggorio, who would not let her call the unfortunate young lady an ambulance. *Why was* he *still here? Did he ever sleep? Could he even show* any *appreciation for what she had just done?* Arlene didn't have time to figure it all out then, as Lumia could have died, choking on her own vomit — or her sudden loss of blood pressure — while waiting for Dr. Ronga, the favored Family practitioner who was ardently insisted upon. Likely the only one who'd be unafraid, Arlene had been first to crash into Urso's room, inexplicably compelled to save a life — only perhaps because she had already taken so many. Turning Lumia so she managed to even keep breathing, Arlene raised her voice to hurry and recruit help easing the girl onto the floor, and screamed for assistance moving away the furnishings *this overdose* could hurt herself upon, while flailing about in such total shock to the drugs in her system. Many there on Villetti's staff did try to help, and the ladies ran to offer assistance, the straps and other loose trappings of — and from under their lingerie, flying like streamers behind them. Gino and Vitale jumped in on the scene at the same time, anxiously anticipating the arrival of The House's preferred doctor. But he made it into The House's chaotic arena shortly, and stabilized little Lucky "LuLu," though Arlene's assistance with that would be overlooked in any official account of the incident, when Greg reported the survivor's "entertainment name" to the doctor. Ronga assessed the new girl, then sent Vitale for bags of intravenous fluids, an errand which for the goombah was even allowed to borrow Greggorio's car to return with. That of course cost The House a tidy sum of money.

"What's the matter with you?" Greg had yelled at Arlene, in probably only the second time she'd ever seen him lose his temper — the first also being that same night when he got into another fight — which wasn't a fight — with his big brother over Lumia. The Irish woman had seen through that charade. But this was real. What was this all about? Now Sega had also been in the eldest brother's room trying to calm Urso down after apparently he'd tried to get both women so high that the pair of them would end up in bed with the eldest Villetti brother. *Naturally. That would be what Urso does.* Maybe he'd even succeeded. However, *he* was now so satisfied — and drugged — that he fell asleep with Sega screaming at him and slept through all that went on now. But Greg had been going on, his new anger directed at Arlene, while he sent the Greek girl away from all of them. "We don't *ever* call an ambulance down here to our business! That's just not done. It brings a lot of unwanted attention to our little operation. I don't want Conway's people here."

"Lumia could have died. Or don't you care?"

"I do care. That one has a great ass. She could make The House plenty of money. I'd figure that's all that you'd care about as well, given your position."

"That's *our* financial position. And we'd have to contend with business falling off from any more bad press. And also, what if someone comes looking for her? From Back East?"

"I've already taken care of all your concerns."

"Oh I'm sure. You're just such the expert in fixing things in that area, aren't you?"

"Why are you worried? Sometimes the girls die. Overdoses happen. We take care of it. There's a price for being in this business. But there's plenty of room left in the river. And I thought that was your area of experience?"

Arlene didn't miss a beat. "Well, I'm saving *a few extra special places*, Greggorio."

"Yeah. I bet you are. Just keep Rose in a place out of the sight of Doctor Ronga for the next couple of hours that he has to spend here," he then said in a tone only slightly over a whisper.

"Why?" Arlene demanded. She did not speak so softly.

"Let's just say the night still has more ways in which it can go wrong if the doc finds out his daughter is a sex addict and has been working *here*. He thinks she's still in Texas at school or something." He glanced down the hall toward the room where the doctor worked on an IV drip for who even *he* would unwittingly call Lucky LuLu, a name she'd no doubt already earned for several more reasons, and it was also where Urso lay content and totally unaware of everything else that went on around him. Naturally.

"And what about a mutual friend of ours in Massachusetts? What is going on with *him?"*

"Why ask me? Or are you only now doing so because you need my little brother's help running this business? But you won't swallow your pride and ask. You and he aren't speaking? Is that it? Did you go and say something stupid? I already knew you wouldn't be up for this task."

He trapped her, because Arlene either admitted to incompetence, or that she was indeed still pining after Taddeo when she knew Greg thought she'd dumped his sibling. And it would be good if he continued thinking this, so that he couldn't use any threats made toward Tad as ammunition against her. She decided risking being charged with incompetence was better than playing this game and risking Tad's life, or at least his being made further fearful and thus distracted, while he was doing whatever he really was doing out there in Massachusetts. But whatever Greggorio meant by what he told McCormick about his little brother being taught some lessons on his trip Back East, the middle brother was not being forthcoming with her. She now might really want to reconsider taking a phone call from her favorite idiot. Just to hear he was okay. But she didn't even need to admit to any incompetence to see that Greggorio was already dismissing, and with his cousins, encroaching on any authority she might have ever held at The Family's bordello.

Arlene almost wished her life was as simple as some of the young women that just came to Villetti's to work and die there. *Wait. That was my original plan as well wasn't it? Well, what's wrong if Roslyn actually* enjoys *what she's doing? Or can't a woman even do that?* She thought she wished she could, as Arlene next busied herself making sure no one encountered anyone that they shouldn't, by setting up shop and doing her paperwork sitting on the ratty carpeting laid out on the upstairs hallway's floor while, watching every room and listening to one couple after another frolicking in their fantasies, packaged and paid for. It almost elicited in her a desire for Taddeo to have already returned to her, for some of his recreation time, save for her being furious with him for not jumping to get back to her from Massachusetts now that she really needed him. But it was hard to ignore all the screaming and angry smacking of flesh against flesh coming from the room occupied by his oldest brother Urso — and Sega of course. She had traversed down the hallway *again* while Arlene was arguing with Greg to go back to Urso and bring *him* back to reality to scream at him some more while Dr. Ronga also had to work in the same damned room to save little LuLu's life. Now *they* were fucking and making up. Could that be what it would eventually be like for her and Taddeo? The appeal of her fantasy where they actually were a couple, staying in Chicago, raising their child — *after she took care of her business for being there* — and then running The Family business, began to rapidly lose its appeal. Meanwhile, Greg wouldn't have any further part in the events presently unfolding, or he was afraid of another confrontation with Urso actually getting dangerously physical for him, while Sega emerged several times, naked, looking bruised, and clutching bedsheets around her until she thought of something else to say and went back into the ongoing fight — looking for even more abuse. Her priorities were just never going to align with Arlene's. So she had Jasmine tending the bar downstairs, and now half-training Gino, while Vitale ran Dr. Ronga's errands, though Villetti's was theoretically closed for the evening now, but under the directive to stay staffed "just in case" someone came in to the lounge looking for more than a nightcap. The temperance movement could put more and more regulations on drinking hole hours of operation, but had nothing on the prostitution business, because that was already outlawed anyway. At last, Greg brought Tancredo in for security when he'd left and then came back upstairs to render assistance — deciding to do that by taking Sega back to the room he'd originally reserved for her that evening and making use of her. Arlene noted he'd been pretty worked up by all the extra activity that had been going on upstairs in The House that busy evening, just as she had. And Arlene still so wished she could have Taddeo there — or at least time for a bath. But that's when Urso finally passed out again, and remained that way — quiet when he found some sleep. Dr. Ronga stayed to allegedly monitor LuLu's recovery, but requested more assistance that Vitale couldn't satisfy. Arlene sent him Daphne.

But Jasmine, the petite brunette-haired girl in the high heels and sparkly green romper, called Arlene downstairs as just one more unexpected event occurred. An older man, but similarly featured to the boy she had assigned Delilah's services to — they both having a long sharp nose in common — came in almost an hour and a half after Dr. Ronga's supplies had arrived; the physician now being aided by Vico and Ignacio, and who still continued to minister some kind of treatment to LuLu in just another one of the most-busy rooms in the Villettis' bordello. It had already been a hell of a long night, as the lounge had suddenly seemed to almost transform into a circus, seeing a huge increase in traffic in very short order, quite later than had been usual, and right after Taddeo had left town. Arlene knew that those two events *could not possibly be related*. Right? Even though New York was still there, the Yankees' series at Comiskey Park would be concluding, as there was no barring of Sunday game play in Chicago. But she had been left at a loss to explain all the rest of the games that now went on in Chi-Town. However, this new fellow who visited the lounge looked familiar somehow. First Arlene remembered he wasn't that new and had visited the establishment at least several times in the recent past, *and she had seen him while she had only been at Villetti's for a couple of weeks by this point*. Which was when her memory recognized Chicago's Representative in the United States Congress, James Mann, from his illustrated picture in the newspaper — the author of the anti-prostitution legislation himself. Naturally. He too had even asked for Delilah. It turned out to be a case of "like father, like son." And he was allegedly only looking for this son, in fact. He stated that as being his reason for being there in the first place to save all that was Christian and holy in his youth — and yet using the same breath he proclaimed what he valued. He asked for Delilah with it. Though with the discretion Villetti's was famous for, Arlene denied having seen anyone fitting Mann's description of his boy. Nor did she proclaim her judgement of him. *But his son must have been the young man little Virginia drove over there that evening.* Only then the Congressman feigned he desired to move on and continue his search for the missing youth, but he had only *suddenly decided* that it was really late and that perhaps he "could afford to stay – just to rest a while." With that excuse, the epitome of the Christian values conservative said he'd patronize her business only because she'd been so kind — and made him feel just so comfortable. And it was the right thing to do. Then *The Honorable* James Mann took a room with Rose, who was "only needed to show him to his accommodation," of course. And of course, that's why he paid a little extra for that room — for "any inconvenience his last-minute arrangements without a reservation could have caused The House or its staffing." But the young madam avoided just one more inconvenience by fulfilling her order to keep *that young woman* out of Roslyn's papa's sight.

Yet Arlene had also long ago decided that she'd seen enough and *nobody* had paid enough. There was a bill to come due and she hadn't made her big move to collect it yet — by way of The House's assets forfeiture coming about in *her*, one sudden, glorious blaze of destruction. Only this moment found her doing everything she could to keep things for The House intact, quiet — and with quite the finesse, she thought. Everything began changing onto the exact opposite course Arlene had originally planned to see things go down. And altogether, she wasn't sure that was such a bad thing. But very soon that would get to be a very expensive thing. Her personal services were going to cost a lot. She herself had been repeatedly raped and abused. That was what she called the "sex" that Urso forcibly coerced, though she didn't count the sex with Stefano that *she* had *actively encouraged* to occur. Arlene filed that as her insurance payment. Still, when she appealed to Greg, he actually told her that she deserved so much *worse* — than even what had already come to her. And that what she really was, would be a murderer, who only by the gross miscalculation of his father, was able to fanagle her position from that of just a whore, to where she actually got to parade around masquerading as The House's operating manager. He said Arlene was just lucky that his old man didn't want to waste any more resources after revealing the evidence the senior Villetti had, that could prove exactly all of what *she* was guilty of. The patriarch merely had no remaining tolerance for Detective Conway continuing any more investigations around his place. So there wasn't any short-term plan for Dulio's body to turn up, that she had to worry about. But Greg warned the Irish woman that her time was coming and that she was definitely going to get all her earnings from everything that she had to account for. Though he said he wasn't ready to touch her himself, he'd be happy to alter the situation if Arlene would just try something — anything. Only she knew better than to let herself be recklessly provoked. Still, she was pretty provoked.

But there were some things the young killer even admitted to herself, were her fault. And there were several she wasn't so proud of. So Arlene knew she had to find McCormick and retrieve her gun, or get into Rinaldo's office and make use of one of his. Only there was one other option — Tad's gun. It should be safe where he hid it back at the laundry — and perhaps even forgotten by the other players in this game while the pitcher was off playing in his. They might not be expecting that. And then as Arlene recollected all her conversations with Mrs. McCormick, and Virginia Hall's appearances running around — and snapping pictures during all the night's crises — a lot of these new developments began to look less and less like coincidences. Arlene found she had a growing deficit of knowledge and the ever-more-determined woman had plenty of debts owed her, that she would now have to catch up being paid on. And much to her greatest surprise, Arlene had such a growing deficit of sleep, that she could not wait to get away so she could visit a Chinese laundry in the middle of the night.

Chapter 42

The next dawn had broken with Greg placing more calls to New York on a Sunday, while he made sure that his cousins Baldavino and Carlo were going to follow Arlene. He hadn't slept again because now he had put yet another plan into motion, and he was concerned that he'd caught the Irish woman meeting with their brother Corrado no sooner than he drove her back from Union Depot on Thursday. Greg had noted that Corry could be all too easy for Arlene to get to, since his interest in her had already been discovered since the first day he ever laid eyes on the bitch. And it remained in spite of her illness he'd witnessed befall her since then, for which he had much reason to worry wasn't an illness in the first place. *So now how was her respone going to affect what* he *was up to?* It was *the* operative question. The past Friday night was already testing the limits of what everyone could handle. Taddeo was away so she'd be more stressed and could act out more impulsively — which was why Arlene could then turn to recruiting Corrado — Greg's closest conspirator and blood cousin. So now Greggorio stressed to the younger Delasandro boys that *two grown men* tailing Arlene had been already sent to their deaths by that crimson-locked killer, so they did not ever want to get caught following her. Also, Greg worried if the hot-headed, egotistical Davino and his brother messed up and *didn't* get themselves murdered, but either somehow got the drop on Arlene, or they had to be lethally and posthumously avenged by their big brother Stefano, Tad could come after *their family* instead of Urso. That would do little to help Greg's machinations. Plus to start with, he'd begun worrying a lot about keeping Corrado obedient as it were. He wasn't sure what had gone down between his closest cousin and that Irish witch. What could she have brewing? And what could she really be hiding by withholding the results of her medical examination by his Uncle Abramo? Greg also hadn't gotten any information he needed out of his aunt's husband, either. What could *she* have to hold over the patriarch of the Delasandros?

But it was past time for the next phase of his primary plan. His own little brother's relationship with Arlene was vulnerable while assets forfeiture coming about in *her*, one sudden, glorious blaze of destruction. Only she was doing everything she could to keep things for The House intact, quiet — and with quite the finesse, she thought. Everything was changing onto the exact opposite course Arlene had originally planned to see things go down. And altogether, she wasn't sure that was such a bad thing. But very soon that would get to be a very expensive thing. Her personal services were going to cost a lot. She herself had been repeatedly raped and abused. That was what she called the "sex" that Urso forcibly coerced, but she didn't count the sex with Stefano that *she* had *actively encouraged* to occur. Still, when she appealed to Greg, he actually told her that she deserved so much *worse* than what had already come to her — that what she really was, would be a murderer who got to masquerade as one of the finest house's respected managers. He said Arlene was just lucky that his father didn't want to waste any more resources proving it, for fear Conway's investigation would blow back on him. But Greg warned the Irish woman that her time was coming and that she definitely earned all she would get. He said he wasn't ready to touch her himself, though he'd be happy to alter the situation if Arlene would just try something — anything. Only she knew better than to let herself be recklessly provoked. Still, she was pretty provoked.

But there were some things the young killer even admitted to herself, were her fault. And there were several she wasn't so proud of. So Arlene knew she had to find McCormick and retrieve her gun, or get into Rinaldo's office and make use of one of his. Only there was one other option — Tad's gun. It should be safe where he hid it back at the laundry — and perhaps even forgotten by the other players in this game while the pitcher was off playing in his. They might not be expecting that. And then as Arlene recollected all her conversations with Mrs. McCormick, and Virginia Hall's appearances running around — and snapping pictures during all the night's crises — a lot of these new developments began to look less and less like coincidences. Arlene found she had a growing deficit of knowledge and the ever-more-determined woman had plenty of debts owed her that she would now have to catch up being paid on. And much to her greatest surprise, Arlene had such a growing deficit of sleep, that she could not wait to get away so she could visit a Chinese laundry in the middle of the night.

distressed and he needed to split those two even further apart so Taddeo might just come back to *him* — his own big brother — for advice, instead of that red-headed bitch that controlled him with her twisted little green cunt. Wouldn't that be just so ironic? He'd already tried to show his little brother that *he* would protect him from Urso, but he couldn't be sure that lesson sunk in. Now Arlene, who had just *and finally* pushed Taddeo away, definitely sought to get him back or she wouldn't be asking questions about him. But Greg and his papa had inadvertenty combined efforts to keep the Tadpole very busy on the East Coast, as if baseball couldn't do that alone. Though Greggorio didn't understand his father's motivations either, *yet*. Only he would suggest that he did — and just enough— to tease his little brother that he possessed the information that the rookie should want. This might buy the naïve Taddeo's allegiance if he felt his woman had abandoned him. No real matter, because on the hunting trip, the way Tad behaved over the mother bear reassured Greg of *what he wanted to make certain he knew about his brother* — of exactly how he'd react if something happened to Arlene, even if he was no longer able to trust and ally himself with her: he'd first become paralyzed, unable to take action. She was a conduit for him to gather his own power with increasing confidence, but Greg now had to make sure she couldn't supply it, or especially misdirect it — in life or even in the event of her death. Tad was too weak to stand on his own and he'd turn to someone else for something — comfort like he had with Sega — until it was past the time for when he'd have to act. But *he* would then only weakly act to defend what he felt was right. Greg could then suggest to Tad the appropriate course of action, possibly convincing him to take that action if Greggorio was careful to make sure his brother didn't thoroughly hate Arlene like he could easily have always hated Urso. Then he could turn Tad on Urso. This was probably what the little leprechaun princess wanted to manage anyway. And it was also way past time for "the new madam" to act like she'd learned that she didn't manage *any* part of Villetti's. However, Greg knew that she *would* fight to gain a stronger position. Arlene represented a very dangerous threat, and likely only the tip of the Irish blade that O'Banion or Weiss wanted to see plunged into the Italians' hearts.

For that reason, he had inspired new pawns to follow her, backed that plan up the same way Corrado had smartly done several times before with a particular eager volunteer, and had already also brought in Greggorio's own new kind of "special agent" from New York to

Chicago. Namely Lumia. And she was still alive — for now — plus all she had to do was lie around naked and remain breathing in order to accomplish her job. To the best of Greg's knowledge, Urso still kept her in a room with him upstairs after Dr. Ronga had revived her. And the latest time this occurred was probably only five minutes ago. Lucky LuLu was quite literally very lucky again, and he too, since she was literally a sleeper agent on Greggorio Villetti's roster, for now. But so had he made Sega. The House's drugs ran through all their veins straight ahead of the blood that he'd spill out from all of them, as the newly rising boss took control of all intravenous lines. And now one agent in particular was about ready for her new operation. Greg smiled to himself. Once in a while, he would enjoy the process besides enjoying the achievement of his desired results.

Chapter 43

So, in concert with the new plan now developing at Villetti's, Mr. Li didn't recognize Baldavino and his younger brother Carlo Delasandro acting as Greggorio Villetti's agents when they entered the Chinaman's laundry later that Sunday morning. They were clean-cut, dark-haired good all-American boys, dressed in fine suits that a man in the clothing business would recognize, but their faces all looked alike to the Asian man. He was regularly open for business seven days a week inside the Maxwell Street Market. Therefore, he would often see new faces, and thought that the youths were customers. Then he noticed they carried nothing that he could service on their persons.

However, a rather inconvenient mistake made by Taddeo Villetti half a week ago could have brought these fellas down upon him — even before they had more than likely followed Arlene, discovering the laundry as *her* destination. He had his doubts about that woman staying with him, and Mr. Li just knew something bad was going to happen, one way or another. It didn't matter whose fault it was now. But Taddeo reasoned likewise, since he'd left money and instructions for Mr. Li, already anticipating the event. The proprietor had warned the athlete to not get caught doing the cleaning. The Villetti boy must have kept with him at least two of the freshened uniforms for he and his buddy from among all those he took his team to change into. No doubt young Taddeo wanted to make a demonstration of his dedication to in-kind reciprocity since it was his fellow ballplayer that was helping him to get around with all their bulky order for the entire rest of the Chicago team. But they could have been seen by any attentive sports fan at Villetti's. And Mr. Li was already familiar with the youth's brothers, and how they operated. It didn't take a mastermind to figure that the young athletes might have changed at the restaurant if their errands would be cause to making them late for their pre-game warm-up exercises the other week — the end of their May home-stand. They wouldn't want to get caught changing in the Cubs' locker room and could instead pretend to their coach that they had already been there, working on practicing something, somewhere. But for practicing this kind of slip up was exactly why Mr. Li would not hire the Villetti boy to practice working there, at his laundry, like the young man had wanted in the first place. Mr. Li did not need this kind of attention drawn down upon his business.

He had other priorities though, for which the old man had decided he could take some risk. The red-haired Irish woman was more careful anyway. Until now. But he had been the one to decide he'd take the risk. And there was money in it for him, as well as other motivations. However, because the younger Delasandros had now discovered something even more important that the proprietor had wanted to hide — *that Mr. Li had a daughter* — he just started feeling like it *definitely* had *not* been worth it at all. Exactly as he'd predicted, the young goombahs from The Villetti House now used poor Zhen's continued well-being to threaten him. They suggested that the thirteen year-old girl might be able to be of service their own brother Tito, who was about her age. But while horrified of specifically what he'd never wanted to let happen — what her discovery could mean for his child — Mr. Li also still felt honor-bound and stayed committed to not giving up any information about Arlene. He should not have been greedy for Villetti's money. Not that the cash was really the reason.

However, the Delasandro boys could not locate *the athlete's woman* when they searched the place, and even after they explained that they were sure she'd been followed there — with another professional's help. Instead of finding her, they had unfortunately seen Zhen Li. But they warned her father that he did not want to meet this other man who now waited outside and that they also now knew that the Irish madam stayed with him. They had seen the old mattress on the large walk-in storage room's floor, and informed the proprietor that now they would most certainly have to come back.

Mr. Li had seen fear on his daughter's face when she was caught for just being curious about the young men and had spied on these visitors during their confrontation with her father. And now Mr. Li's own face was turning red since this was the one area of concern where his emotions could get the better of him. He was normally a relaxed and coldly calculating man of deep reason. But Zhen had quickly disappeared as soon as she was discovered, swiftly relocated by Baldavino and his brother, and then forcibly brought back out so the Li family's visitors could now most seriously confront her elder. But then the girl turned and even ran again, with Carlo Delasandro repeatedly quite interested in where she'd went. However, that interest wavered when Baldavino's second search of the place he'd deemed wise, had by chance come up with a very familiar Smith & Wesson. Mr. Li had hoped they wouldn't find that, and gathered from their conversation, that to the boys, the weapon certainly looked like one of their first cousin Greggorio Villetti's cheaper guns with the muzzle nearly filed off, for close-range assassination. The Villetti Family's middle son liked them that way. But their cousin didn't shoot much — as the Delasandro boys related out loud and to each other, that they'd never heard he'd even killed anyone for certain — and Davino preferred to carry his own Castilli Bodeo. It mattered to his sense of Italian pride or something. But the good fellows explained they'd heard one of the .38s had been delivered to Greg's *brother* by their own older brother Corry, while the pitcher and Arlene were staying at The Sisson. The Delasandros were apparently now retrieving that gun. And they were not happy that Mr. Li was caught playing coy at the least, regarding his recent interactions with Taddeo along with their cousin's woman.

And that's when Arlene did decide to appear. She knew she was making her mistake when she did it, but she could not allow little Zhen to fall into the same fate that had been dealt to her and all of the other girls who were forced to work at the Villettis' bordello. She could distract the Delasandros from searching the place again to find the young Miss Li and reacquire her for only the third time. But did she ever wish they hadn't uncovered that other gun! She'd just arrived to retrieve it but had only decided to make a telephone call from a different location first. And then, as disconcerting as it was to Arlene, she learned that Vitale had gone with the younger boys and it was he who had actually, and successfully, followed her. She had been careless because she was so overtired and so desperately wanting a weapon — any weapon. So, on this Sunday morning, she'd rushed to retrieve one since Katherine McCormick had relieved Arlene of her .45 for some yet-to-be-known reason. And now it was all Arlene's own fault that Mr. Li's once-secretly hidden daughter had now also been put into jeopardy. Arlene silently scolded herself for being so careless that she'd let all the previous nights' goings on wear her out to the point where she'd gotten so sloppy that she underestimated The House only by her assessment of The Family members, and then didn't effectively check for and subsequently lose any other tails — other associates. Somehow, this Vitale had remained undetected by her sonar, but had also remained hidden — in plain sight.

Now she didn't have to try and protect Zhen Li, and she wished she could avoid feeling the way she did about it, but Arlene cared. For some reason that escaped her, she cared. She would do right by someone. But she did it all the while knowing it was the wrong move for an agent such as herself. Yet that was just who she was. She cared about the innocent like she cared about her own unborn baby.

Then to Arlene, Davino passed along the additional great news that since Taddeo was out of town, and the other, older cousin seemed interested to now, always be close around, that he could protect the establishment, and she would have no use for the .38. *Because Urso is so competent? Yeah. Right. Or did they mean Greg? Now what was* he *up to, scheming by using these boys?*

The Delasandros emphasized that point while "the boys" — for they could barely be called young men — looked Arlene over up and down and they really liked what their leering eyes were leering at now. She wished she'd gotten to leave Villetti's at her highest status of alertness and with enough time to have retrieved the Smith & Wesson. Things might have gone differently. That gun still had six bullets. Well, she did leave in order to allow herself enough time, Arlene reminded herself. Only after all the situations she had to handle, back at the bordello, Arlene emotionally broke down and she had to talk to Taddeo. But her next attempt to sort things out with him while he was in Boston, had not gone so well, either. And this time she had to make sure her communication was private, and not surrender any more information to her enemies. Now she would certainly owe Vitale some payback for following her, amongst any other new plans she began to formulate. Obviously, most of the previous ones hadn't gone right thus far. But Arlene had never been very lucky with her fate. Though if she had gotten the gun before she made the phone call, what was she going to do with it? Shoot Baldavino and Carlo? Where would that get her? And what would she do if she had to handle Vitale next? He was a professional it seemed — maybe too professional for The House — which was quite suspicious. And he'd be forewarned that he was confronting an active shooter, in her. Things at the lounge were getting way too crazy. She'd tried and failed to get into Rinaldo's gun collection that he kept locked up over there. But really only as an act so they might never suspect *she* had Tad's new .38. Only now with her failure at the laundry she was completely disarmed. Or was she? Her quick and resourceful mind would not ever let her become despondent. She just needed some more time to readapt her own plans.

But then the younger Delasandros left her alone, at least temporarily still too intimidated by her, or some very subtle delicacy offered by Mr. Li to suggest there was plenty of danger *to them* if they made any move to subjugate Zhen — or Arlene — any further that morning, as they so obviously wished to. Yet they did not leave without reminding Mr. Li that they had plans to come back, maybe with "more friends" — and be properly introduced to Zhen. It did not appear like they would stay intimidated by some old Chinese man — or that the Delasandros held any respect or — dare she say affection for him — as the Villetti brothers might have. As the youngest brother certainly did. So Arlene phoned Taddeo in Boston again. She couldn't reach him even on a Massachusetts Sunday morning? Where could he possibly be? And even for Taddeo, how late could he possibly sleep? Or how mad *at her* could he now be? The relief pitcher was apparently still worth another middle-inning trial until she could close this game. Some part of her desperately needed to hear his voice.

The front desk of the team's Boston hotel they'd stayed at had orders not to disturb the pitcher — as Tad had apparently been out all night. Arlene was furious and called back enough times until the Buckminster's clerk was tired enough from hearing her voice, that he personally went upstairs to Taddeo's room where he knocked lightly, waking Trip, Trevor Bass, and Taddeo, who'd slept on the floor, since Hoff asked him to so he could have a room — even with double beds — all to himself, for the rookie catcher and *a pair* of whores. He'd asked for the favor "since prison life had been so hard on him." For all of the three hundred and sixty minutes he might have spent there — but didn't even spend behind bars. The boys had reluctantly complied with their former minor league team captain just as Tad reluctantly went with the bellhop downstairs to let his friends sleep in some more by leaving their room to keep it quiet. He'd call Chicago and predictably get into one more fight with Arlene where she stayed at the laundry, but from the phone in his hotel's lobby. Taddeo already didn't plan on that going very well — he was on fire with anger in the first place. This time he could've actually described what he felt as pure rage — and with Hoffman, his own best friend. Had he not been in serious danger, Tad might have ran all the way back to Chicago to be there for Arlene in a heartbeat — only he didn't. He couldn't. And now he was stuck owing someone else from

The Family a favor — *another* appointment he'd have to keep. But Hoff was never in real danger or even going to be harmed, unless of course Tad had a mind to do it — and now Taddeo had to listen to his woman bitch at him over how he didn't even care about *her troubles* when nothing could be further from the truth. But there was no pleasing her and he braced himself for the fight while the connection with Chi-Town was made. And when he could finally return, he'd make a connection with his brothers all right. Yes, he'd make sure that he'd connect with *them*, Taddeo Villetti vowed.

Next, and over the phone, his woman told him that Baldavino and Carlo had found her at the laundry where the dirt came in, piled on. That they'd all-but-threatened Zhen Li with initiating the thirteen-year-old girl into The House — in the worst way. And Arlene exaggerated this even more so because she thought it would help her case than because she cared about the woman, when she told Taddeo how Urso had tortured Sega. Arlene *lied* that Urso and Stefan also continued to abuse her as well — though Urso might not be through with her in reality, once he'd had enough of LuLu or her luck ran out and Taddeo's brother's ministrations or that doctor killed the girl first. Tad didn't need to know about her, as Arlene wanted to keep him focused on everything he was already familiar with, going wrong, about right now, back in Chi-Town.

Greg had conveniently disappeared with Sega, as best as she could tell, though Arlene would continue not to really care about that. It might have hurt her income potential by being a possible good little worker down, but the distraction of Sega, and the new little, ditzy bimbo Lumia, did keep both the Villetti brothers away from the Irish woman for maybe more than a day, and maybe at least one good night. Arlene was supposed to be correcting any discrepancies with The House's books anyway. Stefano Delasandro said he had other things to attend to and he trusted her, but what he really meant was that he didn't trust himself *with her* and thought it best that he be with his wife. Sadly, Arlene could control him but worried about his brother. Now Corry appeared to be being prepared to be sent away by Greg on some sort of assignment that required him to travel — some distance too. He was always being kept busy. Maybe deliberately to keep Corrado away from her.

But what Arlene related to her infuriating little paramour out in Boston was that she felt so emotionally distraught, that she even thought about killing herself. This was almost true. She needed

Taddeo back in Chicago. She needed him to show he cared. What she also didn't mention was that in fact, Stefan had caught their skim but felt that what he witnessed happen to the girls now was so wrong that he'd astounded Arlene by letting that slide should she turn that money around and put it to good use helping the other ladies as well as herself. Of course Arlene could never do this even if she cared to. Taddeo had promised some rather expensive payments that already came out of the money she had to make sure she would collect. But she felt that by allowing the twelve-year old Virginia Hall to have free run of the place — with a camera she'd been discovered to be so expertly trained to operate — that *she* was helping the girls by way of helping Katherine McCormick's cause — whatever the feminist power player was up to. Jane Addams would be proud. And Arlene was not accepting of Victoria Moresco's recent declaration that an individual could not be loyal to two mistresses and must therefore choose.

The dark-haired Madame Moresco would also come around once that same day, wearing black and her suspicion of something, as apparently someone had noted McCormick's visiting the lounge the other night and that had gotten back to the madam. She did not exactly plan on speaking to Arlene extensively but Jasmine relayed the impression *she* picked up, that Moresco seemed to want to form her own on-site assessment of Arlene, when the business would be clear of most patrons, at least downstairs. That should not have been too good, because Arlene had gotten no sleep at the laundry after she'd become so mad via her phone conversations with Taddeo. She'd begun slipping up, most notably by getting followed. So she went back to work at the bar. There waiting for her was Victoria Moresco. Surprisingly a jovial-looking middle-aged woman who dressed her slight girth regally, but made one underestimate her by sheer way of her relaxed way she carried herself. Nevertheless, she made sure Arlene heard the unexpectedly treacherous woman's suggestions, intended only for her new, young operative — and that she made one strong impression on the younger lady. There could have been a faint hint of her taking pride in seeing another woman as a business manager — and one who worked with loyalty to her Colosimo family's organization. This almost flattered the Irish woman. But none of this would matter if Moresco only knew, Arlene was already going to be loyal — loyal only to herself.And in the meanwhile, even Taddeo the father of her unborn child, mattered less, if he could not be persuaded to cooperate. *A lot less* — she at least tried to convince herself.

She now expected she would have to make things right all on her own. For no matter what his young woman told him, he would just not abandon his stupid baseball game schedule, and get the hell back home. *That self-centered, inconsiderate* — . She wished she said what she really thought, but realized that wouldn't lure him back to her and rather just continue pushing him away — a horrible mistake she'd begun making since even before his departure, and her singularly deepest regret. She told Tad she wanted to continue hearing he was well and she said she hoped he would be at least smart enough to manage to take care of himself. She said they were both on their own now. But privately she also yearned for him to eventually come back to her side. Well, probably. Maybe. Every time she had to deal with that idiot, he so tried her patience.

But Arlene had other things to pay her attention to right now. Urso was upstairs at Villetti's abusing Lumia or at least still sleeping with her since Dr. Ronga had brought her back to the land of the living. The good doctor took his payment and even had stayed to have his way with another of the girls. After Daphne, he found having Faith to be to his attraction now. And Arlene had alerted Rose to stay out of her father's sight, not act up in rebellion, especially there at Villetti's, publicly. It wouldn't be good for their clients from the Mann family for just one more reason — as if one were needed. She didn't care about why The Family protected the politician. They protected all their clientele's privacy. She just knew the smooth operation of everything would best contribute to her own income. Meanwhile, May next yielded her time to supposedly be with the infamous pursuer of human traffickers now — as he decided "to stay and further study this most important concern of his that the Congressman had just discovered there." *So I guess he's okay with being a bit late for church.* And after she booked that in the meeting minutes, Arlene even managed to get the good doc's daughter completely away from The House, as the girl, all finished with the senior Mann, decided to accept an invitation to go on an extended date with Mr. Torrio's driver and bodyguard, one Frank Nitti. He'd brought Madame Moresco by the place, earlier. Curiously, those two — he and Roslyn — didn't then just spontaneously meet. They seemed to even know each other from some prior encounter they'd had in Texas. But whatever worked in Arlene's favor — .

And even more in her favor still, it seemed like Greg had his hands full, too — with handling Sega. He'd supposedly began staying more than that single night with her upstairs now, but Arlene preferred to avoid him rather than tried too hard to keep track of him. She'd had to come and go to privately contact Taddeo anyway, finally getting away Saturday night — so she could sleep where it was safer for her. But it was true: *she hadn't seen Sega* — for quite a while either, she realized. Greggorio been in charge of the bordello before her, so figuring he could handle that situation and his brother better than she could, especially if someone had to even confront Urso again, she went back to Mr. Li's and stayed there as long as she could Saturday. But she couldn't fall too deeply asleep as the laundry business operated all around her and her presence there eventually invited the Delasandros to show up. She still had to keep the books and cover for her skim. Lady Moresco was expected to come around several times, in person, while New York was visiting Chicago. It was all so frustrating. She'd headed back to the bordello to take a room in which to finally get some sleep. If both those twisted dago brothers had killed each other by the time she had to return, it would suit the Irish woman just fine. Arlene would rather let Greggorio reason out how to handle everything after he hollered at her for thinking she'd call an ambulance for Lumia. Dr. Ronga had proved effective, so nobody had died of an overdose for another few hours at the least. So Greggorio could run things his way as long as he was there. He'd do that anyway and he could have fun with it too, for all she cared.

So Arlene considered that must have been the reason why she wanted to protect Zhen Li, since she had no power to help the other girls like she once thought she could, before the Villetti and Delasandro brothers were frequenting the bordello even more than usual after Tad and his friends from the baseball team left to collect wins in Boston. Arlene just needed to keep a low profile and continue collecting the money. But she'd at least learn if Greg could detect the skim, though she guessed that he wouldn't now — not if Stefano had decided to cover for her. But Arlene wouldn't tell the part to Taddeo about how or especially why Stefan allowed her to keep currency earned from out of the skin trade, sort of — in his own way — though it was all she should truly care about, or be able to assert any control over with any certainty now. She'd prefer Taddeo mad at his cousin besides his brothers, even if the sex she'd shared with Stefano was consensual. That Dally consented to some money disappearing from The Family's bordello was that much more important. Only she couldn't even really keep the change, could she?

But what Tad needed to be was motivated to help her some more — and right away, not furnished with more excuses. She began to hate herself for dismissing him as never being able to help her one minute ago, to pining for him and begging him to reconsider his making a hasty trip back to Chicago in the next. Stefano too had rebelled against something he felt was wrong with The Family. This was also Tad's true nature. He only needed to be reminded of that again. And Greg — whatever he was doing — could soon be discovered to never be too busy to personally audit their every move eventually. She had no doubt he was only temporarily consumed by overseeing his greater preoccupation *upstairs* at Villetti's.

However, Arlene was busy much of the time, too. Only now if Representative Mann got seen there, by and or with his son James Mann, Jr., and their newly bought lady friends, well that would be on Greg. Though Ginny Hall had pictures, just like Katherine McCormick — and maybe even Lady Moresco — wanted her to take. *But that was the scandal that could simply be described in one word, as "Chicago"*. And Arlene would no longer be surprised when Virginia dropped by for another evening after another evening — and always with that camera. This girl would be at it again nearly every night — and that very morning too, when Arlene left Taylor Street for the laundry. No matter. Arlene wasn't responsible for her and what could happen to a female child in such a place. Wishing to stay on Mrs. McCormick's good side until she could settle a score, Arlene did not even think to challenge young Ginny, or even ask a single question of her when she exchanged pleasantries and even poured her another drink at the request of the minor. It seemed this also somehow suited Victoria Moresco's cross-purpose, too. She'd seen the girl on her first visit and done nothing about it either. Arlene could have sworn she saw Victoria even smirk on one occasion. Perhaps this is why the younger madam wanted to protect Zhen Li that much more — because she stood a chance at it. She wouldn't have to defend her in such an environment if she did her best to keep Zhen completely out of it.

But even after repeated questions and much challenge — to his commitment to her — again — Taddeo wouldn't leave Boston to come help run interference for Arlene. Or moreover, now he wouldn't abandon his stupid baseball team, as if the Cubs ever depended upon *his* throwing. But next that Sunday afternoon, he pitched her yet one more excuse. He still had some appointment he had to keep. *What is he hiding?* She told him that she was sick. That she was dealing with a medical condition. But he stressed that she could even use what help she attained from Mr. Li to see her through whatever had afflicted her. She would have to. "Chinese medicine was supposed to be really good." Tad would send him extra money that he borrowed from his friends, attesting that idiot Hoffman already owed him big time, but Arlene should provide some as she had more access to liquid cash than he did, away playing baseball. He hadn't seen any check from Weeghman in his recent history. But Arlene countered that by stating that as long as Tad owed her or her service providers for the medical attention she'd been receiving, that he might want to come back and at least supervise the treatment he was paying for. He refused every sensible reason for leaving his silly baseball team, reminded her that she was originally the one who said that the Cubs were his best deal and he should never abandon them, and she grew irate with Taddeo throwing her own words back at her. He reminded her that she was the one who originally hurt him — by pushing Tad away, first — even before their goodbyes at the train station. He asked for more time to reconsider the situation. Furious, Arlene hung up on him again. She'd deal with the situation she found herself in *without him*. She was originally going to. The Cubs could have Taddeo Villetti. She didn't need some stubborn fool anyhow. Not once before — and not any longer.

Taddeo hung up the phone on his end of the line and sat still for quite a while, looking at the wall of the hotel lobby. The writing was there. He'd made an agreement to do something more while he was on the East Coast. It was part of his deal with his own personal devil — the one he saw in the mirror — and the bargain that had secured Hoff's freedom. He had his stupid friend back, only now had probably lost his perfect girlfriend. *Only Arlene isn't so perfect for me, is she?* Tad would continue wishing things would improve beyond resolving one problem only to find another — and then another one. Did it ever end?

Chapter 44

Greg needed to relieve his own tension and there was nothing like a little sex to help. Later that Sunday morning he had returned upstairs after seeing one of Chicago's shifty Congressmen out. He'd recognized United States Representative James Mann and he presumed Arlene had let that dishonorable hypocrite in there again for his umpteenth visit, this one and any of the previous ones, which could always threaten the legitimate criminal enterprises that were supposed to be protected there. And in addition to that perturbing him, from the hallway he also overheard his older brother at it again, this time slamming the headboard against the wall of his chosen room while he fucked all hell through LuLu once more. It didn't matter if she was conscious, just as long as she was breathing. But after a near death by overdose, Greg didn't need any scandals there ruining the establishment's good reputation, especially as New York's baseball fans remained in town for the Yankees, and while he had a well-connected lawmaker visiting his family-owned brothel. Moreover, he didn't want Arlene influencing the Congressman in any way, if that was even a play she would try for. Greggorio didn't know why, but Johnny Torrio had requested that his father set up a situation so which Colosimo's nephew would have access to the legislator, even though the New Yorker was not a constituent. And meanwhile, Greg needed everything to run smoothly, especially while he had a new lucky girl in The House, and a few more laws to break for his own plans to move forward.

So after Greggorio made sure the Congressman who represented *the Christian righteous* wouldn't be late for church when he left the whorehouse, Greg felt he had no other choice but to force things along and back in the right direction for him, as he made his rounds reevaluating The Family business. He found and also escorted Mann's son and namesake out as well while he went about this. But running it all was even too much stress for him and he needed a release. He lit up a Mexican hopper that Dr. Ronga's daughter had cultivated a different kind of supplier-connection for, and inhaled a deep breath. Bringing the smoking hot Mary-Jane along with him, he found Sega barely conscious in her room. She would do. He appreciated seeing almost all of her naked legs under a new cream-colored dress, likely stolen from Lumia, which had mostly crumpled up beneath her bottom as she rolled around and back onto her back in an "H"-induced bliss — or not exactly how he'd left her after he'd had to repeatedly use one of the hospital bedpans on either side of her, that Dr. Ronga had brought with his *gifts*, originally intended for Lumia. But Greg forgot about that. It was par for the course. He reached out to gently stroke those two lengths of her exposed flesh and then push them further apart, separated enough so he could take in the view while he unbuckled his belt and loosened his own pants to the point where he was comfortable as he turned her over again, mounted her, and slammed himself inside of her. He satisfied himself by using her body, remembering there'd come a moment where he would compensate her for what he had to do with her in just a little bit. In his mind, that justified everything. Greg then rolled her over once more, and opened the top of her dress. It wasn't ever buttoned and appreciated she'd already lost her bra — probably in his brother's room. He took a new smoke from where he'd left MJ in an ashtray on the nightstand. Not ever slowing down, Greggorio then used his mouth and soft kisses, and then his tongue to titillate and then move down the middle of her exposed, naked body and pleasure her with this tongue. With his sobriety and stamina, also maintaining a steady rhythm, Greg was able to multi-task and tie off a tourniquet so he could even inject Sega with The House's preferred *loving-drug* he'd already prepared a needle for from a four-years-vintage, fresh-for-retail-kit while she became slightly more aware of herself to enjoy what was the peak of her climax. She came, an experience she then rapidly settled down from the crescendo of, due to the rapid effect of the injection overtaking her — and then settled into another unconscious slumber with a satisfied smile on her beautiful face as the heroin proceeded to work on her, *as he had*, for going on a second day.

Greg first pumped her full of what more of the drug he trusted he could, and still keep the girl alive with. He bet when he should stop and took Sega within inches of her life while she never knew it. The House had become an effective triage center for any overdoses while Dr. Ronga remained conveniently close by if Greggorio needed him and Vitale's supplies, for another religious revival. But now he beat the living devil out of this girl with his pounding fists — while she seemed not even aware of it — bludgeoning to bruise Sega everywhere!

He'd brought along an extra waste bucket with him so he could repeatedly turn the girl over and made sure she stayed alive by not choking on her own vomit while he fed her veins with new drugs, and supplied her body with new wounds, their pain masked by his former ministrations. Then he shocked himself as he frantically hit her over and over again, suddenly enraged by her appearance resembling his mother. While she was unconscious and wouldn't remember anything, and under his breath, quickened by the exertion it caused Greg to complete his workout on the woman, he told her "Yeah, I know who you are Sega — or *Anna Cumpănas*. You didn't slip past me. In fact, to a great degree, *I* arranged for you to be here. See, I *own* the detectives; they have their own connections *that they own*, for even more sources — even in other law enforcement offices, like East Chicago's — and therefore, now I own the information I need. My papa was a fool to let you into this house without checking the source that sent you to us. Without ever suspecting *me*, or that I'd contacted Cardinella to make his little arrangement work. And Urso was just the fool you would need to take you into his bed and then keep you around the place. You're not any Greek Aphrodite either, but I know exactly who and what you are." Then the scheming middle brother clenched his teeth so hard his jaw trembled, narrowed his glaring eyes, and slowly turned his head from side to side before he took off his belt and whipped her a few times with it, hard, so as to definitely leave some marks. Then he finished up on her in more ways than one and finally carried her nearly naked body to leave her in an alternate room of his choosing. She'd wake, lying nude and on top of a naked Urso and Lumia. He hoped she'd unconsciously defecate again — while with his brother and his latest friend, all in the same bed. But heroin didn't really induce that and he hadn't brewed any coffee. But making this any more entertaining than it already had been didn't really matter. Greg knew "Sega" would awaken in quite a stupor, besides a lot of pain — which he'd blame the unconscious Urso for, and she'd believe him when she came back to him to learn what had befallen her. And Greg re-injected an unconscious Lucky LuLu and his beloved brother as well, just to make certain he'd keep their objections and denials completely out of the picture. Greggorio had been lucky — that during Sega's repeated visits to fight with his brother, she'd been leaving the door unlocked. It was all too easy.

So when the brunette-haired girl did finally rise, Greg had been up all night and into the next day while he waited downstairs for her to stumble into him, crying, bloodied and frazzled — maybe like a lot of other people also experience Mondays in Chicago. But chronic narcolepsy competed with chronic narcissism in Greg, while he fabricated his explanation of how he could never be strong enough to control his brother. And to protect herself, Sega would need to get herself out of there. He reminded her of the fight that the Villetti brothers had fought just that Saturday night, and how Urso had taken Lumia from him. For her safety, he said he could send Sega away while he got some assistance from his father — with which he would definitely need to handle Urso.

And this all occurred as Arlene was not around to either observe or interfere. She must have always seemed to escape the worst of what went on at Villetti's — from Sega's point of view. Those two women did not seem to like one another. But Greg had made sure he'd taken the right steps so that he'd know *exactly* where Arlene would be. She could not escape *him*. He'd paid Vitale a little something extra over what the enforcer made on his father's payroll to make sure the red-haired harbinger of vengeance would be successfully followed just in case his younger cousins bungled the job. He'd seen that too many times already. And he anticipated her going for his old .38, which was probably left behind at the laundry. Vitale had already been on one errand or another for Dr. Ronga so Arlene wouldn't scrutinize his coming and going and she wouldn't suspect him of being the one to follow her to Mr. Li's. But it made sense, as Li was a friend to their family since Tad was a child. Li *would be* someone the little shit would turn to if he were forced to seek help outside of The Family – and clearly demonstrating that he could betray his family. Furthermore, another great possibility was that his bitch's move signaled that Arlene could be running really low on ammunition about now. Well, she'd killed enough already, hadn't she? Plus before his younger brother had left and Greg noted that Taddeo had gotten one or another of his stupid teammates to drive him around, they'd returned to Villetti's with cleaned uniforms. And the scheming middle-brother's first suspicion for where they'd gotten that work done *had been the Chinaman's laundry*. His cousins Baldavino and Carlo had confirmed it, Greg learned by way of Vitale's phone call when they were all on location, and even scouting the family's little pitcher before he was called upon to perform in Boston. And though Greggorio couldn't prove it, he suspected his little brother had also tipped off Mr. Li — a childhood friend to *all the Villetti brothers* — to get rid of Mr. O'Rourke and see him to safety before The House's vengeance could catch up to that stubborn mick butcher. That guy needed to be butchered. But it didn't matter. His father would eventually succeed with that, Greg supposed. But O'Rourke's disappearance had actually worked out to embarrass Greg's competition he imagined for himself in that one, Johnny Torrio. But through his proxies, Greg had now caught on to Mr. Li, and the middle Villetti son had information — and in his daughter he'd tried to hide from the whole House, even a potential hostage that he could use against the slope laundryman — not to mention he'd finally succeeded in keeping track of Arlene.

In the immediacy though, and wrapped in bloodied and tear-stained bedsheets, Sega whimpered in her barstool next to him in the deserted lair of despair, as began another bleak Monday morning for those who were indentured there. Greg poured her another shot of whiskey as he'd told her that the woman's drinks were on The House. He almost admired his own handiwork, but the savagery he'd inflicted on his victim even startled *him* — what he'd become capable of. Not even the young man himself had figured the extent to how far he would go. But no one else did.

"It was never like this when you ran the place. Or even while Taddeo was here. But ever since your youngest brother left with that fucking baseball team, his bitch Arlene has lost control of everything," Sega cried.

He said he knew and was working to rectify it, but none of Urso's siblings had ever been strong enough as his family's first-born, to establish the least bit of authority over *that one*. So Greg would put Sega up at The Lexington in the meanwhile, to let her recover and bring her health back into good standing. He'd already planned to use Lumia's old room that Colosimo thought he was still sponsoring for Greggorio to use for Lu, and for that favor Greg would owe Big Jim. But he wasn't necessarily worried he'd ever have to pay up. He had an idea about how he was going to arrange that, too. For right now, someone else had to pay. He told the woman he was going to help her, but warned Sega that she'd get very sick when she went through withdrawal. So he was posting Gervasio over at the North Side hotel to make sure she got all the attention she needed, but didn't leave or cheat on her recovery.

Greg had the permission, and undoubtedly the supervision of the Irish, as gained by a request he made through Mike Merlo. The man had strangely seemed a bit ill and more pliant than usual. But

Greg gave the Italian immigrants' cause's leader his assurances that Sega would not try to ply her trade near The Loop or anywhere else on the North Side. Though with the way she now looked, Greg couldn't imagine how she could get very far with that anyway. He'd done a good job on Anna Cumpănas and she never knew it was him. Or that he'd learned who the abused single mother really was. And he successfully met with Merlo without his papa's knowledge by inviting him over earlier, out of manufactured concern that the Congressman was reviewing the business of The House. He ingratiated the ailing Italian man with him by also inviting him to review The House's Chastity, that carried on over there. But Rinaldo Villetti was an ardent supporter of the Unione Siciliana, as Colosimo required that. However, with Vitale following Arlene everywhere, and Gervasio gone to babysit Sega at The Lexington, Greggorio's next steps got even more men *more loyal* to his father, away from Taylor Street on an easy and very agreeable assignment. Gino and Vico were encouraged to join their friend toward The Loop if they wanted to switch shifts, but they were under orders to not molest Sega and only tend to anything she might need. This included her cheating on rehabilitation from all the drug usage, to which Greggorio planned to secretly assist, by making sure the associates upped her supply. He knew they would try and use it to coerce her to fuck them. And both The House's underlings jumped at the chance to have an assignment that would ensure their safety while they could enjoy the North Side, anyway. Greg still didn't know exactly how that was possible when O'Banion's people would surely know who the goombahs were and who they worked for. But a ceasefire was continuing to hold, perhaps because they still had Arlene infiltrated on the South Side. There was that, and racketeering and gambling pools required a lot of manpower to maintain control of territories the gangs had etched out in Chicago. Drug distribution was still very smalltime, requiring very specialized import ability after The Harrison Act was passed, and usually went hand-in-hand with prostitution, The Outfit's specialty. But the threat of Anna Cumpănas — however she was connected to this, and the threat of that going well beyond Cardinella, as Greg had considered *that*, was peacefully neutralized anyway; and no one had been killed his way, versus Arlene's established modus operandi. It was even a good thing Taddeo had likely helped O'Rourke escape alive. The shamrocks didn't feel so threatened as it made Johnny The Fox look incompetent. But all this wouldn't happen on its own, under normal circumstances. The Jews must have had something to do with it. *Damned kikes*. Greg still needed more information. If Tadpole came through on his new little assignment on the East Coast, his youngest brother could have even earned the receipt of the intelligence about the Jews that he could use against them. So next Greggorio apologized to Sega for introducing her to drugs, seeing as how she couldn't handle them — *and made her feel more incompetent by the minute*. Greg always had his suspicions about why she'd been there, why she appeared so perfect, like her image was chosen as the exact model for this task, and how such a woman could arrive in such haste, when his father asked for a girl to sidetrack Urso several weeks before. He had a hand in setting that up himself, but feared, Had I been played, too? Perhaps while they drank, Il Diavalo had asked Rinaldo about his late wife, the boys' mother. Then, The Devil had even played Greggorio by tempting his subconscious memories when he'd described Sega's beauty that qualified her for this mission. And soon after that, Anna Cumpănas had arrived to The House as "Sega," only to function as their agent in reserve, so *someone* could win by playing the long game against the Villettis, against The Outfit. The question was "who?" Greggorio did get in position to set up that play himself, only it shouldn't have ever felt right — how easy that was to arrange. No, *he* had been played.

But that was why it was especially obvious that the Greek wench was not going to get along with Arlene, for this and many reasons. Sega already knew why Fire-bush would be there. And Walsh had re-confirmed the Eastern European woman's identity for Greg, just to make sure. For certain, Cardinella had trapped Greggorio in his own game, to use his ambitions to betray his family, and then surely to betray himself. He was going to be double-crossed. Only Greg now thought he had a way to turn hell over on The Devil. So now the middle Villetti son gave Sega — or Anna Cumpănas and formerly Anna Chiolak actually, before she reverted to using her maiden name — hope that if she made it, and could master her own sobriety, and that if she wanted to leave right then — he could send her all the way to New York. There, he knew tentative allies of The Family had taken up station, and actually were Family, according to his father and fading memories from his youth. Greggorio reached out to them before, and found at least one of his estranged uncles to be agreeable to work with. But these good fellas could help Sega make a new name for herself, only secretly and even back where she originally came from. So shortly they'd send for her son to join her Back East when she was sober and ready to once more care for him. Everyone had a price. This should completely meet hers. Except that Back East would also be where she could have Taddeo's "protection" — for as much as she cared to, or to take away Arlene's man completely out of spite for her.

And now his New York relatives also awaited "the fucking Cubs" arrival in The Big Apple. Greg would ultimately send "Sega" to Taddeo. And he could get her to a doctor in Brooklyn if she still had any pain, but in the meanwhile she could see Ronga again, to minister to her wounds, and should she need to, "Dr." Delasandro The Family's pharmacist, who could offer her more "cautious medication" for her pain. But it would be clearly in Tad's nature to help her when she got to New York. Greggorio could easily foresee that. And as retribution for all which had befallen her, Sega would take what was once Arlene's. He told her that all she had to do to keep his protection was stay safe until they were reunited and then of course, get on board for his brother's baseball team. Taddeo's behavior and his interests were well-tested, and his life didn't see him ever really thinking about much of anything else.

* * * * *

And then an even already more sobered Sega took all of Taddeo's Wednesday night only after his team first arrived in Philadelphia. Unfortunately for him, in the city nicknamed the Cradle of Liberty, he spent another weekend night a prisoner — on the phone in his room at The Lorraine with only *another* woman from Chicago, while his friends were celebrating a Cubs' five-game winning streak on the road. But Trevor and Trip saw few more pinch-hitting opportunities and didn't get much more playing time on the field back in Boston, either. They attributed this to the baseball coach not being a major fan of auto racing. Taddeo behaved himself as far as Mitchell knew, but he didn't log any more time on the hill, though he had to continuously report for practice with Hoff. However, all the rookies save for Charlie Hollocher of course, felt like Coach ignored them. But they had to show initiative, for it was all coming together for the veterans *and the rookies* in this ball club. Or most of them anyway.

Only apparently Urso had done his worst. Arlene would not speak to Tad when he tried to call her back at his papa's place and when he returned the call for a *second* conversation with Sega, who was hiding in *The Lexington Hotel* back in Chi-Town, he learned that his so-called woman had all but lost control — in Tad's absence — and that she'd then she'd found some other mysterious priority in hosting strange visitors to the lounge, government types and those from high society who really didn't seem to belong there. And also there was some very young girl who was running around, noticed on several occasions already by all the other ladies, because she was doing her best to avoid all the men — who represented much more of a threat to someone her age. However, the girl was surely a threat to somebody as well. But when gently questioned, this child had suggested everything would be explained later and she offered up small sums of money to be granted secret access into the rooms in which the Villetti girls were taking their tricks. And Arlene had become all but inaccessible to most of the ladies. So there were no answers to be found. But it was also from Sega that Tad could confirm that his woman had fallen into some sort of depression or another because it was *for a fact* that Urso and his cousin Stefano had been abusing her. They'd been debasing her intentionally where knowledge of their acts would weaken the perception of any authority she once briefly held in The House. So Arlene wasn't very conversational with the rest of the girls, but had met with several ladies from *outside The House* as well as even Madam Moresco. This fit with what his woman had told him of why he needed to return and pay for her psychologist. That was for sure. It sounded like she would need one. *And this is getting to be way too much. I'm going to need a shrink myself shortly. While all I ever had wanted was to concentrate on succeeding in baseball.* Taddeo was sure feeling the pressure now — and the irony that he would be almost and just about prepared to give it all up now, to return to Chicago and take back control of everything else that he'd begun working so hard for. But what of how hard he'd worked to get as far as he got in Major League Baseball?

One thing he knew for sure was that Sega had done right by him on their little hunting trip. Tad hadn't forgotten, either. And Greg seemed to have even done something decent for once. His brother was paying *himself* to get her out of the city and send her to get set up some place safer, away from Urso, and with the protection of The Family in New York. Taddeo's team would play there next. Apparently he would as well, specifically per the arrangements he'd been forced to agree to with the captain of the guard, in order to get Hoff out of prison at Charleston. And there was also that Tad felt responsible for Sega since she worked in what his father had now made *his* lounge to run. He finally admitted to himself that he was strongly attracted to the temptation she offered him, and she had once been there *for him* when he'd needed her, on that other Wisconsin road trip.

Taddeo had gotten mixed up in this in the first place for Arlene, but that wasn't working out the way he wished at all. He could do nothing right by her — though she totally failed to appreciate he'd been the one who got her a safe place to hide, a semi-secure position in The House, and a source of income. Like that was nothing? But at every turn their relationship seemed to be doomed to fail from its very inception if he were to be honest with himself about that. And it wasn't like he didn't suspect Greg to have set up whatever lay ahead for him in on his road trip to the East Coast. But nevertheless Tad didn't see any reason not to meet this new girl who kept finding her way into his life. Besides, he'd like to take something away from Urso besides a beating.

Though he traveled with his team and his best friends, while this far away from his papa, he suddenly realized how naked and alone out east, he truly was. Now Sega had known and lived in The House. But it had offered her no comfort either. They had that in common. And he had to live in hotels and on the floor of a Chinese laundry because the journeyman pitcher had no safe home to live his life in either — with Greg sending him on rides to cemeteries with the Genna Brothers, his cousin Corry suggesting he now needed to carry a gun, and the Irish gangs preventing him from attaining something even so simple as a Chicago taxicab ride. Now Dan Griner, Jake Daubert, Burleigh Grimes and the rest of the Robins were waiting for him in Brooklyn. And before that, he'd face Ross Youngs, Kauf, Burns, and Al Demaree in Upper Manhattan. So Taddeo said he knew some people who could help arrange for him to meet the girl in New York next — and he was very motivated and looking forward to this, *some relief*, and the desire for the simple life of living by one's passions. Sega was already proven talented in the way she elicited this from out of him. He remembered a quiet time he felt fleeting relief in her arms when they were in the forest, beneath the shelter of trees and the temptations presented by the possibilities one imagined, looking into an open sky, so far from Chicago — and all their troubles — if it weren't for Tad's brothers also being there. However, there was also that Taddeo had already been further encouraged to make his other rendezvous in New York which he'd been informed he'd be scheduled for — by none other than the Massachusetts' state prison officials — when he'd gotten Hoff out of trouble on The Island. And by making that appointment, Tad would learn exactly how he could retrieve Sega in New York City. And that was probably better than having to try and protect her in Brooklyn. But if they were going to call on him for favors, he would call on *them* — to do likewise. But for who was this really going to be a favor?

Chapter 45

Stephen Orlando Grauley, better known as Sog, reported on the Cubs' visit to Pennsylvania for *The Philadelphia Inquirer*. In short, The Windy City's favorite team blew away the Phillies for a clean sweep, showing some great dominance in the Baker Bowl. After the first afternoon when the Cubs were road-weary but dominant, twenty-eight-year-old Shufflin' Phil Douglas gambled he could pitch a complete shutout game and did so — probably while he was not even sober. Chicago won 3-0 with Dode Paskert and Charlie Deal both hitting homeruns off the beleaguered Mike Prendergast.

Charlie continued to show his renewed worth in the Cubs' lineup with another homerun the second afternoon they played, after taking Friday off competition play for practice in bad weather. This time he got his distance off Carter Bradley Hogg, who watched the ball travel about 390 feet over left-center. Lefty Tyler turned in some great work for Chicago. But amazingly, Georgia-born "Dixie" Hogg only gave up 2 hits to the Cubs, including Deal's homer that earned Chicago's batter 2 RBIs, but he couldn't locate the strike zone and awarded so many bases-on-balls that Mann, Merkle, and Paskert just had to knock the runs in, Merkle's by a sacrifice, for the Cubs to win a second shutout against the 18-and-23 Philadelphia, this time with a score of 6-0!

It was no secret that Sog preferred Athlethics and Pirates baseball to the Phillies, among Pennsylvania's teams. But the Cubs entertained themselves — by winning.

Then on Monday the 10th's game, Chicago's Michael Everston finally got to see some more playing time as by using no less than three different pitchers, Philadelphia had at long last silenced Charlie Deal's bat and Coach Mitchell tried something new to miff the Phillies' Coach, Pat Moran. But all of Flack, Hollocher, Mann, Merkle, and Paskert did their jobs. Even with the 6-hole in the 29-and-12 Cubs' order quelled, the team hit enough to earn Hippo Vaughn another win as the ace ruled from the hilltop in the Baker Bowl and Chicago won again 6-1, with Fred Luderus knocking in Cy Williams for the only Philadelphia run.

Then the Chicagoans were running all the way to Manhattan on a winning streak to face their rivals the Giants, on The Polo Grounds. Only instead of finding celebratory cheer — and the usual drinks and women on the road that go along with the spoils for the victors that his friends all enjoyed, Cub pitcher Taddeo Villetti was running around to find a lot of telephones to make sure that Sega, was safely on her way to rendezvous with him in New York City. Then he soon learned that plan had changed. There would be no rest stop and no run security to hurl forward with, on this gypsy's road. And Tad's golden arm his gun, he would travel on alone, with only it for reassurance. Considering the larger series of games he was going to play in now, he worried it would not be reassurance enough.

Chapter 46

First, on Tuesday the 11th, Taddeo found himself going to prison — again. It had been part of the bargain for him to meet *somebody else* in New York, as well. And since Hoffman owed Taddeo — for a lot, *especially now* — he was supposed to cover for him and help the pitcher hide on the train while everyone else disembarked from their journey from Philadelphia, into Upper Manhattan — the Giants' territory to challenge any visitors. Only right then Tad needed to avoid any questions on his whereabouts — by Coach Mitchell. The rookie pitcher had to ride the railcar dozens of miles further north of The Polo Grounds between Washington Heights and Sugar Hill, where the rest of his teammates would begin their stay at The Theresa Hotel, during the last hours on the 10th of June.

So Tad did take the train further up the line, and then had to catch a cab by the bridge to go the rest of the way from the Cubs' new station by the Harlem River, north, along *the Hudson River*, to a village called Ossining. There in its benevolent wisdom almost one hundred years ago, the State of New York had built four-story brick buildings, prison guard watchtowers — and those behind old double chain and newer barbed wire fences — to reform the land into a maximum security corrections center, called Sing Sing. And there during the darkest part of the middle of that night, young Villetti met the hitman.

First, Warden William H. Moyer was discovered to be quite popular with some of the right inmates, and Taddeo found he was also quite amicable with the well-paid guards, leaving the athlete alone in a conference room into the still-dark skies of the early morning — with DeMarco and Lombardi's alleged assassin. The Sicilian bagmen were not there, or above dry ground anywhere, and the Camorristi probably made some Jewish money manipulators very happy should they have stepped up to replace Mafia associates because trust was weak between some rather diverse groups of northern versus southern Italians, and the Sicilian islanders. Unfortunately, by his point of view, Taddeo's education had to already include such knowledge. He was a Villetti regardless of whether or not he wanted to be one. As such, and while his friends were no doubt drinking and partying, fooling around with wild women, he'd now found himself out here, behind different bars. A lot of them.

But as another one of Tad's charming first cousins explained, continuing Tad's education — unshackled of having any reasons left to keep him from sharing his particular skills he was obviously so proud of, with another member of The Family — prison trips were a small price for Rocco to pay. And he displayed a lack of any emotion about it, even considering the fact he was getting released in just a few more months. *Small price?* Valenti's *younger than Greg but he's been behind bars now for about half the entire time I have been in my teens*. Tad looked his cousin over good. The youth was also four years' Tad's senior but he looked even older than Urso. Prison had turned him pale in just a short time — well he guessed especially compared to people who worked outdoors on a baseball diamond most days — and Rocco's eyes were even sunken in, but still quite animated and definitely neither defeated nor remorseful. But — *indifferent?* He had powerful allies in D'Aquila's organization who could reach through walls and make sure that syndicate members were looked out for on the inside. In turn, Cousin Rocco could reach outside — perhaps even with assistance from Warden Moyer and the entire corrupted system the prison authority had "reformed" — and he had managed to keep The Hoff safe in Charlestown. Powerful, Rocco Valenti might consider *himself*, but just the same, in four more years this was not how Taddeo wanted to see his self.

Rocco assessed his visitor where he was. "My cousin the big baseball player. The Family here on our home turf is *really* looking forward to meeting *you*. Come closer. Have a seat. There's plenty of time. I'm not going anywhere." He laughed at his own joke. "Ya probably don't remember a lot of us back in Brooklyn, as you were pretty little when your papa moved you all out to Chicago. But I once played with your big brother Greggorio, and he's helped keep us up to date with your career."

I bet.

"Anyway, he sure seems to love his baby brother. Like your papa loves you, too. So it didn't really take much doing and some friends of mine got your buddy out of hot water in Boston Harbor and are now helping out some lady friend of yours. Sega?"

Tad blinked. "What?" He should have predicted The Family's street connections were joined with their operatives who went in and out of the prison system on a regularly scheduled basis. So already, far too many dangerous people were involved in Tad's affairs in The Big Apple. *And I thought I got away from all of this shit every time I can get myself out of Chicago. I might want to scratch New York off my list of safe destinations. Boston, too.*

Rocco continued. "So my little cousin's all grown up and got himself a girl?" He smiled.

"Well Sega's not — ." But Tad bit his tongue. A prison inmate, and a murderer, however related he was to Taddeo, knew far too much about him already. *So this is how Greg must want to send Sega to me*. Tad wondered what new angle his brother was playing with this move, would ultimately be. And he now also wondered what condition the poor woman would arrive in. He realized he'd been most likely *very mistaken*, if he thought Greggorio could ever do something nice for his little brother, or anyone, that didn't benefit himself, even if only in this instance.

"Well, how sweet. I can't wait to spend the entire night with a few of my own. Right now, for a price, our East Coast syndicate can fortunately pay for quality *skilled help*, particularly for those *in my line of work*. So the warden allows me *visitors, different kinds of visitors*, in turn for present and future favors. I mean, how can the courts hold me accountable for some fellas conveniently disappearing? I'm right here — in prison — the whole time whenever some new alleged crime happens, right? No one on my cell block can really say if I was in the infirmary or got locked up in solitary because I'm often supposedly a suspect for also carrying out some hit or another *inside* these walls. See the warden always finds something new to blame on me when Tammany Hall stacks my frequent parole hearing boards. So of course I couldn't have been killing somebody on the outside when I sit here accused of killing somebody on the inside, right? But they have to be good to me if they want their dirty work done. So prison's fun. I've never made so much money. And now the warden's bidding on construction contracts for his prisoners qualified for outdoor labor details. It's the system. But ya know a man still wants his freedom. And when I want it badly enough, Moyer better not think he can keep me here against my will, and still let me out to run the larger syndicate's errands — or there will be some swift personnel changes around here. Hey, when you see them, you'll ask The Family for me if they have heard of any good places to lease. I guess I'll have to rent a place real soon when the state can't let me continue staying here."

Taddeo looked his relative over wondering what could turn this young man almost the same age as he was, into the kind of professional killer that Rocco had earned a reputation for being. It was like what he did could not matter the least to Valenti at all. He was just happy to be getting back to it upon each pending release while he repaid what he owed for his comfortable stay in a place like Sing Sing. Taddeo swore he could never see himself becoming like this and he was not going to make it a habit of spending any more time in prisons like some of his family members did. But there he found himself seated and staring at a man he didn't want to let himself become — a murderer — and at the same time he nevertheless wanted to kill his own brother for what Greggorio was doing to him and the women. Couldn't homicide be a short-term hobby?

"Anyway, you'll never tell who, but we got a guard — who before he goes home to his wife — will make sure you reconnect with your lady friend, now that you're both closer to New York City."

Tad felt alarmed at how so many innocent people like his buddy Hoff got affected by their just being around him, because of his relatives associated in this life. "Wait. His wife?"

"Yeah." Rocco laughed. "We know how some men feel about family." Taddeo gulped but then felt confused, as he hoped he'd misinterpreted what Valenti meant. "You know there are lots of fellows who like to do more than a few things before they have to go home to see their wives, and there's a lot of different kinds of insurance policies."

The young visitor was relieved for only a second, as maybe his cousin didn't mean what he initially thought — or perhaps he did? Now Tad definitely worried he didn't know what he should be feeling. Here before him — and even related to him — was this remorseless asshole who could be the pin in the grenade that would start a huge new Mafia-Camorra War. What was going to happen to Sega before he could shelter her? The ideals in life he'd valued, were revealing themselves to *all* be lies. Marriage and the well-being of women weren't even on the table. Not in his family. Or not any longer. Not since his mama's passing. And the whole world was at war even where it looked like it *wasn't* part of the violent struggle between life and death that could be obvious to everyone. The continental United States was every bit as dangerous as Europe. Now Tad hoped this also didn't mean Sega had been abused *after* she got away from Chicago to find him in New York. Or that she still could be being abused. He worried for her and Tad worried about Arlene again — for after all he remembered why he made his original commitment to *her* — and that he was going to have to answer for the skimming plot too, especially if Arlene named him as her accomplice because she got herself caught. He couldn't expect any loyalty from her now. They might even be done, forever, for all he could tell. And that reminded him of rather unpleasant thoughts about how his dear papa might have even treated his mother — and had been behaving well before he even took Arlene, as she'd said their room at The Sisson had already been his father's before she and Tad had taken it over. *But wait a minute. That hotel was not that old*, he once again remembered. *Unfortunately my mother's time on this Earth was done well before the reconstruction on the South Side ever was*. Only in a different way, perhaps that was fortunate. Tad definitely didn't like what this conversation could uncover, or the implications his own thoughts arrived at. However, maybe the facts seemed to vindicate his papa after all. Taddeo wanted them to. But the world was still plotting all around him. It always was. And even Old Man Sisson was in on it. But Tad would rather blame Greg and Urso for everything, than lay it all upon his only parent that remained. He still had *someone*, didn't he? And now — nor before — was he ever particularly fond of anyone else he'd met thus far, who was part of this *Family*.

He also did not like that even here in New York, The Family already had people watching him and directing his life for him, and that not only his papa, but Greg was somehow involved in it. *Of course he would be*.

"Anyway, our inside-man who's on the job just needed to look you over so they can mark who they need to deliver your woman to."

Oh perfect. I had to go to Sing Sing so they can mark me? Now Tad had the thought that The Family didn't need to get parole for their hitman. Taddeo finally saw how he was going to personally practice for the role by killing Hoffman for getting himself locked up in Boston and starting Tad on this prison tour in the first place — when he was actually supposed to be starting on becoming a successful pitcher on stadium tours instead.

However, since Tad would not be getting any sleep that night, Hoff was "very lucky" that Taddeo would spend it behind bars with Rocco versus getting a new woman and maybe pulling Hoff away from one of his because Tad required some privacy for a change. But that would have to change once Taddeo could meet up with Sega, so he could debrief her to gain all the knowledge he could. And Hoff could think whatever he wanted. He was in Tad's debt, not to mention on his blacklist, for the moment. But Tad didn't owe Arlene his fidelity any longer, either. So he guessed. In the meantime, Warden Moyer let the two cousins have the small, cold and spartan conference room all to themselves and thus Taddeo could continue his education and new self-discoveries until early morning, when the trains would begin to run regularly again to get him back to The Polo Grounds.

Tad would be extra groggy at pre-game practice, but he wouldn't be pitching that first game against the Giants more than likely. Claude Hendrix had the start. A right-hander who was more than capable of going the complete game as was customary, plenty of right-handed relief was available with seniority over Taddeo. And Hendrix probably still stood ready to protest over Villetti relieving his duties on the mound at any time, forever after, anyway. That hadn't gone so well the last month. Tad would only be brought in now if the Cubs were losing, and Coach would more than likely use Carter or maybe Douglas if they were ahead — and Phil was sober enough to stand. At least Tad would meet up with Sega sooner than later. And if he were instead actually a lot nicer to his best friend than he felt like being, after even spending another night in prison because of *him*, maybe Hoff would take in Trevor and Mike so he could actually sleep — with Sega — Tad supposed. Actually he hoped. He might gain insight from talking to the older woman, who at twenty-eight, was nearly ten years his senior. But to actually gain some sleep at last wouldn't be a bad thing either. Though his mind wandered to imagining what else he could get from Sega, which also couldn't be bad at all.

He mused whether Cleveland Alexander had as much to worry about when he'd finally get into The War as Taddeo now did with his own special kind of experience pitching for the Cubs — all while dealing with his family, and his conflicting emotions regarding an ever-unsatisfied Arlene. But he thought to himself that if she could be unfaithful, whether or not she'd been forced to be, then so could he. Arlene had been caught hiding the truth from him, or whitewashing it, and she pushed him away from her. In fact, he needed to admit that had truly begun when he'd come home and caught her with that kike in The Sisson. So it wasn't like he owed her any fidelity for that. And now Tad recollected he'd so much as already admitted to himself that he'd been interested in Sega. He knew his brother wanted so badly to continue setting him up, for whatever purpose it could serve. He could try and resist her lust-evoking sensuality. But there wasn't any longer a reason not to take the beautiful Greek girl to bed with him. *Every* fella just couldn't wait to get laid as soon as they got out of prison.

Now by the time Tad did get back to Upper Manhattan, and the fancy hotel, *Theresa*, where the Cubs were being boarded, Hoff was with a couple women in his own room, and Trip and Bass-Man had taken the beds in Tad's room so he would have gotten only about a few hours of sleep — on the floor — before Mitchell wanted them reporting to the visitor's clubhouse at the Giants' stadium. However, his friends were wide awake and waiting for him when he got back — and they were also keeping company — with Sega.

The twenty-eight year old wore a bright red dress — and a lot of black and blue. She sat on Trevor's bed and Tad was immediately alarmed at how beat up this usually beautiful young woman looked. By now the Cubs' wounds their last contact with Brooklyn had left them with, had all mostly healed. Sega had to have been bruised and abused something terrible — and her injuries were still fresh. Her lips were dark, puffy, cracked, and the blood had scabbed in areas that were dark red and black. Her nose was swollen and her eyes, too. And of course he could see the concern in his friends' eyes. There were enough abrasions just on this gal's bare arms and what was exposed of her long, still ever-so-sensually shaped legs, such that Taddeo wondered how she arrived *there*, instead of a hospital. But inexplicably as well as instantly drawn to her, he gathered the young woman in his powerful arms and absorbed her tears into his shirt, where she rested her head directly over his heart. They fell into each other's arms no sooner than they saw one another. Sega looked up into the young man's eyes and her battered, blistered, torn lips were drawn to his, and they met somewhere between relief and the loss of any more denial of passion between them. Mike and Trevor looked at each other amused by the pair's display of familiarity and affection, but then offered much troubled looks to demonstrate their worry as well. Only Tad knew his teammates weren't involved in any of this — and nor should they be. There was nothing in their little naïve-from-being-sheltered lives that could ever compare to the cruelty of the world that the Villettis lived in. And they would never know the anger — no it was rage — and not lust, that Sega elicited in him — when he'd asked who'd done this to her and she whispered in his ear Tad's brother's name. Trip and Trevor reluctantly but luckily agreed on "the new plan now" and departed to go and sleep on the couches in the lobby of The Theresa so this new pair could have some privacy. And after they'd all just gotten Hoff out of prison only a week ago, no doubt another challenge somehow connected to his family's manipulations, Tad could bet on, his teammates were once more giving of themselves, and gave Taddeo Villetti some time in near solitude. So then he too could work on figuring his professional approach toward *his* next big league dream — of murder.

Urso was a monster and needed to be stopped at any cost. What Tad's friends probably assumed would next go on between he and the young woman was no problem to Tad. Actually he still really hoped *that* would go on between them. But Sega had come to New York — and barely holding herself together. And she had actually come there looking for Tad, to inspire him towards something more — *to save her*. She showed faith in him while Arlene had repeatedly rejected multiple offers of his to do the very same for her, only with her tiresome and sarcastic litany of rebukes. But what Arlene didn't know was that Taddeo Villetti had been continuing his practice — of showing great ability at winning saves lately.

And there he was, "Sega's" savior. He looked so young and handsome. For her sake, she would make him so strong. He could be turned on his brother Urso. That man deserved what was coming to him. She only hoped she could make Tad's character strong enough to fight his bastard of a sibling. Then she could be avenged. But that's exactly what Anna supposed Arlene had wanted as well. No matter. The two ladies shared this singular hope. She knew Urso had victimized both women with his assaults. But additionally, Arlene was in her way of accomplishing what that pot-licking bitch had not. Maybe because The Black Hand's agent had been and still felt drugged — and The Family had resupplied her when her train arrived in New York, it was still one big mystery on how success with what she'd originally came out to Chicago for, could still be achieved. Yet it was not a mystery that she had felt attraction for Tad ever since they'd first encountered one another at The Sisson. At the time, she hoped she hadn't let it show. But now she'd felt so bad for him, the way his brothers pushed him and had kept pushing him on that hunting trip Urso had dragged her on for reasons she still had not fathomed. Tad was everything Urso was not. And Arlene had treated Anna so awfully throughout almost the entire time since she'd been dispatched there — when the boys' father had unwittingly created the opportunity when he'd needed to preoccupy his oldest — because he'd decided he would keep Arlene alive for whatever was *his* reason at the time. The Family's patriarch would pay for his mistake and all his sick games he played, too. It was true that Sam Cardinelli had coerced Anna into helping him along with that plan as well, but even Il Diavalo, not so secretly known as The Black Hand, didn't realize what kind of witch's brew he'd stuck his fingers into. And either femme fatale might wind up being the one who would see to Villetti's ending. Chicago did not forgive. Someday, someone was going to teach Cardinelli that, too. But Anna thought it was all that green cunt's fault regarding what had happened to *her*. And she severely missed her own son. Everything she did now was all for her boy. But she would undermine Arlene in every way and steal her success with her mission, as well as her man. The scarlet harlot didn't seem to appreciate him, anyway.

Now as his teammates had departed from their room, she and Taddeo were alone in his suite at The Hotel Theresa. *Someone's* influence was also at work here, putting the Chicago ballclub up in very fine hotels. There were black members of the service staff everywhere, to cater to guests' almost every whim. Hadn't she last spoken to Tad on the phone while he was staying at The Lorraine in Philadelphia? Now he and his friends stayed in a new, thirteen-story construction of terra-cotta style close to the Harlem River. This life of luxury was not typical for young baseball players or the Cubs, who hadn't won the National League Pennant in over ten years. But *Anna Cumpănas* could get used to it like The Lexington, and cater to one whim of Taddeo's that she alone could nurture in his nature — and one that The Theresa's service pool could not.

She loosened her long dark hair and undressed in front of him while under his pretext of assessing her wounds from the assaults and batteries she'd been forced to endure. But she could tell his interest in her peaked. His eyes had wondered all over her trim naked body with its hourglass shape taking form by way of angles that approached her smooth midriff below the twin peaks of her naked breasts. Taddeo looked down at the exposed place between her legs. But in his company, and nude, Anna did not feel vulnerable. Instead she worried if he'd still be attracted to her because of the way his precious Family had left her — and the prison guard — or the men at the café — and any of the latest of these men she had to meet during her long journey from Brooklyn over here to be close to The Polo Grounds. But desire seized him. A protrusion under his pants signaled as much. He was very interested in her. *Then take me as I am. I want you so bad. I want to seek shelter and comfort as you wrap me in your powerful arms and protect me for as long as I can imagine that you actually can.*

Tad couldn't resist temptation any longer. His passion moved him. He'd felt so alone with all he'd been forced to endure already, and so much attraction to Sega. She reminded him of someone, maybe from a long time ago, but Taddeo couldn't place who. Life had been so much simpler when he was just a kid. Right now he wanted her. Bruises and all. He'd always wanted her. If he were a kid and he wanted something, he never hesitated. He learned to just take what he could, since he had such a stubborn father and at least verbally when not physically abusive brothers. So he could and had to just indulge himself. And it made him feel proud that he would take something from Urso who had taken his youngest brother's dignity so many times before. One of his prayers had finally been answered. He stripped out of his clothing he'd come home from prison in. Man and woman's bodies merged together. *Look at this Greek goddess come down from the heavens just for me. Now I am winning this game. This is great!*

Chapter 47

1014 West Taylor Street, Chicago, Illinois, Tuesday, June 4, 1918: 10:45 am CST

One thing was for sure. Rinaldo Villetti's operation was not looking so great. Exactly one week before Taddeo would meet up with one severely bludgeoned Sega, at The Theresa in Upper Manhattan, was when Arlene was about to learn that even Colosimo's Chicago was not rating so well, in New York's sights. Weakness had been seen. A whole web of new entanglements had entwined themselves in possibly more than several other whole webs of their own, older entanglements, to be specific. And they now had attracted new visitors down to Taylor Street — and not just those who were fans of the Yankees.

Then, Madame Moresco arrived to visit the lounge personally, once more late Tuesday morning, on June 4. And she brought her nephew Giovanni Torrio, more popularly known as Johnny The Fox, with her, along with a scathing scouting report, to put it in Tad's terms. Colosimo was not happy with a few too many things the Terranovas saw while the crew from The Morello Family was there in Chicago, with their Jewish money handlers — *or were they more than that?*

Taddeo had succeeded in quietly seeing to it that the young Outfit had failed to even find and punish O'Rourke, who quite the public scene had been made over, because of Urso. The eldest Villetti brother immediately began providing Moresco an inventory of excuses as for why the Irishman had gotten away. Urso felt *he* was being held responsible for making Torrio look like quite the fool. Only Arlene and Mr. Li knew of the young baseball player's involvement in that inning. And so, The Fox had faltered, right in front of New York's big shots, because of it. The direct consequence was one big loss of confidence in Chicago. Privately, somebody must have revealed something like that to Colosimo, but that this conversation *had to have occurred*, would have been obvious to *anyone* who'd be mindful of the state of The House as it were. Arlene had quite the inside view and remembered the young fixer-upper who had visited her in The Sisson a couple weeks ago. Now she did figure the arrogant hymies really had their hand in all things because *that particular Jewish fixer*, had been sent in all the way from New York, and in support of *Irish* interests. Somehow it all connected to her family and Dean O'Banion, who was only allegedly *not* linked to Joseph "Sport" Sullivan, who allegedly was not operating for the Irish — for much larger gains in much larger arenas. *Yeah, riiight.* And her cousins wanted to rob them all while the shylocks were working both sides of the river.

What this would mean — personally for her — was it would be exceptionally stupid of her to endure any more abuse, take any more risks with anyone else's lives, while she waited around Villetti's for a payout. Arlene concluded *that* would not be forthcoming, because now no one had any money. For some reason, she figured that even the Jews held no true liquid assets. Otherwise, they would not be putting this pressure on The Outfit, after having used the internal conflicts in The Mafia, as cause for the Terranovas to make all the introductions in Chicago that she and Taddeo had been observing.

So the young woman knew something big was in the planning. But there was one huge lack of currency that would sooner than later be discovered, where now way too many factions, extremely competitive and distrustful of one another, were involved. And they all were way too invested. She'd personally witnessed the relevant local organizations attempting to be all too stingy with the money, on both sides of the river — *because they no longer had any*. They'd bled out far too much of their resources into whatever was some big collective plan. But she would bet on there being one hell of a war coming once all parties learned that there could be no more funds gained as a reward for their participation — from whatever they now met up together over their worries about investing in. *Arlene* had *inadvertently uncovered evidence that all parties to this from Chicago were way over-extended.* Now she had best find out exactly what was in the works, because Bill Fallon and her other cousin had already positioned her as a pawn in this game — and that was part of her pawn's job. But pawns got sacrificed. Whatever was planned and even already began to get underway, deeply worried her. *And what was Tad facing in Boston because of this?* As far as Arlene knew, he'd then be traveling to Philadelphia. That could temporarily put him out of New York's reach. *But he'd be alone and unprotected. While somehow, all of this was connected.* She wouldn't bother trying *not* to care. He was her child's father.

Greggorio was there on the scene too of course, appearing to try to help his father scramble to make excuses, not just for five killings, three which Arlene knew that *she* was even personally responsible for, but also for a drug overdose while a United States Congressman and his son were on the premises — let alone both of them being there at the same time. This was to be stringently avoided for fear of any leaking of that information while the lawmaker's public approval would be required to be unblemished for the guineas to achieve what they could in the capitol to The Outfit's next benefit. *Which was exactly what?* Bits and pieces of the conversations that Arlene could listen in to suggested that Jim Colosimo even disagreed with some aspects of his own family's vision. And all this had to be happening at nearly the same time as were two high-profile street fights, one being an all-out stadium brawl that required the assistance of not only private security and the police, but the Chicago Fire Department to get control over. The national newspapers even wrote about it in more detail because it involved baseball, which to Arlene, was the singular most boring national pastime there could be — although Chicago's papers only glossed over the riots, no doubt purposely downplaying it by orders for the benefit of the local elected officials. And it protected their city's stupid sport — or the proceeds from it, collected by the gamblers. So in turn, they could buy the politicians. But the representatives of The Outfit who met that morning were wary as Annenberg controlled or influenced much of the press, and he was a Jew. What might be printed, could sway elections like they swayed McKinley's. Johns were always leaving out-of-town newspapers in the brothel's guestrooms, so the competing heads of The Family — and she — saw what was printed in some of Annenberg's other cities his media empire covered. The Jews were in position to easily turn the tables on not only the guineas, but her own people as well. What they published about Chicago's corruption, could curtail any and all the national funding from the Republican Party, thereby overturning the local district and city-wide held seats of Mann and Madsen, as well as Thompson. And Arlene knew firsthand, and by the hands that took care of a dead visitor in her former hotel room, that the shylocks would, because they could, and because they really wanted something in The Windy City as well — and very badly. Plus, now and hopefully never-to-be-forgotten, in what was *not* the printed part of the local lore, was Johnny Torrio's failure to settle down "the leprechaun meat peddler."

So the Irish reasoned that there would not need to be any further attempt to take revenge by any of her people —but neither was it time for a wholesale rebellion by the shopkeepers, against The Outfit. The Italians were embarrassed, and very angry about it all. However, she had been able to overhear that this was one less thing her people would be distracted by, as as had learned the wops, because all the factions' needed to get along right now, their attention needing to be directed somewhere else. But on what? Arlene needed to discern every advantage over these guineas that she could possibly get.

Only then, to top it all off, there was Urso, escalating the disappearance of one of their whores, *Sega the Greek no less*, into a priority missing persons case and threatening the police that he'd hire out-of-state bounty hunters or bring this up to Acting Chief Alcock, if the individuals who were the-usually-depended-upon cops, didn't prioritize the eldest Villetti brother's beck and call to find her, allegedly on behalf of The Family. But Arlene assumed this Detective Conway and his men had always been paid by *Greg* and his father, so the police would naturally have the attitude that *they* could *disrespect* Urso, even if nobody else could. They still had some independent power as long as Mayor Thompson kept up some organized fight to retain it. And the non-cooperation part with Urso was the oldest brother's own fault — but only because he was so cheap. However, ignoring anything Urso demanded could create more problems when and if he could remember what he'd been demanding.

Arlene noted that she might want to scale back on her own experimentation with drug use that with her stress she'd come under, was tempting her to try. She wished she could just bear her burdens sober. She was dealing with her first month of pregnancy on top of everything else — and keeping it a secret, nearly alone in the knowledge — and while she attempted to navigate the guineas' criminal underworld and with nearly no support, to try and figure out what her own family needed her to accomplish there. *"It will become apparent,"* they told her. "It is all very complicated." She envied her — what? *Friends?* As Jasmine and Delilah, more frequently Daphne, although curiously *never* Rose, controlled their ability to want just a little "medicine" to help them get through their nightly routines. Only it would be a cheap vacation she might somehow have to find the opportunity to steal herself away on. Though Arlene doubted she could afford it — that is, letting her guard down.

Urso's complications could certainly steal away more of the

kind of national attention that would not make The Windy City feel locked-down, secure, in only the matter of the time before the press compounded each new scandal with all the rest. And even while there was a world-wide war going on, one Villetti or another would always find a way to get attention — and possibly even beat the family she was born into, at starting the next war in Chicago. However, the few Villettis with any common sense among them, could focus only on the part of the story about "some whore-gone-missing" that Rinaldo or even Greggorio might see the advantage in caring about. That being the part that could garner public sympathy for poor immigrants. And by way of some article that some Jane Addams-trained idealist could get printed — even in the Hearst papers, it would be good for Mike Merlo's fund-raising. Then they would not be entirely dependent on the Jews being happy with their situation, to deal with that story — so that they would *not* kill it to keep the dagos subordinate, as the kikes went about their business with the Irish, while the dagos secretly developed a new source of funding — if they could do it without the Hearst organization learning they'd actually been duped into helping the much-maligned Italians. The wops already had limey and even Irish collaborators. So could Moresco and Torrio even be *that blind* to not see the bigger picture? *Or were they not in on this?* Now it was a fact that the city's "legitimate" and illegitimate both needed more outside funding — and for Chi-Town to attract out-of-town recreational tourism when they were done propping up their next money-earning venture they were so obviously going to be working on. So they really needed a spectacular reputation as "the destination" for vacationers — not the murder capital of the United States. Only Arlene's personal priority was murder — of Rinaldo and any of his sons she didn't personally — what, love?

But perhaps with the help of the occasional opioid shot into her tied-off blood flow, and only released when she was only too ready to receive some much-needed rushing flow *of maybe just one last instant release*, and then numbing of her tortured feelings, Arlene could forget about her sea of conflicting emotions. Yet she was a small creature in a Great Lake full of sharks. The drugs weren't really going to help her escape. However, they surrounded her and presented a temptation that under all of this extreme pressure, she might never be able to resist. It was her undeniable nature to be a realist. Though what Arlene really needed was her gun back to take the right shots. It would be that one real equalizer for her *real family*, that it was originally designed to be.

Now she wondered why was Fallon even coming there? For what? This petty nonsense seemed beneath the Irish inserting a legal professional's effort — even one with such dubious credentials like Billy's. And the dagos', including Taddeo's missteps, certainly shouldn't be worth what she'd been subjected to, as far as her real family should be concerned, *to only determine this*. The Jews had all the money. Arlene knew the Irish didn't; the Italians didn't. So that only left one option. But her brilliant immediate relatives plotted to rob the wrong money train. *Maybe I should let them? It's not like I care*. Taddeo's family should protect him — and perhaps Arlene's child, born into that family. As long as Greggorio could never be allowed to attain power. Plus Urso's priorities were not, or shouldn't ever be, The Family's concern. Only his specific talent for making situations worse could be. The brothers would have to be eliminated. Only now had things in the underworld deteriorated enough that the complications had become the top heads running The Outfit's concern? And not that it had mattered to her, when she'd first accepted the role, but why did the Irish families want a spy in The Outfit to observe and report on all of this? It still seemed trivial save for the heist that would ultimately fail, which was only a plot known to her closest living family, anyway. And Arlene just might let them fail. They deserved to, so far as she was concerned.

Meanwhile, a soldier like Rinaldo did not like having to account for himself in front of Madame Moresco and the far younger Johnny Torrio as he sat with them in his favorite booth, where he was used to commanding the table. No doubt his pedestrian worry was that everything would get straight back to Colosimo, especially *his* negative evaluation. But Chicago would have to get its own house s in order —to meet the New York's financiers' approval — now. But again, what the fuck for? What kind of return were all the different organizations involved, expecting on their investment? Arlene needed to know.

And Sega's disappearing might now have its own special implications for the young madam of The House. Greg made sure he knew that Arlene would also be listening in when, perhaps to calm down his brother, he then announced that there was nothing to worry about, and Sega would be *found* — next week — in New York — *where she'd run away to be with Taddeo*. Though he didn't specify whether or not, she'd be found alive. But he did tell that The Family had helped her, then secured her safe transportation.

Greg took responsibility for it. Only because his older brother had been otherwise busy, he had not been told. That got Arlene fuming, possibly even more than Urso, just like Greggorio surely planned on it doing, with the Irish woman's face turning redder than her hair at this twist in the narrative. And through this move, she knew she could have just lost so much power. The young madam could already imagine why Sega specifically had been sent, by Greg, and what that whore was supposed to do there. Obviously, the woman didn't just run away to disappear all on her own, to only then make this optimally scheduled reappearance. Her constantly plotting rival was always two steps ahead of her and everyone, and he just demonstrated it. Arlene might not ever be able to get Taddeo back when she needed him, now. Not with this move of Greggorio's. She was about to dare to leave her station she worked at over by the bar, to butt in to all the present Family members' usual continued jockeying and scheming to no successful ends, when Victoria Moresco showed a lot more interest in her, just as the topic of the continuing inefficiency with finding the bordello an acceptable, permanent manager came up. The dark-haired woman in her middle-age had left her nephew to represent The Outfit's concerns with the Villettis, while she evaluated what she could overhear from the bar, and then she motioned for Arlene who had been finishing a drink in silence, along with her. The top Lady of The Outfit had taken a seat at the bar and it could look as if Arlene was only serving her a fresh drink while the men thought they worked things out, and made the big decisions around there. Arlene procured herself a second shot and took it down eagerly, then lit a cigarette.

The Irish woman had already been thinking, *Slick moves Greg.* She just knew that *he* overdosed *LuLu* and placed her with Urso so as to cause all the fighting, which then let him make it look like a good idea to send Sega back to The Family in New York — exactly when Taddeo is to be visiting there. And Greggorio had thereby also eliminated Sega as any kind of threat were she another agent infiltrated to act on behalf of Sam Cardinelli and his Black Hand — likely acting to cooperate with The Mafia, allied with the kikes, who for the right money of course, might also work contracts offered from the Irish, that Arlene wouldn't be informed of, but were obviously brokered by the Jews. New York was one dangerous web of one lethal faction in competition with another lethal faction just like Chi-Town — comprised of all too many idiots in every faction. One had to be very sharp and aware of all the players as well as not trip over their next progressively dumber and dumber decisions. But here she was pouring the head Madam a drink at the bar that Rinaldo Villetti had actually been able to open only by the grace of her husband Colosimo, and yet Arlene hadn't any proof — and thus no real reason to think she could achieve something by ratting out Greg Villetti about any of this to Victoria Moresco. *So don't do something idiotic yourself, Arlene. But why would I want to? Because — because I fell in — in love? With Taddeo?* That would be stupid. She arrived quite clear that she wanted to murder them all. Only to then have Taddeo divert her course. But Arlene resolved to keep her edge like a blade, sharp enough to finish what she went south for. Yet Greg was no fool, but perhaps the most dangerous they came. She'd slipped, not foreseen what he'd plotted, and his deeds he did in the dark, now severely threatened her personal mission on the wrong side of Chicago. And now, she still wanted to make sure *her* stupid boyfriend stayed safe while she did this. She knew the man she affectionately could think of as her *personal* idiot, was the papa of her unborn offspring. But tattle-telling on his brother's schemes would accomplish exactly what? Greggorio didn't really do anything wrong against their new Outfit's orders. Though, he sure had set things up to make it look to Moresco and even The Morello Family, that everyone else did.

Arlene knew that she was just jealous of Sega getting her way with the young fool who was after all only another Villetti — although once more, *her Villetti* — and who she now absolutely had to have return to her, to be a true father to her baby. But under the circumstances of how they parted ways, Tad could think it was over between them. No — he would think that. So of course he would take up with Sega. And she was not only rivaling Arlene for her man, but she was in the way of her doing her job at Villetti's. Arlene figured she knew who Sega really was and why Sega had been sent there. She still needed to confirm it. But if Sega was ever on a mission for Cardinelli, or ultimately the Mafia, the other woman had failed — completely. Now, so she would not, Arlene needed to keep Greg, along with Urso and their father Rinaldo, close. So she knew where they all were, when she got her gun back, just as soon as possible.

She thought she'd also come up with a new plan to temporarily control all of them, for now that she knew she was pregnant, her safety would be a far greater concern. She'd considered poison to do her dirty work, though she'd need help to orchestrate that. Arlene didn't have quite a lot of knowledge about such things. And who was there that she could trust presented itself as a problem, maybe at least until she could acquaint herself with that flower on the South Side that the Jew had brought up. Though she didn't think too much on that. Their allegiance would be to the Irish mob, not Arlene's personal mission. And The Family had Dr. Ronga on call. If even one of the Villettis survived her making any attempt on their lives — to even include secretly trying to overdose Urso — they'd probably kill Arlene, regardless if they could *not* prove it was her who had tried to end any one of them. She also knew she couldn't defend herself with a knife once they'd decided to do that. Meanwhile, Cardinelli made bombs, but his planting Sega had been dealt with. So why would the Mafia ever trust *Arlene* — "the princess of all the thieving pot-lickers" — as they'd surely see her — if she tried to approach their suspected agent in Chicago, with the objective of taking Sega's place. And anyway, how *could* an Irish woman ingratiate herself with "Il Diavolo" without losing her soul? Messing with the real Black Hand was too dangerous, and thus off the table for Arlene. Though both her cousins, and Taddeo had noted the Italians — through the Jews — were conspiring something with the Irish. But as long as the Villettis were paying him, why would Cardinelli cut off his own stream of income? And if Greg considered the possibility that Sega was dealing with that devil, *the devil*, then there was no wonder Taddeo's brother acted as fast as he could, no sooner than he could derive even one more benefit from turning her around and getting her out of Chicago. Only when Arlene could ascertain whether Stefan would still be letting her control the bordello's payroll, could she make sure she was now still able to buy police protection. Yet that wouldn't be enough.

Now, additionally, Arlene needed to make sure Greggorio didn't ever arrive too quickly at a point where he could decide he no longer needed Taddeo. Or had he done so already? As frustrating as dealing with her man was, she had to keep in contact with him while he was on the East Coast — with Sega or not — to make sure the rookie pitcher wouldn't be taken out of the game if Greg had arranged that fate instead for his brother, should the middle brother finally be targeted by "the other bitch" while she was still alive, there in Chicago.

Arlene couldn't say what leverage using Taddeo against *her* now brought Greg. After all, he had been trying to drive them apart, as had Rinaldo — or had the latter just been testing her and the strength of the resources at her disposal at the very least — like with Herbert, shot dead — by her, in her former hotel room? Though finally, she thought she knew exactly what each Villetti was responsible for of that which had befallen her and her boyfriend. Arlene saw the light between Rinaldo's and Greggorio's motivations, and where they took different turns acting on them. But Tad might not be mature enough to decide he had to let any of his women go. Now as it appeared he had two of them, as Urso had, his brother setting the example for him as one who treated his women like property and would not let any of them go. Even though the oldest brother had Lumia for now — if she was still alive, as it was hard to know from moment to moment. Arlene usually had to dodge his attention he'd pay her when many times the other woman was unconscious, *and all the while he went about ranting about Sega disappearing from his tender care*. Plus they should all have figured Arlene had been rendered disarmed by now, it having been reported that she'd tried to go for the .38 at the laundry. *Or hadn't everybody been told?* There was so much that she still could learn. Only they all didn't need to learn, if Tad still pined after her and Arlene's relationship with the youngest brother could still be used against either one of them. But everyone had always known, that Taddeo was the easiest to read and predict from among them all and he was good for using nowhere. But maybe the one exception Arlene would secretly grant him, would be to be put to use acting as a father to their unborn child. If he only knew. She would have him fulfill that role.

But what was formerly his weapon, still had all its bullets and had never been fired — even by Arlene. So how could The Family even know what she was capable of doing or had already done? Suspicions didn't count as proof. Now they could easily just decide to "vanish her," but Arlene had made herself useful to all of them, and she still had her best hand to play. True, it was the missing .45 she'd originally brought to the party. But that had only two rounds left, though three notches on the handle that she'd personally carved. However, a gun wasn't the petite young lady's only option, but there was still that she didn't know enough about poison or estimate it'd be fast enough, have a way to meet Cardinelli to learn about how to make a bomb, or think she'd be fast enough or skilled enough to use a knife and take out all of them before they'd overpower her. At present, Arlene didn't have any fast plan. Winning a boxing match with Urso wasn't an option. Plus she was pregnant and had to protect her baby. So the young Irish would-be assassin had to also conclude that what she still really needed was her gun. She was still in the process of developing any other assets.

Now she would be left little choice but to plot out how she would have to use her unborn baby in a way she really didn't care to, in order to coerce any kind of assistance, and betrayal, out of Abramo Delasandro, thus helping her get to his sons. But "the doctor" already didn't want to be a part of this operation, nor have of that for any of his boys. So Arlene would have to figure out how to convince him, and in the meanwhile, didn't need to rat out Greg and place herself in the center of a big fuss — or give Madam Moresco any cause to move any of the Villettis — quite possibly out of Arlene's range, all over bringing up Sega. That would be a worthless effort. And that was final. However, now she was going to have to get her weapon back from Katherine McCormick and then without any hesitation, find Greg, his father, and Urso — and all together — and just shoot the hell out of the whole lot of them. That would put an end to her mission. At least her personal one. Her original plan that had always seemed like the best one.

But it also bothered a lot that now since Sega was making her way to New York, she could also make a better showing of herself to Arlene's own larger family, maybe finish the greater mission that Arlene was supposed to be on — and all from out-of-state and while under Taddeo's protection. Yes, this was that other mission, about which Arlene was supposed to, and unexpectedly needed to, learn everything that she could. And the same one Fallon and her cousin in Louisiana cared more about, as did O'Banion and Sullivan — for the part they were in on — for which had become the reason her work now had her in bed with the Jews. But this job might just yield her a lot of money that she would need, once having decided she would live beyond the end of the month, after all. Now Arlene didn't know that it had to be accomplished in Chicago, though she would've figured so. But on top of that, there was something else she'd come to suspect concerning Sega's role in this. As the Greek woman might actually be an Irish insurance policy, and *not even* the devil's one. Bill Fallon always knew a working woman when he saw one.

However, none of that mattered before when Arlene planned on herself dying. Only now that she carried this baby, she had begun feeling that she would need to live for her unborn child. And she needed the money from the whole Louisiana operation that somehow Sullivan — most likely — along with O'Banion were all planning to get their hands on. *With Fallon then even planning on double-*

crossing them. He had strong ties with the shylocks, too. But she definitely couldn't let Sega take everything away from her if that was what the dark-haired Greek siren was planning — along with taking Taddeo by the opportunity his brother had awarded her. What could be that bitch's original angle in this? It might wind up mattering after all, once she was away from Greg and he could no longer drug her.

Speaking of the need to relax, just a little, Arlene wanted another drink and first poured a second one for Madame Moresco while the two shared company with one another, and each formulated their own plots in the silence. Though she felt the eyes of the Italian matriarch glancing over her many times while they were sharing this moment. Then Arlene had to laugh. In spite of Greg's attempt to leave his little brother *without her* — upon who suspicion of being a very dangerous ally wasn't at all unwarranted — with his choice of sending Sega to Taddeo, he only created another adversary for himself besides the one he was already trying to thwart. The alcohol clamped down on some of the speed the situation raced around at in her mind. But "Yesterday's Aphrodite" would figure Greggorio out, as soon as she got sober. Arlene wouldn't be taking liberties with narcissism to say she was without a doubt smarter and more physically capable than Sega ever would be. Instead, she had suffered far less because she operated more carefully than Sega had. But there was something more to that girl which could be dangerous, and Arlene wouldn't mind learning exactly what. And she also was going to get her baby's father back by her side as well, she swore as an oath to herself — even while Greg assured that Taddeo was on his way to becoming *his* mortal enemy, like Cain was to Abel. And the youngest brother was already changing. So when it was all over, which brother would turn out to be Cain? Which one would survive?

But now Madam Moresco decided she was going to intervene and offer to be Arlene's life coach. They'd drank in silence while Arlene thought and Moresco studied her. "You laughed. The situation is preposterous, isn't it? It's alright to be honest with me. And you can call me Victoria. I'm not worried about us being too familiar becoming a cause for your insubordination. Either you won't be here for long — ."

Arlene held her breath while Victoria paused her speech, worried now as she felt naked without her firearm before the wife of the boss' boss. Or the *real* boss, and even more conspiracies whirled in the wind around her. It was The Windy City after all. And it *was* past time for someone else to die. To become dust in that wind.

But she relaxed when Lady Moresco finished, "Or there will be so many other changes around here that I'll need you to remain in your position as about the only person I will then find competent enough to run this place. Yes, I might see to it that you'll be in charge permanently." Arlene's eyes widened. Victoria began truly mentoring her. "But I'll need your support for that to happen. Virtually everyone isn't finding that this place is running up to standards while it's been under your management. I didn't ask Rinaldo to pass the operation of my husband's place — really *my joint* — off onto his sons, especially his youngest, who would have no experience or sense of business if he were even here to practice at it as much as he practices his baseball game. But now that he left you in control, you should be running things better already. Now I sense you have bad instincts." Arlene frowned as the older woman continued. "In other words: good old-fashioned naughty ones." Victoria smiled. "You did me a great favor by becoming a go-to option for Katherine McCormick. And don't look so surprised. Yes, I know what *she* is doing here, and also what Representative Mann, his son, and his colleague Martin Madden are doing here. You stumbled a little during the whole crisis thing the other week, but ultimately you recovered well and nobody died, that time. But eventually all these men are getting caught in their own hypocrisy if I want them to be — and that's only the ending they're bringing upon themselves." *She* laughed. "And while Missus McCormick doesn't necessarily like me, I don't care and you *are* going to assist her in any which way you can. Because whatever she asks of you, will also help me whether that intolerable, over-opinionated elitist who thinks too much of herself likes it or not. The rest of us have to make a living. She was born into some money and then married into quite a fortunate pile of only more of it. I'd admit she's doing better than I am. So let her ideals cost her what they should. Though ultimately she won't get too far with that even if she does succeed. I have my own plan to do far better, later. I must be patient. But I told you in my sermon Sunday that you cannot succeed by having two mistresses. Only very soon, I will be the ultimate master and her interest here will also serve mine."

"Wait. I got stuck on part of that. You and Mister Colosimo — ?" Arlene risked asking such a personal question. But she had been too quick to catch on to something else, led there by the way Victoria phrased her allusion to things to come.

"Me and my husband are none of your business." That hadn't been wise — to alert the head madam to what Arlene had caught by way of her monologue. "And here you were doing so good with knowing when to just keep your mouth shut while I was testing you by sharing our drinks in silence. For a moment, you had me almost forget how young you are. But my nephew will help me with my marital issues." She nodded over to Rinaldo's favorite booth, where Greg had gotten himself a seat with his father while they conversed with who Arlene knew quite well, was called Johnny "The Fox" Torrio, for good reason. And he had been becoming quite the reason the balance in this place had been turned upside down. Urso was always off balance as it was, but worse now because he thought that Sega had apparently found him so intolerable so as to leave him and go all the way to New York to find Taddeo. Sega might have at least been smart about something, but she shouldn't have had the resources or even the motivation, considering why Arlene thought she was there in Little Italy, to suddenly run to the East Coast. That was obviously Greg's generosity at work.

Urso was always off balance as it was, but worse now because he thought that Sega had apparently found him so intolerable so as to leave him and go all the way to New York to find Taddeo. Sega might have at least been smart about something, but she shouldn't have had the resources or even the motivation, considering why Arlene thought she was there in Little Italy, to suddenly run to the East Coast. That was obviously Greg's work. If Rinaldo suspected who the Greek woman was in the first place, he would have either never taken her into the bordello — especially after the oversight that had seen Arlene arrive there by — or he would have ended her stay there at the river, not in one after another of his son's bedrooms. As even now while the others were trying to have a meeting, Urso was storming about the place shoving furniture, furious as if he should ever be surprised that everyone else and Urso didn't share the same priorities. Arlene was conscious that she was also allowing Sega to become too much of her priority.

But she watched Johnny Torrio's eyes follow the eldest Villetti brother from time to time and what she saw in the Easterner's eyes was new cause for her concern. From across the room, Arlene could spot the wise, mature deliberation of the sort made by a successful businessman around only fifteen years older than herself. And she knew the kinds of decisions this man would make, would result in some major corrective changes for the way business would be handled in Chicago. One way or another, Urso would not survive them. But it having become much more easier to kill since she had already ended three men herself, Arlene preferred it was either she who pulled the trigger, or her own machinations that achieved this to satisfy the revenge that she so desired. She knew she had better step up her own plans and move all the faster. She would not be deprived. She couldn't be. That was blood lust for you, and loyalty to one's own Irish blood. But Johnny Torrio was loyal to his aunt, and Victoria liked her. So Arlene had to now consider that her revenge could actually involve taking the restaurant, lounge and bordello from the Villettis as well, though possibly all that without having to even fire one single additional shot, and not having to flee Chicago. She could be guaranteed income to raise her child on her own, independent of all the men who could come and then die before Arlene would have to. But she wanted Rinaldo to know it was she who had defeated him — and exactly why. And somehow Arlene needed Madame Moresco to leave his youngest son alive and unharmed, so he could still be a father to her baby, his possibly starting a new relationship with Sega notwithstanding. That would be dealt with.

But her child didn't so much need an uncle. Without any word being spoken, or even their mutual introduction, she agreed with exactly what Johnny Torrio must have also been thinking. Urso needed to be ended. *The oaf didn't even think to question his brother Greg on just how his precious Sega could have paid for her train ride? Who helped her get to the station to even take it? In her condition? Or even what did Sega have to be* that *mad about while he still hosted the unconscious Lucky LuLu that he could satisfy himself with while* that *poor little thing had absolutely zero sense of self-awareness*. But Arlene hadn't forced Sega to see any other men yet. And before she'd disappeared, she seemed to prefer to spend her time with Greg when she wasn't fighting with Urso. They might all be finding themselves at one large pity-party in a whorehouse, but even if LuLu couldn't tell, Arlene still had an idea of what the difference between being pimped out and raped was. Sega should, too. There's still a difference, right? Or was there never? I've been working here too long already. Or Katherine McCormick has gotten to me by way of her influence over what had once been a clear vision for my original mission. But now the official one in her eyes, could actually go a few steps beyond what the most-giving philanthropist had stolen out of her purse. Because for the first time, Arlene could clearly see a future for herself — even in Chicago — and she wouldn't need to depend on any man, or even her gun, but rather her head, to realize it.

Victoria lit a cigarette for herself in an elongated and decorated holder, offering a light for the second short smoke of her companion's that she mentored. They took turns smoking and drinking. Quiet once more, until Moresco added, "But in the end you must choose who you ultimately land in bed with, Arlene. You have one choice — between Katherine McCormick or me. I offer you tangible power. The real kind of power I know you so desire. She offers only the empty hope of a ballot, lost in ideals that will be blown away in the winds. The illusion of control. Essentially nothing because the entire system is only becoming more and more corrupted. You will see."

Then Victoria and even Katherine McCormick's other ambitions getting in the way of her own, angered Arlene and she snapped back before she thought about it. "No. I cannot get sidetracked. I've already made a choice. I've chosen myself. That's who deserves my loyalty. And I hope to have a reckoning with the Lady McCormick, very soon. Victoria, you have no idea just who you think you are about to enable. But it doesn't matter because you don't have a better choice. Do you? I just happened along at a time that is opportune for you. Your husband is unfaithful and your nephew, one proven example of ineptitude. And my goals are congruent with yours. Do I have that right? But get this straight: nobody will control me, *Victoria*. And I already have power. Realize." Even after Arlene regretted uttering her display of contempt for it all — she knew she should have kept any more of her thoughts a secret — Lady Moresco was not at all showing any signs of displeasure, but rather surprisingly, she seemed very elated with Arlene's reaction. "Good. I wouldn't expect anyone could subjugate you. That's exactly what I had actually wanted to hear." She managed to confound, then support and even elevate Arlene. "And you *do* already have everything you need to control these men," Victoria Moresco was saying to her. "Because at first glance, favors are traded for money — our revenue, right? That is the basic gist of the *service* business. Only real money just seems to be in short supply at the moment. But favors can also be traded for some gentlemen to be made to succumb to the force of some other *less-than-gentlemen* if that needs to happen. And you can control when that happens. So when sex cannot be the method of coercion, violence can. And those elements combine to bring you power. *Realize*. Other men can be motivated by your relationship to them and your ability to bestow that power. Keep elevating your profile rather than the opposite." She nodded across the lounge to her nephew seated with the Villettis. "Following this plan has made *me* powerful. But I'm watching you Arlene. I know why you are here — your real reasons — and why you came to be here — for certain other people's reasons. And *I* allowed it. Just as I am allowing Lady Katherine to pull off all her shit that she's been up to. She thinks she's so smart. But meanwhile, you just deal with the short-term sacrifices." Then *Lady Moresco* nodded toward Urso. "They will only be temporary inconveniences, I assure you. You are safe where you are already at, and will be only growing stronger. Maintain your patience."

Arlene was still confused and grew skeptical. Only moments ago, she thought she might have been given the opportunity to control something permanently and profitable, making her remaining in Chicago worthwhile. "But then if you know everything about what some others are planning, wouldn't you want to prevent what could mean the collapse of your husband's businesses?" She'd seen the flaw in her own illusion. Victoria was tempting her vain ambitions so she could use her.

"Would I do that?" She looked at Torrio, and Arlene might have felt the only warmness ever emanated from the cold-hearted individual she parlayed with. "These are *my* businesses and some small reorganization might need to be in the works. Chicago really needs a *new* order. And I have so much to gain by what's coming. Much more than those fools who would only figure me for a dumb arm trophy. *I cut off the arms*. And some other parts. Jim had best be good to me. And you'll do well to play your part exactly as I'm sure you are adapting your plan to. I see it making you at least a whole lot better off than you are right now. Me, too. If you give my philosophy serious thought and apply what would naturally be a smart girl like you's conclusion.

"But here's one more bit of advice, Arlene. Of course we are looking for loyalty in our organization. But you know why that's one of my greatest concerns about patronizing you? It's not because you're Irish. *It's because you're not even truly loyal to yourself.* Consider your revenge motivation. Is that what you really want — to throw away a greater opportunity — for money, influence, and power for? Whoever it is you want to avenge, your family members or a lover I'd assume? They're already dead. You are not. You can live. Understand, see, that these men want us, to think they possess us. But they are the ones that are possessed *by us* — and expendable.

There's always more where one or another of them came from. You're young. You still need to grow up some more. And maybe I will help you."

And that concluded their short discussion. Lady Moresco returned with a fresh drink over to the table with the Colosimo Outfit and the men rose to bow to her before they reseated themselves, her alongside her nephew. Arlene put the cork back in the bottle she'd just poured from and admired Victoria's flowing power for those who knew how to see it. And she mused over just what that woman thought she knew about her. Then the phone in the bar rang. Arlene let Faith answer for her. It was Taddeo again. What? Has he been staying up all night in Boston? Or where is he and that stupid team of his playing now? *Philadelphia*, she thought she recalled. Is Sega *not* there yet — keeping him busy? Maybe Greg still hasn't gotten her sober enough to even send her out of Chicago. What's *his* schedule? And when does Tad arrive in New York? That's where members of The Family operated, that could help Greggorio to even do something this creative. And what does *the Tadpole* want? Her foolish paramour wouldn't return from the East Coast when she'd asked him to, even *after* she'd related to him some of the terrible details of that first weekend in which he'd been away from her. Now she'd really been pining to talk to him, and he did ask for Arlene. That's why he would call. Not because he actually cared about taking responsibility in the business. And Arlene almost let herself feel flattered. But Sega could never have arrived out there this soon, alive anyway, so *her* charms couldn't have distracted him, yet. Only Arlene had just been made so furious about all that was going on, so she then took it out on Faith, subordinate — and due to the on-site junior madam's own inability to find forgiveness toward her idiot man-child. It didn't prove too difficult as Arlene knew all too well about exactly which family he came from and her feelings about those people But Taddeo had "something more important that he had to do Back East," did he? Could that be Sega? Who knew? Now Arlene might've absolutely loved him, and really wanted to talk to him, and yet Victoria Moresco's words were not entirely lost on her either. His calling told her that he wasn't dead — for the moment anyway — and he might actually have useful information, following his propensity to offer his pitch-by-pitch recap of every ballgame she was missing. However, Arlene already having so much she needed to consider, didn't know if she could bear it if Taddeo omitted or worse, lied to her about Sega coming there — and so she made the young lady under her own authority explain how the night manager was not presently available.

* * * * *

That was a whole week ago. Then, Arlene had made it clear she had decided she was not speaking with Taddeo. So from Boston, he had traveled on to play in The Baker Bowl in Philadelphia, no less than two maximum security prisons, and now after he'd just arrived in New York last night, it was past seven o'clock this very next morning Tuesday, June 11. And Tad *had* been up the whole night — with Sega — and Michael and Trevor — sitting on the floor of their hotel room between the beds and hearing her out concerning the cold hard truth about the situation back in Chicago. And that, even after he'd just gotten out of prison. Inspecting Sega as a Family asset was important House business he'd told himself, when Trip and Bass-Man headed downstairs and some privacy led to the pair indulging in much-needed sex Taddeo had been denying himself on this road trip. It wasn't like any of his single teammates had denied themselves — and the pitcher couldn't rest. The circumstances that had evolved bothered him so. There in Upper Manhattan he had first, repeatedly tried again to phone the one woman he still truly cared the most for, in Chicago. But at 4 am in her time zone, Arlene would just not talk to him over the widening divide between them. Instead, he only succeeded in aggravating Mr. Li, waking him from his sleep, to get hollered at by the angry Chinaman, and pestering Old Lamont as that one just arrived to work. Then he thought he was being lied to by Jezebel when he called back. Surely, Arlene was at either the bar or the laundry at that hour. Tad would bet she knew he called, but was having someone help her give him the runaround. But the pitcher was unable to retire in Sega's arms after he allowed himself to so easily be seduced there — and on towards other warm places — so he'd gotten up and fetched his friends from downstairs, grateful for the privacy they'd gifted him, but knowing they'd be much more comfortable back in their room versus the hotel lobby. He and Sega could keep their voices down so if his friends found they could catch a few minutes of shut-eye in case any of the rookies had to play in the game against the Giants that afternoon. But secretly, Tad hoped for his closest friends gaining an interest in his own position his family had put him in, and their offering up at least support, if not strategy, for dealing with it. No one really got any sleep.

Taddeo tried two more times to phone the woman he still truly wanted to care for, a few hours later, but Arlene would just not talk to him and a widening divide had really begun to develop between the pair. As payback, and because he felt better in the way he interacted with Sega, the pitcher decided to ignore new and repeated calls from home once she'd apparently decided she'd changed her mind.

Now the hapless young, colored fella who worked as the night clerk, already flustered for too much of his duties on his shift had been relegated to managing the contacts for the Cubs' rookie pitcher, was asked to shrug off even another call from home. Taddeo Villetti was mad at his woman, *again*. It was just the unfortunate fate of the beleaguered Negro to be tasked with heading upstairs and downstairs, upstairs and downstairs, as the personal answering service of the pitcher — a position he never signed on for, because the athlete unplugged his own phone by ripping it out of his guestroom's wall. He was so furious with Urso, when Sega described the true extent of his brother's deprivations, he started tearing up The Theresa worse than he had The Buckminster. While his teammates and he lost some very well-needed sleep, Taddeo had also been left feeling really mad at his old lady, too — for allowing the obvious ill fate that had befallen Sega. How did she let everything that he had set up for her at Villetti's fall apart like this?

He'd previously tried to phone the Irish woman at the laundry and at the bar, but could never seem to reach her. However, he just knew *she* had decided not to take his call, at whichever location she hid. The times he phoned only served to thoroughly irritate Mr. Li. And then when she seemed to change her mind about talking to him, about another half hour later, Tad didn't want to speak with Arlene any longer.

The wounded but still beautiful Greek woman who had regaled the ballplayers in their room with the sad tale she told them next, had put *everyone* in a distraught mood — except for The Hoff of course, who finally came by from his room, where his *two* lady-friends still slept — of course. However, Tad's catcher's excitement over continuing their team's winning streak on The Polo Grounds inadvertently stirred up enough inspiration in Taddeo to suggest to himself a new way that he could still win against his brothers all the way from Manhattan.

He left them all in his room and went down to the lobby once again, so he could have some privacy when he dialed Villetti's this next time. And of course, Arlene wasn't speaking to him, *again* —

if she was even still there — but this time presumably "because *he* didn't answer her call earlier," as some other new girl informed him. But this young lady sounded so drugged that he asked for her to call on someone else to tell him about how things were with Arlene, especially after this girl also told him in her slurred speech that she didn't think she was even supposed to be on the phone. Lumia, he thought she said her name was. But over the telephone, only her softer, feminine voice distinguished her garbled speech from Phil Douglas. *The drunks I have to deal with.*

But following Tad's request, another young lady, Delilah, that he did know of course, did confirm that Arlene was "around," but mad at him, as per usual now. No surprise there. First she was angry. Then she wasn't, and had even discussed it among the girls' inner circle, only next deciding to call. And when he wouldn't answer at The Theresa, Arlene decided to forget about him all over again. For Taddeo, there had been no successfully contacting her for almost a week now, and then she'd changed her mind about that three times in one hour. And then Delilah was told to get off the phone. When Taddeo dialed even another time, he found he couldn't count on Faith. He wished he could reach either Jasmine or Roslyn, but he was told they were both with clients. At least Vickiee offered that as an explanation. And Arlene still just couldn't be bothered.

He'd spent so much time waiting on hold over the telephone, pacing around as far as the phone cord let him, that after nearly a million attempts, he'd finally gotten his chewing gum to stick to the hotel lobby's ceiling. He ignored a few of The Theresa's early guest arrivals or departures who stared at him, for what Taddeo figured must have been their being impressed with the skill exhibited by the athlete's arm. He loved being admired, but his focus was on he and his woman being involved in something potentially very dangerous, and Tad could not believe she was being so immature. So he was really not trying very hard to demonstrate his skill with pitching Wrigley's chewing gum. This game of phone tag was getting ridiculous. So like an adult, the youngest Villetti just stuck his next wad of gum under the tabletop so he could speak clearly. And then he contacted Mr. Li at his laundry again.

The Chinaman was irate, too — and it was much harder to understand *him* this time than even the lush at the bordello, once he got to shouting in his broken English. Taddeo made out something about his being horribly worried over some threat to his daughter. Tad's cousins might have been involved, though it didn't sound like

Stefano or Corrado. But it could have been several of the younger Delasandros. It took a few minutes, but Tad thought he was able to explain that yes, he did understand it was five o'clock in the morning, Chicago time. And then he was at least able to broker a new deal with him. He'd order Arlene "to pay Mr. Li's concerns more tribute" — in the form of favors — so that he could increase his security by way of hiring some additional aid from the enforcers who always hung around his father's place. Specifically, the pair would trade the other working girls' sexual favors for the efforts by the new goombahs. This could convince them to listen to Arlene's orders versus even his papa's or especially Greggorio's. But then this idea proved unacceptable to Mr. Li, as he said the associates would never stand up to Villettis or Delasandros who were Family. The House was their primary employer. Instead, Mr. Li said he was acquainted with *the right people* and Arlene only need bring him the money. Taddeo agreed in spite of being uncomfortable with that, and not knowing exactly who the Chinaman thought were *the right people*, or how he'd manage to get more money. But he expected Arlene would then do her best to reconnect with him — once she got the bill. Ultimately shorting his father, who had to pay Colosimo, not to mention to pay *off*, Cardinella, all in order to pay Li, was actually a terrible idea once Tad thought about it — but only after he agreed to it. So he made a note to himself to stop making all decisions in the future until he had a lot more time to sleep on them. Only now after that, all Tad simply had to do, was figure out was where the money was going to come from. *Simple, right? Uh, yeah.*

He was absolutely proven correct that Arlene would contact him though, just as soon as she learned about the new deal he just agreed upon with the laundryman. He'd barely stepped a few dozen feet away from the public phone, to call for the elevator, before the clerk had received a call from his woman in Chicago. It was being redirected for him to take back on the guest phone since Taddeo declined to have his conversation with Arlene play out in front of all his friends and Sega who were up in his suite right now. And at that particular moment, he really didn't want to explain to The Theresa's staff why the private phone that was originally dedicated to his room, was no longer working. Without a new stick, at least he had some semi-fresh gum stuck under the table that he pulled a chair across the lobby and up to. The clerk watched and Tad stared back at him. "What? Are you going to say something?" The pitcher served the words so softly that they could not have possibly been overheard by the young Negro, but his look he gave the hired help was clear. *Mind you own goddamned business*. Taddeo had enough trouble at the plate.

"Arlene?" He tried to sound friendly, excited. He did his best to fake it anyway, hiding his anger. "Why are you calling so late? You sound upset. Are you okay?"

"I'm just getting raped. Of course I'm okay, Tad." Arlene was fuming. She hadn't been prepared for just how absolutely enraged she'd become upon hearing his voice. It was also crazy at how relieved she was to hear his voice, but she was never going to tell him that. She had everyone else pushing her buttons, while they were dumping their work onto her, and she managed one crisis after another at the bordello. Why would she ever feel upset?

But that bastard had Sega there, surely by now. She was probably in his room right at that very moment. Arlene waited on the telephone for Taddeo to respond. He was surprisingly very quiet for the moment but she could hear him sound like he chewed on some big ball of bubblegum while he chewed on her words. She stayed silent, waiting too. She waited for him to say just one wrong thing, just one, and was she ever ready to fire a salvo down the line.

"I'm so sorry, Arlene. I don't know what I can do. You're sure you don't want me to talk to my father?"

["Hmmm. Let me think about that one, again. Okay. I just reconsidered it. Yes, I'm fucking sure that I don't want you to talk to your goddammed father, Taddeo! Wow. I am so amazed. That you're so dumb it baffles my mind."]

"You haven't spoken to me in going on a week and then you just call now because you want to insult me?"

["I'm having a moment of weakness and I was just experiencing the symptoms of withdrawal from being regularly supplied with more examples of your idiocy over which to berate you. Stupid imbecile."]

"You don't know how much I've missed hearing the sound of your voice. But I was thinking about you and couldn't reach you in The House. So I made a new deal with Mister Li."

["And that's the only reason I'm on a call with you, Genius. Where are you going to come up with that kind of money to hire him, any men? And whose men?"]

"He just wants to protect his daughter, Arlene."

["I'm very well aware of that. Glad you also know. How nice of you to be concerned. But are you aware that you just can't *hire men?* That's why you're not your father. And you are certainly not Colosimo. But they want their cut that's coming to them. And you don't have any money. So I don't know who the hell you think you are. But you're insane, obviously."]

"You're the one going to a psychiatrist."

["*And you're in New York.* Are your eyes open? Do you see how the syndicates work? Who do you think these men back here are going to come to take their payments from? Because if they're actually worth something, it might even see them arriving at The House. I can give them the girls, but even a steady diet of pussy won't feed them. They'll come looking for more — green Taddeo. But not the kind of green with blonde on top. And depending upon who the old Chinaman finds to be in service to him, you might have just started a war. Congratulations Taddeo. You're just fucking brilliant, you know that?"]

"They might not be that emboldened, or we would have seen these guys encroaching on my papa's territory before. Have you considered that maybe the Chinaman's bluffing. The House hires only the *best men* in all South Chicago."

["Who? Like Pepe and Thorello? Suppose Li hires the Genna Brothers from the Near West Side? Or have you thought of that? *He might have*."]

"Only they've got some kind of friendly dealings going on with Greg."

["Well that's just so comforting."] Arlene even laughed out loud.

"So maybe they'll only come to Li looking for the payouts."

["I sleep on Mister Li's floor, Retard! And with all due thanks to you."]

"I thought you were sleeping with Urso, or Stephan. I didn't want to guess who's bed you've now crawled into."

Oh, this really did it. "That situation got really old Taddeo — like a week ago. And if you really minded, I'd have thought I'd see you get back here and doing something about it. So let me see. Moving on, maybe by now I've been through the White Sox, the Yankees, Philadelphia, and at this stage I am about ready to develop new memories of Boston. How's it going for you, Taddeo? Are you seeing any action? Who are *you* sleeping with?"

["Usually Everston and Bass, because Hoff won't share a room."]

Very funny. It's likely the only clever thing that he *can even think of saying. He's not telling me Sega is there. But* I know. *I know*.

["Look, I'll figure out what we're going to do to control Li. There's got to be a way I can come up with more money. You work the girls."]

You're working one for me. I wonder if Sega knows he keeps calling back here. She will not take him from me. But for all the Villettis' sins — including those of my foolish-man-child's — there will be a reckoning. Aphrodite *there is only a symptom of all the hurt and pain his family has caused me all my life, even before* I *ever personally met any one of those guineas. I can't trust my own people, my cousins. What they've done, what they will do, and what they'd ultimately let befall a girl, orphaned way too young. I was just their crazy, suicidal-bitch cousin they could use to further their own plans. Like they'd always been using me. And I will never have the life my parents would have made for me. Not thanks to the Villettis. But I will orchestrate bringing about the life I can make for myself now. And who knows? Maybe this deal, any war it causes, and Mr. Li are going to help me bring that reckoning down on them all. They should not have ever messed with me.* Arlene had no love for Fallon, O'Banion, or any of those on the North Side, either. In fact, she reckoned, she almost had no love left period.

Tad didn't have much time left. It was now past seven in the morning, Eastern Time. He had moved the chair and was pacing in the lobby again, as far as the stretched phone cord allowed him. His chewing gum tasted pretty stale by now and he discarded it under the table once more. "But it's kind of hard to talk right now. I'll get money — somehow. I'll just have to figure out how and to who I'm going to lay the new deal out. Will you answer when I phone you in Chicago?" He got his answer as he heard the sound made by the earpiece being slammed into its station on the microphone stand as Arlene hung up on him.

When Taddeo finally did get to lie down again, he got no rest whatsoever even though Trip and The Bass-Man took breakfast out with Hoff so he could have a bed, and Sega rejoiced she could at last be alone again with Taddeo. The woman worked herself overtime to make sure she won over Taddeo's dedicated, unsaturated support. He'd find no moment to rest and think about things right now. He felt erotically fascinated with the slightly older and much more experienced woman — experienced in the art of creating real passion. It sure beat suffering from the pain of frustration. That it did by a long shot.

Sega pushed his weary body on to one of the beds and straddled him as she lifted her dress above her head and undid her bra to point *her guns* at him. Aroused, his hands found new strength to slide up her smooth thighs helping her lift her deep red, sequin tasseled dress up at least above her waist. He was careful not to put too much pressure on her wounds by his delicate touch. The amount of bruising on her body almost brought his passion to stall, it was so disconcerting. But her hands on his sore shoulders, especially his pitching arm, her pressure she put on it and the other one, felt so good as she used them to brace herself as she pushed her slim, light body up his tight-muscled young chest until her panty's crotch tickled Taddeo's mouth. He knew she was going to look for one to go right up in the center of her strike zone. Even with her cracked lips and fading black eyes, her still youthful smile — missing one tooth, reportedly courtesy of Urso — made her still so irresistibly cute, as she was extremely happy to be with Taddeo, and under his protection. It was quite a change — his being appreciated for once. His stick erect, he easily took a position where he'd be ready to swing at whatever Sega pitched him. If Arlene didn't want to deal with him? Fine. The new couple ripped apart the entire hotel room, playfully enjoying their lust everywhere from on top of the armoire to on top of the heater that Tad laid hotel sheets across and under the woman's tight small ass to protect Sega when the athlete brought his heat for one up and inside. They did things to each other even on the window sill — amazing things, pleasurable things — with the pitcher even hoping The Hoff would be returning back to the hotel to look up and see; then maybe George could show a little consideration and at least keep Trip and Bass-Man in his room for one night so Taddeo could enjoy his in private for once — while his teammates could each contribute to keeping Hoffman out of the prison system for a spell. This would allow Tad to take his liberties for good behavior, with Sega — and he would consider this new arrangement part of George's sentence for his original crime. He even wanted The Hoff to feel jealous of him. He — and Sega — they both had so much physical and emotional pain. Hoffman had even inadvertently contributed to a small part of it, now — and no doubt especially for Arlene. So there ought to be a cost for doing that. And Villettis made sure all prices were paid, didn't they? So the new lovers finally did fall asleep in each other's arms on one of the now-stripped beds when it seemed like only minutes passed — before George came back with one of the other guys' room keys and entered without knocking. "Hey, Taddy-Whacker. Wake up. Get up. It's eleven-forty-five. Get your uniform on. I don't want to dress you. But I gotta get you over to The Polo Grounds and onto the field for practice. We've got a game against the Giants in less than three hours. Coach is going to want to see how all us rookies managed to stay out of trouble our first night in The Big Apple. We wouldn't want to disappoint him now, would we?"

"Yeah. Of course not. We should be just as good as we were for him in Boston."

Hoff just laughed and shook his head. "Ouch. That shot hurt. Stay mad at me if you want, but get yourself ready to bring it — onto the field. But just the same, you better hope they don't pitch or even play uh, maybe *any of us* today."

This Taddeo did indeed hope. He felt like he'd only just fallen asleep — albeit after amazing sex with one slightly older, more experienced real woman, when George was there already calling his balls. As if The Hoff could get any more annoying on this road series. But there were much worse pains Taddeo would learn, that he had only just begun having to face.

Chapter 48

What next got immediately worse for all of the Cubs, was very annoying and inconvenient press — and right in the middle of a seesaw series at The Polo Grounds, home to the very tough and competitive-in-the-standings, New York Giants.

Even with getting no sleep in that he could speak of, Tad was anticipating this incredible opportunity to take the time to appreciate this famous ballpark, with its massive steel and double-deck grandstands that had begun "growing" into the shape of a horseshoe for the largest seating capacity of any Major League stadium of the day. To be sure, entering the enormous ballpark was intimidating even while it was exciting. Home to not only the National League Giants, but the American League's legendary New York Yankees. But for no apparent reason, a scathing sports editorial that bordered on insinuating criminal charges of bribery for the purpose of actually fixing *baseball* — and spoiling any honest game starting *here* — had just made it to print.

One William Barclay Masterson wrote quite a gutsy exposé on Max Flack taking money from gamblers connected to organized crime. In interviews, Masterson, a former lawman who'd made a name for himself as an infamous gunslinger out west in his younger days, was quite the police-interrogator-kind of reporter for the *New York Morning Telegraph.* He got Max to admit that he was twenty-two years old when the ballplayer from Belleville, Illinois lied about his age while signing with Peoria, and instead reported he was only eighteen. "I wanted to be younger. Everyone wanted to be in those days." This could cause his whole contract with the Cubs and everything the team might have achieved by way of his hitting, to be challenged by Major League Baseball.

Masterson suggested that if Flack started out by lying about that, what else was this fella being dishonest about? Max even said he wasn't ever that comfortable in sports and had on occasion expressed doubts about whether he'd make it in the Big Leagues. And with some digging, the cop-turned-investigative-sports-reporter learned that Flack's wife had a young boy with him, and that Chicago's right fielder would never risk injury so he could keep his $5,000 / year contract, he was even now fighting to increase his income on, so that he could support his small family rather than be forced to return to iron-working and making cook-stoves with his father back in the Midwest.

Taddeo had already been nurturing suspicions about Flack and whether he was putting all his work into defending the Cubs' pitching that he could be. Hearing these accusations caused all the Cubs pain. But also Max, a base-stealer who by a different account had a solid reputation, would sometimes be inexplicably caught off the bag, though he didn't seem to ever sacrifice his batting average. However, the young rookie still wasn't sure about these allegations. It could just be that Masterson was biased in favor of the New York team and wanted to slander the Cubs who now had a very tentative lead in the National League, to patronize or increase this reporter's local readership — and who'd be Giants fans, of course.

But during game-time on Tuesday, Tad was witness to more that would bring his teammate into doubt. Young Villetti did ride the bench just as he'd hoped, after being kept up all night in prison, and then with Sega when he was let out of his reorientation-with-society session that he'd completed with Rocco Valenti. But after hiding his lady-visitor from Chi-Town in his hotel room at The Theresa, and with a promise to bring her food and take her out later, he figured he'd have time to sort out his head with everything that had just gone down since his arrival to The Big Apple. In the present, he watched his veteran athlete friends play a baseball game. If he had no other care in the world, this is how he'd have loved to spend his time. Here he was relaxed and he found piece of mind to think. Then it became one heck of an exciting back and forth game that held the audience's — and Tad's — most acute attention, but for very different reasons.

Unless he was mistaken, some of the very same questionable and most-likely extremely threatening characters that he'd seen sitting with his father and Big Jim Colosimo — and even with Tad's team's owner at Weeghman Park — now started walking through the stands from where Taddeo first spotted them, by the Giants' 3rd base dugout. At first, Villetti didn't think much about them being there. That would be expected. Only this one single and bold man, followed up with a whole group of others among Giants partisans, who seemed to be with him, had drawn attention to themselves by moving and upsetting many other spectators. But they were nevertheless shown a lot of courtesy, too much courtesy, for who *those fellas* were. Others who were there only to view the game, and yet almost stood up immediately, regardless of what they were eating, smoking, or drinking, to carefully let these characters pass. Tad lost sight of the suits once they disappeared into the curvature behind home plate but they soon reappeared right next to the edge of the visitors' dugout in which Tad sat against the far right field wall. Coach Mitchell noticed them as well, and the Cubs watched their manager cross in front of the entire bench from where he usually analyzed the game, standing as close as possible to the dish and Bill Klem, who officiated this game. Now, standing in front of Tad so the rookie could not even see the field unless he looked to his left and past The Hoff's smiling satisfied face that he really did not care to see, Fred Mitchell leaned against the same furthest-away dugout wall and listened, as did Taddeo, to the voices of the men in suits and fedoras who gathered there to discuss business.

It was the top of the 3rd inning. The Giants led 1-0.

"Hmmm. Flack's on base," someone said.

"On a walk. And Tesreau balked already. He's in trouble for hell knows what reason and McGraw's warming up Anderson to possibly finish the inning."

Tad looked out across The Polo Grounds and out in left field, exposed to game play, the Giants got their reliever started. That was an uncomfortable position for the bullpen. Of course it wouldn't be any better for the visiting team's side. And everybody wanted to hit down either baseline since it was approximately 260 feet to either outfield wall but 450 out of the horseshoe into dead centerfield. Babe Ruth was one of the only ballplayers who could hit with the kind of power necessary to drive a baseball out there. But on the side of the field, is where the Giants' John Frederick Anderson started warming up his arm for pitching.

Meanwhile, the men who visited by the Cubs' bench continued talking, Mitchell listening. As was young Villetti — trying to hear anything that could also help him identify just who was actually calling this game. "The Jews didn't say whether or not they think Flack should score," the first voice he'd heard added.

"But he's projecting too high of profile, what with "Masterson's View on Timely Topics" in *The Morning Telegraph*. I really couldn't fathom what the shylocks want to be the move here. I really wouldn't care. And Chicago's got their own man out here. What *I* think is that we need to talk to that old leprechaun who's publishing this shit, stirring up trouble."

"You go on and do that Ciro. Or I'd send D'Aquila. That might resolve two problems for us." A new voice spoke. Then it laughed. "But you do realize that the hymie family of *Annenberg* owns *The Telegraph*?"

"You're not scared Giuseppe? Of Masterson. They say that his quick-draw is still just as fast as it was back in his glory days in Arizona."

Was this Ciro, Ciro *Terranova? And was he speaking with* the *Giuseppe "Joe The Boss" Masseria?* Taddeo feared the worst, with *these men* coming over to discuss the game right on top of Chicago's bench — right on top of him. His body began involuntarily shaking.

"The old man is what? Sixty-four. His mouth is sharper than his aim. A situation I want corrected and I don't care how. Let's be clear. I'm not afraid of his guns. I'm just rather busy. If D'Aquila is too much of a coward, send Pagano or the other Valenti. Order it. The latter vouched for his relatives in Chicago being down for this. One of their people's here. He wants to be involved? Let *him* be involved. Or use the connection with the ten-percenters. They write Mister Righteous' checks. There's more than one way to terminate his livelihood."

Wait. Someone from The House followed me *here all the way to Harlem from out of Chicago? So his immediate family had people already prepared to take some kind of action here. Why was* this *even necessary? And who sent them? Had they been in Philadelphia and Boston before that, too?*

"What do you suppose our old Marshal's angle is on this?"

"Masterson? That ancient badge who actually murdered the law?" the voice more than likely belonging to a different underling who entered the conversation.

"*We* don't?"

"Well I never went to Police Academy. But Masterson can smell a good bet when one finds its way under his big nose. And nothing ever needed be legal for him to get himself a piece of that. He made his name in the *athletic world* with boxing. Irish bugs always find themselves a way to infest a crooked ring. So he's *a fine one* to be writing about corruption in professional sports. But this time I'd gamble that his aim is on using his yellow journalism to find his way "in" — likely with Sullivan, striking into baseball for a little change. Actually, now that I just thought better of it, we should settle back and let Rothstein handle it. Let the kikes do some heavy lifting. Plus Mister Big will already be keeping his eyes on 'ol Joe Sullivan. It's a good bet Masterson is here to make *his* move for the big leprechaun."

"But do we do anything about Max Flack?"

"Well, we don't need him in the spotlight right now."

Coach Mitchell suddenly stirred to life from where he'd been leaning against the wall listening and watching as the Giants' Fred Anderson warmed up. "Bass, find your glove. I'm likely putting you in for Flack starting at the bottom of this inning or another, really soon," he said.

That was odd. The change on the lineup card wasn't even being made for a base-hitting situation. Flack was even already *on* base. Taddeo just *knew* that the conversation he and his coach had just overheard had influenced Mitchell's decision. He'd love for his friend to get a chance to play, but Trevor looked like he just woke up when Coach called his name. It would just be Tad's personal preference, but they should sub in Turner Barber. There was no reason to see Bass-Man screw up one of his few chances to play only due to lack of sleep — and that would be Tad's fault there. Now he hated his team's and his experience and his own record in baseball all being messed with like this. And Tad hated New York. But Trevor looked suddenly alive and thrilled to be called upon to play and possibly even stay in for almost a full game, anyway. Tad just hoped he wouldn't get hit with a baseball — especially a batted one, while he napped out there in right field.

So then with an often-dominating battery of Hendrix and Killefer, the Cubs marched on. But New York was going to be giving them their toughest fight, yet.

In the previous innings, Claude had already neutralized their leadoff man, Youngs, only to see Ben Kauff take his slider for a ride out into The Polo Grounds' spacious centerfield. It was exactly the last place Dode Paskert thought New York would hit out toward because it was a shorter distance from home to the walls in either left or right fields — nearly half the distance. Yet nevertheless, Kauff had time to run for two bases, until Paskert could get the ball back to Hollocher as his cutoff. Then George Burns would begin to start his demonstration that he was not afraid of Claude Hendrix, and he also got on base with a single. But it tipped off Charlie's glove as it ripped through the infield and Deal was right behind him, backing him up. Mitchell had coached them well. Hendrix rushed to play 3rd base, as The Polo Grounds were so spacious that if Lester Mann was on time to back up Paskert in that deep pocket at the opening of the big horseshoe, than Deal had to be limber and play shortstop along with Hollocher in the event of this kind of infield hit. Relays from out of the green pastures tested fielders' arms and runners' legs under blue skies and the bright summer's sun. But Hendrix saw no play to help him out in that frame. Kauff was held on the 2-bag, though Bob Emslie called Burns safe at 1st. Zimmerman hit Burns over to 2nd in his first AB. But he was able to hit to the opposite field, intending to help Kauff score. Tad held his breath and forgot all about being sleepy when it was Max Flack's turn to make the play. But the big outfielder returned the ball to Rollie Zeider fast, and Chicago's 2nd baseman's head was in the game. He fired across the diamond to Charlie Deal, who received the ball for a force out even before Kauff took a diving slide to the 3-bag and straight into him. But Deal didn't drop the ball, and Emslie, running around the horn to see the play, yelled "You're outta there!" and the Cubs had their 2nd out.

As a pitcher, Tad knew Claude hoped this would give him a break as his defense backed him up well by cutting down New York's lead runner. But the Giants' shortstop Art Fletcher complicated his life by loading up the bases. Burns was now New York's lead runner at 3rd and he scored standing up as Killefer had to watch him run by when Rollie Zeider tripped over Walt Holke's infield ground ball to have an error recorded against him. While McCarty became the Giants' last out that inning, they had almost gone through their entire batting order. Taddeo, who was already musing over his suspicions about Max Flack, started reconsidering Bunions' handling of a routine ground ball to 2nd base. Tad wasn't sure about anything since he always felt very uncomfortable while dealing with anything to do with New York. Now had it gotten him paranoid where it concerned some of his own teammates?

However, Bill Klem didn't show any favoritism — or maybe it was only racism. But while Chicago couldn't answer New York's offense for the first 2 innings, the ranking and rumored-to-be-unbuyable umpire did with Rodriguez at the dish. "Do not cross my line! I said, 'Do not cross my line you stupid spic. Or I will kick you out of this park so hard that your ass will land all the way back on Cuba."

"Jefe, Chi-Town wasn't even close." The boys on the Cubs' bench were watching this new battle unfold in the bottom of the 2nd.

"He's going to cross the line," Fred Merkle rejoiced. "You know I gotta love seeing Emslie and Klem sticking it to anybody else."

"Yeah, well heads-up Cubbies — and Bonehead. Since *you* especially know who's officiating," Mitchell pitched in.

Uh-huh. The all-mighty dollar as the carrot — or a hospital bill — probably care of The Morello Family, as the stick. Taddeo Villetti could figure for himself.

Rodriguez then did cross Klem's line in a hot-under-the-collar Latin temper tantrum to reengage with him.

"Hey Bean-Bandit: never argue balls and strikes with me. Never ever. You'rrre outta here!" Klem shouted louder than the announcer. Now Tad Villetti thought he should have felt guilty for enjoying any prejudice shown toward any non-Anglo ballplayers, like himself. But he quickly rejected that notion because Rodriguez wasn't on the Cubs — and he played for New York, *of all teams*. So good-bye and "fuck him."

Catching up to the present, the game now in the top of the 3rd, Chicago recovered from being down and even took the lead while no doubt The Morello Family was busy adding their influence to the game. Flack was on with a walk when Hollocher's sacrifice moved him to scoring position as the Terranova brothers — it had to be them — accompanied with who Taddeo was very afraid was definitely Joe Masseria, watched from only inches away from him on the other side of the dugout wall. And no one was complaining they were blocking the view of those who paid for 1st base seats. Masseria sounded as if he came over accompanied by *three* enforcers — around Tad's age — and one of them a really rough looking fellow who Tad saw first. Because when he dared to glance out of the dugout and into the right-field box stands, he saw all these young men standing with their backs to the field and watching the audience as they protected their big Manhattan boss. So Tad could only hope a foul ball hit one of them in the face. But Max Flack remained the subject of everyone else's focus until Coach moved to get Trevor up and ready to replace him *out on the field* in the bottom of *this* inning. But first Flacky scored on a long line-drive single by Lester Mann which got the Cubs' left-fielder on 1st base. Fred Merkle also continued enjoying this game when he got a base hit that scored Mann, but Dode Paskert and Charlie Deal both became outs when McGraw substituted Fred Anderson for Jeff Tesreau on the mound, to handle Chicago's suddenly blossoming offense.

It would take New York an inning and part of another one to tie up the score in the bottom of the 4th, but they were playing like they had a war to win. Harry Hempstead, John T. Brush's son-in-law, wanted to do whatever it took to make New York's "namesake team" win for his wife's father's honor to become undisputed —

after Giants' baseball had been previously associated with Tammany Hall's favorite patron, the developer and Jewish Mob-linked Andrew Freedman. This was just one more thing Tad wished he didn't know, but had decided to pay attention to when his own father had taken sparse moments to talk about baseball during his father-son time with his youngest. Taddeo supposed it was his papa's strained attempt to sort-of talk about baseball and have any sort of relationship with his son — placating his boy's interests after his mama had previously done that, before she passed. But inevitably the sports-talk with his father always digressed into "business talk" and who was doing what in New York. Only this was one of the few times Tad recalled his papa taking an interest in what his son enjoyed. Sort of. Only it also cautioned him about who the Giants were historically linked up with and he had doubts that Hempstead or Brush ever really cleaned up the organization. However, they'd also supported Bill Klem's career it would appear. Only who would really be there to support Tad's career? The young pitcher felt doubt gnawing at him. Why was he doing this? What was he subjecting himself to by staying here? Was he or even any of his friends from the Ansons actually accomplishing anything on their own? Well, plagued by these depressing questions and conditions, Tad watched his buddy from his minor league days in Iowa finally make it out into right field, where Taddeo had a great seat to watch him play. The Bass-Man handled defense capably but didn't turn in any good works at the plate, still adjusting to Major League pitching. The Giants struck for one more run in the 8th, but then Chicago's bats came alive and they retook the entire game to add another victory by a 5-3 score from a terrific performance in the 9th!

Now with Sega back in Tad's room at The Hotel Theresa, Trevor earned himself one of the double beds in Hoff's room, and Trip took the other one for spending time babysitting their Minor League captain in Charleston Prison. George, down two prostitutes and owing credit to his teammates who had to save him from incarceration in Boston, was designated a spot on the floor. For his rescue efforts, or really his papa's connections that saw Hoffman freed, Taddeo had the privacy of his own room in which to stay in The Big Apple with his new woman from Chicago. Since when he was challenged to kill the mother bear, Sega comforted Taddeo in his time of distress, much as she did now. For he alone on his team felt he understood the true threat that Joe Masseria, in command of

The Morello House — the real Mafia, with Arnold Rothstein likely allied, and representing the shylocks — and since dating back to Freedman — and *who knew*, but maybe even Bat Masterson trying to write his way into the story on behalf of Sullivan and the Irish — all represented to the *most-naïve* Chicago Cubs. And so Villetti's team had suddenly earned the attention that earning the winners' spotlight would bring them. It was everything he'd worked toward, and then it suddenly wasn't a very good thing at all.

In Tad's head swirled so many horrible scenarios which he hoped he wasn't about to face when the Cubs were in New York. He'd now have to constantly be thinking fast on his feet in order to just steer his own destiny. He'd only turned around for a minute in Beantown, and forces that wanted to control his destiny had grabbed George and aimed to use his own best friend against him. Trying to figure out how to stay one step ahead of his own family to protect Arlene had already tasked him. But Taddeo vowed that he'd never give up the fight. Just right now instead of exercising his mind to navigate a path toward that victory, he preferred to just think with his other head and how much he was enjoying Sega's entertainment that she provided it. And, she brought in her purse, some new and improved chemistry that she would even inject into Taddeo Villetti's better relations, with her.

First Sega asked if he trusted her. Tad nodded. He really wanted to trust *someone*. Let them drive for a while — at the very least somewhere he actually wanted to go. She asked him to hand her his belt. Then she produced a familiar, slim silver case that opened to allow access to two needles and a vial of something Tad needed so badly to feel again — that disconnect from all his troubles he last resorted to when he had to deal with The Family when going out of town on that hunting trip. Now he only hunted peace of mind, once more. And just for a little while, he begged to God that he could feel this. Soon, after the quick sharp impact into his skin, and an experience that made him think of an icy lightning, immediately radiating out into his veins, he and his angel that the Greek gods sent to him down from the skies — were both quickly drifting into the heavens.

His times in bed with Sega were incredible and Tad hardly wanted to leave, because he had a feeling that the end of his time by the diamond near Harlem would not be quite so happy. Not at all. On June 12, George Burns got the better of Lefty Tyler and the only run scored was actually on Burns' homer out to left field over Les Mann's head. 250-odd feet was an easy distance versus nearly twice that out to center, and New York's left fielder knew all about that. The Giants won a 0-1 game, but not before Hoff got to see some playtime since Coach tried a left-handed bat against Pol Perrit, who pitched New York's complete game. But Tad didn't like it when he saw those he knew were practiced players — for The Mafia — warming up for what he feared, was to deal with *him*.

Furthermore he didn't like it, and he was pretty sure Sega didn't like it either, when The Hoff got his room in The Theresa all to himself for the night, all because he'd played that afternoon. It became the unwritten rule with the former Ansons that if you played — and you didn't screw up either — you earned yourself a victory lap in the hotel the team stayed at during road games. And as the consolation prize, Taddeo received a cup of water on top of his locker that showered him after the game, "because something needed to wash that pussy-cream off his face." The reference to Sega becoming his live-in and the joke were barely humorous, and Tad suspected that George was behind it. But naturally good-natured as he was, Taddeo was moved along the way toward forgiving his best friend for Boston. Sega wasn't as thrilled, but she had become progressively more interested in baseball while rooming with the boys and Trip and Trevor's non-stop chatter about their first away series since being called up. The excitement in their little hotel room was contagious almost every evening and no one was getting a full night's sleep as conversations and drinking went on into the late hours.

In fact it was Sega who refreshed his memory that she'd brought with her something else that could help settle all of them down for one night so they could rest well and be prepared for their next game. From somewhere, this lady of the night now had more new needles — and an opium paste she taught the boys how to heat in a spoon. The grotesque and opaque olive and crusty stew melted down into a liquid that could be suctioned into a syringe. She introduced it as Tad's Uncle Delasandro's revolutionary new product. Only it wasn't very revolutionary. She just wasn't aware that the boys had all seen it before — at Villetti's, before her arrival on the scene there.

And now almost all the roommates didn't indulge, but they did watch as Taddeo, under much more stress than usual, even for him, decided to follow the road that Sega led him down. And Taddeo crashed down, with Sega on the floor, once more retreating into that world of bliss where he was unconcerned and much too happy to care if Trip and Trevor took the beds while Hoff spent the night in the other room with the next, or one of the same whores, as he'd found the first night they'd spent in The Empire State. Everything was easily available in The Big Apple and Tad knew that The Morello Family held the monopoly for supplying it. Nevertheless, he let Sega convince him he should indulge in everything "The Life" had to offer. The blissful life. And she said she had once known it very well. But more importantly, what she *did* know to personally offer, was the affection Taddeo needed so badly. And Sega observed his every reaction to what she was doing to his body. Whereas then of his mind, she playfully inquired "Does Arlene do this for you, Baby? Oh it feels so good. Doesn't it?" There was a lot of truth to that — and that all the Irish girl offered him in abundance of, was criticism and a lot of sarcasm. Sega didn't seem to find any shame in reminding Taddeo of that, but that she continued offering him so much better than what her competition, her rival had, too. "I know a handful of some very good tricks that I bet you that *she* does not."

Then on Thursday, the 13th, that life offered the Cubs — or more likely the gamblers — another victory for their hustle. Bat Masterson had an opinion about that by the time people received delivery of Friday's *Morning Telegraph*. Mitchell had started the twenty-eight-year-old and 6-year veteran Phil Douglas, with both attitude and drinking problems, for the third game of the series to be played that afternoon in Coogan's Hollow, the site of The Polo Grounds. It was already rumored that Hempstead and McGraw were wooing him to sign with the Giants to deprive Weeghman and Mitchell a replacement for Grover Cleveland Alexander in the Cubs' rotation. Masterson insinuated that what this could have inspired was the 3 runs Douglas gave up to the effort by New York that they put into the 2nd inning. Taddeo reluctantly gave the theory some credit, but also suspected Tennessee — and namely its whiskey — might be more responsible for that happy hour, or approximately a fifth of one.

Himself possibly suspicious, and in response to a desire to break up any solidarity among the veterans like Killefer, who Mitchell felt *might even coddle Douglas*, Coach put in Hoffman as a replacement backstop. Tad figured that his manager thought the idealistic rookie that George was, would encourage Shufflin' Phil to play a sober game, which he then did, also encouraged by his growing friendship with Lester Mann, and a lot of coffee the team had ordered in.

But in his column, Masterson insinuated that he was a witness to Hempstead buying Douglas several rounds just before the game and secretly filling his water canteen with bourbon. Apparently Masterson had divorced himself from taking any side in baseball politics and wrote whatever he wanted, and for whatever reason motivated him. While he who had become a gossip slinger brought New York down while he was busy propping up himself, the former gunslinger certainly didn't do Chicago any favors either. Mitchell had to repeatedly be motivated to take Max Flack out of more games and substitute in Trevor Bass — not that Tad's friend from the Ansons minded much.

But Taddeo minded. All this intrigue in professional ball was exactly the type of situation he wanted to escape from in his personal family situation. Did it make no difference, no matter what he did? Young Villetti started to strongly doubt he was making any difference here. Had this life only been a dream? A lie? Only maybe it was back home in Chicago that he actually did have a chance to acquire the power to change some things, anything? And maybe it wasn't his destiny to save Arlene, when all she did was fight with him. *Maybe I am supposed to save Sega?* These were a lot of new, radical thoughts for Taddeo to handle.

Slim Sallee from the Giants' roster handled the duties on the mound for 7 innings of this game until McGraw, determined to regain his lead from when the Cubs tied the Giants 3-3 in the top of the 4th, put in right-hander Fred Anderson in another game again, this time in the bottom of the 8th, after the Cubs had added 3 more runs off Sallee in their previous turn at-bat. Only Anderson couldn't stop Chicago's counter-strike and gave up 1 more run each in the 8th and 9th. Both lefties at the plate, Hoffman and Bass added hits to their personal records and the Cubs won 8-4, *but all by way of the contributions by their veterans* — and Charlie Hollocher — who made sure he reminded everyone that he was there, too. Charlie had indeed finally come out of his slump after Tesreau and Anderson had held him hitless the other afternoon. But he skipped that part in his evaluation of his performance in New York, which he repeated for any Chicago teammate who he could not be sure had heard it over a dozen times, already. Tad ignored all this — and he didn't get to play as Douglas won his second game, and while probably still drunk. So instead he buried his irritation and concentrated on figuring out what he and Trip were going to do about the room arrangements that evening, especially since Tad had Sega staying with him and she didn't have anywhere else to go, but The Bass-Man and Hoff had won their private rooms. This silly tradition had now really taken hold with the former 1917 Ansons, just to give the bored rookies something desirable to compete for with their frustratingly short assignments on their first road trip. With their game performance — if they even got to play — evaluated by their peers — someone could win a private room for the evening. The rest of the rookies would bunk up together, besides being the frequent recipients of practical jokes. It only got complicated when more than one of them got to play in a single game and especially now that Taddeo had a hanger-on who was a refugee from his family's bordello — although both Hoff and Bass were gracious enough to volunteer a space to sleep alongside of them *just for Sega*, but of course. Taddeo declined *for her*, while hoping The Hoff wasn't finally going to become an influence on Trevor. That would be just what the rookies needed.

But while Hoffman found a friend of a lady friend of his to entertain Bass for a while, Tad's friend from the minors came down and got him, Sega, and Trip — the last who just could not stop his anger-filled complaining in the lobby of The Theresa that evening — and let them all back into his assigned room, with Trip taking the floor, his only companion for the evening, being his ongoing attitude problem. But that wasn't going to last. Tad only hoped that for now, Mike realized and appreciated what Trev had done for both of them. It was very kind.

And he hoped the future would quickly look brighter for Everston who never stopped, never gave up on putting the practice work in. And he never stopped complaining either. No, he was all-in. Taddeo wished he still could have felt the same way. But things had already been changing.

The young pitcher might have a suggestion or two, kind of in the form of helpful comments he'd sneak in to help out his friends see even more playing time, but he felt a bit more secure with not even being noticed by Mitchell, versus being poorly evaluated as unnecessarily taking up space on the coach's bench. Now he almost wanted to just clear his head of all of this scheming and get out there again himself, when he finally was going to see a woman — *his new woman* — following his team, if and only if just to root for him. But he liked that Sega was also making friends and getting along with his friends, too. They sure enjoyed one happy hotel party after the next one.

Chapter 49

Approximately twenty-one years from then, give or take a week or two, one of those ballplayers on the 1918 Cubs paused while he recollected that season. The young man — not so young as he was way back then, having now *carefully* survived to actually see his forties — also not so small a feat considering how things went back then — smiled to himself while he watched the black Chrysler New Yorker park outside his family's humble but growing outdoors supply store. Somehow his ever-present good nature had grown in him and then even helped see him escape the very same kind of destruction that became the destiny of some of his teammates he'd been the closest to, from that most-memorable baseball season a long time ago. Only maybe now, at long last, his past, had finally caught up to him.

His visitor, dressed in a black suit which he filled out quite well, was tall and domineering, and even by himself, wouldn't seem to need the two bodyguards, also wearing black suits, who stepped out onto that old, burned-out Missouri street. This young fella especially didn't need that kind of security with him to protect him from the humble supply store operator. The middle-aged observer didn't care so much about his own safety any longer. If it were his time now, after all these years, he might be freed of the stresses of still trying to preserve his family's business as it struggled to stay alive during this Great Depression.

It was now the summer of 1939 and history seemed to be repeating itself. A World War I veteran of the proprietor's generation, one Adolf Hitler, was now the Chancellor of the Weimar Republic in Germany. That charismatic man gathered his own enormous power and there were many who feared him and threats of his aggression toward neighboring Poland and Great Britain, just across the English Channel. The world grew alarmed and then once more started beating the drums of war. The USSR's Joseph Stalin had just been rumored to draft a treaty with Nazi Germany that would divide the rest of Europe up between these growing world superpowers and Mussolini had wisely formed a Pact of Steel during the course of negotiations the previous month, which was intended to limit Germany's expansion into the Mediterranean in at least one country, preserving the dictator's reign.

But this young Italian who came to visit the former ballplayer at his family's store was both on the way toward *his* rise to power, and also solidifying his family's status as second-generation Americans. He was truly one with a mind to build his own empire. Of course, that was his family's tradition.

And this young man, was the spitting image of someone the former Chicago Cubs player knew all too well. The fella now left his bodyguards outside in the sun and made to enter the supply store establishment. When the door that pulled outward like the "PULL" label on it suggested, didn't push in, with one violent thrust, this man in black forced it in. His polished shoes made a tap-down noise as each left the cement outside and hit the synthetic panel floor indoors. He glanced around assessing the operation, hid any possible embarrassment by his awkward trouble at the entrance, and then did not break his stride when he came right up to the customer service counter and wasted no time declaring, "I would have a word with you."

"I know. And I know who you are."

"I'm told that you were a friend to my family."

The man nodded but said nothing.

"I want to know about my father — my real father."

The ex-baseball player nodded again. Actually, he could do nothing to prevent his shuddering or catch the tears that escaped both his reddening eyes. "I knew your parents. Both of them. I knew them well. I loved them."

"Then you'll tell me now. Did my father do it right? Why did the thing he love betray him? I know one version of the story," said the man in black, "but I need to know the truth about what really happened."

"Well, I only played that one season with the Cubs. It wasn't my fate to be a celebrity in the Major Leagues. I had to get out for my own safety. I needed to disappear. Hence this humble lifestyle you see here. But I was there. I witnessed it all. And your papa — he was prepared to love you — with all his heart. And so was your mother. And as a friend of your father's, throughout the most eventful part of any of our entire lifetimes, I swear to you he was *not* betrayed. Not by any of his friends, and not by who I suspect you think. Now I don't know what exactly you were told, but I will do my best to fill you in on what I can. I can't promise you that I will tell you what you want to hear, but I cannot let the truth die with me. You're his son. You're *her* son. You do need to know. *You need to know*."

And then the story was restarted again. A tragedy was unfolding. Told by a veteran who survived it. And at some point, it worked its way into one crescendo or another, at this baseball game or that one. One great season had come and gone, but its full tale, as told by someone who had lived it, still continued on along its course, currently regarding a particular game played out in Coogan's Hollow in June of 1918.

Chapter 50

Friday, June 14, 1918
5:35 pm EST
The Polo Grounds, New York, New York

The 8th Inning
Chicago – ø, Giants - 5

0 Out, 1 On

AB: The New York Giants (30 W – 16 L)
(Fighting to secure 1st place in the National League!)
Arthur "Art" Fletcher (shortstop, Bats: right, Throws: right)
AVG .263, OBP .311
Age: 33, Games: 1,029, Status: 9-year veteran in The Show

On the mound:
Chicago Cubs (32 W – 13 L)
(Fighting to remain in 1st place in the NL)
P: Taddeo "The Shooter" Villetti (R)
(Bats: Right, Throws: Right) 2 W – 3 L, 1 SV, PCT: .460, ERA: 3.0,
SO: 11, HB: 4 x (in 5 games!)
Age: 19, Games: 5, Status: freshman rookie

AND THEN:

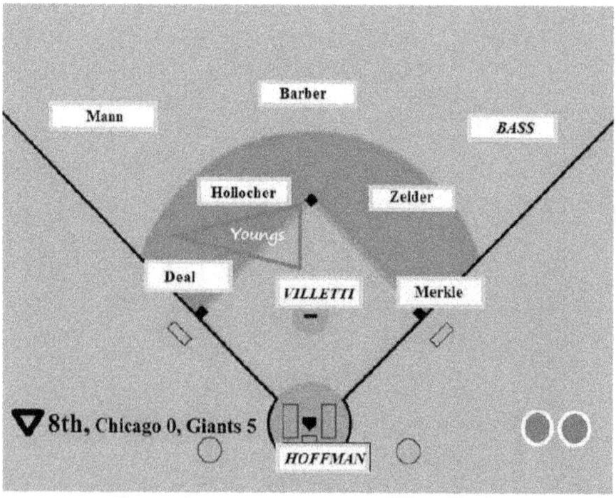

George Hoffman called timeout and ran out to the mound. "Shake it off, Shooter," he said and patted Tad on his left arm. Charlie Hollocher and Charlie Deal ran up for the conference, too. The latter motioned Merkle in to join them. Taddeo was feeling incensed. "Hey, we're down, but that's not on you," his best friend said under his mask. "Ross was a left-hander. Don't let it get to you. McGraw has stacked his lineup well, no matter who we throw. I mean 'Hey — we had Hippo Vaughn out there for seven innings.' "

"No, I should still be pitching better. You know Fellas, I don't think we're going to win this one. Demaree's silenced our bats."

"That's the only reason why you're playing this game."

"Yeah. Thanks for that."

"So I guess New York is just going to have another good day," George said.

"One more good day," Hollocher added.

"Hey, that kind of talk just serves to defeat ourselves, Rookies," Deal coached his younger teammates and gave Hoffman a friendly push to make him smile.

"Yeah, we don't need to get down on ourselves right now *during the game*. We can analyze how it all went to shit, later. We already took two away from them; at best the Giants can leave this series against us with a draw. But *we* still have one at-bat left *this game*. Never mind our drought of runs. Just don't give up!" Fred Merkle led with his veteran experience.

"Okay then. Charlie, you'll have another turn against Al, and we have our big guns like Mann and you Merk, all coming up when we get in our last chance to quench our thirst at the trough. We need to push a fresh start into all of our heads, right now, and approach this like a new game — with our new pitcher," Hoff began encouraging them. "And Tad — *Shooter* — Ross Youngs was a lefty with power. Art Fletcher is a righty with a weak swing. He's getting old, and slower — his best year was in Nineteen-Sixteen. I'm thinking we serve him up our Marshalltown Special."

"Like what you guys had us pull with the Robins last month?" Fred Merkle asked.

"Yup. Well, only sort of."

"Zeider was filling in on the field for me. If you recall, I got beaned bad that game."

"Well Tad, you have a reputation for being an, uh — unconventional or unpredictable pitcher."

"Thanks, I think." But his gratitude had to be insincere. He'd already been wrong. Tad thought that of himself. *Hoff and that incessant optimism of his self-centered world could continue to get more annoying as each day passed. Only hadn't I predicted that? It was the reason I had not wanted to room with my very best friend on our very first away-game trip, in the first place.* Taddeo used to imagine how excited he'd be to be here — playing ball with his closest buddy in the Big Leagues. And on top of it, he finally had a woman right here — in the stands — and even at a road game. This game, as a matter of fact. But this game was not going as he'd envisioned it. He had everything he'd supposedly ever wanted, but had started wondering why he'd wanted this at all.

"I'm just saying, you're a shooter. You launch cannonballs. It's your signature. But it doesn't really matter anymore — in this game. The Giants have a comfortable lead. They expect to win and barring some miracle, they probably will. But that means they're also complacent now. And they think they have *you* already figured out. With Fletcher at the plate and no outs, I bet McGraw calls for him to bunt. But don't hit him. Don't do what they expect you to do when you get flustered out here. Instead, throw him a changeup for the very first pitch, or any after that if his contact lays the ball foul. Really screw with his timing. I'll call for your number one if there's need for it. But you know what I want to set Fletcher up for. And we'll catch them never prepared for it."

"Break it up, Chicago. You're crossing my *patience* now. Let's go! All of you. Chat time's over." Bill Klem hollered at them. "Play ball!"

"Alright. Let's have a little fun and get in some practice. We can always win the next game."

"And the one after that!"

"Go Cubs!"

Taddeo's teammates jogged back to their positions. On the hill, he turned his head to his left and glanced out deep in The Polo Grounds' pasture and smiled, offering a slight nod toward Trevor who was finally on the field at the same time he was, replacing Flack again — though Tad didn't know if Bass could even see the gesture, given "the mileage."

But Art Fletcher did indeed expect the pitch. Sure enough, John McGraw, The Little Napoleon, was in his true battlefield commander form. The Field Marshal wanted to bring home another win for his fans on their home ground by the shore of the Harlem River. But

Fletcher even while he appeared visibly afraid of Villetti hitting him, trusted his coach and pushed his bunt. Even off Tad's changeup, it rolled farther, faster, and stayed fair. Charlie Deal had to wait and watch it come down the baseline and it was too far away, too fast, for Hoff to get it. Holly ran to cover 3rd with Tad moving fast to cover home in the event of a rundown, and to free up Hoffman to chase after whatever he needed to. And Zeider remained at his base for the very same reason, and Mann and Paskert rushed in to cover for any overthrows. But with his leadoff and the time it took to get the ball, Ross Youngs got on the next base standing up and Deal had just enough time to fire the ball to Merkle to get Fletcher to be the first out of the inning. So much for a DP.

Then Kauff got a shallow right field single off Taddeo next. Trevor got the short line drive on the first bounce, but it was positioned just right. There was no chance for even one of his incredible diving catches, and Bass didn't see the need to risk injury from performing one, given the score. Now New York had runners at the corners. And then McGraw signaled Benny Kauff to start driving Tad and Hoff nuts — by taking huge leads off the base. Behind the plate, George signaled a pitch-out and fired his receipt from Villetti's toward a rapidly-growing annoyed Fred Merkle to make an accounting of it. But Kauff dived back to the bag just in time, the infield dirt of the diamond in Coogan's Hollow decorating his New York home game jersey. Then Tad threw his fastball for a gimme first strike on the next Giants batter. With a one-and-one count, Tad cooperated with another plan of Hoff's for a pitchout. George got up in a one-second snap and threw down the infield to Rollie Zeider. It was a great throw! But it wasn't fast enough and Kauff had successfully stolen 2nd to eliminate the possibility of any Cubs' double-play.

At "two-and-one," Tad tried to get the Giant at his plate to chase a slider that moved outside, but McGraw's man exhibited good plate discipline and waited for his pitch. Correctly predicting that a frustrated Taddeo Villetti would either hit him somewhere that hurt, if he was going to walk him — or not take any chances with Bill Klem umpiring so far away from Chicago — and throw him a true strike, Henry Zimmerman — also known as The Great Zim — proved to be great at putting another earned run on Taddeo Villetti's record as he sent his counter-offer back and into shallow left. Almost everybody's hit into the outfield at The Polo Grounds fell shallow in *that* ballpark as it were — and Ross Youngs scored on his single.

Kauff got around to 3rd in the time it took Mann to recover the ball and get it back to Hollocher.

On the mound, Tad started wondering why he was even out there. His eyes wandered around trying to seek out support from meeting up with any of his teammates, but their eyes were looking down at the dirt. Even Hoff's. The Cubs were losing and being shut out by Al Demaree "6 — Nothing." And then Tad did make eye-contact as he turned his feet on the rubber to pitch to Walt Holke, as the Giants' 1st baseman was up next. And when he looked beyond him, he found the gentlemen in the suits on the home team side of The Polo Grounds again — staring straight back at him.

They were the same good fellas who had been over by the visitors' dugout just the other day, intimidating Coach to cause Max Flack not to play 5 complete innings in a row for possibly the whole time the Cubs were in New York. Tad gulped. When he listened in on their conversation from the bench earlier that game, he'd heard them mention "Valenti" and wondered if they had actually referred to his cousin Rocco who walked in and out of Sing Sing — or someone else with that pretty common surname. Then he stopped wondering what *he* was doing out on the mound and remembered that some of these guys had met with his father when his papa had actually turned out for his game versus New York, and played at Weeghman. They were behind the Giants' bench now, but they were behind the Cubs' bench only yesterday. What were they doing? Were they scouting *him?* Why?

Tad grew angrier by the second with New York and all the kinds of games they played. He turned and The Shooter took his shot at Holke, who swung at his first pitch, a predicted fastball, but one Tad threw to sink from high to low and force a ground ball off his bat when the next East Coast asshole switch hit his curveball from the left. Rollie Zeider handled the grounder and finished the assist by a throw to Merkle and there were finally 2 outs.

Now New York's catcher Bill Rariden followed by Jose Rodriguez were next up in the Giants' order. Both were losers with low averages who did not impress Taddeo. Of course, he faced the bottom of the opposing team's order — not that Hippo Vaughn had done well with any part of New York's lineup that afternoon. But Rariden had more experience and already one RBI that game. And from Villetti's perspective, Rodriguez was impatient, had shown a propensity for letting his Latin blood make him quick to anger, and sucked with only a .160 batting average and less than 3 years' experience in The Show. Hoff agreed: the plan was to walk Rariden and load the bases, but take down Rodriguez swinging for the fences — as if he of all people could actually get a hit out of the bathtub bowl that was Coogan's Hollow.

That didn't exactly work.

It was quite the disappointing and embarrassing game, and right in front of Sega, who Tad had gotten a stolen ticket in a great seat — in a clever exchange for a guard's juvenile son to get Bill Killefer's baseball card signed by the player — a signature Tad forged. And then the guard gave his word he'd escort and do what he could to protect Sega in the ballpark. While things went well. Then the game had actually started. It was all downhill from there.

Now that the Cubs were near the end of the road and almost through the bottom of this hateful 8th, Taddeo was touched. Not by greatness of course, but by the warmth of Sega's support. It was all he'd dreamed for it to be: to have a woman in the stands, rooting him on, her voice one distinctive pitch from all the men in New York's audience — and all for him. Tad needed it especially now. That things were not going the Cubs' way was an understatement. But he was so numb it felt almost shocking that it did *not* shock him that he did not even care how this game ended — what misery was left in it.

So as he prepared to just go through the motions, throw his next pitch and the next one after that if he had to, Tad remembered how the silver sparkles shimmered off her new white form-hugging dress and matching hat with its dove feathers as she waved to him from the 1st base field box he'd secured her a seat in. The dress had come in a box and also along with a couple of enforcers from Brooklyn, who'd delivered it and then stood with arms folded across their broad chests, looking intimidating enough to make absolutely sure she'd be safe and not harassed by any man in the stands at The Polo Grounds. Though no one at the gates had dared to stop these guys from getting in, Taddeo had been keeping an eye out for her anyway. Tad craned his neck to look beyond the edge of the visitor's seats as he attempted not to drown in John McGraw's bathtub, and while trying to pay no mind to Coach Mitchell folding his arms across his chest to stare after him, biting his lower lip, trying and failing not to turn his head from side to side. Coach had already taken several drinks from his flask to help him keep his grip over himself this inning. It had to be running on empty because he then lit a cigarette. However, Tad was preoccupied with wondering who ordered his new woman's protection and the change in her wardrobe? All of Chicago's men had enough *other* things to be concerned about regarding that game. But The Mafia seemed to be taking a personal interest in Taddeo. Then at last, with angry jabbing of his finger, Mitchell redirected Tad's attention he paid the previous innings, to what Hoffman was calling from him in the present one. But Villetti couldn't even remember how he'd finished that inning. Only the Giants never needed a last at bat once they'd permanently retired the Cubs.

And after it was all over that afternoon, in the visitors' locker room, Taddeo had hurried to change and didn't wait for the rookies' turn to shower. He just put on his travel suit, eager to get out of there and seek comfort in Sega's arms while he tried to let go of one incredibly bad game, his loss. He just hoped Mr. Mitchell wouldn't keep the Cubs after and review what he thought were their mistakes. Fortunately, Coach had a prepared list and wanted to only meet with certain players like Vaughn, several of the other starting pitchers and Killefer, in addition to several of Chicago's key bats. Tad wasn't on the Mitchell's post-game list this time, but he was nevertheless stirring up one very self-reflective reaction, without his team's manager needing to act as a further catalyst to that.

"I blew it Trevor," he remembered saying to Bass, who he felt comfortable confessing in — as one of his closest friends on the roster — and one he wasn't currently mad at. Some of the team would go on ahead and catch the earlier train to Brooklyn. The others Coach had wanted to speak privately with included Max Flack — no surprise, and Dode Paskert, who Taddeo didn't know what the problem with him was over. These players would travel later.

"Well, you for one, don't need to be so hard on yourself. The Giants' bats were on and ours weren't. Hippo didn't start out so good, but we couldn't give him run-support for seven innings before we then also failed you. There was nothing you could do to save that game Tad," the backup for the backup outfielder said.

"Tell that to Turner. He had a pretty good view of my game getting hammered — by one of New York's — once more."

"Yeah, well he didn't help us out at the plate either," Charlie Hollocher had offered. He patted Taddeo on the back as he moved to take a neighboring seat on the rail car after the veterans got themselves settled. "If he's supposed to be your mentor to get you acclimated, I still can't see how he's helping."

Taddeo nodded, grateful for Holly's support. That had been a nice new change. But no sooner than they would transfer trains and finally arrive in Brooklyn, Tad wanted to take off out of that car to go and find Sega in their hotel. He'd told her to stay close to security so she wouldn't be harassed, not that the security guards or even the New York cops couldn't be a problem themselves. Tad already had experience learning that — but fortunately not the hard way. So he could only just wait to see how Brooklyn's ballclub and its fans would treat him next. He had to find Sega now and try forget about it until he'd have to deal with everyone tomorrow. First he'd had to move her into The Bossert over close by Ebbets Field. The Cubs were staying in Brooklyn Heights, not Flatbush. Though by its good reputation, no one on the team should have any complaints about The Bossert. And a Greek woman utilizing a taxi in any of New York's boroughs, should be not any more uncomfortable than usual. But it shouldn't be any real challenge, seeing as how Sega made it out there to Brooklyn once before.

Yet, it began to really bother Tad that Italian emigrated labor was still constructing more and more expansions to the subway system. It probably was because of things his papa had said, but he didn't want to venture down there when he could avoid it — after so many of his countrymen had died seeing to its development, "paid as the day goes." The blasted molten from the steel parts to the debris from the subterranean carving of the route made Tad shudder to think of how not that many years before the volcanic eruption of Vesuvias in the Motherland, and the Messina Earthquake in 1908, which killed two-hundred thousand Sicilians, caused so much destruction, that it then made it necessary to resettle — for so many of his people who had lost everything in the Old Country. He was only a boy born and already living in the United States when that had happened, but that was the first time he'd ever seen his papa really so sad — stricken in fact. Tad was raised being told The Family was not Sicilian now — they were American. But he knew the Volleros had lost family. If their people weren't killed over there, *living in America*, next killed a good number of them over here. It left all too many people hardened and willing to do anything to survive. So Taddeo preferred Sega take a private taxicab because he preferred she'd survive.

A while earlier, a young and angry Villetti tried to blame everything on Hoffman as they rode the train through northern Manhattan, where they would catch a connection to Brooklyn and get to that fancy fourteen floor Hotel Bossert before their game the next morning. Taddeo had borrowed money from all his fellow rookies again to send Sega there ahead of them by taxi. He'd received no argument from any of his friends; they happily anted up the money because George knew he was on his buddy's shit-list, but moreover, they'd all seen what Tad's brothers had allegedly done to the woman back in Chicago. But they really didn't believe Taddeo's own family members would do that to a woman, and thought that Sega exaggerated her story. George gave his best friend the cab fare, but by this point, Tad was so irritated with him, it did not do well for the two of them to sit together.

For Tad however, her tale just correlated with Arlene's description of events she'd relayed to him, and regardless of the danger in doing so, he really wanted to beat the crap out of Urso and knew he owed Greg something extra. Curiously, his cousin Stefano, too. Taddeo had gained great experience with hurting people from atop the hill, on which he was learning to stand tall, to take command. In fact, he couldn't wait to get back to Chicago and show his family what he had practiced. His own bruises the Robins had given him the last time he played against Brooklyn, were almost all but gone. His recovery emboldened him. He had become one of those hardened people.

But Sega had been on the mend too — ever since being able to relax for once, now that she was safely with Taddeo. And he earned some credit for his skills at protecting a lady friend of his, too. Getting some appreciation for *that* was nice for a change. So the money he and Sega needed to spend seemed to be worthwhile. And she kept him here — on the East Coast. Where somebody would miss him if he didn't stay for now.

Only Tad wondered what kind of money was being spent to put his team up in places like The Bossert, The Theresa before that, The Lorraine, and The Buckminster. Professional athletes played for the sport and the career guys lived in poverty; they weren't treated with that kind of reverence. It was a game. But what kind of game were the Jews and the likes of goombah heavyweights like Joe Masseria playing? And playing together? Possibly with Charlie Weeghman, the Cubs' owner, and one more than rumored to be a leader among the Klansman who hated shylocks and guineas. But while Bat Masterson hounded his team with many others in the press, these unlikely co-collaborators all seemed to manage their getting along with each other over something, and Taddeo had good cause to fear it had something too much to do with him. But now he and Hoff were not getting along — again — and arguing about who had to take on the boarders in their rooms while Sega stayed with Tad.

"So are you still even the same catcher I came up with?"

"If you'd thrown that one harder, I would have made the out with Kauff."

"I did throw it hard. I haven't seen you really catch anything since we got to Chicago — maybe with the exception of probably one disease or another from my papa's bordello."

"That's bullshit and you know it. And today? I identified the threat of the runner, but the bastard had taken one huuuge lead."

"That's good. You can identify one lone and vulnerable runner that made it all the way to first base. I mean it's got to be a lot easier than identifying which girl you last went home with."

"Oh you're funny."

"Yeah, well you're on the couch and taking Trip with you. The Bass-Man gets your room and I get my own with Sega."

"Really?"

"That's fair in our house."

"Not really. And who was that behind the plate? Catching your lousy pitches and helping you with your late inning performance problem? And speaking of catching something from your papa's house — wasn't there a different one only a couple of weeks ago? A different one of *yours*, I mean. Me and Rose helped you move her. What happened? Did you lose your ball with that girl?"

Tad's mouth twitched and he looked away, instantly more troubled than angry. "Yeah, I guess you could say that. I'm not sure what the story is with that one anymore."

Chapter 51

Arlene was also someone with even better reason to feel troubled over her story. Her great plans seemed to always be in a state of flux and just when it appeared like she could be ready to act, the game always changed. In her mind, she reviewed what had happened in the little over a month since she'd taken up her role on the South Side of Chicago. Her own family had put her in place to spy on The Villetti House — a position she pressed and pressed for, in order to be able to volunteer to take — if only so she could turn her gun on those she blamed for the murders of her parents and siblings. Arlene always expected she'd be prepared to die in order to accomplish that. She could have cared less about her future, but then she turns around and she's fallen in love, with and gotten pregnant by Taddeo Villetti, who's also pledging to be protection for her. Though he's naïve and inept — and also the youngest offspring of the family she targeted for destruction. So she waited until he was away on his baseball team's travel games so she could execute her shootings with what little ammunition she had left after having to fire her piece a few times more than planned to escape any more abuse than she'd already taken — and to protect her secret, thereby killing thrice — and no one who was her intended target. She lost any security she'd once had by having at least enough bullets. And now where was her gun? In the worst case scenario, she could turn Taddeo against his own family, but by discovering the possibility of using his jealous cousin Corrado, Arlene could save the life of the father of her unborn baby. Only Greggorio Villetti always seemed one or more steps ahead of her and now he seemed to be the one who sent Corry away somewhere, to thwart that possibility. That one was gone for over a week and a half now.

In the meantime, and before she even knew she was pregnant, she not only planned to spare Tad's life by completing her personal mission for revenge while he was far away, out of town, but she also tried to spare him any grief by staging fights with him to drive him away from her so that he wouldn't become depressed over her death. Right now she was at a good loss to explain how that decision developed. But of course that plan also had to change when she learned about the baby, but not before Greg had decided to discourage her allying with his little brother by using their divide to send Tad a Greek whore. Someone that possibly even Arlene's own family or the Jews had ultimately put into position to make sure that somebody — Sega, if need be — completed what they had wanted out of Arlene, or could take her place. She'd heard rumors about the Sicilian connection to Cardinelli of course, but that one as well, could just trace itself right back to The East, where the shylocks brokered influence for the local islander trash. However, Greg probably knew exactly who Sega was, and thus it probably served him twice-over to get that one out of his way, by sending her all the way back to The Black Hand's East Coast handlers. And she suspected they wouldn't like it once they learned what Greggorio had done. He, or "the someone" who had encouraged him, had originally suggested his father become acquainted with Sega in the first place. Only when she arrived in Chicago and made her moves on Urso, Greg seemed to have once more adapted his plans. That new lush Lumia, must fit into the revised plan somehow. Arlene only hoped that soon, the middle Villetti son would get too smart for his own good. She didn't worry about Taddeo getting smart — at all.

But Arlene had to admit Tad was best off as he was, even if it was in another woman's arms. He was still alive. Now that being the case, and with Greg's plan to keep Corrado from getting into bed with *her* working, Arlene's next best opportunity was with his brother Baldavino Delasandro. He'd already shown interest in her when he and Carlo had driven her to his father's to check on her medical condition — and "the doctor" knew she was pregnant, though he might suspect his son Stefano was the father — especially if she'd lead the oldest Delasandro son to believe that. But Baldavino could prove to be some good secondary insurance. And Arlene felt she was now prepared to do whatever she'd have to, to protect her life — and thereby her baby's. Davino was twenty-three, terribly over-interested in her "woman's private examination" by his father — and thought himself some alleged great gunman. She could possibly manipulate to turn *him* against The Family, as she had hoped to do with Corrado. Victoria Moresco was right; she did have another kind of weapon on her that she could use to coerce that.

The Baller, as his ego asserted to be his preferred call name, was four years her senior, shorter than Taddeo, yet still attractive — as pretty much all the immediately related Villetti men seemed to look alike. Only Arlene long ago realized somebody's personality can make a total difference. This young man in his early twenties was easily enough seduced away from Chastity, and Arlene double-downed on the results she wanted out of having to endure Davino by offering herself to him, should he promise to keep himself and Carlo away from Zhen Li. Arlene really wanted to save that girl. She felt like she could owe her father a debt she might never be able to repay for his taking the young Irish woman in, and exposing his daughter — the most important thing in the world to him — to such risk as were the Villetti and Delasandro families and the permanent sort of damage they could cause the Li's little household. It was long past too late for Arlene. That damage had already been done, a long time ago.

Preparing for what she next had to do, she did take another shot. Arlene copied what, when she was curious, Jezebel once showed her how to do. She used one of Urso's discarded belts he left lying around in the rooms upstairs to tie off her blood flow to her arm. She'd used a match and a spoon from the kitchen to heat up some mash she saved when she'd stolen from The House supply. Then she found a good vein through which her greater plan for an escape would flow.

That was supposed to be a one-time thing — Arlene wanted to keep a clear head — but before the Harrison Act, this was the popular home remedy since Sears had once dominated distribution of the relaxant for a good part of the 20th Century by now. In the immediate moment however, Arlene wished she could have saved herself a little more of the stuff when she found Davino already upstairs. She'd lured him into her trap. But then why did she feel like she was the prisoner? The Delasandro son was all ego but no soul as she got to know what moved through his head, as intimately as possible. He was forceful and abusive with the way he only selfishly satisfied himself with her body she surrendered to him. He ripped her jade green sequined dress and insisted on humiliation sex where Arlene would do things for Baldavino that he couldn't just force her into position for receiving. But this was sex — according to his notion. So from her, and by Arlene's design, he received constant lines that "this" was what his older brothers and cousins were keeping him from enjoying. Arlene continued lying to him and said it wasn't her idea to previously ban him from the bordello unless he paid up like the other johns. Unfortunately, Davino didn't ever bother to attain any knowledge of anyone else who might have conspired to frustrate him. If Arlene couldn't turn him against his cousins, she thought she'd suggest that perhaps he should think about his mother. But Baldavino's ego not his curiosity, was the sole existing thing he wanted to satisfy. She wasn't sure how he could not actually be pleased by the sex she offered him — even as deviant as he preferred it to be. And it was a mystery to Arlene how one such as he, with no ambitions and plans to accumulate power like his cousin Greg, just wanted to be boastful and impress others — inclusive of Baldavino's own brothers — who he would always then put down. But he would puff himself up on nothing but absolutely insignificant examples of any achievement — from the exertion of absolutely no effort. And for the first time Arlene actually felt bad about berating Taddeo for being a loser. At least he tried not to be one every game he played, and moreover, every practice he went out on the field for. And Tad was a great lover who cared about the way she felt. Baldavino was almost a complete disappointment every way around and she cared less if he could be satisfied. She was not. And she only hoped that by her discovering an appeal to his ego was his ultimate weakness, he would yet satisfy Arlene, by fulfilling her new plan she hoped she could use him for. It would definitely require more of that drug because first he had to start thinking paranoid thoughts about what others were doing — or what she could convince them they were plotting — instead of on how wonderful he did everything that he was doing. It wasn't at all wonderful.

Next Arlene cleaned herself up and gathered her girls for a different kind of meeting. There could not be a better time for this than while Sega was gone — and Greggorio had unexpectedly disappeared somewhere, too. There might be no one left to spy on her. Vitale had disappeared as well. But George Herman Ruth, Jr. and the visiting Boston Red Sox arrived to challenge Chicago's American League team. Chicago's other ballplayers, as well as Boston's, were kept busy by day over by Comiskey Park, which attracted most of the rest of the men to the Bridgeport neighborhood northeast of Little Italy instead of onto Taylor Street — during the afternoons anyway. While hosting The Babe continued to get White Sox ticket sales up — along with his own opposing batting and pitching statistics, Arlene wished to ammo-up by getting at least one of her guns back in the first place, and then finally fire off all of her own strikes, now that she thought she could get Davino to play as her backstop in the next inning.

So she planned to head north as well. Much further north to a rally for the Women's Suffrage Movement where Arlene could finally confront Katherine McCormick and demand her own immediate empowerment. And it was long past time for the other ladies to learn to stand up for themselves. Not the middle-class housewives on opioids, paid for by the new bullish war economy, and the spinsters and dykes in spiraling angry cycles of depression, nor the rich-bitch socialites turned philanthropists — only so they could unwittingly fund their own competition. No, Arlene would take along those girls — her working girls, the real women who were those that she could really trust the most — with her on this mission to the North Side. Rose, and Chastity in tow, so she could demonstrate to the latter why she should refrain from gossiping and keep her capably rated mouth shut about what she knew Arlene had done with Baldavino. And Delilah, so that her best friend Jasmine would understand nothing was being kept from *her* — only that Arlene had to leave her most capable help behind to manage the saloon and bordello — and because she might be the only one who could keep Urso from possibly overdosing Lumia and thus prevent the poor girl from meeting her unlucky end. She chose Faith to go with her too, because not only would it relieve one of the youngest girls from having to service Rinaldo Villetti, but she was the one closest to Zhen Li's age. And Daphne would stay behind and be trusted to get familiar with the usual number of Congressmen who came to patronize their true constituency. But together, the five ladies were more than Zhen Li's father wanted to argue with, and she convinced Zhen's old man that she could safely accompany them to the North Side. This would help illustrate the need for some more timely assistance to the ladies on the South Side as long as Katherine McCormick was going to *head down that way* to not-so-secretly collect the offerings from Jane Addams' Hull House philanthropists — and commission her little photographer's contract. Arlene felt that all of that could actually help bolster the young Oriental girl's safety, and little Virginia Hall's. But Arlene also figured that for the cost of a couple of bullets, all women's rights and protection could be advanced a lot faster — in fact just as fast as she could fire them — because her belief in equal opportunity centered around that equal opportunity to commit homicide, which the regal bitch McCormick had deprived her of up until now. America's infamous heiress was so buried in her suffrage movement, that she couldn't see it, or her funds going around in one giant circle, either. Only *the harbinger of death in a dress,* didn't see *her* plan as one for multiple murders. It was true justice. And Arlene intended to teach her working girls the concept, if they were intelligent enough to comprehend it. Zhen Li could lose her innocence about the way the world worked in a different way — a way that could save her. But Juicy Lucy decided to stay behind too, because she just savored sex that much to pass up an opportunity for another john to partner up with for *her* favorite money shot. This was a pity because Lucy might have loved to hear Mary Dennet's speech on women not only enjoying the power of their own bodies, but the pleasure she felt that they had the right to experience with them. Nevertheless, Lucy likely didn't want to also pass up the opportunity to get a disease that her own public platform hadn't adopted, yet.

With Arlene's paranoia taking double the precaution that no one like Vitale followed them, and seeing no hint of him or any other associate of The House, the ladies took a commuter's trolley-style streetcar up to the North Side and to another hotel on the Magnificent Mile in The Loop. There they were met by Nancy who then informed them McCormick could not be present, and Dennet would lead their conference-rally. *Perfect*, Arlene thought. *I have better ways I can take action if only I had one of my guns back, than by making protest demonstration plans for Wilson's continuous inauguration tour.* But she got the idea across to Nancy and then in an admittedly inspiring meeting with Mary Dennet — whose trip out from Boston was so much more exciting than The Babe's — that young ladies like Zhen Li's lives were on the line, right at the infield level of their movement. Women were risking arrest and force-feeding in prison cells while being charged with rioting, some in the government handling them like they were the anarchists who likewise were working to upset the social order. To Arlene, the torture sounded far worse than attending to the personal needs of some old john for less than an hour with opioid party favors and wine, all indulged in by candlelight. She was a pragmatist, not an idealist. And ladies like Juicy Lucy actually chose that to be the perfect life. Arlene just knew better about how it all usually ended. There was still more room in the Chicago River. So it was related that an urgent message would be passed back to McCormick and Arlene would get her meeting sooner than later. The young Irish woman insisted it would be as soon as possible.

Now the most interesting development to come out of this rally and its subsequent group-task-assignment meetings though, was confirmation of McCormick's strategy that Arlene had already suspected. The Washington Senators would be arriving to meet the

White Sox next. Their fans from the District of Columbia would include a majority of the members of the Congressional Committee on Women's Suffrage. They'd enjoy their privilege of holding office by meeting secretly behind closed box doors as they watched the Capitol's baseball team in Chicago and heard off-the-record testimony by McCormick. Meanwhile, Mrs. Dennet relayed that she wanted the bordello girls to enjoy working overtime to help ensure the committee's resolution went down the ladies' way. They had agents in place to make sure there were photographic keepsakes for the Congressmen which she would have copies of such smut for the safe-keeping, hidden by the Christian Women's volunteers of course. Arlene thought of little Ginny Hall, who so successfully evaded much detection or at least thus far, any capture — except for the film she captured of what went on in the Villetti brothel. Only Arlene hoped nothing that she did with Baldavino Delasandro would turn up on those film negatives. Taddeo didn't need to ever see it. Or maybe she'd like him to?

But the Irish woman demonstrated she was willing to get as dirty as the next girl. Villetti's was bouncing. And The House's patrons removed their nametags that identified them as the moral citizens the people elected as Members of Congress, and the girls removed their desire to go to any other church of these heavenly sort of experiences, as their cross necklaces dangled between their naked breasts that they jiggled and pressed into the legislators' faces. Meanwhile, the moral world's leaders' wives, pressed the Congressmen's extra dress shirts where they'd been left behind at their respected homes Back East. Only when Arlene danced the dance, she removed her clothing all in one very seductive performance to only add on to Davino's very complete corruption. She needed to complete it right then to make this young man hers — and before his dangerous cousin Greg returned to The House, or his brother Corry resurfaced from wherever Greggorio had buried him.

* * * * *

Right then, in a very rare venture so far away from the security he felt by way of his position on the South Side, and the comfort he retained by keeping his personal watch over it, Greggorio Villetti had ordered Corrado Delasandro to return most of the distance to join him for their meeting on the Illinois bank of the Mississippi River. Soon Corry would cross the bridge back into the greater St.

Louis area, where he would anonymously slip right under the noses of Egan's Rats once more, and book quiet passage on a riverboat down North America's most impressive interior waterway. On his train trip to meet with his cousin, Greg spent many hours staring out the window of his railcar. He paid for a private sleeper car and used a false name so he would not be disturbed, and so he could think. Greg rarely slept. Now the lands he traversed made no impression on him. They didn't represent the steel peaks and cement canyons that protected the way his family sustained its life in the shadows of Chi-Town. They weren't part of his town. They were beautiful — the golden wheat fields — the blue skies, the birds and the trees, signs of nature. But they were not part of his life. They were somebody else's nature. Control over Chicago was all he really wanted by his nature. He only really took this train trip, versus making a phone call to his cousin, so he could get out and have this alone-time to think. Greg needed to. He still juggled a lot of knives in the air, any one of which could drop to stab him. But one finally nicked a location that didn't wound him, but instead bled the information he needed to get out of New York. It would seem his most appreciated favors he traded for other equally valuable favors from The Family had started to coagulate to strengthen his resistance to bleeding from those that would wound his own plans, that all the others — his papa, his brothers, most of his cousins, Colosimo, the cops, the Genna Brothers, The Mafia, and especially the kikes, the Klan, and all those fucking shamrocks — still had no knowledge of. Maybe only his father suspected him, but the senile fool wouldn't be prepared to do anything — and his papa would only get what he always wanted out of Greg's dealings anyway: that his strongest son would strengthen The House, secure its territory, and enormously expand its earnings. Because Greg was a genius. In his vision, Greggorio Villetti would consolidate the West and South Sides, exile the Irish to only a fraction of what they had controlled on their side of the river, and unleash The Outfit from having to pay any heed to New York — through Cardinella or in any other way except for what the Villettis chose to send, by their way of assistance to their own family — if then there was any reason for any of *them* to remain in Brooklyn or Manhattan.

Then Greg would even supplant his father as being the one who most successfully took care of The Family — for his family. His uncles had always listened to him, been there for him when Greg didn't feel like he could go to his papa, and now Greg felt shocked that his father would allow one of his own brothers to just be carted off to an American prison. Vollero had even just provided his nephew with critical information about the New York professional underground gambling scene. Information he'd been totally lacking beforehand. At the very least, his papa had useful, knowledgeable siblings with experience and foresight, and Greg didn't see it the least bit hypocritical that he demonstrated no loyalty to Urso and Taddeo. *He* was the one with nearly useless brothers. Now he understood everyone's plans in the larger picture that even his papa had deliberately kept him in the dark about — all because his old man didn't trust him. In fact, he knew even more than his papa. So now Greg worked it all out in his mind, including those fantasies of his about how he would do a better job if he were running everything. Soon he would arrive from his trip to personally instruct Corrado and provide him with some privately sourced money to do what he desired his cousin accomplish, by way of Corrado's Mississippi River trip, to secure things downstream in Louisiana. Much more needed to get done — and quickly. It appeared he'd discovered everyone else's big plan just in the nick of time. Now and immediately, Greggorio Villetti had to act. He had to get in on *this*. He had to thwart the Irish; cross their likely double-cross. Then in the near future, some of this money could be used to get Uncle Al out of prison with a new lawyer, and a new trial. While in the present, Greg finally arrived at the only possibly conclusion about *exactly* how all these other players planned to use his little brother Tadpole to achieve their victory.

They just didn't know Greg pitched to himself a better play by with which he'd win at their own game.

Chapter 52

Now Tad wanted to try anything that could kill his anger and frustration with the continuous plotting and suffering that surrounded him, which so far, he knew he had done nothing of consequence to thwart. Worse, he knew he was far too sensitive for this world. And he'd even let his brothers prove it — that he would let every injustice, maybe every little thing, bother him. The bear, bringing Urso's then-woman on the hunting trip, Sega in her condition she'd arrived at his hotel room only a few days past now — this all served to confirm it. Plaguing Taddeo Villetti, were even the great tragedies going on all the way across the Atlantic that he'd never even witnessed, but only heard about. And because of all those awful things happening over there, to all the ones he witnessed getting started by the very powerful men in the stands at the ballpark here — well, Tad could not just blissfully stand by anymore. He once thought that playing professional baseball would bring along with it control over his own destiny. And then Tad could plainly ignore everything else in this world he felt was just not right. But the people he'd met, especially those he'd become close to, didn't need to use words to tell him he could not. He cared about them, their well-being, as well as about himself. However, he knew he'd have to use an ends-justify-any-means-strategy to change anything. The liquid that he felt churning, in fact boiling now — as Taddeo's eyes followed the river water under the bridge that supported his train's track — was comprised of his own blood. Coach Mitchell had definitely not shared anything from *his* flask, let alone stop faking that he still carried it — though that thing was probably empty before the 7th inning of *today's game*. The only thing Coach, or any of the Cubs for that matter had to share at this hour, was failure. However, if Tad hurried to arrive at The Bossert, he might find Sega was there, and she could have more of that "cure" to share, which Taddeo had found once before to relieve all the anxiety and despair that came to one who was stuck in his situation. And maybe he'd actually have a comfortable time-span within which to destroy the next hotel room with Sega, naked, perspiring, and climbing and bouncing off of all the furniture, while the rest of the guys bounced around Brooklyn, or explored the infamous Ebbets Field. But Taddeo wouldn't bother. He'd see the ballpark tomorrow and he didn't bother with taking his shower either, not just to save time, but because he and his new woman would both soon be hot and sweaty together, all over again. It would first be time to enjoy his and hers, alternative athletic abilities. Anything else, he'd take on later. There was a brief distraction for all the rookies as their train's route saw them complete their crossing of the Brooklyn Bridge after one memorable ride, where they took advantage of the long summer daylight to take in the view outside of the windows that showed them everywhere from Harlem to Hell's Kitchen, down to Lower Manhattan. Then they went for a short walk on which they had to carry their own luggage, from the Brooklyn Bridge Station to the street car that would get them to Montague Street. But all that time, Taddeo couldn't forget the memory of that gray water under the bridge and see it churn in his mind. Choppy. As if it signaled that a great storm was coming. He'd so hoped that this evening he would let nothing bother him.

Now with the team making additional stops and people transferring along the commuters' railway, Sega had naturally beat Taddeo to the hotel. But both still arrived while they would be unobserved by the Cubs' manager who was departing from Upper Manhattan on a later train. Upon sighting Tad carrying his travel case and sports bag that nearly weighed him over, she rushed from inside, where she had viewed the team arriving through one of the four fourteen-foot-tall giant arched windows, and then almost glided right through the front double doors — jumping into Taddeo's arms right inside the entrance, completely toppling him into the cold marble floor and onto his back.

"Wait! Watch the pitching arm — and his shoulder." Hoff expressed what he was really concerned the most about. "Oh. Never mind."

"Whoa! Sega. What are you trying to do, kill me?"

"Yeah. Don't do that — yet. We want to make sure Tad's fit enough to give up the winning run again — tomorrow or Monday. Or whenever he next gets around to it."

"Trip, enough already," Trevor pleaded with him.

"Yeah. Looks like a wonderful lobby," the 3rd base substitute retorted as they walked in on the rich red carpeting and stared up giant white columns that each stretched maybe eighteen feet tall and went on as far as the eye could see through the first floor of the building. "I'll go unpack on one of the couches over there." He nodded as a maître d' in a white suit with tightly greased hair and a dark waxed mustache came up immediately upon the group. He looked over Taddeo sprawled out on the floor with Sega on top of him and then Trip, who had removed a new pair of underwear from his travel gear and was holding it up to check its cleanliness in the light of one of the many giant golden chandeliers that decorated the first-floor ceiling. The hotel employee also took in Bob O'Farrell, nodding to a waiter who passed by in thanks for letting him grab an empty cocktail glass off the serving tray with which to spit his tobacco chew into. And he saw The Hoff, with his hand around the backup 3rd baseman's shoulder, as he explained one of his deliquent's plans or another to the disgruntled Everston, who acted like he wasn't at all impressed with the place and was just seeking out a spot to hang his laundry in the lobby. Musicians playing the violin and piano added a soundtrack to all this drama. "Relax, Trip. We're visiting New York City. I know where we can *each* pick up a pair of girls, and I bet we can find a private place to take them while these clowns enjoy their rooms in this dump."

Their envoy from the hotel grew visibly concerned. Other guests looked on while they couldn't help but overhear — not that half a baseball team in their travel suits carrying their bulky luggage and entering the establishment all at once didn't attract a lot of attention in the first place. The maître d' attempted to use a British accent to overcompensate for a German one when he addressed them, but it sounded as cheap and fake as his designer cologne. "Und Zentlemen, *you* hast rezerva'tions *heir*?"

"Uh-huh." Charlie Hollocher replied. "Good place? Your rooms come with broads?"

"No, Zir. Goot Zirs. Ex-kooz mich. Youz are?"

"Chi-Town's finest! We're your Number One Chicago Cubs!" Charlie Deal announced with a huge smile that showed plenty of bright teeth, like everyone in Brooklyn would be charmed by his performance. *When did the veteran become Hoff's understudy?*

Deal should have expected to get only one kind of response from New Yorkers. "Oh yeah? I thought you clowns lost big time today." Some gentleman in a suit nodded toward them while laughing with the other suits he kept company with at a table.

"Yeah. You fellas should be embarrassed for yourselves," said another.

"Hey fuck you!" Rollie Zeider retorted. Several high-society ladies among The Bossert's patrons emitted murmurs that sounded like they were shocked. They didn't know that Bunions knew that kind of language, and furthermore, wouldn't know better than definitely where he was not supposed to be using it.

"Ah, Zentlemen," the maître d's voice interrupted the intellectual conversation. "Youz fur zertain youz are staying hier?"

"Yeah. That's what Coach told us. Though you'd never think Charlie Weeghman would be springing to put us up in this kind of place."

"Right," Tad said from underneath Sega, brushing her shiny, silken brown locks off his face and out of his mouth so he could address their host. "But we're not sleeping on this floor. We got rooms. And I'm the world-famous Taddeo Villetti. The Shooter." As if everyone should be astounded. "Here. Get off me for a minute, Sega. I want to stand up."

"Weze hat no gunfights in hier," the guy in the white monkey suit responded.

"Okay, Villetti. I can tell you impressed him. So now I'll get things settled with this guy and get us our room keys since Coach hasn't yet gotten here." Pete Kilduff finished picking his nose and extended his hand to the maître d,' who folded his own together instead of taking it.

"Zis weg," the German said, and led him toward the hotel's front check-in / check-out counter.

"So where are the working girls at?" Charlie Hollocher asked.

"Come with me out on the town tonight, Junior," Hoff told the shortstop. "I'll show you where the real action in Brooklyn is at, and if I can't find it here, we're headed into New York City!"

Taddeo rolled his eyes and then connected them with those of Trevor Bass. "Are you going with them or enjoying your private room for the night?"

"Not sure. I might read a book while I have some peace and quiet before we're back in the games tomorrow." He glanced at Sega. "Are you staying in and getting some extra sleep? That is if you can avoid any nightmares about Burleigh Grimes and Dan Griner?"

Tad glanced at Sega too, and then smiled toward his friend. "No. I don't know if I'll be getting any extra sleep but I goddamned guarantee you that tonight I won't be thinking about Grimes, or any other one of Wilbert Robinson's would-be wise guys. Though I'll be staying in, too. That's for sure." Taddeo slapped Sega on her small, tight little ass of whose outline wasn't at all hidden by the material of a different striking red dress that she'd adorned especially for their next encounter. "Yup, I'll definitely be staying here," Tad said. His woman giggled. And as soon as Kilduff brought him his room key, he took off for the elevator of the fourteen story Bossert.

"Wait. I need your room for a minute, Buddy. Where am I going to change?" Hoff called running after him.

"Use Bass' suite, beg O'Farrell, or strip naked in the lobby with Mikey. Brooklyn's certainly earned their seeing the full moon as it looks from Chicago. The patrons will love it. But see, I haven't got the time to care, Street Racer. I gotta make up for what I missed while I was in prison." Sega watched him, and smiled, knowingly. Until in one moment, she lost her reason to. "I'm going to be with my new woman, but at some time, I'm gonna have to call Chicago."

" 'bout what's going on with Flack?"

"Much more than that. These aren't games they're hosting us in over here, George. Not anymore. I mean look at this hotel they're putting us up in. I guess we're all overdo for a serious talk. Maybe *you*, more than anybody. But I mean to find out what's really going on. Go have fun tonight."

George didn't know when he was being insulted, or dismissed — or he was always too good natured himself to care. "Well I will certainly do that, Taddeo!" The pitcher had to struggle hard not to smile back at his best friend. It was getting harder to stay mad at him. He and Sega had something better to do together anyway.

For the moment, Anna Cumpănas lay exhausted, dripping wet in the large athlete's arms, staring at his cute boyish face, while her nether regions were pulsating with pleasure beyond her voluntary control over them. But this wild woman just wanted to lose all control. She was safe here for the moment — with her new lover. His maintenance of his body as an asset was to be admired, just as much as it was to be manipulated. But she was also exhilarated — the way she felt with this younger man. She ran her unpainted but taloned fingers over his smooth skin, hairless in his youth, covering bulging, smooth pectorals that stretched up to his powerful shoulder muscles with which he hurled his killer fastballs. And as much as she felt disdain for his presumed fairy leprechaun of a girlfriend, Arlene, the wench had done an impressive job keeping him motivated to stay in shape and win. Today's game with New York was only a tiny setback. That was fine. It was her place to win at her own games. And that was all she could afford to care about. Anna cared not at all for the Irish woman and thought she could take over controlling the Mc-bitch's man-child from here — right now. The young son she protected was her motivation to do just exactly that, surviving all that she had to endure. But first they had to finish destroying the hotel room as they could fit in another go-around after that time that saw most of the team assemble to take their bus to what entertainment could be found in Brooklyn, after checking into their rooms, then departing once more to spend the night out on the town. Though right now what Taddeo needed was a managed release from all his pent-up frustration over the Cubs' crushing loss to the Giants that afternoon. And "Sega's" business there could afford another turn at providing it. She was an animal — and so too could be Tad Villetti. Their bedframe was broke. The second bed's as well, its wooden frame exploded out into its detached panels that had formed its edges, and resting on the feathers from the pillows they ripped apart, along with shreds of their own clothing they tore off one another, stained with certain bodily fluids. She definitely wanted to avail herself of the opportunity to bring his curious, exploring big hands up to her overheating, and now so very sensitive, sweaty breasts, as she commanded his warm, eager bat to instigate another squeeze play up the middle of her home field, just one more time — and with which he'd drive out, one more homerun.

* * * * *

Now Arlene soon found she had a lot to do to manipulate about the score on Taylor Street. But what she had not found, was time to do it in — including the time to figure for exactly what use Victoria had for Katherine McCormick's big movement. What was so important? Though by Friday night on June 14th, she was definitely encouraging Congressmen to move one special interest through the body. That could be a very confusing process, too. Juicy Lucy met an all-too-happy-to-see-her, Michigan Republican Party candidate, Truman Newberry. Man, was he going to be something else. But she had to keep playing.

"Oh my gawd! You're a Washington Senator here for the big league games?"

"Indeed I am," said a fellow who looked like he could have been a hundred-pounds heavier than was even a wax sculpture of Teddy Roosevelt riding his horse. Arlene hated to imagine that sooner than later, he'd look more like President Roosevelt riding a gazelle.

"That is so bugs!" exclaimed the petite brunette in a purple satin short, short-dress with silver chains in her hair attached to three white feathers and only a head full of air flying between her ears beneath them — that kept all this fluff permanently flying. "What position do you play?"

"I mostly like playing backup to the *backed*-up," the fifty-four-year-old Newberry said while winking at the girl. Lucy didn't get the joke. Naturally. But Arlene got it and felt sick from overhearing it and witnessing the light twinkling in the old man's eyes — almost as bright as that which came off the bald spot on top of his head.

And by only another moment's passing, Lumia had then almost fallen down the stairs from Urso's occupied "den of pleasure" on a liquor run and threw up as she too overheard Lucy's squeaky dialogue. Arlene wanted to react the same way, almost immediately, but held her first reflex inside her mouth as LuLu grabbed the bar's wastebasket, leaving only a minimum mess in the restaurant, and Arlene thrust her finger from the extent of her arm, to aim the sick "daughter of The House" to do her business in the kitchen. It couldn't possibly harm the ingredients that the Villettis mixed together for what substituted as nutrition around their place. She then motioned for Tancredo to make himself useful, seeking to have him quit groping the girls that walked passed him — and grab a mop instead.

Finally, Arlene found it in her to next stalk out of the kitchen door and grab Lucy by the arm and pull her out of audio range for any future Senate intelligence report. "You know what you've been paid extra for?"

"Yes'M." Lucy looked surprised and taken aback that Arlene handled her so fiercely.

"Then remember to leave your door unlocked for that Ginny Hall child. Keep Newberry distracted so he doesn't know we're taking pictures. He's in the race against Ford."

"Really? He's a driver, too? Oooo! What kind of car does he own?"

Arlene looked at the saloon's ceiling for a direction to pray for an escape but thought she could see dirt shaking out of it in her direction. She would have even been able to hear the pounding sound that was surely emanating from the rooms upstairs were it not for the black musicians and their ear-throbbing noise. She then realized that she liked so little out of life: not sports, not music, and certainly not stupid people. Had her quest for revenge completely consumed her? The baby would change everything. It gave Arlene a new hope for something better. If she could raise her child safely away from all the worse influences there were in this world. Only here she was, in Villetti's of all places, and Congress was in session. Then Baldavino arrived downstairs, ran his fingers through his neatly straightened brown hair, replacing his fedora above it, adjusted the way his dress shirt tucked into his striped pants under his suspenders, straightened his bowtie, and flashed her his widest smile. She supposed he tried to look like Taddeo, which wouldn't be too hard for him considering they were first cousins. But Arlene wasn't enthusiastic about making a substitution for the pitcher.

* * * * *

Later, and much further east of Chicago, Taddeo Villetti sat next to Trevor Bass on the Cubs' streetcar the boys would take over to Ebbets Field to start practice mid-Saturday morning. He cared greatly for this man's serenity most, among all his less self-disciplined friends' various and constantly fluctuating emotions. Most were understandably solemn today, however — what after their particularly bad loss to New York yesterday. But Tad's entire Friday hadn't ended all that bad after all. Sega created a few happy ending scenarios indeed. Still he didn't need to hear Hoff bragging about all his adventures and Trip struggling to keep up with him or still fight with him, about a game in which he never even got a chance to play. The rest of the team was mostly quiet. Coach Mitchell had actually hailed a private taxi and didn't travel with the rest of them. That was never a good sign. And being left alone under the implied authority held by Bill Killefer certainly created enough apprehension for the other rookies as the streetcar chugged and shuddered along southeast on Atlantic Avenue toward Wilbert Robinson, Dan Griner, Jake Daubert, and Burleigh Grimes, plus Hy Myers and Ernie Krueger, all waiting for the Cubs to arrive on their turf. But Taddeo didn't worry about any of that. His mind was far away from the immediate concerns he ought to have in the present, or even what would be his very first time sighting the infamous Ebbets Field. For almost anyone else, it would be hard to picture a rookie ballplayer *not* being excited by their first opportunity to play in this park.

Taddeo's anticipation centered around playing some entirely different games. What had happened with him and Arlene? Even after everything he'd been enjoying with Sega, his thoughts would return back to her. They were going to be partners. Arlene represented his only hope to get out of this mess — one inclusive of his favor-granting family using their version of a staged prison break with which to hold The Hoff's future hostage over Tad, and his behavior. And yes, all the signs were there. It was definitely his family or someone from it who got George sent to prison without a hearing or trial. Then that meetup with Rocco Valenti in one more prison — a person of great character if there ever was one. Though Tad's brother Greg's duplicitousness and scheming that Taddeo still couldn't even figure, would have any simple killer-for-hire topped. But both those bastards had to have not one heart among either of them to even be capable of their respective missions for The Family — of Greg's mission to only benefit himself. So his sending Sega to Tad in New York wasn't any act of mercy, especially considering the beaten and broken condition she still recovered from. However, together, all of them could even be planning to lead Tad into a trap — to exploit the rift that had grown in Taddeo and Arlene's relationship, that in itself suggesting that Arlene and his working together represented something even more dangerous to somebody. So dangerous that Greg needed to interfere. And so would Tad's family in The Empire State. He just knew it. And the familiar faces that haunted Coogan's Hollow the other evenings did nothing to dispel that notion. Taddeo knew it was not over yet.

He now wished he could reach Arlene. It seemed like only seconds from when they had all these plans and then he turned around and she was gone — or he had to be gone. It all had fallen apart. And now she wasn't speaking to him again — and that had been going on for most of the week. That was *some communication* with his partner. Taddeo just wanted to get things back to some kind of normal. But he was no longer sure that in his life, there had ever been any such thing as normal.

* * * * *

Meanwhile, after all the boys were gone, Anna enjoyed a bath she had drawn in privacy in the suite she shared with Tad at The Bossert. When she'd cleaned up, it would be for about as long as she could stand it before someone connected with The Family was supposed to come and meet her to bring her medicine — what she euphemistically called her fix. What she also now medicated Taddeo with. "Sega" created little waves by moving her naked legs through the water as she ran a sponge with soap bubbles making little snaps that blasted their way around the scrubber's surface. She was surprised when she reflected on them, they reminded her of Cardinelli's bombs that burst every so often across Chicago. Her expression was solemn. She didn't require a mirror to see it. She knew what she was feeling and didn't need to look at her cuts and bruises to be reminded of them either. It was enough that Taddeo told her she was still beautiful and also making quite some progress with her healing. That was the healing someone could see on her outside.

Inside, Anna hoped her toddler son was safe and no one had harmed him or her estranged second husband, Alexander Suciu. Cardinelli had taken issues with some services provided to him by her new spouse, and they had money problems — forcing her to do what she did to help provide for her boy in this new country she was only four years emigrated to, and married in, once divorced in, and all of it way too soon. The Mafia said she'd be safe and that some quite talented people under the leadership of very important men in Manhattan could protect her if she did a job for them in Chicago. They only wanted information — about how and when the Irish planned to betray them — and if The Villetti House, with or without Victoria Moresco — would usurp Colosimo, and then still play ball with New York. *She*, only wanted to return to Indiana and see her boy from her first marriage. She cared nothing about the Villettis and The Windy City's politics, but enjoyed taking one of their sons away from that green bitch, who thought herself just so smart, that Arlene could assert her control over everyone. As that is what Anna saw the Irish doing in America once their first and second generations fought the good fight to get themselves settled in their new country.

Now Anna was actually Romanian, and not at all some Greek woman. But the Austro-Hungarian Empire was at war with the United States and their now-native-born bigots that ran things in this country were more than ever suspicious, if not hateful of most foreigners. Thus it was better if they all thought "Sega" was Greek. Her working name represented nothing more than an Americanized interpretation of Suciu, or "Sage," that could be easily explained to any immigration authorities as only a spelling error, though the average American layman wouldn't be cultured enough to ever figure that out. But truthfully she hated all the complications, and especially being around all these Germans in The Bossert. This was not the experience of any luxury here. Not for her. Not at this kind of stress level. She shifted her trim legs in the bathwater again and raised one arm to wash it with the sponge, watching the water droplets fall off it and into the full basin where she lay relaxing, mostly submerged. But Anna couldn't relax. The Germans were allied with the Hapsburgs and their monarchs had overrun most of her homeland in Europe, forcing many Romanians to flee. And the Italians? They betrayed Otto Van Bismark's plan for an alliance to instead side with Britain, France, and their American allies because these guineas only did what was only in their best interest. They weren't concerned with what happened to the Romanian people, only with territorial gains and who could rape whose farmland. And speaking of rapists, that's what Taddeo's woman did night after night — or organized anyway. Managing the women at the brothel that poorly disguised itself as a lounge to take all of these men's repeated abuse on them. These uncultured boys on this baseball team had the far better disposition than many of Villettis' customers, let alone Urso. But Taddeo was changing. She'd begun to sense he was keeping things from her. There was a side to him that he wouldn't let her see. He was planning something. Anna had a feeling he would avenge her — only she had a bad feeling that the youngest Villetti was going to take that way too far.

She'd made a mistake thinking she could control him when the greater powers that schemed, saw his own father's need to sidetrack Urso as an opportunity to insert *her* into that family's organization. She could have only wished his baby brother had been available. Of course he wasn't. But Arlene was in her way from the get-go.

But Anna wondered if Taddeo really loved the scarlet whore. They fought constantly — perhaps not violently like she and Urso. But it was too bad he was going to be ruined by all his world being just about ready to come crashing down all around him. Anna already knew it would. Only the woman who had arrived in Brooklyn now, wearing the color of bright blood, could care less about the dark, twisting storm cloud that now called herself Villetti's madam. She deserved whatever losses that leprechaun "sporting woman" was going to suffer. However, Anna also knew that woman was a deadly murderer. The men of The House tried to hide it to protect their egos, but they were afraid of her, or she turning other men against them. No sooner than Anna had arrived at The Sisson, the brothers in The Family were investigating dead bodies and missing persons that had only recently had too much to do with Arlene. And the Irish cunt controlled a good amount of the payroll, by way of her managing the bordello — a position Taddeo had secured for her.

Now Anna wouldn't shed any tears if Urso got caught in Arlene's line of fire, but that woman was also very often incompetent or hesitant for reasons her rival couldn't even begin to fathom. But that shamrock bitch was going to be subjected to "Sega's" worst wrath if the opportunity ever arose for it — as she could show them all that she was just as dangerous as the other woman was. And the oldest brother was insignificant. Taddeo could do what he wished to him and Anna would find it sweet, if it were on her behalf. But Rinaldo and Greggorio were *her* priority targets. The Mafia wanted to know what they knew, what they planned. She was sure the Irish employed Arlene for the same reason. Meanwhile, Anna had only just begun the quest for vengeance against Arlene, by taking that paddy princess' young man. And where things were standing, it only saw her hatred growing.

* * * * *

Concurrently, the young Irish woman stood as being plenty subjected to too much Villetti Family interference in her affairs. She had only just dodged multiple advances by Illinois Senator Lawrence Yates Sherman, whom the *other Republicans* at least deferred to, if only because they wanted to make campaign money-raising all "fun and good, *honest games*" in Chicago. It's just that he wasn't even a strong enough presence to avoid having his bill wind up tabled in a whorehouse, where the working women were *supposed* to pay attention to him. Arlene even almost felt *a little bit* of sympathy for the sixty year old two-time widower who just looked so pathetically lonely at a booth by himself in the busy, crowded lounge — which he'd slink back to after each time he'd propositioned her. But Arlene had no more mercy to offer and she was not interested in the partaking of political parlor games on behalf of either Villetti financial interests or Katherine McCormick's schemes and dreams. She had to tend bar because Gino and then Horatio were needed to break up "gentlemen fights" in the lounge, while the seductive Jasmine could be counted on being requested to deliver her special cocktails that she could make — upstairs. And Arlene had only just realized, Vitale was gone again. *When and where had* he *disappeared?* Out of any of the goombah's, that one had shown the slightest competence when he'd followed her and brought The Family down on Zhen Li, so this made him dangerous — and one to keep her eyes on. Only she hadn't done that. But she would inquire of his whereabouts by talking to his friend Gervasio, later. However, the whole place was beginning to spin out of control right now. Only Arlene didn't have time to worry after one goombah — or any other enforcer who could establish a more productive procedure for Congress, because Urso's request for her, personally, could not be ignored. She had to see what that bastard wanted — likely to keep Lumia alive by right about now — and she put Ignacio behind the bar with Vico backing him. She figured the customers could attempt to instruct them on how to make their drinks, but she worried those good fellas couldn't make change with only two cents between them.

On her way, Arlene determined she didn't have any more sympathy to give. But when she finally got upstairs and determined Lucky LuLu was still breathing — and vomiting of course, Arlene was to learn Urso wanted her to strip naked and get on his semen-soaked bedding with the ailing bleach-blonde and his big, naked and hairy body in between them. Sadly, like all Villetti men, she could still see Taddeo in his brother's features. But one of many things the brothers did not share, would be the younger brother's being so easily able to control. So as she had to take Urso's abuse, it only made the absence of her unborn child's father hurt more. And pain gave way to anger and she hate-fucked Urso like Arlene had never done any man. The disillusioned, who would be king, seemed to like it too — her even losing her composure and hitting him — by way of his calling out for her to try and hurt him more, with Urso blowing off a load of any burdens he'd been carrying since Greg had been mysteriously away for a while, and left his older brother in charge of holding The Family's royal scepter.

Chapter 53

"Geez. Let it all out already. You've been protecting your wounds since even before we got lost from Manhattan," Hoff initiated his soft interrogation of Tad, newly arrived in Brooklyn — still less than a day now — as the practice partners stretched it out together before taking a morning jog around Ebbets Field. Taddeo had avoided sightseeing in this iconic ballpark thus far. These grounds alone and their potential for trouble with the home team lineup were only one of Tad's causes for concern. He'd started feeling uneasy no sooner than the taxi he took, since he'd ditched the team's streetcar that morning, pulled up in front of the *triple*-story front to the ballpark at 55 Sullivan Place in Brooklyn's Flatbush neighborhood. Those giant curving archways were intimidating to walk under, as a visiting team member, and alone like he was. Though the architecture was similar to The Bossert, this place felt cold, instead of being lit by warm welcoming lights and Sega leaping into his arms. But this was pregame practice. The fans wouldn't be there for hours. However, Tad felt like Old Rusty was stalking him in the shadows. This was Hy Myers' home. Jake Daubert's territory. Dan Griner's hunting grounds. Taddeo even thought he felt a phantom pain in his face. Later in the afternoon, he and Hoff would start their first game in a new series against these Robins. Though from the bench most likely. He felt truly relieved when he found his best friend, got changed and kept company with him while they prepared to face any challenge — together — and even if he still remained plenty mad at the big idiot. "So what the hell is killing you, Villetti? C'mon. If you can't tell me, who *can* you tell?" As soon as he saw him, Hoff started up the conversation and smiling like nothing had happened and there wasn't any care in the world.

Tad tried to avoid getting caught smiling back at his good buddy's concern. He couldn't keep avoiding him or stay angry with George. But when he thought about coming clean with the truth, his face involuntarily morphed into registering his deep grievance. Taddeo avoided his pal's curious gaze and looked at the ground. He still wouldn't discuss his dilemma, even with The Hoff and all that they had been through. Though it had been feeling more and more uncomfortable, internalizing it. "Aggh." The cold wetness of the grass soaking into his baseball practice pants just adding one more reason for his irritation. But he really did need to talk, so Tad elected to cite the most predictable catalyst for his bad disposition instead. "Dammit. Being shutout, seven to nothin' against the Giants? You mean you don't remember yesterday? What, were you the only one on the team to come out of Coogan's Hollow last night with your ego still intact? I blew one more game — and for Hippo Vaughn. That's not good. I've been too distracted. Plus Killefer looks like he's chewing glass every time he eyes me coming onto the rubber. Trip's always mad. And there's also that even Bass-Man's really not too fond of me right now. He's just good at hiding it."

"Last night wasn't on you. Coach made the call, sending you out there in the 8th. We were already down five-zip anyway — and that's all on Vaughn. Since the first inning. Sometimes even aces have off-days."

"Yeah, but who knew Rodriguez was going to hit me? Not being able to stop those two additional runs from really deciding the game? That hurt the team and went on Trev's sacred personal record, even if it's only on there in his own imagination. He's not fourteen feet tall or something. But that hit most definitely tainted my stats — back in the real world. Still short and limited — as my outings have been. I certainly haven't achieved any ERA to call home about. There's no doubt that would be one more conversation that would *not* end on a positive note, anyway." *When is there not one, lately?*

"Well, Bass's putting salt on his wounds all by himself then. He's big but yeah — he does not stand fourteen feet tall. That's for sure. We've seen some strange times with Mitchell, bringing Trevor out there as he continues making substitutions for Max, and we're on the final rope in the last game of a series, and only nine frames ahead of a rival. Only I think Trevor's kicking himself more over his at-bat, then missing one going over the wall. Besides, Killefer wasn't hitting either. That's why Coach put me in. But you can relax and re-gather yourself. You and Bass seem to be getting along. No fights there that I've seen. He's in a better mood than Trip. That's for sure. And you should plan on having some time off to relax this new series. I know for a fact that Mitchell really does *not* want to throw *you* against Brooklyn. He's thinking — nah, I mean he's praying, 'Please no. Not again.' " Hoff laughed. "So it felt to me more like Coach was trying to school you by making the calls he made yesterday, knowing the game was already lost. So he could see how you can handle the pressure. Bandage a leak. You know relievers don't get to pick if they come out while we're ahead or behind. Especially rookies. *Get you out there before we face the Robins again*. That was Coach's strategy. And it's still quite early in the season, so it couldn't cost the team too much. Right after what, a nine-game winning streak — and all on the road? Ten if you count what we did to Cincinnati before we left Chi-Town. And you have been helping — our team and yourself. Success like what we've experienced? This is crazy. It never lasts forever, let alone a whole second week. So I don't think that can be what's been really eating *you* up. You know you didn't lose that game. It was just dumb luck. And you'll get another chance. Just maybe not *this* series."

The men finished stretching out, left behind them many of the other Cubs who were doing more calisthenics, and started to jog along the third base line of Ebbets Field toward left. His buddy had put him at ease. "All right. I 'spose I'll feel better if I get this off my back sooner than later. It's way past time I could talk to you like I used to, George. I guess — I guess I'm upset over a girl," Tad admitted.

"I knew it. I'd already had that one predicted right," Hoff announced. "What I couldn't figure was whether it's that someone you just met *here* on this road trip, or the badly beaten one from back in Manhattan who you were next rolling around on The Bossert lobby floor with? I wasn't keeping track when I went out with Trip while you elected to stay at the hotel, remember? Maybe she was the same one?"

"Only *you* can work it out to have two or more gals in a single night, Hoff."

"Well as you know, I didn't exactly have a room in Brooklyn Heights this last evening. But I should have — only you're still holding Boston against me. You're breaking our own Marshalltown rules."

Tad shrugged and spit off to his side. "We have two rooms and three of us played yesterday. But only two of our group can manage to play baseball and stay out of prison at the same time."

"That's true. But whatever." Then his friend continued on about his favorite topic, women. "Well if this girl's a new one here, Man, I don't know how you found the time since we practically just got in to Brooklyn and that other one was stalking you. No, wait — it was the one from Manhattan. Right? Had to be. That poor and broken little thing? You worried she caught the right cab or something? Or you came to your senses and broomed her? She *was* the one rolling all over in that mess with you on the floor of The Bossert's lobby? Then you disappeared for the night and then me *and* Mikey actually wanted to stay in *my room* — but Trevor wouldn't let us. Well he knows as do you, with well, how I usually am when we're on the road."

"Just when we're on the road, Hoff?"

"Ha. Only actually I know that you're *all* still mad at me about Boston. But you, my best-friend in the whole wide world, throws me your 'screw-you' ball. And all this because *what's-her-name* showed up?"

"Sega."

"Right."

"I said you and Michael could both lay down on the couches in the lobby."

"Yeah, Trip loved that. So I guess you really *did* need your privacy." Hoff laughed. "No free show? Well I guess I walked in on *that one*, didn't I? The other morning when we were back by Harlem. But I couldn't figure why I then find all four of you needed to be in that room. Just so you could disturb me? Maybe you're all into *that*. I haven't explored everything that is probably offered at your papa's bordello."

"No. No one else here is into *that*. It's just you George."

"But hey. I'll take one for the team." His smile he called on traveled right through the warm middle of his friend's strike zone while the path they ran traversed the outfield. The Hoff scored a timely hit. He was genuinely Taddeo's good friend. Only consistently annoying and perceptive where it came to his best buddy. "But wait. Trip and Bass both said you also disappeared when we were in Philadelphia, too."

"Why? What'd I miss? More auto-racing?"

"Nah. But I'm sure glad the fellas didn't need my room there. Whoah my Philly girl was fine! But did you get yourself another one there, then? I mean, I could see how you'd want one all to yourself, and especially again, now — if Sega's been shared between a fifth of our roster."

"Uh. No. She has not."

"You know *with me* it stays with the team."

"Or within the prison walls."

"Ha! Good one. Nice toss on that. Okay. I deserved it. And that will be one heck of a memory we took away from Boston."

"Well who could forget?"

"You should. Let it go already. But I shouldah known better than to think you were a monk. Well good for you, Taddeo. And don't you worry. This train's leaving for Pittsburgh on Wednesday anyway, and you might be able to sneak out of town to Philly again, once we're back in Pennsylvania and playing so close to her home. The other one's. Closer than Chi-Town anyway. For those midnight trains you'll spend most of your time on. I've got experience with this sort of thing if you need any help. Drop her off, pick her up? Or what? That's *not* a different girl? Or wait. Are you taking the latest one with you? Nah. Really? You *are*, you dog? The one from Upper Manhattan who you kept Trip and Bass-Man up with all last Monday night? Another private conference you don't think I can handle? Or you don't want to obligate *me* for another favor? Do you?"

"Uh." Tad wasn't sure how to answer his ridiculous friend. There was no one plotting against Hoffman. And last of anyone, would be his best friends. "Nice try to turn this around, George. I needed to talk to them and have things be taken seriously. And you weren't there when I went downstairs to fetch Trip and Bass-Man." However, he'd always trusted Hoff. And historically he'd usually felt coming out with the truth was the best policy. Tad was becoming way too suspicious and way too experienced with everyone else's lying now. "Anyway, I'm trying not to," Taddeo responded tone-dead, "— obligate you. Bring any or all of my teammates into my personal life's problems. But she couldn't just leave," he switched to whining. "It's complicated." They continued running.

"Oh. It is still the same broad. You're liking the older woman now. Good. They're more experienced. I can remember — ."

"I'd rather you didn't remember the old times right now. And I'm not talking about 'the same broad' that we were just talking about. Keep up." They still jogged, completing their second whole lap around Ebbets' huge outfield. Reporters had started to be admitted if their bribes had cleared security. And the Robins began to arrive.

"Well you've managed to actually confuse me — about women. And at some time, you really do have to take Trip *and* Bass-Man back into your room. *They* need to leave so I can get some more fun-time in? Pleeease. It sucks being out on the team bus in the middle of the night."

Tad looked at him incredulously while they jogged. "You did not? What? On *our* reserved transportation? That streetcar? And what, was there a driver that parked there who you then let watch you? That's sick, Man. Did you collect a fare from *him?* Where do you find the ladies who would do that? And at the very least you're going to warn me where I shouldn't sit?"

"Oh, yeah. You're alright. I favor Killefer's chosen spot. Or how 'bout Charlie Hollocher's? Please. When it's in the moment, I really don't pay attention to whose seat I'm using."

"That's for sure."

"But whatever and wherever it happened — I mean for you — congratulations. And well, you'll be able to let it all go — or go straighten it all out — in just a few more days." He swatted Tad on his bottom as they ran side-by-side back toward the outfield track. They were in great shape. "So don't sweat it. This is nothing new to me for our road trips. You just have to learn the train schedules. I study 'em like I study opposing batters. I'm a professional. So you should cheer up and look on the bright side. I'm here to help ya. And who could be better at calling your games? You need to only focus on the Robins right now. Don't let *this* distract you. It's going to be a tough fight even without a woman to really mess things up. And they do tend to do that."

"Yeah they do."

"But I noticed her — what's her name? Sega. Down in the hotel lobby when I guess you were finally sleeping. That one came out here all the way from Chicago, huh? She didn't resemble your usual type of girl you keep back home. I thought that was interesting. So I came back in The Bossert to use the men's room. Then I also caught this new one sneaking around buying *some* funny stuff from some guy she meets in our hotel lobby, Friday night. Yeah? But I don't think some nigger from Harlem delivered it. He had his collar up and his hat pulled down low, staying in the shadows. But though my eyes might have fooled me, it looked like she rendezvoused with a wop." He glanced at Taddeo. "I mean a different wop."

"Yeah. Thanks. I got that, George."

"Well it looked like whatever that stuff is that all you people probably like to use. Though I'm not one to question, if that's what makes you feel all right."

But Hoff noticed after he got only the tiniest smile out of his friend, that Tad still couldn't remain the slightest bit relieved by his humor. He muttered, "What do you mean, by 'you people?' Cut out the shit right now. I'm not in the mood. We're in Brooklyn and will have to take too much crap already. Or do you like the way that Hun maître d' at the hotel last night was judging all of us?"

"I don't think he was quite used to the performance you and Sega put on for him at your arrival." But realization of the obvious wasn't too difficult, even for George Hoffman. "Ah. Wait a minute. So it's definitely not your woman *here* that's bothering you."

"No. But right now the one you saw in Manhattan has nevertheless gone missing."

"What? Is that why you were late this morning? And now you're not yet feeling all right about that? Because you think she might be out trying to score another trip?"

"It wouldn't surprise me. Her method of traveling away from it all was just the kind of medical tourism that I needed to indulge in, too. But I'm back now. I wouldn't want to become like one of my uncle's permanent kind of patients. Only Sega needs to do a lot more healing. She's pretty messed up. But it's dangerous for her to be trying to procure that stuff — as a woman on her own in this big city. So that's why I was late. I was sitting with Trevor when I jumped off our car and ran back to The Bossert. At least he knew I was gone."

"Gone mental? Yeah. That's very true. Admission of your problem is like the first step."

Tad looked at the sky but didn't think he should waste a prayer right now.

"But I thought you just said you were also worried about at least one *other* woman?"

"Well, while I have no idea what happened to Sega — what's happening. She didn't want to go to breakfast when we woke up this morning and then she said she was taking a bath when I said goodbye, intending to jump on the same streetcar you all took. At first, I did. Only I found I didn't want to sit with you all this morning. I have a lot of important things on my mind."

"I lost track of you after I saw you actually sitting with Charlie Hollocher. Then the guys were all interested in me starting to tell another story."

"Of course they were. So like I said, I guess you didn't notice when I jumped off after only a few stops. I doubled back while we were just turning off Clinton and I ran back onto Montague. There was something I felt like I'd neglected. Well she wasn't in the room when I arrived back upstairs. And it looked like it had been searched rather hastily. I hope she's all right. And I do hope she comes back."

"I'll bet you do. But like we figured, she probably just went shopping."

"And charging it to my room? Anyway, I can't believe I just missed her like that. And the bathtub was even warm — from very recent use. I've learned to not like it when my friends disappear. So, you know what? For the rest of these road games, you know *you* could help by not troubling me with any additional disappearances or *any* other problems either, George."

"When do I ever do?"

"You need me to answer that? Because I will."

"Oh I'm sure you would." He laughed, exasperated by Taddeo now. They continued jogging. "But maybe the crazy woman's just gone to find her drug connection once again. You're overcomplicating this. It'd be getting to be about that time she'd need a new fix. What's she doing? Injections or simply smoking or eating opioids as edibles?"

"I didn't realize you were a practiced chef with *that menu.* I never thought you were using?"

"I'm not. But I suppose if the moment with that special girl calls for it — ."

"There's a special girl? What I'd really never guess is *that term* would be in George Hoffman's vocabulary." The pair continued panting out their dialog along their morning run, and passing the visiting team's dugout again and then began one more lap while they conversed. Other Cubs started their runs, stretched, or played catch. The Robins were having a meeting. "Only where's Sega so quickly finding a hookup? I'm troubled that associates with my family are the only folks she would know out here. So that through her, they might be still maneuvering my life — and the people in it who I care about, like chess pieces in some twisted, sick game."

"Yeah? Hmmm."

"Yeah, there's something. You just don't wind up in state prison without a trial, George. Who does that? I mean except for you? And what I'm trying to spell out for you is that this only happened to you, because of me."

"Okay, Tad. Thanks for that. But you deflected the question about any *other* woman. So I just made an educated gamble that since the source of your trouble blows from our Windy City, that the rest of your real trouble might also be back in Chicago. Isn't *she?* Now you *are* in trouble."

"Yeah, well more than one of my many troubles might be back there now."

Hoff grinned at him. "More than one of them? I'm loving it."

"Well, at least maybe you guys all *aren't* — in trouble, I mean. I'm not much of a pitcher anymore. At least last night definitely proved that."

"It was *one* game."

"I would normally have to beg Coach to let me up on the hill. But there's some other influence that I'm afraid has been the only cause for him putting me out there — again. And then I blow it for the team — again. And we got it right the first time: Mister Mitchell has no plans — zero plans — for letting me out on the field versus the Robins. That you can bet your entire wage on."

"My wage isn't that much to make it worth my while. None of ours are. We could be organizing a strike. I mean not just the Cubs, but the whole league. Only no. You won't blow it. I mean your game. Not next time. And a whole lot less of the time. You just need more experience. And you've already proven you can save games — even win them. But hey, go back a minute," Hoff said. "What did you mean about *'us guys?' Not being in trouble?* What are you thinking, Tad? Talk to me."

"I started thinking about leaving the team," Tad related to him.

"You what? Oh no you're not. Quitting baseball? You love The Show more than anything. You just need time to adjust to playing at the pro level, that's all."

"*All* it is — *is* that I don't want my friends forced to be involved in something." Tad recollected how his cousin said The Family marked its targets during his conversation at Sing Sing. "Something else, because of me." Of course, The Hoff's behavior and getting him clear of troubles was what led Taddeo to making that bargain and then winding up in Ossining in the first place.

"Wait. No. Tell me your self-doubt did not start all over because of this woman. The one I take it your family sent out here. Or that other one? Oh no. It did, I'm guessing again? That's how this all relates? Wow. That must be some pussy. Tell me you don't want to run full-time protection for her. Or which one? Do I know her?"

Tad had to suppress the instantaneous irritation he felt with the disrespectful manner in which his buddy had just described his lady friend. "It's Arlene," he said.

"The red-headed whore? What — is she a *real* fire bush or something? You're really going to quit playing ball while your arm is only just developing — and all over a whore?"

"Would you stop calling her that? She's an entertainer. And no. I don't have to quit baseball. Maybe I can still get traded, or at least if I continue playing bad enough, get sent to a minor league team — somewhere — back to Marshalltown I'd hope. At least it's familiar. But anywhere away from Chicago would be good," Tad said. "Away from my brothers and my father." He looked at his feet. "And I 'spose I'll take Arlene with me. Once I sobered up, I could see that." Sega had disappeared mysteriously anyway. Though she might turn back up at any most inconvenient time. But that didn't really engender trust in her. Both women kept secrets, but he had a true partnership with Arlene if he really thought about it — and one that he had secretly, already betrayed his family for. And the list of those *he* betrayed included his papa, who'd sent him to his cousin Rocco in the first place. So there was very little cause for trust at all, and Taddeo felt the most alone he had yet.

"*So now it's that one*. As opposed to the one you've been hiding in your hotel rooms throughout most of these road games?"

Tad's mouth hung open. "You don't even know half of it. But you know exactly what I had to be doing when we started out on our tour of The East, don't you Slick? Only you're so innocent of complicating things because you didn't know any better? Right? But if you think you know so much now, why are you still asking me so many questions about this? For your continuing health's sake, you need to stay out of it."

"It was fun making *you* — who are always ever so private — to admit to *all of it*, finally."

"I'm not having fun, Hoff."

"Besides, you didn't say anything when I suggested my ridiculous plan at playing travel agent between you, Philly and Pittsburgh. *And* you filled *my* room with *boarders*. Had to get you back somehow. Forcing me to live with Trip and Bass-Man and their idiosyncrasies."

"Their idiosyncrasies? What about you getting thrown into a maximum security prison?"

"Well, there was that. Again. But heh. I've been there, done that. I mean the balancing act — when we were in the minor leagues and it's not easy to pull off — especially when *you* are starting the next day. So then I'd already figured that *another one* was already with you. Wet and ready for your fastball. Or your spitball if you learned that one during the course of your nights. Especially just now when you acted like you really didn't care *what* you threw — in Coogan's Hollow, or wherever your next outing occurs, I mean — and where the batted balls wind up. You're distracted, Shooter. 'Cause youuu think *you're in luhve*. With her. The one back in Chicago — well

I've done that before, too. It was even before we went to Iowa." Tad blinked at him but Hoff shook his head. "No, not with *your* girl, you idiot. Mine. See, there once was a special one I left behind. Once. And you already admitted about your own Chi-Town gal as it were. I'm just saying the home team girl sometimes works out — *worse* — than the ones on the road. Heh. Yeah. If you ask me, a regular girlfriend means nothing for you but for the regular arrival of big trouble."

"Look, Arlene's in even *more trouble* if she stays there. I mean in Chicago. I think we connected once before. I was almost reaching her. We were forming a real partnership. Then something happened. I've been trying to figure if that was my fault. Only then the Cubs are playing out here and Sega comes and goes. It's all a whirlwind and I don't know what's happening. However what I've come to suspect is — that I'm being set up. Now I've got a prison record to show for it, thank you very much, and I don't think Sega's coming and going all the way out here in Brooklyn is any coincidence. But maybe I at least still have a chance to build a new record with some new club somewhere else more stable. Then maybe that will let me start and earn me *some* additional income from this stupid sport." Tad startled himself that he'd even started talking like Arlene.

"Baseball is not stupid Taddeo and I just told you, that's one wrong girl and one bad game — with mostly Vaughn and Killefer responsible for it on top of everything — and it doesn't make you a bad pitcher, bound for some backseat assignment and some kind of change-of-life episode meant for some kind of really bad person. Now that *would* be stupid. Just look at your record to date, Tad," Hoff pleaded with him.

He finally laughed. "I did. And it's not just *one* bad game."

"So what's going on? You let Arlene get to you. Didn't you?"

"My father's forcing her to work in his stable. The one back in Chicago. I care for her Hoff. I've been buying her time, keeping Arlene booked while trying to hide her from him and my brothers. But my efforts in that endeavor aren't exactly working out either. Bad things happened. And I had gone into business with her. And next thing I know it's started costing me too much money. So actually, you know I could use your help."

"With that luscious red-head? Hey, you just say the word if you can't handle her like a real man and I'll — ."

Tad cut him off. "You'll shut up and listen! And that's almost *all* I'd have you do." He panted a bit more now, but still getting out all his words while he took rapid breaths as the pair of them were *still* jogging. Yet he had to laugh at Hoff's simple carpé diem and nonchalant attitude. But Taddeo looked away, sliding to a halt, as did his friend, who he needed to take him utmost seriously now. "My temporary plan is for *you* to buy some of her time. Don't worry. It both fits with your reputation — and I'll be the one paying for it. Just to keep my family from getting suspicious."

"Hey. What do you mean it fits with *my* reputation?"

"Never mind. I'm uh…I'm directly supervising our lady *employees* now, anyways. It would figure you'd come around more often as it were. I mean with you and I being pals and everything. At least to me, you're kind of like family. If I felt like I had ever had one anyway."

Hoffman made a sound like he just snorted. "Awww. Well hell. Sometimes it's just *so hard* being friends with you, Tad," he said, his sarcasm obvious. "And I'm getting the friend-of-the-family-discount too? Right?" he added.

"Wrong." But his tendency for Hoff's usual joviality aside, Tad imagined his friend *should* have thought he was asking a lot of him — to become involved with this, considering the other man knew just what kind of *family* he'd be playing his next game against. But Hoff always seemed so carefree. So Taddeo almost could've laughed some more over it all. Almost.

"Look. It'll be okay," he said. "Just probably not everything that you're imagining right now." He smiled at his best bud. "I'm going to look for any opportunity to find some more professional help in this area for your relief. But you know the laundry a few blocks away from my papa's place on Taylor Street? Well, it's *you*, so probably not. It's South Side. But you played ball with me there once or twice when we were kids. The back opens up to that old familiar alley by Maxwell, Polk, and Canal. And it's where I got the uniforms cleaned. And you recently helped me move some stuff from the Rainbow Beach hotel over by that alley there? Well it's the same Chinese laundry if you can somehow still be unaware. You were mostly paying attention to Rose if I recall. So I've been renting a corner of Mister Li's extra space there where I thought I could hide Arlene from my father and keep her reasonably safe from everyone else while I'm at it. Safe from my brothers as it were. We were moving her in there for an extended stay when I asked for help from my teammates. And just until I get things all set so Arlene and I can get out of town," Tad explained. "She's my true partner now. Only it didn't take them long to find her there. Now for a moment, Sega made me forget about how difficult it is — what I'm doing — and that my earlier plan hasn't been working out that well at all. But if it weren't for her being here now, *conveniently*, and me feeling like it's my responsibility to take care of *her* and get see to it that she's healthy and gets somewhere safe, then I'd be long gone — headed back to Chicago on my own. I think my brother is deliberately delaying me, based on what I could gather from talking to Sega."

"Wait. Seriously. Aren't you looking at the bigger picture here, Tad?" Hoff asked. "I mean by thinking about leaving the team. Consider this: you're not doing the rest of *us* any favors. We're thirty-two and fourteen right now. The best record in baseball. Though it's only halfway through June. All of us Cubbies need to stick it out for the entire show — keep this team together. Keep the momentum we've got going this season. *And*, keep things balanced in the clubhouse just the way they have been. Sure, we've got our problems, just like every family has its dysfunctions. I know: *we're the rookies*. Though clearly *you'd* be the one to understand something about dysfunctional families more than anyone else on this team."

"Yeah. And I'm going to kill mine, George. I'm going to kill them all."

"You don't mean that. They're your family."

"No I mean it. My brothers. How they've always ridden me. How right now I'm sure they are behind everything that's going bugs on me. How they set us all up with the Genna Brothers. What they did to Old Mister Li. What they did to the poor young woman you met at The Bossert — that *they'd* then sent out here from Chicago. To show me what they could do to those I care for. And you have no idea what Arlene told me they did to her — *my* woman. So I am going to kill my brothers dead when I get back to Chicago."

"Wait a minute. You told me that I'm like your brother."

"Exactly. Don't you see? I want to kill *you* right now." Regarding Hoff made him laugh for a moment.

"That I know you're serious about. But at least they sent Sega to *you*. Maybe that was like their apology? I don't know your family that well. But everyone on the roster now knows each other — and our patterns have gotten all too familiar. At least among ourselves. And no one predicted us Cubs were going to climb right on up to First Place. Soon we'll be halfway through our season before we know it and no one wants to worry a lot about what to expect from any replacements made to the lineup, especially now. We've got to all stick it out to make things happen for the fall. And they all know it's happening for us this year. Finally. That's undeniable and that's why Weeghman went out and put Grover Alexander in our starting rotation."

"For the whole two months he got to stay stateside — and what, the three games that he played."

"And it's why Hendrix is back on the mound today. He's seven and one already. I know somebody who knows somebody that's circulating a rumor that Mister Wrigley is now keeping one eye on the field and the other on his billfold. Exactly *why* I bet Weeghman is spending. He plans to earn a profit. I wouldn't be surprised if he's trying to find our value rising in case he's considering selling his majority stake in the team."

"He needs to. He needs the cash. I hear he's overextended with his diners and everything. And with who *he* probably owes. Do you know who *we're* working for George? Do you really? That fucker Charles Weeghman's *Klan*. Expanding a new network independent of Indiana. And a few years ago, when he opened his short-order diners up, all over? Charlie King, his once-mentor and would-be competition, dies the very same day. You don't still think this is the kind of guy who's worried about your well-being? That's why you were wearing black socks. And he wouldn't let a wop like me on the team if it weren't of some benefit to his bottom line."

"No. I guess not. Or for a favor owed? Didn't your papa move you guys into town just around the time you said King was put out to greener pastures? That's about when Colosimo paid for you guys to move out of the projects on Maxwell because your ma complained those places were making her sick, right?"

"Watch what you're implying. We lived there and moved to better digs *before* Charlie King died and you knew me back in those days. We were already playing street ball. We'd meet when we each took turns as kids sneaking across the river 'fore our parents were any the wiser."

"Or they weren't wise enough to watch out for who they were going to owe. And then we grew up knowing how to recognize funerals when the Irish cops blocked off our roads to send the next one rolling by. Anyway, change is in the air. Maybe change for the better this time. And the guys might not all like you, or Italians. Or me as well — and just the concept of new rookies. But by now they *do know you*, and some of your teammates, like me, think there's still hope we can train you yet, Villetti." Hoff laughed. "Conduct the salvage operation. That is if your malfunctions *are* correctible. You *were* something else back in the minors. *I do remember Iowa.* So don't get all caught up in the problems of some entertainer. Girls who are in that line of work have way too many of them. I know. You can't let them catch up to you, though."

Then how does George explain ever letting himself get so enamored with Rose? You're not pitching what you call for either, Buddy.

The pair completed their fourth lap, put on their gloves and separated a moderate distance apart, as Hoff had also retrieved a practice ball from Ebbets visiting team's dugout for them to begin playing catch with. They separated so as to not interfere with their other teammates who were preparing for the game that day, too. Some of the Robins had also started to now begin their workouts, too. "Now warm up that golden arm of yours Boy, and just be ready to play today. Just in case. And I'll help you out with Arlene. Don't you worry about that, Good Fella. Just help *me* out with my rookie season. I know how lucky I am to be here, on a winning team like Chicago, let alone my just getting called up to the Majors. Favors run both ways, Tad. A Villetti of all people should know that." He laughed again.

Chapter 54

As Tad and Hoff had been on the field since very early, they felt good and warm — from stretching their arms as well as their jaws — and they yielded the practice mound to Claude Hendrix and Bill Killefer, who took The Shooter and The Hoff's places. The veterans had this game to concentrate on getting prepared for. So the reporters who had gathered on the visiting team's side of the field by the Cubs' dugout now only had Villetti and George to concentrate on being prepared for, as this pair had to head back in their direction.

"Hey Hoffman, heard you were considering becoming a race car driver if this stint with baseball doesn't pan out for you. Right?"

"Funny, Guy."

"On assignment from *The Boston Globe* here, Hoffman. Our state correctional workers want to know if you're getting traded? Is Charlestown thinking of starting a new league in the prison system?"

"Don't respond," Tad told his friend, who opened his mouth but held his breath per his pitcher's call on that play.

"Hey, Villetti. Since you're not breaking any speed records, did you ask Hoffman to do it for ya?"

"Oh yeah. And Hoffman, is it true there's scientific evidence that you single-handedly started this rumored Spanish flu epidemic? They said studies are showing that half the single women on the East Coast will come down with it right after the Cubs visit."

"And Villetti, who are you going to plunk in the game today? Is there anyone on the Robins' roster that you haven't hit already?"

"Hey, we heard Robinson might start Dan Griner on short-rest this series. Is there something more personal behind that move? Or are your managers benching both of you for the Brooklyn games and the general public's health and safety?"

"*Chicago Herald* on assignment from your hometown, Pitch. Hey, is Mitchell scared to let you bat because you've started a bean-ball war with the Robins? Is even your fast friend Hollocher safe? We've heard Brooklyn wants to put you all in the hospital. And are the rumors true that not *all* your teammates hate you for that — *yet?* Or is your only friend left Alexander — because he's the honorable one who was sent with the military to the other side of the earth and wouldn't know how you've been stabbing the team in its back, here on the homefront?"

"Hey. *You.* Yeah you. Chicago. We're actually *with the Cubs*, because he's with us, and we're all with Taddeo." Hoffman grew irritated with the heckling already and Tad knew they had a lot more to endure. At least 27 innings of it over the next *four* days that had not yet *even* begun. His friend was usually the good-natured one, but even he hadn't faced the kind of attention like they had brought upon themselves now — for either just being brought up to the Big Leagues — or for other more personal reasons that sort of stung because both ballplayers had to admit, those *were* kind of valid reasons. The rookies did have a propensity to get themselves into a lot of trouble. Tad's anger really began overheating. "So we actually thought we'd try supporting our teammates and winning for a change. How do you think Chicago likes that? And how *are* your newspaper sales?"

"Hey George. How would you like it if we take that warm-up jog again? Get some fresh air until the other guys get back and the press has somebody else to pick on?" Tad asked his friend.

Only then, some reporter just really had to register a strike on Taddeo. It poured a lot of salt on a quite fresh and open wound for which Tad had been trying to do some immediate healing. "Hey Villetti. Good job in Coogan's Hollow. How'd your overrated boys like playing on what'll one day be a *monument field?* Make you think about retiring yourself? That ought to help out all the rest of the guys who actually take baseball seriously. They might find a victory in *something* on the day we see that happen. So tell us, what do you think of New York?"

"Wait. What's that? What do I think of New York?" Taddeo came to a cold stop in his tracks by home plate.

"Yeah."

"Is this for the record? You boys *are* going to write this stuff down?"

"Sure Villetti. You never know if there comes a case where somebody from some rag sheet has to stretch their assignment to fit it to the margin. So c'mon tell us Wise Guy, what do you really think of New York?"

"Well, are you guys ready? To make *me* the voice of Chicago?" The pitcher started grinning.

"Uh-oh," Hoff muttered under his breath.

"Yeah. Sure Rookie. We'll do that."

"All right. Get your pencils and scorecards ready — 'cause the question is, what do I think of New York, right? Well, okay then. What *I think* is — '*Fuck* New York!' And fuck you, too!"

He then immediately started to run around the outside track, tapping Hoff on the elbow as he passed, so his friend would quickly move to catch up with him. And over his shoulder he tossed, "That's what I think. Write that down."

And Taddeo knew better, but he wished the reporters *could* actually print *that* in tomorrow's papers. He felt all their shock follow him as he passed their position in the stands. But a sixth sense told him to make sure he saw who else's eyes followed him. The spectators had begun being admitted in. Tad thought he might just see members of the same company that had held court in the field level seats with his father about three weeks ago in Chi-Town. Yes, indeed. He could've just recognized an individual — or five — who had been watching him play against the Giants as well. It was now *more than the press* that had focused their interest on the young pitcher who was visiting from Chicago.

Chapter 55

"You're not sitting here, you Irish cow-bug."

"From here is where I can keep my best eye on the game. All of it." A new gentleman in a black suit and bowler hat strode down the stairs to the front row of the home plate seating section of Ebbets Field. His broad gray mustache moved when he spoke. It was large enough it might have covered a detestable scowl that would still be given away by how the shifting, evaluating brown eyes regarded each of the Italians — with practiced prejudice. "One of your men will have to move. Now." He clearly did not come to show any respect to Brooklyn's Camorra street boss Salvatore D'Aquila, with his faction's arch rival from New York's true Mafia observing from only a few seats away — and their Jewish bankers sitting like a buffer in between them.

D'Aquila laughed, his bright tan boater hat moving under his shiny, still youthful, smoothly shaven skin — the old school Mustache Pete era as good as gone-by, as far as he was concerned. Things were changing. "Really? Well our friends in Chicago who Vitale here is here representing, don't like your particular brand of sports journalism and what you're printing in *The Morning Telegraph*. They'd prefer it that you would focus more on *the facts* of the game, rather than gossiping on only speculation about the personal lives of Max Flack or other players who I know you have never actually interviewed." Brooklyn's heavyweight boss had decided to throw himself into the role of writing critic versus any other type of challenger for the aged man. "You might want to at least talk to *them*. Now is there some other reason you seem so intent on joining us? Aren't you satisfied by just covering boxing?"

However, Bat Masterson, at even sixty-four years of age, had to be paid some respect. He was the one man, who even if he fired — in this now-full baseball stadium — would still be given the quickest and most comprehensive judgement — that *he* had acted out of righteousness. He could *and had* gotten away with murder according to a great many people. He might do so again. "I sense there could be an interview right here. So I aim to correct any oversight about the job I do — with *this one's* examination coming about very soon. I make sure I get *all* the information I require. And my eyes are on the facts about the real game. That's why I'm sitting here. For this game." He reached his hand into his coat. On the closer side of the Jews to Masterson, Ciro Terranova gulped. But New York City's Joe Masseria didn't flinch. He nodded toward a husky, strong-looking kid that was part of his party, and *Umberto Valenti* observed the reactions in the stands. His brother's man from Chicago inched his hand into his coat, as did Masseria's nearly-a-child-servant hanger-on. But that kid caught Arnold Rothstein's slight shaking of his head, and a taller friend of his, another kid, observed their mentor too, and placed his hand on the first's gun-arm.

Interesting, Masseria's man had some kind of connection to the shylock. Umberto wondered if Sullivan knew. Masseria likely did not, but that wasn't Valenti's concern — though it was likely the newcomer's. But Sally would want to know about this. Only he'd save that secret until he could confirm it, and he could use a reveal of the intel to prove his loyalty, should it become necessary. It often did in this business. Rothstein definitely had taken an interest in this new development, but he clearly had influence over Masseria's young men, but he would *also* want more information and less fighting on this afternoon, especially while they were all in such a public arena.

Umberto knew all too well who the kids were and that Genovese, and his taller yet little buddy Luciano, were not the only ones playing more than one side here. That's what underlings did just to survive in New York's underworld. They learned, and then they betrayed, and then they jockeyed to realize new ambitions of their own. But they were all still children as far as the twenty-eight-year-old Valenti was concerned. He was only being careful by always knowing who anybody and everybody were. Masseria was probably trying to buy their loyalty on the cheap with baseball tickets. It obviously wasn't working. But that might turn out to be Joe The Boss' big problem. One day. Being cheap had its cost.

"And so for starters I'd like to learn exactly what *now* concerns Manhattan about The Windy City or Brooklyn again, for that matter?" Masterson asked.

"The Cubs have improved their record over the Giants. Can't it just be that simple? Tell me, is this an interrogation, Sheriff?"

"I'm retired. This is investigative reporting. It's what I do."

"I heard you're still pretty fast with it," Joe Masseria said unafraid, and obviously unaware that the young men he had with him were *not* going to back him up. Umberto suspected the fat shylock might have plenty to do with that. But Valenti took comfort in his freedom to act — to take both sides when each suited him — but only on behalf of himself.

"I'm just fast with the wire now, back to my paper. I told you that's what I do these days."

"And you're fast at making enemies, too."

"The fastest. I've lived my whole life with having plenty of enemies. Lots and lots of them. But somehow I keep living longer than they ever get to."

"Costello, give him your fuckin' seat. You'll have to stand. Back row. Where you'll stay sharp," Masseria ordered. Another young man, these boys really only teenagers, rushed to do his boss' bidding. Wonderful, that Joe could bribe them with invitations to "the big games." Valenti figured that if The Boss didn't pay better, one day he'd be inviting The Young Turks to his own funeral. One of the other men, German-Jewish by the looks of him with his light complexion and hair, got up and went with this goombah. Without moving a muscle on his face, Arnold Rothstein revealed he looked satisfied by this move. *He definitely has inspired true cooperation with certain individuals in Masseria's organization.* Except that anything could happen to upset the standings this early in the season.

"Masterson, what do you really want?" D'Aquila asked him, not wanting to lose command to Joe Masseria within his own borough. "Out with it. Here I thought you were always a straight shooter."

"I am. And so I want in."

"Into what?"

"Don't fuck with me, Sal. What do I want 'in to?' In to what your planning. What you've been preparing to gamble on."

"On Sullivan's behalf, no doubt," Masseria added. "In case you're too stupid to figure it out, Sally. Isn't that right, Masterson, you old gambler?" The Manhattan boss turned his head to speak to his rival for Peter Morello's throne, but then also looked for a reaction from Arnold Rothstein.

Their financer and the alleged real boss of The Navy Street Gang said nothing. His enforcer Abraham Attell shifted in his seat to look at his leader. It was the only tell Umberto observed among these severely calculated ten-percenters.

A very overconfident Masterson didn't attempt to hide anything. "I'm here only representing myself and my newspaper. But in watching Flack, I've been watching all the Cubs. Your moves you've been ordering. Or benefiting from. I know how. I know *exactly* how. And I bet you just figured out your best option to keep me quiet about it." The famous gunman's hand was still in his suit-coat pocket. "So I'm not just 'some slow, old Irish bug' after all, am I?"

D'Aquila's eyes flickered back to Umberto and the latter seeing that, reflexively drew his breath and held it. He didn't need Masterson — however he found out about it — to expose his ties to his brother in The Windy City whose son was a pitcher on Chicago's team. Right now neither of the men from Brooklyn wanted to fall under Masseria's scrutiny. Manhattan's rising boss who really ran The Morello Borgata could order his jumpy teenage hot-heads like that Genovese fella to take him for a walk outside of the ballpark. Not that Umberto Vilenti doubted his own skills as a killer. Not for one second — especially against any of those inexperienced kids.

But Masterson was in a whole different league. "You don't have a better option to consider." The infamous tough-guy out of Kansas' roughest cattle town and veteran of the truly *wild* West's miners and railroad wars, was neither afraid of the Camorra nor the Mafia. And nobody knew whether or not he worked for the Irish Mob, or only for himself as he asserted. Had he guaranteed some protection to be this bold? He already had a reputation the others should fear.

"Look around you, Sheriff. You're old, surrounded by younger, faster men."

"The reason I'm older now is because I was good enough to survive this long. You should consider that — and that at sixty-four — and with my reputation — I have nothing to lose should you want to open up a ball right here in the stands. And fuck any goodwill you might hold with Brooklyn's people." He addressed the last sentence to D'Aquila. "Because and by the way — you know who's young? I'm very sure you heard Tex Rickard is here. But did you know he's a friend of mine? And that's honest Ernie Quigley umpiring at home plate down there with the voice of a tenor with his pants pulled up too high. He's only thirty-eight and can't be bought — or humiliated. Neither can his good friend Pete Harrison, also down there, calling runners safe and all their hits fair or foul. Lunger. Like Doc Holliday. Both friends of mine. You really want to inhale what you'll ultimately suffocate on? You're not as great as you think at smoking out would-be dangerous men."

"Yeah right. You knew John Holliday?"

"Would you like me to show you what he taught me?"

Masseria laughed, mostly because the Terranova brothers both gulped, but D'Aquila kept a poker face. "I'd rather you save that for later," Arnold Rothstein injected from in between them. A frown flickered on his face and was then hidden as he left his thoughts on the matter in the ballpark's humid and smoky air.

The baseball game had begun uneventfully while everyone was chatting and Masterson had settled himself into the seat that had most likely belonged to one Benjamin Siegel, if Umberto had kept himself up to date with who all the street urchins working as Masseria's enforcers were. It would be his business to. People were shifted around to address the need for caution as well as productive dialogue in the developing situation. Valenti had noted that a solid handful had also apparently moved toward being in position to make secret appeals to Mr. Big as well. Umberto knew Joe The Boss' personal skills were not very endearing, thus not encouraging of much, or even any loyalty, by non-made men. Masseria was still in the process of reorganization. The original captains had founded New York's underworld with the Morello-Terranova Family. And they were still accustomed to being in Peter Morello's clutch. So if Mafia associates like himself weren't sneaking around for D'Aquila or someone allied with the Camorra, then Arnold Rothstein would also be a very appealing and maybe prosperous option. That alone was testimony to why the Jew could even rival Sullivan in the first place. Other ethnicities would need to team up in order to go against the Irish. However, the Camorra seemed more resistant to any adaptation to the changing times, than did their rivals in the Mafia. But there was no competition from either baseball team in the first four innings. Then that too changed.

Chapter 56

Saturday, June 15, 1918
4:22 pm EST
Ebbets Field, Brooklyn, New York

5th Inning
Chicago – 0, Robins – 0

0 Outs, 1 On

AB: The Brooklyn Robins (19 W – 27 L):
Henry Harrison "Hy" Myers (CF, Bats: right, Throws: right)
AVG .256, OBP .292
Age: 29, Games: 475, Status: senior veteran,
6th full season in The Show

On the mound:
Chicago Cubs (32 W – 14 L)
(Fighting to secure the 1st place ranking in the National League)
P: Claude Hendrix (SP)
(Bats: Right, Throws: Right) 8 W – 1 L, PCT: .741, ERA: 2.78, SO: 865,
HB: Ø x (in 8 years)
Age: 32, Games: 268, Status: 8-year veteran

AND THEN:

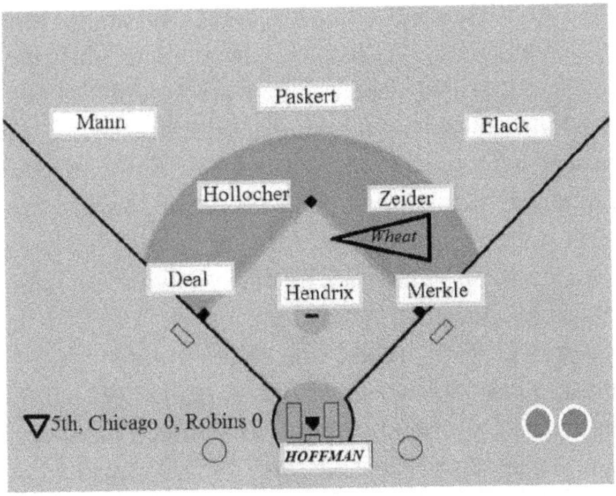

Zack Wheat advanced on the bases like Hell's angel evading Pete Harrison's final judgement. Righty Hy Myers pulled one off Hendrix, who's support was forced deep into Ebbets' back field to catch his flyout. But Wheat had time to tag-up and launch himself toward Rollie Zeider's base. Les Mann only took one hop while he set himself for the long throw, bypassing Charlie Hollocher and going straight for the base. Fred Merkle charged to get behind Zeider and assist locking 2nd down to eliminate any chance of an overthrow. Buck Wheat could see it coming and stretched his legs first to slide in low and got in there under Rollie's tag. "Safe!" came the call and Young Harrison's eagle-eyes were not usually ever called into question. Both he and thirty-eight year old Earnest Quigley, who would rule over the entire field that day, had actually taken their time to meet with both teams before the game and instruct them that these new young umpires did not officiate games like any of the players might have been used to. That included all the types of "players." They would not be intimidated like the old granddads they felt that Major League Baseball all too often dusted off before a game — but with never removing any deep taint of corruption, which had years to fester and rust there — and just stick them into position for business as usual. But there was a new series of games being played now, and whatever else was going on between the Cubs and the Robins, it would not be tolerated so far as the new officials were concerned. A heavier-than-usual police presence at the event, reinforced that condition. In the visitors' dugout, Coach Mitchell threw his hat down to demonstrate how he felt about that this.

But in the stands, Arnold Rothstein enjoyed the game. Umberto saw him nod toward D'Aquila but then clandestinely shake his head side-to-side to direct Brooklyn's street captain not to interfere as he addressed Masseria. "Giuseppe, allow me to illustrate to private citizen-journalist Masterson here an example of what our good 'Sport' Sullivan is so concerned about. Obviously, since our sheriff is here — oh I meant *retired sheriff* — Sullivan's doing his research before he takes any chances betting against me. He's gambling that right now he can get information versus any money off of us. He knows any influence he might have with Tanner Smith and The Marginals doesn't extend to Brooklyn. The Irish cannot dominate every *where* any more. I mean to demonstrate that to Joseph, and to make it clear he has not satisfied my conditions for our cooperating. Only when he does, will I match his investment." To Valenti, and surely to everybody else, it was clear that no one from any organization had yet approached Harrison or Quigley. So if Masterson was not acting as an independent player, as he insisted he was, the Jews and *all* the Italians, would next be sure to catch any move made by any larger Irish organization to attempt to correct their fix on this game — if there was one to be uncovered at all. Or maybe at a future meeting, all of them could agree with the leprechauns, on how they would proceed, working together. And in that case, Sullivan wouldn't be goaded into any hasty bet versus Rothstein right now.

Masseria nodded as the Terranovas looked on glumly, and feeling obviously marginalized themselves. "Vito, help Mister Rothstein here. I want you to go back and join Frankie. Take our guest from The Windy City with you. Then tell Charlie to escort The Outfit's man to Ebbets' front office and have Vitale here find himself a phone. In short order, I want the connection made with Rinaldo Villetti in Chicago, and then have the pretender call his green cop what's-his-name — Bill Conway, I believe — if The Outfit has *bought* him under control. Then he will act as the contact for the Cubs' Coach Mitchell. As I understand it, there is quite a debt still owed. But the end result of this is that I want Villetti's son sent in to substitute for Hendrix. Now. I think good 'ol Claude here is about to give up Brooklyn's first run."

As the younger gentlemen departed to follow orders, Wilbert Robinson first ordered Zack Wheat to steal 3rd, frustrating Charlie Deal, the rookie backstop George Hoffman, and Chicago's current starring pitcher. Wheat went on a breaking ball, waiting for the right toss, and then coming in standing up. That move by Robinson got played unexpected by Hoffman in this instance. And it likely got under the rookie Cubs' catcher's skin because he definitely wouldn't be executing his best play during the opportunity that came up next.

Brooklyn's coach called for Ollie O'Mara to execute a suicide squeeze play. With no score and room to risk a sacrifice out without the payoff, the Robins' 3rd baseman sent a dribbler down his opposite field's line so Merkle had to run in and grab it. Only he overthrew to Hendrix, who rushed to cover 1st and not only was O'Mara safe on Merkle's error, but Wheat put up the first number — one in favor of Brooklyn — onto Ebbets Field's scoreboard. The less-experienced Hoffman, already shaken off balance, might have even dreamed he could get 2, but wound up with nothing. Max Flack once again took his time running in from right field to stop the ball from rolling all the way out there.

Nothing stopped Coach Mitchell's clipboard that he hurled across the Cubs' dugout, furious with his acting-team captain, the right-fielder, and even his starting pitcher. This even before he got a note from a runner in his team's owner's employ, who relayed the next order that afternoon, which came all the way from Chicago. Little did he know it first originated from a Jew right there in Brooklyn — or he would have really lost it.

Now Umberto figured it would have been a tell, had he left to supervise Vitale calling out west to reach his older brother. He waited as long as he could before he excused himself with a general apology that would be indeterminate if it were meant to be directed to D'Aquila or Masseria, and he too headed for Charlie Ebbets' offices. But he kept out of sight to allow both assumed Mafia hanger-on, young Luciano, as well as his brother's man Vitale, to pass by. Then he also phoned Chicago. It was early there and it wouldn't surprise him if good ol' Rinny wasn't around the lounge, but Umberto was accustomed to dealing with his son, a nephew who was practically the same age as he was. That one never slept and practically lived there.

A young lady named Jasmine answered at the bar, once he was connected with Chi-Town. He immediately asked for Greggorio Villetti. She asked him to hold for her manager. After a negligible wait, another woman got on the call, saying her name was Arlene. Curiously he could hear she had a distinct Celtic accent when she informed him that she was the madam, Greg wasn't there either, and now she was in charge. He relayed the message that they needed someone to immediately call for Coach Mitchell in Brooklyn to instruct him that it was Taddeo Villetti's turn to pitch, and certain interests wanted to make sure the Cubs called on him, specifically. With what almost sounded like relief, this Arlene-woman reassured him she would see to it that happened and she would personally call the police to see that justice was done. Curiously, she did not mention if this were the second call to the lounge placed from Brooklyn. Wouldn't she have mentioned it if Umberto's call duplicated Vitale's?

Not too long after that, Valenti returned to his seat in the row alongside both his alleged Camorra and Mafia masters — and saw that his nephew was already pitching. And it *had* apparently impressed the old sheriff that Arnold Rothstein could command how the laws — of baseball — were applied here. Or at least the old hymie thought he could command it. For only giving up 1 run in 5 innings, Claude

Hendrix found himself replaced and Taddeo Villetti had taken the field. For the Robins, Ray Schmandt approached the plate.

Villetti had completed a very standard and uneventful warm-up in the time Quigley allowed him that wasn't worth reporting about. The rookie Hoffman caught for Chicago and together the youths looked really excited about that. The entire league's best-rated defensive catcher had already gotten replaced for a rookie even before this game. Hoffman once more got settled behind the plate, and tossed Chicago's relief pitcher the dead ball game sphere. His record-holding team captain and mentor was apparently assigned guard duty over the Cubs' dugout to not let any potential brawlers from escaping it. This was Brooklyn they were playing. There was 1 out now and the Robins had O'Mara on at 1st. The rookie pretended to drop Hoffman's pitch as a fake late reaction, but he'd been rubbing down his hair under his cap and gathering up some styling grease on his throwing fingers. He let the ball drop so he could rub the greased sphere in the dust, and Villetti did likewise with his left hand with which he picked the ball up, then brought that to his right as he let his glove fall out of its position clutched between his left elbow and the pitcher's side, faking more clumsiness. Then the reliever kicked his mitt with his shoe while he stooped down and picked up a little extra dirt. The Robins fans called out a Bronx cheer and Dan Griner, Jake Daubert, Ernie Krueger, Burleigh Grimes, and even Hy Myers and Ivy Olson — who were on today's lineup card — had already gotten to their feet and were now moving impatiently around their 3rd base dugout when they saw Villetti was the one called on to do the pitching. A tide of brown, black and white fedoras was in motion under the fog of cigar smoke. Quigley and Harrison observed all the goings-on and appeared to look at each other, clench their fists and nod, prepared to do what they would do if things got way out of hand. They *could* control Ebbets Field for about just over another hour, or attempt to — but they had no jurisdiction over Fred Mitchell when he made this move unless he did something that could get him kicked out of the game. But it was only highly irregular, thus suspicious, but not illegal to call upon a rookie battery. Robinson relied on a rookie, too.

So twenty-two year old rookie Ray Schmandt, with no batting average or experience to speak of, stepped into the right-handed batter's box, his legs shaking. He looked toward his bench for his friends' support and Coach Robinson's sign. With 1 on, 1 out, and a rookie batter up, it would be obvious the Brooklyn chief might call for the sacrifice bunt, again.

And with a hand and a ball full of gravel from the pitcher's hill, Taddeo Villetti wound up all tight and coiled, drawing on all his strength and power — then relaxed and offered a slowly descending breaking ball at a ridiculous speed. But as the baseball approached the plate, appearing as if it almost could be regarded as an Italian Rembrandt, the earth on this sphere spun off every which way it could be, ejected along the baseball's rotation — with dirt flying all around *and* right into Ray Schmadnt's eyes. He'd raised up his bat, his last thought to be obedient to Robinson's order, and he closed his eyes. But the ball made a perfect connection with the bat. On 1st, O'Mara — from a good leadoff — started into motion. The pitch, no power behind it to speak of, only caused this ball to drop on the baseline just out of the batting circle, but fair and then motionless, while the Robins' 2nd baseman fell on his butt after the contact, raising his hands to those afflicted eyes. O'Mara couldn't get back to 1st in time. Hoffman grabbed up the ball, tagged Ray Schmandt out and then fired his own fastball to Fred Merkle. Seeing this, O'Mara spun on his left heel and started heading toward the 2-bag again. Zeider came at him and Fred made the toss. Caught in a pickle, Ollie O'Mara attempted to stay alive by heading once more back toward Merkle. But he anticipated the throw and spun again and outran Rollie Zeider toward 2nd base, but Charlie Hollocher attended his duties covering for Rollie. He received the toss from Merk, and put the leather onto O'Mara's leg as he tried to slide in under the Cubs' shortstop's glove. But Harrison ruled him safe! There were then 2, but only 2 outs in the 5th and Villetti and his teammates took down Clarence Mitchell, pinch-hitting for Brooklyn's catcher Otto Miller. With a runner in scoring position, Robinson had preferred to send a left-hander out there versus the Cubs' rookie right-hand, who Mitchell had selected to be pitching — though no one in the Robins' dugout knew that *wasn't* Chicago's coach's idea.

Now Umberto Valenti heard Arnold Rothstein proclaim he wanted to test how young Villetti inspired his teammates to start an offensive that would see Chicago retake the lead and dominate this game. D'Aquila and Masseria, with the Terranova brothers parroting him, all nodded in agreement with one another on this rare occasion, and Bat Masterson looked on. He was curious as well to see if the young son of an almost irrelevant Chicago Outfit associate, had what it took to take command.

Chapter 57

Saturday, June 15, 1918
4:11 pm EST
Ebbets Field, Brooklyn, New York

6th Inning
Chicago – 0, Robins – 1

0 Outs, 1 On

AB: Chicago Cubs (32 W – 14 L)
(Fighting to secure the 1st place ranking in the National League)
Charlie Hollocher (SS, Bats: left, Throws: right) AVG .316, OBP .379
Age: 22, Games: 47, Status: freshman rookie, 1st full season in The Show
M.V.P. in his own mind! — maybe with delusions of god-hood?

On the mound:
Brooklyn Robins (19 W – 27 L)
P: John "Colby Jack" Coombs (SP)
(Bats: switch, Throws: right) 8 W – 14 L, PCT: .364, ERA: 3.81, SO: 1007,
HB: 88 x (in 12 years)
Age: 36, Games: 325, Status: 12-year veteran
Ace pitcher for Philly, injured in 1913 *Never fully recovered!*

AND THEN:

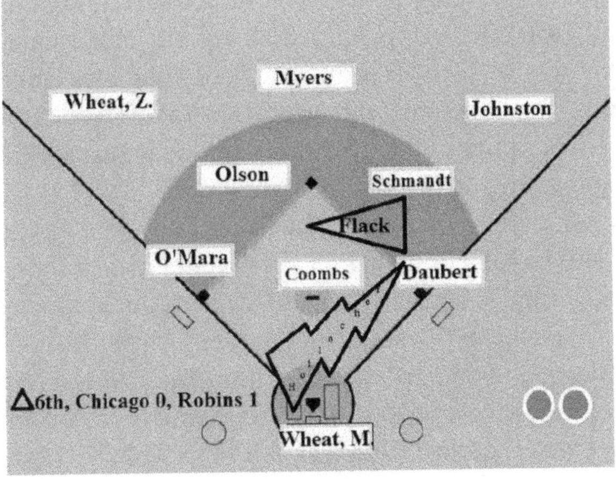

"Alright, let those bats rip, Boys! I know you thought Hendrix was going to complete this game. I did too. But if you get me the runs, I can hold these Brooklyn bastards to the only run they're going to get."

"Then let's 'Go Cubs! Go!' " The team shouted out in unison so the Brooklyn players and fans alike would all hear them.

And as Jack Coombs completed his warm-up tosses to start the inning, Ernie Quigley called for all practice balls in, using some kind of a pitch to his voice that sounded like his own balls needed to be returned to him. Taddeo quickly ran out on to the field and clasped Charlie Hollocher's hand between both of his. "Do it, Holly! Start this."

"You know I will. Go Cubs!" said his former critic, his eyes locked with those of now, he who was his friend.

Things *were* changing. And that's when Chicago's young pitcher spun around and made eye-contact with Sega up in the field box just beyond the 1st base dugout, where Taddeo had secured a seat for her even if she was to be the Cubs' sole fan. But she had made it to the game to cheer him on! Now he pitched for what he knew just had to be a Chicago win all the way out here in Brooklyn. But Giuseppe Masseria's eye had caught her too. Tad found himself staring right at the man the first time when he was on the mound to retire Brooklyn in the 5th. Villetti hoped that he'd shown the Mafia's boss when the tide started turning. *So they all will remember me!* Fuck the Mafia. Fuck New York indeed. And fuck Tad's enemies on the Robins, too. The time was now — for the Cubs to win.

And then it was on. That is Max Flack was on 1st base with a single and Holly's follow-up put him in scoring position. Mann flew out, but Fred Merkle singled with a drive out to left field. Not pulled far enough, Zack Wheat stopped that one on the first bounce and his throw all the way to *Mack* Wheat, Zack's brother, preventing Flacky from scoring. Tad hoped that old Max's hesitation wouldn't screw up this bases-loaded opportunity. *He* was still under suspicion. Villetti had to do something so he could win this game.

Things felt really tense when Dode Paskert ripped one out to Hy Myers and he too got it back in to prevent Flack from going anywhere far from 3rd base. Only with a force-out at any base, the Robins' Ivy Olson inexplicably chased after Charlie Hollocher who danced between 2nd and 3rd, taunting him. But it was a force-out. Only the Robins' shortstop's mistake forgetting *that*, was fine as far as Chicago was concerned. So Flack ran in as Coombs covered the

3-bag because O'Mara saw he had to chase the Cubs' shortstop down since Olson wouldn't throw the ball. They got Holly, but Merkle was now on 2nd and this decision forced the Robins to allow Paskert on 1st.

But during the previous at-bat — Fred Merkle's — Taddeo had been able to see Mitchell was clearly frustrated by Max's cautious base-running — ignoring his manager when he'd been repeatedly been waved home on The Major's hit. Taddeo himself called time, so Harrison would let him cross the field and he ran out to replace George who would bat before Tad, so he could personally coach 3rd base himself. The Hoff got on-deck. Meanwhile, taunts and booing from Brooklyn's audience had rained down on Tad, and some people even threw their garbage at him. But nothing touched him literally and figuratively as he delivered his orders to Chicago's veteran right fielder to run — directly to his face, as that seemed to be necessary. But the Cubs' pitcher had already planned out their strategy to score, with Charlie Hollocher. Exhibiting real leadership now, Taddeo was aware that the Mafia and surely the Camorra watched him. It didn't matter, his "family" was the Cubs. And he hoped his best buddies would get along better with Charlie now because they'd see that rookie playing on the same team as the rest of them. From the stands, and though he couldn't distinctly hear her from this distance, he could see Sega cheering on that team. She was wearing her shimmering white dress again, as if she'd surrendered to Tad's charm.

So next Hollocher came through. And then Charlie Deal did it. He *really* did it.

The man blasted a triple!

"Go! Go! Go!" Tad yelled and in the instant that ball hit to the opposite field landed on a bounce that sent Jimmy Johnston chasing it into the far right corner of the ballpark. Then Merkle was in! Hot on his heels behind him, Paskert ran for all he was worth. Now Johnston had the ball as Dode ran, just about to round 3rd. Taddeo waved him on. "Run Dode, run!" He was so excited he waved and kept waving Paskert on. And he too scored! Chi-Town's boys set fires on the baselines as the ball came back to Schmandt too late to go to 2nd in time to punish Deal for that hit. So Ray Schmandt pivoted and threw home, going after Paskert, even with 2 outs, and allowing Charlie Deal to register that triple! But the Robins failed to stop the third Chicago run of that inning, tagging Dode too late, with dust flying upon the impact, as he dove into home.

"You'rrrrre uh, sssaayfe!" Quigley sang in the voice like the fellas imagined he used as a mating call in a pogue club because he officiated in several different sports, all of which kept him far away from his wife. People wondered about that when they heard his voice — though not usually for much longer after they saw the large, severe no-nonsense looking man. Moreover, his reputation was such that it was never even suggested that the Camorra or the Mafia ever manipulated the new, younger, and otherwise untainted umpire. So far anyway.

But Taddeo didn't need any calls to be made under a "special influence." Coach called upon Rollie Zeider to take the opportunity with now 2 outs to make a suicide squeeze play. The Cubs already had a 2-run lead, anyway. And it was true that Daubert and O'Mara were playing their respective corners very deep — expecting Rollie to try and really launch one. Only now Tad was called back to pick up a bat and get on-deck as Merkle replaced him as the 3rd base coach. The surprise-reliever supposed Mitchell really liked to surprise Wilbert Robinson. Because you didn't order a suicide play with 2 outs. Only Mack Wheat, Coach McGraw's substitution for Otto Miller, who saw Clarence Mitchell, a left-hander pinch-hit in his place against right-hander Villetti, *mis*-handled the ball and overthrew Daubert, leading to Zeider making it on, and Deal scoring from 3rd! It was 4-1 Cubs and Tad could see his own next "squeeze play" materialize in the near future as Sega in that white summer dress, bounced up and down in elation on top of her seat. Tad imagined her bouncing up and down on top of him. Everything was perfect even after poor Hoff flew out on a line drive to Johnston, as he tried to hit to the opposite field to keep the rally going.

Taddeo only wished Arlene would have gone to any of his baseball games when they were right there in Chicago, but she hadn't — and she wasn't here. Sega was. His former woman had even repeated she didn't want to watch baseball. But everything else was — for once — going as great as Taddeo had ever wanted it to.

The sixth inning had passed, but the good times were hardly over yet.

Chapter 58

Saturday, June 15, 1918
5:47 pm EST
Ebbets Field, Brooklyn, New York

9th Inning
Chicago – 4, Robins – 1

0 Outs, 0 On

AB: Chicago Cubs (32 W – 14 L)
(Fighting to secure the 1st place ranking in the National League)
Taddeo "The Shooter!" Villetti (RP, Bats: right, Throws: right)
AVG .500, OBP .500
Age: 19, Games: 6, Status: freshman rookie,
1st full season in The Show

On the mound:
The Brooklyn Robins (19 W – 27 L):
P: John "Colby Jack" Coombs (SP)
(Bats: switch, Throws: right) 8 W – 14 L, PCT: .364, ERA: 3.81,
SO: 1007, HB: 88 x (in 12 years)
Age: 36, Games: 325, Status: 12-year veteran

AND THEN:

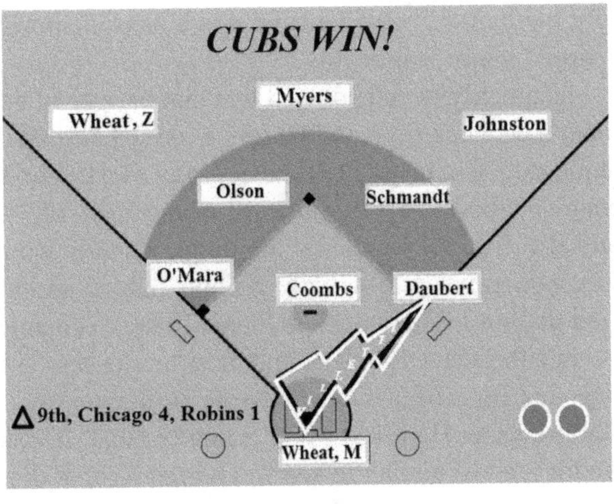

Chicago had employed its Shooter the 6th, 7th, and 8th, as the young talent zeroed in on a much improved ERA — and against his old nemesis, the Robins, too. Then Taddeo got an honest-to-goodness pitch *to hit*. Wilbert Robinson was leaving Jack Coombs on the mound to go the complete game for Brooklyn, it would appear. But it was terribly insulting to think that the Robins' manager would feel so confident that his offense would hit and score off of Taddeo, that he didn't move to a reliever for Brooklyn in the late innings. The Robins were down by 3 runs all the way to the 9th *and Coach Mitchell had switched up Chicago's arms when the Cubs had been only down by 1 in the 5th*. Hoff had made the last out for their offense again, in the 8th inning and following multiple attempts by the whole team to get another Chicago rally going that took them back through the entire batting order. During that time Taddeo, had already thrown his best innings at opposing batters for 3 calls to duty on the mound, and had one non-productive turn at the plate by this point.

He'd still been shaking, hopefully discreetly, when he came up to the dish with McKinley "Mack" Wheat behind him as he stepped into the batter's box. About three weeks ago, Tad had intentionally taken almost half-a-dozen pitches to bean the catcher's brother, who always played left field for this team. And though Taddeo had been hit by New York's pitching before, the Giants and not the Robins had gotten him, so he stood very sure that Brooklyn would also like to. But Tad never knew what pitches "the other Wheat" signaled for, and Jack Coombs never appeared to be purposely trying to hit him but wound up offering him something that he regretted. He let Taddeo's bat take a rip on it, and Chicago's rookie pitcher took one out deep in the field for Hy Myers to hunt down and Taddeo had earned himself a base. Right there, in Ebbets Field, Taddeo Villetti hammered his first truly-earned major league hit!

Only it was quickly overshadowed by what happened next. Coombs must have been tired and he sent a curve ball that didn't break far enough. By adjusting his stance, Max Flack sent it all the 297 feet over Ebbets' right-field wall! *Home run Cubs!* Coach Mitchell and Bill Killefer were now jumping up and down, all smiles and jovial exclamations, arms crazily waving Taddeo and Max Flack around the horn. They touched them all, the excitement was contagious, and Tad waved to Sega and blew her kisses — as well as to Hoff, Trip, and Bass-Man — and Charlie Hollocher — as his feet ran across home plate. He loved every minute of this. It was a rare opportunity for a relief pitcher to score. Though right at that moment, all he thought of was how he was going to score with Sega after this game!

Holly was on deck when Tad ran toward him to return to their team's dugout. They slapped hands as Taddeo ran past, and he raised his to wave to Sega once again. And then rushing in to hugs and pats on the back from his closest friends. Only all that was nothing compared to the reception Max Flack got when the long ball bomber returned to the Cubs' dugout. He even stepped back out onto the grass, removed his cap and took a bow. The audience boo'd and cursed him, and threw produce — prompting security to rush down the steps to try and learn where all the vegetables were. They should have checked the Robins' dugout, Chicago's teammates thought. But Flack was the hero of the hour and everyone from Chi-Town concentrated on that.

In the meantime, Coombs was shaken by Max's hit and walked left-handed Hollocher, though not intentionally. Les Mann got out but moved Charlie into scoring position with a fast, ground ball with a lot of bounce to it. Fred Merkle tried to sort Chicago's situation so there were at least runners at the corners. Coombs and Wheat got him on a pop-up behind the plate and Hollocher couldn't go anywhere.

Then Dode Paskert's single that bounced to Myers in shallow centerfield was returned to the Wheat's brother acting as the Robins' home nest's guard *fast*, so fast that even Charlie, with his speed, didn't gamble that the Cubs could score in that situation. But there were runners at the corners now, ready to run on anything hit by the other Charlie. Only Coombs sent him a speeded-up slider that the tip of Deal's bat connected with to shoot a line-drive right into O'Mara's glove in the hot corner. Hollocher was smart enough to tag up at 3rd and hang on. But Deal's's hit hooked foul by the Robins' dugout and as it soared past Charlie, O'Mara had over-stretched to reach it — and he dropped the ball!

Hollocher charged down the baseline, diving headfirst for homeplate. The catcher's brother ran in as fast as he could to back up O'Mara and sent the baseball cutting back toward the other Wheat. But Brooklyn couldn't harvest a play there and Quigley shouted "Safe!" as Holly popped up, arms up in triumph, the front of his jersey decorated with dirt.

With Chicago runners on 1st and 2nd, but 2 outs, Coombs' infield helped him put away Hoffman, so there wouldn't be a repeat performance of the Cubs' success in the 6th.

And The Shooter took his position on the hill for the Robins' last stand. Then Villetti cut each of them down with some assists from his friends from Chicago. He was through messing around, and Taddeo wrote the final line for the epithet on his first Big League win while on the road.

The Cubs all danced around and shook hands on the Robins' field while in the emptying seats, many distinguished gentlemen wore solemn expressions as they considered what they'd witnessed, and what it meant to them. And they also experienced Bat Masterson's ominous presence finally take its leave of them. The old gunslinger made his next move, one which saw him go to talk with Tex Rickard who he met at the edge of Brooklyn's home team stand. Umberto Valenti watched him depart.

Darting around his celebrating teammates, Taddeo Villetti did his best to keep his eyes on every last one of these gentlemen he recognized from Chicago to Upper Manhattan. If whatever they were up to, had anything to do with him, it wasn't going to be any good. He had no more interest in celebrating — only succeeding.

Chapter 59

Quickly clearing the field, that effort requiring him to dodge all his friends, and keep his eyes on The Mafia, Villetti stayed alert and limber, dodging the press, too. Previously the reporters couldn't be bothered with him except to ridicule the pitcher. Now he wouldn't be bothered, by talking with them. He'd teach these blood hounds something about respect. They'd need to demonstrate a lot more of it if they wanted to talk to him. But Tad wasn't sure he'd reach anyone *he wanted to talk to* at Villetti's. He'd been avoiding the kind of conversation he'd have with Urso or Greg until he could confront them in person — and perhaps take them by surprise — with tremendous newfound strength behind his anger. If he could maintain it — a whole 'nother week on this blasted road trip — Villetti would release pure rage upon his family when he finally returned to Chicago. He had just earned a new victory from atop of the hill. Now he would plan accordingly so no one could slow his momentum. He saw what was going on in the stands, but he was going to be the one solely in control of what went on with his life.

So he also would no longer tolerate his sympathies being toyed with, or lose his focus by once more being rattled and then pressed upon, even by Arlene. She may be his partner, but she offered him no affections, and little more than accusations and overburdening instructions — compared to Sega. But he could not help but care for the Irish woman and Taddeo suspected he always would. In reflection, Tad finally saw them more alike one another than either had cared to see before. But as long as she was in Chicago, how happy could she be when she had to deal with The Family's constant shit? But she wanted to stay there. He thought he still might be able to change Arlene's point of view as he changed into his street clothing in the locker room, and the youngest Villetti found in his pocket, the knife his brother had given him two weeks ago. Suddenly, he remembered he'd always seen the way to carve a new deal — using his game-winning pitch to retire the opposition's attempt to run his field. But he could use Arlene in the position he'd installed her in, to surgically cut far deeper into The Family where it hurt them the most — in their revenue they collected from all their drug, credit and gambling debt collections, and especially their prostitution business. Then Colosimo would turn to The Fox after all, and feed Villetti's nest-mates to the Chicago boss' nephew, perhaps permanently removing them from The Outfit's history. When he'd helped O'Rourke, he'd inadvertently helped his brothers. He would not make that mistake again. But he would still look for a way to protect his father if he could. So Taddeo decided to call for a changeup — and had the operator put him through to Mr. Li's again, from the visiting manager's office in Ebbets Field.

His game could be over on this evening in Brooklyn, but it would still be business hours in Chicago. And Villetti's confidence that he could take care of his own business was definitely on the rise now. Besides, Mr. Li always used to love registering every one of Tad's successes playing baseball. If that could still be true, this one in Brooklyn wouldn't cost him any broken windows.

Only boy did he get screamed at — and he understood barely half of what he got called out on in English, the rest of it coming at him in Chinese — or directed toward someone named *Laowai* — but maybe that name meant *him* — when he reconnected with Chicago. The word probably wasn't a term of endearment. From what he could gather of the situation, everything had really spun out of control now. Then there was something about his daughter again. *Zhen Li*, Tad recalled. It wasn't good. Tad couldn't discern what the Chinaman was saying for certain when he was so upset, but he thought he heard that Mr. Li wanted Arlene out — gone. Taddeo said he needed to talk to her about the situation, if this was indeed a pending eviction, and asked if the laundry owner could instruct her to phone him in Brooklyn at The Bossert no matter what time it was. He'd order the front desk staff to go and wake him. Then he'd do his best to get things settled. He didn't want more interference from his family — which that was exactly what he gathered the reason for *every* trouble must be — to ruin everything he had thought he'd achieved by setting up Arlene with a safe place to stay, a source of income, and employment in such a key role as one he thought would lend her protection from his brothers, and assured by his father. Wasn't *assurances* what he'd gained by humoring the old man and going on that little hunting excursion to gain back his papa's support for him before the pitcher had to leave for Boston? Those victories he was building-upon-victories with suddenly started crumbling right in front of him, on the path that he had paved to walk. He tried to assure Mr. Li that neither one of them were going to stumble into something that the elder man could see his daughter get lost in.

So then the prodigal son did take a chance and he called Villetti's. He thought another new girl answered the phone. He spoke with someone a little more coherent this time, but only barely. She said her name was Lumia. Tad had never heard of her and thought that she must have arrived after he'd left. She sounded very cute, and as if she knew of him, and admired him. But she also sounded sort of young, and scared — or wait — familiar? Taddeo then realized this could actually be the same person he'd spoken with once before. There was something about her accent. That and now she sounded like she could be running out of drugs. Someone had obviously let the business go under-stocked — or someone else was using too much of the supplies. Only the way he could hear her sniffle over the phone, her demeanor suggested that she was also crying and not because of any intention to now come clean — but as revealing an indication that The House was running low on something else since he'd been gone: that boost in morale that he saw happen when at least the ladies on the staff had first reacted to falling under the control of he and Arlene. Apparently there had been a lot of changes that had happened since he left Chicago. He listened to this woman as she described terrible things were suggested to be going on there while he was out of town. He'd now heard this repeatedly from several reliable sources. And *the madam*, which was the manner in which he figured Lumia referred to Arlene, would once again not speak to him. But this "LuLu" was desperate. Her life had been put in danger. They all needed him to return. And then upon it finally registering with her *who he was*, what he might truly care about, the new girl informed Tad that "his lady" knew all about Sega having arrived in Brooklyn since she first united with Taddeo in Upper Manhattan. The madam had become furious at him for that, and at Sega for leaving. So her priorities had changed from making sure Tad's business ran smoothly to whatever new plan she'd been up to. So Tad needed to return immediately to straighten things out. As there had also been repeated problems with Urso, him being severely wasted almost all of the time, and the club was falling under tighter scrutiny from all directions. She reminded Tad that Johnny Torrio was in Chicago. And the business was receiving many unusual visitors. There was a new government presence adding both more funds and more pressure to South Chicago. *So could this actually be Greg's way of dealing with things?* He'd *cultivated The House's relationship with law enforcement, Conway's people. Would he now deliberately attempt to destroy the business?* Then to challenge his brother, Tad might actually have to run it so as to make sure it succeeded. But Lumia then told Tad that Greg had actually left Chicago. Urso came between her and her lover — who was at one time, apparently Greggorio. And maybe that was why he'd left, she put forward. *Somehow I doubt it. He never likes to leave Little Italy to go very far. My brother is definitely up to something. And this naïve little voice over the telephone line did not sound like she'd ever be his brother's type — only just something he would use.* But the unfamiliar girl thought Tad should also know that Corrado had also been long gone, and that she knew there were dangerous people back there in Brooklyn, who now circled the ballplayer. They'd already been watching him and they were even much more of a threat than anyone he'd ever dealt with in Chicago. The young lady said she was from Brooklyn and had little doubt that it was through friends of that nephew of Diamond Jim's that Taddeo had heard of — *indeed I thwarted when I helped O'Rourke escape getting caught at Mr. Li's* — that her travel plans had been arranged. She'd been able to learn this through Rose, who was now dating one of these fellas' cousins back in Chicago. *Hoff will love learning that.* But these men she'd known of had stayed in Chi-Town to watch the Sox play the Yankees after the Cubs had left, and when they weren't at the game, they spent a lot of their time at the lounge. Lumia identified them when she was upstairs with Urso, but had been curious why they came there to meet with Tad's father in his office. In her brief experience at Villetti's, that wasn't what visiting men came upstairs for. Only she related that Arlene didn't seem to notice or care, and now something different preoccupied her, about running the Villetti nightclub business, and other new, seemingly very wealthy and very important men who frequented the bordello. A constant effort to film them was underway, which went all but ignored by The House's staff. Other new gentlemen callers there — the ones who met with Rinaldo Villetti — definitely had noticed this — and did *not* interfere. But then the new girl introduced herself as Lumia once more, also stressing that she hoped he knew that *she* wished him well, and that he would return to the girls in quick time — and all right. He had to. Someone needed to take charge and maintain stability, certainty, in Chicago. Nobody could tell what was going on. He needed to come home and figure this all out.

She whimpered, "Because everything's gone wrong now.

Baldavino is acting as if *he* were in charge. This was never the way it was supposed to be." Tad's cousin didn't know what was going on either, let alone how to run a business. He was reported to spend all his time diverting one of the girls or another upstairs, *to entertain him*, and his brother Carlo. "Mister Villetti, this is not what I came out to visit Chicago for. Greggorio is gone and I don't know where. I've got to try and get sober and get myself out of this place. This is a nightmare. So please stay alive. I sense more big changes are already underway here, and probably for the worse. But I know what the ladies say about you. You're a good man. My only hope now, is for your safe return."

Tad promised the new girl that he would be careful and try and do the best that he could from his station in Brooklyn, but he still expected to have to go to Pittsburgh first, before it would be time for him to be allowed to return to Chicago. The delay would give him time to think, but he'd become frustrated with baseball — and how it caused the loss of the very control over his own life that he'd sought, when he dreamt he'd love making his career in it. Then Lumia related what he thought was her misplaced faith in his brother Greggorio to fix things *if he'd only return*, but Tad didn't see any reason to waste time correcting the girl on that one. Her specific situation seemed inconsequential to him. He'd heard the same song from one or two of the other girls in recent times, already. Nothing had really changed all that much back there. This Lumia had just uncovered the truth. But he was surprised to learn that both Greggorio and Corrado, who usually handled things — including Urso — as best as they could anyway — were also now missing. Taddeo had overheard The Morello Family, to learn at least one of The House's men, came out here to Brooklyn, and his own family had already been messing with him already — since Hoffman's arrest and undoubtedly were up to something, using Sega. But under his papa's or his brother's orders? Tad knew that made a difference. And The Family had been so kind to meet him in the prison system to explain some things — but not enough. What were his closest relatives now planning — a more elaborate rendezvous with him in New York?

And what was really going on back in Chicago? He said his goodbyes to Lumia and left her with the best promises he might not be able to keep, but which he hoped would placate her for a while. Then he when he hung up the phone at the visiting team manager's desk he'd coopted in the Cubs' clubhouse at Ebbets Field, he still

— now more than ever — desperately wanted to hear from Arlene. *What a reversal that is, huh?* But he wouldn't be able to get his woman to help crash the revenues from the bordello now, when it was obvious to everyone the cathouse was turning over four times as many more tricks — and Baldavino, probably Carlo, in addition to Urso — were basically living on the premises. Well, Johnny Torrio should be more than happy with his restaurant review, and it sounded like both Arlene and his papa were cooking up new daily specials. But to Tad it still sounded like the same recipe for the same old shit. Only someone saw that it had been force-fed to him in Brooklyn.

So it would go a little ways toward setting him at ease to also learn wherever Sega had disappeared to as well. Glad to see her make an appearance at the game today, he hoped she found Trip. Or he, who had said he had nothing better to do — found her — in order to be a gentleman, and escort her back to The Bossert following the game. The reporters were definitely not interested in interviewing Mike. But Tad was even going to let him stay in the room with he and Sega that night — if she came back — "just to be fair and show kindness toward one of his closest friends." Trip made his qualifying contribution for sure that day, albeit a different way than on the field. But while Taddeo wished he could be celebrating with his best buddies who all contributed to the Cubs' victory that afternoon, he just couldn't grasp hold of the happiness he'd earned, as whatever happened in Chicago would always bring his high spirits back down again. Something had already compelled him to cut short his celebration on Ebbets' infield after his first away-game win, to call and learn how things were with Arlene — even if he couldn't speak to her — or describe for her that win, inning-by-inning, pitch-by-pitch, as he knew she loved hearing. But Tad knew something felt wrong, like he didn't deserve to be celebrating and hadn't won the real victory yet, but might have rather lost the *last inning* in *the real game*.

Victories came and went, too elusive to hold on to. But Tad knew he needed a win back in Chicago or he'd begin to lose everywhere. He also needed to grab a shower, not even waiting for the veterans to get theirs first — *let them complain, I won* — and then get out of there while most of his friends would still be around and possibly help to protect him from whatever danger Lumia alluded to that might be waiting for him in Brooklyn. While there, he would be on the active sonar of everyone from Dan Griner and Jake Daubert to Vincenzo Terranova and Joe "The Boss" Masseria — and who knew

— in short order the list might include Bat Masterson, too. Young Villetti wasn't taking chances. And Tad also didn't want to chance being on the phone any longer before Coach Mitchell caught him at the team manager's desk and on the team manager's phone.

But Tad moved while the press covering Ebbets Field held the team's boss up, as he knew they would. Mitchell had made some very unusual moves with that pitching change, fielding half a squad of rookies, and also continuing to alter the way he was handling Max Flack's alleged *non*-scandal, especially in light of Chicago's right fielder hitting a home run only a short while ago. Thus Flack couldn't keep himself out of the news even if Coach wanted him to.

However, Tad did not know what he felt right now — about leaving the Cubs on a more permanent basis any sooner than later — like he had been considering only 9 innings ago. He'd come in and *impressively* finished a victorious game for Claude Hendrix, by anyone's standard, and even Killefer had nothing bad to say about his performance. Taddeo had added that to his list of things he'd only hoped for this season. Intoxicated with victory, it clouded his judgement. He still wished that maybe Arlene would speak to him and he could celebrate his victory with her. He'd also just gotten his first base hit in today's game and Mr. Li wouldn't even hear of it. Maybe Tad would call for Old Lamont and tell *him*, later. His papa probably already knew. Taddeo only wished that was comforting — but now something nagging him told him it was not. Greg couldn't ever acquire the authority that would allow him to deal with The Family back in New York, without first getting approval from the brothers' father, could he?

Now even under the current circumstances, Tad began to think about seeing Sega back in his room again, and being thankful that if once more, she could be there for him. Maybe she'd let him try *whatever* Hoffman said she'd been purchasing this time? Today of all days, Taddeo wanted to relax, think about this more *later*, and feel something else other than terrible, in this moment, even after a win. *For I still have one hell of a gauntlet to run my rookie season, don't I?*

Chapter 60

After his shower, he took a few press interviews, as this time they'd be slightly more favorable to Taddeo, if only since his ego was telling him so and some of the newspapers were able to corner him. But with the unorthodox Mitchell, under-investigation Max Flack, and their rush to also get any comment from Claude Hendrix or Bill Killefer all being probably more interesting to their regular readers — Tad made to escape the media press and leave Ebbets Field for the evening. Accompanied by a few more pats on the back from his teammates, the rookie pitcher had tried his best and succeeded at actually evading *everyone* and disappearing long enough to borrow the phone in the visiting club office, and try to check on Arlene back in Chi-Town. Tad had gotten into bed with this woman first, and he and Arlene were each responsible for an equal share of the pair's conspiracy to steal from his father. But he came to a realization that Arlene was the lady that he'd loved first. And he vowed to keep his commitments to her — well, most of them — his affair with Sega notwithstanding. Now he had no idea how he could ever help the young Greek woman, or trust her for that matter, and he had no idea what game she was truly into. But Tad needed to set things right with Arlene. He was already turning over new strategies in his mind for how to rescue his woman in Chicago. He at least always knew where she was. And now there was this new triangle situation and a threat to them both as well as to and one from Mr. Li, who was "through with Laowai" — whatever that meant. But Arlene wasn't likely even close to convinced she should take flight out of The Windy City, and Taddeo didn't know what he could do with her or this mysterious medical condition of hers — especially while he was out of town. Could she hold out until he finished the series with Pittsburgh? He and Arlene still needed the money she was collecting from the ladies so they could eventually have enough when they ran, to stay hidden from his family and succeed with starting over. That would have to come much later than he would have liked — especially if any debts he had to cover now saw him losing all his recently accumulated money from the Cubs' payroll *and managing his father's business —*

what with paying off random doctor house calls in the middle of the night, thanks to Arlene seeing a psychiatrist, and whatever else was going on in Chicago, plus all his friends he'd borrowed from who he still wanted saying good things about him, just in case his name actually came up for a trade. He entertained the thought that if he continued to have success like he did today — with baseball — he might earn himself a raise anyway, doing what he loved best. Only the best thing he could do was reassert his will over his own destiny, by starting to do that once he had resources in Chicago. He'd pull himself together, develop his power and control, and return so much stronger than he reckoned his family would ever be prepared for. Or maybe he still could make the business succeed, with the help of *her*. But in this moment, he wouldn't get very far with neither his thoughts nor his feet, as right outside the locker room, five men in stiff suits, some fashionable with pin striping, were waiting for him. Two blocked Tad's path and two more stepped in behind him, pressing close. They all shared some darker brown or gray flavor of a white man's skin, several sporting bruises, and most with opaque colors for their dark hair, oiled back to lie immobile under their fedoras, flat against their skulls, the bones of which seemed chiseled under hungry tight flesh. This gave them all hard, unyielding appearances. The fifth man stood to Taddeo's side, uncomfortably encroaching on his personal space. Radiating some imposing power about him, he was the first one to speak. "Some people here want to speak to you," he said in a nasally Brooklyn accent.

"They should call my manager's office. Schedule an interview."

"That's very funny. Boys, don't you think that's funny? This guy has a sense of humor." But the man wasn't laughing or smiling.

"Do you know who I am?" Tad tried to sound confident. His survival instincts began drawing upon resources his father had repeatedly impressed upon him, no sooner than he was a boy venturing out in The Windy City's streets, and long before he'd even realized his dream of touring all the National League's baseball stadiums. Even then Tad had always been told that New York could be an especially dangerous place, all the while an attempt was being made to prepare him to survive Chicago.

"Yeah. You're that Cubs pitcher that won the game today," one of the other soldiers said.

But the man by Taddeo's side turned on the other who had spoken. "You. Shut up, Frank. Now! Really."

Now his favorite topic of baseball would always distract the very affable Taddeo. "Hey. It's all right. I'll tell you what. Frank, right? I'll give you *this one* and explain the situation for you." He'd stall and lead them on, while in his mind he went over every option there was to getting himself out of this. "You guys *are* going to write this down, aren't ya?" The men looked at each other perplexed as the pitcher warmed up his delivery. "Well, you sort of know what happened as we were already behind when I came in. And see, *I know* I'm still the rookie. So I didn't really do anything heroic tonight, but Coach probably thought the score safe enough to stretch my arm. As we *were* only down by one run. And that's about all there is to the honest truth of it. I had to hold my own against Jake Daubert and the rest of the Robins, but the other fellas on my squad did most of the heavy lifting. This is their win — with Charlie Deal's triple and Max's home run." At this point, all five of the men he confronted looked around to one another confounded, and definitely not used to getting this kind of reaction when *they* were asked to go meet someone.

"Yeah. Well we're also good at stretching arms." One of the men, the one who let his brown hair grow loose and wavy, was first to recover from his surprise. He looked around at his cohorts for support as he finally spoke up. A brief sound suggested one of them might have chuckled.

However, Taddeo still went on. "But did you guys see what I've learned to do to New York with my sandy? How'd you like that for a comeback at your men who want to work my pitch count? Now *that's* Chicago style." If there was any *humility* in the young pitcher, in order to maneuver to even slightly more solid ground by diluting these men's control over the flow of their interaction, Taddeo was not going to demonstrate it today. But he would also not forget who he'd already imagined he was really dealing with. He'd rather be bragging to Arlene especially, or Mr. Li or Old Lamont, and of course his papa. But Taddeo also knew when he'd been reminded to show off his other credentials. This was such a time when his inheritance actually would play better than whatever he could do for his earned run average. "But you know what else? Why I play so hard? I'm also Rinaldo Villetti's son. Yeah. Rinaldo Villetti. So you need to think carefully about how you're going to handle this — whatever *this* is. Our Chicago family has some powerful allies in New York." By simple probability, Taddeo knew exactly what kind of men had been sent to meet him, and also how ironic it was that it could actually be his father's reputation alone that would save him.

Unless these guys work for Peter the Clutch, of course. Tad's father had insisted upon him and his brothers knowing every detail of the ongoing Manhattan versus Brooklyn rivalry resulting in a continuing Mafia-Camorra War. And about a seasoned veteran gangster named Giuseppe Masseria, the role he played in it — and what that meant to the continued well-being of the Villetti family — if anyone had uncovered anything about the real truth as it applied to these matters. But Tad gambled that these low-level recruits would — and then *did* — demonstrate that they had obviously not.

"Who the fuck is Rinaldo Villetti?" another one of the soldier's associates chose to rudely inquire.

"You can shut up too, Vinny. The senior Villetti is a soldier in the basement of Colosimo's outfit. He thinks he's a rising star because Umberto Valenti's been whispering in D'Aquila's ear, giving him smart ideas about Chicago. And did I just say the basement? I shoulddah probably said the sewer. You'd think they at least woulddah built a good one of those out there. But now that all the bosses have all taken a liking to the shylocks from the Lower East Side because of the money of course, but also 'cause of the stories coming out of there lately, of some Sicilian boy, Luciano, am I right? Well, the protection racket the kid tried to run on the kikes — it backfired badly, but ironically earns him the favor of The Man Uptown. The big Jewish rat himself loves the humor in it and he's rumored to see something in the friendship and non-prejudiced way the young Luciano has partnered up in business with that small fry, what's-his-name? I don't know. Another one of them Hebrews. This skinny punk that stood up to him. And all of us gotta like the kinda big balls *that* took. So five of those youngsters formed a new crew, didn't they? And Joe took them on as *he's* really running Morello's interests. But the Jew gets in with him because his young guns he has for friends attracted some attention. And the kids like this rich Hebrew. Has a cool celebrity court around him and builds them up more than Masseria ever would. Now that doesn't really matter a whole lot to most of us, though it lends some hope that if only immigrants weren't all too busy fighting each other, we'd all do far better with business by fighting the 'ol nativists. At least make some money off *them*. You know, organized cooperation. But I bet all these youngsters will all wind up dead sooner than later anyway. Watch. You should never trust a Jew. This foolish alliance…" he let that thought trail off, its conclusion unspoken.

The man then continued, changing the subject, and Taddeo

assumed the whole monologue might only be *for* his *benefit*. And that now, who the speaker might *not* be, was some low-level flunky Tad would have assumed was sent as only an errand boy — just to catch up with him at the stadium. Instead, this guy was something more. *They are briefing me, staging this conversation for my benefit.* Only then he recalled once more how during some of the more recent games he picked up some bad vibes coming from some of those suits in the stands. Some undesired attention that was pretty hard to avoid especially when one was on the pitcher's mounds in the center of Coogan's Hollow and Ebbets Field. And except for the fact that he wanted to be alone when he called Chicago, he should never have gone about on his own without some protection. Not in this town.

Still, no one had shown him a gun or tried to manhandle him. They were talking to him. From his observations, that was not how these things were usually done. So Tad was not one-hundred percent sure he was in danger. Instead, he'd been involved in a lot of unusual meetings as of the past couple of months. He was still cautious, but a lot less inclined to try and run.

The man who commanded the others he now confronted wielded some power — dangerous power to be sure. And he did not hesitate to offer his opinion about anything and everything. And yet it would seem there remained men much higher up on the food chain than even this one. No decision was going to be made at *this* game. "But since that lucky island trash got himself noticed and then ingratiated with the Jew-rat, some introductions got made, and that let the Jews talk their way into being invited to move in and manage some of the paper side to the business Lombardi and DeMarco have lost." He stared long and hard at Tad, who'd begun to sweat under the scrutiny and was wishing he could take another shower about now. He didn't know who all these people were specifically, but thought he recalled those names mentioned before from the news — some more specifically, from the obituaries. Weren't those the men his cousin was suspected of killing? The more recent victims of his cousin Rocco's anyway. But the gangster that was before Taddeo right now, went on. And Tad tried his best to remember all the names they were dropping so he could collect more information about all the players in this game later, if he even survived. "I should say that *the Sicilians* are losing. This thing's got everyone all twisted around. Wished we were beating up on some of them Jews right now though, fighting *their* muscle, 'stead we're reduced to errand boys picking up one of our own — at their behest. But then again, maybe we're not."

Taddeo frowned, very unsure about who all these people were and where his family's alliances lay. And immediately retrospective now, he definitely did *not* want to have heard all of this information. There were stories about what happened to people "who knew too much." But if something was going to happen to him, it would not ever be fair — because he still didn't even understand most of this in the first place. He had just wanted to play baseball. "We are all still waiting to find out who will lead the new Morello House when all of you-know-what shakes down. So you never know, Boy," the stocky man who spoke jabbed his finger at Tad, "you *might* be among friends. But I really couldn't tell you. Even I've just been tasked with makin' sure you arrive safely to meet the rest of them. Can you believe they wasted *my time* with that? So relax. No one's gonna hurt you, Bright-Eyes. Not yet. You're also quite lucky — that the rest of them jakes seem to have developed some sudden interest in baseball. It might even turn out to be profitable for you. I think you'll soon be glad you went for a ride with us. So now we got to go and play, Pitch." He sighed while he studied the young athlete in a curious manner. "I guess it's time for more introductions on another hill. You'll want to meet these people *most* among any-and-all who might be out there *of your fans*. And *if* time reveals them to be your fans. Plus Mister Bank needs to take a look at you. Which again, only saw me just become some kind of errand boy for the fat Jew, as we come down to the end of things. *You understand how much I detest that?* But that's what my boss ordered. So I wanna get this over with as soon as I can. Now don't waste any more of my time. Let's move!"

But the whole time it's been that one guy talking, Tad thought. Then the suits closed in and shoved Taddeo along and through the stadium passageways used by the players, which were unfortunately deserted at this time. Unfortunate for Tad, who would see no friendly face come to run interference or rescue him. No one to witness how he was leaving the stadium, except for a security guard who was handed cash on the way out to forget he saw anyone from their group except Hugh McCulloch. Everyone else from either team was probably still cleaning up, getting debriefed by their coaches, had left already like Trip, hopefully with Sega — or were kept after being interviewed by the press.

So Tad was continuously pushed forward and out the player entry and exit gates to a waiting Hudson Cruiser, pulled up alongside the edge of the new cement sidewalk. He was definitely not looking forward to *his* next interview that they were escorting him to. As the other men got in on either side of him, they crushed him in tight against their larger frames, and with Tad in *that* press, the car sped off downtown Brooklyn.

A little over ten minutes later, they turned on Navy Street and pulled up to a quaint unassuming café. "Get out, Villetti," the soldier in charge ordered. " 'The Brain' wants to have his look at you."

Tad gulped, wondering what that meant. But he had little doubt that this was the place he'd phoned when he was in Philadelphia and needed help to locate and protect Sega, on her own way to New York. It was only a feeling. Though maybe someone had just called his favor in extremely early, the player's instinct told him he could now very well be facing the real strength in the middle of his New York opposition's lineup. The opposition to him from having any kind of normal career in professional baseball — or normal life for that matter. But these men were beginning to sound like they were the contacts his cousin Rocco told him he'd need to make a rendezvous with when they reached out to him in the first place. His papa had reinforced this impression as well. Though some of the thugs acted as if they'd never heard of Rinaldo Villetti. But this would be another payment added to square up his son's account — the price for getting Hoffman out of prison — and maybe even Sega on her way to safer confines it could seem. Tad hoped. He also had thought — hoped — he would only have these mandatory contacts be over the phone. No such luck.

So when the associate to his right stepped out of the car, Tad followed, relieved to have at least some personal space restored to him, but he was quickly shoved along inside the small eatery and coffee stop.

Inside it was almost eerily deserted save for the proprietor who stood behind the counter, giving him a good look-over, and a large gentlemen in a luxurious white suit cut for quite some refinement, wearing a white fedora, who sat at a table flanked by several young adult males who appeared to be his assistants, or more likely bodyguards. They remained standing, and were either the same age as Taddeo, or less than a handful of years younger. In fact, one might have appeared very familiar. The pitcher suddenly recognized this broad-shouldered one with "the looks" as having been that smug one with Arlene in The Sisson back in Chicago. What was he doing here? And then Tad noticed a slightly older one, still a teenager younger than himself to be sure, but smaller than the others, who hung back in the shadows behind who Tad had assumed were his other pals. All this time, the proprietor was still strangely scrutinizing him — severely. But it was the man who was seated at the table who commanded the room. Tad definitely knew he was familiar with this fella, even if he'd never spoken with him. Only when another rich suit came around a corner from somewhere in the back of the shop, along with his own bodyguard, did Tad sense there was even a possible higher authority in this borough of secrets. The leader of the men who'd gone to fetch the pitcher from Ebbet's Field moved immediately to go whisper something in that gentleman's ear. Then he turned slightly to nod at the proprietor. But the stocky man who the local boss had entered with moved to step in at the side of the seated gentleman in the white suit.

"Taddeo Villetti," the seated man spoke. "My friends here are also friends of your father's. Please don't let any of my men alarm you. We are mostly *all* what you might call, extended family of yours. You are not in any danger here. In fact, you are right where you should be — where things go like they're planned. Because I *make* them happen just as they are planned. As I plan them. And so I'm here in the role some people call, The Fixer. See, I'm good with statistics, probabilities — numbers. So I guess I'm also who you might have heard some people call 'The Brain.' A guy is around for a while and he gets called a lot of names. But I *prefer* you call me Mister Rothstein. And more importantly, you may think of me as The Bank. Possibly, *your* bank, Taddeo Villetti.

"Now this bank is what's going to make your family, and dare I even say your Chicago teammates, very well-to-do. And to think people have suggested there's no money in baseball. Hah! But I'm willing to bank on the fact your father is learning there's no money in bartending. He might be a soldier today, but at the end of the day, he's really only running a small racket, a few whores, and he's a little man in a little place, the strongest thing he's serving just being his drinks. And that's how he'll retire. In just another city, in just another place — like this one." Rothstein spread his arms out with his palms open to emphasize their surroundings in the small café. "Like your uncle's." When Rothstein gestured to him, the man behind the bar cooly nodded toward Taddeo and offered him a somewhat disinterested smile. Something else obviously occupied the man's thoughts more than a family reunion. Taddeo had to admit to himself he had always been a little curious about the rest of his father's family, his papa's younger brothers. But when his mother was alive, she'd discouraged it. Meanwhile, this proprietor made wary eye-contact with the man who led the group that had been sent to fetch Tad from Ebbets Field again, and then he lowered his eyes in regret or shame, as Rothstein continued, demanding the ballplayer's immediate attention. "Now money does come *through* this place, just like your papa's place, but it doesn't stay here either. Perhaps if the operation was just the least bit more profitable, Mister Vollero would have helped himself to the kind of defense that could see him avoid reporting to begin his prison sentence? Hmm. Really." Rothstein's eyes flickered toward the dejected proprietor and a smirk bent his mouth. His gaze fell back on Taddeo, who'd only just realized this storefront they were all meeting in was owned by his uncle. "Or maybe not. It didn't help Morano," Rothstein continued. "But remember young Villetti, money commands loyalty because the desire for it is habit-forming, addicting, and thus it is power. Not simply the kind of power that expands ballpark dimensions, but the kind of power that can one day allow you to really direct your own destiny. Now a *high-ranking* soldier's place is found making his capo money, and yearning that one day he may become a capo, and then a boss, just like D'Andrea always wished to be, held by or holding the undisputed reins of leadership with *lower men*, like Colosimo — and your father." Rothstein's eyes might have shifted toward the other authority figure that the heavy from the stadium had joined. "But your papa lacks the vision to see what benefits a closer partnership with New York could bring him. Meanwhile, your old man is stuck put under Colosimo, and Big Jim lacks the talent, and even the dreams and ambition to attain true control out there in The Windy City. He's too relaxed. Won't come out of his comfort zone. We're watching your own father nipping away at his heels. Like a dog. We already have people in Chi-Town because we've come to feel that some changes may need to be affected in Chicago. Mike Merlo has cancer and D'Andrea's time is waning. Cardinella will get out of control if not clamped down on. And meanwhile the Gennas are strongly in place and getting restless for expansion, plus the Irish seem immovable. Does that about sum up all your home city's basic politics? But you, young Villetti, are in a unique position to see to it that your papa, and eventually yourself and your brothers — who I would expect waste some good amount of their time away just *dreaming* to one day inherit from your insignificant old man — don't have to wait forever to realize that dream. Or bigger ones. We all have been eagerly imagining the day when *that* barrel gets tapped.

I want you to think about that — and imagine what role you might play.

"But this will be just about all for our meeting today. I've been watching you *play* — baseball that is — though that's only part of what I'm talking about. For now I summoned you here because I just wanted to meet you, take a closer measure of you, just because I could, and I also wanted to remind you to start thinking about your personal future. What it is that *you* care about. And I hope I made an impression on you of about just how many men there could be involved here, all helping you to realize that one very bright future. Right now I will soon have another meeting to attend to." He glanced at the Brooklyn street boss, or would-be Camorra captain who probably wanted most to succeed Pellegrino Morano, and then went on with his diatribe. "But in the most immediate of futures, tomorrow — of all ironies — it is Father's Day in America — when you and your teammates will have a one-day break in your busy playing schedule while you're staying in our great City of New York. Ha! You can always count on God's effect on the climate *here* for arranging *that*. And for some of you, it will be your first Father's Day away from your papas, and your dear mamas, too. So I'd like you to consider what a great chance you all could have to bring home to those dearly missed family members of yours, quite the holiday gift from your travels to see your new *East Coast family* that's now also balls-in — behind you."

And just what does he mean by that? Tad wondered uncomfortably.

"And by that I mean *we* are to become Chi-Town's new favorite team's sponsor. So please accept my invitation on behalf of you and a few of your friends on the Cubs' roster that I've pre-selected to come join me for brunch in Manhattan tomorrow and we will discuss some preparations that need to be made for one very memorable baseball season. With Chicago receiving some help from New York, of course. So you'll help them to prepare for and expect my most generous hospitality. I have some new ideas I want to share with your teammates." He nodded to the lead soldier and his associates. "Umberto, when I'm done, please drop Mister Villetti off back at his hotel. And give him that copy of my guest list." To Taddeo he then turned and said, "These invites are not for everyone's knowledge. Handle them discreetly, and do not alter the arrangements in the slightest. You must trust that I and my men already studied and know exactly who *I* want involved." Back to the local soldier again, he continued issuing orders. "Instruct this one on where to go tomorrow, and when he may expect your return to pick him and his specially selected *friends* up, for their trip uptown in the morning. Don't have it going down in front of the Cubs' hotel." To Taddeo once more he said, "And also remember this, should it ever be asked by anyone you don't know, or anyone you don't witness me personally talking to, it is *by your best recollection*, that you were never *here*, and you'll never acknowledge seeing Mister Vollero, err.., or, uh your Uncle Alessandro over there, or his patron, Mister D'Aquila. Who all maybe *also* have somewhere else to report, I'm afraid." Arnold Rothstein nodded to indicate the rather distinguished man standing off to the side of him. "And I hope I don't have to explain *that* any more clearly. But so far, some people have been far luckier than Pellegrino. So far." Then to one of the young men behind him, he ordered, "Get me Fallon on the line. Reach him through Chicago. I will be requiring his counsel." He then rotated his head to return to who Tad was startled to learn was the other boss, and no one else but the infamous Salvatore D'Aquila, acting-Capo of The Camorra.

Taddeo glanced at the even more imposing man who stood backing up Rothstein, and then quickly diverted his glance, when he saw the dark avarice in his eyes, as fear continued gripping the young ballplayer. He shot another look toward the uncle he had not seen since probably back to when he was a little child, if they'd ever met, hoping to catch even an inkling of support now. But he received absolutely none. Mr. Vollero seemed a stranger and terribly preoccupied with something much more personally important to him. Like being locked up in prison soon. And the pitcher's mouth was too dry to utter any kind of an outreach to him anyway.

Then Rothstein once more interrupted Tad's chance to get a grip over what he was feeling about of all this. He continued, "Additionally, on Sunday, we'll be meeting with some more new people you won't know, but they will be definitely among those who never need to know, any details about us speaking with you here, now, beforehand. And you'll avoid any and all questions about *where* and *who* all your real family might be, while we meet in the Terranovas' territory. Giuseppe Masseria is very likely to be there. We all know he's always been wise to what Vincente and Ciro had conspired with us to plan. So you could say it's of *deadly* importance that my instructions are to be followed exactly." The leader of the street enforcers and Tad's uncle looked at each other and then nodded toward Rothstein like he'd appeased their concern.

Both of them? They were both Family? If the tough guy was *Umberto Valenti*, that could mean he was his papa's baby brother, an uncle barely older than Greg, his own brother. All their family names were butchered at Ellis Island. He felt his brother's gift of a knife the enforcers had immediately found, only to then allow him to keep in his pocket for this meeting. Then Taddeo remembered the leaking barrel in his papa's lounge. Apparently butchering had cut its way into The Family's business as well — unless you preferred to drink the coffee, with heroin added — to make you forget. But Tad did not forget Valenti too was a feared assassin — and seemingly even more skilled than Cousin Rocco, for Uncle Bert wasn't the one in prison.

"Yup," the thug who had led the goons that escorted Tad here said. "This is happening. And my brother, your papa, will soon know what *he* needs to know."

"Now here you go, for your time and any discomfort our meeting may have caused," Mr. Rothstein said, reaching for something in his coat's inner pocket and then sliding a stuffed-to-capacity envelope across the table toward Taddeo. The boy couldn't muster any independent thought of his own, such as to even consider the possibility of refusing it. Plus he couldn't deny it — that he needed that cash in order to continue protecting Arlene and his work with the ladies, plus pay Mr. Li and Old Lamont, not to mention his friends. Though he didn't dare count the money right then at *that* table. But he didn't need to be reminded that independent of his father, he'd be broke otherwise.

Next, Rothstein went even further, completely compounding Taddeo's uncomfortable circumstances. "Additionally, I'll either be arriving in Chicago personally and shortly, or I'm sending my associate Mister Attell here to properly appreciate your talent on the mound at home, young man," Rothstein declared. He nodded to the stocky intimidating man, another who'd been standing behind him, whose muscular build could not be mistaken under his business suit, and who had a discernably broken nose, yet appeared as though the ladies might consider him rather handsome, even in spite of it. Tad had prior knowledge of a lightweight boxing champion by that name. Was this what an athlete's retirement in "the business" was reduced to? Then Rothstein said, "Now I've heard some other interesting things about you, Villetti. New York has noticed — and we will be looking further into it.

"And oh yes. I also understand that there are some *Jewish enterprises* in Chi-Town that myself and *my father* do not require *your father* to administrate. Handling this is our purview. So my company will also be looking into *that*." He nodded toward some of the other men around Taddeo's age who stood behind him. "If your father has taught you right, then you should already comprehend and help me explain it to him so there is not any misunderstanding *on his part*. That would be unfortunate. The Villettis must stay out of Rogers Park. And as if this list of points to meet on can't get any longer, it has come to my attention that you're also protecting a young Irish whore? How very unconventional. Mercurial in fact. It's actually so rich. For once I was rewarded with a surprise." He laughed. "I do hope *I* get to meet with *her*. She seems to be very special. I liked the one your house sent to us here already — for that favor you called upon your uncles for. She's staying with your baseball team now? I presume your relatives will help to cover up any infidelity to this other one you're keeping back at home? Your own brother Greggorio helping you with that. Truly amusing."

Tad had wondered what had become of Sega while the Jewish mobster continued. Did Trip get her back to The Bossert? He was trying to protect her. He wanted, no needed, to help her. And what exactly had Greg told them all Back East that they were *all* "helping the pitcher with?" Tad groaned and thought to himself, *No. Not the situation with Hoffman again? George is so dead.*

"What is it with Colosimo's family and whores? They are after all, just whores. Can't get enough blow jobs in The Windy City, eh?" One of Rothstein's conspirators spoke — another "built one" that had originally been with the group that had met Tad at Ebbets Field. He had now moved to guard Mr. D'Aquila. And another now shifted behind him and raised his mouth as if to cover a cough that had surely been a smirk instead. But many of the other men now openly laughed. That included one of his own papa's *brothers* who enjoyed any fun being made at the expense of the Chicago operation. Antagonizing fraternal relationships must be an inherited trait in his immediate, closest family.

Tad had now figured his uncle who'd been commanded to fetch him to be Mr. D'Aquila's man. As he'd been the leader of the Italian thugs that had been sent to the Robins' stadium. How ironic he also turned out to be a relative of Taddeo's — his papa's youngest sibling no less. He'd noticed that this Valenti fellow and the other one, Vollerro — that Taddeo had immediately figured for his uncle — had some sort of relationship going on as well. *They were also brothers*. But it was more than that. They shared a big cover-up. The Valentis, besides the Villettis, were all Volleros and the big shylock knew. *Then that would make* him *also* — . The pitcher's heart skipped a beat as he remembered who visited Arlene at The Sisson and how she might have been inserted into his papa's bordello because Chicago's mob bosses all needed to work on Mayor Thompson, and needed Annenberg and the hymie's newspaper connections to increase their pressure on the Republican. But Rothstein interrupted Tad's quicks thoughts by concluding *he knew* this D'Aquila man would be speaking for his father's personal faction — and soon. Though Tad wished he hadn't already reasoned this. These were some very important people in New York's underworld that he now met with. And they were more than closely connected to his father. Probably the same *family members* Rinaldo Villetti tried to avoid oversight by when he'd decided to relocate to Chicago. They really were Tad's family. He should have no doubt now that he'd witnessed the familiar traits. And so Taddeo Villetti was the nephew of the feared hitman Umberto Valenti — a stone-cold killer who rivaled Cousin Rocco any day he might be furloughed from prison. Yes, there was no doubt Tad now began to see The Family resemblance. But he marveled at how he'd seen the younger brothers had ran his own father — and they'd done enough to run the Villettis, as they were known — right out of New York. That's how The Family came to be in Chicago — but it also meant that there was no rule of succession in The House that said Taddeo must always be subordinate to Urso and Greggorio.

"Well now Taddeo. Don't you worry about anything. Your star is on the rise. When you get back to The Windy City, you'll get to keep your little Irish girl breathing oxygen for a while longer — along with the smell of some real money. And I have a feeling that one way or another, she might be prove very interesting and very useful, too."

"Yeah, real useful." Abe Attell, the boxer laughed from his position behind Rothstein. Even the younger Jew, the tall one from The Sisson, shifted nervously where he leaned against the wall. That's when Taddeo's fear for Arlene was overcome by anger; he felt himself overheat in his own skin, and his pulse accelerate. But his better instinct won out this time and kept his mouth frozen, not even bothering to look at the uncles with whom he had no acquaintance. Apparently, one of the men already had that pending prison sentence to worry about. The other would have told him who he was when he'd first met him at the stadium, if he'd even intended to ever help his nephew out. So Tad would get no support from his immediate *and great* family here. He had to be better, smarter, and more patient than he'd ever been before. The young athlete knew he was alone. And so did Arnold Rothstein.

"In the meantime, we *will* see each other once more, tomorrow, at one of my favorite venue's — Venezia's, in Manhattan — my treat for you, and some of your very cautiously vetted, and shall we say, gifted, teammates. And then you can look forward to even meeting us again, perhaps, at the end of the month, when either I or Abraham plan to make time to go to Chicago to watch you all play some more baseball — in a new way — namely *the way I'm going to coach you in*. So I'll be keeping a close eye on you, Villetti. Meeting your friends and their families. And you should know, while knowing boxing has been my particular specialty, I'm a careful study, and might have some recommendations that may improve some performances in *your competition*." The Jewish mobster laughed. "Don't worry. I'm going to help you. More than you could possibly imagine. Enjoy your new riches I afforded you. Rewards for your smart service to my endeavors." Rothstein nodded at the bulge in the pitcher's pocket where Taddeo had stuffed the cash-containing envelope he wished he could refuse. And then Tad's meeting with this man was finally over.

The pitcher wondered what this all would mean — for his friends and especially him and Arlene. He needed to reconnect with her. And Sega was either gone again — or back at The Bossert. Probably any place she could self-medicate on her drugs. Or was she? Only now it didn't matter. Instead, he definitely wanted to return to Chicago and protect Arlene. And see if he couldn't get her guard down so he could acquire some new knowledge about her and exactly *how* she really came to be working on the South Side in his father's bordello. He could be in one bad partnership with the really wrong woman. *But maybe now I really need to medicate myself on Sega's drugs first?* But the Cubs would have to move on to Pittsburgh and he'd just been coerced into taking the Jew's money with him. And apparently the big shylock determined this to be the same fate of some of his teammates. He worried about his friends. But once he felt the sum of all the means to the end he'd desired most — to escape his family and save Arlene — and now Sega too — right in his suit coat pocket, Tad couldn't bring himself to object. Not that this would be any kind of bright idea on his part, among the obvious kind of company he presently found himself alone with — and all the way out on the East Coast. There was actually Family here, but not the kind of family that would look out for him as his mother once did. All he might have remaining was his papa. But even that wasn't guaranteed. His uncles were subject to D'Aquila and probably Arnold Rothstein, who knew too much and had some people also in with Masseria, obviously. And now his brothers had joined his adversaries, certainly if not cooperatively. All their bases were covered and no one held a position in which to back up Taddeo. He was out on the mound alone. And it had seemed like he'd been made a new contract offer, one that he could not refuse. But for the moment at least, they were all playing nicely. However, now Taddeo Villetti could never escape this game — unless he was prepared for the consequences of betraying them all. So while he actually did consider all the consequences he could think of for doing *that*, he knew for now, he alone had to bear down and *this Cub* would make his immediate stand on the hill — in sole support of his team, and his friends, and in Pittsburgh, if it had to be that way. But Brooklyn's Robins weren't even through with him yet.

Chapter 61

"I'll only be gone a little while," Tad had told his Greek lady-friend when they spoke the morning of Sunday, June 16 before his secret breakfast with his specially selected teammates and Arnold Rothstein in Manhattan for Fathers' Day. He attempted to used his belt to tie off his blood flow on his left arm just below the elbow but found a corner of the hotel bedsheet worked better, pulled tighter. But he added his belt on top of that. Sega helped him locate a vein to inject something to help him relax before his next encounter with Mr. Big. There was one second with pain, the sharp stab of the needle, then chill like liquid ice flowing through him, jolting the pitcher awake fast, like a solid hit should. They were fortunate that they didn't have to cook any mash and the young woman had gotten a brand new and prepared, Sears-brand supply kit from a dealer, somewhere. Then came that wave of relaxation which immediately followed, and Taddeo was beginning to feel prepared and ready to use all his resources. "There's some men who still haven't seen what I can really pitch. There, that's enough juice. I just need to ease my anxiety. Save some for yourself to use while I'm gone." She pulled away the needle and Tad released his belt from constricting his arm. Then he rolled down his sleeve, frowning as he noticed a tiny drop of his blood had just stained it. "But you won't have to worry about anything anymore, Sega. Now that I'm protecting you, Doll." She helped him fasten his cufflink. Taddeo felt not just comforted by the drug, but by the way the Greek woman almost mothered him. He was sincere when he told her he hoped he could hurry through his time he'd be required to spend downtown Manhattan. "The whole time, all I'll be thinking about, is returning back to you. And this. This feels so good."

He knew his words were close to what he'd spoken just before first time she'd left, before his Saturday game, when he'd gone back to the hotel and found she had disappeared. But Sega had come back to him then, even first attending his ball game that day, and was then waiting for Taddeo Saturday night as he hoped she would after another of his team's great games against the Robins — and after that one very awkward and uncomfortable first meeting with Mr. Fixer. But she'd brought that chemical entertainment with her that he wished he hadn't indulged in with her. But he did. Tad would try anything to unwind from all the pressure that his very existence placed upon his shoulders. His trip down Navy Street was not something he enjoyed, but he had some money he could be able to rely on now. Though he wasn't sure he should have taken it. And for some reason he could not explain, his instinct was to not mention he had that envelope, to Sega. Much doubt had followed him back to The Bossert. However, he trusted the needle and after the quick jab of pain, the pleasure he almost instantly felt was amazing. It was becoming a new habit he wasn't entirely unfamiliar with, at least from almost exclusively observing it in his papa's bordello. But it was an escape from the terrible anxiety about his future that Tad felt now. He was certain he had the wherewithal to control how much he used of it. And on the road, he didn't have a direct connection to a supplier, as it were. So his light drug use shouldn't become any problem. Only when the couple used it together, the sex that would follow became more infrequent, but incredible when it did happen, and Taddeo and Sega could've cared less that Trip had brought his own young working-woman with them to share the same room. No one paid attention to what the other side was doing that night. Well, barely.

It was sort of a curious surprise that it became a turn-on to participate in their small voyeuristic orgy. Besides that, it was fun to just forget all one's inhibitions and all the appropriate social conventions — so Taddeo Villetti wouldn't let anything else spoil the victory celebration he felt he totally should have spent his entire evening indulging in — versus that part of it he'd been forced to surrender to Arnold Rothstein. And also on his mind, was his feeling badly for a good friend, who'd gotten out on the field the least this road trip — so far anyway. So Michael found himself a rather breathtaking blonde Irish woman, and Taddeo and Sega shared their room. And then perhaps more, as he'd woken up in a pile of soft bedding that was gathered underneath another pile of all their naked bodies on the floor, their bare skin adhering to one another by some wet, and sticky substances. Only when Sega woke and they softly conversed, neither were terribly shocked by where and how they found themselves — and who else with. So maybe Tad felt it was the drugs that caused him to put forth another promise made, that would unfortunately sooner than later become another promise broken.

Taddeo really meant to keep his word that he'd protect her. But then Sega had a bad pattern of going missing — and she disappeared again Sunday, while Taddeo was away with some of the team for his second meeting with Arnold Rothstein, downtown Manhattan.

There was always a possibility she had gone for good. But when he and his teammates were given return-rides back to their new hotel in Brooklyn after breakfast at Venezia's, and Taddeo learned of her latest disappearance, he hoped she'd find him again. So at first, he wasn't going to run around the entire borough trying to locate her. Tad prayed *she* would find him. She did this vanishing act once before in Brooklyn, and as well as in Upper Manhattan. However, he wouldn't go back on his word to ensure her safety if she'd only make the effort to try and help him versus disappearing *again*. He loved the way she made him feel, or what she added to stimulate his better feelings. So he just knew she'd only gone looking for new drugs. Hoff had warned him about her. Sega had nurtured quite the bad habit and there was evidence it had begun controlling her. That was The Family's doing no doubt, and while to her it might have seemed like she'd escaped The House, the truth was by nurturing her addiction, she might never be free from her slavery now. However, given only an hour coupled with Tad's compassion and the fear he felt for her safety, he betrayed his last resolve to stay put, and Sunday afternoon would see him begin searching for her.

There had never been a note and no indication of where she went or how she left The Bossert. Now the staff in Brooklyn were changing shifts and Taddeo promised himself that he would question every single one who had been on duty that morning when he and some of his teammates had left for Venezia's. He tried to reach every employee before they left work. When he realized that by himself, this couldn't be accomplished fast enough, he tried to enlist his friends' help. But Hoff, Trip and Trevor hadn't gotten any invitation from Arnold Rothstein. This really bothered them, and Taddeo, plus his friends, hadn't seen anything of the young woman either. *Just* other *women no doubt*, Tad thought. He knew what attention toward heavenly experiences they'd be paying for, when given the Sabbath off. He wished he felt he could relax and let Sega find her own way, so he could pay attention to his teammates who he had went and been honest with immediately — that they were not to receive Rothstein's bribes.

But because of his loyalty to his friends, and the other discomforts he felt he was likely and unjustly being put through, no doubt the work of his family with the aid of those shylocks, Tad broke his promise to Mr. Big when it was only hours old. Of course he told his best friends all of what was happening. They were the only ones who he really trusted. Though he knew they'd require motivation to care. And he'd said he would see what he could do for them, in so far as any money allocations went to some additional and very specific players in the Cubs' Rothstein deal. He just asked for them to please give him some time and help him search for Sega. Tad asked them to question all The Bossert's employees at the very least. Meanwhile, he spent all the remaining hours of Sunday afternoon and evening — in between a baseball practice Coach called the team over to in the Flatbush ballpark — visiting all of the shady places he could find where Sega might go to purchase black market drugs. He continued asking for information on the streets, in addition to calling and pleading with his family in New York to help locate her. And he only reached employees who said they knew nothing about who he was talking about when he used the number he'd gotten in prison to call the Navy Street Café. Their reassurances that they'd do their best to keep an eye out for Sega and get a message to his uncle Al to see if he knew anything sounded disingenuous to say the least. Vollero was somehow free on a bond for the 1916 killing of Mafia kingpin Nicholas Morello in the earlier Mafia-Camorra War, and was preparing to go to another trial that very week. This case was just being brought to court now, but his uncle had been released "to continue running his business." Tad could only imagine who else helped arrange that one for their own benefit. And that was just how New York worked. Now the next employee Tad spoke with when he followed up with his last call, was a woman who sounded like she was much more than any simple employee. She sounded as if she'd been paid specifically to flirt with Tad on the line, and suggest that Villetti didn't need to find Sega — and even that she could satisfy his needs as his uncle was more than a little busy worrying about his future and what would become of himself and his business if the prosecutor could move the jury to convict him. But the youngest Villetti had learned to become more than a little suspicious of women flirting with him. Who was *she* anyway? He'd heard his uncle had a very young, new wife. His family was getting to be too much. *My mother warned me.*

So until now, Taddeo had hesitated to use the phone contact he had for Arnold Rothstein but never got to speak with him. Alternately, he reached through one more layer of interference from another lackey for the Jewish mob boss, who Taddeo grew so infuriated with, after repeated phone calls to who-the-hell-knew-where. But when the presumed kike, “Meyer-somebody,” grew too frustrated with stonewalling him any longer, and Tad was put in touch with Rothstein’s street lieutenant, the former champion boxer, Abraham Attell, Taddeo couldn’t help but be excited about an opportunity try and engage the man in conversation about the sports world and his experiences on the phone. He’d been very intimidating in person, but Attell was just not the sociable sort. He said he didn’t answer the phone to chat but curtly demanded to know “why the hell Villetti was trying to contact Rothstein.” And upon being informed it was over the Greek woman, he was told he could not help the young athlete; messages for the boss went up the line but Mr. Big did not take telephone calls from the likes of *him*, and that Villetti was never to call there just about some whore ever again. That was not the Jewish organization’s concern and Attell did not want to have to *reinforce* that lesson.

Chapter 62

Now the effort to locate Sega and see to it that she was no longer in danger was not paying off, at all. The youngest Villetti tried not to lose his control. Instead, Taddeo learned that not even one attempt to help was made on the part of his friends. They were now preoccupied with relaxing and talking about what each was going to do with the Jew's money their buddy was going to secure for them. After practice, they all felt they had nothing better to do since their next game versus the Robins wasn't until Monday. On that next day, which was June 17, Hoff said he'd spring for a good breakfast for the other two fellas from the Iowa farm team, who also had to be so far away from home over the holiday. So in the morning, he took them all out to eat — but most surely to curry favor with Trip and Bass to allow him additional private hotel room nights in Pittsburgh, the Cubs' next destination they would play at. But Sega didn't even show up to eat after any of those concerned would have extended her the offer — perhaps Trip especially after what seemed to have gone on in Tad's room Saturday night. So George figured Sega might have returned on her own while they all were out and she still could have gone out again to meet with her connection for her heroin. He didn't know she hadn't come back all Sunday night. And when they returned to The Bossert after breakfast, he figured they might find her safe in Tad's room that he was still supposed to be sharing with Trip. But she apparently had really disappeared, longer than the last time. She'd likely vanished right after the pitcher returned from his next "big game-day" with the veterans in Lower Manhattan. The game that they learned wasn't being played on a baseball diamond. The other couple they'd shared the room with Saturday night, had woke to find both her and Tad gone anyway — and originally assumed the pair was together. Trip had said those two appeared to be getting close now, and all the boys thought they'd learn where the couple had went once Tad showed up for the afternoon practice that Mitchell had ordered yesterday, since they wouldn't be facing the Robins on a Sunday afternoon. But Tad continued searching for her and had made a point of pestering them to help. It's all Tad spoke of when they practiced his pitches. Then Hoff learned that his friend had gone searching for her again, and not returned over the entire night.

So Hoff had decided to be magnanimous by taking the other two out for his treat — along with whatever-was-her-name who had spent the past night with Hoffman — and who knew, maybe Bass as well, that Monday morning. *Of course* — for this was one wild road trip. He thought Trip was still keeping company with the same young woman he'd met with The Hoff on Friday. She had joined them to eat, too. Only Tad and his inexplicable obsession with Chicago girls was bringing their mood down in New York. But Taddeo learned that on Sunday, when he wound up meeting with all of them again at their hotel before practice — when the youngest pitcher and some of his other fellow teammates had returned from their brunch in Manhattan, what the other rookies had just learned of while they were now readying themselves for that practice — that Sega had already been missing. And for far too long, according to a far too agitated Taddeo.

Tad remembered what had first been on his mind before all of this, and he had pestered and disappointed all his friends. He had been repeatedly apologizing to the veterans for giving up Rodriguez' run batted in at the last Giants game he pitched before the weekend even began. If only the things he had to work on now were just as simple as his baseball skills. However, he knew he should be redeemed — for his performance at Ebbets Field. And he hoped, he would also be rewarded with genuine acceptance by the Chicago squad for the part which saw most of the starters receiving some familiar white envelopes with Rothstein's cash inside of them. Though his best friends on the roster didn't get any of those. But Villetti considered that his deal with the Jewish boss may have been what he really did need to have happen in order to improve his situation. He needed that money more than anyone. Only then Tad was really distracted, ever since realizing he could have now permanently lost his lady friend in Brooklyn while he wasn't paying attention to keeping all his bases covered. Neither were the other rookies, who lost two "situational plays" the other times Sega was found to be missing. Only no one was stopping her from doing whatever she wanted and Taddeo knew it was highly likely she'd been planted there to manipulate him. With the knowledge that Greg had been the one to originally set up her trip back east from Chicago, and of the relationship his brother maintained with Uncles Bert and Al, this wasn't hard to imagine. *And Greg had come along when Papa made his first appearance to watch me play in Chicago. That was no coincidence. Weeghman was there, with his ties to the Irish politicians — and sitting with the shylocks and the Mafia, while I'd been sleeping with Arlene. All along everything's been planned to manipulate my game — and that of all of my teammates. So has my entire life been a lie? And what did I just get my friends into?* Tad needed to get some answers. Sega might be one possible source. But then why wouldn't someone let her return to him, so at least she could report back what he and his teammates decided among themselves about whether they would fulfill their part in Rothstein's deal?

"I asked you to do one thing. *One thing*," Tad had scolded his friends upon his catching up to them Monday morning.

"Well, I'm sorry," George had responded. "I like to get to do stuff, too. And don't forget that I also like being paid."

"Like make your best-friends pay by having to go to prisons for you?" Tad responded. "All these years and I wasn't ever aware that was one of your hobbies. Now I have this *one more situation* to deal with. And it's a big situation. Bigger — and worse than you know. Or could even ever possibly know, you idiot. Thank you very much."

With no luck recruiting help before practice on Monday, Taddeo went out on his own asking questions from those who didn't want to be spoken with, all around Brooklyn. He'd attempted to look into every local pub and market in a desperate effort to locate Sega almost all the way up until noon. The Cubs did have practice but he probably wouldn't be playing in the game today since he'd already pitched in Brooklyn. So Tad reported late, getting chewed out by Coach Mitchell, but only regretting that he couldn't return to Lower Manhattan to seek information about the woman there. His repetitive phoning Venezia's got him nowhere but stonewalled once he learned how he might truly get in touch with Rothstein. Abraham Attell would not take kindly to having his warning ignored though Taddeo took his chances that the man would not get rough with him because the Jews needed him healthy for their plot to work. And as long as Sega was already missing, there was nothing else they could threaten him with. Was there? It's not like he'd care if they suddenly said they were going to hurt Urso, or harm his uncles who hadn't lifted one finger to help him. But his repetitive guess was that Sega was trying to feed her need for salvation with more of the drugs that Hoff had warned him about having seen her purchasing. However, if the hymies knew anything, they definitely did not want to give up any names of drug suppliers in New York that Villetti might approach. To tell the truth, Taddeo wouldn't have minded just one more shot of the juice himself. Just one.

All in all, the search was exhausting and his distemper saw him exhausting all his friends' resistance to their calling *him* out on his continuing to try and make them help. At the risk of several *seasons* more of great friendship, or all of his buddies deciding to beat Tad up, he had *ordered* George, Trevor and Michael to keep searching for her after their workout in Ebbets Field on Sunday. Now he had to promise them money — just because he ordered them, versus asking the lazy bums to make themselves useful. And he already owed them money from what he'd borrowed to provide Sega with her conveniences she'd required to get around New York thus far. That was just another reason why he told them some of their teammates were on the take following that meeting with Rothstein — hoping that they could help him by helping themselves get in on the payout. Then Taddeo planned to explain it would be the reason that he'd owed them less.

But it was all to no avail. He should have known better before he went to the breakfast with Rothstein and the veterans, without her, and then made his friends angry with him over the situation that had then been allowed to develop. Was that so now he'd be *forced* to pay people to align with him? He could have brought Sega and had her wait away from the conspirators' tables, though he supposed Rothstein wouldn't have been too happy about that. And maybe the goombahs he'd sent with Tad's uncle would never have allowed her in one of their cars. Though it wasn't like the whole two lots of the Jewish mob and his relatives in the Camorra didn't know about Sega, already. She came to him from Chicago by way of The Navy Street Café. The Mafia would not know her though. Maybe. But now without money for the rookies, bothering his friends and teammates over his women troubles would leave Taddeo all alone unless he paid them from out of his share that he'd already collected. Whereas then he'd undoubtedly go back to Rothstein to get himself deeper into debt so that he didn't return to Arlene empty-handed. New York had hooked him on their money and now worked to reel him in.

But Taddeo knew that even from miles upon miles away, Greg was the one really pushing him. It had to be his brother. Didn't it? Who else could have orchestrated this? From Coogan's Hollow to Ebbets Field. And why? Greg was the one who exported Sega to New York to begin with. Was he tight with Uncle Bert? Ironically, uncle and nephew were the same age. Or was it with Uncle Al that

Greggorio built a secret relationship? The Villetti boys' great uncle Vollero was in Chicago the night the plumber Dulio was murdered after everyone had witnessed O'Rourke beat him down in that street fight — and right before the butcher's bill was settled for him by The House. Both his brothers began appearing at The Sisson around that time, and Corrado had brought Tad a loaded gun. Then he was sent on that hunting trip by his papa, curious — no suspicious — of who helped O'Rourke escape being caught at Mr. Li's. But the Villetti boys never talked about that, because Greg already knew. But he never said anything. Next, he was definitely Tad's brother responsible for sending Sega halfway across the country to follow his baseball team. So Greg had to be working with the siblings' uncles, and would be the one to make Sega disappear. Had his *great*-uncle ordered that? Did his papa lie about being in control? Perhaps just to protect him? To see to the real situation not frightening him. He was mad he could ever doubt his father and banished the thought of doubting Arlene. He was certain it was others that plotted against him. Now Taddeo saw red every time he thought of his family. Just to use him, these goombahs would hurt so many innocent people. And what for? Why were they doing this? He literally meant to learn the truth. Tad feared what it could mean — now even for his baseball team, and then he made the connection to Urso's gambling, and saw this as reason to literally set him upon killing them. Both of them. Taddeo was so livid, he swore he could find it in him to even torture his brothers to death — as they'd tortured him by bullying him his whole entire life. And now his brothers had no problems with bringing their entire family down on him.

Or was it Arnold Rothstein and his agents that had possibly done this? Only that wouldn't make sense. The fat hymie needed the whole team cooperating with him, and Tad needed to be alive and well and able to be heard when he relayed the Jew's instructions for them. The shylock crime boss was supporting Taddeo, wasn't he? He'd chosen *him* to be the front man in this whole conspiracy. Getting him killed in a confrontation by some civil war within The Villetti Family served no purpose for the Jewish interest.

But having alienated his friends, feeling isolated and alone, and after having gone screaming through the night all over Brooklyn and even to Manhattan — if only he'd gotten the opportunity — and all in a desperate search for Sega, Taddeo had little choice but to resort to trying to call Arlene again. Only she was still not speaking to him. He talked to both Jasmine and Rose at the bar, but neither had much information to pass on to him that Taddeo found to be of any use. Roslyn did come forward with a little prodding and related that his most suspect-brother had made sure Arlene knew about him and Sega. This confirmed what Lumia had told him. *She knows. And she probably hates me for that. Great.* He'd sensed they were broken as a couple long before he allowed himself to take up with Sega. *But it just figures.* Tad already was sure he'd been set up. His brother had played him perfectly. Greggorio wanted to split up he and Arlene. His brother never approved of the alliance between the two lovers that next saw the bordello get taken away from *him*. He had been planning that ever since he was the one who probably encouraged Urso to take Sega, *his woman* at the time, on the brothers' hunting trip — to use *to seduce me*. And that had obviously worked. But now Tad feared what had become of the young woman once Greg had no more use for her — and now that Arlene knew about the affair. Only in trade for that information, Taddeo was pleaded with to return home, again and this time by Rose, as in his absence, all the girls were being forced to service The Family in addition to making their quotas — not to mention being beaten as punishment when they didn't. This was reliable medicine coming from Dr. Ronga's daughter, who to gain his trust, decided to reveal her true name to be Anna, and even that her mother hailed from the British Hughes family. She wasn't one-hundred percent Italian by a longshot — not that Tad really cared anything about genealogy. Everybody had some hidden secret they were keeping. Was she too, up to something? Why not? Everybody else was. But Roslyn was scared and wanted to demonstrate she trusted Taddeo to help. Her new beau Frank, worked for Colosimo, and she'd learned The Outfit was wary about recent developments in their soldier Villetti's house. Johnny Torrio had gathered new associates and planned to invite his protégé, Frank's cousin Al from Back East, to come out and join him in The Windy City.

Taddeo was also told that Urso had some new girl, someone neither Tad nor Arlene had recruited. That had left Sega vulnerable and being forced to work The House when Urso couldn't tie down Arlene — probably literally — and lost interest in the Greek woman for this petite, bleach blonde Italian, 'Lumia.' Tad didn't tell Roslyn that he had already spoken with her. But LuLu's arrival had been mixed into the catalyst for Sega to run off to *him* in New York, and jived with what his now-missing hotel guest had told him. However, the youngest Villetti had grown smarter than to think anything was occurring by coincidence, or especially kindness.

When Taddeo trusted Rose with what Arlene apparently already would know, he added that Sega had been there, but since disappeared. Roslyn suggested that the woman had just run away, and Tad should quit looking for her. Those things happened "in the business." But he could also talk to Jasmine about it if he needed to. She was there by Rose's side while they talked on the phone and concurred with the first woman's opinion. Baldavino was usually on hand if Tad wanted to speak with him, instead. But he didn't want to talk to the other woman or especially his cousin, who should not even be in the lounge upon the revocation of the Delasandros' permission to be anywhere near there. And as much as it was the origin for all his problems, Tad anxiously wanted to get back to Chicago, where he'd straighten all this out — somehow. Some way. No. He desperately wanted to get back right then.

But when he brought up "a personal situation" and offered to pay for his own transportation back to The Windy City, Fred Mitchell utterly refused to hear of such nonsense. Taddeo had thought his work was done in so far as what Rothstein wanted. The Brain had met with the select Cubs he'd wanted to — the starters that could always be counted on to play — and Abraham Attell had introduced himself so they'd know him in Chicago. Young Villetti was a rookie and the Jews and their unlikely joint co-conspirators of both Mafia and Camorra partisans had gotten what they'd really wanted from Villetti — some of the veterans who would most regularly see game play arriving at the point where they would take the shylock's money. Every baseball player wanted more money, especially after the suspicious collapse of the players' union. But as a relief pitcher, and one with mediocre stats, an immaturity problem, and an attitude issue for the record books, there should be no one that needed Taddeo now. The gamblers got the team they really wanted. The Delasandros, Baldavino if not Corrado, were taking back the business in Chicago, most likely to be ran by Greg, operating from the shadows. And it appeared Sega had served her purpose to deprive Arlene any desire to hold out, counting on *that couple's* alliance, with the return of Taddeo. They were no longer a couple. And it would appear that the Cubs' rookie pitcher no longer had anything — to include even what might be left of something to dream for.

However, Tad was informed he still had a contract which effectively stated that he was owned by Mr. Weeghman, who Taddeo could assume was also in on this, so the rookie pitcher was not a free agent who could just go where he wanted any more. He'd become trapped, another enslaved dago with another Anglo master. But with an envelope full of Rothstein's cash in his pocket, Villetti was subject to even another contract, a contract with the Jewish mob, and one Abraham Attell had assured him he'd never get the chance to talk his way out of.

Nor could he call who he wanted either, as Arlene continued refusing to speak to him and was refusing any and all call connections from the East Coast, even when Tad tried to get Trip and Trevor to place the calls for him. George offered too, but Tad said he didn't want to trust him enough to ask anything else of him now. Hoffman's last time failing young Villetti could have cost poor Sega her life — and it apparently had already cost him his relationship with Arlene ever since he had to go and spring his stupid idiot of a best friend from a maximum security prison. This wasn't at all what he ever imagined life was going to be like, playing in the Major Leagues.

Hoff said he could make up for it by stepping up and caring for Arlene when they returned to Chicago, like Taddeo had originally asked. But the rookie pitcher explained in no uncertain terms to all his former Iowa teammates that they needed to wise up and realize who they were really dealing with. It wasn't a game they were playing any more. Maybe he could still get them in on the money coming to the veterans, but Taddeo couldn't get any of his friends to take the threat his *brothers* represented seriously, as they thought that his connecting them with Arnold Rothstein's money was just wonderful, this "Italian thing," and was just the best addition to baseball ever. And Hoffman just continued to annoy him anyway. *My best friend.* The eternal optimist. Hoff could not help but stay unforgiven in Tad's mind because he thought he did everything he could to stay out of trouble since departing for The East. There was far less of a chance anyone could have gotten young Villetti alone to conscript him into this shit if George hadn't gone and gotten himself arrested for illegal street racing in the first place. Blame was being tossed around like a practice ball.

In addition to now the potential loss of friendship with his closest pal who had so angered him he couldn't bring himself to reach out to George — and then Tad feeling like the demands he made of his closest teammates tasking them to look all over New York for Sega Sunday night — and after that turning his wrath on them when they wouldn't bother with such foolish nonsense — young Villetti had made himself a pariah. And he had neither Sega nor the one woman most-special to him who was supposed to be his girlfriend. What he suddenly wished he had, was power and command over others, like his father had; more so like Mr. Rothstein, Mr. D'Aquila, and Giuseppe Masseria had. Rose had even suggested that Arlene hated Sega and the woman was best off never returning to Chicago. *That's just perfect.* Taddeo did not have control over anything, anywhere. Meanwhile, Tad's woman — if she was ever going to play that position — said she did not ever want to talk with him again. So he should fathom she was not "his girl." And in addition to that, she was behaving very strangely and meeting with those who just seemed quite out of place in Little Italy. Ladies of substantial wealth of some sort that Roslyn told him about. And there were additional strangers visiting the family establishment. Government officials. United States Senators — and not from Illinois or the Washington baseball team, either. And there were more women, this very young girl, let alone men of color, presumably hired as entertainers. Things were changing fast on Taylor Street in the short while he'd been gone. When he got back he might not even recognize the place as home. So now more than ever — in Brooklyn or Chicago — Taddeo felt all alone. He was losing everything. He knew it. And there seemed to be less and less that he could do about it.

And it's been no more than three weeks since I left Chicago!

Now, by way of Mitchell's orders, Tad would also be going someplace else he didn't want to be. The Pirates would steal his time next, and all the while he'd have to *buy* his friends back. So the play in Pittsburgh would be first on Taddeo Villetti's calendar.

It seemed like Greg had made sure there was nothing else left on it, that to the young pitcher, could be anything he was looking forward to.

So, with all efforts to find Sega for naught, being in debt to his best friends on his team who were now all extremely irritated with him — and suffering an extremely close loss to the Robins by 1 run on Monday afternoon, Taddeo made plans to ditch his Chicago team. Rothstein had made many new alliances on the roster he could focus on, and there was Family right within the D'Aquila organization that it appeared the shylock could count on. They should have no interest in going after Villetti if he fled now, and maybe even Uncle Bert could discourage them. He was supposed to be Family. And it wasn't like Tad got to pitch a lot as it were — when the Cubs would have many games out of either New York's or Chicago's sphere of influence. *Unless the syndicate owned all the umpires from The Reverend to Bill Klem as well?* Tad should probably account for that in his reasoning out this next move, but he didn't want to. His mind was made up. He'd seemed to have been stripped of everything in his life he truly valued, as the price for only one envelope full of money in his suit pocket. And the one thing it could not buy him, was freedom. So he decided he could not also lose control of even his ability to make the simplest choices about his life as well. Taddeo Villetti had decided he was going to run. He'd go back to Chicago while the team headed on to Pittsburgh on Tuesday, following one last match to split the now-tied series with Brooklyn. He'd find Arlene — who should be grateful he'd finally be bringing her some money. And Tad hoped he could convince her the pair of them could still make the best allies if she would work with him. Then they could make their stand and survive against The Family together. They would make their partnership work. And whatever might have become of Sega, would not have to be the fate of Arlene. The pitcher could make that last save. And just maybe they'd both disappear before Arnold Rothstein could ever find out what happened to *him*. Taddeo Villetti designed his own next play — one in which he would no longer be controlled, and he did not have to stand alone.

Chapter 63

The next call — right on schedule — came in from the East Coast, and it was for Villetti — Rinaldo Villetti — at his home residence, where it wouldn't be reported by anyone else outside of The Family. Urso answered the phone, said hello to his uncle Bert from Brooklyn who he hadn't spoken to for some time, and then passed the phone off to his father. He'd been ordered to come home to his papa for yet another lecture about some problem or another and he longed to get back to the lounge. His old man hadn't even gotten started before the phone rang, but Villetti had already grabbed his son's face and used his fingers to spread Urso's eyes wide to stare into them and determine whether his son's soul was still behind them — or something else. His papa had said, "I thought so," though Urso didn't know what he was thinking. So while his uncle was occupying his father's interest with something regarding the Tadpole, as Urso gathered from overhearing one side of their conversation, he used the opportunity to slip out of the house and head back to the lounge, letting his little brother receive all his papa's attention.

Only when he returned to Taylor Street, he couldn't find LuLu, and Greg hadn't returned for that matter — from wherever he'd gone. Maybe his brother had taken her to rest somewhere else? But Greggorio had been gone for some while. It could have been several days before Urso would have noticed. However, now he did, and he'd make sure his brother learned it wasn't wise to mess with his women the next time he'd catch up with him. Previously, only as an afterthought, Urso recollected that the young lady might've been trying to defeat her demon, beat her addiction. But she was *his* girl, not Greg's. He felt strongly that it would be sort of an inconvenience for him if she'd died. Sort of. Lumia had become *his* addiction. And since when did anything she was trying to do become her decision? He was in charge to decide who tried to do what. But he was previously assured that the young woman's condition had been stabilized. She couldn't be dead. That was also his decision. In support of that conclusion, Dr. Ronga was back there at the lounge waiting to present him with his bill. Though his papa hadn't had time to cover that, so it was likely that's what he'd wanted to talk to his son about. Meanwhile, Urso said the doc would get paid later, after his cousin Stefano did the books and deducted Daphne's fees. Then finally, his papa could approve the reimbursement. Ronga argued with him, saying he was a professional doctor, and protested that he was married and did not indulge in "whatever" he was being charged for. But Urso balled his fingers into a fist and cocked his arm back above the practitioner's head as he informed the good physician that he could see him to the hospital if he really wanted to go that badly, and that Daphne was also to be respected as a professional.

Arlene closed the door behind her to the doctor's former room, as she felt like staying upstairs — if only in the hallway — versus subjecting herself to every responsibility that came with being downstairs in the lounge. One thing Greg had done when he was there, was take some of the pressure off her chest. The removal of Urso from that occupation, literally, was also her best reason for Arlene to hope Lucky LuLu had continued to survive. Presently, Dr. Ronga's latest entertainer was likely off taking her bath to wash the stains away. Then it was rinse and repeat. Only suddenly, Arlene couldn't help herself and the tears escaped her control and started running from her eyes.

As she could still hear Urso and the doctor arguing in the hall, she didn't think she could stand this anymore — and on top of being pregnant. Taddeo was not there and it was still almost a week before his scheduled return; the father of her baby would just not make any exception and take a leave from that stupid team to come back to Chicago for her. Once more Arlene felt she was truly all alone. And there was no one she had told, or could really talk to about her being with child now — and it certainly wouldn't be Dr. Delasandro — still the only person that knew besides the unavailable Katherine McCormick, or possibly her aide, Nancy. But they weren't talking to her because every time she could touch base with someone from their movement, she'd predictably demand they give back her gun and take the vitriol Arlene was very capable of firing at them, even without it. However, she was the one who was refusing to speak to Taddeo — at least she wanted him to feel terrible about that lack of phone communication, so he'd return and talk to her in person. And she felt horrible for Daphne as well.

On the nightstand of a temporarily vacant room that Chastity and Jezebel were preparing for a new customer, was the complimentary dosage. A new needle, as well as what she'd need to light and liquefy her poison with. The House had ran low on vials and their hostesses were all trained well on how to cook "presumably *uncut*" mash. Yet Dr. Delasandro also knew how to fake that. Everything was fake around there, including hope of any escape. Now Arlene stared at the tourniquet that would serve as her last tie to this life. In her pocket, Arlene had already pilfered quite a little handful of additional prepared liquid dosages, the really strong stuff. However, what she still really wanted was her gun back again. *But no. I can't do what I would want, what would be the easiest. I must live for my child now. That I might see my only daughter survive and grow up to own a life I could only dream of. This I will accomplish. Because what if I'm not fast enough? What if I'm not accurate,* just once? *Getting into a firefight with the Villettis could kill my baby, now. And when I have seen to my child's survival, Urso and especially Greggorio and Rinaldo Villetti will be the ones to die. However long it takes. That I will see to with certainty.*

Oh she wanted that .45 back even more each and every passing minute, every hour, and more than the last if that were possible. Adding the provision of a good life, a safe life for her child onto a very short list, she realized that vengeance wasn't just her mission, but it was also her reason for living. It was who she was — the deliverer of death. But Taddeo? Arlene couldn't figure what to make of Taddeo. What would she see become of him? A part of her felt like she didn't want to ever see him again. He didn't come back to help her. His actions, especially with Sega, proved he didn't really care. So she was actually frightened to know how Tad might react if he learned she was pregnant. And Arlene could only hope Baldavino, or his brother Carlo Delasandro, wasn't bothering Zhen Li right then. She didn't know where they were, and she couldn't handle everything by herself — but she thought she remembered asking Faith to give them something both the brothers were wanting of. All she really knew about them was they enjoyed their driving lessons — and that The Baller wasn't even a tenth as skilled as he imagined he was — at anything. She hoped the effort she planned out for also coercing Urso to help her control his cousins would thereby keep the little Oriental girl safe. She wasn't sure after everything, she'd actually gotten somewhere with "The Baller." Arlene wanted to make the little differences, at least while she could. "Use what weapons and power you've got," Victoria Moresco had said. So she had — with Baldavino, though he and Urso together had kept her by the lounge and unable to get back to Mr. Li's. But in the meanwhile, Arlene didn't want to get passed around by every Washington Senator, marked up by everyone who added a rider onto her agenda. Only inventing other work to do in a whorehouse versus whoring herself out, had created a lot of unplanned for delays to Arlene getting a true break from that place. Taddeo would eventually be returning from his baseball team's road trip — but only after he played out his personal calendar. Thus Arlene could think of better things she wanted to do, versus seeing him, save for the relief she knew the pitcher would bring.

Chapter 64

Who Arlene definitely wanted to see was Katherine McCormick. But things would still just not go her way. It suddenly felt like a knot in her stomach kept coiling. She couldn't tell if it was her anxiety or the appearance of actual morning sickness with her child. Hopefully. Dr. Delasandro's other medications had saved her from the Spanish flu. But either way, she wound up seeing the sink much too close up for her taste, and the aftertaste of whatever she'd consumed in the last half-dozen hours. Arlene regurgitated her recent history as she discovered exactly where Lumia had went. Not off with Greg somewhere as everyone who'd actually cared had suspected. Curiously, she had not even seen Urso for a short while now until he'd turned up arguing with the doctor. But then she'd found the newest girl's head — in the toilet bowl. At least it was still attached to her body. One never knew in this sort of place. But while Daphne relaxed and bathed, LuLu was shuddering from her experience with Dr. Ronga's credentials. Or was it "Dr." Delasandro's? It felt close to being the same difference. One doctor was still in The House, and that would barely make any difference. The only positive note: the Brooklyn girl wasn't dead — yet, anyway.

Arlene recovered herself quickly, wishing to set the example she should as the madam if it was the Villetti brothers' intention that this one also became one of The House's entertainers. It could be the only way she could keep herself alive in Chicago. She would reassert her authority. To do so, LuLu would not be allowed to expend all her time in the bathroom. Not when Congress was in session. Arlene wished that the women of the day were able to leave more of a legacy behind them. Although maybe McCormick or at least Moresco could, with their strategy, see that any change actually made, would then be left up to the ladies of the night to initiate, with the United States government, blackmailed from the back of a brothel — and the Christian Women benefitting from the sale of their own sisters' skin. At least the hypocrisy progressed on. Meanwhile, the guineas readied something big they were going to pull, unaware that the assistance of the Irish they'd be supplied with, came with a plan to double-cross them — until Sullivan and O'Banion's people too, got stabbed in the back — by Arlene's cousins. Now the young woman was done with the notion about any ideals getting realized from all of this. She only wanted what wealth and power she hoped it still could yield for her. Resources that would one day protect her child. But LuLu might at least be considerate enough to finish vomiting so she could leave a financial contribution to Arlene even if she left nothing else of value behind her in this whole cruel world. Alternatively, Arlene supposed if Lumia died, she wouldn't continue to leave any financial *burden*. The Irish woman supposed that was something. It would be up to the dagos to clean that mess up and not involve any of those of her own true bloodline — other than the usual Irish for-sale cops if any assistance would even be requested from them with her body. But it left out any chance that funeral would cost the North Side Gang anything, nor any of the Jews. Arlene supposed this was fortunate. Lumia being there had been all Greg's move, after all. The guineas in Chi-Town would pay the price if this girl was also somehow connected Back East and somebody was going to come looking for her.

Victoria had also explained to Arlene that McCormick was only spinning her wheels, never truly heading anywhere. Politics was a self-serving game and right now all the Women's Movement did that *she* cared about, served the real madam's still-hidden interests. Arlene wasn't privy to what they were, but she would make herself be. Meanwhile, the ladies' right to vote had now passed the House of Representatives but stayed held up in the Senate — and people like Congressman Mann had only voted in favor of suffrage for expediency, yet worked tirelessly against it behind the scenes. Political duplicity wasn't Arlene's problem and Victoria was probably right. Once women could vote, the difference they'd make would only serve the worse ends of those who planned to manipulate that vote. A great storm was still coming, yet still just over the horizon. Arlene only couldn't see it clearly yet. So the Congressmen present, who would later be counted upon to convince their friends in the Senate, did little to convince Arlene they were of any value — but for the money they left behind them. But she did see Urso had kept his door closed so he could trap and argue with Dr. Ronga some more, and thus Arlene could slip out of the women's room and proceed unnoticed. Heading downstairs after vomiting, the young madam had much she still did not feel right about. So Arlene might use some of the heroin again, but just take a little dose. In the meanwhile however, she escaped the lounge through the kitchen to go out and smoke a cigarette in the back alleyway. Old Lamont's eyes followed her. And then so did the old man.

"And why are *you* following me? Is there something I can help you with?" she asked him, her tone suggesting she really did not want to be disturbed. Why was he bothering her? They really hadn't interacted much before.

"No, Mademoiselle. But perhaps it is moi who might help you?"

"Yes. Yes actually you could help me. And do you know how? By getting the fuck out of my sight."

"Oh?"

"Wait. I'm sorry. That came out mean. I just really thought I wanted to be alone right now."

"I see. And do you?"

"I still might. But you're Taddeo's friend, aren't you?"

"He considers my advice. Though I will leave you to your thoughts for right now, as that is really what you wished for. You appear to have much to consider yourself. I just ask that you remember, while it all might seem hopeless, you will find you could have a friend in me as well. For now, I think you should call up whoever it is that *you* feel most comfortable talking to."

Is he really trying to charm me? I've been forced to live in one more level of hell in one more hellish week. And what I really need now is to lie down and fuck with some old nigger to make me feel better? Yeah. That's exactly what I need. So is that all he wants? I sure hope he doesn't think I owe him for his assistance scheduling the lounge music. It's a very unhealthy thing to be any kind of man that I owe something to around here.

But she really wanted her gun. However, after only seconds passed, her own reassessment of Lamont's advice-offer, proved to strike a chord with her.

If she couldn't get a weapon, once she got the chance, Arlene would repeat all those ridiculous steps she'd need to make another secret connection to Louisiana without anyone snitching to The Family. She needed to get to Fallon so she could phone and request the funds up front, greater to any amount she couldn't possibly steal from The House in any short amount of time, and then she'd just get the hell out of there. She hoped it would be enough to make a fresh start for her and her baby. She had to acknowledge that Greg's strategy might have beaten her. He'd taken Tad and then Corrado, plus the .38 all away from her — every option that he had knowledge of — or that he could imagine her pursuing. This was in addition to Baldavino barely being help that Arlene could figure she could be able to count on. And she feared that if she even remained on Taylor Street, the possibility was too great that she'd just wind up a tool like Lumia. Being responsible for the safety of a child now, Arlene would never trust her fate to Madam Moresco — or even her own flesh and blood relations. And if *her people* caught her stealing from them, they at least wouldn't kill her and her child — their own kin. But maybe the Villettis would feel the same way? In her womb, she also carried *their* kin. It was her plan that upon having gained knowledge of her pregnancy, she could make *both* the Villettis and the Delasandros think that that from their family came someone who sired her child. There surely wasn't any better reason for her to tolerate Davino Delasandro — or his brother Stefano — or their cousin Urso for certain. That was nearly the only reason she'd fucked Baldavino — except that she wanted to protect Zhen. However, though Arlene had done what she'd could, the Li daughter would be on her own now. She had too much on her plate to handle as it were. However, Stefano could be the one most easily convinced that he was the father — because his own father diagnosed Arlene's pregnancy. Or he'd opt to deny everything to protect his marriage and do anything she asked to protect his secret — yet his father might back up Arlene, Abramo overjoyed to see the first-born of his family's next generation. But if she just disappeared, perhaps in time, they'd forget about her in South West Chicago, and she would make her way somewhere else, someplace else, where she could safely raise a daughter — or prevent a son from inevitably being raised to take his place in the Villetti patriarchy. The rest of them were either bound to get themselves killed anyway, or she would return when they no longer thought of her, and eliminate Rinaldo, Urso, and Greggorio, assassinating them herself, when they were all least expecting it. That's what she owed certain men.

Only now Greggorio had disappeared. She had no idea what he was up to and worried about that all the time. But much to her enormous disappointment, several days later her ever-so-beloved cousin informed Arlene that she should expect nothing in the way of money from her Irish family until she could come up with the information they originally sent her to South Chicago for in the first place. She needed to complete her mission but still had no complete idea of what that was either — only that she had to remain on Taylor Street in her present position and all would become clear soon. She was required to stand by.

That talk left Arlene in several moments of complete despair. She'd spun on Fallon and stabbed her finger into his chest to warn him not to say one more single goddamned thing to her when she left his temporary residence in Lincolnwood, where Arlene went to visit him again — or else his wife would find him laid out cold on the floor. And she promised she'd leave him drugged with her undergarments stuffed into his face. But Arlene felt so denied of any *real money*, she even forgot to make him pay her taxi fare. However, Arlene was after real money, and not just simple change.

Then she remembered her other allies who could help her affect serious change. She didn't trust Victoria Moresco, or her other powerful mentor for that matter. But she might round up the ladies she *could* control, and next take them uptown to rendezvous with Katherine McCormick's people a second time. She recollected what Victoria had said about using all her resources. She would use her own power to gather herself even more. And McCormick's people achieving their objectives could benefit quite nicely from a greater alliance with Arlene's ladies of the night — to get what they wanted, too: namely to control The United States' nativist Congress, right out of an immigrant pauper's brothel. But the Women's Movement also had way more money than she was *not* getting from the family of her own. So she'd call Nancy and arrange a meeting, again. Or try and pass a message through that brat Ginny Hall. Certainly the Christian Women's Temperance Union could see the benefit of turning more men into slaves over their obsession for more and more pussy, if only to replace their other distractions with alcohol and gambling — and the wife-beating that often followed these other refined indulgences. If the haughty uptown bitches didn't play ball, Arlene could easily be in the right position to expose to Jane Addams' do-gooders at The Hull House and the rest of Chicago to exactly how their philanthropy money for immigrant orphaned girls, funded the drug trade so the bosses could stock up the bordellos which laundered their money into the campaign finances of the "progressive candidates." In turn, these beneficiaries made sure that the bosses were never prosecuted and in the meanwhile guarantee women the vote — and thus their reelection. The hypocrisy flowing down the river of dirty money was disgusting. But she had to wonder why the wops' patriarchs would even want that. What were their buried values, and why were her people involved in it, especially when Sullivan really loved gambling and he and O'Banion enjoyed some amicable cooperation among

Irishmen? Were they fixing the next election? Of course that's why they needed the Italians' cooperation in the brothel. And because the guineas allied themselves with the shylocks Back East — another source of money and more importantly, a chance to edit all the Jew-owned newspapers. Or was there still more to it?

It was an insane world, but Arlene's next move would seem to make good simple sense. Others' priorities were far from hers. But protecting her unborn child had become a new personal one. Revenge was still a top cause for a fair amount of Arlene's attention to be paid forward. Only now that too had gotten far more personal — but she was scared for her baby. And she really needed her big payoff for this job, plus a lot more ammunition. She'd take either first, but preferred the money. And she would gladly steal that from Katherine McCormick. For then she would just betray everyone — including herself, her original mission — and skip town leaving her enemies alive — for the meanwhile. But all so her baby would live. Even without their father, this child would have a chance for a good life, Arlene promised herself, and then took a drink to that. And so she also would no longer wait for her baby's father. But she could use him to get her story in the papers, if she had to — presuming he was an "in" through their sports writers. But only if it were really necessary to make good on her threat. Or maybe she would never need Tad again.

Chapter 65

Taddeo was about to take the first step toward his new life. His immediate path would take him only as far as the Atlantic Terminal in the Flatbush neighborhood of Brooklyn, quite close to Ebbets Field. Then he would give Coach and his teammates the slip when they exited the streetcars that would carry all of them off Montague Street and out of the Brooklyn Heights neighborhood. Following that, he'd hide out at the train station until using some of Rothstein's money, he could catch a different route through Detroit that would take him back to Chicago and Arlene — as opposed to the tracks that would direct him south through Staten Island to Allentown and on through to Pittsburgh where Hoffman, Trip, Trevor and all the rest of the Cubs were headed.

When Tad viewed it for the first time, in daylight, outside of his transportation's window, the terminal was massive. Four stories high, it looked as if it dwarfed the Robins' stadium. A monumental byproduct of the Industrial Revolution's Age of Titans. Not that the competition between Ebbets and Brush could ever compare to the one fought by Vanderbilt and Carnegie. Once Taddeo was inside the building again, and this time without a shutout loss to focus on, the young athlete took the time to notice it was largely hollow, with huge arched windows that lit the lobby with natural brightness, that invaded the entire interior's structure in huge beams of light. It was this sort of gothic cathedral architecture's effect that was the cause for the structure to have been designed so large in the first place — with much attention paid to that empty form, over what was absolutely necessary for function. But the tracks actually ran below all this, as the train passengers would next find themselves making their descent into the subway. For this reason, beginning with the 1907 reconstruction of the terminal, New York had begun regulating the trains' emissions so the passengers waiting for their routes to arrive wouldn't be covered in soot by the time they ended their journeys. As a result, upstairs in the ticketing and public waiting areas, these new depots were extraordinary clean, almost modern works of art, with high visibility. He supposed that did serve a good function after all.

Taddeo lagged behind his friends among the other rookies as he carried his sports duffle and second piece of luggage which he feigned like he struggled with more than was actually the case — until theater merged with reality. He was really looking for his first opportunity in which to disappear and hide. Then in truth, perhaps because his own impatience was wearing him down, his luggage started truly becoming cumbersome. He'd also packed up what Sega had left behind to take with him in hopes that maybe one day he could return her belongings if he ever could learn what became the woman. Or he'd bring the items back from Brooklyn to Arlene, as if the most fancy dresses were now examples of his thoughtfulness, bringing her gifts from New York City. But he suspected that she'd be much more appreciative of the money he'd been handed off by Arnold Rothstein. It was so much more than she'd ever expect *he* could earn. And he hoped that would earn her return — to staying by his side.

However, apparently The Bank wanted to make sure the absolute entirety of his investment was insured, to all but guarantee *his* return. As Taddeo fell back from all the rest of the Cubs when they marched through the gigantic terminal, he knew that now was his last opportunity to run. Because as he turned around, there stood Abraham Attell and some of the Young Turks about Tad's age that he'd observed before on Navy Street, to even include "his friend" he'd first encountered at The Sisson, back in Chicago.

Taddeo tried to pretend he didn't see these fellas, and make his turn into an alcove seem natural. That led him to a set of stairs that would take him down an arched tunnel to where the train tracks ran on the floor below him. He sped up his pace once he was sure he was out of sight, hoping he'd lose everyone in the crowd and the closing darkness of the subterranean level, lit less brightly by only electrically generated lighting. However, a ticket-checker noticed him weaving through the commuter lines and demanded to see his boarding pass. Startled, his own anxiety surprising him, Taddeo used his duffle to push the uniformed man out of his way and make a dash toward the train tunnels. It was a spur-of-the-moment thing — not something Tad planned for — but this was happening. The train station employee blew the whistle he wore over his necktie and a new more rapid motion in the crowd helped Tad register additional station security guards in navy blue uniforms, who started parting their way through the people and converging on him.

This did not look good, as anyone could find Taddeo if he got arrested for trying to stow away on a train — and that was never his intention. He had more than the money he needed for a single ticket, and there were just so many fewer places to hide on passenger cars than freight trains in the first place. He was not trying to pull a rookie maneuver. And to top that off, even if he could jump on board, in the subway, without a ticket for any particular train on the time schedule, Tad would have no idea where he was going, except to waste even more time, probably by now having tracked things to go in exactly the wrong direction. He turned about looking to see if he could find a way to evade the guards and slip past the Jewish boss' men. Taddeo planned to reclimb the stairs and get back to the lobby by Ticketing and see if he could stay out of Coach Mitchell's sight, and that of his friends, at least long enough to buy the correct boarding pass to get him out of there. In the worst scenario, he would slide back into the lineup of the Major League Baseball team.

But it was no good going this way! Taddeo saw more of Rothstein's goons at his next turn running the bases, or the men had now split up to encircle him. But as he pivoted to double-back and make sure security wasn't looking in his direction, he turned right into Rocco Valenti! This was it. They'd let his murderous relative out of Sing Sing just to come visit him.

"Taddeo. Wait. Don't run. You'll only make this worse."

"He's right, Little Nephew." As Tad tried to evade Rocco, his youngest Uncle Bert was right there to stop him. "You better not even think about skipping out on Mister Big. Lucky for you, we told him that if that shylock wants to tell our family that he is handling the rest of the kikes, than he better let The Family handle you — not the boxer and the Mafiosos he's using for backup. And now we're here to explain to everyone, this is in an internal Italian house matter, not the half-pricks.' "

Valenti was all of the sudden backed up by those Tad thought he heard were Scalise, Pagano, Mineo and Paragallo. The Camorra. And that was overkill, considering that Rocco was there, and he knew of his uncle Umberto Valenti's reputation. If his family — or more likely Greg — wanted him dead, there was more than enough men here to see to it. And Taddeo was standing right in the middle of two of the most feared killers in any of the five boroughs in that exact moment.

And it was at that moment that Attell and his merry band spotted Villetti and they began to converge from down the station platform. A train just pulled in and the steam curled up and out from its brakes and engine, spreading out to turn the approaching men into what resembled silhouettes of death, descending upon Taddeo and his family members. But as Tad's head and eyes turned on a swivel, looking for some route for escape — the weight of Rothstein's money in his pocket slowing down and just barely *not* paralyzing even a simple action such as that — his friends on the Chicago Cubs arrived. Hoffman led, all of Trip, Trevor Bass, Charlie Hollocher, Turner Barber, Lester Mann, Bob O'Farrell, Charlie Deal and Fred Merkle in bearing down on the whole bunch.

Security now spotted all of this and one of their numbers bolted, probably to call the NYPD and report a brawl in the subway, about to begin — and plead for all backup to come right away.

Then George Hoffman called out, "Hey Shooter. Wondered where you disappeared to. I thought I could help. I've got you your ticket out of here."

"Good. It should be one-way straight to Pittsburgh with no detours for Chicago passengers," Uncle Bert said. He looked across a short distance to meet Abraham Attell's eyes. "We arrived to make *sure* your departure was on the best of terms and to make sure you didn't miss your train," he said to his nephew the baseball player, only without looking at him, though surely loud enough for the hymie thug to hear him. "Be responsible with what are your obligations Taddeo, and maybe we can find your Greek woman you've managed to be phoning everyone about."

"Oh, if only it were that simple," Abraham Attell added, raising his voice. "But this is very serious business, Umberto. And it is now Cosa Nostra's business." He nodded to indicate the boys behind him. They were there for backup, just in case. "Now I hope you haven't forgotten where your loyalties lie? And now that so many are invested, the soft-touch of the Camorra will no longer suffice."

At this point, almost all the station's security guards had all gathered around both the groups from Brooklyn and Manhattan, forming a perimeter but looking very much like they'd all rather be anyplace else.

"Oh yeah? Well, when it comes to how you're treating my friend, who would be these good fellas' teammate," George Hoffman nodded behind him, "you might learn that the Chicago Cubs' bats don't have any kind of a *soft touch* either. We *all* have been training to split some stitches."

To Next Be Continued

in BURIED VALUES: The Fall

- The Cubs have battled all the way to 1st Place. Now will they be able to hold on and make a historic run for the World Series — with all the rookies being able to carry their own weight — and especially with Arnold Rothstein's money in many-a-ballplayer's pocket?

- What *is* Rinaldo Villetti's role in all of this? What has he always been planning? And what might it have to do with his son, his position in Big Jim Colosimo's Outfit, and a Chicago held hostage by the likes of Salvatore Cardinella? The Mafia-Camorra War doesn't appear to be over Back East. And Johnny "The Fox" Torrio might have brought it with him to Chi-Town, along with his protégé, the young Al Capone, with Prohibition shortly to follow.

- And how much of the plans — for just about everything — does Greggorio know? What will the larger conspiracy mean for him in light of his own plotting to take control? The Italians, the Jews, and even more diverse groups of immigrants and other suppressed ethnicities have ideas about how they will advance their own dreams across vintage America, but the Irish stand in their way, struggling so hard to survive with what their people only just gained in the last century. Now Greg's arranging for the elimination of many of *his* competitors, as professional killers surround all, and a lot of people are about to die. But his own brother longs for the day he may return to Chicago — *to kill him instead.*

- Finally, Arlene now carries Taddeo's child. *Or does she really?* But who will she tell that to? And who will find out? Will she then choose fight or flight? And can Tad help his team *and* make a stand to help save his love? Is it even *her?* The decision is especially tough now with Katherine McCormick and Victoria Moresco tempting Arlene with two very different paths to power — that no woman had ever dreamt possible before. Full of crooked twists and turns that will surprise and shock, The Fall will not follow any obvious straight line, but Buried Values nevertheless, always shoots to win.

And fans of the Pittsburgh Pirates, Cincinnati Reds, and St. Louis Cardinals, visits to your home fields in Vintage Americana style, your cities in war time, and the turf of the real Great Gatsby will all be forthcoming. Hope it's an offer you don't want to refuse!

B.V.

And now an Exclusive excerpt from Buried Values: The Fall!

"The wench has my gun!" he yelled.

Urso scrambled to evade the kicks and blows Tad and his friends dealt him ducking under and using the table to partially shield him over and over again, but Corrado's gunshot had barely missed him, too. It was life or death now and he wasn't going to allow it to cost his life. "You carry backup! So back me up!" Urso called. "And never mind the baby. We can't let the whore live now." His brother clasped his fingers together to slam a double-punch into his spine. Urso recovered his breath from the blow and yelled. "If she has time to talk to Taddeo, he learns everything — and he and his teammates could spoil this whole game for everybody!" Then he went for his own weapon as well and fired a shot back up and out through the tabletop. It missed Taddeo by only another inch as he rose from his cover and the sound of the shot left more ringing in everyone's ears. Tad either didn't hear or look, like he reacted to his brother's mention of any baby.

But Arlene caught the look on Corrado's face. He was grinning. And then Urso had started firing carelessly, a reflex triggered by his haphazard instinct for self-preservation. He liked everything simple, black and white, and had now decided in an instant that he wasn't going to be the father of any child with the enemy. However, his cousin was in cahoots with Greg — and they all wanted at least one thing in common now. And that was Arlene shot dead, with it looking like possibly Taddeo, too — though she was determined to survive this. Only then Urso could be betrayed and the order of events covered up, so Rinaldo would never find out. But the Delasandro brother wouldn't turn on Urso and kill him now. Not when Corry needed Urso as backup.

"Yeah? And if I learn exactly *what* about my team?" Tad screamed the question at *his* brother — his volume motivated by both his rage and his inability to even hear himself over all the racket now. "Arlene?"

There he goes again, first and always foremost concerned about baseball — even in the middle of all this. Now the Cubs' brawlers scrambled back, keenly aware that the arms race had just escalated far beyond the firepower their pitcher had intended to have to deploy in this inning. Outside the window, Arlene witnessed the crowd that had gathered to watch the fight fall away in alarm, mindful that multiple stray bullets could find their way outside the Villettis' modest eatery at any minute.

"Here!" Arlene tossed Taddeo the .38 she'd grabbed off Corry only seconds earlier and from her purse withdrew a carved ivory-handled .45 Colt snubby as she and Tad exchanged fire with the latter's family as they covered Mike and Trevor, who attempted to help by throwing more chairs in the direction of the opposing gunmen. One seat went straight through the damaged window, glass flying out and beyond — and *everything* hitting some unlucky spectator. Now all the onlookers started fleeing farther and farther back from the fight, realizing that now *their safety* was in serious jeopardy, too. Even the reporters retreated off the byline from their most exciting story in at least several hours, and Arlene's rescuers began backing up in the opposite direction, beyond the bar, retreating through the doors to the kitchen. Their hastily aimed and exchanged "shots" managing to put down no one but still drain the whiskey.

"Take this!" Tad tossed Everston the hot .38 as he had also brought along a .45 he'd gotten from somewhere Arlene couldn't have guessed. He took another shot at his brother. Something in Taddeo had given way and it no longer inhibited his revenge-motivated actions. His enemies had historically held him down, beaten him, stolen from him his dream for a future with his baseball team, gang-raped his girlfriend, and now presumably killed his best friend. He would try and kill his own family in retribution, and he showed absolutely no sign of hesitation. Arlene felt proud only about what she'd achieved in so far as turning him to *her side*, even at the price it had cost her body and her soul. Only now she was determined it would not cost her baby — and if she could help it, its father, either.

Inside the kitchen, the cooks and dishwashers were yelling out, fleeing and running toward the back exit by the trash dump. Several of the working girls had ducked inside the kitchen with Taddeo and his company, too. Lumia threw up. Bullets flew around them and split apart lit embers as Villetti's boasted the place featured an old-fashioned wood-fueled stove. Now its source of kindling was featured all right, splintered right out of its metallic containment and flying into the laundry. They sparked into the pile of greasy napkins and high-proof alcohol-soaked tablecloths that were always lying around like they were hoping for Taddeo to clean them the next time he got trapped there for punishment. Instead, the situation now made for he and his friends desperately fighting to be paroled — into cleaner air they could breathe, the latest of more urgent priorities, as they were flying by. The flammable material had created a lot more smoke than any real danger of a fire — so far. But they also made for setting the bordello's guests and hostesses who were upstairs into a panic. They too were also trying to make it to the ground level floor and run for the rear exit. No doubt frightened by all the noise, and right into trying to dodge all the bullets, the fleeing customers helped along by Old Lamont, who was actually moving up toward the fighting group. "Go. Go! Rose, Vickie, Sega! Sin-die, Jasmine. Delilah. Chastity. May. LuLu! Get out of here!" he called out to them. Suddenly a stream of girls and their horny patrons in various stages of undress from their business on the second floor started fleeing out of the building through the employee access into the kitchen, constantly startled by more gunshots and growing more fearful of a fire. Poor Faith was lost as she fell, hit by an off-target shot. More bullets flew and new stains were added to the colors already on Villetti's kitchen floor, beneath the newest, scarlet ones. Trip saw this and tried hiding his emotions from the others by directing his look of sorrow toward the ground. But his shock by the girl's loss was already picked up on by the others closest to him. It didn't even need to be, because it wouldn't take long to morph into violent anger, a weapon that was always within his reach.

Most of the ladies were really screaming now. Some man in a suit that Taddeo should have only had time to figure for an early customer, was felled next. He must have also panicked and tried to escape last, from all of the group that came by way of the stairs. That guy might have remained safe if he'd only stayed put. However, Arlene knew that one needed to hide his identity and presence especially *there* of all places. But the smoke had likely started to permeate the hallway and suffocate the guestrooms. But wait: *had* Taddeo also just seemed to recognize him?

What was this crisis if not educational? *However, Katherine McCormick might be happy about the politician's son's fate,* Arlene thought. Because Arlene also knew exactly who the downed man was. She'd witnessed the scene earlier when that young fellow had demonstrated exactly what their family really cared about. Though Arlene wondered if that was what his father would have cared for him to die for. But it was just as likely his father would have lost his life gambling with his chances at getting off with something from Villetti's. Reinforcing her original thought, this crisis was a major learning opportunity. For some, it would come to them the hard way. But as it happened, Urso and Corry started to really use more caution when aiming their shots. In seconds, ammunition could start to run low. But it was already too late to matter. The real firefight started to take form. The smoke grew thicker and now red and yellow fingers could be seen through it, reaching for the ceiling.

Yet Tad paid only cursory attention to all of this. He appeared to be searching for someone among the women as they all ran past. He'd grab each by their shoulders and spin them around to bring their face close to his. Arlene didn't care that she sounded insulted. "Taddeo. I'm right here! Oh no! You do not go looking for that bitch right now!" She fired again but missed Corrado. She thought she might have even been able to actually shoot Sega if she saw her in all of this, but Arlene didn't have any bullets to spare and thought the Greek witch had already been evacuated. The young madam loathed the fact that woman had ever returned in the first place. Was Sega up to doing something worse than she'd done already? Or were Arlene's eyes played tricks on her, showing her the worst of what she did *not* want to see? And right under her nose in The House she had supposed authority to run. Had she become both blind and paranoid? Everything was happening so fast.

Taddeo ignored his girlfriend. Return fire streaked over his and his friends' heads. Mr. Li's daughter wasn't there. He shouted to Bass. "Trev, you're nearest the door. The stairs up top to the private quarters are closer to us than they are to my brother and his guns. I'll cover for you. Make for the foyer. Then I need you to get upstairs and get me a girl."

"I'm fucking right here, Taddeo!" Arlene screamed, fired, and withdrew .45 ammunition from her purse, began to reload, dropped that weapon in frustration, the Bodeo she'd taken off Baldavino useless without .9mm cartridges, and then fired another shot out across the dining area with her Colt to keep Urso and Corrado pinned down. "I've not completely run out of ammunition, yet. Only this is hardly the time!"

Tad had finally taken notice of everything his old woman was armed with. "Geez Arlene! What the heck are you sporting?"

"Nothing for you, I'd bet. But ya want to have a quick inning right now, Pitch? Is that your last wish?" Trev called out, interrupting, before Arlene could answer — if she even would.

"I need you to do something. Now Bass-Man!"

"I want to get out of here! Alive — if you don't mind."

A glance over the serving counter revealed Urso also carried a 1911 Colt semi-automatic pistol from which he unleashed a couple of its deadly rounds. Things crashed and burst apart in the kitchen behind them as the bullets made contact. The volume of everything kept escalating.

"We are *all* getting out of here. When I say run, you run. Upstairs. Find the China-girl." Arlene whipped her head around to look at him curiously.

"There still could be a lot of girls upstairs *here*, Tad. How will I know which one's from China? I can't speak Chinese."

"God you are a stupid idiot ball jockey!" Arlene quipped while she grabbed the .38 out of Trip's hands, giving him the empty Bodeo only to trade shots with Urso, who now fired his Beretta, but with one gun they could see in *each* of the Villetti brother's hands. "You'll know if you can ever bring yourself to look at a woman above her shoulders!" she hollered back at Trevor Bass.

"She's the slant, you dumb-ass!" Trip vomited out.

"Take this." Tad passed Bass-Man the gun that had finished Hoff only less than an hour ago. They were all desperate. "You've got only one shot left. But save it if you can. I want that bullet back. I've got something special planned involving where that one goes."

"Who's guaranteed any choice in all of this? But a China-girl? Wow. Your Papa's place gets more and more exotic every time I come around here, Tad," Trevor remarked.

"You're not here to write a restaurant review. Your blood and your ghost is going to permanently reside here if you don't go right now! Do as I told you. Go! I've only got two shots left. Arlene, I won't ask why you've got all those pieces, but how are you fixed for ammo?"

"I could have only a couple left in your cousin's gun. I'm not carrying another reload for that and this uses something close to forty-fours." She nodded at what Tad thought looked like his other cousin Baldavino's gun, now in Trip's hand as they'd all ducked behind a food prep counter. The lettuce was getting shredded as heads were cut up in the gunfire, carving out a new salad medley where blood could make an optional topping. "But I wasn't ever planning on making a long enough stand for the time it takes for you to find a new girlfriend. Only it looks like if your family even allows you to survive this, you are definitely going to need one!"

"I'm trying to rescue — ."

"Sure you are! And I'm so fucking mad at you right now, Taddeo. I might just kill you."

"I will have your ammo up for you in a heartbeat, Mademoiselle," Old Lamont spoke up in his French accent. "Your other gun was already reloaded. Here's this for now." He passed up something he'd palmed in his hand to her. "And now you have a deuce more for your Colt, than you have fired yet."

"Oh, screw this shit!" Tad yelled. "Wait. You're bringing us reloads?" he asked Lamont.

"I was given some more to hide for you here and instructed to help out only if you really needed me," Lamont was trying to explain to Arlene. "Looks like you really need me."

"What?" Tad looked back at the old Negro like he was crazy. "That your new boyfriend?"

"You have got to be kidding me," Arlene exclaimed.

"No, Mademoiselle. You see — ."

"Are you two going to do this right now?" Trip hollered out the question, trying to be heard in all the racket.

"Aggh! I don't care right now," she told the older man. "Tell me later — if we live." She fired several more rounds off covering Trevor Bass for reasons she couldn't understand, nevertheless, trusting Taddeo for reasons she also didn't understand. She just hoped that somehow they meant to rescue Zhen Li. That was what she wanted, too. "Hurry up with my reload!" she yelled. Her cohorts didn't need to know she would have called for the very same plan.

"Yes, Mademoiselle." Lamont shuffled back, staying low as a stray bullet flew back through the serving window now and then, until he had to get on a defective stepstool that wobbled on uneven legs further destabilized by Lamont's imbalance that came with his age. He pulled down a canned vegetable container from a high shelf that rattled with the noise like tin makes when clanked against more tin. More bullets flew around him, whistling through the air inches from his ears. "New rounds coming up!"

Arlene and Taddeo both grabbed for the can as Lamont stepped down, ducking for cover, and opened it up for them. Their fingers touched while they reached inside grabbing for more ammunition. Then both lovers' eyes met as they ejected spent cartridges, reloaded .45s and fired again while Trev burst back through the kitchen doors and dove for the stairway. He made it through the first door, while a shot chased him and shattered the glass. They heard Bass' footfalls grow softer as they moved farther away until they went pounding across the ceiling above them. Then the sounds of doors slamming open and closed and screaming from above reached them in addition to the ringing in their ears caused by all the gunfire in the enclosed area. But Urso and Corry's rate of fire got slower, more cautious. They had to be conserving ammo as well. Lucky for Taddeo and Arlene, they were all equally as terrible of shots. And equally lucky, the rookies' team stood with fresh reserves. Then Lamont passed another larger object forward to Arlene. "Your backup piece, M'Lady. I was given this to keep for you, as well." He handed her a new .45 that completed a matching set with the one already in her hand.

"So why the hell are you saving weapons and ammunition for me?" Arlene yelled back her question at Lamont. "How did you even know I had a gun before we ever met?"

"I just explained I was sent to take the job here so I could help you."

Of course — The *cook* was her other secret contact. Not the flower on the South Side. But The *flour*. "By who though? Why?"

"Let's just say we're related," the old black man said.

"Yeah. I noticed our resemblance," Arlene retorted while she exchanged a shot with Corrado.

"Wait. A spy — or spies in my own house?" Taddeo suddenly woke up to just one more issue he now had to deal with.

"Very perceptive. Now the smart one's catching on," Arlene commented, then called back to Lamont. "Do I have to shoot him, too?"

"Really? Then now would be the time, Woman. I'm running out." But Old Lamont didn't say anything and let Taddeo alone respond to that.

"I'm out too," Mike's voiced carried to them between the weapons fire noise. And the crackling of the fire could be heard during that seconds pause.

"That's because I didn't think you'd know what to do even if I did give you a loaded gun, Ball Jockey."

"Why don't you try me?"

"This isn't spring ball, Trip — but the real game. Only now and once again, I think we could use those fire hoses. Dan Griner has nothing on my brother. Do you have thirty-eight cartridges too, Lamont?" Tad called in his question with a strong voice so that he could be heard over the next round of gunfire — in addition to the snappy retorts his friends exchanged.

"No. Nobody suspectin' we'd get to smuggle in *two* different types of weapons for our use, here. The Smith and Wesson piece was your brother's. Nor was there anybody tellin' me I'd be the quartermaster."

"Lamont. You'll pay attention to me. Now I don't want to shoot him, old man. I just need him to shut up, already," Arlene said with a sidelong glance to indicate to Tad she wanted to make sure he heard. "Understand?"

"*My boss* says you need to shut up," Lamont told Taddeo.

"Yes. And you don't need ammo. I do. I will deal with your brother, Taddeo. But that piece you had seem familiar, hot shot?" Arlene asked him.

"The thirty-eight I gave to Bass-Man?"

To the black man she explained, "I stole my loverboy's gun a while back and had another of my own special-delivered to me. See, I'm usually rather thoroughly searched," Arlene rolled her eyes, "at your family's pleasure." She finished the sentence with an accusatory glance at the athlete. "So I take the opportunity to hide weapons and forge alliances everywhere I go. It's how I've managed to stay alive. Now please tell me you also have a plan." Tad's mouth fell open until he gagged on the smoke. Opposing sides traded more shots. A pot of something the cooks had boiling was dislodged off an open range and its grease splatter on the walls showered by embers sparked by near misses, caused what was another small cooking fire to reach out towards the ceiling with its many fingers. If Tad's group had been coughing before on a small problem with the air quality — that had been spreading out enough to alarm the upstairs occupants of the bordello — they really started heaving and choking on the smoke now. Behind him, the young woman said, "No. Of course you don't. Well I didn't mean to make for it going down this messy. All this is because the other two Villetti boys took the thirty-eight away from me some while back and apparently may have done something with it to upset the ball jockeys here," she informed her ally. Lamont got his update from over her shoulder.

"You're crossing a line, Arlene," Trip yelled his warning at her.

"You really are," Tad added. "You don't get to go there, Honey. *You* could even be a collaborator." But he knew Arlene could not have known what happened to Hoff. Could she? Why? And what was going on? The heat had really turned up on her — actually on them all because the place was on fire and they couldn't fight the flames and his family members who were trying to kill them. But Urso could have bragged to her. *I'm surrounded on all sides by lies and distortions. And then more lies and distortions. What I need to fight for now, is the truth!*

"Ha! By all means, if you don't like my company any more, why don't you get up and leave?" she said as return fire from their enemies' weapons kept them all pinned down close to the floor.

"Funny."

"Keep arguing and they get a chance to keep reloading, Mademoiselle. I just thought I might point that out," Lamont said. "And also that the kitchen's on fire." The flames had sparked an apron and the fire leapt up onto more of the dirty dishrags, soaked with enough liquor and cooking oil to also ignite. "You have to decide right now if you're going to work with him."

"Like I have a choice anymore?"

Shadows flickered on the front wall around where there once had been windows. The hanging lamps above the staircase would backlight figures descending the stairs, angling their shadows into the lounge through the foyer. "Here they come!" Tad shouted. "Arlene, give me that gun. My friends will need some cover. I'll protect you."

She coughed from the smoke. "Sure you will, Ace. And there's absolutely no way I'm giving up this gun! It's a classic piece. An heirloom to my family."

"You're a classic piece of something," Tad answered her back. "But I promise to always love you if you just don't let my friends down now!"

"Like I've ever been able to say 'no' to you, Taddeo." Arlene popped up and fired over the serving counter, her shots breaking apart lamps, plates, and glasses; splintering wood; and forcing Urso and Corry to drop and crouch down. "My forty-four and thirty-eight are empty. Lamont, I know there's one more gun. Top shelf. Behind the cooking spices. Fallon thought Rinaldo might want me to cook for him." Bass and Mr. Li's daughter in a purple dress embroidered with twin golden dragons were a flash as they sped through the doorframe as Arlene fired her last shot she'd loaded.

"Something's sure cooking," Everston said as he helped them pass.

"You guys are fixing lunch at a time like this?" Bass asked as he sped past to then force Zhen Li down undercover beneath a food prep table.

"Wait. You were going to kill my papa?"

"Now's definitely not the time, Big-Brains," she retorted, with flames sparking behind her. One of the walls had lit up good now and smoke started to obscure the ceiling. At least Zhen was safe. For maybe only a few minutes longer.

"Does anybody have any more ammo?" Mike called out the prevailing question. Everyone shrugged, except Taddeo who crouched there in a stupor, pondering over the next bit of information about his father that he'd just received.

"I still have one shot," Trevor reported, realizing he'd actually made it back to the kitchen with Zhen Li and they were both still alive. He reacted naturally *for him* as he looked around the place, still feeling his chest and his stomach to check for wounds. He'd checked out their surroundings, too. "Hey, do you guys want a snack?"

"You keep that handy." Lamont, dodging two more bullets, had gotten on another work stool and started looking for the other gun while he responded to Bass.

"He meant the bullet in the thirty-eight. But if you really want to, you *can* fix *me* a sandwich," Arlene said.

"We're in a sandwich right now!" Trip yelled back.

Pick up BURIED VALUES: The Fall,

To find out who gets fed their fate next!

SPECIAL THANKS
&
ACKNOWLEDGEMENTS

There are so many friends and professionals who have helped me bring Buried Values to life and who I would like to thank for the contributions they have made along the way as this novel series develops, that I could not possibly name everyone here, all at once.

Please look to my acknowledgements feature on www.BuriedValues.com and let me know if I've mistakenly forgotten you. I will do my best to personally thank everyone. The acknowledgement page will be continuously updated and new aspiring writers may find useful links to many industry professionals who might help them publish their own works as well. Online you will find many connections to these professional services I hope will be useful for you, and that have helped tremendously, toward bringing Buried Values out for everyone.

About the Author

Joshua Adam Weiselberg was born in Chicago and brought up growing the closest to his ever-supportive grandpa, a lifelong Cubs fan who would have loved to have seen 2016's victorious season. However, it might be interesting to note that the baseball-themed novels in the Buried Values series were not in response to that incredible year Chicago had on the diamond, but were actually always planned out to connect the previously established characters from Louisiana with The Outfit. They were already two years under development as works-in-progress before the Cubs even showed any sign of how they'd perform, only the season almost immediately prior to when publication could happen! What luck, huh? Baseball is anything but predictable. Or is it? Reading some more offerings out of the sports world of Buried Values *might influence your opinion about that.*

A labor of love, the complete story is told in three volumes now — the operating plan to originally release one book quarterly. It had to be perfectly coordinated with the larger Buried Values legacy, that on-going mystery in society about "where are we now, where did we come from, and where we are going?" so this novel never got to see release in 2016 or '17 as it was originally hoped. But before you now lays the author's hope that you have enjoyed this adventure, released exactly 100 years after the incredible amount of actual true events included this fiction-novel, really did happen. It is hoped that you will look forward to finding out what happens next.

Meanwhile, Josh continues to enjoy playing baseball in recreational leagues, a practice he began way back when he was only 7 years old in Little League in California and then on into his school years.

In San Diego, as a Padres season-ticket holder, Josh had multiple turns taking batting practice at Petco Park, a highlight in his fandom of the sport — to play in a real big league stadium, as was his fond memories of an on-the-grass and on-deck experience at Wrigley Field. Trips to Spring Training in the Cactus League and Boston's Fenway Park are awesome memories, as was spending much time living near Anaheim Stadium and going to the Angels' games (and Disneyland). It's fair to say Josh loves baseball and adding sports fiction and research back to the time of some true legends, also to include certain heavy-hitters *off* the diamonds, and the vintage cars, the music, the famous hotels, and infamous gambling and other crime organizations with "all kinds of players," have hopefully been as fascinating to the reader, as it was for the writer/researcher.*

And there's always more to come!

* In the Cubs' 2016 Champion Season Josh returned to attend games in Chicago and visit all the actual locations in Chi-Town where the adventure you just enjoyed took place. [photos by Sergio Peña added above and to include more on Buried Values' Facebook page, website, and with the author shown here at the L station at Addison and Clark St., and on-deck at Wrigley Field (Weeghman Park in those days) in authentic 1918 fashion.]

BURIED VALUES
THE TREASURE
BURIED VALUES
THE LIBRARY
JOSHUA ADAM WEISELBERG